The POLITY & GOVERNANCE COMPENDIUM

For IAS Prelims General Studies

CSAT Paper 1, UPSC & State PSC EXAM

• **Corporate Office :** 45, 2nd Floor, Maharishi Dayanand Marg, Corner Market, Malviya Nagar, New Delhi-110017

Tel. : 011-49842349 / 49842350

Chief Editor : Satya Prakash
Editor : Ratan Sharma

Typeset by Disha DTP Team

Printed at Repro Knowledgecast Limited, Thane

For further information about the books from DISHA,
Log on to **www.dishapublication.com** or email to **info@dishapublication.com**

CONTENTS

CONSTITUTIONAL FRAMEWORK AND CITIZENSHIP

Chapter 1

What is Constitution?

- Constitution is the organic and fundamental law of a nation or state.
- It may be written or Unwritten.
- It establishes the character and conception of its government.
- It lays the basic principles to which the internal life of a nation is to be conformed.
- It organizes the government, regulates, distributes and limit the functions of different organs of government.
- It prescribes the extent and manner in which the sovereign powers of a nation is to be exercised.

Why do we need a Constitution?

- Constitution provides a set of basic rules that allow for minimal co-ordination amongst members of a society.
- Constitution specifies who has the power to make decisions in a society. It decides how the government will be constituted.
- Constitution set some limits on what a government can impose on its citizens. These limits are fundamental in the sense that government may never trespass them.
- Constitution enable the government to fulfill the aspirations of a society and create conditions for a just society.
- A Constitution expresses the fundamental identity of a people. The constitution sets authoritative constraints upon what one may or may not do.

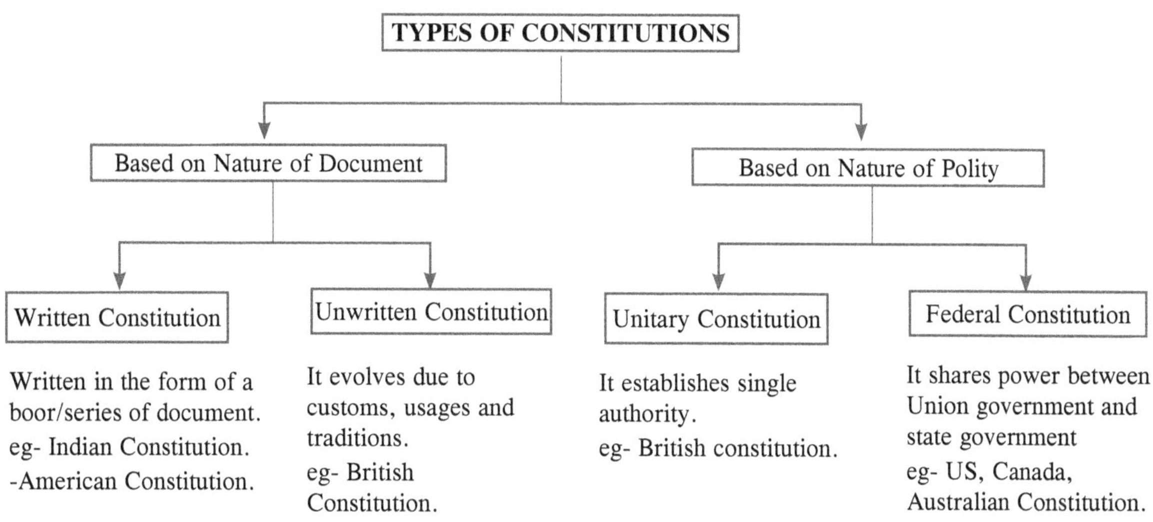

Different types of Governments

- Republic – A government whose authority is based on citizen voters, which are represented by elected or nominated officials chosen in free electrons.
- Democracy – Democracy means 'rule of the people'. The term today refers to a political system in which the people of their elected representatives govern themselves.
- Theocracy – A government where priests rule in the name of God or by officials who are regarded as divinely guided, or consistent with the principles of a particular religion.
- Autocracy – A government controlled by absolute power and in the hands of a single person with minimal restraints on the decisions & lack of any mechanisms of popular control.
- Technocracy – A government where scientists and technical experts are in control of the state & where rulers are selected on the basis of their knowledge/skill rather than wealth/power.
- Fascism – A way of ruling that advocates total control of the people and seeks to promote the ancestral and cultural values & eradicate foreign influences.
- Anarchy – Anarchy is a state of absence of law, a state of lawlessness and disorder (usually resulting from a failure of government).
- Monarchy – A government where supreme authority is vested in a single and usually hereditary figure, such as a king, & whose powers can vary from absolute to none at all.
- Oligarchy – Rule of the few. This is a form of power structure in which power effectively rests with a faction of persons or families.
- Plutocracy – Government ruled by the rich or power provided by wealth, often used to describe a wealthy class ruling a government, often from behind the scenes.
- Tyranny – Government or authority of an absolute ruler; the purposes of government/approved by law and justice.
- Totalitarian – A totalitarian system is one in which a single political authority regulates total control over state. that is centralized and dictatorial.
- Federation – A political organization characterized by a union of small states, groups or parties, which are self-governed in internal affairs and are united under a central government.
- Communism – As a system of government, communism is when the state owns and operates industry on behalf of the people.
- Junta – A junta refers to a group or coalition that takes control of the state after overthrowing a government. Usually, this is done by military groups.
- Dictatorship – A form of government where the power rests entirely on one person or a group of persons. This rule could be acquired by inheritance or force and is usually oppressive.

The Philosophy of the Indian Constitution

- Indian Constitution is liberal, democratic, egalitarian, secular and federal, open to community values, sensitive to the needs of religious and linguistic minorities as well as historically disadvantaged groups.
- Indian Constitution is committed to building a common national identity.
- Indian Constitution has a pretty strong liberal character and freedom of expression is an integral part of the Indian constitution.
- The liberalism of the Indian Constitution differs from the classical liberalism that always privileges rights of the individuals over demands of social justice and community values.
- Indian Constitution does not see religion merely as a 'private matter concerning the individual.
- Indian Constitution reinforces and reinvents forms of liberal individualism.
- Out Constitution upholds the principle of social justice without compromising on individual liberties.
- Despite the unitary bias of the Indian Constitution there are important constitutionally embedded differences between the legal status and prerogatives of different sub-units within the same federation.
- Out Constitution constantly reinforces a common national identity. It tries to balance the various identities.
- The Indian Constitution reflects a faith in political deliberation. It reflects a spirit of compromise and accommodation.

History of Constitution of India

324 B.C. – 185 B.C.	Emperor Ashoka established Constitutional Principles, Engraved then in major rocks, Pillar and on minor rocks for public (Edicts of Ashoka).
1599 A.D. – 1765 A.D.	East India Company takes total administrative control by gaining rights of taxation in Bengal after Battle of Plassey (1757).
1765 A.D. – 1947 A.D.	East India Company takes total unified control over the whole of India from a single centre in Calcutta. But its rule ended with the revolt of 1857.
1858 A.D. – 1947 A.D.	This period of the British Raj was the time when the constitution of India took shape.
1950 A.D.	Finally a constitution was enacted and adopted by India. This constitution was written by the free people of India and was adopted on 26, November 1949.

- Before 1947, India was divided into two main entities. The British India which consisted of 11 provinces and the princely states ruled by Indian princes under subsidiary alliance policy. The two entities merged together to form the Indian Union, but many of the legacy systems of British India is still followed.
- The historical underpinnings and evolution of the India Constitution can be traced to many regulations and acts passed before Indian Independence.
- The process of the evolution of the constitution began many decades before 26 Jan/1950 and has continued unabated since. Its origin lie deeply embedded in the struggle for independence from Britain and in the movements for responsible and constitutional government in the princely states.

HISTORICAL BACKGROUND

Constitutional Developments	Important Provisions
Regulating Act, 1773	• British government to regulate affairs of East India Company. • Designated Governor of Bengal as Governor General of Bengal. Warren Hastings was the first Governor General of Bengal. • Established a Supreme Court at Calcutta (1774).
Pitts India Act, 1784	• Indian affairs under direct control of British government. • Board of Control was established to manage political affairs.
Charter Act of 1793	• Salary of company to drawn from the Indian exchequer. • The Governor General and governors to override the decision of Councils. • Company got monopoly of trade with India for another 20 years.
Charter Act of 1833	• Governor General of Bengal became Governor General of India. • Lord William Bentinck was the first Governor General of India. • The Act centralized British rule in India. • Created Government of India, with authority over all of British India. • East India Co. lost its monopoly of tea trade and China trade. • The Indian Civil Services was founded.
Charter Act of 1853	• Separated legislative & executive functions of Governor General's Council. • Civil Services was thrown open to Indians also. • Patronage of the directors of the company ends. • It introduced local representation in the Indian (Central) Legislative Council. • It abolished the East India Company.
Government of India Act: 1858	• This Act is known as the Act for the Good Government of India. • Designation of Governor-General of India was changed to that of Viceroy of India. • Lord Canning became the first Viceroy of India. • It created a new office of Secretary of State for India. • It abolished the Board of Control and Court of Directors. • The Secretary of State was responsible ultimately to the British Parliament.
Indian Councils Act: 1861	• Viceroy should nominate some Indians as non-official members of his expanded council. • It initiated the process of decentralization by restoring the legislative powers to Bombay and Madras Presidencies. • It provided for establishment of new legislative councils for Bengal, NWFP and Punjab. • It recognized the 'Portfolio' system, introduced by Lord Canning in 1859.
Indian Councils Act: 1892	• It added the number of non-official members in the central and provincial legislative councils. • The act made a limited and indirect provision for the use of elections.

Indian Councils Act: 1909 (*Morley-Minto Reforms*.	• Lord Morley was then the secretary of state for India and Lord Minto was then the viceroy of India). • It increased the size of the legislative councils, both central and provincial. • It enlarged the deliberative functions of the legislative councils of both the levels. • It introduced a system of communal representation for Muslims by accepting the concept of 'separate electorate'. • Lord Minto is known as the Father of Communal Electorate. • It also provided for association of Indians with the executive councils of the Viceroy and Governors.
Government of India Act: 1919/ *Montague - Chelmsford Reforms*.	• Montague was the secretary of state for India and Lord Chelmeford was the viceroy of India. • This Act is also known as Act of Devolution. • It demarcated and separated the central and provincial subjects. • Provincial subjects were divided into transferred and reserved subjects. • It provided for the establishment of a Public Service Commission. • It created a new office of the High Commissioner for India in London. • Transferred subjects were administered by Governor with the help of ministers who were responsible to the legislature. • Reserved subjects were administered by Governor and Executive Council who were not responsible to the legislature. • *Dyarchy/ Dual system* of government was introduced. • *Bicameral legislature* with upper and lower houses were formed with direct elections. • Majority of members in both houses were directly elected. • 3 of the 6 members of governor-general's council had to be Indians.
Simon Commission: (1927)	• 7 members Statutory Commission Constituted to report o the Condition of India under its new Constitution. • The Commission recommended the abolition of dyarchy, extension of responsible government in the provinces. • Establishment of a federation of British India and Princely states was recommended but it never came into existence. • A white paper on constitutional reforms was prepared based on the recommendations of Simon Commission.
Communal Awards: (1932)	• Announced by the British Prime Minister Ramsay MacDonal. • It announced a scheme of representation of the minorities, which came to be known as the Communal Award.
Poona Pact: (1932)	• Gandhiji undertook fast undo death in Yeravada jail against the extension of Communal Award. • At last there was agreement between the leaders of the Congress and the depressed classes.
Government of India Act: 1935	• It provided for the establishment of an all-India Federation consisting of provinces and princely states as units. However such a federation never came into existence. • It abolished dyarchy in the provinces and introduced 'provincial autonomy'. • It provided for the adoption of dyarchy at the centre. • It introduced bicameralism in six out of eleven provinces. • It extended the principle of communal representation by providing separate electorates for depressed classes (Scheduled Castes), women and labour (workers). • It abolished the Council of India. • It provided for establishment of a Federal Court. • It provided for the establishment of a Federal Public Service Commission. • It provided for the establishment of *Reserve Bank of India*. • Introduced responsible governments in provinces.

The August Offer, 1940	• Establishment of an Advisory War Council. • A "Constitution making Body" shall be appointed immediately after the war. • The number of Indians in the Viceroy's Executive Council to be increased.
Cripps Mission: 1942	• The Constitution of India was to be framed by an elected Constituent Assembly by the Indian People. • India to get a Dominion states. • There shall be on Union of India comprising all the British provinces and princely states. • The British provinces and princely states would be free to retain their existing constitutional position.
C.R. Formula, 1944	• The Muslim League would support the Congress's demand for complete freedom. • As the end of was a Commission would demarcate these contiguous areas in NWFP and NEI where Muslims were in majority.
Wavell Plan: 1945	• A new Executive Council was to be formed at the Centre. • Except the Viceroy and the Commander in Chief, all other members of the new Executive Council are to be Indians. • All portfolios except the Defence would be held by the Indian Members.
Lord Attlee's Announcement, March 1946	• On 15 March 1946, Lord Attlee declared that as the tide of nationalism was surging ahead in India, it was in British interest to take positive action.
Cabinet Mission Plan: 1946	• Objective of the Mission was to help India achieve its independence as early as possible. • The Cabinet Mission rejected the claim for a separate Constituent Assembly and a separate state for the Muslim. • There was to be a Union of India, comprising both British India and the states having jurisdiction over the subjects of Foreign Affairs, Defence and Communication. • All residency powers were to be vested in the Provinces and the states. • The Union was to have an executive and a legislature consisting of representatives of the Provinces and the states. • A Constituent Assembly should be set up to draw up the future Constitution of the country.
Indian Independence Act, 1947	• It abolished the office of Viceroy and provided for each dominion a governor general. • It empowered the constituent Assemblies of the to dominions to frame and adopt any constitution for their respective nations. • It abolished the office of the Secretary of State for India. • It granted freedom to the Indian princely states either to join the Dominion of India or Dominion of Pakistan or to remain independent. • Declared India as independent & sovereign state. • Established responsible government at the Centre & Provinces. • Designated Governor General of India & Provincial Governors as Constitutional heads or nominal heads. • Lord Mount batten became the first Governor General of free India. The first & last Indian Governor General was C. Rajagopalachari.

Interim Government (1946)

S. No.	Members	Portfolio
1.	Pt. Jawaharalal Nehru	External Affairs and Commonwealth Relations
2.	Sardar Vallabhbhai Patel	Home, Information and Broadcasting
3.	Dr Rajendra Prasad	Food and Agriculture
4.	Dr John Mathai	Industries and Supplies
5.	Jagijvan Ram	Labour
6.	Sardar Baldev Singh	Defence
7.	CH Bhabha	Works, Mines and Power
8.	Liaquat Ali Khan	Finance
9.	Abdur Rab Nishtar	Posts and Air
10.	Asaf Ali	Railways and Transport
11.	C Rajagopalachari	Education and Arts
12.	II Chundrigar	Commerce
13.	Ghaznafar Ali Khan	Health
14.	Joginder Nath Mandal	Law

First Cabinet of Free India (1947)

Members	Portfolio
Pt. Jawaharlal Nehru	Prime Minister, External Affairs and Commonwealth Relation; Scientific Research
Sardar Vallabhbhai Patel	Home, Information and Broadcasting; States
Dr. Rajendra Prasad	Food and Agriculture
Maulana Abul Kalam Azad	Education
Dr. John Mathai	Railways and Transport
RK Shanmugham Chetty	Finance
Dr. BR Ambedkar	Law
Jagjivan Ram	Labour
Sardar Baldev Singh	Defence
Raj Kumari Amrit Kaur	Health
C.H. Bhabha	Commerce
Rafi Ahmed Kidwai	Communication
Dr. Shyama Prasad Mukherji	Industries and Supplies
V.N. Gadhil	Works, Mines and Power

Sources of Indian Constitution

India constitution has borrowed its provisions from following sources.

Country	Provisions Borrowed
Government of India Act, 1935	• Federal scheme. • Emergency powers. • Ordinance defining the power of the President and Governors. • Office of the Governor. • Judiciary. • Administration at the Centre and state level.
United Kingdom	• Parliamentary system. • Bicameral parliament. • Prime minister. • Council of ministers. • Single citizenship. • Office of CAG. • Writ jurisdiction of courts. • Rule of law.
USA	• Written Constitution. • Fundamental rights. • Supreme Court. • President as executive head of the state. • Impeachment of the President, removal of SC and HC judges. • Vice President as chairman of Rajya Sabha. • Judicial review, independence of judiciary.
Australia	• Concurrent list. • Cooperative federalism. • Joint sitting of two houses of parliament.
USSR	• Fundamental duties.
Weimer Constitution of Germany	• Suspension of fundamental rights during emergency. • Ballot system.
Canada	• Federal system. • Residuary powers. • Appointment of Governor. • Advisory jurisdiction of SC.
South Africa	• Procedure of constitutional amendment. • Electing member to Rajya Sabha.
Ireland	• Concept of directive principles of state policy. • Nomination of members to Rajya Sabha by the President. • Presidential election.

MAKING OF INDIAN CONSTITUTION

- The Constitution of India Bill (1895) was the first non-official attempt at drafting a constitution for India.
- The idea of Constituent Assembly for making the Constitution was first mooted by *M. N. Roy in 1934*.
- Indian National Congress (INC) officially demanded the formation of Constituent Assembly in 1935.
- The demand was accepted, in principle, for a Constituent Assembly in August offer of 1940.
- Under the Cabinet Mission Plan, 1946 a Constituent Assembly was constituted in Nov. 1946 for framing the Indian Constitution.
- While the cabinet mission plant rejected the idea of two constituent assemblies, the provisions made by it, more or less satisfied the Muslim League.

Composition of the Constituent Assembly

- The total strength of the Constituent Assembly was to be 389. (296 seats were allotted to British India and 93 seats to be Princely states).
- Each province and princely state were to be allotted seats in proportion to their respective population.
- Seats to each British province were to be divided among the Muslims, Sikhs and General.
- Voting was to be held by the method of proportional representation by means of single transferable vote.
- The members from princely states were to be nominated by the heads of the princely states.
- Therefore the Constituent Assembly was partly elected and partly nominated.
- Although the Constituent Assembly was not directly elected by the people of India on the basis of adult franchise, the Assembly comprised representative of all sections of Indian society.

- First meeting of Constituent Assembly was held on Dec 9, 1946.
- Muslim League boycotted the Constituent Assembly.
- Dr. Sachidanand Sinha, the senior most member of the assembly, was elected as the temporary president of the assembly.
- Dr. Rajendra Prasad was elected as the permanent president of the Assembly.
- Sir B. N. Rau was appointed as the legal advisor to the Assembly.
- An *Objective Resolution'* was moved by *Jawaharlal Nehru* on *Dec. 13, 1946*, which later became the Preamble to the Constitution.
- On the 26th November, 1949 the Constitution was declared as passed after the President of the Assembly signed the document. Thus on *26th November, 1949* the Constitution of India was *adopted*. The commencement of the Constitution began on 26th Jan. 1950.
- Provisions relating to citizenship, elections, provisional parliament, and temporary provisions became effective from 26th November, 1949.
- On January 24, 1950 the Constituent Assembly held its final session. It had continued as a provisional parliament from 26 January, 1950 till the formation of new parliament in May, 1952.
- First '*Draft Constitution of India*' was published in Feb, 1948. It was prepared by Sir B. N. Rau, Constitutional Advisor to the Constituent Assembly.
- **Dr. B. R. Ambedkar is considered the father of the Indian Constitution.**
- **The Constituent Assembly took almost 3 years (2 years, 11 months & 18 days) to draft the Constitution for Independent India.**
- It held *11 sessions* covering a total of 165 days.

Objective resolution

On *January 22, 1947*, the Constituent Assembly adopted Objective Resolution proposed by Jawahar Lal Nehru. The Objectives Resolution contained the fundamental propositions of the Constitution and set forth the political ideas that should guide its deliberations.

The main principles of the resolution were:

(i)　India shall be an Independent, Sovereign, Republic;

(ii)　India shall be a Union of erstwhile. British Indian territories, Indian states and the parts outside British India and Indian states as are willing to be a part of the Union.

(iii)　Territories forming the Union shall be autonomous units and exercise all powers except those assigned to or vested in the Union.

(iv)　All powers and authority of sovereign and independent India and its Constitution shall flow from the people.

(v)　All people of India shall be guaranteed and secured social, economic and political justice; equality of status and opportunities before law; and fundamental freedoms of talk, expression, belief, faith, worship, vocation, association and action - subject to law and public morality.

(vi)　The minorities, backward and tribal areas, depressed and other backward classes shall be provided adequate safe guards.

(vii)　The territorial integrity of the republic and its sovereign rights on land, sea and air shall be maintained according to justice and law of civilized nations.

(viii)　The land would make full and willing contribution of the promotion of world peace and welfare of mankind.

Important Committees	
COMMITTEE	CHAIRMAN
Drafting Committee Members: ● Alladi Krishnaswamy Ayyar ● N. Gopala Swami Ayyangar ● Dr. KM Munshi ● Syed Mohammad Saadullah ● N Madhava Rao ● TT Krishna Machari	Dr. B.R. Ambedkar (Father of the Indian Constitution)
Flag Committee	J. B. Kriplani
Union Constitution Committee	Jawaharlal Nehru
Provincial Constitution Committee	Sardar Vallabh Bhai Patel
Union Powers Committee	Jawaharlal Nehru
Committee on Fundamental Rights and Minorities	Sardar Vallabh Bhai Patel
Special Committee to Examine the Draft Constitution	(Chairman: Alladi Krishnaswamy Iyer)
Finance & Staff Committee	Dr. Rajendra Prasad
Ad-hoc Committee on Supreme Court	S. Varadachariar
Ad-hoc Committee on National Flag	Dr. Rajendra Prasad
Committee on Chief Commissioners' Provinces	B. Pattabhi Sitaramayya

Other functions performed by Constituent Assembly :

- Adoption of the National flag on July, 22, 1947.
- Ratification of India's membership of the Commonwealth in May 1949.
- Adoption of the National Anthem on Jan. 24, 1950.
- Adoption of the National Song on Jan. 24, 1950.

Criticism of the Constituent Assembly

- It was not a representative body as its members were not directly elected by the people of India on the basis of Universal adult franchise.
- It was not a Sovereign Body as it was created by the proposals of the British government.

- It was dominated by Congress. In fact the Assembly was the Congress and the Congress was India.
- It was dominated by Hindus.

Sources of Indian Constitution

- The Constitution of India is remarkable for many outstanding features even though it has been prepared after ransacking all the known constitutions of the World and most of its provision are substantially borrowed from others.
- Indian Constitution has borrowed various provision from different Constitutions existing at that time.

SALIENT FEATURES OF INDIAN CONSTITUTION

(i) Bulkiest Constitution of the World

Indian Constitution is the one of longest Constitution in the world. Originally it contained 395 Articles, 22 Parts and 8 Schedules. After amendments till date, there are more than 447 Articles, 24 Parts and 12 Schedules.

(ii) Combination of Rigidity and Flexibility

The Indian Constitution is a combination of rigidity and flexibility. While some provisions of the Constitution can be amended by the Parliament by a simple majority, others require a two-third majority of the members of the parliament as well as ratification of not less than one-half of the state legislatures (Article 368). Again, some provisions of the Constitution can be amended by the parliament alone by a two-third majority.

(iii) Parliamentary System of Government

The Constitution provides for a parliamentary system of government under which the real executive power rests with the Council of Ministers and the President is only a nominal head. The Council of Ministers stay in office as long as they enjoy the confidence of the Parliament.

The framers of the Constitution decided to adopt a parliamentary system of government for several reasons. *Firstly*, the system was already in existence in India and people were well acquainted with its working.

Secondly, the vast size of the country and the diversity of its culture necessitated the adoption of a parliamentary form of government.

Thirdly, the desire to avoid conflicts between the Executive and the Legislature, which was a common features in America, also induced the members of the Constituent Assembly to opt for a parliamentary system.

(iv) Federal System with a Unitary Bias

The Indian Constitution provides for a federation with a strong centre. It is noteworthy that the Constitution has not used the word '*federation*', anywhere, and has described India as a **'Union of States'** which implies that the Indian federation is not the result of any agreement among the units and the *units cannot secede* from it. India possesses most of the federal features but also several of the unitary features. The Indian federal structure acquires a unitary character during emergency, when the normal distribution of powers between the centre and the states undergoes vital changes.

For KC Wheare India has a *quasi federal* **set up.**

Morris Jonnes called it as **Bargaining Federalism & Granville Austine** called it as **Cooperative Federalism.**

- **India is a distinct federation with following characteristics:**
  - Division of power.
  - Bicameral legislature.
  - Supremacy of the constitution.
  - Written constitution.
  - Independency of Judiciary.
- **Constitution has a unitary bias:**
  - Appointment of Governors by the centre.
  - Parliament's power to legislate in national interest.
  - Parliament's power to form new states, change their names and alter boundaries of existing states.
  - Emergency provisions.
  - Single constitution.
  - Single citizenship.
  - Integrated judiciary.
  - Office of CAG.

(v) Fundamental Rights

The Constitution contains an elaborate list of Fundamental Rights. The state cannot make laws which takes away or abridge any of the fundamental rights of the citizens. If it does so, the courts can declare such a law as *unconstitutional*. It may be noted that the fundamental rights granted by the Constitution are not absolute and are subject to certain restrictions. In other words, the Constitution seeks to strike a balance between individual liberty and societal interests.

(vi) Fundamental Duties

The constitution also contains a list of *11 fundamental duties*. While ten of these duties were added to the Constitution by the *Forty Second Amendment* in *1976*, the eleventh duty was added by the 86th Constitutional Amendment Act (2002). These duties serve as constant reminders to the citizens that they have to observe certain basic norms of democratic conduct.

(vii) Directive Principles of State Policy

The Constitution outlines certain Directive Principles of State Policy which the government has to keep in mind while formulating any policy. These principles seek to provide social and economic basis for democracy and the establishment of a welfare state. Unlike the Fundamental Rights, the Directive Principles of State Policy are **non-justiciable**, which implies that no action can be brought against the State before a court of law for its failure of implementing the Directive Principles of States policy.

(viii) Secular State

The Constitution makes India a secular state. This means that there is no state religion and the state is completely detached from religious dogmas. It also implies that citizens are free to profess, practise and propagate any religion. However, freedom of religion is not absolute and the same can be regulated in the interest of the public.

(ix) Independent & Integrated Judiciary

The Constitution provides for an independent judiciary which ensures that the government is carried on in accordance with the provisions of the Constitution. Judiciary acts as the guardian of the liberties and fundamental rights of the citizens. It also determines the limits of the powers of the centre and the states.

The Constitution provides a single integrated judiciary with the Supreme Court at the top. Below the Supreme Court, there are high Courts at the state level. Under the High Court, there are Subordinate courts.

(x) People as Source of Authority

The Constitution draws its authority from the people and has been promulgated in the name of the people. This is evident from the Preamble which states 'We, the people of India… do hereby adopt, enact and give to ourselves this Constitution.'

(xi) Universal Adult Franchise

The Constitution introduces universal adult franchise and accords the right to vote to all citizens above 18 years of age without discrimination. However, it makes reservation of seats for Scheduled Castes and Scheduled Tribes to provide them adequate representation.

(xii) Emergency Provisions

The Constitution vests extraordinary powers in the President during emergencies arising out of **armed rebellion** or **external aggression**; emergency due to the **breakdown of constitutional machinery** in the state; and **financial emergency** when the credit of the country is threatened. In fact, during emergency the federal Constitution can virtually be converted into a unitary Constitution.

(xiii) Single Citizenship

It provides single citizenship. All persons residing in different parts of the country are treated as Indian citizens and are entitled to the same rights of citizenship. There is no separate citizenship of states.

(xiv) Bicameral Legislature

It provides a bicameral legislature at the Centre consisting of the Lok Sabha and the Rajya Sabha. The former contains representative of the people, while the latter contains representatives of the states.

(xv) Special Provision of Minorities

The Consitution makes special provision for minorities, Scheduled Castes, Scheduled Tribes, etc. It not only reserves seats for them in the Parliament and State legislatures, but also grants them certain special rights and privileges.

(xvi) Panchayati Raj

The Constitution provides constitutional basis to Panchayati Raj institutions as well as urban local bodies. This was achieved through the **seventy-third** and **seventy-fourth amendments** to the Constitution carried out in December 1992.

(xvii) Synthesis of Parliamentary Sovereignty and Judicial Supremacy:

- The doctrine of Sovereignty of Parliament is associated with the British Parliament while the principle of judicial supremacy with that of the American Supreme Court.

- The American Constitution provides for 'due process of law' against that of 'procedure established by law' contained in the Indian Constitution. The Supreme Court through its power of judicial review can declare the laws passed by the Parliament as unconstitutional. On the other hand, the Parliament can amend major portions of the Constitution.

(xviii) Basic Structure Doctrine.

Certain features of the Constitution are beyond the amending powers of the Parliament. All laws and constitutional amendments which transgress the basic structure are liable to be struck down. Some of the major features of the basic structure include; supremacy of the Constitution, republican form of government, secularism, federal character, sovereignty of the country, parliamentary democracy, fundamental rights, directive **principles etc.** *In Kesavananda Bharati Vs State of Kerala case 1973, Supreme Court propounded the Doctrine of Basic Structure of the Constitution.*

Parts of Constitution

Parts	Subject Matter	Articles Covered
I	The Union and its territory	1 to 4
II	Citizenship	5 to 11
III	Fundamental Rights	12 to 35
IV	Directive Principles of State Policy	36 to 51
IV-A	Fundamental Duties	51-A
V	The Union Government	52 to 151

Schedules in Constitution of India

Numbers	Subject Matter	Articles Covered
First Schedule	1. Names of the States and their territorial jurisdiction 2. Names of the Union Territories and their extent.	1 and 4
Second Schedule	Provisions relating to the emoluments, allowances, privileges and so on :	59, 65, 75, 97, 125, 148, 158, 164, 186 & 221
	1. The President of India 2. The Governors of States 3. The Speaker and the Deputy Speaker of the Lok Sabha 4. The Chairman and the Deputy Chairman of the Rajya Sabha 5. The Speaker and the Deputy Speaker of the Legislative Assembly in the states 6. The Chairman and the Deputy Chairman of the Legislative Council in the states 7. The Judges of the Supreme Court 8. The Judges of the High Courts 9. The Comptroller and Auditor-General of India	
Third Schedule	Forms of Oaths or Affirmations for:	75, 84, 99, 124, 146, 173, 188 and 219
	1. The Union ministers	
	2. The candidates for election to the Parliament	
	3. The members of Parliament	
	4. The judges of the Supreme Court	
	5. The comptroller and Auditor-General of India	
	6. The state ministers	
	7. The candidates for election to the state legislature	
	8. The members of the state legislature	
	9. The judges of the High Courts	
Fourth Schedule	Allocation of seats in the Rajya Sabha to the states and the union territories	4 and 80
Fifth Schedule	Provisions relating to the administration and control of scheduled areas and scheduled tribes	244
Sixth Schedule	Provisions relating to the administration of tribal areas in the states of Assam, Meghalaya, Tripura and Mizoram.	244 and 275
Seventh Schedule	Division of powers between the Union and the States in terms of List I (Union List), List II (State List) and List III (Concurrent List). Presently, the Union List Contains 100 subjects (originally 97), the state list contains 61 subjects (originally 66) and the concurrent list contains 52 subjects (originally 47).	246
Eighth Schedule	Languages recognized by the Constitution. Originally, it had 14 languages but presently there are 22 languages. They are: Assamese, Bengali, Bodo, Dogri (Dongri), Gujarati, Hindi, Kannada, Kashmiri, Konkani, Mathili (Maithili), Malayalam, Manipuri, Marathi, Nepali, Oriya, Punjabi, Sanskrit, Santhali, Sindhi, Tamil, Telugu and Urdu. Sindhi was added by the 21st Amendment Act of 1967; Konkani, Manipuri and Nepali were added by the 71st Amendment Act of 1992; and Bodo, Dongri, Maithili and Santhali were added by the 92nd Amendment Act of 2003.	344 and 351
Ninth Schedule	Acts and Regulations (originally 13 but presently 282)[19] of the state legislatures dealing with land reforms and abolition of the Zamindari system and of the Parliament dealing with other matters. This schedule was added by the 1st Amendment (1951) to protect the laws included in it from judicial scrutiny on the ground of violation of fundamental rights. However, in 2007, the Supreme Court ruled that the laws included in this schedule after April 24, 1973, are now open to judicial review.	31-B

Tenth Schedule	Provisions relating to disqualification of the members of Parliament and State Legislatures on the ground of defection. This schedule was added by the 52nd Amendment Act of 1985, also known as Anti-defection Law.	102 and 191
Eleventh Schedule	Specifies the powers, authority and responsibilities of Panchayats. It has 29 matters. This schedule was added by the 73rd Amendment Act of 1992.	243-G
Twelfth Schedule	Specifies the powers, authority and responsibilities of Municipalities. It has 18 matters. This schedule was added by the 74th Amendment Act of 1992.	243-W

PARTS OF CONSTITUTION

Preamble

The term Preamble refers to the introduction or preface to the Constitution.

It provides a key to the understanding and interpretation of the Constitution, it has, therefore, been described as the soul of the Constitution. In cases of doubt the Supreme Court has referred to the Preamble to elucidate vague aspects of the Constitution.

The Constitution of India is preceded by a Preamble which

(i)   indicates the source from which it derives authority; and

(ii)   state the objective which the constitution seeks to achieve.

It has been amended by the 42nd Amendment Act 1976 which added 3 new words– Socialist, Secular & Integrity.

'We, the people of India having solemnly resolved to constitute India into a *sovereign, socialist, secular democratic republic* and to secure to all its citizens:

JUSTICE social, economic and political;

LIBERTY of thought, expression, belief, faith and worship;

EQUALITY of status and of opportunity and to promote among them all ;

FRATERNITY assuring the dignity of the individual and the unity and integrity of the nation.

In our Constituent Assembly this twenty-sixth day of November, *1949* we do hereby *adopt, enact* and *give* to ourselves this Constitution.

- Supreme Court has pronounced that Preamble is an integral part of the Constitution. The importance and utility of the Preamble has been highlighted in several decision of Supreme Court.

- The word *sovereign* means that India is both internally as well as externally free and is not dependent upon any outside authority.

- The term '*socialist*' in the Preamble refers to elimination of inequality in income and status and standards of living.

- *Secularism* implies that the state is only concerned with relations between various citizens and is not concerned with relations of man with God. Further, it means that the state has no religion of its own.

- The term *Democratic* implies that the government draws its authority from the people. The rulers are elected by the people and are accountable to them.

- The word *republic* implies that the head of the state in India shall be an elected person and shall hold office for a fixed term. The President of India is the *chief executive* head of India.

Justice

The preamble speaks of *social, economic,* and *political* justice. *Social justice* implies that discrimination on the basis of caste, race, sex or religion should cease.

Economic justice implies that the gap between the rich and the poor is bridged, and that exploitation ceases.

Political justice implies that all citizens should have equal opportunity to participate in the political system.

Liberty

Derived from latin word 'liber' means freedom. Certain minimal rights must be enjoyed by every person in a community for a free and civilised existence.

Equality

All citizens are equal before law and enjoy equal protection of the laws of the land.

Fraternity

Fraternity means a sense of *brotherhood*. Fraternity is also sought to be promoted by ensuring equal rights to all. Fraternity is not possible unless the dignity of each individual is presented and respected.

Significance of the Preamble

- The Preamble embodies the basic philosophy and fundamental values – Political, Moral and Religious on which the Constitution is based.

Views on Preamble

- "The Preamble to our Constitution expresses what we had thought or dreamt so long". – Sir Alladi Krishnaswami Iyer

- "Preamble is the 'horoscope of our Sovereign democratic republic". – K. M. Munshi

- "Preamble is key to the constitution. It is the soul of the Constitution". – Pandit Thakur das Bhargava
- "Preamble is the 'Key-note' to the Constitution. – Sir Ernest Barker

Preamble as part of the Constitution

- The current opinion held by the Supreme Court that the Preamble is a part of the Constitution.
- However it should be noted that :
1. The Preamble is neither a source of power to legislature nor a prohibition upon the powers of legislature.
2. It is non-justifiable, that is, its provisions are not enforceable in courts of law.

Whether Preamble can be amended?

- The Supreme Court held that the Preamble is a part of the Constitution.
- Preamble can be amended, subject to the condition that no amendment is done to the 'basic features'.
- The Preamble has been amended only once so far in 1976, by the 42nd Constitution Amendment Act, which has added three new words – Socialist, Secular and Integrity to the Preamble.

The Union and its Territory

Part 1 of the Constitution comprises four Articles concerned with the territory of India. **Article 1** stipulates that *India, that is Bharat*, shall be a Union of States. The states and territories of India are to be specified in the *First Schedule*. It is to be noted that the expression, 'Union of India', is not synonymous with 'the territory of India'; the 'Union' includes only the States which are members of the federal system and share a distribution of powers with the Union while the 'territory of India' includes the entire area over which the sovereignty of India extends.

The makers of the Indian Constitution, gave the Union Parliament the power to reorganise the States by a simple procedure. In the original Constitution there were four categories of States and Territories. But since the Seventh Amendment Act, 1956, all the States (except for Jammu and Kashmir) belong to one class and all the constitutional provisions relating to States apply to all of them in the same manner. As for the administration of the certain Scheduled Areas and Tribal Areas within the States, the provisions are specially listed in the Fifth and Sixth Schedules. The Union Territories are centrally administered according to provisions contained in Part VII of the Constitution. They are governed by the President through an administrator appointed by him. At present, there are 29 states & 7 Union Territories.

Reorganisation of States

Article 2 empowers Parliament to admit into the Union, or establish, new States on such terms and conditions as it thinks fit. By **Article 3**, Parliament has the power to form a new State from the territory of any State or by uniting two or more States, increase or decrease the area of any State, or alter the boundaries or the name of any State. The only conditions laid down for making such a law is

(i) such a Bill must be introduced only on the recommendation of the President, and

(ii) Before recommending the Bill, the President has to refer it to the concerned State Legislature which would express its views within a specified period. The President is not, however, bound by the views of the State Legislature. However, **in the case of Jammu and Kashmir, the consent of the State Legislature is required before a Bill on such alterations is introduced in Parliament. A simple majority and ordinary legislative procedure is enough for Parliament to form new States or alter existing State boundaries.** Thus the will of the Union Executive and Legislature prevails in matters of altering or redistributing the territories of the units of the federation.

The Constitution authorises the Parliament to form new States or alters the areas, boundaries or names of the existing states without their consent.

- Therefore the territorial integrity or continued existence of any state is not guaranted by the Costitution.
- This is why India is described as "an indestructible union of destructible states".

Article-4 declares that laws made for admission or establishment of new states under (Article-2) and formation of new states and alteration of areas, boundaries or name of existing states (under Article-3) are not to be considered as amendments of the Constitution under Art.-368.

- Therefore such a law can be passed by a simple majority and by the ordinary legislative process.

Note:

1. Indian territory can be ceded to a foreign state only by amending the Costitution under Article-368.
2. The Settlement of a boundary dispute between India and another country does not require a costitutional amendment.

Reorganisation of States

The Government appointed a commission under S.K. Dhar to examine the feasibility of reorganisation of States on a linguistic basis. The **S.K. Dhar Commission** preferred reorganisation for administrative convenience rather than on a linguistic basis.

The Dhar Commission's report created much resentment and led to the appointment of another Linguistic Provinces Committee in **December 1948** to examine the **Linguistic** basis of States reorganisation. This Committee consisted of J.L. Nehru, Vallabhbai Patel and Pattabhi Sitaramayya and hence was popularly known as **JVP Committee.**

In October 1953, the Government of India created the first linquistic state, known as Andhra state by separating the Telugu Speaking areas from the Madras State.

- The creation of Andhra state intensified the demand from other regions for creation of State on linquistic basis.

This compelled the Govt. of India to appoint a 3 member States Reorganization Commission in **1953** to look into the question of redrawing of the boundaries of States. This **commission was chaired by Fazal Ali.**

The States Re-organisation Commision (SRC) submitted its report in September 1955 and broadly accepted language as the basis of re-organisation of states. But the SRC rejected the theory of 'one-language-one state'.

- The Commission suggested the abolition of the four-fold classification of states under the original Constitution and creation of 16 states and 3 centrally administered territories.

- By the States Re-organisation Act (1956) and the 7th Constitutional Amendment Act (1956), the distinction between Part-A and Part-B states was done away with and Part-C states were abolished.

- As a result, 14 States and 6 Union Territories were created on November 1, 1956.

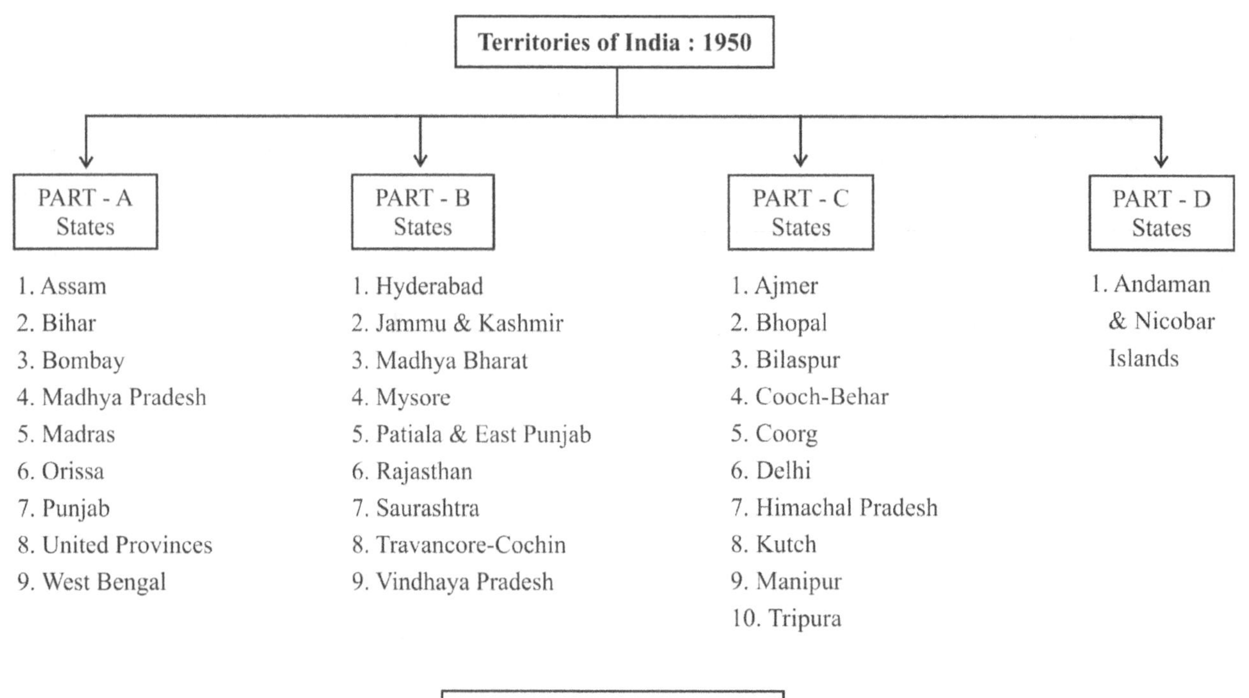

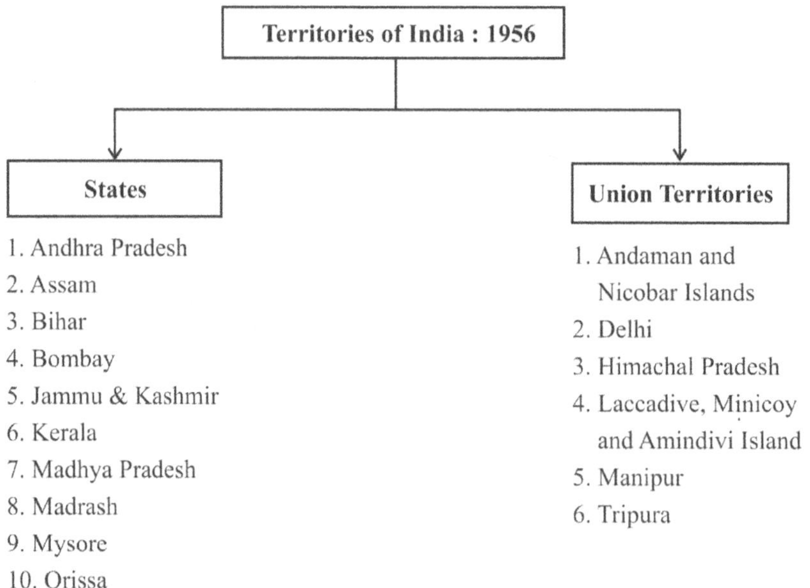

Territory of India 2018

	(STATES)		
1.	Andhra Pradesh	16.	Manipur
2.	Arunachal Pradesh	17.	Meghalaya
3.	Asom	18.	Mizoram
4.	Bihar	19.	Negaland
5.	Chhattisgarh	20.	Odisha
6.	Goa	21.	Punjab
7.	Gujarat	22.	Rajasthan
8.	Haryana	23.	Sikkim
9.	Himachal Pradesh	24.	Tamil Nadu
10.	Jammu and Kashmir	25.	Telangana
11.	Jharkhand	26.	Tripura
12.	Karnataka	27.	Uttarakhand
13.	Kerala	28.	Uttar Pradesh
14.	Madhya Pradesh	29.	West Bengal
15.	Maharashtra		

Union Territories

1. Andaman & Nicobar Islands
2. Chandigarh
3. Dadra and Nagar Haveli
4. Daman and Diu
5. Delhi (National Capital Territory)
6. Lakshadweep
7. Puducherry

Formation of states after 1950s

Andhra Pradesh	Formed by the State of Andhra Pradesh Act, 1953 by carving out some areas from the State of Madras.
Kerala	Formed by the State Reorganisation Act, 1956. It comprised Travancore and Cochin areas.
Karnataka	Formed from the princely state of Mysore by the state Reorganisation Act, 1956, It was renamed Karnataka is 1973 from Mysore.
Gujarat and Maharashtra	The State of Bombay was divided into two states namely, Maharashtra and Gujarat by the Bombay (Reorganisation) Act, 1960.
Nagaland	State of Nagaland Act, 1962 created the State of Nagaland, which was carved out of Assam (now Asom).
Haryana	It was carved out from the State of Punjab by the Punjab (Reorganisation) Act, 1966.
Himachal Pradesh	State of Himachal Pradesh Act, 1970 elevated the Union Territory of Himachal Pradesh to the status of state.

Meghalaya	First carved out as a sub-state within the State of Assam by 23rd Constitutional Amendment, 1969. Later, in 1971, it received the status of full-fledged State by the North-Eastern Areas (Reorganisation) Act, 1971.
Manipur and Tripura	Both these states were elevated from the status of Union Territories by the North-Eastern Areas (Reorganisation) Act, 1971.
Sikkim	Sikkim was first made an associate state by the 35th Constitutional Amendment Act, 1974. 36th Amendment Act, 1975, uplifted its status to a full state in 1975. From 1947 to 1974, Sikkim was a **protectorate** of India, with India being responsible for its defence, external affairs and communications.
Mizoram	It was given the status of a full state by the State of Mizoram Act, 1986.
Arunachal Pradesh	It received the status of a full state by the State of Arunachal Pradesh Act, 1986.
Goa	It was separated from the Union Territory of Goa, Daman and Diu and was made a full-fledged state by the Goa, Daman and Diu Reorganisation Act, , 1987. But, Daman and Diu remained as Union Territory till date.
Chhattisgarh	Created, as 26th State of India, by dividing Madhya Pradesh on 1st November, 2000.
Uttarakhand	It was formed by dividing Uttar Pradesh on 9th November, 2000. In January 2007, the name of the state was officially changed from **Uttaranchal** to **Uttarakhand**. It is 27th state of the Union of India.
Jharkhand	Created as 28th State, in 2000, by dividing Bihar on 15th November, 2000.
Telangana	Created as 29th State on 2nd June, 2014. It was separated from Andhra Pradesh with Hyderabad as the capital of both state for a period of 10 years. Telangana was created on the recommendation of **Shri Krishna Committee Report.**

Citizenship

Meaning of Citizenship

The population of a state is divided into two classes – Citizens and aliens. While citizens enjoy full civil and political rights, aliens do not enjoy all of them. Citizens are members of the political community to which they belong.

Citizens are full members of the Indian state and owe allegiance to it. They enjoy all civil and political rights.

Part II of Constitution (Articles 5-11) contains provisions relating to citizenship of India. In brief:

Article 5 - citizenship at the commencement of the Constitution.

Article 6 - rights of citizenship of certain persons who have migrated to India from Pakistan.

Article 7 - rights of citizenship of certain migrants to Pakistan;

Article 8 - right of citizenship of certain persons of India origin residing outside India.

Article 9 - Persons voluntarily acquiring citizenship of a foreign state not be citizens.

Article 10 - continuance of the rights of citizenship.

Article 11 - parliament to regulate the right of citizenship by law.

- The Constitution of India provides for **single citizenship**. All persons residing in different parts of the country enjoy Indian citizenship (*Article 5*). There is no separate citizenship of states. According to the Constitution, the following three categories of persons are entitled to citizenship:
  1. Person domiciled in India,
  2. Refugees who migrated to India from Pakistan,
  3. Indians living in other countries.

- *Domiciled* persons include those with permanent homes in India, persons born in India, persons either of whose parents was born in Indian territory, and persons ordinarily residing in India for at least five years before the commencement of the Constitution, provided they had not voluntarily acquired the citizenship of some foreign country.

Acquisition and Termination of Citizenship

Rules regarding acquisition and termination of Indian citizenship have been laid down in the *Citizenship Act of 1955*. A person can acquire citizenship of India in five ways.

1. Citizenship by Birth

A person born in India on or after January 1950 is treated as citizen of India by birth.

2. Citizenship by Descent

A person who was residing outside India on or after 26 January 1950 is treated as a citizen of India by descent if his father was citizen of India at the time of his birth.

3. Citizenship by Registration

The following categories of persons can be registered as citizens of India on application by the prescribed authority:

(a) Persons of Indian origin who are ordinarily resident in India for five years before filing of application for registration.

(b) Persons of Indian origin who are ordinarily resident in of any country or place outside India.

(c) Women who are married to citizens of India.

(d) Minor' children of persons who are citizens of India.

(e) Persons of full age and capacity who are citizens of Commonwealth countries or the Republic of Ireland.

4. Citizenship by Naturalisation

A person can acquire citizenship of India through naturalisation if he (a) belongs to a country where the citizens of India are allowed to become subjects or citizens of that country by naturalisation;

(b) renounces the citizenship of his country and intimates the renunciation to the government of India;

(c) has been residing in India or serving the government for 12 months before the date of making application for naturalisation;

(d) possesses a good character;

(e) possesses workable knowledge of an Indian language;

(f) intends to reside in India or to serve under the Government of India after naturalisation. However, the Government of India can waive any or all of the above conditions in case of a person who has rendered distinguished service in the cause of philosophy, science, art, literature, world peace and the like.

5. By Incorporation of Territory

If any new territory is added to India, the Government of India can specify the persons of the territory who shall be citizens of India by reasons of their connection with that territory.

Citizenship can be terminated in three ways

(a) A citizen may voluntarily renounce his citizenship by making necessary declaration to this effect in the prescribed form. Usually citizenship is renounced by a citizen who wants to become the national to another country.

(b) The citizenship can be terminated if a person voluntarily acquires the citizenship of any other country by naturalisation, registration or otherwise.

(c) The Central Government can deprive a naturalised citizen of his citizenship, if it is satisfied that the citizenship was acquired by *fraud*, *false* representation or *concealment* of material facts; or if the person shows disloyalty towards the Indian Constitution or indulges in trade with enemy countries during war; or if the person has been sentenced to imprisonment for a period of two years or more within five years of his registration of naturalisation or if he has been continuously residing out of India for more than seven years.

Amendment of Citizenship Act

In *1986, the Citizenship Act* was amended and acquisition of citizenship by persons coming to India as refugees from Bangladesh, Sri Lanka and other countries was made difficult. It provided that persons born in India

(a) on or after January 26, 1950 but prior to 26 November 1986, (b) on or after the commencement of the Amending Act, 1986, shall be citizens of India by right only if either of their parents is a citizen of India at the time of his birth. It increased the period for acquisition of citizenship through registration from six months to five years.

In *December 2003 the Citizenship Act 1955* was amended to facilitate the re-acquisition of the Indian citizenship by persons of full age who are children of Indian citizens and former Indian citizens. However, the Act made the acquisition of Indian citizenship and naturalisation more stringent to prevent illegal migrants from becoming eligible for Indian citizenship.

Commonwealth Citizenship

Every person who is a citizen of a Commonwealth country, by virtue of that citizenship enjoys the status of Commonwealth citizenship in India. The Indian Citizenship Act 1955 empowers the Central Government to make provisions on the basis of reciprocity for the enforcement of all or any of the rights of a citizen of India on the citizens of U.K. Australia, Canada, Ceylon (Sri Lanka), New Zealand, Pakistan, and other Commonwealth countries.

Single Citizenship

Another notable feature of the Indian citizenship is that the Constitution recognises only one citizenship, viz. that of India. There is no separate state citizenship as in other federal countries. This implies that every citizen has same rights, privileges and immunities, no matter in which state he resides.

Dual Citizenship for People of India Origin (PIOs)

- In *December 2003* a new law was passed which permits the people of Indian origin residing in 16 countries, viz. Australia, Canada, Finland, France, Greece, Ireland, Israel, Italy the Netherlands, New Zealand, Portugal, Cyprus, Sweden, Switzerland, UK and United States, to have dual citizenship status. This will enable them to participate in the economic activities and acquire real estate.
- As of *January, 2006*, the Indian government has introduced the *"Overseas Citizenship of India" (OCI)* so as to allow a limited form of dual citizenship. A citizenship (Amendment) ordinance 2005, was promulgated in June 2005 and an Act was passed in August 2005. The amended Act enables the central government to register, as an Overseas *Citizen* of India (OCI), any person of full age and capacity.

- Who is a citizen of another country now, but was a citizen of India at the time of, or at any time after the commencement of the Constitution of India on 26th January 1950.
- Who is a citizen of another country, but was eligible to become a citizen of India at the time of common cement of the Constitution.
- Who is a citizen of another country, but belonged to a territory that became a part of India after the 15th of August 1947.
- Who is child or a grand child of such a citizen; or a minor child of a person mentioned in all the above. No person who is or has been citizen of Pakistan or Bangladesh shall be eligible to be registered as an OCI.

Pravasi Bharatiya Divas (PBD)

It is celebrated on 9th January every year to mark the contribution of Overseas Indian Community in the development of India. 9th January, was chosen as the day to celebrate this occasion, since **it was on this day in 1915 that Mahatma Gandhi, returned to India from South Africa**.

PBD conventions are being held every year, since 2003. These conventions provide a platform to the overseas Indian community to engage with the government and people of the land of their ancestors for mutual beneficial activities.

The decision to celebrate the Pravasi Bharatiya Divas was taken in accordance with recommendations of the High Level Committee (HLC) on the Indian Diaspora set-up by Government of India under the Chairmanship of **Dr. LM Singhvi**.

The 14th edition of Pravasi Bhartiya Divas held in Bengaluru with the theme "Redefining Engagement with the Indian Diaspora".

- The 15th Pravasi Bhartiya Divas will be held in the holy city of Varanasi from January 21 - January 23, 2019. Its theme will be "Role of Indian Diaspora in building a new India".

Exercise -1

1. Constituent Assembly was framed on the recommendation of:
   (a) Indian Independence Act
   (b) Government of India Act, 1935
   (c) Cabinet Mission Plan - 1946
   (d) Queen's Proclamation

2. ______________ headed the Drafting Committee of the Constituent assembly?
   (a) Sachchidanand Sinha
   (b) B.N. Rao
   (c) Jawaharlal Nehru
   (d) B.R. Ambedkar

3. ______ is borrowed from the Weimar Constitution of Germany by the India Constitution
   (a) A federation with a strong centre
   (b) System of presidential elections
   (c) Directive Principles of State Policy.
   (d) Suspension of fundamental rights during Emergency

4. Preamble borrows the ideals of "liberty, equality and fraternity from:
   (a) Russian Revolution (b) Irish Revolution
   (c) French Revolution (d) American Constitution

5. Preamble enshrines ideals spelt out in:
   (a) Speech by Nehru on the banks of Ravi calling for Purna Swaraj.
   (b) Nehru Report
   (c) Resolution adopted at the Karachi session of the Congress Party
   (d) Objectives Resolution of the Constituent Assembly

6. States Reorganisation Act created ___ states and ___ Union Territories.
   (a) 14; 7   (b) 14; 6
   (c) 15; 7   (d) 15; 6

7. The Constitution bestows __ citizenship on Indian citizens.
   (a) Single   (b) dual
   (c) Federal   (d) Three

8. Pravasi Bharatiya Diwas coincides with:
   (a) Gandhiji's becoming a lawyer in South Africa
   (b) Gandhiji's return from South Africa
   (c) Beginning of civil disobedience movement
   (d) India's proclamation as a republic

9. Which portfolio was held by Dr. Rajendra Prasad in the Interim Government formed in the year 1946?
   (a) Defence
   (b) External Affairs and Commonwealth Relations
   (c) Food and Agriculture
   (d) None

10. Which of the following is correctly matched?
    (a) 1909 Act   -   Principle of election
    (b) 1919 Act   -   Provincial autonomy
    (c) 1935 Act   -   Dyarchy in states
    (d) 1947 Act   -   Responsible government

11. Statutory recognition to the portfolio system was accorded by:
    (a) Indian Councils Act of 1892
    (b) Indian Councils Act of 1871
    (c) Indian Councils Act of 1861
    (d) Indian Councils Act of 1882

12. Which act provided for direct control of Indian affairs by the British Government?
    (a) Charter Act of 1858
    (b) Regulating Act of 1773
    (c) Pitts India Act of 1784
    (d) Charter Act of 1833

13. Which one of the following pairs is correctly matched?
    (a) 1919 Act   -   Dyarchy at the Centre
    (b) 1861 Act   -   Portfolio system
    (c) 1935 Act   -   Bicameralism
    (d) 1853 Act   -   Governor-General of India

14. The Constituent Assembly, which framed the Indian Constitution, was set up in
    (a) 1945   (b) 1946
    (c) 1947   (d) 1949

15. Which one of the following pairs is not correctly matched?
    (a) States Reorganization : Andhra Pradesh Act
    (b) Treaty of Yandabu : Assam
    (c) State of Bilaspur : Himachal Pradesh
    (d) Year 1966 : Gujarat becomes a state

16. Constitutional government stand for
    (a) limited government
    (b) a government limited by the desires and capacities of those who exercise power.
    (c) a government run according to general laws known to the people
    (d) a government run by people's representatives.

17. Which items is wrongly matched?
    (a) December 9, 1947   Constituent Assembly's First meeting
    (b) November 26, 1949   The people of India adopted, enacted and gave to themselves the Constitution
    (c) January 24, 1950   The Constitution was signed by the members of the Constituent Assembly
    (d) January 26, 1950   the date of commencement of the Constitution

18. Which features and source are WRONGLY matched?
    (a) Judicial review   -   British practice
    (b) Concurrent List   -   Australian Constitution
    (c) Directive Principles   -   Irish Constitution
    (d) Fundamental Rights   -   US Constitution

19. Which one among the following has the power to regulate the right of citizenship in India?
    (a) The Union Cabinet   (b) The Parliament
    (c) The Supreme Court   (d) The Law Commission

20. What is extradition?
    (a) Delivering a national of another country for the trial of offences
    (b) To block the trade of other countries with a particular country
    (c) Forcing a person to leave the country of which he is a citizen
    (d) To force foreign national to leave the country

21. "Referendum" has an integral relationship with
    (a) Indirect democracy
    (b) Limited monarchy
    (c) Direct democracy
    (d) People's courts
22. Which of the following statements best describe in systems of liberal democracy?
    (a) Liberal democratic political systems only occur in highly industrialised societies.
    (b) The same political party holds power continuously in liberal democratic regimes.
    (c) Liberal democratic governments prevent their citizens from travelling abroad.
    (d) Liberal democratic governments protect basic civil liberties.
23. The mention of the word 'justice' in the preamble to the constitution of India expresses
    (a) social, political and religious justice
    (b) social, economic and cultural justice
    (c) social, economic and political justice
    (d) economic and political justice
24. In which case the Supreme Court evolved the concept of 'Basic Structure of Constitution'?
    (a) Golak Nath case
    (b) Shankari Prasad case
    (c) Kishana Nanda Bharti case
    (d) Minerva Mills case
25. By which amendment of the constitution, the Word 'Socialist' was incorporated in the preamble of the constitution?
    (a) 42nd Amendment   (b) 44th Amendment
    (c) 25th Amendment   (d) 24th Amendment
26. Which one of the following rights has been described by Dr. Ambedkar as 'The heart and soul of the constitution'?
    (a) Right of Equality
    (b) Right to freedom
    (c) Right to property
    (d) Right to Constitutional Remedies
27. Which schedule of Indian Constitution is related to Panchayti Raj?
    (a) II Schedule   (b) VIII Schedule
    (c) X Schedule   (d) XI Schedule
28. Which term is not used in the preamble of the Indian constitution?
    (a) Republic   (b) Integrity
    (c) Federal   (d) Socialist
29. The source of the basic structure theory of the constitution of India is
    (a) the constitution
    (b) opinion of jurists
    (c) Judicial interpretation
    (d) parliamentary statutes
30. The provision of the sixth schedule shall not apply in which one of the following states?
    (a) Meghalaya   (b) Tripura
    (c) Mizoram   (d) Goa
31. Which of the states of Indian federation has a separate constitution?
    (a) Goa
    (b) Tamil Nadu
    (c) Jammu & Kashmir
    (d) Himachal Pradesh

32. Which one of the following is not a part of the 'basic structure' of the Indian constitution?
    (a) Rule of law
    (b) Secularism
    (c) Republican form of government
    (d) Parliamentary form of government
33. The philosophical foundation of the Indian constitution is
    (a) Directive principle of state policy
    (b) Fundamental rights
    (c) Federal Structure
    (d) Preamble
34. Which article of Indian constitution declares Hindi in Devanagri Script as an official language of India?
    (a) Article 343   (b) Article 348
    (c) Article 154   (d) Article 156
35. Which of the following gave the idea of constituent Assembly for India?
    (a) Simon Commission
    (b) Rajaji Formula
    (c) Cabinet Mission Plan
    (d) Wavell Plan
36. Who amongst the following was not a member of the drafting committee of the constitution?
    (a) Mohammod Sadullah
    (b) K.M. Munshi
    (c) A.K. Ayyar
    (d) J.L. Nehru
37. The tenth schedule of Indian constitution deals with
    (a) Anti-defection Legislation
    (b) Panchayti Raj
    (c) Land Reforms
    (d) Distribution of powers between the union and states
38. The number of official languages recognized under 8th schedule of the Indian Constitution is
    (a) Sixteen   (b) Seventeen
    (c) Twenty   (d) Twenty Two
39. The feature of Indian constitution borrowed from South African constitution is:
    (a) Procedure established by law
    (b) Procedure for amendment of constitution and election of Rajya Sabha members
    (c) Method of election of President
    (d) Joint Sitting of the Parliament
40. The words justice in the form of social, economic and political justice present in the Preamble has been taken from
    (a) American Revolution (b) French Revolution
    (c) Russian Revolution   (d) None of the above
41. The terms not introduced in the Preamble through the 42nd amendment are:
    (a) Socialist   (b) Secular
    (c) Integrity   (d) None of the above
42. Which case determined that the Preamble is a part of the constitution?
    (a) Berubari Union case
    (b) Kesavananda Bharati case
    (c) Golaknath case
    (d) Minerva Mills case

43. (a) Originally the constitution had 14 languages in the 8th schedule.
    (b) Currently there are 22 languages with the last amendment being the 92nd amendment.
    (c) Both (a) & (b)
    (d) None of the above
44. Which statements are correct?
    (a) Article 2 of the constitution gives the right to the government to create new states into the Union of India which are not part of India already.
    (b) Article 3 gives the power to the government to change the boundaries of the state within India.
    (c) Both (a) & (b)
    (d) None of the above
45. The parliament can make any law for the whole or any part of India for implementing international treaties?
    (a) with the consent of all the states
    (b) with the consent of majority of states
    (c) with the consent of state concerned
    (d) without the consent of any state.
46. Under which one of the following constitution amendment act, four languages were added to the eighth schedule of the constitution of India?
    (a) 90th Amendment Act
    (b) 91st Amendment Act
    (c) 92nd Amendment Act
    (d) 93rd Amendment Act
47. Who among the following was the advisor of the Drafting Committee of the Constituent Assembly?
    (a) B. Shiva Rao   (b) Dr. B.R. Ambedkar
    (c) Sachidananda Sinha (d) B.N. Rao
48. The idea of including the Emergency provisions in the Constitution of India has been borrowed from the
    (a) Constitution of Canada
    (b) Weimar Constitution of Germany
    (c) Constitution of Ireland
    (d) Constitution of the USA
49. Which one of the following Schedules of the Constitution of India includes the disqualification of a Legislator on grounds of defection?
    (a) 8th Schedule   (b) 7th Schedule
    (c) Schedule   (d) 10th Schedule
50. Which schedule of the Constitution of India contains the three lists that divide powers between the Union and the sates?
    (a) Fifth   (b) Sixth
    (c) Seventh   (d) Eigth
51. In which part of the Constitution, details of citizenship are mentioned?
    (a) I   (b) II
    (c) III   (d) IV
52. Who among the following was the first Law Minister of India?
    (a) Jawaharlal Nehru
    (b) Maulana Abdul Kalam Azad
    (c) Dr BR Ambedkar
    (d) T Krishnamachari
53. Who among the following was the Finance Minister of India in the Interim Government during 1946-1947?
    (a) R K Shanmukham Chetty
    (b) John Mathai
    (c) Liaquat Ali Khan
    (d) Chintamanrao Deshmukh

54. Which one of the following rights conferred by the Constitution of India is also available to non-citizens?
    (a) Freedom of speech, assembly and form association
    (b) Freedom to move, reside and settle in any part of the territory of India
    (c) Freedom to acquire property or to carry on any occupation, trade or business
    (d) Right to constitutional remedies
55. Which one among the following statements is not correct? The word 'socialist' in the Preamble of the Constitution of India read with
    (a) Article 39 (d), would enable the court to uphold the constitutionality of nationalisation laws
    (b) Article 14, would enable the court to strike down a-statute which failed to achieve the socialist goal to the fullest extent
    (c) Article 25, would enable the court to ensure freedom guaranteed under that Article
    (d) Article 23, would enable the court to reduce inequality in income and status
56. The Constitution of India is republican because it
    (a) provides for an elected Parliament
    (b) provides for adult franchise
    (c) contains a bill of rights
    (d) has no hereditary elements
57. The Preamble is useful in constitutional interpretation because it
    (a) uses value loaded words
    (b) contains the real objective and philosophy of the constitution makers
    (c) is a source of power and limitation
    (d) gives an exhaustive list of basic features of the Constitution
58. Which one among the following was **not** a proposal of the Cabinet Mission, 1946?
    (a) The Constituent Assembly was to be constituted on the democratic principle of population strength
    (b) Provision for an Indian Union of Provinces and States
    (c) All the members of the Constituent Assembly were to be indians
    (d) British Government was to supervise the affairs of the Constituent Assembly
59. 'The Draft Constitution as framed only provides a machinery for the government of the country. It is not a contrivance to install any particular party in power as has been done in some countries. Who should be in power is left to be determined by the people, as it must be, if the system is to satisfy the test of democracy'.
    The above passage from Constituent Assembly debates is attributed to
    (a) Pandit Jawaharlal Nehru
    (b) Dr B R Ambedkar
    (c) Maulana Abdul Kalam Azad
    (d) Acharya J B Kriplani
60. Which among the following features of a federal system is **not** found in the Indian Political System?
    (a) Dual citizenship
    (b) Distribution of powers between the Federal and the State Governments
    (c) Supremacy of the Constitution
    (d) Authority of the Courts to interpret the Constitution

61. The Sixth Schedule of the Indian Constitution contains provisions for the administration of Tribal areas. Which of the following States is not covered under this Schedule?
 (a) Assam (b) Manipur
 (c) Meghalaya (d) Tripura

62. In the following quotation,
 "WE THE PEOPLE OF INDIA, having solemnly resolved to constitute India into a Sovereign Socialist Secular Democratic Republic and to secure to all its citizens:
 JUSTICE, social, economic and political; LIBERTY of thought, expression, belief faith and worship;
 EQUALITY of status and of opportunity: and to promote among them all; FRATERNITY assuring the dignity of the individual and the unity and the integrity of the Nation.
 In our Constituent Assembly this 'X' do hereby adopt, enact and give to ourselves this Constitution.",
 'X' stands for:
 (a) twenty-sixth day of January, 1950
 (b) twenty-sixth day of November, 1949
 (c) twenty-sixth day of January, 1949
 (d) None of the above

63. Which one of the following schedules of the Constitution of India contains provisions regarding anti-defection laws?
 (a) Second Schedule (b) Fifth Schedule
 (c) Eighth Schedule (d) Tenth Schedule

64. The Constitution of India recognises:
 (a) only religious minorities
 (b) only linguistic minorities
 (c) religious and linguistic minorities
 (d) religious, linguistic and ethnic minorities

65. Which one of the following statements correctly describes the Fourth Schedule of the Constitution of India?
 (a) It lists the distribution of powers between the Union and the states
 (b) It contains the languages listed in the Constitution
 (c) It contains the languages listed in the Constitution
 (d) It allocates seats in the Council of States

66. If a new state of the Indian Union is to be created, which one of the following schedules of the Constitution must be amended?
 (a) First (b) Second
 (c) Third (d) Fifth

67. The Ninth Schedule to the Indian Constitution was added by:
 (a) First Amendment
 (b) Eighth Amendment
 (c) Ninth Amendment
 (d) Forty Second Amendment

68. Which one of the following schedules of the Indian Constitution lists the names of states and specifies their territories?
 (a) First (b) Second
 (c) Third (d) Fourth

69. Which one of the following statements correctly describes the Fourth Schedule of the Constitution of India?
 (a) It contains the scheme of the distribution of powers between the Union and the States
 (b) It contains the languages listed in the Constitution
 (c) It contains the provisions regarding the administration of tribal areas
 (d) It allocates seats in the Council of States

70. Which Schedule of the Constitution of India contains : Special provisions for the administration and control of Scheduled Areas in several States?
 (a) Third (b) Fifth
 (c) Seventh (d) Ninth

71. The distribution of powers between the Centre and the States in the Indian Constitution is based on the scheme provided in the
 (a) Morley-Minto Reforms, 1909
 (b) Montagu-Chelmsford Act, 1919
 (c) Government of India Act, 1935
 (d) Indian Independence Act, 1947

72. The provisions in Fifth Schedule and Sixth Schedule of the Constitution of India are made in order to
[IAS Prelims 2015]
 (a) protect the interests of Scheduled Tribes
 (b) determine the boundaries between States
 (c) determine the powers, authority and responsibilities of Panchayats
 (d) protect the interests of all the border States

73. The Montague-Chelmsford Proposals were related to
 (a) social reforms **[IAS Prelims 2016]**
 (b) educational reforms
 (c) reforms in police administration
 (d) constitutional reforms

74. Which one of the following is not a part of the Directive Principles of State Policy as enshrined in the Constitution of India? **[NDA-2018]**
 (a) Equal justice and free legal aid
 (b) Protection of monuments and places and objects of national importance.
 (c) Protection of personal law
 (d) Separation of Judiciary from Executive

75. The word socialist was inserted into the preamble to the constitution of India through which one of the following Amendment Acts? **[NDA-2018]**
 (a) 41st Amendment Act
 (b) 42nd Amendment Act
 (c) 43rd Amendment Act
 (d) 44th Amendment Act

76. Which one of the following objectives is not embodied in the Preamble to the Constitution of India?
[IAS Prelims 2017]
 (a) Liberty of thought (b) Economic liberty
 (c) Liberty of expression (d) Liberty of belief

77. The mind of the makers of the Constitution of India is reflected in which of the following? **[IAS Prelims 2017]**
 (a) The Preamble
 (b) The Fundamental Rights
 (c) The Directive Principles of State Policy
 (d) The Fundamental Duties

78. Which one of the following rights was described by Dr. B.R. Ambedkar as the heart and soul of the Constitution?
[IAS Prelims 2002]
 (a) Right to Freedom of Religion
 (b) Right to Property
 (c) Right to Equality
 (d) Right to Constitutional Remedies

Exercise -2

Statement Based MCQ

1. With reference to the constitution of India consider the following statements:
   1. Constitution gives us a moral identity.
   2. The Indian constitution was never subjected to a referendum.

   Which of the above given statement is/are correct.
   (a) 1 only
   (b) 2 only
   (c) Both 1 and 2 only
   (d) None of the above

2. Consider the following statements:
   1. Executive council of four members to assist the governor general of Bengal.
   2. Establishment of a supreme court at Calcutta.
   3. Establishment of dyarchy in provinces.

   Which of the above statements is/are among the provisions of Regulating Act of 1773:
   (a) 1 and 2 only
   (b) 2 and 3 only
   (c) 1 and 3 only
   (d) 1, 2, and 3 all

3. Which of the following statements is are true regarding Proportional Representation System of election:
   1. Voters exercise their preference for a party and not a candidate.
   2. More than one representative may be elected from one constituency
   (a) 1 only
   (b) 2 only
   (c) Both 1 and 2
   (d) None of the above

4. With reference to Government of India Act; 1858; consider the following statements:
   1. It abolished the East India Company.
   2. It ended the system of double government.
   3. It created a new office, secretary of state for India.
   4. It established new legislative council for Bengal.

   Which of the following is/are correct.
   (a) All 1, 2, 3 and 4
   (b) 1, 2 and 4 only
   (c) 1, 2 and 3 only
   (d) 1, 3 and 4 only

5. Consider the following statements:
   1. Naturalised citizens are not eligible for the office of President in India.
   2. Cultural and educational rights are available only to citizens in India.

   Which of the above given statements is/are true.
   (a) 1 only
   (b) 2 only
   (c) Both 1 and 2
   (d) Neither 1 nor 2

6. Which of the following ingredients or components is/are revealed by The Preamble of the Constitution.
   1. Nature of Indian State.
   2. Source of authority of the constitution.
   3. Objectives of the constitution.
   4. Date of adoption of the constitution.
   (a) 1, 2 and 3 only
   (b) 2, 3 and 4 only
   (c) 1, 3 and 4 only
   (d) All the above

7. Consider the following statements with reference to the Government of India Act. 1919
   1. Dyarchy was introduced in provinces.
   2. Provincial Legislative councils were expanded.
   3. Voting rights was further curtailed.

   Select the correct answer from the codes given below.
   (a) 1 and 2 only
   (b) 2 and 3 only
   (c) 1 and 3 only
   (d) 1, 2 and 3 all

8. Which among the following found place in the Motilal Nehru Report, 1928;
   1. Dominion status for India.
   2. Separate electorates for Muslims
   3. Linguistic provinces.
   4. Certain fundamental rights.

   Select the correct answer from the codes given below.
   (a) 1 and 2 only
   (b) 2 and 3only
   (c) 1, 3 and 4 only
   (d) All the above

9. Which of the following language is not listed in the eighth Schedule of the constitution.
   (a) Konkani
   (b) Kashmiri
   (c) Himachali
   (d) Santhali

10. Consider the following statements with reference to preamble of the constitution.
    1. The preamble to the Indian Constitution is based on the 'Objective Resolution' drafted and moved by Pandit Nehru.
    2. Three new words secular, integrity and fraternity were added by 42nd Constitutional Amendment Act (1976).

    Which of the above given statement is are correct.
    (a) 1 only
    (b) 2 only
    (c) Both 1 and 2
    (d) None of these

11. Consider the following statements:
    1. The citizens in India owns allegiance only to the Union.
    2. The right of outsiders to enter, reside and settle in tribal areas is restricted.
    Which of the above statements is/are correct:
    (a) 1 only
    (b) 2 only
    (c) Both 1 and 2
    (d) Neither 1 nor 2

12. With reference to the Government of India Act of 1858, Consider the following statements :
    1. The British Governor-General of India was given the title of viceroy.
    2. It established 20 member council which was an advisory body.
    3. |It abolished the Board of control and court of Directors.
    Select the correct statement/statements using the code given below:
    (a) 1 only
    (b) 2 and 3 only
    (c) 1 and 3 only
    (d) 1 , 2 and 3

13. With reference to August offer 1940, Consider the following statements:
    1. It proposed dominion status for India.
    2. It proposed the expansion of Viceroy council.
    3. It proposed the appointment of a constitution making body, immediately after war.
    Select the correct statement/statements using the code given below:
    (a) 1 only
    (b) 2 and 3 only
    (c) 1 and 3 only
    (d) 1 , 2 and 3

14. Which of the following is one of the ways in which a person can lose Indian citizenship.
    1. By voluntarily renouncing his/her Indian citizenship.
    2. By voluntarily acquiring the citizenship of another country.
    3. Compulsory termination of Indian citizenship by the central government.
    Select the correct answer using the codes given below:
    (a) 1 and 2 only
    (b) 2 and 3 only
    (c) 1 and 3 only
    (d) All 1, 2 and 3

15. Which of the following is not a feature of the GOI Act of 1909 (Morley-Minto Reforms):
    1. It increased the size of legislative councils.
    2. It provided for a system of communal representation for Muslims.
    3. It provided for association of Indians with the executive councils of the Viceroy and Governor.
    4. It provided for separate electorates for Sikhs.

16. With reference to Preamble consider the following statements:
    1. Preamble is a part of the constitution.
    2. Preamble can be amended subjected to certain conditions.
    Which of the above given statements is/are correct.
    (a) 1 only
    (b) 2 only
    (c) Both 1 and 2
    (d) None of the above

17. Which of the following functions was/were performed by the Constituent Assembly.
    1. Adoption of national flag.
    2. Ratification of India's Membership of the Common-wealth.
    3. Adoption of national anthem.
    4. Election of first president of India.
    Select the correct answer from the codes given below
    (a) 1, 2 and 3 only
    (b) 2 and 3 only
    (c) 2, 3 and 4 only
    (d) All the above

18. With reference to the constitution of the constituent assembly, consider the following questions:
    1. It was constituted under the scheme formulated by the Cripps Mission.
    2. Representatives of princely states were to be elected by the people of princely states.
    3. Each province and princely state were to be alloted seats in proportion to their respective population.
    Which of the above given statements is/are correct:
    (a) 1 and 2 only
    (b) 2 and 3 only
    (c) 3 only
    (d) 1, 2 and 3 all

19. Indian Constitution establishes a secular state meaning that:
    1. State treats all religions equally
    2. Freedom of faith and worship
    3. Educational bodies can impart religious instructions
    4. State does not discriminate on the basis of religion
    Which of the above statements is/are correct?
    (a) 1 and 2
    (b) 1, 2 and 3
    (c) 2, 3 and 4
    (d) 1, 2 and 4

20. What facts emerges from the Preamble?
    1. When the Constitution was enacted
    2. Ideals that were to be achieved .
    3. System of government
    4. Source of authority
    Which of the above statements is/are correct?
    (a) 2, 3 and 4
    (b) 1 and 2
    (c) 1, 2 and 3
    (d) 1, 2, 3 and 4

21. Which statement is correct?
    1. Territory of the constituents of the Indian federation may be altered by the Parliament by a simple majority.
    2. Consent of the State Legislature is necessary before the Parliament alters boundaries.
    3. President's recommendation is necessary for introducing any Bill on redrawing the boundary of a State.
    4. President must have State's opinion before altering the name of the State.
    Which of the above statements is/are correct?
    (a) 1 only   (b) 1 and 2
    (c) 1, 3 and 4   (d) 1 and 3

22. _____ gives the Indian Constitution a unitary bias?
    1. Rigidity of the amendment process
    2. Written Constitution
    3. Same Constitution for Centre and States
    4. Fixed State boundaries
    Which of the above is/are correct?
    (a) 2 and 4   (b) 1, 2 and 4
    (c) 3 and 4   (d) 3 only

23. Consider the following statements :
    1. The Charter Act 1853 abolished East India Company's monopoly of Indian trade.
    2. Under the Government of India Act 1858, the British Parliament abolished the East India Company altogether and undertook the responsibility of ruling India directly.
    Which of the statements given above is/are correct?
    (a) 1 only   (b) 2 only
    (c) Both 1 and 2   (d) Neither 1 nor 2

24. The salient features of the Government of India Act, 1935 are:
    1. All India Federation
    2. Provincial Autonomy
    3. Dyarchy at the Centre
    4. Abolition of Dyarchy in the states
    Which of the above is/are correct?
    (a) 1 and 2   (b) 1, 2 and 3
    (c) 2,3 and 4   (d) 1, 2, 3 and 4

25. The features of Government of India Act of 1858 includes:
    1. Replacement of Company rule by the Crown rule.
    2. Establishment of a Board of Control over the Court of Directors.
    3. Reaffirmation of the system of open competition.
    4. Separating the legislative and executive functions of the Governor-General.
    5. Creation of a new office of the Secretary of State for India.

    Which of the above statements is/are correct?
    (a) 1,3 and 4   (b) 1,2 and 4
    (c) 1 and 5   (d) 1, 3 and 5

26. The features of Indian parliamentary system are:
    1. Independent judiciary.
    2. Collective responsibility of the executive to the legislature.
    3. A written Constitution.
    4. Presence of de jure and de facto executives.
    5. Individual responsibility of the executive to the legislature.
    Which of the above statements is/are correct?
    (a) 2, 3 and 4   (b) 1, 2 and 4
    (c) 2, 4 and 5   (d) 1, 2, 4 and 5

27. Which of the following are the federal features of the Indian Constitution?
    1. Rigid Constitution 2. Bicameralleg legislature
    3. Office of the CAG   4. Collective responsibility
    5. Office of the Governor
    (a) 1, 2 and 3   (b) 1, 2 and 5
    (c) 1, 2, 3 and 4   (d) 1 and 2

28. The forms of oaths or affirmations for which of the following officials are mentioned in the third schedule of the Indian constitution?
    1. The Comptroller and Auditor General
    2. The Chief Election Commissioner
    3. The Chief Justice of a High Court
    4. The Attorney General
    Select the correct answer using the codes given below:
    (a) 1 and 2 only   (b) 1, 2 and 3 only
    (c) 2, 3 and 4 only   (d) 1 and 3 only

29. Which of the following provisions of the constitution reveal the secular character of the Indian State?
    1. The state shall not deny to any person equality before the law.
    2. No religious instruction shall be provided in any educational institution maintained by the state.
    3. The state shall endeavour to secure for all citizens a uniform Civil Code.
    4. Any section of the society shall have the right to conserve its distinct language.
    (a) 1, 2, 3 only   (b) 2 only
    (c) 2 & 3 only   (d) 1, 2, 3 & 4

30. Which of the following feature/s of the constitution of India has/have been borrowed from GOI Act 1935?
    1. Office of the Governor.
    2. Emergency Provisions.
    3. Legislative Procedure.
    4. Bicameralism.
    5. Federation with a strong center.

(a) 1, 2 & 4 only

(b) 1, 3, 4 & 5 only

(c) 1 & 2 only

(d) None of the above options are correct

31. Which of the following terms was/were added to preamble by the 42ⁿᵈ Amendment act?

1. Socialist   2. Secular

3. Republic

(a) 1 & 2 only   (b) 1 only.

(c) 2 & 3 only   (d) 1, 2 & 3

32. Which of the following statements are incorrect?

1. The Preamble is a prohibition on the powers of the legislature.

2. Preamble is not a part of the constitution.

3. Preamble cannot be amended, as it is a part of the basic structure of the constitution.

(a) 1 & 2 only   (b) 2 & 3 only.

(c) 1 & 3 only   (d) 1, 2 & 3

33. Which of the following statement/s is/are correct?

1. Indian territory can be ceded to a foreign state without amending the constitution as mentioned in article 368.

2. Resolution of boundary dispute between India and another country does not require constitutional amendment.

Select the correct answer using the codes given below

(a) 1 only   (b) 2 only

(c) Both   (d) None

34. Choose the correct statements from below:

1. The Regulating Act of 1773 was the first step by British govt to regulate the East India Company.

2. The Pitt's India Act setup the Supreme Court in Calcutta.

3. The Charter Act of 1833 first recognized the company's territories in India as British possessions.

4. Pitt's India Act created the Board of Control to look after political affairs.

(a) Only 1,2,3 is correct   (b) Only 1,3,4 is correct

(c) Only 1,4 is correct   (d) All are correct

35. Choose the correct answer

1. Charter Act of 1833 created the post Governor General of India.

2. Charter Act, 1833 deprived the Governors of Bombay and Madras their legislative powers.

3. Charter Act, 1853 introduced open competitive system for recruitment of civil servants.

4. Macaulay Committee on the Indian Police Service was formed in 1854 and it drafted the Indian Police Act,1861.

(a) Only 1,2 is correct   (b) Only 1,3 is correct

(c) Only 1,2,3 is correct   (d) 1,2,3,4 is correct

36. Consider the following statements:

1. An amendment to the Constitution of India can be initiated by an introduction of a bill in the Lok Sabha only.

2. If such an amendment seeks to make changes in the federal character of the Constitution, the amendment also requires to be ratified by the legislature of all the States of India.

Which of the statements given above is/are correct?

(a) 1 only   (b) 2 only

(c) Both 1 and 2   (d) Neither 1 nor 2

37. Which among the following statements is/are the features of a Federal state?

1. The power of the central and the state (Constituent Unit) Government are clearly laid down.

2. It has an unwritten constitution.

Select the correct answer using the code given below:

(a) 1 only   (b) 2 only

(c) Both 1 and 2   (d) Neither 1 nor 2

38. Which of the following statements is/are not violative of the principle of federalism?

1. The President of India takes over administration of provinces under the emergency provisions.

2. The Parliament of India has exclusive power to make any law with respect to any matter not enumerated in the Concurrent List or State List.

3. The distribution of powers between the Union and Provinces is done through three different lists enumerated in the Constitution of India.

Select the correct answer using the code given below:

Code:

(a) 1 and 2   (b) 2 and 3

(c) 3 only   (d) 1 and 3

39. Which of the following statements with regard to the Federal System is/are correct?

1. In a federation, two sets of governments co- exist and there is distribution of power.

2. There is a written constitution.

Select the correct answer using the code given below:

(a) 1 only   (b) 2 only

(c) Both 1 and 2   (d) Neither 1 or 2

40. Which of the following statements regarding the Preamble of the Constitution of India is/are correct?

1. The Preamble is an integral part of the Constitution.

2. The words 'secular' and 'socialist' have been a part of the Preamble since its inception.

Select the correct answer using the code given below:
(a) 1 only (b) 2 only
(c) Both 1 and 2 (d) Neither 1 nor 2

41. Consider the following statements
1. A person who was born on January, 26th, 1951 in Rangoon, whose father was a citizen of India by birth at the time of his birth is deemed to be an Indian citizen by descent.
2. A person who was born on July, 1st 1988 in Itanagar, whose mother is a citizen of India at the time of his birth but the father was not, is deemed to be a citizen of India by birth.
Which of the statements given above is/are correct?
(a) Only 1 (b) Only 2
(c) Both 1 and 2 (d) Neither 1 nor 2

42. Under which of the following conditions can citizenship be provided in India?
1. One should be born in India.
2. Either of whose parents was born in India
3. Who has been a resident of India for not less than five years.
Select the correct answer using the codes given below
(a) 1, 2 and 3 (b) 1 and 2
(c) 2 and 3 (d) None of these

43. 1. A written Constitution is the formal source of all Constitutional Laws in the country and the unwritten Constitution is not the formal source.
2. A written Constitution is entirely codified whereas an unwritten Constitution is not.
Select the correct answer using the codes given below
(a) Only 1 (b) Only 2
(c) Both 1 and 2 (d) Neither 1 nor 2

44. Consider the following statements
1. In India, only two Union Territories have Legislative Assemblies.
2. Mizoram, Nagaland and Meghalaya, have only one seat each in the Lok Sabha.
Which of the statement(s) given above is/are correct?
(a) Only 1 (b) Only 2
(c) Both 1 and 2 (d) Neither 1 nor 2

45. The Government of India Act, 1919
1. Established a bicameral legislature at the centre.
2. Introduced dyarchy in the provincial executive.
3. Introduced a Federal System of Government in India.
Select the correct answer using the codes given below
(a) 1 and 3 (b) 2 and 3
(c) 1,2 and 3 (d) 1 and 2

46. Among the following ideals and philosophy, identify those enshrined in the Preamble to the Constitution of India.
1. Sovereign democratic republic.
2. Socialism and secularism.
3. Capitalism and free trade.
Select the correct answer using the codes given below
(a) 1 and 2 (b) 1 and 3
(c) 1,2 and 3 (d) 2 and 3

47. The citizenship means
1. full civil and political rights of the citizens.
2. the right of suffrage for election to the House of the People (of the Union) and the Legislative Assembly of every state.
3. the right to become a Member of the Parliament and Member of Legislative Assemblies.
Select the correct answer using the codes given below
(a) 1 and 2 (b) 1 and 3
(c) 2 and 3 (d) All of these

48. Which of the following statement(s) is/are not correct for the Ninth Schedule of the Constitution of India?
1. It was inserted by the first amendment in 1951.
2. It includes those laws which are beyond the purview of judicial review.
3. It was inserted by the 42nd Amendment.
4. The laws in the Ninth Schedule are primarily those which pertain to the matters of national security.
Select the correct answer using the code given below:
(a) 1 and 2 (b) 2 and 3
(c) 3 and 4 (d) 3 only

49. Which of the following statements is/are not true for the category of the Overseas Citizens of India (OCI) inserted by the amendment to the Citizenship Act of India in 2003?
1. It gives dual citizenship to Persons of Indian Origin (PIO) who are citizens of another country.
2. It gives Persons of Indian Origin (PIO) who are citizens of another country, an OCI card without citizenship.
3. It permits the OCI to vote in general elections in India.
4. It allows the OCI to travel to India without visa.
Select the correct answer using the code given below:
(a) 1 and 2 (b) 1 and 3
(c) 3 only (d) 2 and 4

50. Consider the following statements:
1. Article 371 A to 371 I were inserted in the Constitution of India to meet regional demands of Nagaland, Assam, Manipur, Andhra Pradesh, Sikkim, Mizoram, Arunchal Pradesh and Goa.
2. Constitution of India and the United States of America envisage a dual policy (The Union and the States) but a single citizenship.
3. A naturalized citizen of India can never be deprived of his citizenship.
Which of the statements given above is/are correct?
(a) 1, 2 and 3 (b) 1 and 3
(c) 3 only (d) 1 only

51. Consider the following statements:
1. The Constitution of India has 40 parts.
2. There are 390 Articles in the Constitution of India in all.
3. Ninth, Tenth, Eleventh and Twelfth Schedules were added to the Constitution of India by the Constitution (Amendment) Acts.
Which of the statements given above is/are correct?
(a) 1 and 2 (b) 2 only
(c) 3 only (d) 1, 2 and 3

52. Which of the following provision(s) of the Constitution of India became effective from 26th November 1949?
    1. Elections **[NDA-2018]**
    2. Citizenship
    3. Emergency provisions
    4. Appointment of the Judges
    Select the correct answer using the code given below:
    (a) 1 only   (b) 1 and 2 only
    (c) 1, 2 and 3   (d) 2 and 4

53. Which among the following Acts were repealed by Article 395 of the Constitution of India?   **[CDS 2016]**
    1. The Government of India Act, 1935
    2. The Indian Independence Act, 1947
    3. The Abolition of Privy Council Jurisdiction Act, 1949
    4. The Government of India Act, 1919
    Select the correct answer using the code given below.
    (a) 1 and 2 only   (b) 1 and 3 only
    (c) 1, 2 and 3 only   (d) 1, 2, 3 and 4

54. On 26th November, 1949, which of the following provisions of the Constitution of India came into effect?
    1. Citizenship   **[CDS 2016]**
    2. Elections
    3. Provisional Parliament
    4. Fundamental Rights
    Select the correct answer using the code given below.
    (a) 2, 3 and 4   (b) 1, 2 and 3
    (c) 1 and 3 only   (d) 1 and 2 Only

55. Which of the following statements regarding the Constituent Assembly of India is/are correct?   **[CDS 2016]**
    1. The Assembly was elected indirectly by the members of the Provincial Legislative Assemblies.
    2. The elections were held on the basis of Universal Adult Franchise.
    3. The scheme of election was laid down by the Cabinet Delegation.
    4. The distribution of seats was done on the basis of the Mountbatten Plan.
    Select the correct answer using the code given below.
    (a) 1 only   (b) 1, 2 and 3
    (c) 2 and 4   (d) 1 and 3 only

56. A citizen of India will lose his or her citizenship if he or she
    1. renounces Indian citizenship   **[CDS 2016]**
    2. voluntarily acquires the citizenship of another country
    3. marries a citizen of another country
    4. criticizes the Government
    Select the correct answer using the code given below.
    (a) 1, 2 and 3   (b) 2, 3 and 4
    (c) 1 and 2 only   (d) 1 and 4

57. The Sixth Schedule of the Constitution of India pertains to the administration of tribal areas in which of the following States?   **[CDS 2016]**
    (a) Assam, Meghalaya, Tripura and Mizoram
    (b) Meghalaya, Tripura, Manipur and Mizoram
    (c) Assam, Manipur, Meghalaya and Tripura
    (d) Manipur, Meghalaya, Tripura and Arunachal Pradesh

58. Which one of the following statements with regard to the Ninth Schedule of the Constitution of India is not correct?   **[CDS 2016]**
    (a) It was inserted by the Constitution (First Amendment) Act, 1951.
    (b) The Acts and Regulations specified in the Ninth Schedule shall become void on the ground that it violates a fundamental right in Part III of the Constitution.
    (c) The Supreme Court has the power of judicial review of an Act included in the Ninth Schedule on the doctrine of basic structure.
    (d) The appropriate Legislature can repeal or amend an Act specified in the Ninth Schedule.

59. Which of the following statements is/are correct regarding the Preamble of the Indian Constitution?   **[CDS 2017]**
    1. The Preamble by itself is not enforceable in a Court of Law.
    2. The Preamble states the objectives which the Constitution seeks to establish and promote.
    3. The Preamble indicates the source from which the Constitution derives its authority.
    Select the correct answer using the code given below.
    (a) 1, 2 and 3   (b) 1 and 2 only
    (c) 1 and 3 only   (d) 2 only

60. Match the following

	List-I (Schedule in the Constitution of India)	List-II (Subject)
A.	Tenth Schedule	1. Languages
B.	Eighth Schedule	2. Provisions as to disqualification on the grounds of defection
C.	First Schedule	3. Validation of certain Acts and Regulations
D.	Ninth Schedule	4. The States

Codes:

	A	B	C	D
(a)	4	3	2	1
(b)	2	1	4	3
(c)	4	1	2	3
(d)	2	3	4	1

61. Match the following

	List-I (Provision of the Constitution of India)	List II (Source)
A.	Amendment of the Constitution	Constitution of Germany
B.	Directive Principles	Constitution of Canada
C.	Emergency Power of the President	Constitution of South Africa
D.	The Union-State Relations	Irish Constitution

Codes :

	A	B	C	D
(a)	1	2	4	3
(b)	3	4	1	2
(c)	1	4	2	3
(d)	3	7	4	2

62. Match the following

	List-I (Act)	List-II (Feature)
A.	The Indian Councils Act, 1892	Introduction of provincial autonomy
B.	The Indian Councils Act, 1909 Indian	Introduction of the principle of election
C.	The Government of India -Act, 1919	Introduction of diarchy in provinces
D.	The Government of India Act, 1935	Introduction of separate electorate for the Muslims

Codes:

	A	B	C	D
(a)	2	4	3	1
(b)	1	3	4	2
(c)	2	3	4	1
(d)	1	4	3	2

63. Match the following

	List-I (Person)	List-II (Role in making of the Constitution of India)"
A.	Rajendra Prasad	1. Member. Drafting Committee
B.	T T Krishanamachari	2. Chairman Constituent Assembly
C.	H C Mukherjee	3. Chairman. Drafting Committee
D.	B R Ambedkar	4. Vice Chairman. Constituent Assembly

Codes:

	A	B	C	D		A	B	C	D
(a)	2	1	4	3	(b)	2	4	1	3
(c)	3	4	1	2	(d)	3	1	4	2

64. Match List I (Acts of colonial Government of India) with List II (Provisions)

	List I		List II
(A)	Charter Act, 1813 Britain to fully East	(1)	Set up a board of control of regulate the India company
(B)	Regulating Act	(2)	Company's trade monopoly in India was ended
(C)	Act of 1858	(3)	The power to govern was transferred from East Indian the Company the to British Crown
(D)	Pitt's India Act	(4)	The Company's directors were asked to present to the British Government all correspondence and documents pertaining to the administration of the company

(a) A – 2 ; B – 4 ; C – 3 ; D – 1
(b) A – 1 ; B – 3 ; C – 4 ; D – 2
(c) A – 2 ; B – 3 ; C – 4 ; D – 1
(d) A – 1 ; B – 4 ; C – 3 ; D – 2

65. Match List-I with List-II and select the correct answer:

	List-I (Item in the Indian Constitution)		List-II (Country from which it was derived)
A.	Directive Principles of State Policy	1.	Australia
B.	Fundamental Rights	2.	Canada
C.	Concurrent List in Union-State Relations	3.	Ireland
D.	India as a Union of States with greater powers to the Union	4.	United Kingdom
		5.	United States of America

Codes:

(a) A-5, B-4, C-1, D-2 (b) A-3, B-5, C-2, D-1

(c) A-5, B-4, C-2, D-1 (d) A-3, B-5, C-1, D-2

Hints and Explanations

EXERCISE-1

1. (c)   2. (d)   3. (d)   4. (c)   5. (d)
6. (b)   7. (a)   8. (b)   9. (c)   10. (d)
11. (c)   12. (c)   13. (b)   14. (d)   15. (d)
16. (a)   17. (a)   18. (a)
19. (b)   The parliament may regulate the right of citizenship of India through the amendment of citizenship act.
20. (a)   21. (c)
22. (d)   Civil liberties are the rights held by citizens of a country. In liberal democracies citizens have rights such as freedom of speech, freedom of association e.g. to join a trade union, freedom to choose their political representatives.
23. (c)   The mention of the word 'justice' in the preamble to the constitution of India expresses social, economic and political justice.
24. (c)   25. (a)   26. (d)   27. (d)   28. (d)
29. (c)   30. (d)
31. (c)   The state of Jammu & Kashmir of Indian federation has a separate constitution. Article 370 of the Indian constitution, which is of a temporary nature, grants special status to Jammu and Kashmir. Under Part XXI of the Constitution of India, which deals with "Temporary, Transitional and Special provisions", the State of Jammu and Kashmir has been accorded special status under Article 370.
32. (d)   33. (d)   34. (a)
35. (c)   Cabinet mission plan gave the idea of constituent Assembly for India. In 1946, British Prime Minister Clement Attlee formulated a cabinet mission to India to discuss and finalize plans for the transfer of power from the British Raj to Indian leadership as well as provide India with independence under Dominion status in the Commonwealth of Nations. The Mission discussed the framework of the constitution and laid down in some detail the procedure to be followed by the constitution drafting body.
36. (d)
37. (a)   The tenth schedule of Indian constitution deals with anti-defection Legislation. Tenth Schedule (Articles 102(2) and 191(2))—"Anti-defection" provisions for Members of Parliament and Members of the State Legislatures.
38. (d)   39. (b)   40. (c)   41. (d)
42. (b)   43. (c)   44. (c)
45. (d)   Act 253- Parliament has power to make any law for the whole or any part of the country or territory of India for implementing any treaty, agreement or convention with any other country or any decision made at any international conference, association or other body without the consent of any state.
46. (c)   Under the constitutional (Ninety-second amendment) Act, four languages Bodo, Dogri, Santhali and Maithali were added to languages under the eight schedule of the constitution of India thereby raising the total number of languages listed in the schedule to 22.
47. (d)   The advisor of the drafting committee of the constituent assembly was Sir B.N. Rao.
48. (b)   the idea of including the emergency provisions in the Constitution of India has been borrowed from the Weimar Constitution of Germany.
49. (d)   The 10th Schedule to the Indian Constitution is known as Anti-Defection Law. It was inserted by the 52nd Amendment Act 1985 to the Constitution. It sets the provisions for disqualification of elected members on the grounds of defection to another political party.
50. (c)   7th Schedule gives allocation of powers and functions between Union & States. It contains 3 lists:
Union List (97 Subjects)
States List (66 subjects)
Concurrent List(52 subjects)
51. (b)   Details of Citizenship are mentioned in part ll(Article 5-11) of the constitution.
52. (c)   Jawaharlal Nehru took charge as the first Prime Minister of India on 15 August 1947, and chose 15 other members for his cabinet in which B. R. Ambedkar was the first law minister of India.
53. (c)   Liaquat Ali Khan became the first Finance Minister of India in the Interim Government during 1946-1947.
54. (c)   Freedom to acquire property or to carry on any occupation trade or business is also available to non citizens.
55. (d)   Traffic in human beings and beggars and other similar forms of forced labour are prohibited and any contravention of this provision shall be an offence punishable in accordance with law . The terms 'Socialist' was added by the 42nd Amendment and assert that the government must adopt socialistic policies to ensure decent life for all Indian citizens. Thus, the word Socialist in the preamble of the Constitution of India read with Article 23.
56. (a)   The constitution of India is republican because it provides for an elected parliament.
57. (b)   The preamble is useful in constitutional interpretation because it contains the real objective and philosophy of the constitution makers.
58. (d)   The Cabinet mission arrived on March 24, 1946. The objective of this mission was to:
- Devise a machinery to draw up the constitution of Independent India.
- Make arrangements for interim Government.

- Thus the mission was like a declaration of India's independence.
- British Government was to supervise the affairs of the constituent Assembly, was not the aim of the mission.

59. **(b)** On 29 August 1947, the Drafting Committee was appointed with Dr B. R. Ambedkar as the Chairman along with six other members assisted by a constitutional advisor. These members were Pandit Govind Ballabh Pant, K M Munshi, Alladi Krishnaswamy Iyer, N Gopala swami Ayengar, B L Mitter and Md. Saadullah. A Draft Constitution was prepared by the committee and submitted to the Assembly on 4 November 1947. This is Ambedkar's second argument rested on the legitimacy of the democratic system.

60. **(a)** Dual Citizenship is not found in the Indian political system. The Indian Constitution does not allow dual citizenship. Automatic loss of Indian citizenship covered in Section 9(1) of the Citizenship act 1955, provides that any citizen of India who by naturalisation or registration acquires the citizenship of another country shall cease to be a citizen of India. Indian Government has started OCI (Overseas citizen of India) Scheme in 2005. According to the scheme if you are already a Person of Indian origin (POI) and have taken up citizenship abroad, you can take up benefits of OCI scheme, which gives you the same travel and residence privileges like other Indians but you are not allowed to vote and take up jobs in Government sector.

61. **(b)** Tribal areas generally mean areas having preponderance of tribal population. However, the Constitution of India refers tribal areas within the States of Assam, Meghalaya, Tripura & Mizoram, as those areas specified in Parts I, II, IIA & III of the table appended to paragraph 20 of the Sixth Schedule.

62. **(b)** The Constitution of India was enacted on Nov. 26, 1949 but it was commenced on Jan. 26, 1950.

63. **(d)** Tenth schedule was added by the 52nd Constitutional Amendment Act, 1985. It provides for anti-defection law.

64. **(c)** The Constitution of India recognizes religious and linguistic minorities under article 29 and 30 (Cultural and Educational rights). However it does not define the term Minority.

65. **(d)** Fourth schedule allocates seats in the Council of States i.e. Rajya Sabha.

66. **(a)** First schedule contains names of the States and UTs, that's why it should be amended, if a new state is created.

67. **(a)** Ninth Schedule was added by First Amendment Act of 1951, which relates to Land Reforms.

68. **(a)** The 'First Schedule' of the constitution deals with list of States and Union Territories.

69. **(d)** Fourth schedule allocates seats in the Council of States i.e. Rajya Sabha (Upper House of Parliament).

70. **(b)** Fifth schedule relates to the control and administration of scheduled areas in states other than Tripura, Assam, Meghalaya and Mizoram. While Sixth Schedule deals with administration and control of tribal areas in the state of Assam, Meghalaya, Mizoram and Tripura.

71. **(c)** Distribution of power between the Centre and the States in the Indian Constitution is based on the Government of India Act. 1935.

72. **(a)** The Fifth Schedule of the Constitution of India deals with administration and control of scheduled areas and scheduled tribes in these areas. The Sixth Schedule to the Constitution of India contains provisions concerning the administration of tribal areas in the States of Assam, Meghalaya, Tripura and Mizoram.

73. **(d)** (i) The Montagu–Chelmsford Reforms were reforms introduced by the British Government in India to introduce self-governing institutions gradually to India. The reforms were outlined in the Montagu-Chelmsford Report prepared in 1918 and formed the basis of the Government of India Act 1919.
(ii) They're related to Constitutional reforms.
Ref: Disha's Crack CSAT Paper-1, 2016(4th Edition) Page H-228.1

74. **(c)** 75. **(b)**

76. **(b)** Read the preamble given in any school textbook: "We, the people of India,....LIBERTY of thought, expression, belief, faith and worship..."So, "B" is the answer.

77. **(a)** Sir Alladi Krishnaswami Iyer, a member of the Constituent Assembly, had said 'The Preamble to our Constitution expresses what we had thought or dreamt so long." So "A" is the answer.

78. **(d)** Right to Constitutional Remedies under article 32 is a Fundamental Right. It was called the very soul of Indian constitution and very heart of it, by B.R. Ambedkar.

EXERCISE-2

1. **(c)** Some countries have subjected their constitution to a full-fledged referendum, where all the people vote on the desirability of a constitution.

   The Indian constitution was never subjected to such a referendum, but nevertheless carried enormous public authority because it had the consensus and backing of leaders who were themselves popular.

   Therefore the authority of people who enact the constitution helps determine in part its prospects for success.

   – Constitutional norms are the overarching framework within which one pursues individual aspirations, goals and freedoms.

- The constitution sets authoritative constraints upon what one may or may not do. It defines the fundamental values that we may not trespass. So the constitution also gives one a moral identity.

2. (a) Dyarchy or the Act of devolution was introduced by Govt. of India Act of 1919.

The Regulating Act of 1773 also strengthened the control of the British Government over the company by requiring the Court of Directors (governing body of the company) to report on its revenue, civil & military affairs in India.

- Remember: The Regulating Act of 1773 was the first step taken by the British Government to control and regulate the affairs of the East India company.

Source: M. Lakshmikant

3. (c) In Proportional Representation System voters exercise their preference for a party and not a candidate. The seats in a constituency are distributed on the basis of votes polled by a party. Thus, representatives from a constituency would and do belong to different parties. And more than one candidate can be elected from one constituency.

Source: N.C.E.R.T. (Std. XIth) (Polity–Chapter 3)

4. (c) The Govt. of India Act: 1858 was enacted in the wake of the Revolt of 1857. Important features of the Act:

- Governor General of India was made Viceroy of India.

- It ended the system of double government by abolishing the Board of control and court of directors.

- It abolished the East India Company.

- It established a 15 member council of India to assist the Secretary of State for India.

Note: Indian Councils Act of 1861 provided for establishment of new legislative councils for Bengal, NWFP and Punjab.

5. (b) In India both a citizen by birth as well as a naturalised citizen are eligible for the office of president while in USA, only a citizen by birth and not a naturalised citizen is eligible for the office of president.

- Cultural and educational rights are available only to citizens in India and not to aliens (Article-29 and Art.-30).

6. (d) 1. The preamble states that the constitution derives its authority from the people of the India.

2. It declares India to be a Sovereign, Socialist, Secular democratic and republican polity.

3. It specifies justice, liberty, equality and fraternity as the objectives.

7. (a) Voting rights were also given to womens through the Governments of India Act. 1919. Thus the scope of franchise was expanded.

Dyarchy ie rule of Two-executive councillors and popular ministers was introduced. The governor was to be the executive head in the province.

8. (c) In 1928, the congress appointed a sub committee under the chairmanship of Motilal Nehru to draft a Constitution.

The major recommendation of the Nehru Report were:

- Dominion status on lines of self governing dominions as the form of government desired by Indians.

- Rejection of separate electorates which had been the basis of constitutional reforms so far, instead it demanded for joint electorates with reservation of seats for Muslims

- Linguistic provinces.

- Nineteen fundamental rights including equal rights for women right to form unions and universal adult suffrage.

- Responsible government at the centre and in provinces.

9. (c) At present the eighth schedule of the constitution specifies 22 languages (originally 14 languages).

These are

1. Assamese	12. Manipuri
2. Bengali	13. Marathi
3. Bodo	14. Nepali
4. Dogri (Dongri)	15. Oriya
5. Gujarati	16. Punjabi
6. Hindi	17. Sanskrit
7. Kannada	18. Santhali
8. Kashmiri	19. Sindhi
9. Konkani	20. Tamil
10. Mathili (Maithili)	21. Telugu
11. Malayalam	22. Urdu

10. (a) – Statement 1 is correct Pt. Nehru introduced the "Objective Resolution" in the constituent Assembly which on Dec.13, 1946. This resolution as accepted by the constituent Assembly forms the basis of the Indian Political System. It guided the constitution making process.

11. (c) Though the Indian constitution is federal and envisages a dual polity (centre and states), it provides for only a single citizenship, that is Indian citizenship. The citizens in India are allegiance only to the union. There is no separate state citizenship.

- The freedom of movement and residence (under Article-19) is subjected to the protection of interests of any schedule tribe.

- In other words, the right of outsiders to enter, reside and settle in tribal areas is restricted. This is door to protect the distinctive culture, language, customs and manners of schedule tribes and to safeguard their traditional vocation and property against exploitation.

12. (c) In August 1858, the British parliament passed an act that set an end to the rule of the company. It ended the system of double government by abolishing the Board of control and court of Directors. This act established a 15-member council of India to assist the secretary of state for India. The council was an advisory body.

13. (d) To get Indian Cooperation in the war effort, the viceroy announced the August offer. The Congress rejected the August offer. Nehru said," Dominion status concept is dead as a door mail.

14. (d) The Citizenship Act, 1955 prescribes three ways of losing citizenship whether acquired under the Act or prior to it under the constitution viz, renunciation, terminations and deprivation.

    1. Any citizen of India of full age and capacity can make a declaration renouncing his Indian Citizenship.

    2. When an Indian citizen voluntarily acquires the citizenship of another country, his/her Indian citizenship automatically gets terminated.

15. (d) The principle of communal representation by providing separate electorates for Sikhs, Indian Christians and Anglo-Indians and Europeans was provided by the government of India Act: 1919 (Montagu-Chelmsford Reforms)

    – All other statements are true regarding the Government of India Act: 1909.

16. (c) The supreme court held that the Preamble is a part of the constitution. The court held that Preamble can be amended, subject to the condition that no amendment is done to the 'basic features'.

    In other words, the court held that the basic elements or the fundamental features of the constitution as contained in the preamble cannot be altered by an amendment under Article-368.

17. (d) In addition to the making of the constitution and enacting of ordinary laws, the constituent assembly also performed the given functions. (as mentioned in the question)
Besides the constituent assembly also adopted National Song on Jan. 24 ; 1940.

18. (c) The Constituent Assembly was constituted in Nov.-1946 under the scheme formulated by the Cabinet Mission Plan. (and not the Cripps Mission)

    – Each province and princely state were to be allotted seats in proportion to their respective population.

    – Voting was to be done by the methods of proportional representation by means of single transferable vote.

    – The representation of princely states was to be nominated by the heads of the princely states.

19. (d)   20. (d)   21. (d)   22. (d)   23. (b)
24. (d)   25. (d)   26. (c)   27. (d)

28. (d) The forms of oaths or affirmations, in the third schedule of the Indian constitution, are mentioned for the given officials. Third Schedule (Articles 75(4), 99, 124(6), 148(2), 164(3), 188 and 219).

29. (d)   30. (c)   31. (a)   32. (d)   33. (b)
34. (c)   35. (c)   36. (d)   37. (a)

38. (b) The Parliament of India has exclusive power to make any law with respect to any matter not enumerated in the Concurrent List or State List. The distribution of powers between the Union and Provinces is done through three different lists enumerated in the Constitution of India.

39. (c) Federal government is the common government of a federation. There is more than one level of government which run according overlapping and shared power is prescribed by a constitution.

40. (a) The preamble to the Constitution of India is a brief introductory statement that sets out the guiding purpose and principles of the document.

41. (a) A person born in India on or after 26th January 1950 but before 1st July 1987 is a citizen of India by birth irrespective of the nationality of his parents, considered citizen of India by birth if either of his parents is a citizen of India at the time of his birth. The citizenship of India is mentioned in Articles 5 to 11 (Part II).

42. (a) Under article 5 of the Indian Constitution Citizenship at the commencement of the Constitution every person who has his domicile in the territory of India and

    (i) who was born in the territory of India; or

    (ii) either of whose parents was born in the territory of India; or

    (iii) who has been ordinarily resident in the territory of India for not less than five years preceding such commencement, shall be a citizen of India.

43. (c) A written constitution is one which is found in one or more than one legal documents duly enacted in the form of laws. It is precise, definite and systematic and codified. An unwritten constitution is one in which most of the principles of the government have never been enacted in the form of laws. It consists of customs, conventions, traditions and some written laws bearing different dates. It is not codified. It is unsystematic, indefinite and unprecise. So, Written Constitution is the formal source of all constitutional laws and Unwritten Constitution is not the formal source.

44. (a) Delhi and Puducherry have their own elected legislative assemblies and the executive councils of ministers.

45. (d) This act made the central legislature bicameral. The first house which was central legislature with 145 members (out of which 104 elected and 41 nominated) was called central Legislative Assembly and second with 60 members (out of which 33 elected and 27 nominated) was called Council of States. It introduced Diarchy in the provincial executive. Federal system of Government was introduced in India by The Government of India Act 1935.

46. (a) According to the preamble of Indian Constitution, India is a Sovereign, Socialist, Secular and Democratic Republic. Capitalism and free trade is not enshrined in the preamble of the Indian constitution.

47. (d) All statements are true. Citizenship is covered in Part II of the Indian constitution (articles 5-11).

48. (a) The Ninth Schedule was added by the 1st Amendment 1951 to protect the laws included in it from judicial scrutiny on the ground of violation of fundamental rights. However in 2007 Supreme Court ruled that the laws included in it after 24 April 1973 are now open to judicial review.

49. (c) It does not permit the OCI to vote in general election in India. On the occasion of first Pravasi Bhartiya Diwas on 9th January 2003, former Prime Minister Atal Bihari Vajpayee had made an announcement for grant of dual citizenship to PIOs. The necessary Legislation was introduced by the Government of India in Parliament in May 2003.

50. (d) Article 371 A to I deals with special provisions to -Nagaland, Assam, Manipur, Andhra Pradesh, Sikkim, Mizoram, Arunachal Pradesh and Goa. The Constitution of India envisages a single policy for both Union and the States. A naturalized citizen is one who acquires citizenship either by Naturalization or by Registration. They can be deprived of citizenship if they acquired citizenship by using fraudulent means.

51. (c) The Constitution of India has 24 parts, 12 schedules and more than 444 articles at present. In the original constitution, there were 22 parts, 8 schedules and 395 articles. Ninth Schedule was added by 1st Constitutional Amendment Act, 1951. Tenth Schedule was added by 52nd Constitutional Amendment Act, 1985. Eleventh Schedule was added by 73rd Constitutional Amendment Act, 1992. Twelfth Schedule was added by 74th Constitutional Amendment Act, 1992.

52. (b)

53. (a) The Government of India Act, 1935 and The Indian Independence Act, 1947, together with all enactments amending or supplementing the latter act, but not including the abolition of Privy Council jurisdiction act, 1949 are hereby repealed by Article 395 of the Constitution of India.

54. (b) The constitution came into force on 26 January 1950, but some provisions relating to Citizenship, Elections, provisional parliament, temporary & transitional provisions were given immediate effect on 26 November 1949.

55. (d) The members of the Constituent assembly were indirectly elected by the members of the provincial assemblies by method of single transferable vote system of proportional representations. The membership plan was roughly as per suggestions of the Cabinet Mission plan. The basis of divisions of seats was "population" roughly in 1:10 Lakh ratio.

56. (c) The citizenship cannot be deprived merely on the ground of marriage with a foreigner and criticizing the Government.

57. (a) The Sixth Schedule of the constitution of India pertains to administration of tribal areas in states of Tripura,Meghalaya,Mizoram and Assam.

58. (b) Article 31-B was inserted by the First Constitutional (Amendment) Act 1951 which states that without prejudiced to the generality of the provisions contained in Article 31-A, none of the Acts and Regulations specified in the Ninth Schedule of the constitution of India nor any of the provisions thereof shall be deemed to be void.

59. (a) Preamble is a brief introductory statement to the Constitution of India which sets out the guiding purpose and principles of the document, and it indicates the source from which the document derives its authority, meaning, the people. Preamble is not an integral part of the Indian constitution and therefore it is not enforceable in a court of law.

60. (b) Schedule X was added by 52nd amendment in 1985. It contains provisions of disqualification on the grounds of defection.
Schedule VIII contains List of 22 languages of India recognized by Constitution.
Schedule 1 deals with the List of States & Union Territories.
Schedule X Contains acts & orders related to land tenure, land tax, railways, and industries. Added by Ist amendment in 1951. Laws under Schedule IX are beyond the purview of judicial review even though they violate fundamental rights enshrined under part III of the Constitution.

61. (b) Constitution of India is unique in itself. Many features of our constitution are borrowed from various sources around the world.
1.Amendment of the constitution - Constitution of South Africa
2.Directive Principles- Irish Constitution
3.Emergency Powers of the President- Constitution of the Germany
4.The Union State Relations- Constitution of Canada

62. (a) The Indian Council Act 1892- Introduction of the principle of election
The Indian Council Act 1909- Introduction of separate electorate for the Muslims
The government of India act 1919- Introduction of diarchy in provinces
The government of India Act 1935- Introduction of provincial autonomy.

63. (a) The Constitution of India was drafted by the constituent assembly and it was set up under the cabinet Mission plan on 16 May 1946. Dr. Rajendra Prasad became the President of the Constituent Assembly. Tiruvellore Thattai Krishnamachari was a member of drafting committee. Mookerjee was the Vice-president of the Constituent Assembly. Bhimrao Ambedkar was appointed Chairman of the Constitution Drafting Committee.

64. (a)

65. (d) Borrowed features from different countries are correct.

FUNDAMENTAL RIGHTS, FUNDAMENTAL DUTIES AND DIRECTIVE PRINCIPLES OF STATE POLICY

Chapter 2

FUNDAMENTAL RIGHTS

- Fundamental rights under Articles 15, 16, 19, 29 & 30 are applicable to Indian citizens.
- Fundamental rights under Articles 14, 20, 21, 23, 25, 26, 27 and 28 are available to all resident of India both citizens and foreigner.
- Some fundamental rights are negatively worded as prohibitions on the State like Articles - 14, 15(1), 16(2), 18(1), 20, 22(1) and 28(1)
- Fundamental rights which impose *absolute limitations upon the legislative power* cannot be regulated by the legislature are covered by Articles 15, 17, 18, 20 and 24.
- All fundamental rights are guaranteed against state action.
- If Rights under Article 19 and Article 21 are violated by an individual, legal remedies but not Constitutional remedies are available.
- Article 12 defines the State which includes:
  1. Government and Indian parliament *i.e.* executive and Legislature of the Union.
  2. Government and legislature of the states.
  3. All local and other authorities within the territory of India.
  4. All local and other authorities under the control of GOI.
  5. All other statutory or non-statutory authorities like LIC, ONGC, SAIL etc.

According to the Supreme Court, even a private body or an agency working as an instrument of the state falls within the meaning of the 'state' under Article-12.

- Article 13 confers the power of judicial review to the courts of all legislative acts.
- Supreme Court of India and State High Courts have this power under Article 32 and 226. They can declare a law unconstitutional if it is inconsistent with Part III of the Constitution.
- Power of judicial review is derived from Article - 13.
  The term 'Law' in Article-13 includes:

(i) Permanent laws enacted by state Legislature/Parliament.

(ii) Temporary laws i.e, ordinances issued by the President or Governor.

(iii) Statutory instruments in the nature of delegated legislation.

(iv) Non-legislative sources of law.

Article-13 declares that a Constitutional amendment is not a law and hence can not be challenged.

However as per the Supreme Court's ruling in the Kesavananda Bharti case (1973), a constitutional amendment can be challenged on the ground that it violates a fundamental right that forms a part of the 'basic structure' of the constitution and hence can be declared null and void.

ARTICLE-14: Equality before law/Equal protection of Laws

- Equality before law and equal protection of laws are different.

Equality Before Law	Equal Protection of Law
Negative concept	Positive concept
Absence of special privilege due to birth, creed or like in the favour of any person. There is equal treatment before law.	Right to equality of treatment in similar circumstances.
Dicey's concept of rule of law.	Treated as due process of law.
Established law in England.	An American concept.

'Rule of Law' is the "Basic Feature" of the Constitution which cannot be destroyed even by constitutional amendment under Article 368.

Exception to the Rule of Law

Art	Explanation
361	Immunity to the President of India and State Governors.
361(1)	President of India and state Governors are not answerable to any court for exercise and performance of their powers and duties.

361 (2)	No criminal proceedings can be initiated against President of India and state Governors during their term of office.
361 (4)	No civil proceeding can be instituted during the term of office in respect of any act done by President of India and State Governor in their personal capacity before or after they enter office till 2 months after the notice has been delivered to the President.
	The foreign ambassadors and diplomats enjoy immunity from criminal and civil proceedings. The UNO and its agencies enjoy the diplomatic immunity.

- Concept of equality provides protection against arbitrariness.
- Concept of equality promotes natural justice.
- Right to Equality incorporates Equal pay for equal. work [Art 39(d)]. This is not a fundamental right but a constitutional goal under Articles 14, 16 and 39(d).

ARTICLE 15: Prohibition of discrimination on certain grounds:

15 (1)	No discrimination on grounds of religion, race, caste, sex or place of birth can be made. It applies to matters under the control of the state.
15 (2)	Prohibits discrimination at public places (shops, public hotels, restaurants, well, tanks, bathing ghats etc.) and applies both to state and private individual.
15 (3)	Provisions for protection of women & children.
15 (4)	Provisions to protect interests of backward classes, 1st amendment Act, 1951.

There are 3 exceptions to the rule of non-discrimination:
1. The state can make any special provision for women and children.
2. The state can make any special provision for the advancement of any socially and educationally backward classes of citizens.
3. The state is empowered to make any special provision for the advancement of any socially and educationally backward classes of citizens.

Note: This provision was added by the 93rd Amendment Act of 2005.

Creamy Layer

Children of certain categories of people belonging to this group among OBCs and thus will not get the quota benefit. e.g. persons holding constitutional posts, Group A officers etc.

ARTICLE 16: Equality of opportunity in public employment

16 (1)&(2)	No discrimination in public employment on grounds of religion, race, caste, sex, descent, place of birth or residence.
16 (3)	Residence within a state is a qualification for appointment for any government post.
16 (4)	For reservation of posts in govt. jobs in favour of any backward class.
16 (5)	Provides for the incumbent of any office, in connection with the affairs of any religious or denominational institution or any member of the governing body shall be a person professing a particular religion or belonging to a particular denomination is not a violation of the Constitution.

Mandal Commission

The Second Backward Classes Commission was appointed under the chairmanship of B. P. Mandal in 1979 to investigate the conditions of the socially and educationally backward classes and suggest measures for their advancement.

The Mandal Commission in its report indentified as many as 3743 castes as socially and educationally backward classes.

The Mandal Commission recommended for reservation of 27% government jobs for the other Backward classes (OBCs).

Subsequently Ram Nandan Committee (1993) was appointed to indentify the Creamy Layer among the OBCs.
- National commission for Backward classes was established in 1993 by an act of Parliament.

Note: The 76th Amendment Act of 1994 has placed the Tamilnadu Reservations Act of 1994 in the Ninth Schedule to protect it from judicial review as it provided for 69 percent of reservation for exceeding the 50 percent ceiling.

ARTICLE 17 & 18: Abolition of Untouchability and Titles

17	Abolition of Untouchability. The parliament has passed protection of civil rights act, 1955 to abolish untouchability.
18	Abolition of Titles except military and academic titles, *i.e*, Bharat Ratna, Padma Vibhushan, Padma Shri and National Awards.

The Supreme Court held that the right under Article-17 is available against private individuals and it is the constitutional obligation of the state to take necessary action to ensure that this right is not violated.

In 1996, Supreme Court upheld the constitutional validity of the National Awards – Bharat Ratna, Padma Vibhushan, Padma Bhusan and Padma Shri i.e. the court held that these awards do not amount to 'titles' within the meaning of Article-18.

ARTICLE 19
- Provides for 6 fundamental rights in the nature of freedoms. These are guaranteed to Indian citizens with reasonable restrictions.

Freedom		Restrictions imposed	
19 (1) (a)	Speech & Expression Freedom of Press & Media. People's Right to Information	19 (2) 8 Grounds	Integrity and sovereignty of India
			Security of the state
			Friendly relations with foreign states
			Public order
			Decency and morality
			Contempt of court
			Defamation
			Incitement to an offence
19 (1) (b)	Freedom to assemble peacefully	19(3) 3 Grounds	Assembly must be peaceful.
			Assembly must be unarmed
			Restriction under Art 19 (3): Sovereignty and integrity of India Public order
19 (1) (c)	Form Freedom to Associations	19 (4) 3 Grounds	Sovereignty and integrity of India
			Public order
			Morality
19 (1) (d)	Freedom of Movement	19 (5) 2 Grounds	Interest of general public
			Protection of interests of any Scheduled Tribe
19 (1) (e)	Freedom of Residence	19 (5) 2 Grounds	Interest of general public
			Protection of interests of Scheduled Tribe.
19 (1) (f)	Freedom of Profession, Occupation, Trade or Business	19 (6)	By the state making any law relating to: Protecting Public interest.
			Establishing professional/ technical qualifications for a profession/ occupation, trade or business.
			Enabling state to conduct any trade or business excluding citizens wholly or partially.

These six rights are protected against only state action and not private individuals.

Freedom of speech and expression includes:

- Freedom of the Press.
- Right to Telecast.
- Freedom of Silence.
- Right aganist bundh called by a political party.
- Right to demonstration or picketing but not right to strike.
- With reference to freedom of Association the Supreme Court held that the trade unions have no guaranteed right to effective bargaining or right to strike or right to declare a lock-out.

The freedom of movement has two dimensions, i.e. internal (right to move inside the country) and external (right to move out of the country and right to come back to the country).

- Article-19 protects only the first dimension. The second dimension is dealt by Article-21 (right to life and personal liberty).
- With reference to freedom of profession, no objection can be made when the state carries on a trade, business, industry or service either as a monopoly to the exclusion of citizens or in competition with any citizen.

ARTICLE 20 : Protection in respect of conviction for offences

- Provides 3 safeguards to persons accused of crimes:
  - **Article 20 (1): Ex-Post facto law** – no person shall be convicted of any offence except for the violation of 'law in force'. Such protection does not apply in case of Preventive Detention.
  - **Article 20 (2): Double Jeopardy** – no person shall be prosecuted and punished for the same offence more than once.
  - **Article 20 (3): Prohibition against Self Incrimination** – no person accused of an offence shall be compelled to be a witness against himself.

An ex-post-facto law is one that imposes penalties retrospectively, that is upon acts already done or which increases the penalties for such acts.

- A civil liability or a tax can be imposed retrospectively.

ARTICLE 21 and 22 : Protection of Life and Personal Liberty

- Constitution provides for a two fold guarantee:
  - No person shall be deprived of his life and personal liberty except according to the law **(Article 21).**
  - Safeguards against arbitrary arrest and detention **(Article 22).**
- Prior to Menaka Gandhi Case (1978), Article 21 guaranteed the Right to Life and Liberty against arbitrary action of the executive. Article 21 now protects Right to Life and Personal Liberty even from legislative action. It includes –
- Right to live with human dignity.
- Right to livelihood.
- Right to privacy.
- Right to shelter.
- Right to health and Medical Assistance.
- Right to free legal aid.
- Right against solitary confinement.
- Available to 'citizens' and 'non-citizens'.
- **Right to Education is a Fundamental Right under Article 21-A (86th Constitutional Amendment 2002).**
- Provision of Compensation if Article 21 is violated.
- Right to Death is not a fundamental right under Article 21.

ARTICLE 22: Protection against Arrest and Detention

Article 22 grants protection to persons who are *arrested* or *detained*. Detention is of two types – *punitive* and *preventive*. **Punitive Detention** is to punish a person for an offence committed by him after trial and conviction in a Court. **Preventive** means detention of a person without trial and conviction by a person for a past offence, but to prevent him from committing an offence in the near future.

- It includes
  - Right to be informed about the ground of arrest.
  - Right to be defended by a lawyer of his own choice.
  - Right to be produced before a magistrate within 24 hours.
  - No detention beyond 24 hrs except by order of the magistrate.

No law providing for preventive detention shall authorize the detention of a person for a longer period than 3 months unless - an advisory board consisting of persons who are qualified to be appointed as judge of a High Court has reported before the expiration of the said period of 3 months that their is in its option sufficient cause for such detention.

- This right is not available to an enemy, an alien and a person arrested and detained under Preventive Detention.

The 44th Amendment Act of 1978 has reduced the period of detention without obtaining the opinion of an advisory board from three to two months.

It is noteworthy that no democratic country in the world has made preventive detention as an integral part of the constitution as has been done in India.

ARTICLE 23 and 24: Right Against Exploitation

- **Article 23:** protects individual against actions of the state and private citizens. This right is available to both citizens and non-citizens.
- **Article 23(i):** prohibits traffic in human beings and forced labour,
- **Article 23(ii):** nothing in this article shall prevent state from imposing compulsory services for public purpose and in imposing such service the state shall not make any discrimination on grounds of religion, race, caste or class or any of them.
- **Article 24:** prohibits employment of children below 14 years of age in a dangerous occupation, factory and mines.

The expression 'traffic in human beings' include :

(a) Selling and buying of men, women and children like goods.

(b) Immoral traffic in women and children.

(c) Devadas is.

(d) Slavery.

Article-23 also permits the state to impose compulsory service for public purpose, as for example military service or social service.

The child Labour (Prohibition and Regulation) Act, 1986 is the most important law to enforce the rights granted under Article-24.

In 2006, the government banned the employment of children as domestic servants or workers in business establishments like hotels, dhabas, restaurant.

ARTICLE 25 and 28: Right to Freedom of Religion

- India, under the Constitution, is a **"Secular State"**, *i.e.* a state which observes an attitude of neutrality and impartiality towards all religions.
- **There is no "State religion" in India.** State will not establish a religion of its own, nor will it patronize any religion. This is implicit from:
  - State will not compel any citizen to pay any tax for promotion or maintenance of a religion or religious institution **(Article 27).**
  - No religious instruction shall be provided in an educational institution run completely by government funds.
  - Religious instruction can be imparted in educational institutions recognized by or receiving aid from the state, no person attending such institution shall be compelled to receive such religious instructions **(Art 28).**
- **Article 25** guaranteed the Freedom of Conscience and Freedom to Profess, Practice and Propagate personal religion
- Right to 'Propagate' under Article 25 gives the right only to disseminate the tenets of religion but it would not include the *Right to Convert*.
- States have made it a penal offence to convert or attempt to convert a person by means of *"force, fraud or allurement'*.
- Volunteer conversion with free consent is allowed.
- **Article 26** provides rights to every religious group or denominations:-
  - To establish and maintain institutions for religious and charitable purposes.
  - To manage its own religious affairs.
  - To own and acquire movable and immovable property.
  - To administer such property in accordance with national laws.

Article-25 covers not only religious beliefs (doctrines) but also religious pratices (rituals).

Aricle-26 protects collective freedom of religion. Like the rights under Article-25, the rights under Article-26 are also subject to public order, morality and health but not subject to other provisions relating to the Fundamental Rights.

Article-27 lays down that no person shall be compelled to pay any taxes for the promotion or maintenance of any particular religion or religious denomination.

In other words the state should not spend the public money collected by way of tax for the promotion or maintenance of any particular religion.

Cultural and Educational Rights

- **Article 29 (1)** guarantees to citizens having a distinct language, script or culture of its own, the right to conserve the same.

- **Article 30** provides for the right to religious and linguistic minorities to establish and maintain educational institution to conserve their language, script or culture.
- **Article 30 (2)** prohibits the state from discriminating against any educational institution in grant of aid. No citizen shall be denied admission to educational institutions maintained by the state or receiving aid out of state funds on grounds of religion, race, caste and language. It is compulsory for unaided private institutions to give reservations to backward classes. Minority institutions are exempted from such obligation.
- Article 29 applies only to citizens.
- Article 30 applies to both citizens and non-citizens.

ARTICLE 31-A, 31-B & 31-C

Art	Relates To	Amendment
31 A	Facilitate agrarian reforms	1st Amendment, 1951
31 B	None of the acts mentioned in 9th Schedule shall be deemed to be void on the ground that they are inconsistent with Part III of the Constitution. Legislature is competent to amend and repeal these acts.	1st Amendment, 1951
31 C	Empowers legislature to enact laws for implementing Directive Principles of State Policy under Articles 39 (b) & (c). Only Articles 39(b) & (c) have over-riding effect over fundamental rights.	25th Amendment, 1971

- Supreme Court has viewed that *9th Schedule* must come under Judicial Review. Sates have passed acts regarding reservations, and placed them under Schedule 9 to make them non-justiciable.
- Right to Property which was a fundamental right under Article 31, was repealed by 44th Constitutional Amendment, 1978. It was made a Constitutional Right under ordinary law under Article 300-A.

ARTICLE 32: Right to Constitutional Remedies

Article-32 confers the right to remedies for the enforcement of the fundamental rights of an aggrieved citizen. In other words, the right to get the Fundamental Rights protected is in itself a fundamental right.

- It empowers a person to approach the Supreme Court directly for the enforcement of his Fundamental Rights.
- Right to Constitutional Remedies cannot be suspended except otherwise provided in the Constitution, *i.e.* during Emergency.
- Dr. Ambedkar calls this article **"the very soul and heart of the Constitution."**

Writs Under Article 32	
Habeas corpus means *'to produce the body of*	Order to the person who has detained another to produce the detainee before the court. This is issued to let the court know the grounds of confinement. This protects *individual liberty*. It is a powerful safeguard against arbitrary Acts not only of *private individual* but also of the *Executive*.
Mandamus means *'a Command'*	Commands a public or quasi-public legal person to perform his duty. The writ of mandamus can be issued by the court to enforce Fundamental Rights: whenever a public officer or a Government has committed an Act violating a person's Fundamental Rights, the court can restrain that authority from enforcing such orders or committing such an act.
Prohibition means *'to forbid'*	Issued by Supreme Court or High Court to a lower court forbidding it continue proceedings in a case beyond its jurisdiction or exercise jurisdiction which is not vested with it legally. The Supreme Court can issue the writ only where a Fundamental Right is affected because of jurisdictional defect in their proceedings.
Certiorari means *'to be certified'*	Issued to a lower court after a case has been decided by it quashing the decision or order. It ensures that the jurisdiction of an inferior court or tribunals is properly exercised. While prohibition is available during the pendency of the proceedings and before the order is made, certiorari can be issued only after the order has been made under similar circumstances.
Quo Warranto means *'what is your authority'*	Issued by the court to enquire into the legality of claim which a person asserts to a public office. The writ of quo warranto enables the public to see that a public office is not usurped by an unlawful claimant.

- **Article 226** gives power to High Court to issue writs.
- **Article 32** is used for the enforcement of fundamental rights only, Article 226 is helpful for "any other purpose" also.

While the Supreme Court can issue writs only for the enforcement of fundamental rights, whereas a High Court can issue writs not only for the enforcement of Fundamental rights but also for any other purpose.

Therefore the writ jurisdiction of the High Court is wider than that of Supreme Court in this respect.

However the territorial jurisdiction of the Supreme Court for the purpose of issuing writs is wider than that of a High Court.

Parliament can empower any other court to issue directions, orders and writs of all kinds. Any other court does not include High Courts.

Also constitution provides that the President can suspend the right to move any court for the enforcement of the fundamental right during a National Emergency (Article-359).

- Courts also issue Injunction, which is not mentioned in the Constitution. It is issued against private persons.
- **Public Interest Litigation (PIL)**
  The traditional rule to apply for redressal of breach of fundamental rights. The person whose right has been breached can approach the court (locus standi).
- **Public Interest Litigation (PIL), borrowed from USA, is being applied for achieving larger public interest. Any public-spirited person can go to the court for redressal of breach of fundamental rights.**

Right to Information

The right to information has been granted to citizens under **the Information Act passed by the Indian Parliament in 2005**. The Act entitles every citizen to have access to information controlled by public authorities of both the Union and the State governments. The main objective of this right is to make the government open, transparent, responsive and accountable to the people. According to this law people can seek any information from the government, which is duty bound to provide the requisite information within a specified period of 30 days. If the concerned authorities do not provide correct and timely information, complaint can be lodged with the Central Information Commission/State Information Commission. If the requested information is denied to a person, he/she must be informed of the reasons for refusal. It may further be noted that the law does not apply to Jammu and Kashmir, or security agencies like IB, RAW and BSE. The other areas which have been excluded from the jurisdiction of the law include cabinet papers, legal advice relating to decision making, information likely to breach the privileges of the Parliament and state legislatures, etc.

Applicablity of Fundamental Rights to Armed Forces

Article-33 empowers the Parliament to restrict or abrogate the fundamental rights of the members of armed forces, para-military forces, police forces, intelligence agencies.

The power to make laws under Article-33 is conferred only on Parliament and not on state legislatures. Efficicacy of these rights.

- FRs are stated in a vague, indefinite and ambigous manner.
- Judicial process is too expensive and hinders the common man from getting his rights enforced through the court.
- Critics assert that the provision for preventive detention (Article-22) takes away the spirit and substance of fundamental rights.

Suspension of Fundamental Rights

- Fundamental rights are not absolute and have limitations regarding their exercise. The limitations strike a balance between individual liberty and social need.

- **Article 358** provides that during national emergency, President under Article 352, fundamental freedoms guaranteed by Article 19 are suspended and cannot be revived during emergency. Things done during emergency cannot be challenged even after it is over.
- **Article 359** empowers the President to suspend the Right to move a Court for the enforcement of rights conferred by Part III of the Constitution (except Article 20 & 21) during an emergency.
- Under Article 358, rights conferred by article 19 are suspended. Suspension under article 359 can only be by an order of the President.

Can Fundamental Rights be Amended

- Whether fundamental rights are amendable is debatable.
- In Golaknath case, 1967, Supreme Court questioned the validity of amendments to the Constitution by the parliament. It held the amendments to be invalid.
- 24th Amendment 1971, added word 'Power' to Article 368 and described specifically the power of Parliament to amend the Constitution and laid down procedures.
- This was challenged in Keshavanand Bharati case (1973) in which *"Basic Structure"* doctrine was established by the Supreme Court. Parliament had the power to amend the Constitution without harming its Basic structure. But as to what forms the basic structure is not clear.
- 42nd **Amendment** was passed by the parliament in 1976. It was called the **"Mini Constitution"**. It gave unlimited amending powers to the Parliament. The validity of this amendment was tested in Minerva Mills case, 1980. The basic structure of the Constitution has been pronounced by the Supreme Court.
- The Parliament is not authorized to limit the operation of Articles 14, 19 and 21 which form the part of basic structure of the Constitution.

Exception to Fundamental Rights

- Article-31(A) saves five categories of laws from being challenged and invalidated on the ground of contravention of the fundamental rights conferred by Article-14.
- Article-31(B) saves the acts and regulations included in the Ninth Schedule from being challenged and invalidated on the ground of contravention of any of the faundamental rights.
- No law that seeks to implement the Directive Principles Specified in Article-39(b) or (c) shall be void on the ground of contravention of the fundamental rights conferred by Article-14.

Criticism of Fundamental Rights

- FRs are subjected to innumerable exceptions, restrictions, qualifications and explanations.
- FRs mainly consists of political rights and lacks in economic and social rights.
- FRs are not sacrosanct as the Parliament can curtail or abolish them.
- The suspension of the enforcement of FRs during the National Emergency is another blot on the

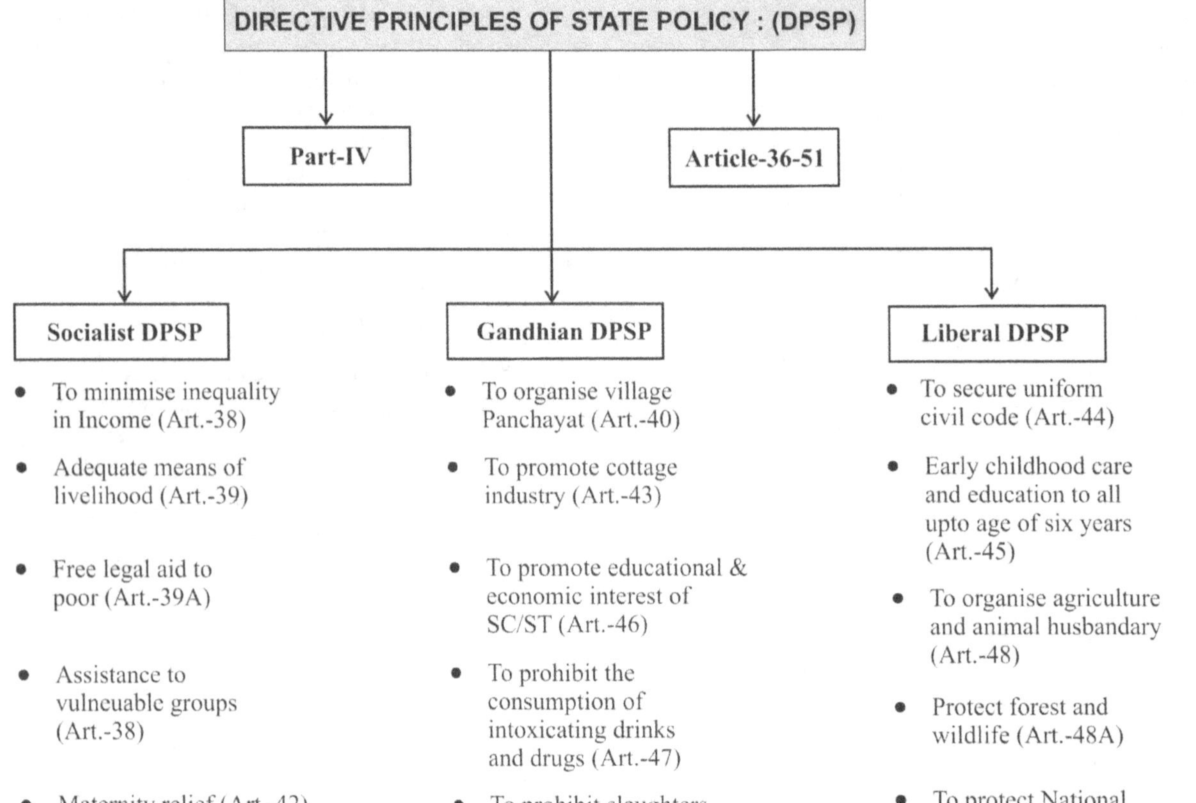

Brief Note of DPSP

- India borrowed the concept of Directive Principles from the Irish Constitution of 1937, who in turn copied it from the Spanish Constitution.
- The DPSP are enumerated in Part-IV of the Constitution from Article 36 to 51.
- Directive Principles are the ideals that the state should strive to achieve. Therefore states should keep these principles in mind while formulating policies and enacting laws.
- The term 'state' in Part-IV has the same meaning as in Part-III dealing with Fundamental Rights.
- The Directive Principles resemble the 'Instrument of Instructions' enumerated in the Government of India Act of 1935.
- DPSP embody the concept of a s'welfare state' and not that of a 'police state', which existed during the clolonial era.
- The Directive Principles are non-justiciable in nature, that is, they are not legally enforceable by the courts for their violation.
- While fundamental rights aim at political freedom, DPSP aim at securing economic and social justice through appropriate state action.
- They impose obligations on the state and give directions to take positive action to promote social welfare.
- Articles 38 & 39 embody the Jurisprudential doctrine of "Distributive Justice".
- 42nd Amendment Act (1976) added Articles 39-A, 43-A, 48-A. Provision for "Creation of Opportunities for healthy development of children" in Article 39 (A).

Article	Relates To
38	Social order based on justice and to minimise inequalities in income, status, facilities and opportunities.
39	Principles of policy to be followed by the State for securing economic justice in the form of: • Means of Livelihood to all. • Use of resources for common good. • Prevention of concentration of wealth. • Equal pay for equal work. • Protection of workers. • Protection of children and youth.
39 A	Equal justice and free legal aid to the poor. Legal aid and speedy trial are fundamental rights under Article 21 of the Constitution available to all prisoners and are enforceable by the courts.
40	Organization of village panchayats.
41	Right to Work, Education and Public assistance in some cases.
42	Just and humane conditions of work.
43	Living wage for workers. Living wage and not minimum wage.
43 A	Participation of workers in management.
44	Uniform civil code.
45	Free and compulsory education for children.
46	Educational and economic interests of SC, ST and weaker sections.
47	Standard of living and improvement in health.
48	Agriculture and animal husbandry.
48 A	Protection of environment, forests and wildlife.
49	Protection of monuments, places and objects of national importance.
50	Separation of judiciary from the executive.
51	Promotion of international peace and security.

Directive Principles added by Amendments

The 42nd Amendment Act : 1976 added four new Directive Principles to the original list.

1. To secure opportunities for healthy development of children (Art.-39)
2. To promote equal justice and to provide free legal aid to the poor. (Art.-39A)
3. Participation of workers in the management of industries. (Art.-48A)
4. To improve the environment and to safeguard forests and wild life (Art.-48 A).

The 44th Amendment Act of 1978 added one more Directive Principle, which requires the state to minimise inequalities in income status, facilities and opportunities (Art.-38).

Directives in other Parts of the Constitution

Besides the directives in part IV, there are certain other Directives in the Constitution, which are also non-Justiciable. These include **Article 350 A** which calls upon the state to provide adequate facilities for instruction in mother tongue at primary school level to children from linguistic minority groups. **Article 351** calls upon the Union to promote the spread and development of Hindi to enable it to become the medium of expression of all the parts of the composite culture of India. **Article 335** supports the claims of the Scheduled Castes and Scheduled Tribes to appointments in government service, subject to the maintenance of efficiency of administration.

Fundamental Rights and Directive Principles: Difference

There is no doubt that both the Fundamental Rights and the Directive Principles of State Policy are important feature of the Constitution. However, they differ from each other in certain ways.

Differences –

(i) The Fundamental Rights seek to protect the individual from state encroachment and thus they are enforceable; the Directive Principles are aimed at the promotion of the general welfare of society and they are not enforceable.

(ii) The Fundamental Rights constitute limitations upon State action; The Directive Principles are positive instructions to the government to take steps to establish a just social, economic and political order.

FUNDAMENTAL DUTIES

- Covered under **Article 51-A** (PART IV A) of the Constitution.
- **Added to the Constitution by 42nd amendment, 1976.**
- **Added on the recommendations of "Swaran Singh Committee."**
- Originally there were **10 duties,** but Art-51-A (k) was added by 86th Amendment Act, 2002. (93rd amendment bill) to add one more fundamental duty.
- Borrowed from the Constitution of **USSR**.

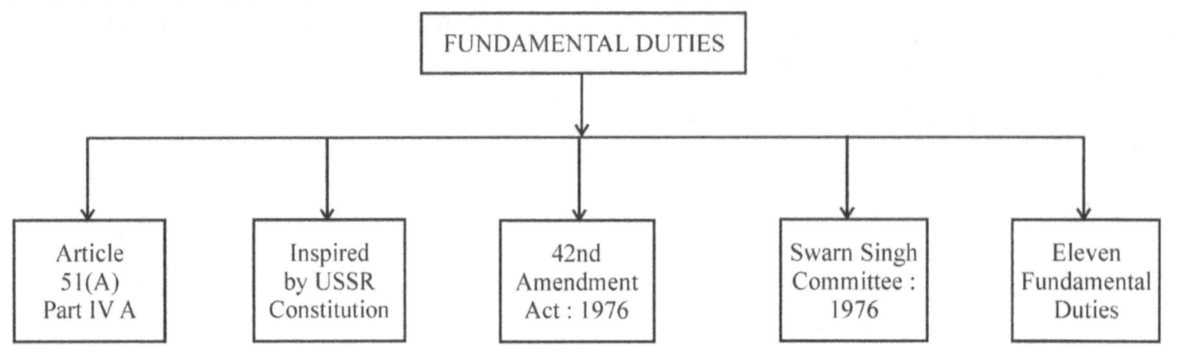

Article - 51 (A)	ELEVEN FUNDAMENTAL DUTIES
(a)	To abide by the Constitution and respect its ideals and institution, the National Flag and the National Anthem.
(b)	To cherish and follow the noble ideals that inspired the national struggle the sovereignty, unity and integrity of India.
(c)	To uphold and protect the sovereignty unity and integrity of India.
(d)	To defend the country and render national service when called upon to do so.
(e)	To promote harmony and the spirit of common brotherhood.
(f)	To value and preserve the rich heritage of country.
(g)	To protect the natural environment including forests.
(h)	To develop scientific temper, humanism and the spirit of inquiry and reform.
(i)	To safeguard public property and to abjure violence.
(j)	To strive towards excellence in all spheres.
(k)	To provide opportunities for education to his child or ward between the age of six and fourteen years.

Characteristic features of Fundamental Duties

- Some of them are moral duties while others are civic duties.
- Speaks of those values/norms which have been integral part of Indian tradition, mythology, religions and practices.
- The Fundamental Duties are confined to citizens only and do not extend to foreigners.
- The Fundamental Duties are non-justiciable.
- There are not legal sanction against the violation of Fundamental Duties.

Verma Committee on Fundamental Duties

In 1999, the Verma Committee on Fundamental Duties of the citizens identified and pointed out the legal provisions for the enforcement of certain Fundamental Duties. The following are some of them:

(a) The Prevention of Insults to National Honour Act (1971) prevents disrespect to the Constitution of India, the National Flag and the National Anthem.

(b) The Indian Penal Code declares the imputations and assertion prejudicial to national integration as punishable offences.

(c) The Wildlife (protection) Act 1972 prohibits trade in rare and endangered species.

(d) The Representation of People Act (1951) has provided for the disqualification of members of the Parliament or a State Legislature for indulging in corrupt practice of soliciting votes on the ground of religion or promoting enmity between different sections of people on grounds of religion, caste, race and language, etc.

Exercise -1

1. The Verma Committee on Fundamental Duties of the citizens (1999) identified the existence of legal provisions for the implementation of some of the fundamental duties. Which among the following is not one among them.
   - (a) The protection of Civil Rights Act (1955)
   - (b) The Indian Penal Code (IPC)
   - (c) The representation of People Act (1951)
   - (d) The Government of India Act (1935)

2. Which provision of the Present Indian Constitution resembles closely to the "Instrument of Instructions" enumerated in the Government of India Act of 1935–
   - (a) Fundamental Rights
   - (b) Emergency Provisions
   - (c) Directive Principles of State Policy
   - (d) Other than those given in the options

3. Which of the following is not a fundamental duty of the citizens as listed in Article-51 (A):
   - (a) To strive towards excellence in all spheres.
   - (b) To promote harmony and the spirit of common brotherhood.
   - (c) To pay taxes and oblige to other financial rules.
   - (d) To defend the country and render national services when called upon to do so.

4. Recently Art-28(1) of the constitution was in news. Art-28(1) pertains to
   - (a) Freedom to manage religious affairs.
   - (b) Freedom of conscience and free profession, practice and propagation of religion.
   - (c) Freedom as to payment of taxes for promotion of any particularly religion.
   - (d) Restrictions on religious instruction in state funded institutions.

5. Which of the following is not a fundamental rights available to a person who is not a citizen of India but residing in any part of India:
   - (a) Equality of opportunity in matters of public employment.
   - (b) Protection in respect of conviction for offence.
   - (c) Protection of life and personal liberty.
   - (d) Right to elementary education.

6. In context of Fundamental right of equality before law, the Indian Constitution makes exceptions in the case of
   - (a) President or a Governor
   - (b) Foreign sovereigns only
   - (c) President only
   - (d) None of the above

7. Constitution permits preventive detention but stipulates that:
   - (a) no one should be detained beyond three months unless an Advisory Board authorises further detention.
   - (b) grounds for detention should be conveyed to the person before arresting him
   - (c) the person must be produced before a magistrate within 24 hours of the arrest
   - (d) All of the above

8. Who can impose reasonable restrictions on Fundamental Rights?
   - (a) Supreme Court
   - (b) Parliament
   - (c) President on the advice of the Council of Ministers
   - (d) None of these as restrictions are provided in the Constitution

9. Enforcement of Directive Principles depends on
   - (a) Judiciary
   - (b) Effective opposition in the Parliament
   - (c) Resources available to the Government
   - (d) Public cooperation

10. If the State implements a Directive Principle calling for equitable distribution of material resources it
    - (a) is put in the Ninth Schedule
    - (b) is not void even if it violates the rights in Articles 14 and 19
    - (c) can be struck down by the Supreme Court on grounds of violating Fundamental Rights
    - (d) is not void if it violates a fundamental right

11. Which of the following Constitutional Amendment Act added a new fundamental duty in Part-IVA and Article-51(A) of the Constitution?
    - (a) Forty-Second   (b) Forty-Fourth
    - (c) Eighty-Sixth   (d) Ninety-Second

12. Right to Information Act, 2005 is :
    - (a) A fundamental right under the Constitution
    - (b) Available only to citizens
    - (c) Applicable for all public and private bodies
    - (d) Applicable for all states

13. Which Article of the Constitution of India says, 'No child below the age of fourteen years shall be employed to work in any factory or mine or engaged in any other hazardous employment'?
    - (a) Article 24   (b) Article 45
    - (c) Article 330   (d) Article 368

14. The Fundamental Duties were added to the Constitution
    - (a) to make the fundamental rights more effective
    - (b) to check anti-national, subversive and unconstitutional agitations
    - (c) to accord priority to the directive principles over fundamental rights
    - (d) to achieve all the above objectives

15. A fundamental Right guaranteed in the Indian Constitution can be suspended only by
(a) a proclamation of national emergency
(b) an Act passed by the Parliament
(c) an amendment of the Constitution
(d) the judicial decision of the Supreme Court

16. "The state shall strive to promote the welfare of people by securing and protecting as effectively as it may, a social order in which justice–social, economic and political–shall inform all the institutions of the national life." This provision is contained in which of the following articles of the Indian Constitution?
(a) Article 39 (b) Article 46
(c) Article 38 (d) Article 37

17. The Directive Principles of State Policy are incorporated in
(a) Part III (Articles 36-51)
(b) Part IV (Articles 36-51)
(c) Part V (Articles 19-21)
(d) Part II (Articles 36-56)

18. A writ of prohibition is an order issued by the supreme court or high court which
(a) affects the production and consumption of liquor
(b) prohibits the police from arresting a person
(c) forbids the administrative authority from taking a particular action
(d) prohibits a quasi-judicial authority from proceeding with a case

19. The 44th Amendment of the Indian Constitution withdrew the Fundamental Right:
(a) to freedom of religion
(b) to constitutional remedies
(c) to property
(d) against exploitation

20. Which one of the following pairs is not correctly matched?
(a) Power of Parliament : Creating a new State
(b) Power of State Legislature : Altering the name of a State
(c) Equality before the law : Both Indian and non-Indian citizens
(d) Equality of opportunity : Indian citizen

21. Which one of the following is not included in Article 19 of the constitution of India, pertaining to the Right to Freedom?
(a) Right to reside and settle in any part of the territory of India
(b) Right to form associations or unions
(c) Right of minorities to establish and administer educational institutions
(d) Right to assemble peacefully and without arms

22. Which of the following best explains the Directive Principles of state policy, contained in the Constitution?
(a) The main objectives of the framers of the Constitution
(b) The principles that are expected to guide the state in the governance of the country

(c) The ideals of a Welfare State that should be acceptable to all right-thinking persons.
(d) Social rights are opposed to personal rights, enumerated in Part III.

23. Which one of the following is not a correct statement in relation to the provisions of the Indian Constitution?
(a) No person shall be convicated of any offence except for violation of law in force at the time of commission
(b) No person shall be denied bail
(c) No person shall be punished for the same offence more than once
(d) No person accused of an offence shall be compelled to be a witness against himself

24. Which of the following is/are among the list of fundamental duties enumerated in our Constitution?
(a) To abide by the Constitution and respect its ideals and institutions, the National Flag and the National Anthem
(b) To cherish and follow the noble ideals which inspired our national struggle for freedom
(c) To uphold and protect the sovereignty, unity and integrity of India
(d) All of the above

25. Which one of the following is incorrect?
(a) Our Constitution does not discriminate against any citizen on the ground of his religion, in matters of employment to public services or holding public offices
(b) Our Constitution does not prohibit the imparting of religious instruction in educational institutions run by the Government
(c) The Constitution of India guarantees to all the citizens of India the right to profess, practise and propagate a religion of their choice
(d) No person can be made to pay taxes for the promotion of any particular religion under our Constitution

26. Article 21 declares that –
"*No person shall be deprived of his life or personal liberty except according to procedure established by law.*"
This protection under article 21 is:
(a) Against arbitrary legislative action.
(b) Against arbitrary executive action.
(c) Both (a) & (b)
(d) None

27. Which of the following writs can be issued against administrative authorities?
(a) Prohibition, Certiorari & Mandamus.
(b) Certiorari & Mandamus.
(c) Prohibition & Mandamus.
(d) Prohibition & Certiorari.

28. The Preventive Detention Act has a restraining effect on:
(a) Right of Equality
(b) Right to Freedom
(c) Right to Religion
(d) Right to Constitutional Remedies

29. Reasonable restriction on the rights of Indian citizens can be imposed by:
   (a) the President　　(b) the Parliament
   (c) the Supreme Court　(d) None of the above
30. Which Article empower an individual to move to the Supreme Court in case of violation of his/her Fundamental Rights?
   (a) Article 13　　　(b) Article 14
   (c) Article 32　　　(d) Article 34
31. Freedom of speech under the Indian constitution is subject to reasonable restriction on the grounds of protection of
   (a) sovereignty and integrity of the country
   (b) the dignity of the office of the Prime Minister
   (c) both (a) and (b)
   (d) none of the above
32. Cultural and Educational rights include:
   (a) Right of minorities to establish and administer their educational enstitutions
   (b) Right of minorities to promote their language
   (c) Right against discrimination for admission to educational institutions on the grounds of religion, race or caste
   (d) All of these
33. The fundamental right aims to ensure?
   (a) an independent judiciary
   (b) socialistic government
   (c) individual liberty
   (d) none of these
34. Which fundamental right is pertains to with abolition of social distinctions?
   (a) Right to equality
   (b) Right against exploitation
   (c) Right to life and liberty
   (d) Cultural and educational rights
35. The Fundamental Rights have the sanction of:
   (a) the Supreme Court　(b) the Constitution
   (c) majority opinion　(d) the Government
36. How can the Fundamental Rights be suspended?
   (a) If Parliament passes a law by two-thirds majority
   (b) If the Supreme Court orders it
   (c) If the President orders it in the time of National Emergency
   (d) They can never be suspended
37. Which one of the following writs literally means 'we command'?
   (a) Habeas Corpus　(b) Mandamus
   (c) Quo Warranto　(d) Certiorari
38. In India, Mandamus will lie against:
   (a) officers bound to do a public duty
   (b) Government
   (c) both officers and the Government
   (d) none of these
39. The writ of prohibition issued by the Supreme Court or a High Court is issued against:
   (a) judicial or quasi-judicial authorities
   (b) administrative and judicial authorities
   (c) administrative authorities only
   (d) administrative authorities and government

40. Under the Constitution of India, which one of the following is not a fundamental duty ?
   (a) To vote in public elections
   (b) To develop the scientific temper
   (c) To safeguard public property
   (d) To abide by the Constitution and respect its ideals
41. The authority to issue writs for the enforcement of Fundamental Rights rests with whom?
   (a) All the courts in India
   (b) The Parliament
   (c) The Supreme Court
   (d) The President of India
42. How can the Fundamental Rights be protected by a citizen?
   (a) By approaching the Supreme Court which will issue appropriate writs against the authority
   (b) Parliament will take note of such violations and tell the courts
   (c) The Executive will inform the Courts
   (d) It is automatically protected
43. Right to participate in government and equal opportunity to occupy the highest office based on qualification gives the citizens:
   (a) national liberty　(b) political liberty
   (c) natural liberty　(d) civil liberty
44. A citizen's freedom of speech and expression may be subjected to reasonable restriction on the grounds of all except:
   (a) sovereignty of India (b) public order
   (c) contempt of court　(d) unbecoming criticism
45. The Indian Constitution declares that protection of life and liberty:
   (a) can never be taken away in any condition
   (b) can be taken away only according to procedure established by law
   (c) can be taken away during the Emergency through Presidential order
   (d) none of the above
46. 'Economic Justice' as one of the objectives of the Indian Constitution has been provided in
   (a) the Preamble and the Fundamental Rights
   (b) the Preamble and the Directive Principles of State Policy
   (c) the Fundamental Rights and the Directive Principles of State Policy
   (d) None of the above
47. Which of the following Articles of the Constitution of India makes a specific mention of village panchayats?
   (a) Article 19　　　(b) Article 21
   (c) Article 40　　　(d) Article 246
48. The Instrument of Instructions of the Government of India Act 1935 has been incorporated in the Constitution of India as
   (a) Fundamental Rights
   (b) Directive Principles of State Policy
   (c) Fundamental Duties
   (d) Emergency Provisions

49. Freedom of the press in India is
    - (a) available to the people under the law of the Parliament
    - (b) specifically provided in the Constitution
    - (c) implied in the right of freedom of expression
    - (d) available to the people of India under executive order

50. Right to Information in India is a
    - (a) Fundamental Right
    - (b) Legal Right
    - (c) Both Fundamental and Legal Right
    - (d) Neither Fundamental nor Legal Right

51. Which one among the following statements is correct ? The press in democracy must
    - (a) be free and impartial
    - (b) be committed to the policies of the government
    - (c) highlight the achievement of the government without criticizing its policies
    - (d) criticize the policies of the government

52. Which of the following would be construed as a reasonable restriction of the right to freedom'?
    - (a) When the state disallows a candidate from securing votes in the name of religion
    - (b) When the state disallows citizens from forming a club out of State funds that denies access to women
    - (c) When the Government of Nagaland disallows temporary residents to buy immovable property in Nagaland.
    - (d) All of the above

53. Which one of the following is not a correct description of the Directive Principles of State Policy?
    - (a) Directive Principles are not enforceable by the courts
    - (b) Directive Principles have a political sanction
    - (c) Directive Principles are declaration of objective for State Legislation
    - (d) Directive Principles promise equal income and free health care for all Indians

54. Which one of the following International Human Rights Instruments has been signed by India but not yet ratified?
    - (a) Convention on the right of the child.
    - (b) Convention on the Elimination of all forms of discrimination against women
    - (c) Convention on the political rights of women
    - (d) Convention on the nationality of married women

55. Which one of the following is a human right as well as a Fundamental Rights under the Constitution of India?
    - (a) Right to Information (b) Right to Education
    - (c) Right to Work   (d) Right to Housing

56. Which one of the following Fundamental Rights is also available to a foreigner on Indian soil?
    - (a) Prohibition of discrimination on grounds of religion, race, caste, sex or place of birth
    - (b) Equality of opportunity in matters of public employment
    - (c) Protection of life and personal liberty according to procedure established by law
    - (d) To practice any profession or to carry on any occupation, trade or business

57. Which one among the following statements regarding the constitutionally guaranteed Right to Education in India is correct?
    - (a) This right covers both child and adult illiteracy and therefore, universally guarantees education to all citizens of India.
    - (b) This right is a child right covering the age group of 6 to 14 years and becomes operational from the year 2015.
    - (c) This right has been taken from the British Constitution which was the first Welfare State in the world.
    - (d) This right has been given to all Indian children between the ages of 6 to 14 years under the 86th Constitutional Amendment Act.

58. Which one among the following is not guaranteed by the Constitution of India?
    - (a) Freedom to move freely throughout the country
    - (b) Freedom to assemble peacefully without arms
    - (c) Freedom to own, acquire and dispose property anywhere in the country
    - (d) Freedom to practice any trade or profession

59. The purpose of Directive Principles of State Policy is to
    - (a) lay down positive instructions which would guide State Policy at all levels.
    - (b) implement Gandhiji's idea for a decentralised state
    - (c) check the use of arbitrary powers by the government
    - (d) promote welfare of the backward sections of the society

60. According to the Constitution of India, which of the following are fundamental for the governance of the country?
    - (a) Fundamental Rights
    - (b) Fundamental Duties
    - (c) Directive Principles of State Policy
    - (d) Fundamental Rights and Fundamental Duties

61. Which one among the following is a Fundamental Duties of citizens under the Constitution of India?
    - (a) To provide friendly co-operation to the people of the neighbouring countries
    - (b) To protect monuments of national importance
    - (c) To defend the country and render national service when called upon to do so
    - (d) To know more and more about the history of India

62. Which one among the following writs literally means to have the body of?
    - (a) Certiorari   (b) Habeas Corpus
    - (c) Mandamus   (d) Quo Warranto

63. Which one among the following is not a fundamental duty of the citizen of India?
    - (a) To develop scientific temper, humanism and the spirit of inquiry and reform
    - (b) To safeguard public property and to abjure violence
    - (c) To uphold and protect the sovereignty, unity and integrity of India
    - (d) To practice family planning and to control population

64. The writ of Prohibition is issued by a superior court
    (a) to prevent an inferior court or tribunal from exceeding its jurisdiction or acting contrary to the rules of natural justice
    (b) to an inferior court or body exercising judicial or quasijudicial functions to transfer the record to proceedings in a case for its review
    (c) where it can call upon a person to show under what authority he/she is holding the office
    (d) to an authority to produce an illegally detained person before the court for trial

65. Which one among the following is not included in the Fundamental Rights embodied in the Constitution of India?
    (a) Right to Equality
    (b) Right to Freedom
    (c) Right against Exploitation
    (d) Right to Information

66. Which one among the following is a Fundamental Duties of citizens under the Constitution of India?
    (a) To provide friendly cooperation to the people of the neighbouring countries
    (b) To visit the monuments of national importance
    (c) To defend the country and render national service when called upon to do so
    (d) To know more and more about the religions of India

67. Which one among the following statements is not correct?
    (a) The right conferred by Article 32 cannot be suspended except by virtue of Article 359 (1) of the Constitution of India
    (b) The enforcement of Articles 20 and 21 cannot be suspended
    (c) Punishments can be prescribed by a State Legislation for offences under Part III of the Constitution of India
    (d) The Fundamental Rights can be abrogated by law made by the Parliament with regard to members of the forces charged with the maintenance of public order

68. Which of the following freedoms is not specifically mentioned in the Constitution of India as a Fundamental Right but has been subsequently upheld by the Supreme Court as such?
    (a) Freedom of trade, occupation and business
    (b) Freedom to reside and settle in any part of the country
    (c) Freedom of association and union
    (d) Freedom of the press

69. Which one of the following categories of persons is not treated at par so far as the availability of Fundamental Rights is concerned ?
    (a) Members of the armed forces
    (b) Members of the forces charged with the responsibility of maintenance of public order
    (c) Members of the forces employed in connection with the communication systems set up in the country
    (d) Members of the forces employed in connection with the communication systems set up for maintenance of public order

70. Which of the following is not true of Article 32 of the Indian Constitution ?
    (a) It gives the Supreme Court and the High Courts the power to issue writs for the enforcement of Fundamental Rights.
    (b) It is included in Part III of the Indian Constitution and is therefore itself a Fundamental Right.
    (c) Dr. Ambedkar called it the 'very soul of the Indian Constitution'.
    (d) An aggrieved person has no right to complain under Article 32 where a Fundamental Right has not been violated.

71. The purpose of the inclusion of Directive Principles of the State Policy in the Indian Constitution is to establish:
    (a) political democracy
    (b) social democracy
    (c) Gandhian democracy
    (d) social and economic democracy

72. In the Constitution of India, promotion of international peace and security is included in the **[IAS Prelims 2014]**
    (a) Preamble to the Constitution
    (b) Directive Principles of State Policy
    (c) Fundamental Duties
    (d) Ninth Schedule

73. The ideal of Welfare State' in the Indian Constitution is enshrined in its　　　**[IAS Prelims 2015]**
    (a) Preamble
    (b) Directive Principles of State Policy
    (c) Fundamental Rights
    (d) Seventh Schedule

74. Which one among the following is not a Fundamental Right under the Constitution of India?
    (a) Right to equality
    (b) Right to freedom
    (c) Right to citizenship
    (d) Right against exploitation

75. Which one of the following is not a part of the Directive Principles of State Policy as enshrined in the Constitution of India?
    (a) Equal justice and free legal aid
    (b) Protection of monuments and places and objects of national importance.
    (c) Protection of personal law
    (d) Separation of Judiciary from Executive

76. The Right to Education was added to the fundamental Rights in the Constitution of India through the　　　**[CDS-2016]**
    (a) Constitution (86th Amendment) Act, 2002
    (b) Constitution (93th Amendment) Act, 2005
    (c) Constitution (87th Amendment) Act, 2003
    (d) Constitution (97th Amendment) Act, 2011

77. According to the provisions of the Constitution of India, which one of the following is not a fundamental duty?

[CDS-2016]

(a) To respect the National Flag
(b) To defend the country
(c) To provide education to one's child
(d) To promote village and cottage industries

78. Which one of the following statements relating to the Directive Principles of State Policy is not correct?

[CDS-2017]

(a) The provisions contained in Part IV of the Constitution of India shall not be enforceable by any Court.
(b) The Directive Principles of State Policy are fundamental in the governance of the country.
(c) It shall be the duty of the State to apply the Directive Principles in making laws.
(d) The Directive Principles are directed in making India an advanced capitalist country of the world.

79. Right to Privacy is protected as an intrinsic part of Right to Life and Personal Liberty. Which of the following in the Constitution of India correctly and appropriately imply the above statement?

(a) Article 14 and the provisions under the 42nd Amendment to the Constitution
(b) Article 17 and the Directive Principles of State Policy in Part IV
(c) Article 21 and the freedoms guaranteed in Part. III
(d) Article 24 and the provisions under the 44th Amendment to the Constitution

Exercise -2

Statement Based MCQ

1. In context of Fundamental Rights consider the following statements:
   1. Fundamental Rights are absolute Rights.
   2. Government can put reasonable restrictions on the exercise of fundamental rights.

   Select the correct statements.

   (a) 1 only
   (b) 2 only
   (c) Both 1 and 2
   (d) None of the above

2. Consider the following statements:
   1. In the original constitution the subject of local government was assigned to the states.
   2. Local government was mentioned in DPSP as one of the policy directives to all governments in the country.

   Select the correct statement/statements using the codes given below:

   (a) 1 only
   (b) 2 only
   (c) Both 1 and 2
   (d) Neither 1 nor 2

3. Which of the following statements stands true with reference to the constitution of India?
   1. The policy of reservation shall not be seen as a violation of the right to equality.
   2. Right to shelter and livelihood is a Fundamental Right.

   Select the correct answer using the codes given below:

   (a) 1 only
   (b) 2 only
   (c) Both 1 and 2
   (d) None of the above

4. Consider the following statements:
   1. The Fundamental Duties are confined to citizens only and do not extend to foreigners.
   2. Fundamental Duties are non-justiciable.
   3. There is no legal sanction against the violation of fundamental duties.

   Select the correct statement/statements using the codes given below:

   (a) 1 and 2 only
   (b) 2 and 3 only
   (c) 1 and 3 only
   (d) 1, 2 and 3 all

5. Consider the following statements with reference to fundamental rights:
   1. There is a clear tension between right to life and personal liberty and the provision for preventive detention.
   2. Any genuine protest against an act or policy of government by the people can not be denied permission.

   Choose the correct statements using the codes given below.

   (a) 1 only
   (b) 2 only
   (c) Both 1 and 2
   (d) None of these

6. Which of the following is/are not the socialist directive principle as enshrined in part-IV of the constitution:
   1. Organise Village Panchayats.
   2. Equal pay for equal work for men and women.
   3. To prohibit the consumption of intoxicating drinks and drugs.
   4. Maternity relief and humane conditions of work.

   (a) 1, 2 and 3 only
   (b) 1 and 3 only
   (c) 2 and 4 only
   (d) All the above

7.　With reference to the constitution of India which of the following statements is/are correct.

1.　The government can interfere in religious matters for rooting out certain social evils.

2.　One can persuade people to convert from one religion to another.

(a)　1 only　　　　　(b)　2 only

(c)　Both 1 and 2　　(d)　None of the above

8.　Which of the following statements are correct regarding the Directive Principles of State Policy-

1.　They impose a moral obligation on the state authorities for their application.

2.　Public Opinion is the real force behind the application of D.P.S.P.

(a)　1 only　　　　　(b)　2 only

(c)　Both 1 and 2　　(d)　None of the above

9.　Which among the following Directive Principles were added to the constitution through 42nd Amendment Act of 1976.

1.　Free legal aid to poor.

2.　Agriculture and animal husbandry.

3.　To safeguard forests and wildlife.

4.　To promote international peace.

Select the correct answer using the codes given below:

(a)　2 and 4 only

(b)　1, 2 and 3 only

(c)　1 and 3 only

(d)　All the above

10.　Which of the following is/are exceptions to Fundamental Rights:

1.　Amalgamation of corporations.

2.　Land Reforms.

3.　Acquisition of estates and related rights by the state.

Select the correct answer using the code given below:

(a)　1 only

(b)　2 and 3 only

(c)　1, 2, 3 all

(d)　1 and 3 only

11.　Which of the following are examples of implementation of directive principles:

1.　Tenancy reforms.

2.　The Minimum Wages Act (1948)

3.　The wild life (protection) Act, 1972.

4.　Community Development Programme (1952)

(a)　1 and 2 only　　(b)　2 and 3 only

(c)　1, 2, 3 only　　(d)　All the above

12.　Which of the following is/are among the Fundamental Right as possessed by an Indian citizen.

1.　Right to telecast.

2.　Right to strike.

3.　Right against bandh called by a political party/ organization.

4.　Right to know about government activities.

Select the correct answer using the codes given below:

(a)　1, 2, 3 only　　　(b)　1, 3, 4 only

(c)　2, 3, 4 only　　　(d)　All the above

13.　The rights included in Part III of the Constitution are called 'fundamental' because?

1.　They are available to both citizens and aliens

2.　They are above ordinary law

3.　They are fundamental to governance.

4.　They are not absolute

Which of the above is/are correct?

(a)　2 and 4　　　　　(b)　1, 2 and 3

(c)　1, 3 and 4　　　(d)　3 only

14.　Which among the following rights comes under Right to Equality?

1.　Non-discrimination by State on grounds of religion or race

2.　Equal protection before law

3.　Equal pay for equal work

4.　Equality of opportunity in employment provided by the State

Which of the above is/are correct?

(a)　1, 2 and 3　　　(b)　2, 3 and 4

(c)　2 and 4　　　　　(d)　1, 2 and 4

15.　Which of the following is/are wrongly matched?

1.　Habeas corpus – 'to have a body'

2.　Mandaums – we command

3.　Quo warranto – 'by what authority'

4.　Prohibition - issued to a lower court quashing a decision or order

Which of the above statements is/are correct?

(a)　2, 3 and 4　　　(b)　1 and 2

(c)　3 only　　　　　(d)　3 and 4

16.　Which among the following is/are 'Socialistic' Directive Principle as mentioned in Part-IV of the Constitution?

1.　Prevention of concentration of wealth

2.　Right to work

3.　Separation of judiciary and executive

4.　Organising agriculture along scientific research

Which of the above is/are correct?

(a)　1 and 2　　　　　(b)　1, 2 and 3

(c)　2 and 4　　　　　(d)　1, 2, 3 and 4

17.　Which statement does not indicate the difference between Fundamental Rights and Directive Principles?

1.　Directive Principles aim at promoting social welfare, while Fundamental Rights protect individuals from State encroachment

2.　Fundamental Rights put limitations on State action but Directive Principles are positive instructions to the Government to move towards a just socio-economic order

3. Fundamental Rights were the terminate six months at most the period till the date for presidential election is notified included in the original constitution, but Directive Principles were added by the first amendment
4. Fundamental Rights can be amended but Directive Principles cannot be amended

Which of the following statements is/are correct?
(a) 1 and 2   (b) 2 and 3
(c) 3 and 4   (d) 1, 2 and 4

18. Which are among the Fundamental Duties in the Constitution?
1. To preserve the heritage of our composite culture
2. To abide by the Constitution
3. To strive for excellence in scientific research
4. To render national service

Which of the above is/are correct?
(a) 1, 2 and 3   (b) 1 and 2
(c) 1, 2 and 4   (d) 1, 2, 3 and 4

19. Consider the following statements :
1. Free and compulsory education to the children of 6-14 years age group by the State was made a Fundamental Right by the 76th Amendment to the Constitution of India.
2. Sarva Shiksha Abhiyan seeks to provide computer education even in rural areas.
3. Education was included in the Concurrent List by the 42nd Amendment, 1976 to the Constitution of India.

Which of the statements given above are correct?
(a) 1, 2 and 3   (b) 1 and 2
(c) 2 and 3   (d) 1 and 3

20. Which of among the following is/are true with reference to the Directive Principles of State policy?
1. They are borrowed from the Irish Constitution.
2. They are incorporated in Part V of the Constitution.
3. They seek to provide social and economic base to democracy.
4. The state must compulsorily implement them.
5. All of them are Gandhian in nature.

Select the correct answer using the codes given below:
(a) 1, 2, 3 and 5   (b) 1, 3 and 5
(c) 1,3,4 and 5   (d) 1 and 3

21. Consider the following statements with reference to the Fundamental Rights:
1. They are enforceable in the court of law.
2. These rights are absolute.
3. They can be suspended during national emergency, except some.
4. They are available only to Indian citizens.
5. They are contained in Part IV of the Constitution.

Which of the above statements is/are correct?
(a) 1, 3, 4 and 5   (b) 1, 2, 3 and 5
(c) 1 and 3   (d) 1, 3 and 5

22. Which of the following are envisaged by the right against exploitation in the constitution of India?
1. Prohibition of traffic in human beings and forced labour
2. Abolition of untouchability
3. Protection of the interests of minorities
4. Prohibition of employment of children in factories and mines.

Which of the above statements is/are correct?
(a) 1 and 2   (b) 1 and 3
(c) 2, 3 and 4   (d) 1 and 4

23. Which of the followings is/are among the Fundamental Duties of citizens laid down in the Indian Constitution?
1. To preserve the rich heritage of our composite culture
2. To protect the weaker sections from social injustice
3. To develop the scientific temper and spirit of inquiry
4. To strive towards excellence in all spheres of individual and collective activity

Select the correct answer using the codes given below :
(a) 1 and 2 only   (b) 2 only
(c) 1, 3 and 4 only   (d) 1, 2, 3 and 4

24. In which of the following cases the six rights guaranteed by article 19 can be suspended?
1. External Aggression.
2. Internal Emergency.
3. When Martial Law is in force.

Select the correct answer using the codes given below :
(a) 1 only   (b) 2 & 3 only
(c) 1 & 3 only   (d) 1, 2 & 3

25. Which of the following rights is/are available to foreigners in India.
1. Right to Education.
2. Right to Information.
(a) 1 only   (b) 2 only
(c) Both   (d) None

26. Which of the following statement/s is/are correct:
1. Right to Information is a fundamental right enshrined in article 19 (1) of the constitution.
2. Supreme Court of India is not under the purview of RTI act.

Select the correct answer using the codes given below :
(a) 1 only   (b) 2 only
(c) Both   (d) None

27. Article 32 confers the right to remedies for the enforcement of the FR of an aggrieved citizen. Consider the following statements *w.r.t* article 32.
1. Parliament can suspend this right during national emergency.
2. Only SC shall have the power to issue writs for the enforcement of any of the FR.

Select the correct answer using the codes given below:
(a) 1 only   (b) 2 only
(c) Both.   (d) None

28. Which of the following right(s) is/are enshrined in Article 21 – "No person shall be deprived of his life or personal liberty except according to procedure established by law."
    1. Right to speedy trial.
    2. Right against delayed execution.
    Select the correct answer using the codes given below :
    (a) 1 only   (b) 2 only
    (c) Both   (d) None

29. The directive principles were made non – justifiable and legally non – enforceable because:
    1. The country did not possess sufficient financial resources to implement them.
    2. There was widespread backwardness in the country that could stand in the way of implementation.
    Select the correct answer using the codes given below :
    (a) 1 only   (b) 2 only
    (c) Both   (d) None

30. Which of the following statement/s is/are correct.
    1. The directive principles are meant to establish *Political Democracy*.
    2. The directive principles are meant to establish *Social Democracy*.
    3. The directive principles are meant to establish *Economic Democracy*.
    Select the correct answer using the codes given below :
    (a) 1 only   (b) 2 & 3 only
    (c) 1 & 3 only   (d) 1, 2 & 3

31. Which of the following statement/s is/are correct.
    1. Fundamental Rights enjoy legal supremacy over Directive principles.
    2. The Parliament can amend the Fundamental Rights for implementing the directive principles.
    Select the correct answer using the codes given below :
    (a) 1 only   (b) 2 only
    (c) Both   (d) None

32. Which of the following statements is/are correct?
    Article 26 of the Constitution of India states that subject to public order, morality and health, every religious denomination or any section thereof shall have the right.
    1. to establish and maintain institutions for religious and charitable purposes.
    2. to manage its own affairs in matters of religion.
    3. to own and acquire movable and immovable property.
    Select the correct answer using the codes given below
    (a) Only 1   (b) 1 and 3
    (c) 1 and 3   (d) All of the above

33. Consider the following statements.
    1. Article 46 of the Constitution of India provides for free legal aid to Scheduled Castes and Scheduled Tribes.
    2. Article 14 of the Constitution of India provides for equality before law.

Which of the statements given above is/are correct?
(a) Only 1   (b) Only 2
(c) Both 1 and 2   (d) Neither 1 nor 2

34. In which of the following years the Fundamental Duties have been added to the existent Fundamental Rights in the Constitution of India?
    (a) 1965   (b) 1976
    (c) 1979   (d) 1982

35. Which of the following statements regarding the Fundamental Duties contained in the Constitution of India are correct?
    1. Fundamental Duties can be enforced through writ jurisdiction.
    2. Fundamental Duties have formed a part of the Constitution since its adoption.
    3. Fundamental Duties became a part of the Constitution in accordance with the recommendations of the Swaran Singh Committee.
    4. Fundamental Duties are applicable only to the citizens of India.
    Select the correct answer using the codes given below
    (a) 1 and 2   (b) 2 and 4
    (c) 2 and 3   (d) 3 and 4

36. Which of the following statements is/are correct?
    1. In India, the constitutional remedy under Article 32 is available only in case of Fundamental Rights, not in the case of rights which follow from some other provision in the Constitution.
    2. Both the Supreme Court and High Courts can issue the writs of habeas corpus, mandamus, prohibition, certiorari and quo warranto only for the purpose of enforcement of Fundamental Rights.
    Select the correct answer using the codes given below
    (a) Only 1   (b) Only 2
    (c) Both 1 and 2   (d) Neither 1 nor 2

37. Which of the following statements regarding *writ of certiorari* is/are correct?
    1. There should be court, tribunal or an officer having legal authority to determine the questions of deciding Fundamental Rights with a duty to act judicially.
    2. Write of certiorari is available during the tendency of proceedings before a subordinate court.
    Select the correct answer using the codes given below
    (a) Only I   (b) Only 2
    (c) Both 1 and 2   (d) Neither 1 nor 2

38. Which of the following are envisaged as being part of the 'Right against Exploitation' in the Constitution of India?
    1. Prohibition of traffic in human beings and forced labour.
    2. Abolition of untouchability.
    3. Protection of the interests of the minorities.
    4. Prohibition of employment of children in factories and mines.
    Select the correct answer using the codes given below
    (a) 1 and 2   (b) 1 and 3
    (c) 1 and 4   (d) 2, 3 and 4

39. Which among the following conditions are necessary for the issue of *writ of quo warranto*?
    1. The office must be public and must be created by a Statute or by the constitution itself.
    2. The office must be a substantive one and not merely the function or employment of a servant at the will and during the pleasure of another.
    3. There has been a contravention of the Constitution or a Statute or Statutory Instrument, in appointing such person to that office.
    Select the correct answer using the codes given below
    (a) 1 and 2
    (b) 1 and 3
    (c) 2 and 3
    (d) All of these

40. The Rights to Information means and includes
    1. Inspection of documents.
    2. Taking out files from office to any place desired by the applicant.
    3. Taking photograph of files.
    4. Obtaining information in tapes.
    Select the correct answer using the codes given below
    (a) 1 and 3
    (b) 1, 2 and 3
    (c) 2 and 4
    (d) All of these

41. Which among the following provisions of the Constitution of India is/are fulfilled by the National Social Assistance Programme launched by the Government of India?
    1. Fundamental Rights
    2. Fundamental Duties
    3. Directive Principles of State Policy
    Select the correct answer using the codes given below:
    (a) 1 and 2
    (b) 1 and 3
    (c) Only 3
    (d) All of these

42. Consider the following statements
    1. Forming a cooperative society is a Fundamental Right in India.
    2. Cooperative societies do not fall within the ambit of the Right to Information Act, 2005.
    Which of the statements given above is/are correct?
    (a) Only 1
    (b) Only 2
    (c) Both 1 and 2
    (d) Neither 1 nor 2

43. Which of the following is/are included in the Directive Principles of the State Policy?
    1. Prohibition of traffic in human beings and forced labour
    2. Prohibition of consumption except for medicinal purposes of intoxicating drinks and of other drugs which are injurious to health
    Select the correct answer using the codes given below:
    Code:
    (a) 1 only
    (b) 2 only
    (c) Both 1 and 2
    (d) Neither 1 nor 2

44. Consider the following provisions under the Directive Principles of State Policy as enshrined in the Constitution of India :
    1. Securing for citizens of India a uniform civil code
    2. Organizing village Panchayats
    3. Promoting cottage industries in rural areas
    4. Securing for all the workers reasonable leisure and cultural opportunities
    Which of the above are the Gandhian Principles that are reflected in the Directive Principles of State Policy?
    (a) 1, 2 and 4 only
    (b) 2 and 3 only
    (c) 1, 3 and 4 only
    (d) 1, 2, 3 and 4

45. Which of the following provisions of the Constitution of India have a bearing on Education?
    1. Directive Principles of State Policy
    2. Rural and Urban Local Bodies
    3. Fifth Schedule
    4. Sixth Schedule
    5. Seventh Schedule
    Select the correct answer using the codes given below :
    (a) 1 and 2 only
    (b) 3, 4 and 5 only
    (c) 1, 2 and 5 only
    (d) 1, 2, 3, 4 and 5

46. Which of the following is/are among the Fundamental Duties of citizens laid down in the Indian Constitution?
    1. To preserve the rich heritage of our composite culture
    2. To protect the weaker sections from social injustice
    3. To develop the scientific temper and spirit of inquiry
    4. To strive towards excellence in all spheres of individual and collective activity
    Select the correct answer using the codes given below :
    (a) 1 and 2 only
    (b) 2 only
    (c) 1, 3 and 4 only
    (d) 1, 2, 3 and 4

47. Consider the following statements regarding the Directive Principles of State Policy:
    1. The Principles spell out the socio-economic democracy in the country.
    2. The provisions contained in these Principles are not enforceable by any court.
    Which of the statements given above is / are correct?
    (a) 1 only
    (b) 2 only
    (c) Both 1 and 2
    (d) Neither 1 nor 2

48. Which of the following fundamental rights as enshrined in the Constitution of India belong only to the citizens? **[CDS 2017]**
    1. Article 19 (Protection of right to freedom of speech)
    2. Article 21 (Protection of life and personal liberty)
    3. Article 15 (Prohibition of discrimination)
    4. Article 16 (Equality of opportunity)
    Select the correct answer using the code given below.
    (a) 1, 2 and 3
    (b) 2, 3 and 4
    (c) 1, 3 and 4
    (d) 1 and 4 only

49. Which of the following statements is/ are correct regarding Right to Education in India? **[CDS 2017]**
    1. Free and compulsory education should be provided to all children of the age of six to fourteen years.
    2. The imperative of the provision of the Right to Education Act, 2009 is that schools must have qualified teachers and basic infrastructure.
    3. There should be quality education without any discrimination on the ground of economic, social and cultural background.
    Select the correct answer using the code given below.
    (a) 1, 2 and 3   (b) 1 and 2 only
    (c) 1 and 3 only   (d) 3 only

50. Which of the following statements is/are correct?
    [CDS 2017]
    1. The Directive Principles of State Policy are meant for promoting social and economic democracy in India.
    2. The Fundamental Rights enshrined in Part III of the Constitution of India are ordinarily subject to reasonable restrictions.
    3. Secularism is one of the basic features of Constitution of any country.
    Select the correct answer using the code given below.
    (a) 1 only   (b) 2 only
    (c) 1 and 2 only   (d) 1, 2 and 3

51. Consider the following statements :
    1. As per the Right to Education (RTE) Act, to be eligible for appointment as a teacher in a State, a person would be required to possess the minimum qualification laid down by the concerned State Council of Teacher Education.
    2. As per the RTE Act, for teaching primary classes, a candidate is required to pass a Teacher Eligibility Test conducted in accordance with the National Council of Teacher Education guidelines.
    3. In India, more than 90% of teacher's education institutions are directly under the State Governments.
    Which of the statements given above is/are correct?
    [IAS Prelims 2018]
    (a) 1 and 2   (b) 2 only
    (c) 1 and 3   (d) 3 only
    Difficulty: Tough because such technical details about RTE act are not covered in routine books.

Matching Based MCQ

DIRECTIONS (Qs. 52 to 56) : Match List-I with List-II and select the correct answer using the codes given below the lists.

52.
List-I (Writs)		List-II (Provisions)
(A) Habeas Corpus	(1)	directs public servant to perform some public duty refused to have been performed by him
(B) Mandamus	(2)	directs an individual (private or executive) to produce a detainee before the court
(C) Prohibition	(3)	issued by high court forbidding an inferior court from continuing proceedings in a particular case
(D) Certiorari	(4)	enquires into the legality of the claim which a party asserts to a public office
	(5)	Issued to a lower court quashing its decision in a particular case

(a) A – 5; B – 1; C – 3; D – 2; E – 4
(b) A – 2; B – 1; C – 3; D – 5; E – 4
(c) A – 4; B – 2; C – 3; D – 1; E – 5
(d) A – 3; B – 4; C – 5; D – 2; E – 1

53.
List-I (Writs)		List-II (Literal meanings)
(A) Mandamus	(1)	'By what warrant or authority'
(B) Habeas Corpus	(2)	'We command'
(C) Quo warranto	(3)	'To be certified'
(D) Certiorari	(4)	'You may have the body' or 'To have the body of

(a) A – 2; B – 3; C – 4; D – 1
(b) A – 2; B – 4; C – 3; D – 1
(c) A – 1; B – 4; C – 2; D – 3
(d) A – 2; B – 4; C – 1; D – 3

54. Which one of the following pairs is not correctly matched?
(a) Power of Parliament	:	Creating a new State
(b) Power of State Legislature	:	Altering the name of a State
(c) Equality before the law	:	Both Indian and non-Indian citizens
(d) Equality of opportunity	:	Indian citizen

55. Match List-I (Article of Indian Constitution) with List -II (Provisions) and select the correct answer using the codes given below the lists:

List-I (Article of Indian Constitution)		List-II (Provisions)
A. Article 16 (2)	1.	No person shall be deprived of his property save by the authority of law
B. Article 29 (2)	2.	No person can be discriminated against in the matter of public appointment on the ground of race, religious or caste
C. Article 30 (I)	3.	All minorities whether based on religion or language shall have to establish and administer educational institutions of their choice

D. Article 31 (I)   4. No citizen shall be denied admission into any educational institution maintained by the State, or receiving State aid, on grounds of religion, race, caste, language or any of them

Codes :

(a) A-2, B-4, C-3, D-1   (b) A-3, B-1, C-2, D-4

(c) A-2, B-1, C-3, D-4 (d) A-3, B-4, C-2, D-1

56. Match List I (Articles of the Constitution of India) with List II (Provision) and select the correct answer using the codes given below the lists:

List-I	List-II
A. Article 14	1. The State shall not discriminate against any citizen on grounds only of religion, race, caste, sex place of birth or any of term.

B. Article 15   2. The State shall not deny to any person equality before the law or the equal protection of laws within the territory of India.

C. Article 16   3. 'Untouchability' is abolished and its practice in any form is forbidden.

D. Article 17   4. There shall be equality of opportunity for all citizens in matters relating to employment or appointment to any office under the State.

Codes:

(a) A-2, B-4, C-1, D-3 (b) A-3, B-1, C-4, D-2

(c) A-2, B-1, C-4, D-3 (d) A-3, B-4, C-1, D-2

Hints and Explanations

EXERCISE-1

1. **(d)** The Government of India Act is not relevant in this context.

   Besides the legal provisions given in the question, there are certain other provisions like

   – The wildlife (protection) Act of 1972

   – The forest (conservation) Act of 1980

   – The unlawful Activities (prevention) Act of 1967

2. **(c)** In the words of Dr. B.R. Ambedkar 'The Directive principles are like the "instrument of instructions", which were issued to the Governor-General and to the Governors of the colonies of India by the British Government under the Government of India Act, 1935.

3. **(c)** To pay taxes is not a fundamental duties but a legal obligation for those people who fall under the tax bracket as decided by the government.

   There are 11 fundamental duties mentioned in the constitution. The 11th fundamental duty was added by the 86th Constitutional Amendment Act, 2002.

4. **(d)** Article-28 (1) states that no religious instruction shall be provided to an institute wholly run out of state funds.

   Recently the supreme court questioned a revised education code followed by the central government run Kendriya Vidyalayas, which make students to recite Sanskrit and Hindi verses with folded palms and closed eyes during morning assemblies.

   It raises an important issue where a Secular State, which is supposed to have no religion, is counselling students drawn from diverse faiths, beliefs, minority communities and many other rationalist families.

   Source: N.C.E.R.T- XIth [Indian Constitution at - work]

5. **(a)** Fundamental Rights available to both citizens and foreigners are those provided in Article- (4, 20, 21, 21A, 22 and 23). Fundamental Rights available only to Indian citizens are those provided in Art- 15, 16, 19, 29 and Art-30.

6. **(a)**   7. **(a)**   8. **(b)**   9. **(c)**

10. **(b)**   11. **(a)**   12. **(b)**

13. **(a)** Article 24 of the constitution states that, no child below the age of fourteen years shall be employed to work in any factory or mine or engaged in any other hazardous employment.

14. **(b)**   15. **(a)**   16. **(c)**   17. **(b)**   18. **(d)**

19. **(c)** The 44th Amendment of the Indian constitution removed the right to property from the list of fundamental right and made it an ordinary right.

20. **(b)** In the case of altering the name of a state, requires approval of Union Cabinet and Parliament under article 3 and 4 of the constitution.

21. **(c)**   22. **(b)**   23. **(b)**   24. **(d)**   25. **(b)**

26. **(c)**   27. **(b)**   28. **(b)**   29. **(b)**   30. **(c)**

31. **(a)**   32. **(d)**   33. **(c)**   34. **(a)**   35. **(b)**

36. **(c)**   37. **(b)**   38. **(c)**   39. **(a)**

40. **(a)** To vote in public elections is not a fundamental duty.

41. **(c)**   42. **(a)**   43. **(a)**   44. **(d)**   45. **(b)**

46. **(b)** The Preamble to the Constitution of India in its introductory statement says- "Justice- Social,

47. (c)

48. (d) The instrument of instructions on the government of India act 1935 has been incorporated in the constitution of India in the year 1950 as an emergency provisions.

49. (c) Freedom of the press in India is implied in the right of Freedom of Expression.

50. (a)

51. (a) A press in democracy must be free and impartial.

52. (d)

53. (d) The Directive Principles of State Policy are guidelines for creating a social order characterized by social, economic, and political justice, liberty, equality, and fraternity as enunciated in the constitution's preamble. It does not promise equal income and free healthcare for all Indians.

54. (d) Convention on the nationality of married women has been signed by India but not yet ratified.

55. (b) The Constitution (86th Amendment) Act, 2002 inserted Article 21-A in the Constitution of India to provide free and compulsory education of all children in the age group of six to fourteen years as a Fundamental Right. This is recognized in the International Covenant on Economic, Social and Cultural Rights as a human right that includes the right to free, compulsory primary education for all.

56. (c) According to article 21 of the Indian Constitution, no person shall be deprived of his life or personal liberty except according to procedure established by law. The Supreme Court of India on 19 June 2013 in its decision established that right to life and liberty, enshrined under Article 21 of the Constitution, is available to foreign nationals also.

57. (d) The 86th amendment to the Constitution approved in 2002 providing free and compulsory education to all children age 6 to 14 years has been notified. It included Article 21(a) in the Indian constitution making education a fundamental right.

58. (c) The Indian Constitution does not recognize property right as a fundamental right. In the year 1978, the 44th amendment eliminated the right to acquire, hold and dispose of property as a fundamental right.

59. (a) The purpose of Directive Principle of State Policy is to lay down positive instructions which would guide State Policy at all levels. The Directive Principles of State Policy contained in Part IV, Articles 36-51 of the Indian constitution. The Directive Principles may be said to contain the philosophy of the constitution. The Directive principles are broad directives given to the state in accordance with which the legislative and executive powers of the state are to be exercised.

60. (c) Directive Principles of State Policy are guidelines to the central and State government of India to be kept in mind while framing laws and policies. DPSPs aim to create social and economic conditions under which the citizens can lead a good life. They also aim to establish social and economic democracy through a welfare state. They act as a check on the government. It is a yardstick in the hands of the people to measure the performance of the government. It shall be the duty of the state to apply these principles in making laws.

61. (c) The Forty Second Constitution Amendment Act, 1976 has incorporated ten Fundamental Duties in Article 51(a) of the constitution of India. The 86th Constitution Amendment Act 2002 has added one more Fundamental Duty in Article 51(a) of the constitution of India. As a result, there are now 11 Fundamental Duties of the citizen of India.

62. (b) *Habeas corpus* writs literally means you should have the body. It is writ that a person may seek from a court to obtain immediate release from an unlawful confinement.

63. (d) To practise family planning and to control population, is not a fundamental duty of the citizen of India. The Fundamental Duties of citizens were added to the Constitution by the 42nd Amendment in 1976. Originally ten in number, the Fundamental Duties were increased to eleven by the 86th Amendment in 2002, which added a duty on every parent or guardian to ensure that their child or ward was provided opportunities for education between the ages of six and fourteen years.

64. (a) The writ of Prohibition is an order from a superior court to a lower court or tribunal directing the judge and the parties to cease the litigation because the lower court does not have proper jurisdiction to hear or determine the matters before it.

65. (d) RTI act was passed by Parliament on 15 June 2005 and came fully into force on 12 October 2005.

It has been given the status of a fundamental right under Article 19(a) of the Constitution. Article 19 (a) under which every citizen has freedom of speech and expression and have the right to know how the government works, what role does it play, what are its functions and so on.

66. (c) One of the fundamental duties is to "defend the country and render national service when called upon to do so."

67. (c) The State shall not make any law which takes away or abridges the rights conferred by this Part III and any law made in contravention of this clause shall, to the extent of the contravention, be void.

68. (d) The constitution of India does not specifically mention the freedom of press. Freedom of press is implied from the Article 19(a)(a) of the Constitution.

69. (a) Members of Armed Forces are not treated at par so far as the availability of Fundamental Rights is concerned.

70. (d) Under Article 226,a High Court can issue these writs not only for the purpose of enforcement of the fundamental rights but also for the redressal a of any other injury or illegality, owing to contravention of the ordinary law.

71. (d) The purpose of Directive Principles of State Policy is to establish the social and economic democracy. Political democracy is established by the Fundamental Rights.

72. (b) Promotion of international peace and security is included in the Directive Principles of State as Article 51 of constitution that mentions to promote international peace and security and maintain just an honourable relations between nations between nations; to foster respect for international law and treaty obligations, and to encourage settlements of international disputes by arbitration.

73. (b) Directive Principles of State Policy (DPSPs) aim to create social and economic conditions under which the citizens can lead a good life. They also aim to establish social and economic democracy through a welfare state. The Directive Principles of State Policy are guidelines/principles given to the central and state governments of India, to be kept in mind while framing laws and policies.

74. (c) 75. (c)

76. (a) In 2002, through the 86th amendement act, the Right to Education was added to the Fundamental Rights.

77. (d) The fundamental duties include to abide by the Constitution and respect its ideals and institutions, the National Flag and the National Anthem; to uphold and protect the sovereignty, unity and integrity of India; to defend the country and render national service when called upon to do so; to provide opportunities for education to his child or, as the case may be, ward between the age of six and fourteen years.

78. (d) The Directive Principles of State Policy are a set of guidelines for central and state governments of India for framing laws and policies. These are contained in Part IV (Article 36-51) in Indian Constitution, and though not enforceable, the principles, are fundamental in the governance of the country. They aim to promote social and economic democracy through a welfare state.

79. (c) The Supreme Court ruled that "the right to privacy is protected as an intrinsic part of the right to life and personal liberty under Article 21 and as a part of the freedoms guaranteed by Part III of the Constitution" so Option C is right. [Ref: IndianExpress 2017-August]
Let's also look at the wrong options:

- Article 14- Gives the Right to Equality. 42nd Constitutional Amendment Act 1976, is known as mini constitution.
- Article 17- Related to the Abolition of Untouchability. It is part of Right to Equality. Part IV- Directive Principles of State Policy, does not have any mention about the Privacy.
- Article 24- Prohibition of employment of children in factories, et(c) 44th Constitution Amendment- 44th amendment of the Constitution was enacted by the Janata Government mainly to nullify some of the amendments made by the 42nd Amendment Act, 1976.

EXERCISE-2

1. (b) Judiciary has the powers and responsibility to protect the fundamental rights from violations by actions of the government.
Executive as well as legislative actions can be declared illegal by the judiciary if these violate the fundamental rights or restrict them in an unreasonable manners.
However fundamental rights are not absolute or unlimited rights. Govt. can put reasonable restrictions on the exercise of our fundamental rights.

2. (c) When the constitution was prepared, the subject of local government was assigned to the states. It was also mentioned in the directive principles as one of the policy directives to all governments in the country (Article-40).
However the Directive Principles of State Policy being non-justiciable, the establishment of Panchayati Raj institutions remain primarily advisary in nature.

3. (c) Article 16(4) of the constitution explicitly clarifies that a policy like reservation will not be seen as a violation of right to equality.
The supreme court has ruled that (Article-21) also includes right to live with human dignity, free from exploitation.
 – The court has held that right to shelter and livelihood is also included in the right to life because no person can live without the means of living, that is means of livelihood.

4. (d) All the above given statements are true regarding the fundamental duties. There is no legal sanction against the violation of fundamental duties. Howver parliament is free to enforce them by suitable legislation. Also fundamental duties are non-justiciable that is they are not enforceable in the court.

5. (a) According to the provision of the preventive detention (Art-22), a person can be arrested simply out of an apprehension that he or she is likely to engage in unlawful activity and imprisoned for some time without following the established procedure. Therefore it comes in conflict with the right to life and personal liberty.

The Rights provided by Art-19(i) i.e. right to freedom of speech and expression is subjected to certain restrictions. Such as public order, peace and morality etc.

Therefore any genuine protest against an act or policy of government by the people may be denied permission.

Source: N.C.E.R.T XIth [Indian Constitution at Work]

6. (b) To organise village panchayat (Art-40) and prohibition of consumption of intoxicating drugs (Art-47) are Gandhian directive principles (not the Liberal).

7. (c) Freedom of religion becomes a matter of political controversy for many reasons.

The constitution has guaranteed the right to propagate one's religion (Art-25). This includes persuading people to convert from one religion to another. However the constitution does not allow forcible conversions. It only gives us the right to spread information about over religion and thus attracts others to it.

Rights provided under Article-19(i) are not absolute. The govt. can impose restrictions on the practice of freedom of religion in order to protect public order, morality and health. The government can interfere in religious matters for rooting out certain social evils.

Source: N.C.E.R.T (XIth); Indian constitution at work.

8. (c) Article-37 makes it clear that Directive Principles are fundamental in the governance of the country and it shall be the duty of the state to apply these principles in making laws.

Alladi Krishna Swamy Ayyar observed in the constituent Assembly that "No minister responsible to people can afford to overlook directive principles.

9. (c) The 42nd Amendment Act of 1976 added four new Directive principles to the original constitution.

– Opportunity for healthy development of children (Art-39)

– Equal justice and free legal aid to poor (Art-39 A)

– Participation of workers in the management of industries. (Art-43 A)

– Improve the environment and safeguard forests and wildlife (Art-48 A)

10. (c) Following are the exceptions to Fundamental Rights.

1. Saving of Laws providing for Acquisition of estates, etc.

2. Validation of certain acts and regulations.

3. Saving of law giving effect to certain directive priciples.

All the above given statements are true with reference to question.

11. (d) All the above mention are the examples of implementation of D.P.S.P besides many other like Maternity Benefit Act (1961), Child Labour Prohibition and Regulation Act (1986), 3-tier Panchayati Raj System etc.

12. (b) The Supreme Court held that the freedom of speech and expression includes following:

– Freedom of the press.

– Right to telecast (i.e the government) has no monopoly on electronic Media)

– Right against tapping of telephonic conversation.

– Right against bandh called by a political party or organisation.

– Right to know about government activities.

– Right to demonstration or picketing but not right to strike.

13. (d)	14. (d)	15. (d)	16. (a)	17. (d)
18. (d)	19. (c)	20. (d)	21. (c)	22. (d)
23. (c)	24. (c)	25. (a)	26. (a)	27. (d)
28. (c)	29. (c)	30. (b)	31. (c)	

32. (d) Article 26 of the Indian Constitution states freedom to manage religious affairs subject to public order, morality and health, every religious denomination or any section thereof shall have the right-

(a) to establish and maintain institutions for religious and charitable purposes;

(b) to manage its own affairs in matters of religion;

(c) to own and acquire movable and immovable property; and

(d) to administer such property in accordance with law

33. (b) Article 46 deals with Promotion of educational and economic interests of the weaker sections of the people, and in particular, of the Scheduled Castes and the Scheduled Tribes and shall protect them from social injustice and all forms of exploitation. It does not provide free legal aid to them. According to Article 14, "the State shall not deny to any person equality before the law or equal protection of the laws within the territory of India".

34. (b) The Fundamental Duties were added to the Constitution by the 42nd Amendment in 1976 on the recommendations of the Swaran Singh Committee. They were originally ten in number, but by the 86th Amendment in 2002 they were increased to eleven.

35. (d) The fundamental duties are defined as the moral obligations of all citizens to help promote a spirit of patriotism and to uphold the unity of India. The Fundamental Duties of citizens were added to the Constitution by the 42nd Amendment in 1976, upon the recommendations of the Swaran Singh Committee. The fundamental duties are contained in Art. 51A Part IV(a). The fundamental duties however are non-justifiable in character. This means that no citizen can be punished by a court for violation of a fundamental duty.

36. (c) According to Article 32, when an individual feels that he has been "unduly deprived" of his fundamental rights, he can move the Supreme Court and seek justice. Apart from the Supreme Court, the High Courts also have the power to protect fundamental rights. Like the apex court, they also can issue

writs for the enforcement of fundamental rights of the citizens. Both courts can issue five different writs - *Certiorari, Habeas Corpus, Mandamus, Prohibition*, and *Quo Warranto*.

37. (b) If a lower court or tribunal gives its decision but based on wrong jurisdiction the affected party can move this writ to a higher court like supreme court or High Court. The writ of certiorari issued to subordinate judicial or quasi judicial body when they act.
    - Without or in excess of jurisdiction
    - In violation of the prescribed procedure
    - In contravention of principles of natural justice
    - Resulting in an error of law apparent on the face of record.

38. (c) Articles 23 and 24 of the Indian Constitution safeguard women and children and others against exploitation of various forms.
    Article 23 declares slave trade, prostitution and human trafficking a punishable offence.
    Article 24 of the Indian Constitution prohibits employment of children below the age of 14 years in dangerous jobs like factories and mines.

39. (d) All the conditions given in the question are necessary for issuing writ of quo warranto. The conditions necessary for the issue of a writ of quo warranto are as follows :
    (i) The office must be public and it must be created by a statute or by the constitution itself.
    (ii) The office must be a substantive one and not merely the function or employment of a servant at the will and during the pleasure of another.
    (iii) There has been a contravention of the constitution on or a statute or statutory instrument, in appointing such person to that office.

40. (c) The right to information includes
    - Any document, manuscript and file
    - Any microfilm, microfiche and facsimile copy of a document;
    - Any reproduction of image or images embodied in such microfilm (whether enlarged or not).
    - Any other material produced by a computer or any other device
    It does not include taking photograph of files.

41. (c) The National Social Assistance Programme(NSAP) represents a significant step towards the fulfilment of the Directive Principles in Article 41 of the Constitution. It came into effect from 15th August 1995.

42. (c) With the enactment of the 97th amendment to the Constitution of India and its inclusion in Part IX of the Constitution, formation of cooperative societies has become one of the fundamental rights of an Indian citizen. Cooperative societies have thus come under the ambit of The Right to Information Act. Cooperative societies normally include cooperative banks, credit societies, sugar factories, distilleries, handloom-power loom factories, distilleries, milk producing societies, water supply societies etc.

43. (b) Statement 1 is incorrect as it is a Fundamental Right under article 23 of Part III of the constitution. Statement 2 corresponds to Directive Principles of State Policy under Article 47 under Part IV of the Constitution.

44. (b) Organizing village Panchayats and promoting cottage industries in rural areas are the Gandhian principles that are reflected in the Directive Principles of State Policy.

45. (c) 1, 2 and 5 are correct.

46. (c) All the statements except 2 regarding the Fundamental Duties of citizens are correct.

47. (c) The directive principles ensure that the State shall strive to promote the welfare of the people by promoting a social order in which social, economic and political justice is informed in all institutions of life. The provisions of The Directive Principles of State Policy are not enforceable by any court, but the principles laid down therein are considered fundamental in the governance of the country, making it the duty of the State to apply these principles in making laws to establish a just society in the count.

48. (c) Article 21 (Protection of life and personal liberty) is available to foreigners and Citizens both.

49. (a) Right of Children to Free and Compulsory Education (RTE) Act, 2009 was enacted on 4 August 2009, which focuses on free and compulsory education for children between 6 and 14, quality of education, no discrimination in education based on socio-economic and cultural background, schools with qualified teachers with basic infrastructure, standards relating to pupil teacher ratios, etc.

50. (c) The Directive Principles of State Policy are meant for promoting social and economic democracy in India. The Fundamental Rights enshrined in Part III of the constitution of India are ordinarily subject to reasonable restrictions.

51. (b)
    · Under RTE Act section 23, National Council for Teacher Education (NCTE) decides the minimum qualification. So, #1 is wrong.
    · After RTE it is mandatory that only those people may be appointed as teachers who are able to clear TET. So, #2 is right. Thus by elimination, we get the correct answer B: only 2.

52. (b)   53. (d)

54. (b) In the case of altering the name of a state, requires approval of Union Cabinet and Parliament under article 3 and 4 of the constitution.

55. (a) These are Fundamental Rights under Part III of the Constitution, runs from Art 14 – 32.

56. (c) These are Fundamental rights under Part III of the Constitution.

UNION GOVERNMENT

Chapter 3

Introduction

- Union Government (or Government of India) has three organise, namely the executive, Legislature and the judiciary.
- Part-V of the Constitution deals with the Union Government.

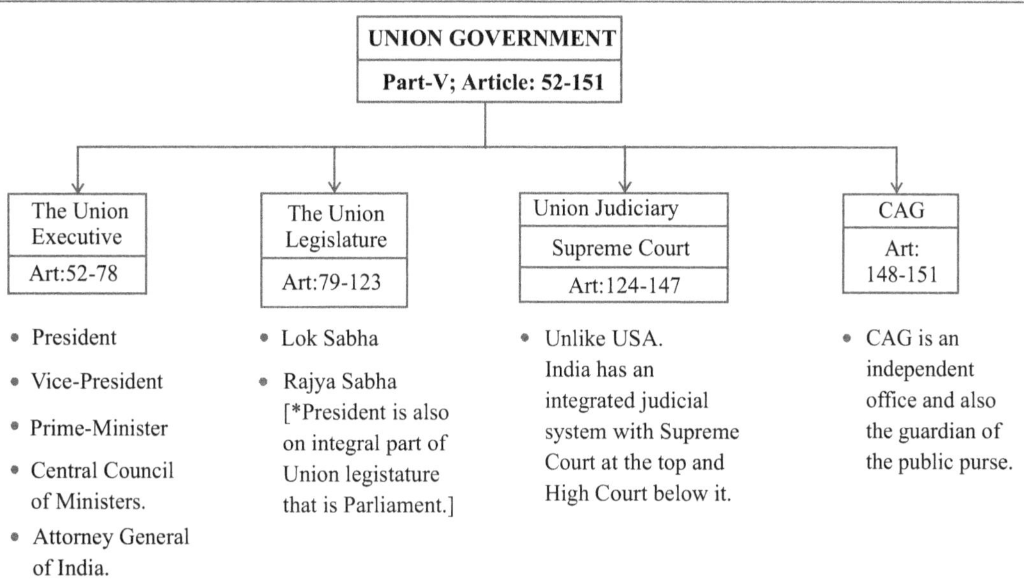

UNION EXECUTIVE

The President

- **Article 52:** There shall be a President of India. He shall be the head of the state.
- **Article 53:** Executive powers of the Union shall be vested in the President (and shall be) exercised by him either directly or through the officers subordinate to him in accordance with the constitution.

Election of the President (Articles 54 & 55)

- **Article 54** provides that President shall be elected by the members of an electoral college consisting of:-

(a) Elected members of both houses of parliament; and

(b) Elected members of the legislative assemblies of the states.

- In Art-54 & Art - 55 the word "State" includes "National Capital Territory of Delhi" and UT of Pondicherry (Puducherry). This was added by 70th Amendment Act, 1992.

Members of legislative councils (in case of the bicameral legislature in state) do not participate in presidential election.

Nominated members of both the Houses at the Centre and the States do not participate in the election of the President.

- **Article- 55 (1) :** There shall be uniformity in the scale of representation of the different states at the election of President.
- **Article- 55 (3) :** states that the election of the President shall be held in accordance with the system of proportional representation by means of single transferable vote & the Voting is done through secret ballot.
- To secure uniformity among states and parity between the Union and states following formula is adopted:

$$\text{Value of the vote of an MLA} = \frac{\text{Total population of the state}}{\text{Elected members of the state legislative assembly} \times 1000}$$

$$\text{Value of vote of an MP} = \frac{\text{Total value of votes of all MLAs of all states}}{\text{Total Nos. of elected MPs}}$$

- Population data used for these calculations are of 1971 census. 42nd amendment, 1976 froze the "last preceding census" to 1971, till the first census after 2000.
- In 2000, the Union cabinet decided to extend the freeze on fresh delimitation of parliamentary and assembly constituencies up to 2026.
- After calculating the value of vote of MLAs and MPs, a complex system of calculating the quota of individual candidates is used which is based on the order of preference of candidates.

Disputes on election of the President

- Article 71 provides that all doubts and disputes arising out of the election of President or Vice-President shall be 'inquired' into and 'decided' by the Supreme Court whose decision shall be final.
- If the election of President is declared void by the Supreme Court, the acts performed by President before the date of such decision of court remain valid.
- Article 71(4) declares that the election of President or Vice-President cannot be challenged on the ground that electoral college was incomplete.

Qualification for election as President :

A person to be eligible for election as President should fulfil the following qualifications:

- He should be a citizen of India.
- He should have completed 35 years of age.
- He should be qualified for election as a member of the Lok Sabha.
- He should not hold any office of profit under union or state government.

Note: A sitting President or Vice-President of the Union, the Governor of any state and a Minister of Union or State is not deemed to hold any office of profit and hence qualified as a Presidential candidate.

Conditions of president's office:

(a) Under Article 59, the President cannot be a member of either house of parliament or any state legislature. If such a member is elected President, he shall be deemed to have vacated his seat in that house on the date which he enters the office of President.

(b) His emoluments, allowances and privileges are determined by the parliament by law. His Salary and allowances cannot be diminished during his term of office.

(c) Oath or affirmation of President's office is administered by the Chief Justice of India (Article 60) or by the senior most judge of the Supreme Court.

(d) Term of office of President is 5 years from the date on which he/she enters upon his/her office. **The president is eligible for re-election.**

(e) He may be elected for any number of terms.

Vacancy in the President's office:

A vacancy in the President office can occur in any of the following ways:

- On the expiry of his tenure of five years.
- By his resignation.
- On his removal by the process of impeachment.
- By his death.
- When his election is declared void.

Note: Any person i.e. Vice-President, Chief Justice of India acting as a President or discharging the functions of the President enjoys all the powers and immunities of the Presidents.

Impeachment against the President

- Impeachment is a quasi-judicial procedure in the parliament in (Article 61).
- Impeachment charge against the President can be initiated by either houses of the parliament.
- If the vacancy is caused by ending of the term, election to fill the vacancy must be completed before the expiry. Outgoing President continues to hold office even if his/her term has expired until his/her successor enters his/her office.
- **If there is some other reason of vacancy other than expiry of term, election to fill the vacancy must be held within the 6 months from the date of occurrence of vacancy. The Vice-President shall act as President [Article 65(1)].**
- If the President is temporarily unable to discharge his/her duties due to an absence from India, illness or any other such cause, Vice-President shall discharge his functions until the President resumes his duties [Article 65(2)].
- In case the office of Vice-President is vacant, the Chief Justice of India (or if his office is also vacant, the senior most judge of the Supreme Court available) acts as the President or discharges the functions of the President.
- When any person, i.e Vice-President, Chief Justice of India, or the seniormost judge of the Supreme Court is acting as the President or discharging the functions of the President, he enjoys all the powers and immunities of the President and is entitled to such emoluments, allowances and privileges as are determined by the Parliament.

Impeachment Process

Charge must be in the form of a proposal/ resolution signed by not less than 1/4th of the total members of the house that turned the charges and 14 days' advance notice should be given to the president.

↓

This resolution must be passed by a majority of not less than $2/3^{rd}$ of the total membership of the initiating house.

↓

Charge is then investigated by the other house. The President has right to appear and to be represented at such investigation.

↓

If the other house, after investigations, passes a resolution by 2/3rd majority of the total membership declaring that the charge is proved, the President is removed from the office from the date on which the resolution is passed.

In this context, two things should be noted:

(a) the nominated members of either House of Parliament can participate in the impeachment of the President though they do not participate in his election;

(b) the elected members of the legislative assemblies of states and the Union Territories of Delhi and Pondicherry do not participate in the impeachment of the President though they participate in his election.

No President has so far been impeached.

Privileges of the President (Article 361)

(a) He is Not answerable to any court for the exercise of powers and duties of his office.

(b) During his term of office, no criminal proceedings, no process for arrest or imprisonment can be undertaken.

(c) No civil proceeding until:-

(a) A notice in writing has been given to the President two months in advance.

(b) The notice states the nature of proceeding, cause of action, name, residence and description of the party taking the proceedings and the relief claimed.

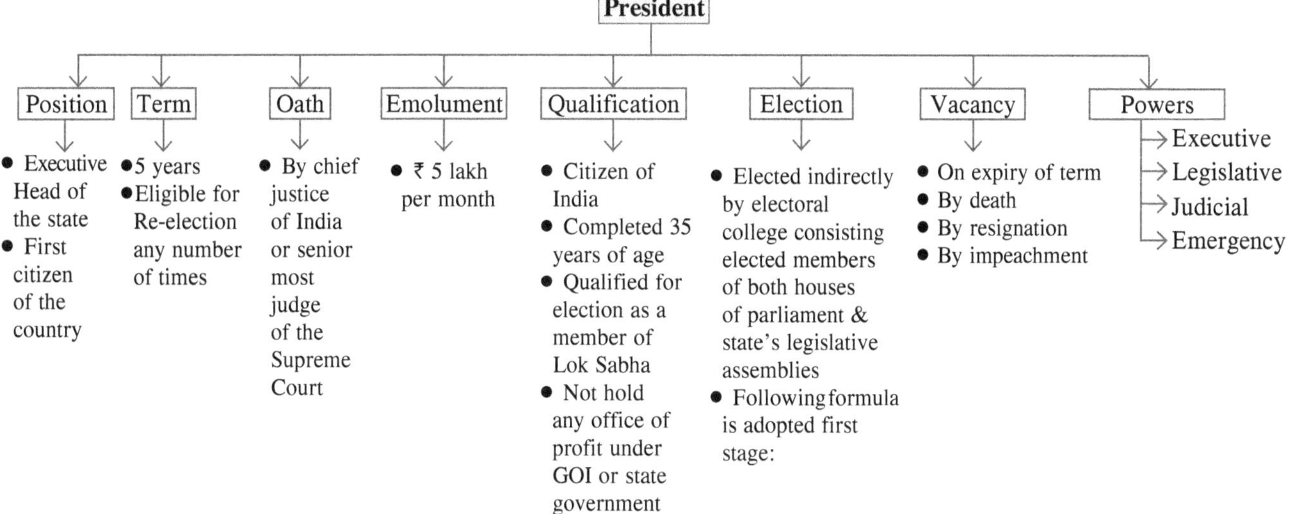

Powers and Functions of the President

• "Executive power of the Union shall be vested in the President" (Article 53).

• All executive powers are exercised by the President with the advice of the Council of Ministers [Article 74(1)].

• After the 42nd Constitutional Amendment it became obligatory for the President to seek advice of Council of Ministers. 44th Amendment gave him the power to send back the advice for reconsideration. But if the Council of Ministers sent back the same advice, President had to act according to such advice.

• "Executive Power" refers to the power exercised by the Council of Ministers in the name of the President. The Council of Ministers is the *"real executive"*.

• The Prime-minister and other minister holds office during his pleasure.

• He appoints the Attorney Gernal of India. The AGI holds office during the pleasure of the President.

  ▪ He apoint:

  ▪ The Comptroller and Auditor General of India,

  ▪ The Chief Election Commissioner and other election commissioners,

  ▪ The Chair-man and members of the UPSC,

  ▪ Chairman of Finance Commission,

- ▪ The Governors of State.
- ▪ He can declare any area as scheduled area.

Legislative Powers

- President is an integral part of the Parliament. He exercises legislative powers with ministerial advice [Article 74(1)].
- When a bill is presented to the President for his consent, he can take following 3 steps:
  - (a) He may **give his assent** to the bill.
  - (b) He **can withholds his ascent** to the bill.
  - (c) He may (in case of bills other than money bills) **return the bill for reconsideration** of the parliament.
- **A money bill cannot be returned for reconsideration.**
- But if a bill (other than money bill) is passed again by both houses of Parliament with or without amendment and again presented to President, he has to give assent to it.
- In case of state bills reserved by Governor for consideration of President, President has power of absolute veto, i.e. withholding of assent to the bill. Reservation is compulsory in the case where the law in question would derogate the powers of the High Court under the Constitution.
- In case of money bill of states so reserved, President may either declare his assent or withhold his assent.
- He has power to summon, prorogue the Parliament and he can dissolve the Lok Sabha (Article 85).
- He shall have the power to summon a joint sitting of both houses of Parliament in the case of deadlock over an ordinary bill presided over by Speaker (Article 108).
- Addresses both houses of Parliament assembled together, at first session after each general election to the Lok Sabha and at the commencement of first session of each year.
- President has right to address either house or their joint sitting at any time, and to require the attendance of members for this purpose. President has right to send messages to either house of parliament either in regard to any pending bill or to any other matter.
- He nominates 12 members of the Rajya Sabha from amongst persons having special knowledge or practical experience in literature, science, art and social service. [Aricle-80(1)]
- He can nominate two members to the Lok Sabha from the Anglo-Inidan community. (Aricle-331)
- He decides on questions of disqualification of MPs in consultation with the Election Commission.
- He lays certain reports and statements before Parliament like: Reports of CAG, UPSC, Finance Commission, Special Officers for SCs/STs, Linguistic minorities, Commission on backward classes and Annual Financial Statement (Budget).
- Prior recommendation of President for introducing legislation is required on:
  - (i) Bill for formation of new states or alteration of boundaries of existing states (Article 3).
  - (ii) Money bill [Article 117(1)].
  - (iii) Bill involving expenditure from consolidated fund of India even though it may not be a money bill.
  - (iv) State bills restricting Freedom of Trade (Article 304).
- **Presidential veto's can be of following types:**
  The Veto power enjoyed by the executive in modern states can be classified into the following four types
  1. **Absolute Veto**

     It is the power to say no to a Bill passed by both Houses of Parliament. Such as Bill never becomes an act. The power cannot be overridden by the legislature. The Indian President has this power in relation in Bills except Money Bills.
  2. **Suspensive Veto**

     The President exercises this veto, when he returns a Bill for reconsideration of the Parliament. However, if the Bill is passed again by the Parliament, with or without amendments and again presented to the President, it is obligatory for the President to give his assent to the Bill.
  3. **Pocket Veto**

     In this case, the President neither assents nor rejects nor returns the Bill, but simply keeps the Bill pending for an indefinite period. This power of the President not to take any action (either positive or negative) on the Bill is known as the **Pocket Veto.** Since, the Constitution of India does not specify a time limit for the President to give assent to a Bill, the Indian President can exercise Pocket veto.
  4. **Qualified Veto**

     It is the power of veto which can be overridden by the legislature by a higher majority. The American President may return a Bill within 10 days specifying his objections to the Bill. If both the houses pass the Bill again with 2/3rd majority (present and voting) the veto is overridden. If the requisite majority cannot be mustered, the veto stands. In India, there is no Qualified veto.
- **President of India enjoys Absolute, suspensive and pocket veto.**

Financial Powers

- He causes to be laid before the Parliament the "Annual Financial Statement" or the "Budget".
- Money Bill can be introduced in the Parliament only with his prior recommendation.
- No demand for grant can be made except on his recommendations.
- He can make advances out of the Contingency Fund of India to meet any unforeseen expenditure.
- He constitutes a "Finance Commission" after a gap of 5 years to recommend the distribution of revenues between Centre and states.

Executive Powers

- All executive actions of GoI are performed in the name of the President.
- He appoints the Prime Minister and on his advice ministers of the Union; judges of the Supreme Court and high courts, Governors of the states, Attorney General, Comptroller & Auditor General, Chairman and members of Public Service Commission, members of the Finance Commission, other official commissions, special officers for SCs & STs, commission to report on administration of scheduled areas, Inter state council, Commission to investigate the condition of backward classes, special officers for linguistic minorities.
- These officials hold their office during the pleasure of the President. They can be removed by following the procedure laid down in the Constitution. He/she exercises these powers with the advice of Council of Ministers.
- He makes rules specifying the manner in which the orders and other instruments made and executed in his name shall be authenticated.
- He directly administers the Union Territories through administrators appointed by him.
- He appoints the Chief Justice and the other judges of Supreme Court and high courts.
- He can seek the advice of the Supreme Court on questions of law or fact Such advice tendered by the Supreme Court is not binding on him.
- He can appoint an inter-state council to promote centre state operation.
- He can declare any area as sheduled area and has power with respect to the administration of scheduled areas and tribal areas.

Judicial Powers

- He appoints the Chief Justices and the other judges of Supreme Court and high courts.
- He can seek the advice of the Supreme Court on questions of law or fact. Such advice tendered by the Supreme Court is not binding on him.
- Under Article 72, President has the power to grant:
  - **Pardons** which completely absolve the offender from all punishments.
  - **Reprieves** or stay on the execution of the sentence for a temporary period.
  - **Respites** or awarding lesser punishment on special grounds.
  - **Remission** or reduction of sentence without changing it's character.
  - **Commutation** or substitution of one form of punishment for another form which is lighter.
- To suspend, remit or commute the sentence of any person convicted of any offence –
  - By court martial.
  - An offence against any law relating to any matter to which executive power of the union extends.
  - In all cases of death sentence.
- He is the only authority for commuting a death sentence.
- Pardoning powers on the President is to correct possible judicial errors.
- Power of President is an executive power and independent of judiciary. He is not a court of appeal and cannot be compelled to give a hearing to a petitioner. Courts cannot interfere in the exercise of this power.
- The President uses his pardoning powers on the advice of Union Government.

Military Powers

President is the supreme commander of the armed forces of the country. The exercise of this power is regulated by law (Article 53). He appoints the chiefs of the Army, Navy and Air force. He can declare war or conclude peace subject to the approval of the parliament.

Diplomatic Powers

He represents India in international forums. He sends and receives ambassadors and diplomatic representatives. All treaties and international agreements are negotiated and concluded in his name though subject to approval of the Parliament.

Emergency Powers

- The President can proclaim emergency in the entire country or in any part of it on the grounds of war, external aggression or armed rebellion.
- Term 'armed rebellion' was inserted by the 44th constitutional amendment act (1978), replacing the original term 'internal disturbance'.
- The President can proclaim this emergency only after receiving a written recommendation from the cabinet.
- The proclamation of emergency must be approved by the parliament (both houses) within one month. If approved, the emergency shall continue for six months.
- It can be extended for an indefinite period with an approval of the parliament for every six months.
- **A national emergency has been proclaimed three times so far in 1962, 1971 and 1975.**

President can impose three types of emergencies :

(a) National Emergency (Article-352)

(b) President's Rule (Article-356 & 365)

(c) Financial Emergency (Article-360)

- During national emergency President can
  - Give directions to any state with regard to the manner in which its executive power is to be exercised.
  - Extend the normal tenure of the Lok Sabha by one year at a time.
  - Modify the pattern of the distribution of financial resources between the union and the states.

- ▪ Suspend the fundamental rights of citizens except the right to life and personal liberty (article 21) and the right to protection in respect of conviction for offences (article 20). Moreover, the right to six freedoms (article 19) can only be suspended in case of external emergency (i.e. on the grounds of war or external aggression) and not in case of internal emergency (*i.e.* on the grounds of an armed rebellion).
- The Parliament can make laws on items mentioned in the State List during the period of national emergency. Such laws become ineffective six months after the emergency.
- If a notice in writing signed by not less than 1/10th of total members of Lok Sabha describing their intention to disapprove the continuation of emergency, served to Speaker of House or to President if house is not in session, special sitting shall be held within 14 days from date of such notice.
- Satisfaction of President can be challenged on grounds of malafide intention.
- In Minerva Mills Vs Union of India it was held that there is no bar to judicial review of the validity of proclamation of emergency issued by President under Article 352(1). But court's powers are confined to check whether limitations conferred by constitution are complied with or not.

State Emergency/President's Rule

- Also known as a constitutional emergency, it can be proclaimed by the President on the following grounds:
  - (i) **Failure of constitutional machinery in the states (article 356) or**
  - (ii) Failure to comply with or to give effect to directions given by the union (article 365)
- Imposed when the President is satisfied (on the basis of either a report of the state governor or otherwise), that the governance of a state cannot be carried on in accordance with the provisions of the constitution.
- **The above proclamation in a State should be approved by the Parliament (both houses) within two months. If approved, it remains in force for six months. It can be extended for a maximum period of three years with the approval of parliament every six months.** However, beyond one year, it can be extended by six month at a time only when the following two conditions are fulfilled.
  - (i) Proclamation of national emergency should be in operation in the entire country, or in the whole or any part of the concerned state; and
  - (ii) The election commission must certify that the general elections to the concerned state cannot be held on account of difficulties.
- The President acquires the following extraordinary powers during state emergency:-
  - (i) Assign to himself all or any of the functions of the state government and powers of the governor.
  - (ii) Declare that the powers of the state legislature shall be exercisable by or under the authority of the parliament.
  - (iii) Authorize (when the Lok Sabha is not in session) expenditure from the consolidated fund of the state pending the sanction of such expenditure by the parliament.
  - (iv) Promulgate ordinances for the administration of the state when the parliament is not in session.
- In brief, the President dissolves the state council of ministers headed by the chief minister and the state legislature. The parliament passes the state budget and legislation bills. The state Governor, on behalf of the President, carries on the state administration of the state with the help of advisors appointed by the President.
- However, the President can't assume to himself power vested in high court/ suspend operation of any provision relating to high court.
- In S.R. Bommai Vs UOI case, Supreme Court said that the satisfaction of President can be scrutinized by the courts.
- First time proclaimed in Punjab in 1951 followed by PEPSU in 1953 and A.P. in 1954.

Financial Emergency

- The President can proclaim financial emergency if he is satisfied that the financial stability or credit of India or any part thereof, is threatened. Such a proclamation must be approved by the parliament within two months.
- President acquires the following extraordinary powers:-
  - ▪ He can give directions to the states to observe the canons of financial propriety.
  - ▪ He can require that all money bills and other financial bills passed by the state legislature be reserved for his consideration.
  - ▪ He can issue directions for the reduction of salaries and allowances of all or any class of person serving in connection with the affairs of the union and the states, including the judges of the Supreme Court and high courts.
- Financial Emergency has been imposed in India.

Miscellaneous Powers/Residuary Powers

- Can make rules and regulations relating to matters not mentioned in the Constitution.
- He has final legislative power for all Union Territories except Pondicherry and Delhi.
- He has special power for Scheduled Areas, Tribes and Tribal Areas.

Ordinance Making Power of the President (Article 123)

- Ordinances can be issued when both the houses of parliament are not in session and the President is satisfied that circumstances exist which make it necessary to take 'immediate action'.
- This power is exercised on the advice of Council of Ministers.

- It is the most important legislative power of the President.
- Ordinances issued by the President have the force of an act of the Parliament. Ordinance can be retrospective, may amend or repeal any act of the parliament or a previous ordinance itself.
- Ordinances must be laid before both houses of the parliament and shall not operate at the expiry of 6 weeks from the date of re-assembly of the Parliament, unless disapproved earlier by the Parliament. If the houses are summoned to re-assemble on different dates, the period of 6 weeks is counted from the later of those dates.
- Though the ordinance making power of the President is coextensive with legislative power of the Parliament, it is not a parallel power of legislation. It is the power to meet emergent needs for legislation when the Parliament is not in session.
- An ordinance is void if it makes a provision which under the Constitution is beyond the competence of the Parliament.
- An ordinance cannot violate fundamental rights. Judicial interference is possible to check any malafide intention in an ordinance.
- Ordinance making power is a relic of Act of 1935.
- Ordinance making powers of President (Article 123) & Governor (Article 213) are corollary to each other.

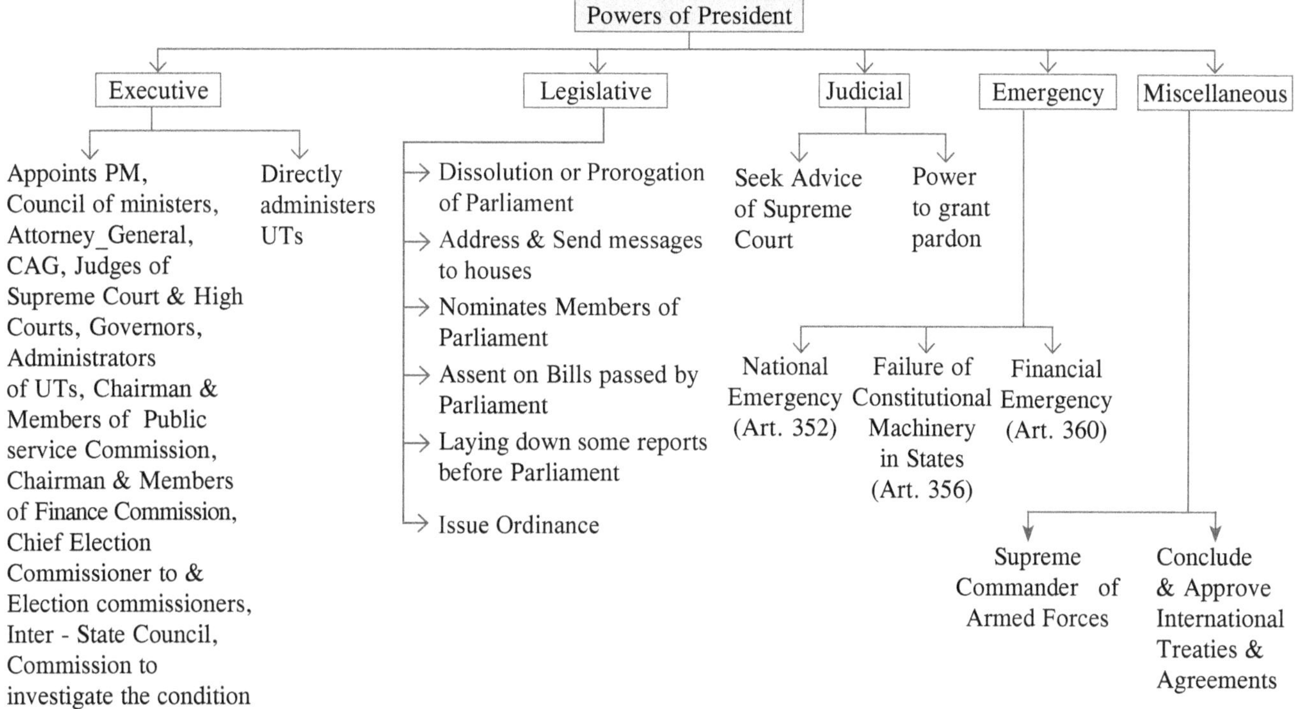

Position of Indian President

The position of the Indian President is somewhat difficult to categorise. Like the American president, he is elected for a fixed term, and like his American counterpart he is removable by the legislature through the process of impeachment. But the Indian Constitution makers preferred not to go completely the American way because absence of coordination between the legislature and the executive is a source of weakness of he American political system. Political analysts prefer to use the more dignified term of "Constitutional head" the president has thus been made a formal or constitutional head of the executive and the real executive powers are vested in the Ministers or the Cabinet.

List of President of India

Name	Tenure		Important Facts
	From	To	
Dr. Rajendra Prasad	26.01.1950	13.05.1962	First President and also had the longest tenure (12 years).
Dr. S. Radhakrishnan	13.05.1962	13.05.1967	Was also the first Vice-President of India.
Dr. Zakir Hussain	13.05.1967	03.05.1969	Shortest tenure; First Muslim President; First President to die in harness

V.V. Giri	03.05.1969	20.07.1969	First acting President of India.
Justice M Hidayat-ul-lah	20.07.1969	24.08.1969	Was also the Chief Justice of India.
V.V. Giri	24.08.1969	24.08.1974	—
F. Ali Ahmed	24.08.1974	11.02.1977	Died in Office
BD Jatti	11.02.1977	25.07.1977	Acting President
N Sanjeeva Reddy	25.07.1977	25.07.1982	Youngest President (64 years)
Giani Zail Singh	25.07.1982	25.07.1987	First Sikh President
R Venkataraman	25.07.1987	25.07.1992	Oldest President (76 years)
Dr SD Sharma	25.07.1992	25.07.1997	—
KR Narayanan	25.07.1997	25.07.2002	First Dalit President
Dr APJ Abdul Kalam	25.07.2002	25.07.2007	First Scientist to become President
Mrs Pratibha Patil	25.07.2007	25.07.2012	First Woman to become President
Pranab Mukherjee	25.07.2012	17.07.2017	—
Ram Nath Kovind	17.07.2017	Till Date	—

Vice President

- Article 63 of the Constitution provides that there shall be a Vice-President of India.
- Article 66 says that the Vice-President is elected by the member of both houses of Parliament in a joint session by secret ballot with the system of proportional representation by means of single transferable vote. States have no role to play in his election.
- Qualifications of the Vice-President are same as those of President except that **he must be eligible for election to Rajya Sabha.**
- His term of office is 5 years. He may resign from his office before the expiry of normal term by writing to the President.
- He can be removed from the post of the Vice President by a resolution of the Rajya Sabha, passed by a majority of all the members of the house and agreed to by a simple majority of the Lok Sabha. Such a resolution can be moved only after giving 14 day's notice of the intention to move the resolution.
- While resolution for impeachment of the President can be moved in the either of the houses, the resolution for the removal of Vice-President can only be moved in the Rajya Sabha.

- Vice-President gets a salary and other emoluments as chairman of Rajya Sabha.

Functions of The Vice President

- No functions are attached to the office of the Vice President.
- He is the **ex-officio chairman of Rajya Sabha** (Article 64).
- He presides over the meetings of Rajya Sabha but is not a member of Rajya Sabha. He has no right to vote.
- During his discharge of his functions as a President, in case that post falls vacant on account of the death, resignation or removal of the President (Article 65).
- He is entitled to such emoluments, allowances and privileges as may be determined by parliament by law, mentioned in Second Schedule.

Vice-Presidents of India

Vice-Presidents	Tenure
Dr. Sarvapalli Radhakrishnan	1952-1962
Dr. Zakir Hussain	1962-1967
Varahagiri Venkatagiri	1967-1969
Gopal Swarup Pathak	1969-1974
BD Jatti	1974-1979
Justice Mohammad Hidayat-ul-lah	1979-1984
R Venkataraman	1984-1987
Dr Shanker Dayal Sharma	1987-1992
KR Narayanan	1992-1997
Krishan Kant (Died)	1997-2002
Bhairon Singh Shekhawat	2002-2007
Mohammad Hamid Ansari	2007-2017
M. Venkaiah Naidu	2017-Till Date

The Prime Minister and Council of Ministers

- Vice President can act as President only for a maximum period of six month within which a new President has to be elected.
- While acting as the President, the Vice-President shall have all powers and immunities of the President.
- While acting as President or discharging the function of President, the vice president does not perform the duties of the office of the Chair-man of Rajya Sabha.
- While Vice-President is acting as President the duties of Chair-man of Rajya Sabha are performed by the Deputy Chairman.

Parliamentary democracy in India envisages the presence of a nominal and real executive. They are the President and the Prime Minister respectively.

- Prime Minister is the 'Real Chief Executive'. The office of the Prime Minister first originated in England and was borrowed by the framers of the Constitution.

The Prime Minister

Appointment & OATH :

- The Constitution does not contain any specific procedure for the selection and appointment of the Prime Minister.
- Article-75(1) of the Constitution provides that the Prime Minister shall be appointed by the President.
- A person can be appointed as Prime-Minister, even if he is not a member of either house of Parliament and may continue to be so upto a period of six months.
- The Prime Minister by virtue of Article-75(4) is required to take two types of Oath in the presence of the President which are as follows:
  1. Oath of office.
  2. Oath of secrecy.

Generally the President has no choice in the appointment of the Prime Minister and invites the leader of the majority political party in the Lok Sabha for this office. The Prime Minister theoretically holds office during the pleasure of the President. But the Prime Minister actually stays in office as long as he enjoys the confidence of the Parliament especially the Lok Sabha. *The normal term is five years* but it is automatically reduced if the Lok Sabha is dissolved earlier.

SALARY:

- The Prime Minister gets the same salary and allowances which are paid to the members of Parliament. He also receives a constituency allowance like other MPs. In addition, he is also entitled to a sumptuary allowance, free official residence, free travel medical facilities, etc.
- **Powers of Prime Minister.** The Prime Minister enjoys extensive powers which are as follows-
  1. The President convenes and prorogues all sessions of the Parliament in consultation with him.
  2. He can recommend the dissolution of Lok Sabha to the President before expiry of its normal term.
  3. All the members of the Council of Ministers are appointed by the President on the recommendations of the Prime Minister.
  4. He allocates portfolios among the various ministers and reshuffles them. He can ask a minister to resign and can even get him dismissed by the President.
  5. He presides over the meetings of the Council of Ministers and exercises a strong influence on its decisions.
  6. He exercises general supervision over the working of other ministers and ensures that they work as a team.
  7. The Prime Minister can bring about the fall of the Council of Ministers if he resigns. He is the *pivot* around which the Council of Ministers revolves.
  8. The Prime Minister is the chief channel of communication between the President and the Council of Ministers and keeps the former informed about all the decisions of the Council.
  9. He assists the President in the appointment of all high officials.
  10. He can recommend to the President, with the concurrence of other cabinet ministers, to proclaim a state of emergency on grounds of war, external aggression or armed rebellion.
  11. He advises the President about imposition of Presidential Rule in the states on grounds of breakdown of constitutional machinery or imposition of an emergency due to financial instability.
  12. He is the chairman of the NITI Aayog, National Development Council & Inter-State Council.

List of Prime Ministers

Name	Tenure		Note	Party (Alliance)
	From	To		
Jawarharlal Nehru	15.08.1947	27.05.1964	First Prime Minister of India, died in office; also had the longest tenure (17 years)	INC
Gulzari Lal Nanda	27.05.1964	09.06.1964	First Acting Prime Minister	INC
Lal Bahadur Shastri	09.06.1964	11.01.1966	Only Prime minister to die abroad during an official tour	INC
Gulzari Lal Nanda	11.01.1966	24.01.1966	First to become Acting Prime Minister twice	INC
Indira Gandhi	24.01.1966	24.03.1977	First woman Prime Minister of India; First Prime Minister to lose an election	INC
Morarji Desai	24.03.1977	28.07.1979	Oldest Prime Minister (81 years) and the first to resign from office	Janata Party
Charan Singh	28.07.1979	14.01.1980	Only Prime Minister who did not face the Parliament	Janata Party (Secular) with INC
Indira Gandhi	14.01.1980	31.10.1984	First Prime Minister to be assassinated	INC

Rajiv Gandhi	31.10.1984	01.12.1989	Youngest Prime Minister (40 years)	INC
VP Singh	21.12.1989	10.11.1990	First Prime Minister to step down after vote of no-confidence	Janata Dal (National Front)
Chandra Shekhar	10.01.1990	21.06.1991	—	Samajwadi Party with INC
PV Narasimah Rao	21.06.1991	16.05.1996	First Prime Minister from Southern India	INC
Atal Bihari Vajpayee	16.05.1996	01.06.1996	Shortest tenure of a Prime Minister	BJP
HD Deva Gowada	01.06.1996	20.04.1997	—	Janata Dal (United Front)
IK Gujral	21.04.1997	19.03.1998	—	Janata Dal
Atal Bihari Vajpayee	19.03.1998	13.10.1999	—	BJP (NDA)
Atal Bihari Bajpayee	13.10.1999	22.05.2004	—	BJP (NDA)
Dr Manmohan Singh	22.05.2004	26.05.2014	First Sikh Prime Minister, longest tenure after JL Nehru	INC (UPA)
Narendra Modi	26.05.2014	Till date	First PM born after Independence	BJP (NDA)

Council of Ministers

- "There shall be a Council of Ministers with Prime Minister as its head to aid and advice the President, who shall in exercise of his functions act in accordance with such advice" [(Article 74(1)]
- **The Prime Minister is appointed by the President, Ministers are appointed by the President on advice of the Prime Minister [Article 75(1)].**
- The ministers hold office during the pleasure of President [Article 75(2)].
- There is no constitutional bar for a nominated member to be appointed as a union minister.
- There is no bar on the appointment of a person from outside the legislature as minister, but he cannot continue as minister for more than 6 months unless he secures a seat in either house of Parliament by election or nomination. [Article 75(5)].
- The salaries and allowances of ministers are determined by the Parliament.
- Constitutional duties of the Prime Minister as provided in Article 78 is to communicate to the President "all decisions" of the Council of Ministers relating to:
  - Administration of the affairs of the Union.
  - Proposal for legislation.
  - To furnish information relating to the administration of affairs of the Union and proposals for legislation as the President may call for.
  - If the President so requires to submit for the consideration of Council of Ministers any matter on which a decision has been taken by a minister but which has not been considered by the council.
- Allocation of the portfolios among ministers is done by the Prime Minister.

Powers of Council of ministers:

The Council of Ministers formulates and implements the policy of the country. It introduces most of the important bills and resolutions in the Parliament and steers them through. It prepares and presents the budget to the Parliament for its approval.

The foreign policy of the Government is determined by the Council of Ministers. It advises the President with regard to appointments of diplomats.

Collective Responsibility

- **Council of Ministers are collectively responsible to the Lok Sabha [Article 75(3)].** The ministry resigns if it loses the confidence of the Lok Sabha.
- Vote of no confidence passed against any minister leads to the resignation of the entire Council of Ministers.
- They work as a team and swim and sink together.

Individual Responsibility

- The principle embodied in Article 75(2) is that of individual responsibility. It says that the minister shall hold office during the pleasure of the President.
- Hence a minister can be dismissed even if the ministry has the confidence of legislature.

Legal Responsibility

The system of legal responsibility of a minister is not prescribed in the Indian Constitution. Further the courts are barred from inquiring into the nature of advice rendered by the ministers.

Composition of Council of Ministers

There are 3 categories of Ministers:

1. Cabinet ministers
2. Minister of state
3. Deputy ministers

- **Cabinet ministers** head ministries in the Government. They are members of the Cabinet, attend its meetings and decide policies.
- **Ministers of state** can have an independent charge or can be attached to cabinet ministers. They are not members of the cabinet nor do they attend its meetings unless invited.

- **Deputy ministers** have no separate charges. They assist the ministers with whom they are attached and perform administrative duties.
- There are also parliamentary secretaries with no department under their control. They assist senior ministers in discharging parliamentary duties. Since 1967, no parliamentary secretaries have been appointed.
- **Cabinet is an extra-constitutional body based upon conventions. It is the supreme policy making body.**
- Kitchen cabinet is an extra-constitutional body consisting of the Prime Minister and a few influential colleagues in whom he has faith and with whom he can discuss issues.

Council of Ministers (At Centre and State level): Composition

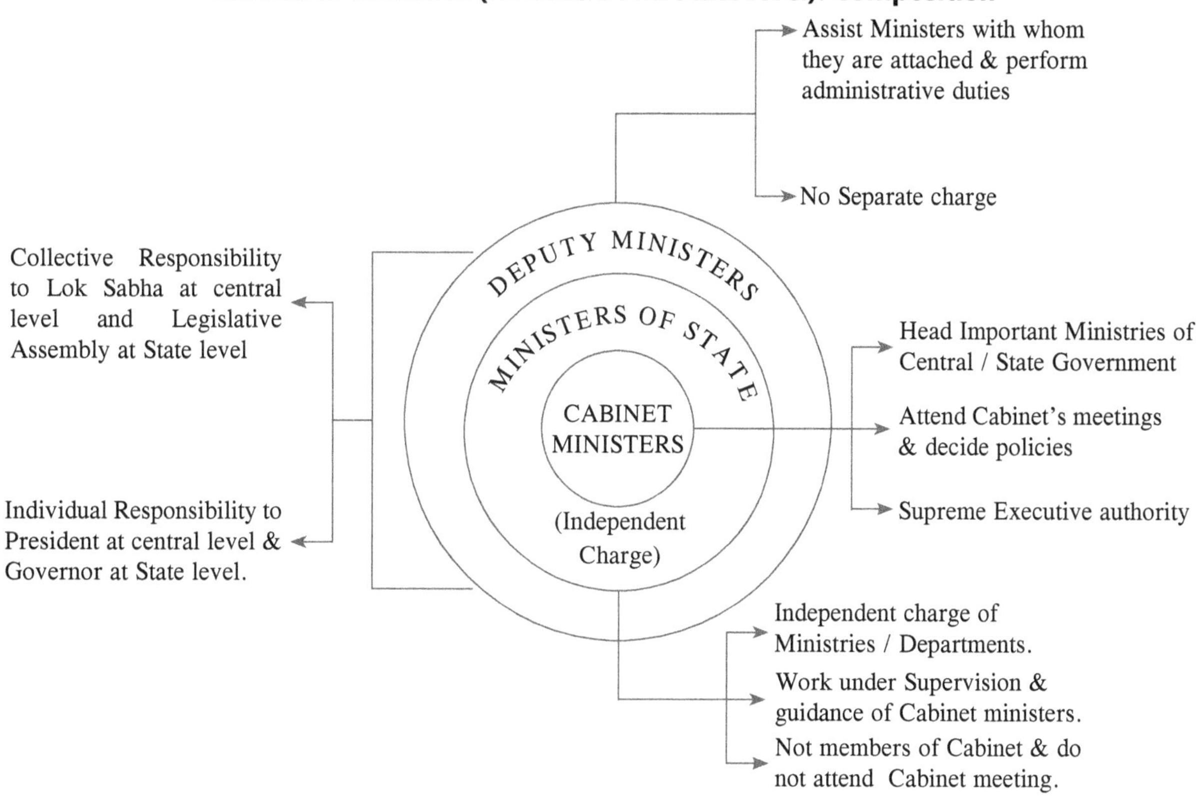

Council of Ministers vs Cabinet

Council of Ministers	Cabinet
It is a wider body consisting of 60 to 70 ministers.	It is a smaller body consisting of 15 to 20 Ministers.
It includes all the three categories of ministers, i.e. Cabinet Ministers, Ministers of State and Deputy Ministers.	It includes the cabinet Ministers only. Thus, it is a part of the Council of ministers.
It does not meet, as a body, to transact government business. It has no collective functions.	It meets as a body frequently, to deliberate and take decisions regarding the transaction of the government business. Thus, it has collective functions.
It is vested with all powers, but in theory.	It exercises, in practice, the power of the Council of Ministers.
Its functions are determined by the Cabinet.	It directs the Council of Ministers by taking policy decisions which are binding on all ministers.
It implements the decisions taken by the Cabinet.	It supervises the implementation of its decisions by the Council of Ministers.
It is a constitutional body, dealt in detail by the **Articles 74** and **75** of the Constitution. Its size is determined by the Prime Minister according to the exigencies of the time, Its classification into a three-tier body is based on the conventions	The word 'cabinet' was inserted in the **Article 352** of the Constitution in 1978 by the **44th Constitutional Amendment Act**. Thus, it did not find a place in the original text of the Constitution. Even, now Article 352 defines the cabinet saying that, it is "the council consisting the

to the parliamentary form of government as developed in Britain. It has however, got a legislative sanction. Thus, the Salaries and Allowances Act of 1952 defines a 'Minister' as a "Member of the Council of Minister", by whatever name called and includes a Deputy Minister.	Prime Minister and other Ministers of Cabinet rank appointed under Article 75" and does not describes its powers and functions. In other words, its role in our politico-administrative system is based on the conventions of the parliamentary form of government as developed in Britain.
It is collectively responsible to the Lower House of the Parliament.	It enforces the collective responsibility of the Council of Ministers to the Lower House of the Parliament.

ATTORNEY GENERAL AND SOLICITOR GENERAL OF INDIA

The Constitution (Article-76) has provided for the office of the Attorney General for India. He is the highest law officer in the country.

He is appointed by the President and holds office during his pleasure. To be eligible for appointment as Attorney General of India, a person must possess the qualifications prescribed for a judge of the Supreme Court. He is entitled to such salary and allowances as may be determined by the President. The Attorney General is entitled to **audience in all courts** in the country and **can take part in the proceedings of the Parliament** and its committees. However, **he is not given the right to vote**.

The team of office of the Attorney General is not fixed by the Constitution. Further, the Constitution does not contain the procedure and grounds for his removal.

> Attorney General can be removed from office by the President at anytime.
>
> The remuneration of the Attorney General is not fixed by the Constitution.

Functions

He is the chief legal adviser of the Government of India and gives it advice on all such legal matters which may be referred or assigned to him by the President.

He also performs such other legal duties as are assigned to him by the President from time to time.

The Attorney General appears before the Supreme Court and various High Courts in cases involving the Government of India.

Attorney General of India (AGI) does not fall in the category of Government servants. Further, he is not debarred from private legal practice.

In addition to the AGI, there are other law offices of the Government of India. They are the Solicitor General of India and additional Solicitor General of India.

They assist the AGI in the fulfilment of his official responsibilities.

Note: K.K. Venugopal is the current Attorney General of India.

The Parliament

The Parliament is the Union Legislature of India. It consists of the President and two houses the Lok Sabha (house of people) and Rajya Sabha (council of states). Article 79 to 123 in Part-V deals with the provisions of the Parliament.

Functions of Parliament

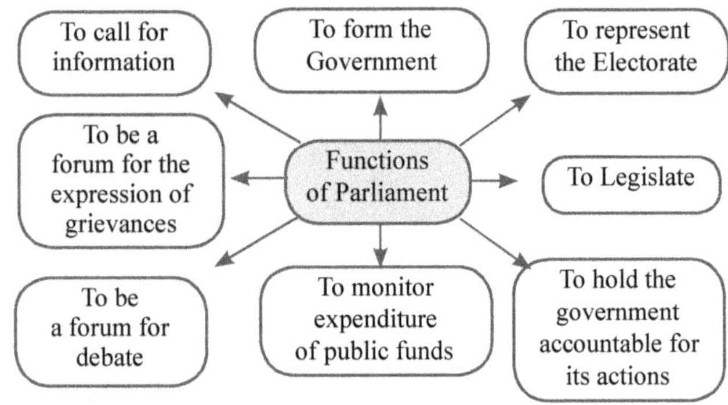

Lok Sabha

Lower House of the Parliament and also known as the first Chamber.

- Members of Lok Sabha are directly elected by the people.
- Total membership is fixed at 552 by the Constitution. Their distribution among the States and Union Territories are:
  - 530 representatives from the states.
  - 20 members from the Union Territories.
  - 2 Anglo Indian members nominated by the President if such community has not been adequately represented.
- The mode of election of the Lok Sabha is:
  - State representatives are elected directly by the people of the state.
  - Union territory representatives are elected in the manner prescribed by parliament by law.
  - Every citizen of India of 18 years and above and is not disqualified on the grounds of non-residence, unsoundness mind, crime or corrupt or illegal practices is entitled to vote (Art 326).
- Constitution 61st Amendment Act (1987) has reduced the age of voting from 21 to 18 years.
- Term of Lok Sabha is normally 5 years but it can be dissolved earlier by the President.
- Its term can be extended beyond 5 years by the Parliament. This can be done during the proclamation of emergency (Under Art 352). But this extension can not be done for a period exceeding one year at a time and such extension cannot continue beyond a period of 6 months after proclamation of emergency ceases to operate.

Territorial Constituencies for Lok Sabha

- For conduct of elections, each state is divided into territorial constituencies. Art 81(2) provides for the uniformity of representation in 2 respects (after 7th Amendment Act 1956) :
  - as between different states
  - as between different constituencies in same state
- Each state has been allotted a fixed number of seats keeping the ratio between the number of seats and the population.
- Each state has been divided into territorial constituencies such that the ratio between the population of the state and the number of seats allotted to it remains almost the same.
- Art 82 stipulates delimitation of territorial constituencies to the Lok Sabha.
- Delimitation of Constituencies is done after each Census by a designated authority and in a manner as the Parliament by law determines. 1971 census data is being used now. The number of seats has been freezed till 2026 to maintain the share of states where the rate of population growth is declining.
- Constitution provides for proportional representation for Rajya Sabha and not for Lok Sabha and legislative assemblies.

Offices of Speaker and Deputy Speaker of Lok Sabha

- The Speaker presides over the Lok Sabha.
- Speaker and Deputy Speaker are elected by the members of Lok Sabha.
- Deputy Speaker performs the duties of the speaker if the office of the speaker falls vacant. If the office of the Deputy Speaker is also vacant, duties of the Speaker shall be performed by a member of the house appointed by the President.
- They vacate their office the moment they cease to be a member of the house. The Speaker continues in his office even if Lok Sabha is dissolved. He/she holds the office till the new Lok Sabha meets.
- They can be removed by a resolution of the Lok Sabha with a majority of all the then members of the house. However a 14 days' notice is necessary to move such a resolution.
- To ensure the independence of the Speaker, his/her salary is paid from the Consolidated Fund of India and is not subject to the annual vote of the Parliament.
- He/ she cannot be removed from the office except by a resolution passed by a special majority.
- If the Speaker wants to resign, the letter of resignation should be addressed to the Deputy Speaker and vice-versa.

- Upto the 10th Lok Sabha, both the Speaker and Deputy Speaker were usually from ruling party. Since the 11th Lok Sabha there has been a consensus that Speaker comes from the ruling alliance and post of Deputy Speaker goes to the main opposition party.

List of Speaker

Speakers	Tenure
Ganesh Vasudev Mavalankar (Died)	1952-1956
M. Ananthasayanam Ayyangar	1956-1962
Hukam Singh	1962-1967
Neelam Sanjiva Reddy (Resigned)	1967-1969
Gurdial Singh Dhillon (Resigned)	1969-1975
Bali Ram Bhagat	1976-1977
Neelam Sanjiva Reddy (Resigned)	1977-1977
KS Hegde	1977-1980
Bal Ram Jakhar	1980-1989
Rabi Ray	1989-1991
Shivraj V. Patil	1991-1996
PA Sangma	1996-1998
GMC Balayogi (Died)	1998-2002
Manohar Gajanan Joshi	2002-2004
Somnath Chatterjee	2004-2009
Ms. Meira Kumar	2009-2014
Ms. Sumitra Mahajan	2014-till date

Pro Tem Speaker

As provided by the Constitution, the Speaker of the last Lok Sabha vacates his office immediately **before the first meeting of the newly-elected Lok Sabha.** Therefore, **the President appoints a member of the Lok Sabha as the speaker *Pro Tem*.** Usually, the senior most member is selected for this. The President himself administers oath to the speaker Pro Tem.

The speaker Pro Tem has all the powers of the speaker. He presides over the first sitting of the newly-elected Lok Sabha. His main duty is to administer oath to the new members. He also enables the house to elect the new speaker.

When the new speaker is elected by the house, the office of the speaker Pro Tem ceases to exist. Hence, this office is a temporary office, existing for a few days.

Rajya Sabha

The Rajya Sabha is the second chamber or Upper House of the Parliament. It consists of representatives of the states. The maximum strength of the Rajya Sabha is **250**. Of these, 238 represent the states and union territories and the rest are nominated by the President. The nominees are persons who have distinguished themselves in the field of literature, art, science, social service and so on. Representatives of the states are elected by members of state legislative assemblies on the basis of proportional representation through a single transferable vote. It is noteworthy that in the Rajya Sabha, the states have been provided representation on the basis of their population.

- Rajya Sabha is a permanent house and is not subject to dissolution.
- Its members are elected for a period of 6 years but 1/3rd of its members retire after every 2 years.

As regards qualifications for membership of the Rajya Sabha, the candidate must –

- be a citizen of India.
- be 30 years of age or more.
- be a parliamentary elector in the state in which he is seeking election.
- possess such other qualifications as may be prescribed by the Parliament from time to time.

Chairman and Deputy Chairman of Rajya Sabha

- The Vice-President of India is the ex-officio chairman of the Council of States.
- Deputy chairman is elected by the Rajya Sabha. He shall be a member of Rajya Sabha.
- Office of Deputy Chairman terminates if he ceases to become the member of the Council.
- Deputy Chairman can also resign, submitting his resignation to the Chairman in writing. He can also be removed from his office by a resolution of the Rajya Sabha, passed by a majority of all the then members of the Council. But such a resolution can only be moved by giving at least 14 days notice in advance.
- If the office of Chairman is vacant, Deputy Chairman discharges his functions. But if the office of Deputy chairman is also vacant, the duties of his office shall be discharged by such a member of the Rajya Sabha as the President may appoint for the purpose.
- The sitting of the house is presided over by the Chairman and in his absence, by the Deputy Chairman. But if both of them are absent then such person as may be determined by the rule of procedure of the Council shall preside over the sitting of the house.

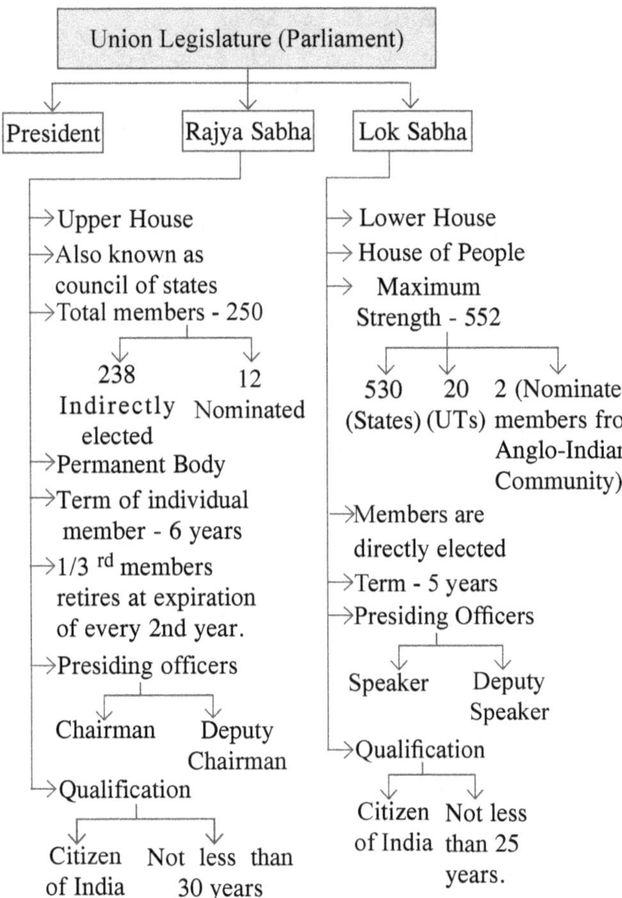

Qualifications for the Membership of Parliament (Art 84)

- The individual should be a citizen of India.
- He should be at least 30 years of age for Rajya Sabha and 25 years for Lok Sabha.
- He should possesses such other qualifications as prescribed by the Parliament.
- His name should be registered as a voter in any parliamentary constituency.
- No minimum educational qualification has been prescribed.
- He/she must not hold any office of profit under the Union or state government.
- He must be a member of a scheduled caste or scheduled tribe in any state or union teritony, if he wants to contest a seat reserved for them.

Disqualification from Membership of Either House of Parliament

- If the individual holds an office of profit under GOI or a state government. Some posts have been exempted from it.
- If the individual is of unsound mind which has been declared so by a competent court.
- If the person is undischarged or insolvent.

- The individual is not a citizen of India and has voluntarily acquired citizenship of a foreign country or has allegiance to a foreign power.
- If he is so disqualified by or under any law made by the Parliament (Art 102).
    - President has to obtain the opinion of the Election Commission before disqualifying a member, (Art 103).
    - Representation of people's act also provides additional grounds for disqualifications.
    - A member can also be disqualified on the grounds of defection.
- Conditions when a member of parliament shall vacate his seat (Art 101)
    - If he has obtained membership of both houses of the Parliament, he needs to vacate one of the seats.
    - If elected to both to the Parliament and state legislature, he needs to resign from the state legislature.
    - If he is disqualified under Art. 102.
    - If he resigns in a voluntary manner.
    - If he remains absent from all meetings of the house for a period of 60 days without prior permission of the house.
    - Detention of a person under a preventive detention law is not a disqualification.
    - The question of disqualification under the tenth schedule is decided by the Chair-man in case of Rajya Sabha and Speaker in the case of Lok Sabha (and not by the President of India).

Powers, Privileges and Immunities of Parliament and its Members

- Both the houses of the Parliament and state legislature have same privileges.
- Art 105 (1) & (2) and Art 194 (1) & (2) state the privileges to both the houses of parliament and state legislature.
- Supreme Court has held that if there is any conflict between the privileges of the Parliament and fundamental rights of citizens, the former shall prevail.
- Privileges can be classified into two categories:
    - Individual privileges.
    - Collective privileges of Lok Sabha and Rajya Sabha.

Individual Privileges

- Freedom from arrest in civil cases. There would be arrest in criminal cases or under preventive detention.
- Freedom from attendance as a witness: a member cannot be summoned by a court to give evidence as a witness while the Parliament is in session.
- Freedom of speech: A member of the Parliament is not liable in any court for anything said in Parliament or any of its committees.

Collective Privileges of Each House

- Right to publish debates and proceedings.
- Right to restrain publications by others.
- Right to exclude others like withdrawal of strangers from any part of the house. The Speaker and the Chairman have the right to order such action.
- Right to regulate internal affairs of the house and to decide matters within its walls.
- Right to punish any parliamentary misbehavior.
- Right to punish members and outsiders for breach of privilege.

Joint Session of the House

- **Art 108 provides** that when a bill is passed by one house is sent to the other. The other house may:
    - Reject the bill altogether.
    - Disagrees on it and returns it with some amendments which are not ultimately considered by the originating house.
    - Takes no action and more than 6 months time has passed.
    - The President in such a case may summon a joint sitting of both the houses.
- **At a joint sitting of two houses, the Speaker of the Lok Sabha and in his absence, the Deputy Speaker, or if he is also absent, Deputy Chairman of the Council of States and if he is also absent, such person as may be determined by the members present in the sitting presides. Lok Sabha by its numerical majority prevails over the joint sitting.**
- **This provision does not apply to money bill.**
- There cannot be a joint sitting for Constitution Amendment bills. Nor do such bills require previous sanction of the President.
- President cannot summon a joint sitting if the bill has lapsed by reason of a dissolution of Lok Sabha.

Special Powers of Lok Sabha with respect to Rajya Sabha

- A Money Bill can be introduced only in the Lok Sabha and not in the Rajya Sabha. Rajya Sabha cannot amend or reject a Money Bill. It should return the bill to the Lok Sabha within 14 days with or without recommendations. The Lok Sabha can either accept or reject fall or any of the recommendations of the Rajya Sabha. In both cases, the Money Bill is deemed to have been passed by the two houses.
- A Financial Bill, not containing solely the matters of **Article 110,** can be introduced only in the Lok Sabha and not in the Rajya Sabha. But, with regard to its passage, both have equal powers. The final power to decide whether a particular bill is a Money Bill is vested in the Speaker of the Lok Sabha. The Speaker of Lok Sabha presides over the joint sitting of both the houses.

- The Lok Sabha with a greater number wins the battle in a joint sitting except when the combined strength of the ruling party in both houses is less than that of opposition parties.
- Rajya Sabha can only discuss the budget, but cannot vote on the demands for grants. A resolution for the discontinuance of the national emergency can be passed only by the Lok Sabha and not by the Rajya Sabha.
- The Rajya Sabha cannot remove the Council of Ministers by passing a No-Confidence Motion. This is because the Council of Ministers is collectively responsible only to the Lok Sabha.

Special power of Rajya Sabha with respect to Lok Sabha

As a federal chamber, it can initiate Central intervention in the State Legislative field. Article 249 of the Constitution provides that the Rajya Sabha may pass a resolution, by a majority of not less than two-thirds of the members present and voting, to the effect that it is necessary or expedient in the national interest that Parliament should make laws with respect to any matter enumerated in the State List. If such a resolution is adopted, Parliament will be authorised, to make laws on the subject specified in the resolution, for the whole or any part of the territory of India.

Such a resolution will remain in force for such period, not exceeding 1 year, as may be specified therein, but this period can be extended by 1 year at a time by passing further resolutions.

Sessions of the Parliament

- A 'Session' of the parliament is the period spanning between the first sitting of a House and its prorogation (or dissolution in case of Lok Sabha) During a session the House meets everyday transact business.
- **Parliament normally meets in three sessions in a year:-**
  - **Budget Session: February - May**
  - **Monsoon Session: July - August**
  - **Winter Session: November - December**

Delimitation Commission

Pursuant to the enactment of the Constitution (Eighty-fourth Amendment) Act 2001, the Delimitation Act, 2002 was enacted. The Delimitation Commission was constituted on July 12, 2012 under the provisions of the Delimitation Act, 2002 with justice Kuldip Singh, a retired judge of the Supreme Court as its chairperson. The main task of the Commission is to readjust the division of territorial constituencies of the House of the people allocated to each state and readjust the division of territorial constituencies of the Legislative Assembly of each state. The Commission will also refix the seats reserved for the Scheduled Casts and the Scheduled Tribes. Earlier the census figures of 1991 were to be the basis, but after the eighty seventh Amendment Act, the census figure of 2001 are to be the basis.

Devices of Parliamentary Proceedings :	
Question hour	<ul><li>First hour of every parliamentary sitting.</li><li>Starred questions are answered orally and supplementary questions can follow.</li><li>Unstarred questions are answered in writing.</li><li>Short notice questions are asked giving less than 10 days notice.</li></ul>
Zero hour	<ul><li>Starts immediately after the question hour.</li><li>Any matter can be discussed during the zero hour.</li></ul>
Half-an-hour discussion	<ul><li>To clear fact on matters of public importance on which lot of debate has occurred.</li></ul>
Short duration discussions	<ul><li>To discuss urgent matters.</li><li>Also known as two hour discussion.</li></ul>
Calling attention motion	<ul><li>Moved to call the attention of a minister to matters of public importance.</li></ul>
Adjournment motion	<ul><li>To draw attention of parliament to a matter of urgent public importance.</li><li>Motion needs the support of 50 members for admission.</li><li>Rajya Sabha cannot move this motion.</li></ul>
No Confidence motion	<ul><li>Moved to prove the confidence of Lok Sabha in the Council of Ministers.</li><li>If No Confidence motion is passed, council of Ministers has to resign.</li><li>No Confidence motion needs the support of 50 members to be admitted.</li><li>Can be moved only in Lok Sabha.</li></ul>
Censure Motion	<ul><li>This motion seeks to censure the government for its lapses. It can be moved against an individual minister or a group of minister or the entire Council of Ministers.</li><li>If it is passed in the Lok Sabha, the Council of Ministers need not resign from the office.</li></ul>
Closure Motion	Moved by a member to cut short the debate on a matter before the House. If the motion is approved by the House, debate is stopped forthwith and the matter is put to vote.
Privilege Motion	Moved by a member when he/she feels that a minister has committed a breach of privilege of the House. The puspose of privilege motion is to censure the concerned minister.

Motion of Thanks	The first session after each general election and the first session of every financial years is addressed by the President. This address of the President is discussed in both the House of Parliament on motion called the 'Motion of Thanks'.
Point of Order	A member can raise a point of order when the proceedings of the House do not follow the normal rules of procedure. No debate is allowed on a point of order.

Legislative Procedure in Parliament

- The legislative procedure is identical in both the Houses of Parliament. Every bill has to pass through the same stages in each House. A bill is a proposal for legislation and it becomes an act or law when duly enacted.
- Bills introduced in the Parliament are of two kinds: *public bills* and *private bills* (also known as government bills and private members' bills respectively). Though both are governed by the same general procedure and pass through the same stages in the house, they differ in various respects. Public bill can introduced by a minister which requires seven days notice. It reflects the policies of the Government and its rejection by the House shows non confidence of ruling party in Parliament and may leads to its resignation while private bill introduce by any member of Parliament and requires one month notice. Its rejection has no implication on parliamentary confidence.
- The bills introduced in the Parliament can also be classified into four categories:
  1. *Ordinary bills,* which are concerned with any matter other than financial subjects.
  2. *Money bills*, which are concerned with the financial matters like taxation, public expenditure, etc.
  3. *Financial bills*, which are also concerned with financial matters (but are different from money bills).
  4. *Constitution amendment bills*, which are concerned with the amendment of the provisions of the Constitution.

The Constitution has laid down separate procedures for the enactment of all the four types of bill.

Ordinary Bill

- This is a bill other than money bill and finance bill.
- An ordinary bill may originate in either house of the Parliament.

First Reading

At this stage the title of the bill is read and a brief speech regarding the aims and objective of the bill is made. Opponents of the bill also make a brief speech at this stage and after a formal vote, the bill is published in gazette.

Second Reading

At this stage the general principles of the bill as a whole are discussed and decision regarding reference of the bill to the appropriate committee is taken. No amendments are possible at this stage.

Committee Stage

After the second reading, the bill is referred to the appropriate committee where its provisions are thoroughly discussed. The committee can also make suitable suggestions for improvement of the bill and suggest necessary amendments.

Report Stage

The committee submits its report to the House, where it is thoroughly discussed. The members of the House hold a clause-by-clause discussion and vote thereon. At this stage, they can also propose fresh amendments, which are accepted by majority vote.

Third Reading

A general discussion on the bill takes place and formal voting for the acceptance or rejection of the bill is held. No amendments can be proposed at this stage.

After a bill has been passed by one house it is transmitted to the other house, where it goes through all these stages once again. After the bill has been passed by the other house, it is sent to the President for assent. However, if the other house proposes certain amendments which are not acceptable to the originating house, it may lead to a deadlock. The deadlock is resolved by convening a joint-sitting of the two houses where the decision is taken by majority vote.

The President can either accord his assent or return the bill for reconsideration of the Parliament. But if the Parliament repasses the bill, the President has to accord assent to it.

Money Bill (Article 110)

- **Whether a bill is a money bill or not is decided by the speaker of the Lok Sabha.**
- Art 109 says that a money bill can only be introduced in Lok Sabha and not in Rajya Sabha and only with the prior recommendation of the President.
- When a money bill is passed by the Lok Sabha, it is sent to Rajya Sabha for its recommendations. Rajya Sabha must return the bill with or without any recommendations, within 14 days from the date of receipt of bill. It is the discretion of the Lok Sabha whether to accept or reject recommendations of Rajya Sabha. The bill now is deemed to be passed by the Lok Sabha and is sent to the President for his/her assent.
- President cannot withhold his/her to a money bill (Art 111).
- There is no provision for a joint sitting in the case of a money bills as the Lok Sabha has a final say in the matter.

Financial Bills

- They are of 3 kinds-
  1. Money bills
  2. Other financial bills
  3. Bills involving expenditure
- A financial bill will deal with matters mentioned in Art 110 (1). A money bill deals with other matters also. **Therefore all money bills are financial bills but all financial bills are not money bills.**
- All financial bills are introduced only in the Lok Sabha after the recommendations of the President.

- A financial bill is passed like an ordinary bill.
- Joint session can be held for a finance Bill.

Constitutional Amendment Bill (Article 368)

- Certain provisions of the Constitution can be amended by the Parliament by **simple majority**. These include provisions relating to the creation of new states, reconstitution of existing states, creation or abolition of upper chambers in the state legislature, etc.
- Some provisions can be amended by Parliament by a **two-third majority** and also require the **approval of the legislatures of not less than one-half of the states**, (There is no time limit within which the states should give their consent to the bill). Provisions that can be amended this way include election of the President, powers of the Union and state executive, Union judiciary, High Courts, representation of states in Parliament, amendment procedure, etc.
- But a major portion of the Constitution can be amended by a **two-third majority in Parliament**. This must also be the clear-cut majority of the total membership of each house. The provisions which can be amended in this ways are F. R., D.P.S.P, etc.
- It may be noted that provisions which affect the federal character of the Constitution can be amended only with the approval of the states.
- A notable feature of the amendment procedure in India is that the initiative rests with the Centre and the states cannot initiate any amendments.

Comparisons among different bills

Ordinary Bill	Money Bill	Financial Bill	Constitutional Amendment Bill
Can be introduced in either house of parliament.	Only in Lok Sabha.	Only in Lok Sabha.	In either house of parliament.
Does not need President recommendation for introduction.	Need President recommendation for introduction.	Need President recommendation for introduction.	Does not need President recommendation for introduction.
Passed by simple majority.	Passed by simple majority.	Passed by simple majority.	Passed by simple or special majority (by both houses separately) and or approval of legislatures of not less than one-half of the states.
Equal legislative jurisdiction of both houses of parliament.	RS has only recommendatory power (14 days)	Equal legislative jurisdiction of both houses of Parliament.	Equal legislative jurisdiction of both houses of Parliament.
Joint session can be held.	Joint session cannot be held.	Joint session can be held.	Joint session cannot be held because if one house rejects the bill, it comes to an end.
President has three options: Absolute veto, suspensive veto, pocket veto.	President has choice of withholding or giving assent to the bill, but by convention he can not withhold the assent.	President has three options: Absolute veto, suspensive veto, pocket veto.	President has to give assent to the bill.

Public and Private Bills

Public Bills

A public bill is introduced by minister in the Parliament or state legislature which reflects the policies of the rulling party or the government. A public bill generally has greater chance of approval by the Parliament unlike a private bill. The rejection of a public bill by the house amounts to the expression of want of parliamentary confidence in the government and may lead to its resignation. This bill is drafted by the concerned department in consultation with the law department and its introduction in the house requires seven days' notice.

Private Bill

A private bill is introduced by any member of Parliament other than a minister which reflects the stand of opposition party on public matter. A private bill rejection by the house has no implication on the parliamentary confidence in the government or the resignation. The introduction of a private bill requires one month's notice and has lesser chance of parliamentary approval. A private bill's drafting is the responsibility of the member concerned.

Youth Parliament

On the recommendation of the fourth all India whips conference a scheme of youth parliament was started in 1960s with the objectives of:

(a) acquainting the younger generation with parliamentary practices and procedures;

(b) imbibing the spirit of discipline and tolerance in the minds of youth; and

(c) in calculating the basic values of democracy in the student community and enabling them to acquire a proper perspective on the functioning of democratic institutions. The youth parliament scheme was first introduced in the schools in Delhi in 1966-67.

Annual Financial Statement – Budget (Article 112)

The Constitution refers to budget as the 'annual financial statement'. The team 'budget' has nowhere been used in the Constitution.

The budget is a statement of the estimated receipts and expenditure of the government of India in a financial year. The government presents the budget on the first day of February, so that it could be materialized before the commencement of new financial year in April.

Railway budget has been merged with the union budget since the financial years 2017-18.

- Over all, the budget contains the following:
  1. Estimates of revenue and capital receipts.
  2. Ways and means to raise the revenue.
  3. Estimates of expenditure.
  4. Details of the actual receipts and expenditure of the closing financial year.
  5. Economic and financial policy of the coming year that is taxation proposals, prospects of revenue etc.
- The Railways budget was separated from the General budget in 1921 on the the recommendations of the Acworth Committee.
- President shall lay before each house of parliament, an annual financial statement (known as budget)- Article 112
- No demand for a grant shall be made except on recommendation of President- (Article 113).
- Rajya Sabha has no power to vote on demand for grants.
- No money shall be withdrawn from Consolidated Fund of India except under appropriation made by law- (Article 114).
- Money Bill cannot be introduced in Rajya Sabha.
- Rajya Sabha should send Money Bill within 14 days to Lok Sabha.
- No tax can be levied except by authority of law- (Article 265)

Types of Budget		
Budget Type	**Given By**	**Relates To**
Performance Budgeting	First Hoover Commission, USA. Introduced in India in 1968 on recommendations of Administration Reforms Commission	Emphasis on 'purpose' of expenditure
Zero-Based Budgeting	Phyrr, USA	Every scheme critically reviewed & re-justified totally from zero (or scratch)
Line-Item Budgeting	Developed in 18th century. Traditional system prevailed in India.	Emphasis on items of expenditure & not its purpose. Sole objective is control over expenditure.

Stages In Enactment of Budget

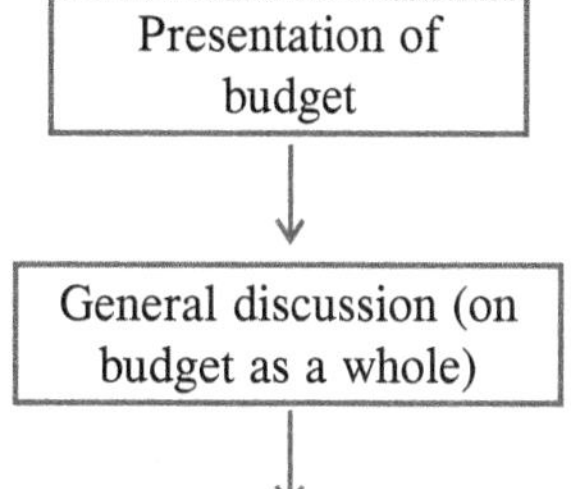

Other Grants

Supplementary grant	It is granted when the amount authorized by the Parliament through the appropriation act for a particular service for the current financial year is found to be insufficient of that year.
Additional grant	It is granted when a need has arisen during the current financial year for additional expenditure upon some new service not contemplated in the budget for that year.
Excess grant	It is granted when money has been spent on any service during a financial year in excess of the amount granted for that service in the budget for that year. It is voted by the lok sabha after the financial year.
Vote of credit	It is granted for meeting an unexpected demand for the service, the demands cannot be stated with the details in the budget. It is like a blank cheque given to the executive by the lok sabha.
Exceptional grant	It is granted for a special purpose and forms no part of the current service of any financial year.

Token grant	It is granted when funds to meet the proposed expenditure on the new service can be made available by re-appropriation. A demand for the grant of token sum of ₹ 1 is submitted to the vote of Lok Sabha and if assented, funds are made available.

Various Cut Motions as Moved in Lok Sabha	
Policy cut	Disapproval of policy. It states that amount of demand be reduced to ₹ 1.
Economy cut	Demand be reduced by a specified amount.
Token cut	Demand is reduced by ₹ 100.

Parliamentary Terms

Summoning

The president from time to time sumons each House of Parliament to meet. But, the maximum gap between two sessions of Parliament cannot be more than six months. In other words, the Parliament should meet at least twice a year.

Adjournment

A sitting of Parliament can be terminated by adjournment or adjournment *sine die* or prorogation or dissolution (in the case of the Lok Sabha). An adjournment suspends the work in a sitting for a specified time, which may be hours, day or weeks.

It is the period between the prorogation of the parliament and its re-assembly is a new session.

Adjournment Sine Die

- Adjournment *sine die* means terminating a sitting of Parliament for an indefinite period.
- The power of adjournment as well as adjournment *sine die* lies with the presiding officer of the House. He can also call a sitting of the House before the date or time to which it has been adjourned or at any time after the House has been adjourned *sine die*.

Prorogation

The presiding officer (Speaker or Chairman) declares the House adjourned *sine die*, when the business of a session is completed. Within the next few days, the President issues a notification for prorogation of the session. However, the President can also prorogue the House while in session.

Dissolution

Rajya Sabha, being a permanent House, is not subject to dissolution. Only the Lok Sabha is subject to dissolution. Unlike a prorogation, a dissolution ends the very life of the existing House, and a new House is constituted after general elections are held. The dissolution of the Lok Sabha may take place in either of two ways:

1. Automatic dissolution, that is, on the expiry of its tenure of five years or the terms as extended during a national emergency; or

2. Whenever the President decides to dissolve the House, which he is authorised to do. Once the Lok Sabha is dissolved before the completion of its normal tenure, the dissolution is irrevocable.

When the Lok Sabha is dissolved, all business including bills, motions, resolutions, notices, petitions and so on pending before it or its committees lapse. They (to be pursued further) must be reintroduced in the newly-constituted Lok Sabha. However, some pending bills and all pending assurances that are to be examined by the Committee on Government Assurances do not lapse on the dissolution of the Lok Sabha. The position with respect to lapsing of bills is as follows:

1. A bill pending in the Lok Sabha lapses (whether originating in the Lok Sabha or transmitted to it by the Rajya Sabha).

2. A bill passed by the Lok Sabha but pending in the Rajya Sabha lapses.

3. A bill not Passed by the two Houses due to disagreement and if the president has notified the holding of a joint sitting before the dissolution of Lok Sabha, does not lapse.

4. A bill pending in the Rajya Sabha but not passed by the Lok Sabha does not lapse.

5. A bill passed by both Houses but pending assent of the President does not lapse.

6. A bill passed by both Houses but returned by the President for reconsideration of Houses does not lapse.

Quorum

Quorum is the minimum number of members required to be present in the House before it can transact any business. It is one-tenth of the total number of members in each House including the presiding officer. It means that there must be at least 55 members present in the Lok Sabha and 25 members present in the Rajya Sabha, if any business is to be conducted. If there is no quorum during a meeting of the House, it is the duty of the presiding officer either to adjourn the House or to suspend the meeting until there is a quorum.

Funds

Indian Constitution provides three kinds of funds for Central Government

1. Consolidated Fund of India
2. Public Accounts of India
3. Contingency Fund of India

Consolidated Fund of India

- Article 266 provides the Parliament to have a 'Consolidated Fund of India'. It is a fund to which all receipts are credited and all payments are debited. In other words,
  - all revenues received by the Government of India.
  - all loans raised by the Government by the issue of Treasury Bills, loans or ways and means of advances.
  - all money received by the government in repayment of loans for the Consolidated Fund of India.
- All the legally authorised payments on behalf of the government are made out of this fund. No money out of this fund, can be appropriated (issued or drawn) except in accordance with a Parliamentary Law.

Public Account of India

All other public money received by Government of India on or on behalf of it, shall be credited to the Public Accounts of India. It includes departmental deposits, remittances, judicial deposits, provident fund deposits, etc. Payments from this account can be made by without parliamentary appropriation as these payments are mostly in the nature of banking transactions. It is covered in **Article 266 (1)**.

Contingency Fund of India

The Constitution authorised the Parliament to establish a 'Contingency Fund of India' (Under Article 267), into which amounts determined by law are paid from time-to-time. Accordingly, the Parliament enacted the **Contingency Fund of India Act** in 1950.

This fund is placed at the disposal of the President and he can make advances out of it to meet unforeseen expenditure pending its authorisation by the Parliament.

Charged Expenditure

The budget consists of two types of expenditure—the expenditure 'charged' upon the Consolidated Fund of India and the expenditure 'made' from the Consolidated Fund of India. The charged expenditure is non-votable by the Parliament, that is, it can only be discussed by the Parliament, which the other type has to be voted by the Parliament. The list of the charged expenditure is as follows:

1. Emoluments and allowances of the President and other expenditure relating to his office.

2. Salaries and allowances of the Chairman and the Deputy Chairman of the Rajya Sabha and the Speaker and the Deputy Speaker of the Lok Sabha.

3. Salaries, allowances and pensions of the judges of the Supreme Court.

4. Pensions of the judges of high courts.

5. Salary, allowances and pension of the Comptroller and Auditor General of India.

6. Salaries, allowances and pension of the chairman and members of the Union Public Service Commission.

7. Administrative expenses of the Supreme Court, the office of the Comptroller and Auditor General of India and the Union Public Service Commission including the salaries, allowances and pensions of the persons serving in these offices.

8. The debt charges for which the Government of India is liable, including interest, sinking fund charges and redemption charges and other expenditure relating to the raising of loans and the service and redemption of debt.

9. Any sum required to satisfy any judgement, decree or award of any court or arbitral tribunal.

10. Any other expenditure declared by the Parliament to be so charged.

Parliamentary Committees

Parliamentary Committees are of two kinds–**Adhoc Committees** and the **Standing Committees**. Adhoc Committees are appointed for a specific purpose and they cease to exist when they finish the task assigned to them and submit a report. The principal Adhoc Committees are the Select and Joint Committees on Bills.

Apart from he Adhoc Committees, each House of Parliament has Standing Committees like the Business Advisory Committee, the Committee on Petitions, the Committee of Privileges and the Rules Committee.

The Committee on Subordinate Legislation, the Committee on Government Assurances, the Committee on Estimates, the Committee on Public Accounts and the Committee on Public Undertakings and the Departmentally Related Standing Committees (DRSCs). play an important role in exercising a check over Governmental Expenditure and Policy Formulation.

Estimates Committee

- This Committee originated in 1921. This Committee consists of *30 members* by the Lok Sabha every year from amongst its members. A minister is not eligible for election to this committee. **The term of the committee is 1 year**. The function of the Committee are as follows:
  - To report what economies, improvements in organisation, efficiency and administrative reform consistent with the policy underlying the estimates, can be affected.
  - To suggest alternative policies in order to bring about efficiency and economy in administration.
  - To examine whether the money is well laid out within the limits of the policy implied in the estimates.
  - To suggest the form in which the estimates are to be presented to the Parliament.
- This committee was constituted in 1950 on the recommendation of **John Mathai**.

The Principles of Proportional Representation by means of a Single Transferable Vote is used in election of the members. The Chairman of this Committee is appointed by the Speaker from amongst its members and he is invariably from the ruling party.

Committee on Public Undertakings

- This committee was created in 1964 on the recommendation of the **Krishna Menon Committee**. The Committee on Public Undertakings consists of 15 members elected by the Lok Sabha; 7 members of the Rajya Sabha are also associated with it. A minister is not eligible for election to this committee. The term of the committee is 1 year. The functions of the Committee on Public Undertakings are as follows:
  - To examine the reports and accounts of Public Undertakings;
  - To examine the reports, if any, of the Comptroller and Auditor General on the Public Undertakings.
  - To examine, in the context of the autonomy and efficiency of the Public Undertakings, whether the

affairs of the Public Undertakings are being managed in accordance with sound business principles and prudent commercial practices.

- The Chairman of the Committee is appointed by the Speaker, from amongst its members who are darwn from the Lock Sabha only.

Committee on Public Accounts

This committee was first set-up in 1921 under the provisions of the Government of India Act, 1919. This committee consists of 22 members (15 from Lok Sabha and 7 form Rajya Sabha). A minister is not eligible for election to this committee. The term of the committee is 1 year. The main duty of the committee is to ascertain whether the money granted by Parliament has been spent by government 'within the Scope of the Demand.'

Rules Committee

It considers matters of procedure and conduct of business in the house and recommends any amendments or additions to the Rules of Procedure and Conduct of Business in Lok Sabha that are considered necessary.

Presentation of States & Union territories in 'Lok Sabha' and 'Rajya Sabha'

States	Lok Sabha (No. of Seats)	Rajya Sabha (No. of Seats)
Andhra Pradesh	25	11
Assam	14	7
Goa	2	1
Haryana	10	5
Jammu & Kashmir	6	4
Kerala	20	9
Maharashtra	48	19
Meghalaya	2	1
Odisha	21	10
Rajasthan	25	10
Tamil Nadu	39	18
West Bengal	42	16
Mijoram	1	1
Jharkhand	14	6
Uttar Pradesh	80	31
Bihar	40	16
Gujarat	26	11
Himachal Pradesh	4	3
Karnataka	28	12
Madhya Pradesh	29	11
Manipur	2	1
Nagaland	1	1
Punjab	13	7
Sikkim	1	1
Tripura	2	1
Arunachal Pradesh	2	1
Uttarakhand	5	3
Chattisgarh	11	5
Telangana	17	7

Union Territories	Lok Sabha (No. of Seats)	Rajya Sabha (No. of Seats)
Delhi	7	3
Chandigarh	1	Nil
Dadra and Nagar Haveli	1	Nil
Daman and Diu	1	Nil
Andaman and Nicobar	1	Nil
Puducherry	1	1
Lakshadweep	1	Nil

Exercise -1

1. The term of the legislative assembly can be extended during the period of national emergency by a law of parliament for
   (a) One year at a time (for any length of time)
   (b) 6 months at a time (for any length of time)
   (c) 9 months at a time (for any length of time)
   (d) 3 months at a time (for any length of time)
2. Which of the following is not a discretionary power of president:
   (a) Appointment of prime minister when no party has a clear majority in the Lok Sabha.
   (b) Dismissal of the council of ministers when it cannot prove the confidence of the Lok Sabha.
   (c) Removal of a judge of supreme court.
   (d) Dissolution of the Lok Sabha if the council of ministers has lost its majority.
3. Which of the following is not a condition when parliament can legislate on the matters of state list:
   (a) When Rajya Sabha declares that it is necessary for parliament to make laws on matter of state list.
   (b) During the proclamation of national emergency in the state.
   (c) When two or more states pass resolutions in this regard.
   (d) When there is no clear majority in the state legislative assembly.
4. The President takes an oath before taking office in the presence of Chief Justice of India. If the Chief Justice is not available, he takes the oath in the presence of the
   (a) Vice-President
   (b) Senior-most Judge of the Supreme Court
   (c) Attorney-General
   (d) Election Commissioner
5. who elects the Vice-President?
   (a) Electoral college which elects the President
   (b) Members of the Rajya Sabha and Lok Sabha
   (c) Electoral college consisting of members of Parliament
   (d) Members of Parliament in a joint meeting
6. Candidate for Vice-presidential election must possess the qualifications prescribed for a Presidential candidate except that he must be:
   (a) a citizen of India
   (b) over 35 years of age
   (c) hold no office of profit under the Government
   (d) Qualified to be a member of the Rajya Sabha
7. A resolution for impeaching the President can be moved after 14 days' notice signed by
   (a) not less than 50 members of the House
   (b) not less than one-third of the total number of members of the House
   (c) not less than one-fourth of the total number of members of the House
   (d) at least 100 members of Lok Sabha and 50 members of Rajya Sabha
8. If a resolution impeaching the President is passed, the President is considered to have been removed
   (a) from the date on which the resolution is passed
   (b) when the Chief Justice of India passes such an order
   (c) notification in the Gazette of India
   (d) once a new incumbent is elected
9. Which of the following powers are exercised both by the President and the Governors?
   (a) Power to pardon a sentence by court martial
   (b) Power to remit a sentence in an offence relating to matters on the State List
   (c) Power to commute a death sentence
   (d) Power to remit a sentence by court martial
10. Legislative powers of the President EXCLUDES the power to :
    (a) summon or prorogue the Houses of Parliament
    (b) call a joint sitting of the Houses to resolve deadlocks
    (c) nominate 12 members to the Lok Sabha
    (d) address either House at any time
11. An ordinance promulgated by the President :
    (a) has an indefinite life
    (b) effective only if the Lok Sabha is dissolved
    (c) must be laid before the Parliament when it meets
    (d) is a parallel power of legislation available to the President even when Parliament is in session
12. Which among the following bills require previous sanction of the President before its introduction?
    (a) Money bill
    (b) Bill affecting taxation in which States are interested
    (c) State bills imposing restrictions upon freedom of trades
    (d) All of the above
13. If the President returns a bill to the legislature for reconsideration:
    (a) a re-passage of the bill by two-thirds majority forces him to give his assent
    (b) a re-passage of the bill by a majority will make him give an assent
    (c) joint sitting of the parliament is needed to pass the bill.
    (d) legislature must accept the amendments proposed by the President
14. If the Chairman of Rajya Sabha becomes acting President, his duties as a Chairman are performed by
    (a) Speaker.
    (b) A newly elected Chairman
    (c) Deputy Chairman
    (d) None of the above
15. Military powers of the President EXCLUDES
    (a) Supreme command of the armed forces
    (b) President's power to declare war or peace is subject to control by the Parliament
    (c) President needs the sanction of Parliament to approve training and maintaining of armed forces
    (d) President is independent of all legislative control
16. President does NOT APPOINT the
    (a) Finance Commission
    (b) Planning Commission
    (c) Commission on Official Languages
    (d) UPSC
17. Post of the Prime Minister of India:
    (a) is based on conventions
    (b) has been created by the Parliament
    (c) has been created by the Constitution
    (d) is less powerful than that of the President
18. In case of resignation or death of the Prime Minister
    (a) Council of Ministers is dissolved
    (b) General elections are held
    (c) Cabinet elects another leader
    (d) Lok Sabha is dissolved

19. Prime Minister holds his office during the pleasure of the President & continue as long as he enjoys the confidence of the
    (a) Electorate
    (b) Lok Sabha
    (c) Party to which he belongs
    (d) Parliament

20. In parliamentary democracy the
    (a) Executive controls the Legislature
    (b) Executive and Legislature are separate
    (c) Judiciary controls both legislature and Executive
    (d) Legislature controls the Executive

21. According to the Constitution
    (a) Prime minister allocates work amongst ministers based on specific guidelines
    (b) Number of ministers, including the prime minister should not be more than 15% of total number of members of Lok Sabha
    (c) a member of either House of Parliament from any political party who is disqualified under the, Anti-Defection Act appointed a minister during that term even if elected again
    (d) all of the above are correct

22. Money Bill
    (a) cannot be introduced in the Rajya Sabha
    (b) has to be certified by the President
    (c) can be amended by the Council of States
    (d) both (a) and (b)

23. Amendments cannot be put up in either House to
    (a) Annual Financial Statement
    (b) Appropriation Bill
    (c) Demand for grants
    (d) Any of the above

24. Privileges of the members of Parliament include:
    (a) Freedom from arrest in all cases
    (b) Freedom of attendance as witness if Parliament is in session
    (c) Total freedom of speech
    (d) All of the above

25. Parliament does not have the power to remove:
    (a) Comptroller and Auditor General
    (b) Supreme Court Judges
    (c) Chairman of UPSC
    (d) High Court Judges

26. Which among the following is not a committee of the Parliament?
    (a) Public Accounts Committee
    (b) Estimates Committee
    (c) Committee on Public Under-takings
    (d) Rules Committee

27. Members of Rajya Sabha are:
    (a) Elected indirectly
    (b) All are nominated
    (c) Elected both directly and indirectly
    (d) Elected by members of State Legislative assemblies and Legislative Councils

28. A dissolution does not affect:
    (a) A bill that originated in the Rajya Sabha and is with Lok Sabha the President calls upon it to do so
    (b) Rajya Sabha passes a resolution by simple majority that it is necessary in national interest
    (c) Speaker certifies the need
    (d) There is a national emergency

29. Parliament can legislate on a subject in the State List if:
    (a) The President calls upon it to do so
    (b) Rajya Sabha passes a resolution by simple majority that it is necessary in national interest

    (c) Speaker certifies the need
    (d) There is a national emergency

30. Who/which among the following ensures that no unauthorized money is spent out of the Consolidated Fund of a State.
    (a) Public Accounts Committee
    (b) Comptroller and Auditor-General of India
    (c) Finance Commission
    (d) None of the above

31. If the Prime Minister of India Belonged to the Upper House of Parliament
    (a) he will not vote in his favour in the event of a no-confidence motion
    (b) he will not speak on the budget in the Rajya Sabha
    (c) he can make statements only in the Lok Sabha
    (d) he has to become a member of the Lower House within 6 months after being sworn as the Prime Minister

32. Which among the following duties is not performed by the Comptroller and Auditor General of India?
    (a) Expenditure from the Consolidated Fund of India
    (b) Expenditure from the Contingency Funds and Public Accounts
    (c) Trading, manufacturing, profit and loss accounts
    (d) Receipt and issue of public money, and to ensure that public revenue is lodged in the exchequer

33. Parliament can legislate for the country or part of it for implementation of international treaties. For this consent of all the:
    (a) States is required
    (b) State/States concerned needs to be taken
    (c) Legislation has to be ratified by at least half of the States of India
    (d) No consent is required

34. Among the following Presidents of India, who was also the Secretary General of Non-Aligned Movement for some period ?
    (a) Dr. Sarvepalli Radhakrishnan
    (b) Varahagiri Venkatagiri
    (c) Giani Zail Singh
    (d) Dr. Shanker Dayal Sharma

35. Which one of the following devices calls the attention of minister towards a matter of public importance?
    (a) Half-an-hour discussion
    (b) Calling attention notice
    (c) Short duration discussion
    (d) Adjournment motion

36. Which of the following is not a condition of admissibility of cut motions in the Parliament?
    (a) It should not make suggestions for the amendment of existing laws.
    (b) It should not relate to expenditure charged on the Consolidated Fund of India.
    (c) It should relate to more than one demand.
    (d) It should not raise a question of privilege.

37. Which of the following statements about President's ordinance-making power is not correct?
    (a) It is co-extensive with legislative power of Parliament.
    (b) Laid down in Article 123.
    (c) Shall cease to operate on expiry of six weeks from the reassembly of the Parliament.
    (d) Cannot be withdrawn at any time by the President.

38. The President of India is elected by an electoral college consisting of :
    (a) Members of Parliament and state legislatures
    (b) Elected members of Parliament and state legislatures
    (c) Elected members of Parliament and state legislative assemblies
    (d) Elected members of Lok Sabha and members of Rajya Sabha and state Legislative Assemblies

39. Disqualification on grounds of defection for a member of Parliament will not apply
    (a) in case of a split in the original political party to which he is elected
    (b) if he has voluntarily given up his membership of a political party
    (c) if the abstains from voting in the house contrary to the direction of the political party
    (d) if a nominated member of a house joins a political party after 6 months

40. The Rajya Sabha has exclusive jurisdiction in
    (a) approving a proclamation of emergency
    (b) the creation and abolition of states
    (c) the election of the Vice-President
    (d) authorizing Parliament to legislate on a subject in the state list

41. The Vice-President of India can be removed from the office
    (a) by a resolution initiated in the council of states and approved by the Lok Sabha
    (b) by a resolution in the Lok Sabha agreed by the council of states
    (c) by a resolution adopted by the two house meeting in a joint session
    (d) by following a formal process of impeachment

42. According to Art. 81 of the Constitution, as amended by the 87th Amendment, the population figures to be considered for dividing each state into territorial constituencies for Lok Sabha elections are of ____ census
    (a) 1971   (b) 2001
    (c) 1991   (d) 2011

43. The amendment of the Constitution can be initiated in
    (a) the Lok Sabha only
    (b) the Rajya Sabha only
    (c) the Legislative Assemblies of states
    (d) either house of the Parliament

44. When a Money Bill is introduced in the Lok Sabha whose recommendation is necessary?
    (a) Lok Sabha Speaker   (b) Union Finance Minister
    (c) Leader of the Lok Sabha (d) The President

45. Who is empowered by the Constitution to dissolve the Lok Sabha before the expiry of its term?
    (a) The Prime Minister
    (b) The President
    (c) The President of India on the advice of the Prime Minister
    (d) The Chief Election Commissioner

46. With reference to the passage of Money Bill in Indian Parliament, which one of the following statements is correct?
    (a) The decision of the Union Finance Minister is final on the question whether a bill is Money Bill or not
    (b) A Money Bill can be introduced only in the Lok Sabha
    (c) After a money bill is passed by Lok Sabha and transmitted to Rajya Sabha, it should be returned within one month
    (d) When Rajya Sabha returns the Money Bill with its recommendations, the Lok Sabha has to accept such recommendations

47. In the absence of both the President of India and the Vice-President, who shall act as the President of India?
    (a) Prime Minister
    (b) Speaker of the Lok Sabha
    (c) Chief Justice of the Supreme Court
    (d) Deputy Chairman of Rajya Sabha

48. Which one of the following statements is not correct ?
    (a) All the expenditure other than that which is charged on the Consolidated Fund of India is to be submitted to the Lok Sabha in the form of demands for grants
    (b) No demand for a grant is made except on the recommendation of the President of India
    (c) The Lok Sabha can refuse assent to any demand for grant
    (d) The Lok Sabha can suggest an increase in the expenditure

49. Article 75 of the Constitution of India provides that the Council of Ministers of the Union shall be collectively responsible to
    (a) the House of the People
    (b) both the Houses of Parliament
    (c) the President only
    (d) the President and both the Houses of the Parliament

50. The Union Executive of India consists of:
    (a) The President; Vice-President, Lok Sabha Speaker and the Council of Ministers
    (b) The President, Deputy Chairman of the Rajya Sabha, Lok Sabha Speaker and the Prime Minister
    (c) The President and the Council of Ministers only
    (d) The President, Vice-President and the Council of Ministers only

51. When an ordinary Bill is referred to a joint sitting of both the Houses of Indian Parliament, it has to be passed by a
    (a) simple majority of the total number of members of both the Houses present and voting
    (b) two-third majority of the total number of members of both the Houses
    (c) simple majority of the total number of members of both the Houses
    (d) two-third majority of the total number of members of both the Houses present and voting

52. Which one of the following statements about a Money Bill is not correct?
    (a) A Money Bill can be tabled in either House of Parliament
    (b) The Speaker of Lok Sabha is the final authority to decide whether a Bill is a Money Bill or not
    (c) The Rajya Sabha must return a Money Bill passed by the Lok Sabha and send it for consideration within 14 days
    (d) The President cannot return a Money Bill to the Lok Sabha for reconsideration

53. Which one of the following duties is not performed by Comptroller and Auditor general of India?
    (a) To audit and report on all expenditure from the Consolidated Fund of India
    (b) To audit and report on all expenditure from the Contingency Funds and Public Accounts
    (c) To audit and report on all trading, manufacturing, profit and loss accounts
    (d) To control the receipt and issue of public money, and to ensure that the public revenue is lodged in the exchequer

54. What is a 'charged expenditure'?
    (a) An expenditure which has been incurred already and for the bills which are pending for payment
    (b) Expenditure on the essential aspects of adminstration
    (c) The expenditure that can be incurred by the president without the approval of the parliament.
    (d) The expenditure from the Consolidated Fund of India for which the approval of the Parliament is not necessary, according to the Constitution.

55. Which of the following statements is not correct?
    (a) The president shall not be answerable to any court for the exercise and performance of the powers and duties of his office
    (b) Parliament can initiate, in accordance with the procedure laid down in the Constitution, impeachment proceedings against the President during the term of his office
    (c) Civil proceedings can be instituted against the President, in respect of any act done in his personal capacity before he entered upon his office as President, during the term of his office
    (d) No criminal proceedings shall be instituted or continued against the President in any Court during his term of office

56. The Comptroller and Auditor General of India
    (a) Can be appointed as a member of U.P.S.C. after his retirement
    (b) Can be appointed as Chairman of the State Public Service Commission
    (c) Shall not be eligible for any further office either under the government of India or under the Government of any State after his retirement
    (d) Can be appointed to any office after his retirement

57. Which one of the following is not a main feature of the Cabinet system of government as it prevails in India?
    (a) The members of the Council of Ministers are chosen by the president and not by the Prime Minister
    (b) The proceedings of the Cabinet are kept secret
    (c) The Prime Minister presides over the Cabinet meetings
    (d) All of the above

58. Which one of the following is not a department in the ministry of Human Resource Development?
    (a) Department of Elementary Education and Literacy
    (b) Department of Secondary Education and Higher Education
    (c) Department of Technical Education
    (d) Department of women and child development

59. The Comptroller and Auditor General is appointed by the president. He can be removed
    (a) by the president
    (b) on an address from both Houses of Parliament
    (c) on the recommendation of the president by the supreme court
    (d) by CJI

60. Which one of the following expenditure is not charged on the consolidated fund of India?
    (a) Salary and allowances of the president of India
    (b) Salary and allowances of the vice president of India
    (c) Salary and allowances of the justice of the supreme court of India
    (d) Salary and allowances of the speaker of the Lok Sabha

61. Who has the right to seek advisory opinion of the supreme court of India, on any question of law?
    (a) Prime Minister
    (b) President
    (c) Any of the high courts
    (d) All of the above

62. Recommendations to the President of India on the specific Union state fiscal relation are made by the
    (a) Finance Minister
    (b) Reserve Bank of India
    (c) Planning Commission
    (d) Finance Commission

63. Who amongst the following is not entitled to take part in the activities of Lok Sabha?
    (a) The Comptroller and Auditor General of India
    (b) The Attorney General of India
    (c) The solicitor General
    (d) The secretary to president of India

64. A bill presented in Parliament becomes an Act after
    (a) It is passed by both the Houses
    (b) The president has given his Assent
    (c) The Prime minister has signed it
    (d) The Supreme Court has declared it to be within the competence of the Union Parliament

65. Which one of the following statements about the parliament of India is not correct?
    (a) The constitution provides for a parliamentary form of Government
    (b) The foremost function of the parliament is to provide a cabinet
    (c) The membership of the cabinet is restricted to the lower house
    (d) The cabinet has to enjoy the confidence of the majority in the popular chamber

66. The 'Contingency Fund' of the state is operated by
    (a) The Governor of the state
    (b) The Chief Minister of the state
    (c) The State Finance Minister
    (d) None of the above

67. The office of the President does not characterize the combination of governmental systems of
    (a) Parliamentary and Federal
    (b) Republican and Parliamentary
    (c) Presidential and Republican
    (d) Democratic and Republican

68. The system of Proportion of representation as an electoral mechanism ensures
    (a) Representation of minorities
    (b) Rule of majority
    (c) Stability in government
    (d) Common political thinking

69. Who is the highest civil servant of the Union Government?
    (a) Attorney General
    (b) Cabinet Secretary
    (c) Home Secretary
    (d) Principal Secretary of the P.M.

70. The speaker's vote in the Lok Sabha is called
    (a) Casting vote   (b) Sound vote
    (c) Direct vote   (d) Indirect vote

71. The Parliamentary Committee which scrutinizes the report of the CAG of India is
    (a) Estimates Committee
    (b) Select Committee
    (c) Public Accounts Committee
    (d) None of these

72. What is the period of appointment of the comptroller and Auditor General of India?
    (a) 6 years
    (b) upto 65 years of age
    (c) 6 years or 65 years of age, whichever earlier
    (d) upto 64 years of age

73. In order to be recognised as an official opposition group in the parliament, the minimum strength required is
    (a) $1/3^{rd}$ of the total strength
    (b) $1/4^{th}$ of the total strength
    (c) $1/6^{th}$ of the total strength
    (d) $1/10^{th}$ of the total strength

74. Who among the following is the chairman of the National Integration council?
    (a) The President   (b) The Vice-president
    (c) The Prime Minister (d) The Chief Justice of India
75. Who advises the Government of India on legal matters?
    (a) Attorney General
    (b) Chief justice of supreme court
    (c) Chairman, Law Commission
    (d) None of these
76. The Committee of parliament on official language comprises the members
    (a) 20 from Lok Sabha, 10 from Rajya Sabha
    (b) 10 from Lok Sabha, 20 from Rajya Sabha
    (c) 10 from Lok Sabha, 10 from Rajya Sabha
    (d) 20 from Lok Sabha, 20 from Rajya Sabha
77. In case the President wishes to resign, to whom is he to address his resignation letter?
    (a) Chief Justice of India
    (b) Secretary of Lok Sabha
    (c) Vice President
    (d) Prime Minister
78. Who among the following Indian Prime Ministers resigned before facing a vote of no-confidence in the Lok Sabha?
    (a) Chandra Shekhar
    (b) Morarji Desai
    (c) Chaudhary Charan Singh
    (d) V.P. Singh
79. 'Zero Hour' in political Jargon refers to
    (a) Suspended motion
    (b) Question hour
    (c) Adjourned time
    (d) Question-answer session
80. Which of the following types of authorities are attributed to the President of India?
    (a) Real and Popular
    (b) Titular and de jure
    (c) Constitutional and Nominal
    (d) Both (b) and (c)
81. When the offices of both Speaker and Deputy Speaker falls vacant –
    (a) The members of Lok Sabha immediately elect a Speaker.
    (b) The senior most willing member of Lok Sabha becomes the speaker.
    (c) The President appoints any member of Lok Sabha as speaker.
    (d) The Deputy Chairman of Rajya Sabha presides over till the next speaker is elected.
82. With Regard to Constitutional Amendment Bill –
    (a) The President can reject the bill but cannot return the bill.
    (b) The President cannot reject the bill but can return the bill.
    (c) The President can neither reject the bill nor return the bill.
    (d) The President can either reject the bill or return the bill.
83. The Vice President can be removed from office before completion of his term in which of the following manner?
    (a) She/he can be impeached in similar manner as President.
    (b) A Resolution of Rajya Sabha passed by special majority and agreed to by the Lok Sabha.
    (c) A Resolution of Rajya Sabha passed by simple majority and agreed to by the Lok Sabha.
    (d) A Resolution of Rajya Sabha passed by an absolute majority and agreed to by the Lok Sabha.
84. The office of the 'Whip' is mentioned in:
    (a) Constitution of India.
    (b) Rules of the house.
    (c) In a separate Parliamentary Statute.
    (d) None
85. The office of the Leader of the opposition is mentioned in:
    (a) Constitution of India
    (b) Rules of the house
    (c) A separate Parliamentary Statute
    (d) None of these
86. A minister who is not a member of either house (Note: A person can remain a minister for six months, without being a member of either house of parliament):
    (a) Can participate in the proceedings of Lok Sabha only.
    (b) Can participate in the proceedings of Rajya Sabha only.
    (c) Can participate in the proceedings of either house of parliament.
    (d) Cannot participate till he becomes a Member of either house of parliament.
87. The first reading of the Bill in a House of Parliament refers to :
    (a) The motion for leave to introduce a Bill in the House
    (b) The general discussion on the Bill as whole where only the principle underlying the Bill is discussed and not the details of the bill.
    (c) The general discussion on the Bill where the bill is discussed in details.
    (d) The state when the Bill is referred either to select committee of the House or to the joint committee of the two houses.
88. Department of official languages is subordinate office of which ministry?
    (a) Ministry of social justice and Empowerment
    (b) Ministry of Home Affairs
    (c) Ministry of Rural Development
    (d) Ministry of Culture
89. Which one of the following is part of the Electoral College for the election of the president of India but does not form part of the forum for his impeachment?
    (a) Lok Sabha
    (b) Rajya Sabha
    (c) State Legislative Councils
    (d) State Legislative Assemblies
90. The speaker can ask a member of the House to stop speaking and let another member speak. This phenomenon is known as?
    (a) Decorum   (b) Crossing the floor
    (c) Interpolation   (d) Yielding the floor
91. Which one of the following Bills must be passed by each House of the Indian parliament separately, by special majority.
    (a) Ordinary Bill   (b) Money Bill
    (c) Finance Bill   (d) Constitution Amendment Bill
92. Department of Border management is a department of which one of the following Union Ministers?
    (a) Ministry of Defense
    (b) Ministry of Home Affairs
    (c) Ministry of Shipping, Road Transport and Highways
    (d) Ministry of Environment and Forest.

93. What will follow if a Money Bill is substantially amended by the Rajya Sabha?
    (a) The Lok Sabha may still proceed with the Bill, accepting or not accepting the recommendations of the Rajya Sabha
    (b) The Lok Sabha cannot consider the bill further
    (c) The Lok Sabha may send the Bill to the Rajya Sabha for reconsideration
    (d) The President may call a joint sitting for passing the Bill

94. Which one of the following is the largest Committee of the Parliament?
    (a) The Committee on Public Accounts
    (b) The Committee on Estimates
    (c) The Committee on Public Undertakings
    (d) The Committee on Petitions

95. Who among the following decides whether a bill is a Money Bill or not ?
    (a) Union Finance Minister
    (b) Speaker of Lok Sabha
    (c) Union Minister of Parliamentary Affairs
    (d) President of India

96. While Proclamation of Emergency is in operation, the term of the Lok Sabha can be extended for a period not exceeding?
    (a) Six weeks   (b) Three months
    (c) Six months   (d) One year

97. What is the term of a Member of the Rajya Sabha ?
    (a) Three years   (b) Four years
    (c) Five years   (d) Six years

98. The Union Executive of India consists of:
    (a) The President; Vice-President, Lok Sabha Speaker and the Council of Ministers
    (b) The President, Deputy Chairman of the Rajya Sabha, Lok Sabha Speaker and the Prime Minister
    (c) The President and the Council of Ministers only
    (d) The President, Vice-President and the Council of Ministers only

99. Who among the following chooses the Speaker of the House of People?
    (a) The Prime Minister of India
    (b) The Union Minister of Parliamentary Affairs
    (c) The Leader of the Opposition in the Lok Sabha
    (d) The House of People

100. In the Union Government, under whose charge is the Cabinet Secretariat?
    (a) The Minister of Parliamentary Affairs
    (b) The President of India
    (c) The Prime Minister of India
    (d) The Union Home Minister

101. If any question arises whether a Bill is a Money Bill or not, whose decision shall be final?
    (a) The Supreme Court of India
    (b) The President of India
    (c) The Speaker of the Lok Sabha
    (d) Joint Parliamentary Committee

102. The Speaker of the Lok Sabha can resign his office by addressing his resignation to
    (a) the President
    (b) the Prime Minister
    (c) the Deputy Speaker of the Lok Sabha
    (d) the Chief Justice of India

103. Who can initiate impeachment proceedings against the President of India ?
    (a) Only Lok Sabha
    (b) Only Rajya Sabha
    (c) Either House of the Parliament
    (d) Any Legislative Assembly

104. The Government Bill means a bill introduced by a
    (a) Member of the Treasury bench in the Lok Sabha
    (b) Member of the Parliament who is not a Minister
    (c) Minister in the Lok Sabha
    (d) Minister in any House of the Parliament.

105. When an ordinary Bill is referred to a joint sitting of both the Houses of Indian Parliament, it has to be passed by a
    (a) simple majority of the total number of members of both the Houses present and voting
    (b) two-third majority of the total number of members of both the Houses
    (c) simple majority of the total number of members of both the Houses
    (d) two-third majority of the total number of members of both the Houses present and voting

106. Which one among the following features of the Constitution of India is indicative of the fact that the real executive power is vested in the Council of Ministers headed by the Prime Minister?
    (a) Federalism
    (b) Representative legislature
    (c) Universal adult franchise
    (d) Parliamentary democracy

107. Normally the Parliament can legislate on the subjects enumerated in
    (a) the Union List
    (b) the Concurrent List
    (c) the State List
    (d) the Union as well as Concurrent List

108. Vice-President of India is elected by an electoral college consisting of
    (a) members of both Houses of Parliament
    (b) members of Rajya Sabha only
    (c) elected members of both Houses of Parliament
    (d) elected members of Lok Sabha only

109. Joint Parliamentary Sessions in India are chaired by the
    (a) President of India
    (b) Vice-President of India who is the Chairman of the Rajya Sabha
    (c) Speaker of the Lok Sabha
    (d) Prime Minister of India

110. Which of the following is not a Parliamentary Committee?
    (a) Demands for Grants Committee
    (b) Committee on Public Accounts
    (c) Committee on Public Undertakings
    (d) Committee on Esti mates

111. Who was the President of India at the time of proclamation of emergency in the year 1976?
    (a) V.V Giri   (b) Giani Zail Singh
    (c) Fakhr-ud-din Ali Ahmad   (d) Shankar Dayal Sharma

112. Who among the following determines the authority who shall readjust the allocation of seats in the Lok Sabha to the states and division of each State into territorial constituencies?
    (a) The President of India
    (b) The Parliament of India
    (c) The Chief Election Commissioner of India
    (d) The Lok Sabha alone

113. In India the Supreme Command of the Armed Forces is, vested in the President. This means that in the exercise of this power
    (a) he/she cannot be regulated by law
    (b) he/she shall be regulated by law
    (c) during war, the President seeks advice only from the Chiefs of the Armed Forces
    (d) during war the President can suspended the Fundamental Rights of citizens

114. The quorum for Joint Sitting of the Indian Parliament is
    (a) One- twelveth of the total number of members of the House
    (b) One-sixth of the total numbers of members of the House
    (c) One-tenth of the total number of members of the House
    (d) Two-third of the total number of members of the House
115. Identify the correct sequence of passing a Budget in the Parliament
    (a) Vote on Account, Finance Bill, Appropriation Bill Discussion on Budget
    (b) Finance Bill, Appropriation Bill, Discussion on Budget, Vote on Accounts
    (c) Discussion on Budget, Vote on Account, Finance Bill, Appropriation Bill
    (d) Discussion on Budget, Appropriation Bill, Finance Bill, Vote on Account
116. The function of a Protem Speaker is to
    (a) conduct the proceeding of the House in the absence of the Speaker
    (b) officiate as Speaker when the Speaker is unlikely to be elected
    (c) swear members and hold charge till a regular Speaker is elected
    (d) scrutinize the authenticity of the election certificates of members
117. If the Prime Minister is a member of the Rajya Sabha
    (a) He/she has to get elected to the Lok Sabha within 6 months
    (b) He/she can declare the government's policies only in the Rajya Sabha
    (c) He/she cannot take part in the voting when a vote of no confidence is under consideration
    (d) He/she cannot take part in the budget deliberation in the Lok Sabha
118. The impeachment of the President of India can be initiated in
    (a) either house of the Parliament
    (b) a joint siting of both houses of the Parliament
    (c) the Lok Sabha alone
    (d) the Rajya Sabha alone
119. The President of India is elected by a proportional representation system through single transferable vote. This implies that
    (a) each elected MP or MLA has an equal number of votes
    (b) MPs and MLAs of a State have the same number of votes
    (c) all MPs and MLAs have one vote each
    (d) MPs and MLAs of different States have different numbers of votes
120. With reference to the conduct of government business in the Parliament of India, the term 'closure' refers to
    (a) suspension of debate at the terminafan of a day's sitting of the Parliament
    (b) a rule of legislative procedure under which further debate on a motion can be hatted
    (c) the termination of a Parliamentary session
    (d) refusal on the part of tie Government to have the opposition look at important documents
121. While a proclamation of emergency is in operation the duration of the Lok Sabha can be extended for a period
    (a) not exceeding three months
    (b) not exceedng nine-months
    (c) of one year at a time
    (d) of two years at a time
122. With regard to the powers of the Rajya Sabha, which one among the following statements is not correct?
    (a) A money bill cannot be introduced in the Rajya Sabha
    (b) The Rajya Sabha has no power either to reject or amend a money bill
    (c) The Rajya Sabha cannot discuss the Annual Financial Statement
    (d) The Rajya Sabha has no power to vote on the Demands for Grants
123. In the Rajya Sabha, the states have been given seats
    (a) in accordance with their population
    (b) equally
    (c) on the basis of population and economic position
    (d) on the basis of present economic status
124. The Speaker of the Lok Sabha may be removed from office by
    (a) the majority party in the house adopting a no-confidence motion
    (b) a resolution passed by not less than half of the total membership of the house
    (c) a resolution passed by at least two-thirds of the total membership of the house
    (d) a resolution passed by a majority of all the members of the house
125. Which one among the following committees of the Parliament of India has no members of the Rajya Sabha?
    (a) Public Accounts Committee
    (b) Estimates Committee
    (c) Public Undertakings Committee
    (d) Departmentally Related Standing Committee on Finance
126. Besides representation, the Parliament of India is also a deliberative body with diverse functions.
    Which one among the following is not a function of the Parliament of India?
    (a) Ventilating the grievances of the people
    (b) Executing major policy decisions
    (c) Holding the government accountable for its actions and expenditure
    (d) Amending the Constitution
127. Which of the following statements is not correct?
    (a) A Money Bill shall not be introduced in the Council of States
    (b) The Council of States has no power to reject or amend a Money Bill
    (c) the Council of Ministers is responsible to the House of the People and not to the Council of States
    (d) The House of the People has special powers with respect to the State List compared to the Council of States
128. Who among the following have the right to vote in the elections to both the Lok Sabha and the Rajya Sabha?
    (a) Elected members of the Lower House of the Parliament
    (b) Elected members of the Upper House of the Parliament
    (c) Elected members of the Upper House of the State Legislature
    (d) Elected members of the Lower House of the State Legislature
129. Which one of the following statements about the duties of Prime Minister is correct?
    (a) Is free to choose his minister only from among members of either House of the Parliament
    (b) Can choose his cabinet after consulting the President of India.
    (c) Has full discretion in the choice of persons who are to serve as ministers in his cabinet
    (d) Has only limited power in the choice of his cabinet colleagues because of the discretionary powers vested the President of India

130. If the Prime Minister of India belonged to the Upper House of Parliament:
    (a) he will not be able to vote in his favour in the event of a no-confidence motion
    (b) he will not be able to speak on the budget in the Lower House
    (c) he can make statements only in the Upper House
    (d) he was to become a member of the Lower House within six months after being sworn in

131. Which one of the following statements about a Money Bill is not correct?
    (a) A Money Bill can be tabled in either House of Parliament
    (b) The Speaker of Lok Sabha is the final authority to decide whether a Bill is a Money Bill or not
    (c) The Rajya Sabha must return a Money Bill passed by the Lok Sabha and send it for consideration within 14 days
    (d) The President cannot return a Money Bill to the Lok Sabha for reconsideration

132. The Parliament can make any law for whole or any part of India for implementing international treaties
    (a) with the consent of all the States
    (b) with the consent of the majority of States
    (c) with the consent of the States concerned
    (d) without the consent of any State

133. The term of the Lok Sabha:
    (a) cannot be extended under any circumstances
    (b) can be extended by six months at a time
    (c) can be extended by one year at a time during the proclamation of emergency
    (d) can be extended for two years at a time during the proclamation of emergency

134. Which one of the following Articles of the Indian Constitution provides that 'It shall be the duty of the Union to protect every State against external aggression and internal disturbance'?
    (a) Article 215   (b) Article 275
    (c) Article 325   (d) Article 355

135. Which one of the following Bills must be passed by each House of the Indian Parliamentary separately by special majority?
    (a) Ordinary Bill
    (b) Money Bill
    (c) Finance Bill
    (d) Constitution Amendment Bill

136. With reference to Indian Parliament, which one of the following is not correct?
    (a) The Appropriation Bill must be passed by both the Houses of Parliament before it can be enacted into law
    (b) No money shall be withdrawn from the Consolidated Fund of India except under the appropriation made by the Appropriation Act
    (c) Finance Bill is required for proposing new taxes but no additional Bill/Act is required for making changes in the rates of taxes which are already under operation.
    (d) No Money Bill can be introduced except on the recommendation of the President

137. Which of the following special powers have been conferred on the Rajya Sabha by the Constitution of India?
    (a) To change the existing territory of a State and to change the name of a State
    (b) To pass a resolution empowering the Parliament to make laws in the State List and to create one or more All India Services
    (c) To amend the election procedure of the President and to determine the pension of the President after his/her retirement
    (d) To determine the functions of the Election Commission and to determine the number of Election Commissioners

138. The Parliament can make any law for the whole or any part India for implementing international treaties:
    (a) with the consent of all the State
    (b) with the consent of the majority of States
    (c) with the consent of the States concerned
    (d) without the consent of any State

139. In what way does the Indian Parliament exercise control over the administration?
    (a) Through Parliamentary Committees
    (b) Through Consultative Committees in various ministries
    (c) By making the administrators send periodic reports
    (d) By compelling the executive to issue writs

140. Which one of the following statements is correct?
    (a) Only the Rajya Sabha and not the Lok Sabha can have nominated members
    (b) There is a constitutional provision for nominating two members belonging to the Anglo-Indian community to the Rajya Sabha
    (c) There is no constitutional bar for a nominated member to be appointed as a Union minister
    (d) A nominated member can vote both in the Presidential and Vice Presidential elections

141. Which one of the following statements is not correct?
    (a) In the Lok Sabha, a no-confidence motion has to set out the grounds on which it is based
    (b) In the case of a no-confidence motion in Lok Sabha, no conditions of admissibility have been laid down in the Rules
    (c) A motion of no-confidence once admitted, has to be taken up within ten days of the leave being granted
    (d) Rajya Sabha is not empowered to entertain a motion of no-confidence

142. The resolution for removing the Vice-President of India can be moved in the:
    (a) Lok Sabha alone
    (b) Either House of Parliament
    (c) Joint Sitting of Parliament
    (d) Rajya Sabha alone

143. The authorization for the withdrawal of funds from the Consolidated Fund of India must come from
    (a) The President of India
    (b) The Parliament of India
    (c) The Prime Minister of India
    (d) The Union Finance Minister

144. In the Parliament of India, the purpose of an adjournment motion is
    (a) to allow a discussion on a definite matter of urgent public importance
    (b) to let opposition members collect information from the ministers
    (c) to allow a reduction of specific amount in demand for grant
    (d) to postpone the proceedings to check the inappropriate or violent behaviour on the part of some members

145. The Prime Minister of India, at the time of his/her appointment
    (a) need not necessarily be a member of one of the Houses of the Parliament but must become a member of one of the Houses within six months
    (b) need not necessarily be a member of one of the Houses of the Parliament but must become a member of the Lok Sabha within six months

(c) must be a member of one of the Houses of the Parliament
(d) must be a member of the Lok Sabha

146. What will follow if a Money Bill is substantially amended by the Rajya Sabha?
(a) The Lok Sabha may still proceed with the Bill, accepting or not accepting the recommendations of the Rajya Sabha
(b) The Lok Sabha cannot consider the bill further
(c) The Lok Sabha may send the Bill to the Rajya Sabha for reconsideration
(d) The President may call a joint sitting for passing the Bill

147. Certain Bills can not be introduced or proceeded with unless the recommendation of the President is received. However, no recommendation is required in some other cases. In which one of the following cases such recommendation is not required? **[IAS Prelims 2014]**
(a) For introduction of Bills and for moving amendments relating to financial matters
(b) For introduction of a Bill relating to formation of new states or of alternation of areas of existing states
(c) For moving of an amendment making provision for the reduction or abolition of any tax
(d) For introduction of a Bill or moving of an amendment affecting taxation in which states are interested

148. After a Bill has been passed by the Houses of the Parliament, it is presented to the President who may either give assent to the Bill or with hold his assent. The President may
[IAS Prelims 2014]
(a) assent within six months
(b) assent or reject the Bill as soon as possible
(c) return the Bill as soon as possible after the Bill is presented to him with a message requesting the House to reconsider the Bill
(d) with hold his assent even if the Bill is passed again by the Houses

149. The Annual Financial Statement of the Government of India in respect of each financial year shall be presented to the House on such day as the **[IAS Prelims 2014]**
(a) Speaker may direct
(b) President of India may direct
(c) Parliament may decide
(d) Finance Minister may decide

150. When a bill is referred to a joint sitting of both the Houses of the Parliament, it has to be passed by **[IAS Prelim 2015]**
(a) a simple majority of members present and voting
(b) three-fourths majority of members present and voting
(c) two-thirds majority of the Houses
(d) absolute majority of the Houses

151. The Parliament of India acquires the power to legislate on any item in the state list in the national interest if resolution to that affect is passed by the **[IAS Prelims 2016]**
(a) Lok Sabha by a simple majority of its total membership
(b) Lok Sabha by a majority of not less than two-thirds of its total membership
(c) Rajya Sabha by a simple majority of its total members.
(d) Rajya Sabha by a majority of not less than two-thirds of its members present & voting

152. Which among the following can attend the meeting of both Houses of Parliament while not being a member of either House? **[NDA 2017]**
(a) The Solicitor General of India
(b) The Vice-President of India
(c) The Comptroller and Auditor General of India
(d) The Attorney General of India

153. Which one of the following statements with regard to the Comptroller and Auditor General (CAG) of India is NOT correct? **[NDA 2018]**
(a) He is appointed by the President of India
(b) He can be removed from office in the same way as the judge of the Supreme Court of India
(c) The CAG is eligible for further office under the Government of India after he has ceased to hold his office
(d) The salary of the CAG is charged upon the Consolidated Fund of India

154. Every Judge of the Supreme Court of India is appointed by
[NDA 2018]
(a) the Supreme Court Collegium
(b) the Cabinet
(c) the President of India
(d) the Lok Sabha

155. Who among the following is the ex officio Chairman of the North Eastern Council? **[NDA 2018]**
(a) The President of India
(b) The Prime Minister of India
(c) The Union Home Minister
(d) The Union Minister of State (Independent Charge), Ministry of Development of North Eastern Region

156. The Parliament of India acquires the power to legislate on any item in the State List in the national interest if a resolution to that effect is passed by the
[IAS Prelims 2016]
(a) Lok Sabha by a simple majority of its total membership
(b) Lok Sabha by a majority of not less than two-thirds of its total membership
(c) Rajya Sabha by a simple majority of its total membership
(d) Rajya Sabha by a majority of not less than two-thirds of its members present and voting

157. Which of the following are not necessarily the consequences of the proclamation of the President's rule in a State? **[IAS Prelims 2017]**
1. Dissolution of the State Legislative Assembly
2. Removal of the Council of Ministers in the State
3. Dissolution of the local bodies
Select the correct answer using the code given below:
(a) 1 and 2 only (b) 1 and 3 only
(c) 2 and 3 only (d) 1, 2 and 3 only

158. The main advantage of the parliamentary form of government is that **[IAS Prelims 2017]**
(a) the executive and legislature work independently.
(b) it provides continuity of policy and is more efficient.
(c) the executive remains responsible to the legislature.
(d) the head of the government cannot be changed without election.

159. Out of the following statements, choose the one that brings out the principle underlying the Cabinet form of Government:
[IAS Prelims 2017]
(a) An arrangement for minimizing the criticism against the Government whose responsibilities are complex and hard to carry out to the satisfaction of all.
(b) A mechanism for speeding up the activities of the Government whose responsibilities are increasing day by day.
(c) A mechanism of parliamentary democracy for ensuring collective responsibility of the Government to the people.
(d) A device for strengthening the hands of the head of the Government whose hold over the people is in a state of decline.

160. The Parliament of India exercises control over the functions of the Council of Ministers through.
   1. Adjournment motion **[IAS Prelims 2017]**
   2. Question hour
   3. Supplementary questions
   Select the correct answer using the code given below:
   (a) 1 only
   (b) 2 and 3 only
   (c) 1 and 3 only
   (d) 1, 2 and 3

161. With reference to the Parliament of India, consider the following statements: **[IAS Prelims 2017]**
   1. A private member's bill is a bill presented by a Member of Parliament who is not elected but only nominated by the President of India.
   2. Recently, a private member's bill has been passed in the Parliament of India for the first time in its history.
   Which of the statements given above is/are correct?
   (a) 1 only
   (b) 2 only
   (c) Both 1 and 2
   (d) Neither 1 nor 2

162. For election to the Lok Sabha, a nomination paper can be filed by **[IAS Prelims 2017]**
   (a) anyone residing in India.
   (b) a resident of the constituency from which the election is to be contested.
   (c) any citizen of India whose name appears in the electoral roll of a constituency.
   (d) any citizen of India.

163. Consider the following statements: **[IAS Prelims 2017]**
   1. In the election for Lok Sabha or State Assembly, the winning candidate must get at least 50 per cent of the votes polled, to be declared elected.
   2. According to the provisions laid down in the Constitution of India, in Lok Sabha, the Speaker's post goes to the majority party and the Deputy Speaker's to the Opposition.
   Which of the statements given above is/are correct?
   (a) 1 only
   (b) 2 only
   (c) Both 1 and 2
   (d) Neither 1 nor 2

164. Which one of the following statements is not correct regarding the Office of the Vice President of India?
   [CDS 2017]
   (a) The Vice President is elected by an electoral college consisting of the elected members of both the Houses of the Parliament.
   (b) The Vice President is elected in accordance with the system of proportional representation by means of single transferable vote.
   (c) The Vice President shall not be a member of either House of the Parliament or of a House of the Legislature of any State.
   (d) The Vice President of India shall be ex officio Chairman of the Council of States and shall not hold any office of profit.

165. Which one of the following Schedules of the Constitution of India has fixed the number of Members of the Rajya Sabha to be elected from each State? **[CDS 2017]**
   (a) Fifth Schedule
   (b) Third Schedule
   (c) Sixth Schedule
   (d) Fourth Schedule

166. A Money Bill passed by the Lok Sabha can be held up by the Rajya Sabha for how many weeks? **[CDS 2017]**
   (a) Two
   (b) Three
   (c) Four
   (d) Five

167. Which one of the following cannot be introduced first in the Rajya Sabha? **[CDS 2017]**
   (a) Constitutional Amendment
   (b) CAG Report
   (c) Annual Financial Statement
   (d) Bill to alter the boundaries of any State

168. Every Judge of the Supreme Court of India is appointed by
   (a) the Supreme Court Collegium **[NDA 2018]**
   (b) the Cabinet
   (c) the President of India
   (d) the Lok Sabha

169. Who among the following is the ex officio Chairman of the North Eastern Council? **[NDA 2018]**
   (a) The President of India
   (b) The Prime Minister of India
   (c) The Union Home Minister
   (d) The Union Minister of State (Independent Charge), Ministry of Development of North Eastern Region

170. The Parliament of India acquires the power to legislate on any item in the State List in the national interest if a resolution to that effect is passed by the **[IAS Prelims 2016]**
   (a) Lok Sabha by a simple majority of its total membership
   (b) Lok Sabha by a majority of not less than two-thirds of its total membership
   (c) Rajya Sabha by a simple majority of its total membership
   (d) Rajya Sabha by a majority of not less than two-thirds of its members present and voting

171. The main advantage of the parliamentary form of government is that **[IAS Prelims 2017]**
   (a) the executive and legislature work independently.
   (b) it provides continuity of policy and is more efficient.
   (c) the executive remains responsible to the legislature.
   (d) the head of the government cannot be changed without election.

172. Out of the following statements, choose the one that brings out the principle underlying the Cabinet form of Government:
   [IAS Prelims 2017]
   (a) An arrangement for minimizing the criticism against the Government whose responsibilities are complex and hard to carry out to the satisfaction of all.
   (b) A mechanism for speeding up the activities of the Government whose responsibilities are increasing day by day.
   (c) A mechanism of parliamentary democracy for ensuring collective responsibility of the Government to the people.
   (d) A device for strengthening the hands of the head of the Government whose hold over the people is in a state of decline.

173. For election to the Lok Sabha, a nomination paper can be filed by **[IAS Prelims 2017]**
   (a) anyone residing in India.
   (b) a resident of the constituency from which the election is to be contested.
   (c) any citizen of India whose name appears in the electoral roll of a constituency.
   (d) any citizen of India.

Exercise -2

Statement Based MCQ

1. Regarding the Loksabha and Assembly elections in India consider the following statements:
   1. The winning candidate need not secure a majority of the votes.
   2. Constitution prescribes a plurality system as the method of election.
   Which of the above is/are correct.
   - (a) 1 only
   - (b) 2 only
   - (c) Both 1 and 2
   - (d) None of the above

2. Consider the following statements:
   1. A minister can only be a member of the Lok Sabha.
   2. The ministers are collectively responsible to the Parliament.
   Select the correct statement/statements using the codes given below.
   - (a) 1 only
   - (b) 2 only
   - (c) Both 1 and 2
   - (d) Neither 1 nor 2.

3. With reference to the veto powers of the President of India, consider the following statements:
   1. He possess suspensive veto in the case of money bills.
   2. President has no veto power in respect of a constitutional amendment bill.
   Select the correct statement/statements using the codes given below:
   - (a) 1 only
   - (b) 2 only
   - (c) Both 1 and 2
   - (d) Neither 1 nor 2

4. Article - 74 speaks of a council of minister to aid and advise president of India. Such a ministerial advice has been made binding on the president through:
   - (a) 44th Constitutional Amendment
   - (b) 42nd Constitutional Amendment
   - (c) 91st Constitutional Amendment
   - (d) 61st Constitutional Amendment

5. Which among the following is/are demerits of the parliamentary system:
   1. No guarantee of a stable government.
   2. Not conducive for the formulation and implementation of long-term policies.
   3. The cabinet exercises nearly unlimited powers.
   4. It is against separation of powers between legislature and the executive.
   Select the correct answer using the codes given below.
   - (a) 1, 2 and 3 only
   - (b) 2, 3 and 4 only
   - (c) 1, 2 and 4 only
   - (d) All 1, 2, 3 and 4

6. Consider the following questions:
   1. Proportional Representation System is a complicated system and more suitable for a small country.
   2. The First Post the Post system offers voters a choice not simply between parties but between specific candidates also.
   Select the correct statement/statements using the codes given below.
   - (a) 1 only
   - (b) 2 only
   - (c) Both 1 and 2
   - (d) None of these

7. Consider the following statements:
   1. The Governor cannot return a Money Bill for re-consideration of the state legislature.
   2. When a money bill is reserved for consideration of president, he/she can return the bill for the re-consideration of the state legislature.
   With reference to state-legislature, which of the above given statement is/are correct.
   - (a) 1 only
   - (b) 2 only
   - (c) Both 1 and 2
   - (d) Neither 1 nor 2

8. Which of the following is/are instrument through which legislature holds executive accountable:
   1. Deliberation and discussion.
   2. Approval or Refusal of laws
   3. Financial control.
   4. No confidence motion
   5. Question Hour.
   Select the correct answer using the codes given below:
   - (a) 1, 2 and 3 only
   - (b) 2, 3 and 4 only
   - (c) 1, 2, 3 and 4
   - (d) 1, 2, 3, 4 and 5

9. Consider the following statements:
   1. A formal impeachment is not required for removal of vice-president.
   2. No ground has been mentioned in the constitution for removal of vice-president.
   Select the correct statement/statements using the codes given below:
   - (a) 1 only
   - (b) 2 only
   - (c) Both 1 and 2
   - (d) Neither 1 nor 2

10. Consider the statements regarding the Lok Sabha elections.
    1. All citizens have right to stand for election and become representatives.
    2. A person who has undergone imprisonment for two or more years cannot contest election.
    3. There are no restrictions of income, education or class or gender on the right to contest elections.
    Choose the correct statements:
    (a) 1 only   (b) 1 and 3 only
    (c) All 1, 2 and 3   (d) 2 and 3 only

11. Consider the following statements:
    1. A speaker protem is appointed by president.
    2. The chairman of Rajya sabha is a member of Rajya sabha.
    Select the correct statement/statements from the codes given below:
    (a) 1 only   (b) 2 only
    (c) Both 1 and 2   (d) Neither 1 nor 2

12. Consider the following statements:
    1. Constitution provides for reservation of seats for SCs/STs in Lok Sabha and State Assemblies.
    2. Constitution provides for reservation of seats for SCs/STs in Rajya Sabha.
    Which of the above statements are correct.
    (a) 1 only   (b) 2 only
    (c) Both 1 and 2   (d) None of the above

13. The electoral college for the election of vice-president consist of
    1. Elected members of both houses of parliament.
    2. Nominated members of both the houses of parliament.
    3. Elected members of the state legislative assemblies.
    Select the correct answer using the codes given below:
    (a) 1 and 2 only   (b) 2 and 3 only
    (c) 1 and 3 only   (d) 1, 2 and 3

14. Consider the following statements:
    1. Elections to members of Rajya-Sabha is done through secret ballot system.
    2. An elector belonging to a political party has to show the ballot paper after marking his vote to a nominated agent of that political party.
    With reference to elections to the Rajya Sabha which of the following is/are incorrect:
    (a) 1 only   (b) 2 only
    (c) Both 1 and 2   (d) None of these

15. 1. In 'Separate electorates' members of a particular community only are eligible to vote.
    2. In 'Reserved constituencies' all voters in a constituency are eligible to vote.
    Select the correct statements.
    (a) 1 only   (b) 2 only
    (c) Both 1 and 2   (d) None of the above

16. Which of the following is one of the conditions to be recognised as a National Political Party
    1. Six percent of valid votes polled in any four or more states at a general election to Lok sabha.
    2. Two percent of seats in the Lok sabha at a general election.
    3. Recognition as a state party in four states.
    Select the correct answer from the codes given below
    (a) 1 and 2 only
    (b) 1 and 3 only
    (c) 2 and 3 only
    (d) All the above are correct

17. Consider the following statements:
    1. Before a bill is introduced in parliament, there cannot be a debate on the need for introducing such a bill.
    2. A money bill can be introduced either in Lok Sabha or Rajya Sabha.
    Select the correct statement/statements from the codes given below:
    (a) 1 only   (b) 2 only
    (c) Both 1 and 2   (d) Neither 1 nor 2

18. With reference to the "Administrator" appointed by the President in Union Territories (UT) consider the following statements.
    (i) Every UT is administered by the President through an "Administrator" appointed by him.
    (ii) The administrator may also be designated as chief commissioner.
    (iii) The "Administrator" is just a representative of the President and not the constitutional head of the UT.
    Which of the statement/statements given above is/are correct?
    (a) (i) and (ii)   (b) all are correct
    (c) (ii) and (iii)   (d) (i) and (iii)

19. Which of the following is a ground of disqualification for being elected as a member of parliament:
    1. Holding any office of profit under the union or state.
    2. Being an undischarged insolvent.
    3. Losing the citizenship of India.
    4. Detention under a preventive detention law.
    Select the correct answer using the codes below:
    (a) 1, 2 and 3 only   (b) 2, 3 and 4 only
    (c) 1, 2 and 4 only   (d) 1, 2, 3 and 4

20. Consider the following statements with reference to the central council of ministers:
    1. The total number of ministers (including Prime Minister) shall not exceed 10% of the total strength of Lok sabha.
    2. The ministers shall hold office during the pleasure of the prime-minister.
    Select the correct statement/statements using the codes below:
    (a) 1 only   (b) 2 only
    (c) Both 1 and 2   (d) Neither 1 nor 2

21. Consider the following statements:
    1. The Rajya Sabha cannot initiate, reject or amend money bills.
    2. The Council of Ministers is responsible only to Lok-Sabha.

    Select the correct statement/statements using the codes below:
    (a) 1 only
    (b) 2 only
    (c) Both 1 and 2
    (d) Neither 1 nor 2

22. Recently, the issuing of whip by political parties on multiple issues has been questioned. Consider the following statements with reference to the office of whip.
    (i) Whip is an assistant floor leader appointed by every political party.
    (ii) The office of whip, in India, is mentioned in the constitution and in the rules of the house.
    (iii) Whip has the responsibility of ensuring the attendance of his party members and securing their support in favour of or against a particular issue.
    (iv) Whip regulates and monitors the behaviour of party members in the Parliament.

    Which of the statement/statements given above is/are correct?
    (a) (i), (iii) and (iv) only
    (b) (iii) and (iv) only
    (c) (i) and (ii) only
    (d) All the above are correct

23. Consider the following statements:
    1. Members of Rajya Sabha are elected by system of proportional representation by means of single transferable vote system.
    2. Rajya Sabha can criticise the government but cannot remove it.

    Select the correct statement/statements using the codes given below:
    (a) 1 only
    (b) 2 only
    (c) Both 1 and 2
    (d) Neither 1 nor 2

24. Consider the following statements:
    1. Holding any office of profit under union or state government.
    2. Detention of a person under a preventive detention law.
    3. Acknowledgement of allegiance to a foreign state.
    4. Failure to lodge an account of election expenses.

    Which of the above given could be a reason for disqualification of a member of parliament?
    (a) 1, 2 only
    (b) 1, 2 and 3 only
    (c) 1, 2 and 4 only
    (d) All the above

25. Which committee was appointed by the government in 1975 to enquire whether the parliamentary systems should be continued or should be replaced by the presidential system?
    (a) R.K.V. Committee
    (b) Ashok Mehta Committee
    (c) Swaran Singh Committee
    (d) Justice Shah Committee

26. Who among the following constitutes the electoral college of the President?
    1. All Members of Parliament
    2. Members of State Legislative Assemblies
    3. Elected members of State Legislative assemblies
    4. Elected members of State Legislative Councils.

    Which of the above is/are correct?
    (a) 1 and 3
    (b) 4 only
    (c) 1 only
    (d) 3 only

27. ________President can declare?
    1. Emergency due to armed rebellion
    2. Financial Emergency
    3. President's Rule in a State

    Which of the above is/are correct?
    (a) 1 only
    (b) 3 only
    (c) All of the Above
    (d) None of the Above

28. Who can be appointed as Prime-minister?
    1. the leader of the majority party in the Lok Sabha
    2. anyone he thinks fit
    3. the person who can win the confidence of the majority in Lok Sabha
    4. Leader of the party with a majority in either Lok Sabha or Rajya Sabha

    Which of the following statements is/are correct?
    (a) 1 only
    (b) 1 or 3
    (c) 3 or 4
    (d) 1, 3 or 4

29. Consider the following statements about the office of Attorney-General of India?
    1. He is a member of the Cabinet.
    2. He can address either House of Parliament and vote.
    3. He must have qualification of a judge of the Supreme Court.
    4. Salary of Attorney General is fixed by Parliament.

    Which of the above statements is/are correct?
    (a) 2 and 4
    (b) 1, 2 and 4
    (c) 3 only
    (d) 3 and 4

30. Which statements about Financial Bill is CORRECT?
    1. It is same as a money bill
    2. It can be introduced only in the Lok Sabha
    3. It can be amended by the Rajya Sabha.
    4. It can only be introduced agreement of the President

    Select the correct answer using the codes given below:
    (a) 1 only
    (b) 2 and 4
    (c) 2, 3 and 4
    (d) 3 and 4

31. Both Houses of Parliament enjoy equal power in all spheres except:
    1. financial matters
    2. responsibility of the Council of Ministers
    3. amendment procedure
    4. presidential election
    Select the correct answer using the codes given below
    (a) 3 and 4   (b) 2, 3 and 4
    (c) 1, 2 and 3   (d) 1 and 2

32. Which factor can restrict the power of Parliament in India?
    1. A written Constitution prescribing the scope of operation
    2. Supreme Court can strike down unconstitutional laws passed by Parliament
    3. Parliament is limited by the Fundamental Rights provided by the Constitution
    Which of the above statements is/are correct?
    (a) 1, 2 and 3
    (b) 1 and 3
    (c) 2 only
    (d) None, as Parliament is sovereign

33. Which of the following are the principles on the basis of which the parliamentary system of government in India operates ?
    1. Nominal executive head
    2. Vice-President as the chairman of the upper house
    3. Real executive authority with the council of ministers
    4. Executive responsibility to the lower house
    Which of the above statements is/are correct?
    (a) 1, 2 and 4   (b) 1, 2 and 4
    (c) 1, 3 and 4   (d) 2, 3 and 4

34. Consider the following statements :
    1. The Chairman of the Committee on Public Accounts is appointed by the Speaker of the Lok Sabha.
    2. The Committee on Public Accounts comprises Members of Lok Sabha, Members of Rajya Sabha and a few eminent persons of industry and trade.
    Which of the statements given above is/are correct?
    (a) 1 only   (b) 2 only
    (c) Both 1 and 2   (d) Neither 1 nor 2

35. With reference to Union Government, consider the following statements :
    1. The Ministries/Departments of the Government of India are created by the Prime Minister on the advice of the Cabinet Secretary.
    2. Each of the Ministries is assigned to a Minister by the President of India on the advice of the Prime Minister.
    Which of the statements given above is/are correct ?
    (a) 1 only   (b) 2 only
    (c) Both 1 and 2   (d) Neither 1 nor 2

36. The correct statements about calling attention notice are :
    1. It is a device of calling the attention of a minister to a matter of urgent public importance.
    2. Its main purpose is to seek an authoritative statement from the minister.
    3. It does not involve any censure against government.
    4. It is an Indian innovation in the parliamentary procedure since 1952.
    5. It is not mentioned in the Rules of Business and Procedure.
    Which of the above statements is/are correct?
    (a) 1, 2, 3 and 4   (b) 4 and 5
    (c) 1, 2, 3 and 5   (d) 1, 2 and 3

37. Which of the following statements are true of Adjournment Motion?
    1. It is an extraordinary procedure which sets aside the normal business of the House.
    2. Its main object is to draw the attention of the House to a recent matter of urgent public importance.
    3. The Rajya Sabha can make use of this procedure.
    4. It must be supported by not less than 50 members for introduction.
    5. It involves an element of censure against government.
    Which of the above statements is/are correct?
    (a) 1, 2, 4 and 5   (b) 2, 3 and 5
    (c) 2, 3 and 4   (d) 1, 2 and 4

38. In parliamentary countries, like India, the legislative control over administration is considerably reduced and restricted in effectiveness due to which of the following reasons?
    1. The expansion in the volume and variety of administrative work.
    2. Frequent use of Guillitone.
    3. The large size of the legislature
    4. The members of the legislature are laymen.
    5. The financial committees do post mortem work.
    Which of the above statements is/are correct?
    (a) 1, 2 and 5   (b) 2, 3 and 4
    (c) 2, 3, 4 and 5   (d) 1, 2, 3, 4 and 5

39. Which of the following documents are presented to the legislature along with the budget?
    1. An explanatory memorandum on the budget
    2. A summary of demands for grants
    3. An Appropriation Bill
    4. A Finance Bill
    5. The economic survey
    Select the correct answer using the codes given below:
    (a) 1,3 and 5   (b) 1,2 and 3
    (c) 2,3 and 5   (d) 1,2, 3 and 4

40. Which of the following statements are incorrect?
    1. Appropriation Bill cannot be amended while the Finance Bill can be amended.
    2. Finance Bill cannot be amended while Appropriation Bill can be amended.
    3. Same procedure governs both the Appropriation Bill and the Finance Bill.
    4. Appropriation Bill and the Finance Bill are governed by different procedures.
    5. Appropriation Bill cannot be rejected by the Rajya Sabha while Finance Bill can be rejected by it.
    Select the correct answer using the codes given below:
    (a) 2 and 4   (b) 2, 4 and 5
    (c) 1 and 3   (d) 1, 3 and 5

41. Which of the following are not correct about CAG of India?
    1. He is appointed by the President for a period of five years.
    2. His salary and conditions of service are determined by President.
    3. He shall vacate office on attaining the age of 60 years.
    4. He can be removed by the President on his own.
    5. He is responsible for maintaining the accounts of Central and state governments.
    Which of the above statements is/are correct?
    (a) 1,4 and 5   (b) 2,3 and 4
    (c) 1,2,3,4 and 5   (d) 3,4 and 5

42. Which of the following are the functions of the Public Accounts Committee of Parliament?
    1. To examine, in the light of CAG's report, the accounts showing the appropriation of sums granted by the Parliament.
    2. To examine, in the light of CAG's report, the statement of accounts of state corporations, trading and manufacturing projects except of those as are allotted to the committee on public undertakings.
    3. To examine the statement of accounts of autonomous and semi-autonomous bodies, the audit of which is conducted by the CAG.
    4. To examine if any money has been spent on any service during a financial year in excess of the amount granted by house of people for that purpose.
    Which of the above statements is/are correct?
    (a) 1, 2 and 4   (b) 1, 2, 3 and 4
    (c) 1, 2 and 3   (d) 1, 3 and 4
43. The Indian President's veto power is a combination of:
    1. Pocket veto   2. Absolute veto
    3. Suspensive veto   4. Qualified veto
    Select the correct answer using the codes given below:
    (a) 2 and 3   (b) 1, 3 and 4
    (c) 2,3 and 4   (d) 1,2 and 3
44. The correct statements regarding the difference between the pardoning powers of President and Governor are:
    1. The Governor can pardon sentences inflicted by court martial while the President cannot.
    2. The President can pardon death sentence while Governor cannot.
    3. The Governor can pardon death sentence while the President cannot.
    4. The President can pardon sentences inflicted by court martial while the Governor cannot.
    Which of the following statements is/are correct?
    (a) 1 and 2   (b) 2 and 4
    (c) 1 and 3   (d) 3 and 4
45. Consider the following statements about the Attorney General of India:
    1. He is appointed by the President of India
    2. He must have the same qualifications as required for a judge of the Supreme Court.
    3. He must be a member of either House of Parliament.
    4. He can be removed by impeachment by Parliament.
    Which of the above statements is/are correct?
    (a) 1 and 2   (b) 1 and 3
    (c) 2, 3 and 4   (d) 3 and 4
46. Which of the following are included in Article 78 of the Indian Constitution, defining the duties of Prime Minister?
    1. To communicate to the President all decisions of the council of ministers relating to the administration of the affairs of the union and proposals for legislation.
    2. To take prior presidential sanction for the budget before submitting it in the Parliament
    3. To furnish the information called for by the President regarding administration of affairs of the union
    4. If the President so requires, to submit for consideration of the council of ministers a matter on which a minister has taken a decision without submitting the same for consideration by the council beforehand.
    Which of the above statements is/are correct?
    (a) 1 and 2   (b) 1, 3 and 4
    (c) 2 and 4   (d) 1 and 3

47. Which of the following corporations, for the purpose of auditing, are kept completely out of the purview of CAG of India ?
    1. Industrial Finance Corporation
    2. Food Corporation of India
    3. Central Warehousing Corporation
    4. Life Insurance Corporation of India
    5. Reserve Bank of India
    Which of the above statements is/are correct?
    (a) 1, 2 and 5   (b) 1, 2, 4 and 5
    (c) 2, 3 and 4   (d) 2, 4 and 5
48. According to the Constitution of India, it is the duty of the President of India to cause to be laid before the Parliament which of the following?
    1. The Recommendations of the Union Finance Commission
    2. The Report of the Public Accounts Committee
    3. The Report of the Comptroller and Auditor General
    4. The Report of the National Commission for Scheduled Castes
    Select the correct answer using the codes given below :
    (a) 1 only   (b) 2 and 4
    (c) 1, 3 and 4   (d) 1, 2, 3 and 4
49. In India, other than ensuring that public funds are used efficiently and for intended purpose, what is the importance of the office of the Comptroller and Auditor General (CAG)?
    1. CAG exercises exchequer control on behalf of the Parliament when the President of India declares national emergency/financial emergency.
    2. CAG reports on the execution of projects or programmes by the ministries are discussed by the Public Accounts Committee.
    3. Information from CAG reports can be used by investigating agencies to press charges against those who have violated the law while managing public finances.
    4. While dealing with the audit and accounting of government companies, CAG has certain judicial powers for prosecuting those who violate the law.
    Which of the above given above is/are correct?
    (a) 1, 3 and 4   (b) 2 only
    (c) 2 and 3   (d) 1, 2 and 3
50. With reference to Indian public finance, consider the following statements:
    1. Disbursements from Public Accounts of India are subject to the Vote of the Parliament
    2. The Indian Constitution provides for the establishment of a Consolidated Fund, a Public Account and a Contingency Fund for each State
    3. Appropriations and disbursements under the Railway Budget are subject to the same form of parliamentary control as other appropriations and disbursements
    Which of the statements given above are correct?
    (a) 1 and 2   (b) 2 and 3
    (c) 1 and 3   (d) 1, 2 and 3

51. With reference to Indian Parliament, consider the following statements :
    1. A member of the Lok Sabha cannot be arrested by police under any case when the Parliament is in session.
    2. Members of Indian Parliament have the privilege of exemption from attendance as witnesses in the law courts.
    Which of these statements is/are correct ?
    (a) 1 only   (b) 2 only
    (c) Both 1 and 2   (d) Neither 1 and 2

52. Consider the following statements:
    1. The President of India cannot appoint a person as Prime Minister if he/she is not a member of either Lok Sabha or Rajya Sabha.
    2. The candidate for the office of Prime Minster must have the support of the majority members of both Lok Sabha and Rajya Sabha.
    Which of the statements given above is/are correct ?
    (a) 1 only   (b) 2 only
    (c) Both 1 and 2   (d) Neither 1 nor 2

53. Which among the following statements with respect to the Comptroller and Auditor General of India is/are correct?
    1. The procedure and grounds for his removal from the office are the same as of a Judge of Supreme Court.
    2. He prescribes the form in which accounts of the Union and the States are to be kept.
    Select the correct answer using the code given below
    (a) 1 only   (b) 2 only
    (c) Both 1 and 2   (d) Neither 1 nor 2

54. Which of the following statements about a parliamentary committee in India are correct?
    1. It is appointed or elected by the house or appointed by the speaker/chairman.
    2. It works under the direction of the speaker/chairman of the house.
    3. It presents its report to the president.
    Select the correct answer using the codes given below:
    (a) 1 and 2 only   (b) 2 and 3 only
    (c) 1 and 3 only   (d) 1, 2 and 3

55. Which of the following features of the Indian Government system are the essential features of the parliamentary Government system?
    1. Presence of nominal and real executives
    2. Membership of the ministers in the legislature
    3. Separation of powers between the Union and State government
    4. Independent judiciary system
    Select the correct answer using the codes given below:
    (a) 1 and 2 only   (b) 1, 2 and 3 only
    (c) 2 and 3 only   (d) 1, 2, 3 and 4

56. Which of the following committee(s) is/are not exclusively the committee of the lower House of the Parliament of India?
    1. Estimate committee
    2. Committee on public undertaking
    3. Committee on the welfare of Scheduled Castes and STs
    4. Committee on Empowerment of women
    Select the correct answer using the codes given below:
    (a) 1 and 2 only   (b) 2, 3 and 4 only
    (c) 1 only   (d) 2 and 4

57. Though the Rajya Sabha and Lok Sabha are constitutent part of Parliament, on some subject they have unequal powers which of the following matters depict the difference of powers between these two houses?
    1. No confidence motion
    2. Power to vote on Demand for Grants
    3. Impeachment of judges of the High Court
    4. Passing of laws in the national interest on the subject enumerated in state list
    5. Creation of all India services.
    Select the correct answer by using the codes given below:
    (a) 1, 3 and 4 only   (b) 2, 3 and 5 only
    (c) 1, 2, 4 and 5 only (d) 1, 2 and 5 only

58. Which among the following have the right to vote in the elections to both the Lok Sabha and the Rajya Sabha?
    1. Elected members of the Lower House of the Parliament
    2. Elected members of the Upper House of the Parliament
    3. Elected members of the Upper House of the State Legislature.
    4. Elected members of the Lower House of the State Legislature.
    (a) 1 and 2 only   (b) 1, 2 and 3 only
    (c) 3 and 4 only   (d) 4 only

59. Consider the following statements:
    1. The chairman of the committee on public accounts is appointed by the speakers of the Lok sabha
    2. The committee on public Accounts comprises members of Lok Sabha, members of Rajya sabha and a few eminent persons of industry and trade
    Which of the statements given above is/are correct?
    (a) 1 only   (b) 2 only
    (c) Both 1 and 2   (d) Neither 1 nor 2

60. Consider the following statements regarding 'No confidence motion'
    1. Only a motion expressing want of confidence in the council of ministers as a whole is admitted and one expressing lack of confidence in an individual minister is out of order
    2. A no confidence motion needs to set out grounds on which it is based.
    3. Any no confidence motion once moved can't be withdrawn
    4. Rajya Sabha is not empowered to entertain a motion of no confidence
    Which of the following given above are not correct?
    (a) 1 and 2 only   (b) 1, 2, and 3 only
    (c) 2 and 3 only   (d) 1, 2, 3 and 4

61. When the House of people clearly and conclusively determines that the government does not command its support, the government has to resign. By which of the ways parliamentary confidence in the government may be expressed by the House of People?
    1. Defeating the government on a major issue of policy.
    2. Passing an adjournment motion
    3. Defeating the government on finance issues
    4. Passing a motion of no confidence in the council of ministers.
    (a) 1 and 3 only   (b) 2, 3 and 4 only
    (c) 2 and 3 only   (d) 1, 2, 3 and 4

62. With reference to Union Government consider the following statements:
    1. The ministries/Departments of the government of India are created by the PM on the advice of the cabinet secretary.
    2. Each of the ministries is assigned to a minister by the president of India on the advice of the PM.
    Which of the statements given above is/are correct?
    (a) 1 only
    (b) 2 only
    (c) Both 1 and 2
    (d) Neither 1 nor 2

63. Consider the following facts about Comptroller and auditor general of India, and choose the correct answer:
    1. CAG is a constitutional Body.
    2. CAG has absolute power to audit accounts of all the functionaries of Central and States' governments as well as of private corporate bodies.
    (a) Only 1 is correct
    (b) Only 2 is correct
    (c) 1 and 2 both are correct
    (d) Neither 1 nor 2 is correct

64. Which of the following statements are correct about Indian Government?
    1. Rajya Sabha represents the local interests of the States.
    2. A member of Rajya Sabha must be a resident of the State from which he is elected.
    3. Number of seats allotted to a State has to be proportionate to its population.
    4. The term of a member of Rajya Sabha is same as that of Senator in the US.
    Codes:
    (a) 2, 3 and 4
    (b) 1, 2 and 3
    (c) 1, 3 and 4
    (d) 1 and 2

65. Which of the following situation will bring about the collapse of the council of ministers of a state.
    1. Resignation by Chief Minister.
    2. Death of Chief Minister.
    (a) 1 only
    (b) 2 only
    (c) Both
    (d) None

66. Which of the following statements are correct:
    1. President can nominate 2 members from the Anglo – Indian community if not adequately represented in LS.
    2. Governor can nominate 2 members from the Anglo – Indian community if not adequately represented in LA.
    (a) 1 only
    (b) 2 only
    (c) Both.
    (d) None

67. Corrects statement/s with regard to UTs is/are:
    1. The parliament can make laws on any subject of three lists for the UT except Delhi and Puducherry.
    2. The Lt. Governor of Delhi is not empowered to promulgate ordinances.
    (a) 1 only
    (b) 2 only
    (c) Both
    (d) None

68. Which of the following statement/s is/are correct with regard to Joint State Public Service Commission (JSPS(c):
    1. President can provide for a JSPSC on the request of the state legislatures concerned.
    2. JSPSC will be considered as a constitutional body with all the powers of a SPSC.

    (a) 1 only
    (b) 2 only
    (c) Both
    (d) None

69. Which of the following are quasi judicial bodies:
    1. Finance Commission.
    2. Central Vigilance Commission
    3. National Human Rights Commission.
    4. Central Information Commission.
    5. Competition Commission of India.
    6. Union Public Service Commission.
    7. National Commission for SCs.
    (a) All except 1, 2 & 6
    (b) All except 2, 4 & 6
    (c) All except 6
    (d) None of the above options are correct

70. Which of the following official(s) is/are appointed by the President by Warrant under his hand and seal.
    1. CAG.
    2. Chairperson of National Commission of SCs.
    3. Attorney General of India.
    4. CVC
    (a) 1, 2 & 4 only
    (b) 2 & 3 only
    (c) 1 & 3 only
    (d) 1, 2 & 3

71. Which of the following funds/authorities/bodies can be audited by CAG:
    1. Consolidated funds of India, States & UTs having legislative assembly.
    2. Contingency funds of India.
    3. Public account of States.
    4. Receipts and expenditures of PPP.
    5. Local bodies.
    (a) 1, 2 & 3 only
    (b) 1, 2 & 5 only
    (c) 1, 3, 4 & 5 only
    (d) All

72. Which of the following statement(s) is/are true with regard to the Attorney General of India:
    1. He/she is the highest law officer of the country.
    2. He/she can be removed by the President on same grounds and in the same manner as a judge of the SC.
    (a) 1 only
    (b) 2 only
    (c) Both
    (d) None

73. Which of the following statement/s is/are true with regard to the Attorney General of India:
    1. He/she can be a member of a Parliamentary committee.
    2. He/she is debarred from private legal practice.
    (a) 1 only
    (b) 2 only
    (c) Both
    (d) None

74. The correct statement/s with regard to Ordinance making power of President is/are -
    1. The President cannot promulgate an ordinance to amend tax laws.
    2. The President cannot promulgate an ordinance to amend the constitution.
    (a) 1 only
    (b) 2 only
    (c) Both
    (d) None

75. The 'Council of Ministers' does not consist of:
    1. Deputy Ministers.
    2. Parliamentary Secretaries.
    3. Deputy Chairman – Planning Commission.
    (a) 1, 2 & 3
    (b) 2 only
    (c) 3 only
    (d) None of these

76. The Representatives of states & UT in the Rajya Sabha are elected by:
    1. The members of the State Legislative Assembly only.
    2. The elected members of the State Legislative Assembly only.
    3. The system of proportional representation by single transferrable vote.
    4. The system of proportional representation by List.
    (a) 1 & 3   (b) 1 & 4
    (c) 2 & 3   (d) 2 & 4

77. Which of the following criteria is laid down by the constitution for a person to be chosen a member of parliament:
    1. If a candidate is to contest a seat reserved for SC / ST, he must be a member of a SC / ST in any state or Union Territory.
    2. He/she must not have been punished for preaching and practicing social crimes such as untouchability, dowry & sati.
    3. He/she must not have any interest in government contracts, works or services.
    (a) 1 only   (b) 2 & 3 only
    (c) 1, 2, & 3   (d) None of these

78. Which of the following statements are correct.
    1. If a MLA is elected to be a MP, his seat in parliament becomes vacant if he does not resign his seat in the state legislature within 14 days.
    2. If a person is elected to two seats in a house, he should exercise his option for one. Otherwise both seats become vacant.
    (a) 1 only   (b) 2 only
    (c) Both   (d) None

79. When the Lok Sabha is Dissolved:
    1. A bill passed by Lok Sabha pending in Rajya Sabha does not lapse.
    2. A bill pending in Rajya Sabha & not passed by Lok Sabha does not lapse.
    (a) 1 only   (b) 2 only
    (c) Both   (d) None

80. Consider the following statements with regard to Calling Attention motion and Zero Hour:
    1. Both are Indian innovation in the parliamentary procedure.
    2. Both are not mentioned in the rules of procedure.
    3. Only Zero hour is Indian innovation.
    4. Only Zero Hour is not mentioned in the rules of procedure.
    The correct statements is/are:
    (a) 1 & 2 only   (b) 3 & 4 only
    (c) 2 & 3 only   (d) 1 & 4 only

81. Which of the following motion/s if passed leads to the defeat of the government:
    1. Censure Motion.
    2. Cut Motion.
    (a) 1 only   (b) 2 only
    (c) Both   (d) None

82. The decision whether a bill is money bill or not is decided by the speaker, this decision cannot be questioned by:
    1. Any court of law.
    2. Lok Sabha.
    3. President of India.
    (a) 1 & 2 only   (b) 2 & 3 only
    (c) 2 only   (d) None of these

83. Which of the following condition may lead to the resignation of the government:
    1. Defeat of an ordinary bill introduced by a minister.
    2. Defeat of a money bill.
    (a) 1 only   (b) 2 only
    (c) Both   (d) None

84. Which of the following is/are correct:
    1. A Money bill can be introduced only in Lok Sabha.
    2. A Money bill is also a Financial Bill.
    3. All Financial bills can be introduced only on the recommendation of the President.
    (a) 1 only   (b) 1 & 2 only
    (c) 1, 2 & 3   (d) None of these

85. Which of the following Expenditure is/are the expenditure 'Charged' on the Consolidated fund of India:
    1. Emoluments and allowances of President & Vice President.
    2. Salaries, allowances and pensions of the Judges of the Supreme Court & high court.
    (a) 1 only   (b) 2 only
    (c) Both   (d) None

86. Which of the following officials take the Oath that has the following lines: "To preserve protect and defend the constitution"
    1. President
    2. Governor
    3. Chief Justice of India
    (a) 1 only   (b) 1 & 2 only
    (c) 1, 2 & 3   (d) None of the above

87. Consider the following statements : Attorney General of India can
    1. take part in the proceedings of the Lok Sabha
    2. be a member of a committee of the Lok Sabha
    3. speak in the Lok Sabha
    4. vote in the Lok Sabha
    Which of the statements given above is/are correct?
    (a) 1 only   (b) 2 and 4
    (c) 1, 2 and 3   (d) 1 and 3 only

88. In the context of India, which of the following principles is/are implied institutionally in the parliamentary government?
    1. Members of the Cabinet are Members of the Parliament.
    2. Ministers hold the office till they enjoy confidence in the Parliament.
    3. Cabinet is headed by the Head of the State.
    Select the correct answer using the codes given below.
    (a) 1 and 2 only   (b) 3 only
    (c) 2 and 3 only   (d) 1, 2 and 3

89. Consider the following statements:
    1. The Council of Ministers in the Centre shall be collectively responsible to the Parliament.
    2. The Union Ministers shall hold the office during the pleasure of the President of India.
    3. The Prime Minister shall communicate to the President about the proposals for legislation.
    Which of the statements given above is/are correct?
    (a) 1 only   (b) 2 and 3 only
    (c) 1 and 3 only   (d) 1, 2 and 3

90. Consider the following statements:
    1. The Chairman and the Deputy Chairman of the Rajya Sabha are not the members of that House.
    2. While the nominated members of the two Houses of the Parliament have no voting right in the presidential election, they have the right to vote in the election of the Vice President.
    Which of the statements given above is/are correct?
    (a) 1 only (b) 2 only
    (c) Both 1 and 2 (d) Neither 1 nor 2

91. Consider the following statements :
    1. The President shall make rules for the more convenient transaction of the business of the Government of India, and for the allocation among Ministers of the said business.
    2. All executive actions of the Government of India shall be expressed to be taken in the name of the Prime Minister.
    Which of the statements given above is/are correct?
    (a) 1 only (b) 2 only
    (c) Both 1 and 2 (d) Neither 1 nor 2

92. Consider the following statements :
    A Constitutional Government is one which
    1. places effective restrictions on individual liberty in the interest of State Authority
    2. places effective restrictions on the Authority of the State in the interest of individual liberty
    Which of the statements given above is/are correct?
    (a) 1 only (b) 2 only
    (c) Both 1 and 2 (d) Neither 1 nor 2

93. Which of the following is/are the function/functions of the Cabinet Secretariat?
    1. Preparation of agenda for Cabinet Meetings
    2. Secretarial assistance to Cabinet Committees
    3. Allocation of financial resources to the Ministries
    Select the correct answer using the code given below.
    (a) 1 only (b) 2 and 3 only
    (c) 1 and 2 only (d) 1, 2 and 3

94. Consider the following statements:
    The parliamentary Committee on public accounts
    1. consists of not more than 25 Members of the Lok Sabha
    2. scrutinizes appropriation and finance accounts of the Government
    3. examines the report of the Comptroller and Auditor General of India.
    Which of the statements given above is/are correct?
    (a) 1 only (b) 2 and 3 only
    (c) 3 only (d) 1, 2 and 3

95. Consider the following statements:
    1. The President of India cannot appoint a person as Prime Minister if he/she is not a member of either Lok Sabha or Rajya Sabha.
    2. The candidate for the office of Prime Minster must have the support of the majority members of both Lok Sabha and Rajya Sabha.
    Which of the statements given above is/are correct ?
    (a) 1 only (b) 2 only
    (c) Both 1 and 2 (d) Neither 1 nor 2

96. Consider the following statements:
    1. It is on the advice of the Speaker of Lok Sabha that the President of India summons and prorogues Parliament and dissolves Lok Sabha .
    2. The resignation of the Prime Minister means the resignation of the entire Council of Ministers.
    3. A vote of confidence against one Minister. in Lok Sabha means the vote of confidence against the entire Council of Ministers.
    Which of the following statements given above are correct?
    (a) 1 and 2 only (b) 2 and 3 only
    (c) 1 and 3 only (d) 1, 2 and 3

97. Consider the following statements:
    1. Salary and allowances of the Speaker of Lok Sabha are charged on the Consolidated Fund of India.
    2. In the Warrant of Precedence, the Speaker of Lok Sabha ranks higher than all the Union Cabinet Ministers other than Prime Minister.
    Which of the statement given above is/are correct?
    (a) 1 only (b) 2 only
    (c) Both 1 and 2 (d) Neither 1 nor 2

98. Which one of the following statements is/are correct with regard to the Vice-President of India?
    1. He must be a member of Parliament.
    2. He is elected by proportional representation.
    3. He is Ex-officio Chairman of the Rajya Sabha.
    Select the correct answer unsing the code given below:
    (a) 1 only (b) 1 and 3
    (c) 2 and 3 (d) 1 and 2

99. In which among the following cases, the joint session of both the Houses of Parliament can be summoned?
    1. To amend the Constitution.
    2. When a Bill has been pending with one House for more than six months after it was passed by the other
    3. When both the Houses disagree on the amendments to be made in a Bill.
    4. When a bill is passed by one House and is rejected by the other.
    Select the correct answer using the codes given below.
    (a) 1, 2 and 3 (b) 2, 3 and 4
    (c) 2 and 3 only (d) 1 and 4

100. Consider the following statements
    1. A Money Bill cannot be introduced in the Council of States.
    2. The Council of States cannot reject a Money Bill nor amend it.
    Which of the statements given above is/are correct?
    (a) Only 1 (b) Only 2
    (c) Both 1 and 2 (d) Neither 1 nor 2

101. Which one of the following statements is not correct?
    (a) The Vice-President of India holds office for a period of five years
    (b) The Vice-President of India can be removed by a simple majority of votes passed in the Rajya Sabha only
    (c) The Vice-President of India continues to be in office even after the expiry of his term till his successor takes over
    (d) The Supreme Court of India has to look into all disputes with regard to the election of the Vice-President of India

102. Consider the following statements:
 1. The Annual Appropriation Bill is passed by the Lok Sabha in the same manner as any other Bill.
 2. An amendment to the Constitution of India can be initiated by an introduction of a Bill in either Lok Sabha or Rajya Sabha.
 Which of the statements given above is/are correct?
 (a) Only 1   (b) Only 2
 (c) Both 1 and 2   (d) Neither 1 nor 2

103. Consider the following statements:
 1. When the Vice-President of India acts as the President of India, he performs simultaneously the functions of the Chairman of Rajya Sabha.
 2. The President, of India can promulgate ordinances at any time except when both Houses of Parliament are in session.
 Which of the statements given above is/are correct?
 (a) Only 1   (b) Only 2
 (c) Both 1 and 2   (d) Neither 1 nor 2

104. Consider the following statements:
 1. The Union Executive consists of the President and the Council of Ministers with the Prime Minister as the head.
 2. The President may, by writing under his hand addressed to the Vice-President, resign his office.
 3. Executive power of the Union is vested in the Prime Minister.
 Which of the statements given above is/are correct?
 (a) 1 and 3   (b) 2 and 3
 (c) 1, 2 and 3   (d) Only 2

105. Consider the following statements:
 1. Ministry of Parliamentary Affairs constitute Consultative Committees of Members of both the Houses of Parliament.
 2. The main purpose of these Committees are to provide a forum for formal discussions between the Government and Members of Parliament on polices and programmes of the Government.
 Which of the statements given above is/are correct?
 (a) Only 1   (b) Only 2
 (c) Both 1 and 2   (d) Neither 1 nor 2

106. Consider the following statements on Parliamentary Committees:
 1. Members of the Rajya Sabha are not associated with the Committees on Public Accounts and Public Undertakings.
 2. Members of the Committee on Estimates are drawn from both the Lok Sabha and the Rajya Sabha.
 Which of the statements given above islare correct?
 (a) Only 1   (b) Only 2
 (c) Both 1 and 2   (d) Neither 1 nor 2

107. Consider the following statements:
 1. The Ministries Departments of the Union Government are created by the Prime Minister.
 2. The Cabinet Secretary is the Ex-officio Chairman of the Civil Services Board.
 Which of the statement given above is/are correct?
 (a) Only 1   (b) Only 2
 (c) Both 1 and 2   (d) Neither 1 nor 2

108. Consider the following Vice-Presidents of India:
 1. V.V Giri   2. M Hidayatullah
 3. BD Jatti   4. GS Pathak
 Which one of the following is the correct chronology of their tenures?
 (a) 1, 4, 3, 2   (b) 2, 1, 3, 4
 (c) 3, 2, 1,4   (d) 4, 1,3, 2

109. According to the Constitution (Fifty Second Amendment Act, 1985 as amended in 2003, a legislator attracts disqualification under the 10th Schedule if
 1. he voluntarily gives up the membership of the party on whose ticket he was elected.
 2. he votes or abstains from voting contrary to any direction issued by his political party.
 3. as a result of split, less than one third of the members formed a new group or party in the house.
 4. a member who has been elected as a independent member joins any political party.
 Select the correct answer using the codes given below.
 (a) 2 and 3   (b) 1, 2 and 4
 (c) 1 and 3   (d) All of these

110. Under which of the following conditions security deposits of a candidate contesting for a Lok Sabha seat is returned to him/her?
 1. The nomination made by the candidate if found to be invalid.
 2. The candidate has withdrawn his/her nomination even though it is found valid.
 3. The candidate lost the polls but secured 1/6th of the total number of valid votes polled in that election.
 Select the correct answer using the codes given below
 (a) 1 and 2   (b) Only 3
 (c) 2 and 3   (d) All of these

111. Consider the following statements
 1. The total elective membership of the Lok Sabha is distributed among the States on the basis of the population and the area of the State.
 2. The 84th Amendment Act of the Constitution of India lifted the freeze on the delimitation of constituencies imposed by the 42nd Amendment.
 Which of the statements given above is/are correct?
 (a) Only 1   (b) Only 2
 (c) Both 1 and 2   (d) Neither 1 nor 2

112. Which of the following statements is/are correct?
 1. A registered voter in India can contest an election to Lok Sabha from any constituency in India.
 2. As per the Representation of the People Act, 1951, if a person is convicted of any offence and sentenced to an imprisonment of 2 years or more, he will be disqualified to contest election.
 Select the correct answer using the codes given below
 (a) Only 1   (b) Only 2
 (c) Both 1 and 2   (d) Neither I nor 2

113. Which of the following Committees are the Committees of Parliament?
 1. Public Accounts Committee
 2. Estimates Committee
 3. Committee on Public Undertakings
 Select the correct answer using the code given below
 (a) 1 and 2   (b) 1 and 3
 (c) 2 and 3   (d) 1, 2 and 3

114. Consider the following statements about the powers of the President of India
 1. The President can direct that any matter on which decision has been taken by a Minister should be placed before the Council of Ministers.
 2. The President can call all information relating to proposals for legislation.
 3. The President has the right to address and send messages to either House of the Parliament.
 4. All decisions of the Council of Ministers relating to the administration of the Union must be communicated to the President.
 Which of the statements given above are correct?
 (a) 1,2 and 3 (b) 1 and 3
 (c) 2 and 4 (d) 1,2, 3 and 4

115. Consider the following statements relating to the procedure of the election of the Speaker and the Deputy Speaker of the Lok Sabha
 1. The election of a Speaker shall be held on such date as the Prime Minister may fix and the Secretary General shall send to every member. notice of this date.
 2. The election of a Deputy Speaker shall be held on such date as the Speaker may fix and the Secretary General shall send to every member notice of this date.
 3. At anytime before noon on the day preceding the date so fixed, any member may give notice in writing of a motion that another member be chosen as the Deputy Speaker of the House.
 Which of the statement(s) given above is/are correct?
 (a) 2 and 3 (b) Only 2
 (c) 1 and 3 (d) All of these

116. Which of the following pairs of constitutional authority and procedure of appointment is/are correctly matched?
 1. President : Elected by an electoral college consisting of elected MLAs and MPs
 2. Vice-President: Elected by an electoral college consisting of MLAs and MPs
 3. Speaker : The House of People chooses after its first sitting
 Select the correct answer using the codes given below
 (a) 1, 2 and 3 (b) Only 1
 (c) 1 and 3 (d) 2 and 3

117.

Council of states	House of the People
Not more than 250 members	Not more than 552 members
"Not more than 238 representatives of States and Union Territories"	Not more than 530 representative of states plus not more than 2 nominated Anglo-Indians plus X

 Which one of the following will fit in the place marked 'X'?
 (a) Ministers who are not members of Parliament but who have to get themselves elected to either House of Parliament within six months after assuming office
 (b) Not more than 20 nominated members
 (c) Not more than 20 representative of Union Territories
 (d) The Attorney General who has the right to speak and take part in the proceedings of either House of the Parliament

118. Which of the following are/is stated in the Constitution of India?
 1. The President shall not be a member of either House of Parliament
 2. The Parliament shall consist of the President and two Houses
 Choose the correct answer from the codes given below:
 (a) Neither 1 nor 2 (b) Both 1 and 2
 (c) Only 1 (d) Only 2

119. Consider the following statements:
 1. The joint sitting of the two houses of the Parliament in India is sanctioned under Article 108 of the Constitution
 2. The first joint sitting of Lok Sabha and Rajya Sabha was held in the year 1961
 3. The second joint sitting of the two Houses of Indian Parliament was held to pass the Banking Service Commission (Repeal) Bill
 Which of the above statements is/are correct?
 (a) 1 and 2 (b) 2 and 3
 (c) 1 and 3 (d) 1, 2 and 3

120. With reference to the Union Government, consider the following statements:
 1. The Constitution of India provides that all Cabinet Ministers shall be compulsorily be a sitting members of Lok Sabha only.
 2. The Union Cabinet Secretariat operates under the direction of the Ministry of Parliamentary Affairs.
 Which of the statements given above is/are correct?
 (a) 1 only (b) 2 only
 (c) Both 1 and 2 (d) Neither 1 nor 2

121. According to the Constitution of India, it is the duty of the President of India to cause to be laid before the Parliament which of the following?
 1. The Recommendations of the Union Finance Commission
 2. The Report of the Public Accounts Committee
 3. The Report of the Comptroller and Auditor General
 4. The Report of the National Commission for Scheduled Castes
 Select the correct answer using the codes given below :
 (a) 1 only (b) 2 and 4 only
 (c) 1, 3 and 4 only (d) 1, 2, 3 and 4

122. Consider the following statements:
 1. While members of the Rajya Sabha are associated with Committees on Public Accounts and Public Undertakings, members of Committee on Estimates are drawn entirely from the Lok Sabha.
 2. The Ministry of Parliamentary Affairs works under the overall direction of Cabinet Committee on Parliamentary Affairs.
 3. The Minister of Parliamentary Affairs nominates Members of Parliament on Committees, Councils, Board and Commissions etc. set up by the Government of India in the various ministries.
 Which of these statements are correct?
 (a) 1 and 2 (b) 2 and 3
 (c) 1 and 3 (d) 1, 2 and 3

123. Consider the following statements:
    1. The Rajya Sabha alone has the power to declare that it would be in national interest for the Parliament to legislate with respect to a matter in the State List.
    2. Resolutions approving the proclamation of Emergency are passed only by the Lok Sabha.
    Which of the statement(s) given above is/are correct?
    (a) 1 only   (b) 2 only
    (c) Both 1 and 2   (d) Neither 1 nor 2

124. Consider the following statements in respect of financial emergency under Article 360 of the Constitution of India:
    1. A proclamation of financial emergency issued shall cease to operate at the expiration of two months, unless before the expiration of that period it has been approved by the resolutions of both Houses of Parliament.
    2. If any proclamation of financial emergency is in operation, it is competent for the President of India to issue directions for the reduction of salaries and allowances of all or any class of persons serving in connection with the affairs of the Union but excluding the Judges of Supreme Court and the High Courts.
    Which of the statements given above is/are correct?
    (a) 1 only   (b) 2 only
    (c) Both 1 and 2   (d) Neither 1 nor 2

125. Consider the following statements:
    1. The Chairman of the Committee on Public Accounts is appointed by the Speaker of the Lok Sabha.
    2. The Committee on Public Accounts comprises Members of Lok Sabha, Members of Rajya Sabha and few eminent persons of industry and trade.
    Which of the statements given above is/are correct?
    (a) 1 only   (b) 2 only
    (c) Both 1 and 2   (d) Neither 1 nor 2

126. Who among the following have held the office of the Vice-President of India?
    1. Mohammad Hidayatullah
    2. Fakhruddin Ali Ahmed
    3. Neelam Sanjiva Reddy
    4. Shankar Dayal Sharma
    Select the correct answer using the code given below:
    Codes:
    (a) 1, 2, 3 and 4   (b) 1 and 4 only
    (c) 2 and 3 only   (d) 3 and 4 only

127. With reference to Union Government, consider the following statements:
    1. The Ministries and Departments of the Government of India are created by the Prime Minister on the advice of the Cabinet Secretary.
    2. Each of the ministries is assigned to a Minister by the President of India on the advice of the Prime Minister.
    Which of the statements given above is/are correct?
    (a) 1 only   (b) 2 only
    (c) Both 1 and 2   (d) Neither 1 nor 2

128. Regarding the office of the Lok Sabha Speaker, consider the following statements:
    1. He/She holds the office during the pleasure of the President.
    2. He/She need not be a member of the House at the time of his/her election but has to become a member of the House within six months from the date of his/her election.
    3. If he/she intends to resign, the letter of his/her resignation has to be addressed to the Deputy Speaker.
    Which of the statements given above is /are correct?
    (a) 1 and 2 only   (b) 3 only
    (c) 1, 2 and 3   (d) None

129. A deadlock between the Lok Sabha and the Rajya Sabha calls for a joint sitting of the Parliament during the passage of
    1. Ordinary Legislation
    2. Money Bill
    3. Constitution Amendment Bill
    Select the correct answer using the codes given below :
    (a) 1 only   (b) 2 and 3 only
    (c) 1 and 3 only   (d) 1, 2 and 3

130. In the context of India, which of the following principles is/are implied institutionally in the parliamentary government?
    1. Members of the Cabinet are Members of the Parliament.
    2. Ministers hold the office till they enjoy confidence in the Parliament.
    3. Cabinet is headed by the Head of the State.
    Select the correct answer using the codes given below.
    (a) 1 and 2 only   (b) 3 only
    (c) 2 and 3 only   (d) 1, 2 and 3

131. Consider the following statements:
    1. The Council of Ministers in the Centre shall be collectively responsible to the Parliament.
    2. The Union Ministers shall hold the office during the pleasure of the President of India.
    3. The Prime Minister shall communicate to the President about the proposals for legislation.
    Which of the statements given above is/are correct?
    (a) 1 only   (b) 2 and 3 only
    (c) 1 and 3 only   (d) 1, 2 and 3

132. Consider the following statements:
    1. The Chairman and the Deputy Chairman of the Rajya Sabha are not the members of that House.
    2. While the nominated members of the two Houses of the Parliament have no voting right in the presidential election, they have the right to vote in the election of the Vice President.
    Which of the statements given above is/are correct?
    (a) 1 only   (b) 2 only
    (c) Both 1 and 2   (d) Neither 1 nor 2

133. Consider the following statements:
    In the electoral college for Presidential Election in India,
    1. the value of the vote of an elected Member of Legislative Assembly equals

$$\frac{\text{State Population}}{\text{Number of Elected MLAs of the State}} \times 100$$

    2. the value of the vote of an elected Member of Parliament equals to total value of the votes of all elected MLA's and total number of elected MP's
    3. there were more than 5000 members in the latest elections.
    Which of these statements is/are correct?
    (a) 1 and 2   (b) Only 2
    (c) 1 and 3   (d) Only 3

134. Consider the following statements:
     1. The Speaker of Lok Sabha has the power to adjourn the House sine die but, on prorogation, it is only the President who can summon the House
     2. Unless sooner dissolved or there is an extension of the term, there is an automatic dissolution of the Lok Sabha by efflux of time, at the end of the period of five years, even if no formal order of dissolution is issued by the President
     3. The Speaker of Lok Sabha continues in office even after the dissolution of the House and until immediately before the first meeting of the House
     Which of the statements given above are correct?
     (a) 1 and 2   (b) 2 and 3 .
     (c) 1 and 3   (d) 1, 2 and 3

135. The functions of the committee on estimates, as incorporated in the Constitution of India, shall be to   **[CSAT–2014]**
     1. report what economies, improvements in organisation, efficiency or administrative reform may be effected.
     2. suggest alternative policies in order to bring about efficiency and economy in administration.
     3. examine whether the money is well laid out within the limits of the policy implied in the estimates.
     4. examine the reports, if any, of the Comptroller and Auditor General on the public undertakings.
     Select the correct answer using the codes given below
     (a) 1 and 2   (b) 2 and 3
     (c) 1, 2 and 3   (d) 3 and 4

136. The subject matter of an adjournment motion in the Parliament   **[CSAT–2014]**
     1. must be directly related to the conduct of the Union Government.
     2. may involve failure of the Government of India to perform its duties in accordance with the Constitution.
     Select the correct answer using the codes given below
     (a) Only 1   (b) Only 2
     (c) Both 1 and 2   (d) Neither 1 nor 2

137. The principle of "collective responsibility' under parliamentary democracy implies that   **[CSAT–2014]**
     1. a motion of no-confidence can be moved in the Council of Ministers as a whole as well as an individual minister.
     2. no person shall be nominated to the cabinet except on the advice of the Prime Minister.
     3. no person shall be retained as a member of the Cabinet if the Prime minister says that he shall be dismissed.
     Select the correct answer using the codes given below
     (a) Only 1   (b) Only 2
     (c) Only 3   (d) 2 and 3

138. The Committee on Public Accounts under the Constitution of India is meant fox   **[CSAT–2014]**
     1. the examination of accounts showing the appropriation of sums granted by the House for the expenditure of the Government of India
     2. scrutinising the report of the Comptroller and Auditor-General
     3. suggesting the form in which estimates shall be presented to the Parliament
     Select the correct answer using the codes given below

     (a) Only 1   (b) Only 2
     (c) 1 and 2   (d) All of these

139. Which of the statements relating to the Deputy Speaker of the Lok Sabha is/are correct?   **[CSAT–2014]**
     1. The office of the Deputy Speaker acquired a more prominent position after the enforcement of the Constitution of India in 1950.
     2. He/She is elected from amongst the members.
     3. He/She holds office until he/she ceases to be a member of the House.
     Select the correct answer using the codes given below
     (a) Only 1   (b) 1 and 2
     (c) 1, 2 and 3   (d) 2 and 3

140. Which of the following principles is/are taken into consideration by the Speaker while recognising a parliamentary party or group?   **[CSAT–2014]**
     1. An association of members who have an organisation both inside and outside the House
     2. An association of members who shall have at least one-third of the total number of members of the House
     3. An association of members who have a distinct programme of parliamentary work
     Select the correct answer using the codes given below
     (a) 1, 2 and 3   (b) Onfy 1
     (c) 1 and 3   (d) 2 and 3

141. Which of the following statements in the context of structure of the Parliament is/are correct? **[CSAT–2014]**
     1. The Parliament of India consists of the President, the Council of States and the House of the People.
     2. The President of India is directly elected by an electoral college consisting of the elected members of both the Houses of the Parliament only.
     Select the correct answer using the codes given below
     (a) Only 1   (b) Only 2
     (c) Both 1 and 2   (d) Neither 1 nor 2

142. Which of the following statements are correct regarding Joint Session of the Houses of the Parliament in India?
     1. It is an enabling provision, empowering the President to take steps for resolving deadlock between the two Houses.
     2. It is not obligatory upon the President to summon the Houses to meet in a join sitting.
     3. It is being notified by the President.
     4. It is frequently resorted to establish the supremacy of the Lok Sabha.
     Select the correct answer using the codes given below
          [CSAT–2014]
     (a) 1 and 2   (b) 1, 2 and 3
     (c) 2 and 3   (d) 3 and 4

143. Consider the following statements :   **[CSAT–2014]**
     1. The President shall make rules for the more convenient transaction of the business of the Government of India, and for the allocation among Ministers of the said business.
     2. All executive actions of the Government of India shall be expressed to be taken in the name of the Prime Minister.
     Which of the statements given above is/are correct?
     (a) 1 only   (b) 2 only
     (c) Both 1 and 2   (d) Neither 1 nor 2

144. With reference to the Union Government, consider the following statements : **[CSAT–2015]**
    1. The Department of Revenue is responsible for the preparation of Union Budget that is presented to the Parliament.
    2. No amount can be withdrawn from the Consolidated Fund of India without the authorization from the Parliament of India.
    3. All the disbursements made from Public Account also need the authorization from the Parliament of India.
    Which of the statements given above is / are correct?
    (a) 1 and 2 only   (b) 2 and 3 only
    (c) 2 only   (d) 1, 2 and 3

145. Consider the following statements: **[CSAT–2015]**
    1. The Rajya Sabha has no power either to reject or to amend a Money Bill.
    2. The Rajya Sabha cannot vote on the Demands for Grants.
    3. The Rajya Sabha cannot discuss the Annual Financial Statement.
    Which of the statements given above is / are correct?
    (a) 1 only   (b) 1 and 2 only
    (c) 2 and 3 only   (d) 1, 2 and 3

146. Consider the following statements:
    1. The Executive Power of the Union of India is vested in the Prime Minister.
    2. The Prime Minister is the ex officio Chairman of the Civil Services Board.
    Which of the statements given above is / are correct?
    (a) 1 only   (b) 2 only
    (c) Both 1 and 2   (d) Neither 1 nor 2

147. Which of the following statements is/are correct?
    1. A Bill pending in the Lok Sabha lapses on its prorogation
    2. A Bill pending in Rajya Sabha, which has not been passed by the Lok Sabha, shall not lapse on dissolution of the Lok Sabha.
    Select the correct answer using the codes given below
    [CSAT–2016]
    (a) 1 only   (b) 2 only
    (c) Both 1 and 2   (d) Neither 1 nor 2

148.
List-I	List-II
(Form of government)	**(Essential features)**
(A) Cabinet government	(1) Separation of powers
(B) Presidential government	(2) Collective responsibility
(C) Federal government	(3) Concentration of powers
(D) Unitary government	(4) Division of powers
	(5) Administrative law

    (a) A – 3 ; B – 4 ; C – 2 ; D – 1
    (b) A – 2 ; B – 1 ; C – 4 ; D – 3
    (c) A – 3 ; B – 4 ; C – 1 ; D – 2
    (d) A – 4 ; B – 3 ; C – 2 ; D – 5

149.
List-I	List-II
(A) The council of ministers shall be collectively responsible to the House of People.	(1) Article 74
(B) Duties of the Prime Minister towards the President.	(2) Article 77
(C) Council of ministers to aid and advise the President.	(3) Article 76
(D) All executive action of the Government of India shall be taken in the name of the President.	(4) Article 75
	(5) Article 78

    (a) A – 4 ; B – 5 ; C – 1 ; D – 3
    (b) A – 3 ; B – 2 ; C – 4 ; D – 1
    (c) A – 4 ; B – 5 ; C – 1 ; D – 2
    (d) A – 3 ; B – 4 ; C – 1 ; D – 2

150.
List-I	List-II
(A) Chief Election Commissioner	(1) Elected by Rajya Sabha
(B) Deputy Chairman of Rajya Sabha	(2) Elected by Lok Sabha
(C) Chairman of Lok sabha	(3) Appointed by Lok Sabha Speaker
	(4) Appointed by the president

    (a) A-4, B-1, C-3   (b) A-2, B-3, C-4
    (c) A-1, B-4, C-2   (d) A-4, B-1, C-2

151. Match list I with list II and select the correct answer using the codes given below the lists :
List I	List II
(Functionaries)	**(Oaths or affirmations)**
A. President of India	1. Secrecy of Information
B. Judges of Supreme Court	2. Faithful discharge of duties
C. Members of Parliament	3. Faith and Allegiance to the constitution of India
D. Minister for the Union	4. Upholding the constitution and the law

    Codes:
    (a) A-3, B-4, C-1, D-2
    (b) A-4, B-3, C-2, D-1
    (c) A-3, B-4, C-2, D-1
    (d) A-4, B-3, C-1, D-2

152. Match List I with List II and select the correct answer:
List-I	List-II
(Functionaries)	**(Oaths or affirmations)**
A. President of India	1. Secrecy of information
B. Judges of Supreme Court	2. Faithful Discharge of duties
C. Members of Parliament	3. Faith and Allegiance to the Constitution of India
D. Minister for the Union	4. Upholding the Constitution and the law

    Codes:
    (a) A-3, B-4, C-1, D-2
    (b) A-4, B-3, C-2, D-1
    (c) A-3, B-4, C-2, D-1
    (d) A-4, B-3, C-1, D-2

153. Match List-I with List-II and select the correct answer using the codes given below the lists:

List-I (Article of the Constitution)		List-II (Content)
A.	Article 54	1. Election of the President of India
B.	Article 75	2. Appointment of the Prime Minister
C.	Article 155	3. Appointment of the Governor of a State
D.	Article 164	4. Appointment of the Chief Minister and Council of Ministers of a State
		5. Composition of Legislative Assemblies

Codes:
(a) A-1, B-2, C-3, D-4
(b) A-1, B-2, C-4, D-5
(c) A-2, B-1, C-3, D-5
(d) A-2, B-1, C-4, D-3

154. Which of the following statements relating to the powers of the President of India is/are correct? **[CDS 2017]**
   1. The executive power of the Union shall be vested in the President.
   2. The executive power shall be exercised by the President only through officers subordinate to him.
   3. The supreme command of the defence forces of the Union shall be vested in the President.
   Select the correct answer using the code given below.
   (a) 1, 2 and 3   (b) 1 and 2 only
   (c) 1 and 3 only   (d) 3 only

155. A Joint Sitting of the Parliament is resorted to, for resolving the deadlock between two Houses of the Parliament for passing which of the following Bills? **[CDS 2017]**
   1. Money Bill
   2. Constitutional Amendment Bill
   3. Ordinary Bill
   Select the correct answer using the code given below.
   (a) 1 only   (b) 2 and 3 only
   (c) 3 only   (d) 1, 2 and 3

156. The President of India is elected by an Electoral College comprising of elected members of which of the following? **[CDS 2017]**
   1. Both the Houses of the Parliament
   2. The Legislative Assemblies of States
   3. The Legislative Councils of States
   4. The Legislative Assemblies of NCT of Delhi and Puducherry
   Select the correct answer using the code given below.
   (a) 1 and 2 only   (b) 1, 2 and 3
   (c) 1, 2 and 4   (d) 3 and 4

157. A person is disqualified for being chosen as, and for being, a Member of either House of the Parliament if the person **[CDS 2018]**
   1. holds any office or profit under the Government of India or the Government of any State other than an office declared by the Parliament by law not to disqualify its holder
   2. is an undischarged insolvent
   3. Is so disqualified under the Tenth Schedule of the Constitution of India
   4. Is of unsound mind and stands so declared by a competent Court
   Select the correct answer using the code given below.
   (a) 1, 2 and 4 only   (b) 1, 2, 3 and 4
   (c) 3 and 4 only   (d) 1, 2 and 3 only

158. Which of the following are not necessarily the consequences of the proclamation of the President's rule in a State? **[IAS Prelims 2017]**
   1. Dissolution of the State Legislative Assembly
   2. Removal of the Council of Ministers in the State
   3. Dissolution of the local bodies
   Select the correct answer using the code given below:
   (a) 1 and 2 only   (b) 1 and 3 only
   (c) 2 and 3 only   (d) 1, 2 and 3

159. The Parliament of India exercises control over the functions of the Council of Ministers through.
   1. Adjournment motion   **[IAS Prelims 2017]**
   2. Question hour
   3. Supplementary questions
   Select the correct answer using the code given below:
   (a) 1 only   (b) 2 and 3 only
   (c) 1 and 3 only   (d) 1, 2 and 3

160. With reference to the Parliament of India, consider the following statements: **[IAS Prelims 2017]**
   1. A private member's bill is a bill presented by a Member of Parliament who is not elected but only nominated by the President of India.
   2. Recently, a private member's bill has been passed in the Parliament of India for the first time in its history.
   Which of the statements given above is/are correct?
   (a) 1 only   (b) 2 only
   (c) Both 1 and 2   (d) Neither 1 nor 2

161. Consider the following statements: **[IAS Prelims 2017]**
   1. In the election for Lok Sabha or State Assembly, the winning candidate must get at least 50 per cent of the votes polled, to be declared elected.
   2. According to the provisions laid down in the Constitution of India, in Lok Sabha, the Speaker's post goes to the majority party and the Deputy Speaker's to the Opposition.
   Which of the statements given above is/are correct?
   (a) 1 only   (b) 2 only
   (c) Both 1 and 2   (d) Neither 1 nor 2

Hints and Explanations

EXERCISE-1

1. (a) During the proclamation of national emergency, the team of the assembly can be extended by a law of parliament for one year at a time (for any length of time).

   However, this extension cannot continue beyond a period of six months after the emergency has ceased to operate.

2. (c) A judge of the supreme court is removed from his office, only on the grounds of proved misbehaviour or incapacity. Parliament is empowered to regulate the procedure for the investigation and proof of such misbehaviour or incapacity. Whatever the procedure, each house will have to pass a resolution supported by two-thirds of the members present and voting and a majority of the total membership of the house and address it to the president. The president will then issue orders for removal of the judge.

3. (d) Parliament can legislate on the matters of state list on the situations mention in options (a), (b) and (c).

   – Lack of majority in the state assembly is no ground for parliament to make laws on state list.

4.	(b)	5.	(b)	6.	(d)	7.	(c)	8.	(a)
9.	(b)	10.	(c)	11.	(c)	12.	(d)	13.	(b)
14.	(c)	15.	(d)	16.	(b)	17.	(c)	18.	(a)
19.	(b)	20.	(d)	21.	(b)	22.	(a)	23.	(b)
24.	(b)	25.	(c)	26.	(d)	27.	(a)	28.	(b)
29.	(d)	30.	(b)	31.	(a)	32.	(d)	33.	(d)
34.	(c)	35.	(b)	36.	(c)	37.	(d)	38.	(c)
39.	(a)	40.	(d)	41.	(a)	42.	(c)	43.	(d)

44. (d) Money bill can be introduced by the prior permission of President only. The proposal is money bill or not it is decided by Lok Sabha speaker.

45. (c) President can dissolve the Lok Sabha on the advice of Prime Minister. The time duration of Lok Sabha is 5 years.

46. (b) Under Article 109, special procedure in respect of Money Bill has been given, a Money Bill shall not be introduced in the council of state, it can be introduced in only Lok Sabha. After a money bill is passed by Lok Sabha and send to Rajya Sabha, it should be returned within 7 days.

47. (c) In the absence of both the President of India and the vice president, the chief justice of India (or in his absence, the senior-most judge of the supreme court available) shall act as the president of India.

48. (d)

49. (a) According to the Article 75 of Indian Constitution the Council of Ministers of the Union shall be collectively responsible to the House of the People.

50. (c) The Union Executive of India, as in parliamentary type of government, consist of president and the council of ministers.

51.	(a)	52.	(a)	53.	(d)	54.	(d)	
55.	(c)	56.	(c)	57.	(a)			

58. (d) Department of women and child development is not a department under Ministry of Human Resource Development. Human Resources Development (HRD) as a theory is a framework for the expansion of human capital within an organization through the development of both the organization and the individual to achieve performance improvement.

59. (b) The comptroller and Auditor General can be removed on an address from both Houses of Parliament. The Comptroller and Auditor General (CAG) of India is an authority, established by the Constitution of India under Chapter V, who audits all receipts and expenditure of the Government of India and the state governments, including those bodies and authorities substantially financed by the government. The CAG is also the external auditor of government-owned companies.

60. (d) Salary and allowances of the speakers of the Lok Sabha is not charged on the Consolidated fund of India. Consolidated fund or the consolidated revenue fund is the term used for the main bank account of the government in many of the countries in the Commonwealth of Nations. All tax revenue is paid into the fund unless Parliament has specifically provided otherwise by law. Any money received by the government which is not taxation, and is not to be retained by the receiving department (for example, fines), is classed as a Consolidated Fund extra receipt (CFER). These are to be paid into the Consolidated Fund as soon as they are received.

61.	(b)	62.	(d)	63.	(d)	64.	(b)	
65.	(c)	66.	(a)	67.	(c)	68.	(a)	

69. (b) Cabinet Secretary is the highest civil servant of the Union Government. The Cabinet Secretary is the senior-most civil servant in the Government of India. The Cabinet Secretary is the ex-officio head of the Civil Services Board. The Cabinet Secretary is under the direct charge of the Prime Minister. Though there is no fixed tenure, the average tenure of the Cabinet Secretary has been less than 3 years. His or her tenure however, can be extended.

70. (a) The speaker's vote in the Lok Sabha is called casting vote. A casting vote is a vote given to the presiding officer of a council or legislative body to resolve a deadlock and which can be exercised only when such a deadlock exists.

71. (c) The parliamentary Committee which scrutinizes the report of the CAG is public accounts committee. The Comptroller and Auditor General (CAG) is an authority, established by the Constitution of India under Chapter V, which audits all receipts and expenditure of the Government and the state governments, including those bodies and authorities substantially financed by the government.

72. (c) 73. (d)

74. (c) The prime minister is the chairman of the National Integration council. The National Integration Council originated in a conference convened by Prime Minister Jawaharlal Nehru in September–October 1961. The purpose was to find ways to counter problems that were dividing the country including attachment to specific communities, castes, regions and languages.

75. (a)   76. (a)   77. (c)

78. (c) Chaudhary Charan Singh was the Prime Minister resigned before facing a vote of no-confidence in the Lok Sabha. Chaudhuri Charan Singh was the fifth Prime Minister, serving from 28 July 1979 until 14 January 1980.

79. (d) 'Zero Hour' in Political jargon refers to question answer session. Zero Hour in Parliament starts at 12 noon during which members raise matters of importance, especially those that cannot be delayed.

80. (d)   81. (c)   82. (c)   83. (d)

84. (d)   85. (c)   86. (c)

87. (a) The first reading of the bill in a house of parliament refers to motion for leave to introduce the bill in the House.If a motion for leave to introduce a Bill is opposed, the Speaker, after permitting, if he thinks fit, brief statements from the member who opposes the motion and the member who moved the motion, may, without further debate, put the question: provided that where a motion is opposed on the ground that the Bill initiates legislation outside the legislative competence of the House, the Speaker may permit a full discussion thereon. Provided further that the Speaker shall forthwith put to vote the motion for leave to introduce a Finance Bill or an Appropriation Bill.

88. (b) Department of official languages is subordinate office of the Ministry of Home affairs. It deals with the implementation of the provisions of the Constitution relating to official languages and the provisions of the Official Languages Act, 1963.

89. (d) State legislature assemblies, both houses of the parliament form part of the electoral college for the election of the president. An electoral college is a set of electors who are selected to elect a candidate to a particular office. Often these represent different organizations or entities, with each organization or entity represented by a particular number of electors or with votes weighted in a particular way.

90. (d) Decorum = Parliamentary etiquette
Crossing the floor = Changing the party
Interpolation = Seeking clarification through ruling
Yielding the floor = Respecting speaker's order

91. (d) The Constitutional amendment bill must be passed by each house of the Indian Parliament separately by special majority.

92. (b) Department of border management is a department of ministry of Home affairs of the union minister. Department of Border Management is dealing with management of borders, including coastal borders.

93. (a) When a money bill returns to the Loksabha with amendments made by the Rajyasabha, it is open to Loksabha to accept or to reject any or all of the recommendations. When the Loksabha chooses to accept or decline the money bill with or without the recommendation, the money bill is deemed passed in both houses.

94. (b) The largest Committee is Estimates, given its 30 members

Committee on	No. of members
Public Accounts	22
Estimates	30
Public Undertakings	22
Petitions	LS(15) , RS(10)

95. (b) Article 110 of Indian constitution defines a Money Bill. The speakers decision as to whether a bill is a Money Bill is final.

96. (d) While proclamation of Emergency is in operation be extended by parliament by law for a period not exceeding one year at a time and not extending in any case beyond a period of six months after the proclamation has ceased to operate [Article 83 (2)]

97. (d) The Rajya Sabha is a permanent house, not subject to disolution, one third of its members retiring after every two years. Thus every member enjoys a 6-year tenure.

98. (c) The Union Executive of India, as in parliamentary type of government, consist of president and the council of ministers.

99. (d) The presiding officer of the Lok Sabha is the Speaker who is elected by the member from amongst themselves.

100. (c) Cabinet Secretariat is under the charge of the Prime Minister of India.

101. (c) If any question arises whether a Bill is a money bill or not, the decision of the Speaker of the Lok Sabha shall be final under the article 110 of the constitution of India.

102. (c) The speaker of the Lok sabha can resign from his office by addressing his resignation to the deputy speaker of the Lok Sabha.

103. (c) Either house of the parliament can initiate impeachment proceedings against the president of India.

104. (d)

105. (a) Joint session is presided over by the speaker of Lok Sabha or in his absence by the Deputy Speaker.

106. (d)

107. (b) The Concurrent List or List-III is a list of 52 items (previously 47 items) given in Part XI of the Constitution of India, concerned with relations between the Union and States. This part is divided between legislative and administrative powers.

108. (a) Members of both houses of parliament.

109. (d)

110. (a) Demands for Grants Committees are Departmentally Related Standing Committees.After the General Discussion on the Budget is over, the House is adjourned for a fixed period. During this period, the Demands for Grants of the Ministries/ Departments are considered by the Committees. It is not a parliamentary committee.

111. (c) In India, "the Emergency" refers to a 21-month period in 1975-77 when Prime Minister Indira Gandhiunilaterally had a state of emergency declared across the country.Fakhruddin Ali Ahmed was the President at that time.

112. (b) According to article 82 of Indian Constitution, the parliament of India shall readjust the allocation of seats in the Lok Sabha to the states and division of each state into territorial constituencies.

113. (b) According to Article 53(b) of the Indian Constitution the supreme command of the Defence Forces of the Union shall be vested in the President and the exercise thereof shall be regulated by law.

114. (c) The quorum to constitute a joint sitting shall be one-tenth of the total number of members of the Houses.

115. (d) The correct sequence is, Discussion on Budget, Appropriation Bill, Finance Bill, Vote on Account.

116. (c) Protem Speaker performs the duties of the office of the Speaker from the commencement of the sitting of the new Lok Sabha till the election of the Speaker. Protem speaker is mainly an operating and temporary speaker.

117. (c) He/she cannot take part in the voting when a vote of no confidence is under consideration.

118. (a) Under Article 61, the President of India can be removed from the office by a process of impeachment for the violation of the Constitution. The impeachment is to be initiated by either House of Parliament.

119. (c) Irrespective of the fact that a number of seats may have to be filled, this system postulates one vote for each voter with the reservation that this single vote is transferred to other candidates. This is the reason why this system is known as "single transferable vote system."

120. (a) "Closure" is one of the means by which a debate may be brought to a close by a majority decision of the House, even though all members wishing to speak have not done so.

121. (c) While a proclamation of emergency is in operation, this period may be extended by Parliament by law for a period not exceeding one year at a time.Under Article 352 the president can declare a national emergency when the security of India or part of it is threatened by war or external aggression or armed rebellion.

122. (c) A Money Bill cannot be introduced in Rajya Sabha. Rajya Sabha has no power either to reject or amend a Money Bill. It can only make recommendations on the Money Bill. Whether a particular Bill is a Money Bill or not is to be decided by the Speaker of Lok Sabha. Rajya Sabha may discuss the Annual Financial Statement. It has no power to vote on the Demands for Grants.

123. (c) In the Rajya Sabha the states have been given seats on the basis of population and economic position.

124. (d) The Speaker of Lok Sabha may be removed from his office by a resolution of the House of the People passed by a majority of all the then members of the House. No resolution for the purpose of removal of the Speaker or the Dy. Speaker shall be moved unless at least fourteen days notice has been given of the intention to move the resolution.

125. (b) The Estimates Committee is a Parliamentary Committee consisting of 30 Members, elected every year by the Lok Sabha from amongst its Members. The Chairman of the Committee is appointed by the Speaker from amongst its members. The term of office of the Committee is one year.

126. (b) Our Parliamentary system blends the legislative and the executive organs of the State in as much as the executive power is wielded by a group of Members of the Legislature who command majority in the Lok Sabha.

127. (d) The Constitution empowers Parliament of India to make laws on the matters reserved for States (States List). However, this can only be done if Rajya Sabha first passes a resolution by two-thirds supermajority granting such a power to the Union Parliament. The union government cannot make a law on a matter reserved for states without an authorisation from Rajya Sabha.So the House of People does not have special powers with respect to the state list.

128. (d) As Indian follows Universal Adult Suffrage elected members of the Lower House of the State Legislature *i. e.*, Las have the right to vote in the elections to both the Lok Sabha and Rajya Sabha. The State Legislature besides making laws also has one electoral power in electing the President of India. Elected members of the Legislative Assembly along with the elected members of Parliament are involved in this process.

129. (c) PM has complete discretion to choose his ministers in the Cabinet not necessarily from the two Houses of Parliament but can also choose any other person. That person should become member of either house within 6 months from the date he enters the office.

130. (a) Because no-confidence motion can be moved only in Lok Sabha (not in RS) by the opposition.

131. (a) A Money bill can be introduced only in LS (not in RS) that too on the recommendation of the President.

132. (d) Parliament has exclusive power to make law with respect to any of the matters enumerated with the Union List. According to entry no 14 in the Union List it reads- 'entering into treaties and agreements with foreign contries and implementing of treaties, agreement and convention with foreign countries'.

133. (c) The term of the LS can be extended by not more than one year at a time during the proclamation of national emergency under Article 352.

134. (d) According Article 355, it shall be the duty of the Union to protect every State against external aggression and internal disturbance and to ensure that the government of every State is carried on in accordance with the provisions of this Constitution.

135. (d) According to Article 368 an amendment of this Constitution may be initiated only by the introduction of a Bill for the purpose in either House of Parliament, and when the Bill is passed in each House by a majority of the total membership of that House present and voting, it shall be presented to the President who shall give his assent to the Bill and thereupon the Constitution shall stand amended in accordance with the terms of the Bill.

136. (a) Appropriation Bill is a money bill. In case of money bill, RS has only recommendatory power and need not to be passed by RS.

137. (b) The Constitution of India empowering the Parliament to make laws in the State List and to create one or more All India Services.

138. (d) It is the sole prerogative of Parliament under Article 253 of the Constitution.

139. (a) Parliamentary Committees are formed to dispose off the large volume of work in time but with detailed scrutiny. Their appointment, terms of office as well as functions etc are regulated by provisions under Article 118(1). These are of 2 kinds: Standing Committees and Ad-hoc Committees.

140. (c) In Rajya Sabha, 12 members are nominated by the President from the persons who have special knowledge in art, science, literature and social service. In Lok Sabha, 2 members are nominated by the President from the Anglo-Indian community (Art 331). A nominated member can vote only in the Vice-Presidential elections.

141. (a) In case of a No-confidence motion, there is no need to set out the grounds on which it is based. No-Confidence motion is introduced only in the Lok Sabha by the opposition and needs a support of not less than 50 members of LS for its introduction. Rule 198 of the Lok Sabha specifies the procedure for a motion of no-confidence. Any member may give a written notice; the speaker shall read the motion of no-confidence in the House and ask all those persons to rise who favours that the motion be taken up. If there are 50 MPs in favour, the speaker allots a date for discussing the motion.

142. (d) Article 67(b) in the Constitution of India states, a Vice President may be removed from his office by a resolution of the council of States passed by a majority of all the then members of the council and agreed to by the House of the People; but no resolution for the purpose of this clause shall be moved unless at least fourteen days notice has been given of the intention to move the resolution.

143. (b) Parliament shall have power to authorise by law the withdrawal of moneys from the Consolidated Fund of India for the purposes for which the said grants are made.

144. (a) Adjournment motion :
   (i) It is introduced in the Parliament to draw attention of the house to a definite matter of urgent public importance and needed to support of 50 members to be admitted.
   (ii) It is regarded as an extraordinary device, because it interrupts the normal business of the house.
   (iii) It involves an element of censure against the government and Rajya Sabha is not permitted to make use this device.
   (iv) The discussion an adjournment motion should last for not less than two hours and thirty minutes.

145. (a) Article 75(I) of the Indian Constitution provides that the Prime Minister shall be appointed by the President. The Constitution permits a person to be appointed PM without his\her being a member of either House of the Parliament at the of appointment.

Before expiry of this time, he has to become a member of either the Rajya Sabha or the Lok Sabha.

146. (a) When a money bill returns to the Loksabha with amendments made by the Rajyasabha, it is open to Loksabha to accept or to reject any or all of the recommendations. When the Loksabha chooses to accept or decline the money bill with or without the recommendation, the money bill is deemed passed in both houses.

147. (c) The recommendation of the president is required for introduction of money bills or for moving amendments to acts relating to financial matters, except those making provision for the reduction or abolition of any tax. So, for option (c) president's recommendation is not required.

148. (c) Article 111 of the Indian constitution stipulates that the President shall give assent to a bill passed by both houses of the parliament or return the bill as soon as possible for reconsideration with his recommendation.

149. (b) According to article 112,the President shall in respect of every financial year cause to be laid before both the Houses of Parliament a statement of the estimated receipts and expenditure of the Government of India for that year, in this Part referred to as the annual financial statement.

150. (a) In India, if a bill has been rejected by any house of the parliament and if more than six months have elapsed, the President may summon a joint session for purpose of passing the bill. The bill is passed by a simple majority of a joint sitting.

151 (d) Given verbatim in *Disha Publications Crack CSAT Paper-1, 2016 (4th Edition) Page p-101*
   • When Rajya Sabha Passes a Resolution If the Rajya Sabha declares that it is necessary in the national interest that Parliament should make laws on a matter in the State List, then the Parliament becomes competent to make laws on that matter. Such a resolution must be supported by two-thirds of the members present and voting.

152. (d)   153. (c)   154. (c)   155. (c)

156. (d) Given verbatim in Disha Publications Crack CSAT Paper-1, 2016 (4th Edition) Page p-101
   • If the Rajya Sabha declares that it is necessary in the national interest that Parliament should make laws on a matter in the State List, then the Parliament becomes competent to make laws on that matter. Such a resolution must be passed by the Rajya Sabha by a majority of not less than two-third of its members present and voting.

157. (b) MIND IT: you've to find the wrong statements here- they're the right answers.
   • when the President's Rule is imposed in a state, the President dismisses the state council of ministers headed by the chief minister. The state governor, on behalf of the President, carries on the state administration with the help of the chief secretary of the state or the advisors appointed by the President. Meaning "2" is definitely the consequence of proclamation. Hence all options involving "2" are wrong. Hence by elimination we are left with answer "B": 1 and 3 only.

158. (c) New NCERT, Std. 11, Introduction to Indian Constitution, page 91: Parliamentary system is also known as Cabinet Government. It provides for collective responsibility of the executive to the legislature.Hence answer "C".

159. (b) NCERT Class 9: Democratic Politics: Chapter 5: Working of the institutions, page 87
   - Since it is not practical for all ministers to meet regularly and discuss everything, (hence) the decisions are taken in Cabinet meetings. That is why parliamentary democracy in most countries is often known as the Cabinet form of government. Hence "B" is the answer.

160. (d) The Parliament exercises control over the ministers through various devices like question hour, discussions, adjournment motion, no confidence motion, etc. and Supplementary questions can be asked during the question hour.Therefore, all three are correct.

161. (d) Private member's bill as a bill introduced by any member of the parliament who's not a minister. Hence first statement is wrong.
   - The Indian Express report in 2016 says only 14 private members bill have been passed since 1952. So statement 2 is also wrong.

162. (c)

163. (d) New NCERT, Std. 11, Introduction to Indian Constitution Chapter 3: Election and Representation, Page 57: India has first past the post system wherein a candidate who wins the election may not (need to) get majority (50%+1) votes. Statement #1 is wrong.
   Upto the 10th Lok Sabha, both the Speaker and the Deputy Speaker were usually from the ruling party. Since the 11th Lok Sabha, there has been a consensus that the Speaker comes from the ruling party (or ruling alliance) and the post of Deputy Speaker goes to the main opposition party.Meaning it's an 'informal consensus' among political parties, and not Constitutional provision. Hence, statement 2 is wrong.

164. (a) Vice-President is elected by an Electoral College, which consists of the members of the Lok Sabha and Rajya Sabha (both elected and nominated members). He/she is the ex officio Chairperson of the Rajya Sabha. The qualification for getting elected as Vice president is that he/she should be more than 35 years of age and should not hold any office of profit.

165. (d) The Fourth Schedule to the Constitution provides for allocation of seats to the States and Union Territories in Rajya Sabha. The allocation of seats is made on the basis of the population of each State. Consequent on the reorganization of States and formation of new States, the number of elected seats in the Rajya Sabha allotted to States and Union Territories has changed from time to time since 1952.

166. (a) A Money Bill after having been passed by the Lok Sabha, and sent to Rajya Sabha for its recommendations, has to be returned to Lok Sabha by the Rajya Sabha, with in a period of fourteen days from the date of its receipt, with or without recommendations.

167. (c) The Rajya Sabha cannot discuss the Annual Financial Statement.

168. (a)   169   (c)

170. (d) Given verbatim in Disha Publications Crack CSAT Paper-1, 2016(4th Edition)Page p-101
   - If the Rajya Sabha declares that it is necessary in the national interest that Parliament should make laws on a matter in the State List, then the Parliament becomes competent to make laws on that matter. Such a resolution must be passed by the Rajya Sabha by a majority of not less than two-third of its members present and voting.

171. (c) New NCERT, Std. 11, Introduction to Indian Constitution, page 91: Parliamentary system is also known as Cabinet Government. It provides for collective responsibility of the executive to the legislature.Hence answer "C".

172. (b) NCERT Class 9: Democratic Politics: Chapter 5: Working of the institutions, page 87
   - Since it is not practical for all ministers to meet regularly and discuss everything, (hence) the decisions are taken in Cabinet meetings. That is why parliamentary democracy in most countries is often known as the Cabinet form of government. Hence "B" is the answer.

173. (c)

1.   (c) In India the method of election followed for the General elections and assembly elections is First Past the Post (FPTP) system. In this system whoever has more votes than all other candidates is declared elected. The winning candidate need not secure a majority of the votes.
   - This is the method of election prescribed by the constitution.

   Source: N.C.E.R.T. (Std. XIth) (Chapter 3

2.   (b) A minister can be a member of either of the two houses i.e. Lok-Sabha and Rajya Sabha. A person cannot be a minister without being a member of the parliament. The constitution stipulates that a minister who is not a member of the parliament for a period of 6 consecutive months ceases to be a minister.
   - The Ministers are collectively responsible to the parliament in general and to the Lok Sabha in particular (Art.-75). They act as a team and Swim and Sink together.

3.   (b) Suspensive veto-when president returns a bill for reconsideration of the parliament.
   President does not possess suspensive veto in the case of money bills. The president can either give his assent to a money bill or withhold his assent to a money bill but cannot return it for the reconsideration of the parliament.
   President has no veto power in respect of a

constitutional amendment bill. The 24th constitutional Amendment Act of 1971 made it obligatory for the president to give his assent to a constitutional amendment bill.

4. (b) After the 42nd Constitutional Amendment (1976), ministerial advice has been made binding on the president, but no such provision has been made with respect to the governor.

5. (d) All the above given statements are among demerits of the parliamentary system. Also the parliamentary system is not conducive to administrative efficiency as the ministers are not experts in their fields.

6. (c) Proportional Representation is a complicated system which may work in a small country, but would be difficult to work in a sub-continental country like India. The reason for the popularity and success of the FPTP system is its simplicity.

Also the FPTP system offers voters a choice not simply between parties but between specific candidates.

7. (a) When a Money Bill is presented to the governor, he may either give his assent, withhold his assent or reserve the bill for presedentical asset but cannot return the bill for re-consideration of the state legislature.

When such a Money Bill is reserved for the consideration of the president, the president may either give his assent to the bill or withhold his assent to the bill but cannot return the bill for reconsideration of the state legislature.

8. (d) The legislature in parliamentary system ensures executive accountability at various stages: policy making, implementation of law or policy during and post-implementation stage.

The legislature does this through the use of a variety of devices:

– Deliberation and discussion

– Approval or Refusal of laws

– Financial Control

– No Confidence Motion

– Question Hour.

– Zero Hour

– Adjournment motion

– The most powerful weapon that enables the parliament to ensure executive accountability is the no-confidence motion.

9. (c) A formal impeachment is not required for the removal of vice-president. He can be removed by a resolution of the Rajya sabha passed by an absolute majority. Notably no ground has been mentioned in the constitution for his removal.

The vice-president can hold office beyond his term of five years until his successor assumes charge. He is also eligible for re-election to that office. He may be elected for any number of times.

10. (c) All the above given statements are correct. In order to stand for Lok sabha or Assembly election, a candidate must be at least 25 years. There are some restrictions but at general level our system of election is open to all citizens.

11. (a) As provided by the constitution, the speaker of the last Lok Sabha vacates his office immediately before the first meeting of the newly elected Lok Sabha.

Therefore, the president appoints a member of the Lok sabha as the speaker protem. He presides over the first sitting of the newly-elected Lok-sabha. His main duty is to administer oaths to the new members. He also enables the house to elect the new speaker.

The vice-president of India is the ex-officio chairman of the Rajya sabha.

Unlike the speaker (who is a member of the house), the chairman is not a member of the House. But like the speaker, the chairman also cannot vote in the first instance.

12. (a) 1. Constitution provides for reservation of seats in the Lok Sabha and State Legislative Assemblies for the Scheduled Castes and Schedule Tribes. This provision of reservation has been extended upto 2020.

2. There is no constitutional provision for reservation of any kind in the council of states or the upper house, which has members elected by the State Assemblies as distinct from the directly elected Lok Sabha.

3. Art-330 provides for reservation of SC/STs in Lok Sabha but no mention of reservation in Rajya Sabha.

13. (a) The electoral college for the election of the vice-president is different from that of president in two respects.

1. It consists of both elected and nominated members of the parliament.

2. It does not include the members of the state legislative assemblies.

14. (a) In 2003, certain changes were made with respect to elections to the Rajya Sabha:

1. Domicile or residency requirement of a candidate contesting an election to the Rajya Sabha was removed.

2. Instead of secret ballot system, open ballot system was introduced for elections to Rajya Sabha. This was done to curb cross-voting and to wipe out the role of money power during Rajya Sabha.

Source: M. Lakshmikant

15. (c) Separate electorate means that for electing representative from a particular community, only those voters would be eligible who belong to that community.

However in case of reserved constituency all voters in a constituency are eligible to vote but the candidates must belong to only a particular community or social section for which seat is reserved.

16. (c) At present, a party is recognized as a national party (2009) if any of the following conditions is fulfilled.

1. If it secures 6% of valid votes polled in any four or more states at a general election to Lok sabha or to legislative assembly and in addition it wins four seats in the Lok sabha from any state/states. Therefore statement one is incomplete and fulfills only half the condition.

2. If it wins two percent of seats in the Lok sabha at a general election and these candidates are elected from three states. OR

3. If it is recognized as a state party in four states.

17. (d) Even before a bill is introduced in the parliament there may be a lot of debate on the need for introducing such a bill. A political party may pressurise the government to initiate a bill in order to fulfill its election promises or to improve its chances of winning forthcoming elections.

A money bill can only be introduced in the Lok sabha, once passed there, it is sent to the Rajya Sabha. Rajya Sabha can either approve a money bill or suggest changes but cannot reject it. If it takes no action within 14 days the bill is deemed to have been passed.

18. (b) All the statements given in the question are correct. The powers and functions of administrator are defined under Article 239 and 239 AA of the constitution. The administrator may be designated as Leiutenant Governor, Chief Commissioner or Administrator.

19. (a) For being eligible to be elected as a member of parliament, a person must not have been convicted for any offence resulting in imprisonment of two or more years.

But the detention of a person under a preventive detention law is not a disqualification.

20. (d) The total number of ministers, including the prime-minister, in the council of ministers shall not exceed 15% of the total strength of the Loksabha. The provision was added by the 91st Amendment Act of 2003.
   - The ministers shall hold office during the pleasure of the president.
   - The council of ministers shall be collectively responsible to the Lok Sabha.
   - The Salaries and allowances of ministers shall be determined by the parliament.

21. (c) There are certain powers which are enjoyed by Lok-Sabha only. Rajya Sabha cannot initiate, reject or amend money bills. However Rajya Sabha can suggest amendments to the Money Bills.
   Lok -Sabha is not bound to accept such suggestions Also since most of its members are drawn from Lok-Sabha, the council of ministers is responsible to Lok-Sabha only. Other reason for this unequal distribution of power is that government/executive sits in Lok-Sabha and not in Rajya Sabha.

22. (a) Statements (i), (iii) and (iv) are correct. Besides, the office of whip, in India is mentioned neither in the constitution nor in the rules of the house, nor in the parliamentary statutes. The members are supposed to follow the directives given by the whip. Failing to do so can invite disciplinary actions like disqualification from party membership or expulsion under the Anti-Defecation law.

23. (c) The representatives of states in the Rajya Sabha are elected by the members of state legislative assemblies. The election is held in accordance with the system of proportional representation by means of single transferable vote.
   - The Rajya Sabha cannot initiate, reject or amend money bills. Also the council of Ministers is responsible to the Lok Sabha and not Rajya Sabha. Therefore Rajya Sabha can criticise the government but cannot remove it.

24. (d) Grounds of disqualification of a member of parliament:
   - If he holds any office of profit under the union or state government.
   - If he is of unsound mind.
   - If he is an undischarged insolvent.
   - If he is not a citizen of India.
   - If he is so disqualified under any law made by parliament.

   Besides these, the parliament has laid down many other grounds for disqualification in the Representation of People Act (1951).

25. (c) Whether the parliamentary system should be continued or should be replaced by the presidential system has been a point of discussion and debate in our country since the 1970s.
   This matter was considered in detail by the Swaran Singh Committee appointed by the Congress government in 1975.
   The committee opined that the parliamentary system has been doing well and hence there is no need to replace it by the presidential system.

26.	(d)	27.	(d)	28.	(b)	29.	(c)	30.	(c)
31.	(d)	32.	(a)	33.	(c)	34.	(a)	35.	(b)
36.	(d)	37.	(a)	38.	(d)	39.	(d)	40.	(b)
41.	(c)	42.	(b)	43.	(d)	44.	(b)	45.	(a)
46.	(b)	47.	(d)	48.	(c)	49.	(c)	50.	(b)
51.	(d)	52.	(d)	53.	(c)						

54. (c) All the members of the Lok Sabha, except two members may be nominated by the President from Anglo-Indian Community.

55. (b) Parliamentary committee in India presents its report to the speaker/Chairman of the house. The work done by the Parliament in modern times is not only varied and complex in nature, but also considerable in volume. The time at its disposal is limited. It cannot, therefore, give close consideration to all the legislative and other matters that come up before it. A good deal of its business is, therefore, transacted in Committees of the House, known as Parliamentary Committees.

56. (d) A no confidence motion does not need to set out grounds on which it is based. The withdrawal of the notice of no confidence motion by a member may be made when he is called upon by the speaker to ask for leave of the House.

57. (c) Both the Houses have been enshrined with equal powers on the matter of impeachment of judges of the High Courts. Soumitra Sen is a retired judge of the Calcutta High Court. He was the first judge in independent India to be impeached in India's Rajya Sabha for misappropriation of funds.

58. (d) Article 80 states that the state legislature participates in the election of the members of Rajya Sabha and also of the president (Art.54)

59. (a) 'Committee on public Accounts' consists of 22 members, 15 from the Lok Sabha and 7 from Rajya Sabha. A Lok Sabha member from a major opposition party is appointed its chairman. The Public Accounts Committee (PAC) is a committee of selected members of Parliament, constituted by the Parliament of India, for the auditing of the expenditure of the Government of India.

60. (d) A no-confidence motion does not need to set out grounds on which it is based. The withdrawal of the notice by a member may be made when he is called upon by the speaker to ask for leave of the House.

61. (d) The government may be expressed by the House of People by all the statements given. So the all statements are correct.

62. (b) The government of India consists of a number of ministers/departments for its administration, each ministry assigned to a minister who runs it with the assistance of a secretary in charge of the particular ministry.

63. (a) 64. (c) 65. (c) 66. (a) 67. (d)
68. (d) 69. (c) 70. (a) 71. (d) 72 (a)
73. (a) 74. (b) 75. (d) 76. (c) 77. (d)
78. (c) 79. (b) 80. (d) 81. (b) 82. (d)
83. (c) 84. (b) 85. (a) 86. (b)

87. (c) The Attorney General of India has a post parallel to any minister in Parliament. He can take part in the proceedings of either house. He can be a member of any committee of Parliament. He has the right to speak in the Parliament but he has no right to vote.

88. (a) Minister/ministers can be removed by issuing no confidence motion in the parliament. All cabinet members are mandated by the constitution to be the member of either house of the parliament of India. Cabinet is headed by the cabinet secretary not by the Head of the State.

89. (c) The Council of Ministers shall be collectively responsible to the parliament; the Prime minister shall communicate to the president about the proposals for legislation but the union. If a President were to dismiss the Council of Ministers on his or her own initiative, it might trigger a constitutional crisis. Thus, in practice, the Council of Ministers cannot be dismissed as long as it commands the support of a majority in the Lok Sabha.

90. (b) The nominated members of the Rajya Sabha have the right to vote in the election of the Vice President so far none from them has been inducted in the Council of Ministers.

91. (a) Clause (3) of Article 77 "Conduct of Business of the Government of India" of the Constitution of India lays down as follows: "The President shall make rules for the more convenient transaction of the business of the Government of India, and for the allocation among Ministers of the said business.
The Constitution of India mentions that All executive action of the Government of India shall be expressed to be taken in the name of the President. Therefore, only option (a) is correct.

92. (c) A constitutional Government needs to balance between individual liberty viz a viz State Authority.

93. (c) The functions of the Cabinet Secretariat are preparation of agenda for Cabinet Meetings & Secretarial assistance to Cabinet Committees. However Allocation of financial resources to the Ministries as per the provisions in budget is prepared by finance ministry.

94. (b) The committee consists of 15 members of Lok sabha not 25 members. The function of the committee is to examine the accounts showing the appropriation of the sums granted by Parliament to meet the expenditure of the government of India and such other accounts laid before the House as the committee may think fit. Apart from the Reports of the Comptroller and Auditor General of India on Appropriation Accounts of the Union Government, the Committee also examines the various Audit Reports of the Comptroller and Auditor General on revenue receipts, expenditure by various Ministries/Departments of Government and accounts of autonomous bodies.

95. (d) 96. (b)

97. (c) Parliament may by law fix the salaries and allowances of the officers of Parliament (Article 97). The salaries are charged on the consolidated fund of India.

98. (c) 99. (c)

100. (c) Money Bills can be introduced only in Lok Sabha. Money bills passed by the Lok Sabha are sent to the Rajya Sabha.Rajya Sabha(Council of States) cannot reject or amend this bill. It can only recommend amendments.

101. (b) According to Article 67, a Vice-President may be removed from his office by a resolution of the Council of States passed by a majority of all the then members of the Council and agreed to by the House of the People.

102. (b) The Appropriation Bill is intended to give authority to Government to incur expenditure from and out of the Consolidated Fund of India. The procedure for passing this Bill is the same as in the case of other money Bills. An amendment of the Constitution can be initiated only by the introduction of a Bill in either House of Parliament. The procedure of amendment in the constitution is laid down in Part XX (Article 368) of the Constitution of India.

103. (b) Article 65 of the Indian Constitution says that while acting as president or discharging the functions of president, the Vice President does not perform the duties of the office of the chairman of Rajya sabha.
Article 123 of the Constitution grants the President certain law making powers to promulgate Ordinances when either of the two Houses of Parliament is not in session and hence it is not possible to enact laws in the Parliament.

104. (d) The Union executive consists of the President, the Vice-President, and the Council of Ministers with the Prime Minister as the head to aid and advise the President.He may, by writing under his hand addressed to the Vice-President, resign his office (Article 61). According to article 52,executive power of the Union is vested in the President.

105. (c) The Ministry of Parliamentary Affairs handles affairs relating to the Parliament of India and works as a link between the two chambers, the Lok Sabha and the Rajya Sabha. It constitutes consultative committees of members of Parliament and makes arrangements for holding their meetings, both during and between sessions.

106. (d) Committee on Public Accounts and Committee on Public Undertakings consist of 15 members elected by the Lok Sabha and 7 members of the Rajya Sabha. Committee on Estimates consists of 30 members who are elected by the Lok Sabha every year from amongst its members.

107. (b) The Government of India (Allocation of Business) Rules, 1961 are made by the President of India under Article 77 of the Constitution for the allocation of business of the Government of India. The Ministries/Departments of the Government are created by the President on the advice of the Prime Minister under these Rules. The Cabinet Secretary is the ex-officio Chairman of the Civil Services Board of the Republic of India.

108. (a) Correct chronological order of the Vice-Presidents of India is as follows:
1. V.V. Giri – 1967
2. G.S. Pathak –1969
3. B.D. Jatti –1974
4. M. Hidayatullah – 1979

109. (d) The Tenth Schedule (Anti-Defection Act) was included in the Constitution in 1985 by the Rajiv Gandhi ministry and sets the provisions for disqualification of elected members on the grounds of defection to another political party.

110. (b) The deposit made by a candidate shall be returned if the following conditions are satisfied:-
   (i) the candidate is not shown in the list of contesting candidates, that is to say, either his nomination was rejected or after his nomination was accepted, he withdrew his candidature; or
   (ii) he dies before the commencement of the poll; or
   (iii) he is elected; or
   (iv) he is not elected but gets more than 1/6th of the total number of valid votes polled by all the candidates at the election.

111. (c) The total elective membership of the Lok Sabha is distributed among States in such a way that the ratio between the number of seats allotted to each State and population of the State is, as far as practicable, the same for all States. The 84th Amendment to the Constitution (which was numbered as the 91st Amendment Bill before it was passed in Parliament) lifted the freeze on the delimitation of constituencies, as stipulated by the 42nd Constitution amendment of 1976, and allowed delimitation within States on the basis of the 1991 Census.

112. (b) A registered voter in India can contest an election to Lok Sabha from any constituency in India except autonomous Districts of Assam, Lakshadweep and Sikkim. According to Section 8 of Representation of Peoples Act 1951,a person convicted of any offence and sentenced to imprisonment for not less than two years [other than any offence referred to in sub-section (a) or sub-section (b)] shall be disqualified from the date of such conviction and shall continue to be disqualified for a further period of six years since his release.

113. (d) There are three Financial Committees in the Indian Parliament mentioned below:
   1. Estimates Committee- This Committee consists of 30 members who are elected by the Lok Sabha every year from amongst its members. The term of the Committee is one year.
   2. Committee on Public Undertakings- The Committee on Public Undertakings consists of 22 members (15 members from Lok Sabha and 7 members from Rajya Sabha). The term of the Committee is one year.
   3. Public Accounts Committee- This Committee consists of 22 members (15 members from Lok Sabha and 7 members from the Rajya Sabha). The term of the Committee is one year.

114. (d) According to Article 78 it shall be the duty of the Prime Minister-
   (a) to communicate to the President all decisions of the council of Ministers relating to the administration of the affairs of the union and proposals for legislation;
   (b) to furnish such information relating to the administration of the affairs of the Union and proposals for legislation as the President may call for;
   (c) if the President so requires, to submit for the consideration of the Council of Ministers any matter on which a decision has been taken by a Minister;

115. (d) ● Election of Speaker shall be held on such date as the President may fix, and the Secretary-General shall send notice of this dateto every member.
   ● The election of a Deputy Speaker shall be held on such date as the Speaker may fix and the Secretary-General shall send notice of this dateto every member.
   ● At any time before noon on the day preceding the date so fixed, any member may give notice in writing, addressed to the Secretary-General, of a motion that another member be chosen as the Deputy Speaker of the House and the notice shall be seconded by a third member and shall be accompanied by a statement by the member whose name is proposed in the notice that he is willing to serve as Deputy Speaker, if elected.

116. (c) The Vice-President is elected by an Electoral College, which consists of the members of the Lok Sabha and Rajya Sabha (both elected and nominated members).

117. (c) The maximum strength of the House envisaged by the Constitution of India is 552, which is made up by election of up to 530 members to represent the states; up to 20 members to represent the Union Territories and not more than two members of the Anglo-Indian Community to be nominated by the President of India, if, in his/her opinion, that community is not adequately represented in the House.

118. (b) Statement 1 is correct as per provisions under Article 59. Statement 2 is correct as according to Article 79, Parliament shall consist of the President and two Houses.

119. (d) So far three joint sittings have been held, First was held on Dowry Prohibition Bill, 1961, Second was held on Banking Service Commission (Repeal) Bill, 1978 and Third was held on Prevention of Terrorism Bill, 2002. The presiding officer of joint sitting is Speaker of the Lok Sabha.

120. (d) Statement 1 is incorrect as members of RS can become cabinet ministers. Statement 2 is incorrect as Cabinet secretariat is under the direct charge of the PM.

121. (c) It is not the duty of the President of India to cause to be laid report of public Accounts Committee before the Parliament.

122. (a) The PAC is formed every year with a strength of not more than 22 members of which 15 are from Lok Sabha, the lower house of the Parliament, and 7 from Rajya Sabha, the upper house of the Parliament.

The term of office of the members is one year. The Estimates Committee, constituted for the first time in 1950, is a Parliamentary Committee consisting of 30 Members, elected every year by the Lok Sabha from amongst its Members. The Ministry of Parliamentary Affairs renders secretarial assistance to the Cabinet Committee on Parliamentary Affairs, which, inter-alia recommends prorogation of both the Houses of the Parliament, Govt's stand on Private Members' Bills and Resolutions. Option 3 is not correct.

123. (a) Statement 1 is correct as per provisions under Article 249. Statement 2 is incorrect as resolutions approving the proclamation of Emergency are passed by both Houses of Parliament (not only LS).

124. (a) Statement 1 is correct as under Article 360, any Proclamation of Financial Emergency issued shall cease to operate at the expiration of two months, unless before the expiration of that period it has been approved by the resolutions of both Houses of Parliament. If approved by both Houses, then it operates for 6 months.
Statement 2 is incorrect as it is excluding Judges of SC and High Courts; but under the provisions of effects of article 360, Judges of SC and HCs are included.

125. (a) Statement 2 is incorrect as Public Accounts Committee consists of 22 members: 15 from Lok Sabha and 7 from Rajya Sabha.

126. (b) Mohd. Hidayatullah (1979-84); Shankar Dayal Sharma (1987-92)

127. (b) According to Article 70 the Prime Minister shall be appointed by the President and the other Ministers shall be appointed by the President on the advice of the Prime Minister.

128. (b) If the Lok Sabha Speaker wants to resign, the letter of his / her resignation has to be addressed to the Deputy Speaker.

129. (a) Only 3rd and 4th are correct, thus the option (b) is right.

130. (a) Minister/ministers can be removed by issuing no confidence motion in the parliament. All cabinet members are mandated by the constitution to be the member of either house of the parliament of India. Cabinet is headed by the cabinet secretary not by the Head of the State.

131. (c) The Council of Ministers shall be collectively responsible to the parliament; the Prime minister shall communicate to the president about the proposals for legislation but the union. If a President were to dismiss the Council of Ministers on his or her own initiative, it might trigger a constitutional crisis. Thus, in practice, the Council of Ministers cannot be dismissed as long as it commands the support of a majority in the Lok Sabha.

132. (b) The nominated members of the Rajya Sabha have the right to vote in the election of the Vice President so far none from them has been inducted in the Council of Ministers.

133. (b) The value of a MP's vote is calculated by dividing the total value of all MLAs' votes by the number of MPs.
Value of an MP vote =

$$\frac{\text{The sum of vote value of elected members of all the Legislative Assemblies}}{\text{The sum of elected members of both the house of Parliament}}$$

134. (b) Option 2 and 3 are correct. But as to option 1 there are special provisions. The Speaker shall determine the time when a sitting of the House shall be adjourned sine die or to a particular day, or to an hour or part of the same day: provided that the Speaker may, if he thinks fit, call a sitting of the House before the date or time to which it has been adjourned or at any time after the House has been adjourned sine die. It is not the President.

135. (c) The Committee on Public Undertakings examines the reports of the Comptroller & Auditor General on public undertakings.

136. (b) The subject matter of the motion must have a direct or indirect relation to the conduct or default on the part of the Union Government and must precisely pinpoint the failure of the Government of India in the performance of its duties in accordance with the provisions of the Constitution and Law.

137. (d) Collective responsibility of cabinet is a tradition in parliamentary governments in which the prime minister is responsible for appointing the cabinet ministers. It is the Prime Minister who enforces collective responsibility amongst the Ministers through his ultimate power to dismiss a Minister. No person shall be nominated to the cabinet except on the advice of the Prime Minister. In India, a Motion of No Confidence can be introduced only in the Lok Sabha.

138. (c) The Public Accounts Committee (PAC) is a committee of selected members of Parliament, constituted by the Parliament of India, for the auditing of the expenditure of the Government of India. Its chief function is to examine the audit report of Comptroller and Auditor General (CAG) after it is laid in the Parliament.

139. (c) The Deputy Speaker of the Lok Sabha is the vice-presiding officer of the Lok Sabha. He/She is elected from amongst the members. It acquired a more prominent position after 1950. He holds office till either he ceases to be a member of the Lok Sabha or he himself resigns.

140. (c) In recognizing a parliamentary party or group, the speaker shall take into consideration the following principles:
An association of members who propose to form a parliamentary party:
1. Shall have an association of members who have a distinct programme of parliamentary work
2. Shall have an organization both inside and outside the house
3. Shall have at least a strength equal to the quorum fixed to constitute a sitting of the house i.e one tenth of the total number of members of the house.

141. (a) Article 79- There shall be a Parliament for the Union which shall consist of the President and two Houses to be known respectively as the Council of States and the House of the People.
Article 54 - The President shall be elected by the members of an electoral college consisting of the elected members of both Houses of Parliament; and the elected members of the Legislative Assemblies of the States.

142. (b) Article 108 of the Constitution empowers the President to summon a joint session of both houses "for the purpose of deliberating and voting on the Bill". In India,

if a bill has been rejected by any house of the parliament and if more than six months have elapsed, the President may summon a joint session for purpose of passing the bill. If at the joint sitting the Bill is passed with or without amendments with a majority of total number of members of the two Houses present and voting, it shall be deemed to be passed by both the Houses.

143. (a) Clause (3) of Article 77 "Conduct of Business of the Government of India" of the Constitution of India lays down as follows: "The President shall make rules for the more convenient transaction of the business of the Government of India, and for the allocation among Ministers of the said business.

The Constitution of India mentions that, "All executive action of the Government of India shall be expressed to be taken in the name of the President." Therefore, only option (a) is correct.

144. (c) All revenues received by the Government by way of taxes like Income Tax, Central Excise, Customs and other receipts flowing to the Government in connection with the conduct of Government business i.e. Non-Tax Revenues are credited into the Consolidated Fund constituted under Article 266 (1) of the Constitution of India. No amount can be withdrawn from the Fund without authorization from the Parliament.

145. (b) A Money Bill cannot be introduced in Rajya Sabha. Rajya Sabha has no power either to reject or amend a Money Bill. It can only make recommendations on the Money Bill. It has no power to vote on the Demands for Grants.

146. (d) The Executive powers of the Union of India is vested in the President. The Cabinet Secretary (and not the Prime Minister) is the ex-officio head of the Civil Services Board.

147 (b) • prorogation doesn't affect the bills of any other business pending before the house so 1st statement is wrong.
• A bill pending in the Rajya Sabha but not passed by the Lok Sabha does not lapse if the president has notified the holding of a joint sitting before the dissolution of Lok Sabha.

148. (b)   149. (c)   150. (c)

151. (b) President- Upholding the constitution and the law; Judge of the supreme court- Faith and allegiance to the constitution of India; Members of Parliament- Faithful Discharge of Duties; Minister for the Union-Secrecy of Information.

152. (c) Oath or affirmation by the President under article 60; Oath or affirmation by Judge of SC, Members of Parliament, Ministers for the Union comes under Third Schedule of the Constitution.

153. (a)

154. (c) The President of India is the head of the executive of the Union Government and all executive powers are exercised by him/her either directly or through the subordinate officers. President can appoint the important officers in Central Government including the Attorney-General for India. The supreme commander of all the defense services is the President.

155. (c) A joint sitting of parliament is resorted to for resolving the deadlock between two houses of the parliament for passing of only Ordinary Bill and Finance Bill , not for Constitution amendment and Money Bill.

156. (c) The President is elected by the members of an electoral college consisting of the elected members of both the Houses of Parliament and the elected members of the Legislative Assemblies of States and the Union Territories of Delhi and Pondicherry.

157. (b) A person shall be disqualified for being chosen as, and for being, a member of either House of Parliament-(a) if he holds any office of profit under the Government of India or the Government of any State, other than an office declared by Parliament by law not to disqualify its holder; (b) if he is of unsound mind and stands so declared by a competent court; (c) if he is an undischarged insolvent; (d) if he is not a citizen of India or has voluntarily acquired the citizenship of a foreign State, or is under any acknowledgment of allegiance or adherence to a foreign State; (e) if he is so disqualified by or under any law made by Parliament. A person shall be disqualified for being a member of either House of Parliament if he is so disqualified under the Tenth Schedule.

158. (b) MIND IT: you've to find the wrong statements here- they're the right answers.
• when the President's Rule is imposed in a state, the President dismisses the state council of ministers headed by the chief minister. The state governor, on behalf of the President, carries on the state administration with the help of the chief secretary of the state or the advisors appointed by the President. Meaning "2" is definitely the consequence of proclamation. Hence all options involving "2" are wrong. Hence by elimination we are left with answer "B": 1 and 3 only.

159. (d) The Parliament exercises control over the ministers through various devices like question hour, discussions, adjournment motion, no confidence motion, etc. and Supplementary questions can be asked during the question hour. Therefore, all three are correct.

160. (d) Private member's bill as a bill introduced by any member of the parliament who's not a minister. Hence first statement is wrong.
• The Indian Express report in 2016 says only 14 private members bill have been passed since 1952. So statement 2 is also wrong.

161. (d) New NCERT, Std. 11, Introduction to Indian Constitution Chapter 3: Election and Representation, Page 57: India has first past the post system wherein a candidate who wins the election may not (need to) get majority (50% + 1) votes. Statement #1 is wrong. Upto the 10th Lok Sabha, both the Speaker and the Deputy Speaker were usually from the ruling party. Since the 11th Lok Sabha, there has been a consensus that the Speaker comes from the ruling party (or ruling alliance) and the post of Deputy Speaker goes to the main opposition party. Meaning it's an 'informal consensus' among political parties, and not Constitutional provision. Hence, statement 2 is wrong.

JUDICIARY

The Indian Judicial System is one of the oldest legal systems in the world today. Inspite of India adopting the features of a federal system of government, the Constitution has provided for the setting up of a **single integrated system of courts** to administer both Union and State Laws.

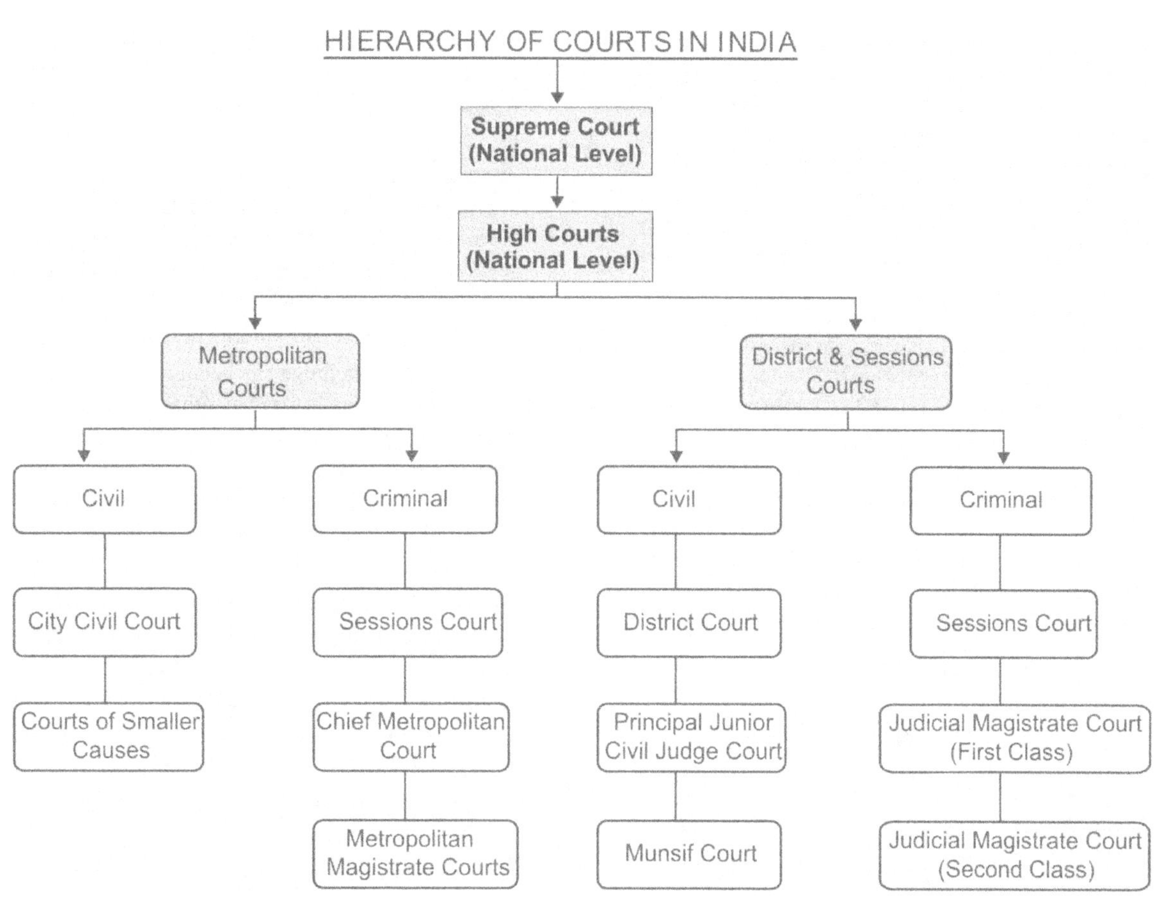

Union Judiciary
Evolution of Judicial System in India :

The concept of Nyaya can be traced back to the religious scriptures like Ramayan, Mahabharat, Smriti and Vedas.

Law cannot be understood properly when divorced from its historical background and spirit of the nation whose law it is.

- Ancient scriptures like Dharmashastra of Manu, Smriti of Narad, Arthashastra by Kautilya gives enough evidence that the coherent judicial system was existing in ancient India.
- Panchayat was the smallest unit of the judicial system in Ancient India.
- The Final Court in the system was the King's court, assisted by the Chief Justice in (Ancient and Medieval times).
- During Mughal period, each community had its own personal law and it was interpreted and administered through its own agents.

British Rule and the Judicial System in India

- Warren Hastings deserves substantial credit for stream lining Judicial system. He implemented judicial plan of 1772.
- The Regulating Act of 1773 created Supreme Court at Calcutta. The judges of the Supreme Court were the lawyers appointed by the Crown.

Supreme Court (Articles 124-147)

- **The Supreme court of India was inaugurated on January 28, 1950.** It succeeded the Federal Court of India, established under the Government of India Act of 1935.
- **Article 124 to 147 in part V of the Constitution** deal with the organisation, independence, jurisdiction, powers, procedures and so on of the Supreme Court. The Parliament is also authorised to regulate them.
- **Supreme Court is the final interpreter and guardian of our Constitution. It is also the guardian of Fundamental rights of the people.**
- It decides the disputes between Centre and States regarding encroachment of power, thus maintains the supremacy of the Constitution.
- It is the **highest court of appeal in India.**
- Originally, the strength of Supreme Court was fixed at Eight (Including one Chief Justice and Seven other Judges. Presently the maximum strength of 31).
- Constitution does not provide for minimum no. of judges who will constitute a bench for hearing cases. Largest bench constituted so far has been of 13 Judges in Keshavanand Bharati vs. Union of India case in 1973.

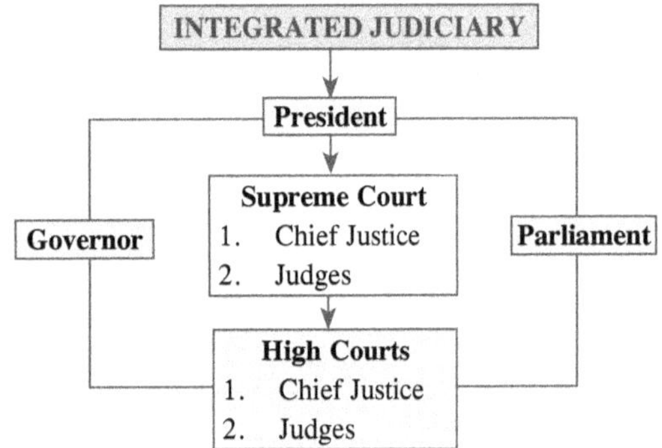

Appointment and Removal of Judges

Qualifications to be appointed as a judge of Supreme Court:

- He must be a citizen of India.
- He must either be a distinguished jurist, or one who has been a High Court judge for at least 5 years or an advocate of a High Court (or 2 or more such courts in succession) for at least 10 years (Article 124).
- No minimum age is fixed for the appointment of a judge.
- **The Chief Justice of India is appointed by the President.** In this matter, the President shall consult such judges of the Supreme Court and the high courts as he may deem necessary. A 9 Judges bench of the SC has laid down that the senior most Judge of Supreme Court should be appointed as Chief Justice of India.
- **In the appointment of other judges, the President shall always consult the Chief Justice of India. He 'may' consult other judges of SC and high courts as he may deem necessary [Article 124(2)].**
- The consultation with the Chief Justice is obligatory in the case of appointment of a judge other than Chief Justice.
- Power of appointment is exercised by the President on the advice of Council of Ministers.
- There is no fixed period of office for Supreme Court judges. Once appointed, they hold office till the age of 65 years. He can quit office earlier by submitting his resignation to the President.
- He can be removed by an order of President only on the grounds of proved misbehavior or incapacity. The order of President in this regard can only be passed after it has been addressed to both houses of parliament in the same session, by special majority (majority of the membership of house and majority of not less than $2/3^{rd}$ of members of that house present and voting). [Article 124 (4)].
- A Supreme Court judge can become Chief Justice of India but cannot practice before any other court or act as a Judge before any other authority. But there is one exception. This is regarding the retired SC judge appointed as a judge of the Supreme Court for a temporary period by the Chief Justice of India with the previous consent of President [Article 128].
- Salaries of Judges are determined by the Parliament by law. These cannot be varied to their disadvantage during their term (except during financial emergency). Their salaries and expenses are charged on the Consolidated Fund of India. Salary of Chief Justice - ₹ 2,80,000/month Salary of Judges - ₹ 2,50,000/month
- **Seat of the Supreme Court is in New Delhi.** However it can be shifted elsewhere in India or more benches of SC can be established in India by Chief Justice of India in consultation with the President.
- According to Article 129, Supreme Court is a **"Court of Record"**. It means:-

Court records are admitted to be of evidentiary value.

It can punish for contempt of the court-

- Contempt is of 2 type: Criminal and Civil.
- Judges can be liable for the contempt of their own court.

Collegium System in India Judiciary

It is the system of appointment and transfer of judges that has evolved through judgements of the supreme court and not by an Act of Parliament or by a provision of the Constitution.

- The Supreme Court Collegium is headed by the Chief Justice of India and comprises four other senior-most judges of the court.
- Judges of the higher judiciary are appointed only through the Collegium System and the government has a role only after names have been decided by the collegium.
- The Collegium System has its genesis in a series of judgment called judges cases. The Collegium came into being through interpretations of pertinent constitutional provisions by the Supreme Court in the judges cases.
- Critics argue that the Collegium System is non-transparent since it does not involve any official mechanism of Secretariat.
- It is seen as a closed-door affair with no prescribed norms regarding eligibility criteria or even the selection procedure.
- The NDA government has tried twice (unsuccessfully) to replace the Collegium System with a National Judicial Appointments Commission (NJAC).

Adhoc and Acting Judges

- Article 127 says that if there is no Quorum of the Supreme Court Judges to hold or continue any session of the court, the Chief Justice of Indian (CJI), with the previous consent of the President and in consultation with the Chief Justice of the High Court concerned, can request in writing a Judge of the High Court, who is qualified to be a Judge of the Supreme Court, to function as an *adhoc* Judge of the Supreme Court.
- While so attending as the Judge of the Supreme Court, he shall have all the Jurisdiction, powers and privileges and shall discharge the duties of a Judge of the Supreme Court.

Appointment of acting Chief Justice

When the office of Chief Justice of India is vacant or when the Chief Justice is by reason of absence or otherwise unable to perform the duties of his office, the duties of the office shall be performed by such one of the other judges of the court as the President may appoint for the purpose.

Jurisdiction of the Supreme Court

- It extends to the cases originating in Supreme Court alone. No other court has power to try such cases.
- Therefore Supreme Court is a federal court. These are between:

(i) GOI on one side and one or more states on the other.

(ii) GOI and one or more States on one side and other states on the other

- However such jurisdiction does not apply to the disputes arising out of a treaty or agreement which is in operation or wherein provided for such exclusion. These matters are:-

(i) Exclusion of Jurisdiction of Supreme Court by Parliament in case of use, distribution or control of water of any inter-state river valley (Article 262).

(ii) Financial matters between Centre and states (Article 280).

(iii) Adjustment of expenses between Centre and states (Article 290).

Attendance of retired Judges at sittings of the Supreme Court

Notwithstanding anything in this chapter the Chief Justice of India may at any time, with the previous consent of the President, request any person who has held the office of a judge of the Supreme Court or High Court to act as a Judge of the Supreme Court and. Every such person so requested shall, while so sitting and acting be entitled to such allowances as the President may by order determine and have all the jurisdiction , power and privileges of, but shall not otherwise be deemed to be a judge of that court.

Appellate Jurisdiction

- Appeal lies with the Supreme Court against the High Courts in the following 4 categories of cases:

  (a) Constitutional matters (civil, criminal or others) – Article 132

  (b) Civil matters (except Constitutional) – Article 133

  (c) Criminal matter (except Constitutional) – Article 134

  (d) Special leave to appeal – Article 136

- Special leave to appeal is issued by Supreme Court in its discretion. It cannot be issued in case of judgment passed by a court or tribunal of armed forces.
- It can be granted in any judgement whether final or interlocutory.
- It may be related to any matter — constitutional, civil, criminal, income-tax, labour, revenue, advocates, etc.
- High Court can certify a case involving substantial question of law as to the interpretation of the Constitution and thus refer it to Supreme Court.

Advisory Jurisdiction

- Article 143 of the Constitution provides that if it appears to the President that:

  1. A question of law or fact has arisen or is likely to arise.

  2. Any dispute arising out of any pre-constitution treaty, agreement, covenant, engagement or other similar instruments is in question.

He may refer such question for the advisory opinion of the Court and the Court may after such hearing as it thinks fit, report to the President its opinion thereon.

- Supreme Court is not bound to give advisory opinion on the matters of political significance and may refuse to do so.
- The Court, however, is bound to give its advisory jurisdiction on the matters relating to disputes arising out of a treaty or agreement entered into before the commencement of the Constitution.
- The advice is not binding on the President and he may accept or reject it.
- Law declared by the Supreme Court is binding on all the courts in India (Article 141). But Supreme Court itself is not bound by its own decisions. Article 137 empowers Supreme Court to review its own judgment.
- Under Article 139A (inserted by 44th amendment Act 1978) Supreme Court may transfer to itself cases from one or more high courts if these involve substantial question of law or that great significance. Supreme Court may transfer cases from one High Court to another in the interest of justice.

Power of Judicial Review

Judicial review is the power of the Supreme Court to examine the constitutionality of legislative enactments and executive orders of both the Central and state governments. On examination, if they are found to be violative of the Constitution (*ultra-vires*), they can be declared as illegal, unconstitutional and invalid (null and void) by the Supreme Court. Consequently, they cannot be enforced by the Government.

Judicial review is needed for the following reasons:

(a) To uphold the principle of the supremacy of the Constitution.
(b) To maintain federal equilibrium (balance between Centre and states).
(c) To protect the fundamental rights of the citizens.

The Supreme Court used the power of judicial review in various cases, as for example, the *Golaknath case (1967), the Bank Nationalisation case (1970), the Privy Purses Abolition case (1971), the Kesavananda Bharati case (1973), the Minerva Mills case* (1980) and so on.

Though the phrase 'Judicial Review' has nowhere been used in the Constitution, the provisions of several articles' explicitly confer the power of judicial review on the Supreme Court. The constitutional validity of a legislative enactment or an executive order can be challenged in the Supreme Court on the following three grounds:

(a) it infringes the Fundamental Rights (Part III),
(b) it is outside the competence of the authority which has framed it, and
(c) it is repugnant to the constitutional provisions.

From the above, it is clear that the scope of judicial review in India is narrower than that of what exists in USA, though the American Constitution does not explicitly mention the concept of judicial review in any of its provisions. This is because, the American Constitution provides for 'due process of law' against that of 'procedure established by law' which is contained in the Indian Constitution. The difference between the two is: 'The due process of law gives wide scope to the Supreme Court to grant protection to the rights of its citizens. It can declare laws violative of these rights void not only on *substantive grounds* of being unlawful, but also on *procedural grounds* of being unreasonable.

Supreme Court, while determining the constitutionality of a law, however examines only the *substantive question i.e.,* whether the law is within the powers of the authority concerned or not. It is not expected go into the question of its reasonableness, suitability or policy implications.'

The exercise of wide power of judicial review by the American Supreme Court in the name of due process of law' clause has made the critics to describe it as a *'third chamber'* of the Legislature, a super-legislature, so on. This American principle of judicial supremacy is also recognised in our constitutional system, but to a limited extent. Nor do we fully follow the British Principle of parliamentary supremacy. There are many limitations on the sovereignty of Parliament in our country, like the written character of the Constitution, the federalism with division of powers, the Fundamental Rights and the judicial review. What exists in India is a synthesis of both that is, the American principle of judicial supremacy and the British principle of parliamentary supremacy.

Other Powers

- Besides the above, the Supreme Court has numerous other powers:
- It decides the disputes regarding the election of the President and the Vice-President. In this regard, it has the original, exclusive and final authority.
- It enquires into the conduct and behaviour of the chairman and members of the Union Public Service Commission. If it finds them guilty of misbehaviour, it can recommend to the President for their removal. The advice tendered by the Supreme Court in this regard is binding on the President.
- It is authorised to withdraw the cases pending before the High Courts and dispose them by itself. It can also transfer a case or appeal pending before one High Court to another High Court.
- The Supreme Court's jurisdiction and powers with respect to matters in the Union List can be enlarged by the Parliament. Further, its jurisdiction and powers with respect to other matters can be enlarged by a special agreement of the Centre and the states.

Due Process of Law Vs. Procedure Established by law: The U.S. Constitution (Constitutional Amendments) provides that a person should not be deprived of his right to liberty and property except according to due process of law. The Indian Constitution, however, lays down that a man may not be deprived of his rights to liberty except according to the procedure established by law. The due process of law gives wide scope to the Supreme Court to grant protection to the rights of its citizens. It can declare laws violative of these rights void not only on substantive grounds of being unlawful, but also on procedural grounds of being unreasonable. Our Supreme Court, while determining the constitutionality of a law, however is expected to examine only the substantive question, i.e, whether the law is within the powers of the authority concerned or not. It is not expected to go into the question of its reasonableness, suitability or policy implications. The Supreme Court pronounces its judgement on a specific case through a specific petition. It does not give its opinion or advice on a general reference. There should be an aggrieved person who petitions the Court to challenge the constitutionality of the statute which has adversely affected his rights. He has to show that he has sustained or is in immediate danger of sustaining some direct injury as a result of the enforcement of the statute, and that the injury complained of is justiciable.

Jurisdiction of Supreme Court

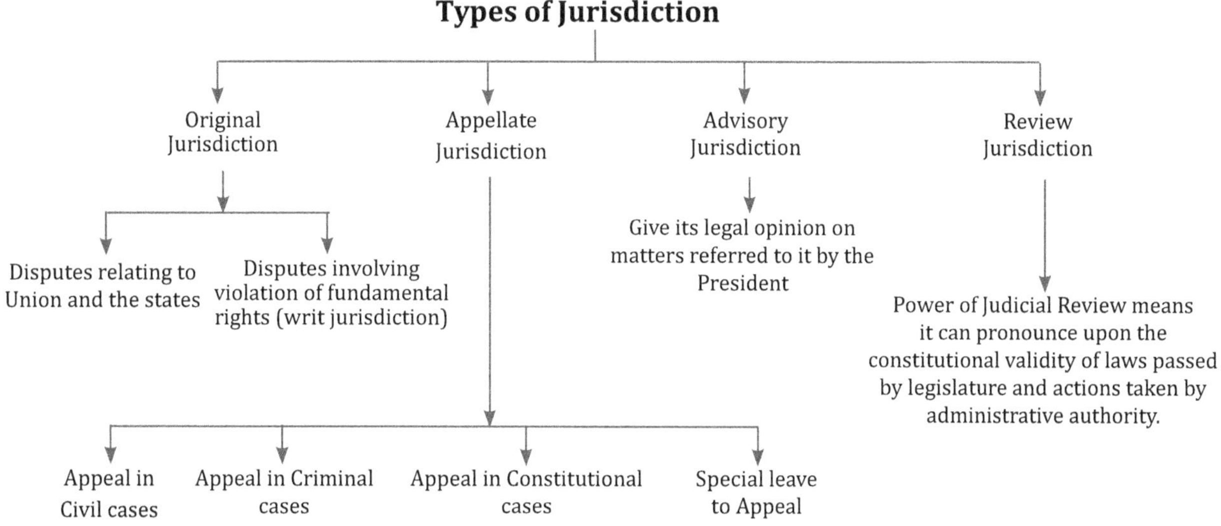

Chief Justice of India (Since, 1951)

S. No.	Name	Took Office	Left Office
1.	HJ Kania	15th Aug, 1947	16th Nov, 1951
2.	MP Sastri	16th Nov, 1951	3rd Jan, 1954
3.	Mehr Chand Mahajan	3rd Jan, 1954	22nd Dec, 1954
4.	BK Mukherjee	22nd Dec, 1954	31st Jan, 1956
5.	Sudhi Ranjan Das	31st Jan, 1956	30th Sep, 1959
6.	Bhuvaneshwar Prasad Sinha	30th Sep, 1959	31st Jan, 1964
7.	PB Gajendragadkar	31st Jan, 1964	15th Mar, 1966
8.	AK Sarkar	16th Mar, 1966	29th June, 1966
9.	K Subba Rao	30th June, 1966	11th April, 1967
10.	Kailash Nath Wanchoo	12th April, 1967	24th Feb, 1968
11.	M Hidayatullah	25th Feb, 1968	16th Dec, 1970
12.	Jayantilal Chhotalal Shah	17th Dec, 1970	21st Jan, 1971
13.	SM Sikri	22nd Jan, 1971	25th April, 1973
14.	AN Ray	25th April, 1973	28th Jan, 1977
15.	Mirza Hameedullah Beg	29th Jan, 1977	21st Feb, 1978
16.	YV Chandrachud	22nd Feb, 1978	11th July, 1985
17.	PN Bhagwati	12th July, 1985	20th Dec, 1986
18.	RS Pathak	21st Dec, 1986	6th June, 1989
19.	ES Venkataramiah	19th June, 1989	17th Dec, 1989
20.	S Mukherjee	18th Dec, 1989	25th Sep, 1990
21.	Ranganath Mishra	25th Sep, 1990	24th Nov, 1991

22.	Kamal Narain Singh	25th Nov, 1991	12th Dec, 1991
23.	MH Kania	13rd Dec, 1991	17th Nov, 1992
24.	Lalit Mohan Sharma	18th Nov, 1992	11th Feb, 1993
25.	MN Venkatachaliah	12th Feb, 1993	24th Oct, 1994
26.	AM Ahmadi	25th Oct, 1994	24th Mar, 1997
27.	JS Verma	25th Mar, 1997	18th Jan, 1998
28.	MM Punchhi	18th Jan, 1998	9th Oct, 1998
29.	AS Anand	10th Oct, 1998	1st Nov, 2001
30.	SP Bharucha	2nd Nov, 2001	6th May, 2002
31.	BN Kirpal	6th May, 2002	11th Nov, 2002
32.	GB Pattanaik	11th Nov, 2002	19th Dec, 2002
33.	VN Khare	19th Dec, 2002	2nd May, 2004
34.	S Rajendra Babu	2nd May, 2004	1st June, 2004
35.	RC Lahoti	1st June, 2004	1st Nov, 2005
36.	YK Sabharwal	1st Nov, 2005	14th Jan, 2007
37.	KG Balakrishnan	14th Jan, 2007	11th May, 2010
38.	SH Kapadia	12th May, 2010	28th Sep, 2012
39.	Altamas Kabir	29th Sep, 2012	18th July, 2013
40.	P Sathasivam	19th July, 2013	26th April, 2014
41.	Rajendra Mal Lodha	27th April, 2014	27th Sep, 2014
42.	HL Dattu	28th Sep, 2014	02nd Dec, 2015
43.	T.S.Thakur	03rd Dec, 2015	4th Jan, 2017
44.	Jagdish Singh Khehar	4th Jan, 2017	27 Aug, 2017
45.	Dipak Mishra	28 Aug, 2017	2nd Oct, 2018
46.	Ranjan Gagoi	3rd Oct, 2018	Present

Public Interest Litigation (PIL)

The Supreme Court in the early 1980s devised a mechanism of PIL.

Through PIL, the judiciary has also shown readiness to take into consideration rights of those sections who cannot easily approach the courts. For this purpose, the judiciary allowed public spirited citizens, social organisations and lawyers to file petitions on behalf of the needy and the deprived. **Justice Krishna Iyer and Justice Bhagwati were champions of the concept of PIL in India.**

In other words, Public-interest Litigation is a legal contest fought judicially, to armor the public interest. It is introduced in a court of law, not by the court itself or by any other private party.

It is not necessary, for the exercise of the court's jurisdiction, that the person who is the victim of the violation of his or her right should personally approach the court.

PIL is essentially a new legal ambit in which court of law can initiate and enforce action to serve and secure significant public interest.

- However the person filling the PIL must prove to the satisfaction of the court that the petition is being filed for a public interest.

Judicial Activism

It means the assertive role played by the judiciary to force other organs of the state namely the Executive and Legislature to discharge their duties properly, as assigned to them by the Constitution. The Judiciary has played an activist role in the recent 2G Scam Case, CVC Case, Jharkhand Legislative Assembly Case, Cancellation of Coal Blocks Case.

Judicial activism means that instead of judicial restraint, the Supreme Court and other lower Courts become activists and compel the authority to act and direct the government to take certain actions.

Judicial activism has arisen mainly due to the failure of the executive and legislature to act at certain instances.

Secondly it has arisen due to the fact that there is a doubt that the legislature and executive have failed to deliver the goods.

Landmark Judgements of the Supreme Court

AK Gopalan Case, 1950

The case corresponds to the charges of violation of Fundamental Rights to freedom under the **Preventive Detention Act**. The court was approached over the validity of the act.

- The Supreme Court held that the constitutional validity of a law cannot be verified by the judiciary and the judiciary has only the capacity to verify whether the procedure according to the law has been followed.

Champakam Dorairajan Case, 1951

- The case challenged the reservations given to backward classes in educational institutions in Tamil Nadu.
- First Amendment Act was inserted as Article 15(4) in the Constitution.

Shankari Prasad Case, 1952

The First Constitutional Amendment Act, providing for reservations, was challenged on grounds that it violated Fundamental Rights. The court held that Parliament has the power to amend the Constitution.

Berubari Case, 1960

While ceding a part of Indian Territory to an alien state, the court in an advisory opinion held that such process cannot take place unless a Constitutional Amendment to that effect is made.

Golaknath Case, 1967

The Supreme Court held that Constitutional Amendment cannot be extended to infringement of Fundamental Rights.

Keshvananda Bharati Case, 1973

The Supreme Court propounded the Basic Structure Doctrine and held that certain basic features of the Constitution cannot be amended while others can be done, so without having a sweeping change in the Constitution.

Minerva Mills Case, 1980

The Supreme Court held that Fundamental Rights and Directive Principles of State Policy are complementary to each other and any law enacted to implement the Directive Principle could not curb the Fundamental Rights.

Shah Bano Case, 1985

The Supreme Court held that Muslim women also have right to get maintenance from their husbands when they are divorced.

Sto Stephen's College Case, 1992

The Supreme Court held that atleast 50% of seats in minority institutions should be reserved for non- minority students.

Indira Sawhney Case, 1993

In this case, the Supreme Court declared that reservation cannot exceed 50% and introduced the *'creamy layer'*.

SR Bommai Case, 1994

The Supreme Court held that Federalism is a part of Basic Structure and State Governments cannot be arbitrarily dismissed by a Governor. The case laid down the guidelines in proving a majority under Article 356.

Chandra Kumar Case, 1997

The Supreme Court upheld that judicial review is a part of basic structure of the Constitution.

TMA Pai Case, 2002

The Supreme Court held that the right to administer minority educational institution is not absolute and the state can regulate the institutional affairs in the interest of educational standards.

2G Spectrum Scam, 2008

The Supreme Court declared allotment of spectrum as 'unconstitutional and arbitrary' and quashed all the 122 licenses issued in 2008 during tenure of A Raja, the main official accused in the 2G scam case.

Black Money, 2012

The government refused to disclose details of about 18 Indians holding accounts in LGT Bank, Liechtenstein evoking a sharp response from a bench comprising Justice B Sudershan Reddy and SS Nijjar. The court ordered the SIT to probe the matter.

Right to Reject, 2013

The Supreme Court directed the Election Commission to introduce a 'None of the Above' (NOTA) button on electronic voting machines and ballot papers which can be used by the voters to reject all the candidates contesting elections in a constituency.

Re-Opening Dance Bars, 2013

Eight years after the Maharashtra Government banned dance bars in Mumbai, the Supreme Court on 16th July gave its go-ahead to their re-opening in the city and elsewhere in the state.

Supreme Court Recognises Transgenders as 'Third Gender, 2014

In a Landmark judgement the Supreme Court recognised the transgender persons as third gender.

IMPORTANT SUPREME COURT JUDGEMENTS IN 2016-17

Date	Judgment	Parties
04-02-2016	SC observed that the request of the information seeker about the information of his answer sheets and details of the interview marks can be and should be provided to him by Public Service Commission under RTI Act but not about examiners.	Kerala Public Service Commission vs. State Information Commission.
18-03-2016	SC Allows Photos of CMs, Governors, and Ministers in Government Advertisements.	Request by Centre, W. Bengal & T. Nadu govts. To Supreme Court.
30-03-2016	SC approved guidelines of Union Government to protect Good Samaritans from police, who help road accident victims.	SC's Committee & Transport Ministry for road safety.
28-04-2016	SC ordered to conduct the National Eligibility Cum Entrance Test (NEET) 2016 in Two Phases, for academic year 2016-17 for admission to MBBS, BDS and like Courses of medical colleges throughout the country.	Sankalp Charitable Trust vs. UoI.
02-05-2016	SC appointed RM Lodha Panel to oversee functions of Medical Council of India.	SC appointed Panel on its own.
11-05-2016	SC ruled that Telecom Regulatory Authority of India TRAI's Penalty on Tel-companies for Call Drops is Illegal.	Cellular Operators Association of India vs. TRAI.
11-05-2016	SC issued landmark guidelines for disaster /drought management. The writ petition was filed by Swaraj Abhiyan.	Swaraj Abhiyan vs. UoI.
12-05-2016	SC asked the SpiceJet Ltd to pay Rupees Ten Lakhs to Jeeja Ghosh, an eminent activist involved in disability rights, for forcibly de-boarding her by the flight crew, because of her disability.	Jeeja Ghosh vs. UoI.
30-06-2016	SC directed the Union Government and State Governments to treat only transgender & not Lesbians, Gays and Bisexuals as socially and educationally backward classes and provide them quotas in admission to educational institutions and public appointments.	Transgender vs. Govt.

08-07-2016	**SC** ruled that security forces cannot use excessive and retaliatory force in disturbed areas under the Armed Forces (Special Powers) Act (AFSPA), 1958.	Verdict on PIL filed by Extra Judicial Execution Victim Families Association.
18-07-2016	**SC** accepted recommendations of the Lodha Committee on reforms to the BCCI, including a bar on ministers and civil servants and those above 70 from becoming its members.	BCCI vs. Lodha Committee Recommendations.
19-07-2016	**SC** can transfer cases from Jammu & Kashmir Courts to courts outside it and vice versa.	Anita Kushwaha vs. Pushpa Sudan.
01-08-2016	**SC** held that former Chief Ministers are not entitled for government accommodation for lifetime.	Lok Prahari vs. State of Uttar Pradesh.
09-08-2016	**SC** ruled that persons in Govt/judicial service need not resign to participate in District Judge Selection Process. SC held that Article 233(2) of the Constitution of India only prohibits the appointment of a person as District Judge, who is already in the service of the Union or the State, but not the selection of such a person.	Vijay Kumar Mishra and Anr vs. Patna High Court.
22-08-2016	**SC** held that all Tribunals are not necessary parties to the proceedings where legality of its orders challenged.	S. Kazi vs. Muslim education society.
05-09-2016	**SC** ordered Karnataka to release 15000 cusecs of water to Tamil Nadu, Later on a plea by state of Karnataka; it was modified to 12000 cusecs.	State of Karnataka vs. State of Tamil Nadu.
07-09-2016	**SC** directed Union & state govts. To upload FIRs in Police Websites.	Youth Bar Association of India vs. Union of India.
19-09-2016	**SC** in case of Tattu Lodhi, (child rapist and murderer) in an "judicial innovation", stripped Lodhi of his right to apply for release from prison on remission for the next 25 years.	Child's Parent vs. Tattu Lodhi.
28-09-2016	**SC** observed that providing social security to the legal profession becomes an essential part of any legal system which has to be effective, efficient and robust to enable it to provide necessary service to the consumers of justice.	Cardamom Marketing Corporation & Anr. vs. State of Kerala & Ors.
06-10-2016	**SC** held that persistent effort of the wife to constrain her husband to be separated from the family constitutes an act of 'cruelty' to grant divorce.	Narendra vs. K.Meena.
07-10-2016	**SC** stayed the commercial release of Genetically Modified (GM) mustard crop till October 17, 2016.	On petition filed by Aruna Rodrigues vs. Govt. of India.
10-10-2016	**SC** widened the scope of the Domestic Violence Act by ordering deletion of the words "adult male" from it, paving the way for prosecution of women and even non-adults for subjecting a woman relative to violence and harassment.	Hiral P Harsora and ors vs. Kusum Narottamdas Harsora.
21-10-2016	**SC** Freezes BCCI's Transactions with State Cricket Bodies.	BCCI vs. Lodha Committee.
11-11-2016	**SC** upheld the constitutional validity of Entry Tax imposed by States on goods coming in from other states.	Jindal Stainless Ltd. vs. State of Haryana.
30-11-2016	**SC** ordered all cinema halls across India to play the National Anthem before the screening of films.	Shyam Narayan Chouksey vs Union of India.
03-12-2016	**SC** ruled that horse racing per se is not animal cruelty. It held that it is different from Jallikattu, which metes out specific methods of torture to bulls.	Animal Welfare Board of India vs A. Nagaraja & Ors
15-12-2016	• **SC** set aside a Rajasthan High Court order which had directed the Union Government to exempt judges of the high court from pre-embarkation security checks, i.e. High Court judges not exempted from airport frisking.	• Union of India vs. Rajasthan High Court and Ors.
	• **SC** passed an order to ban all liquor shops on national as well as state highways across the country as a measure to control the road mishaps. • **SC** ruled that the Indian Air Force (IAF) personnel cannot sport a beard on religious grounds. • **SC** refused to quash the March 2015 resolution by both houses of Parliament against Justice Markandey Katju for describing Gandhi as a British agent and Netaji as a Japanese agent in a blog.	• State of Tamil Nadu vs. K. Balu • Mohammed Zubair and Ansari Aaftab Ahmed vs. IAF authorities. • Justice Markandey Katju vs. the Lok Sabha.

Date	Judgment	Case
16-12-2016	• **SC** held that Jammu and Kashmir has "no vestige" of sovereignty outside the Indian Constitution and its own, while the citizens of the state are "first and foremost" citizens of India. • **SC** has referred constitutional validity of demonetization to a constitutional bench.	• State Bank of India vs. Santosh Gupta & Anr. Etc. • A batch of cases vs. GoI.
02-01-2017	• **SC** ruled out that no politician can seek votes in the name of caste, language, region or religion & it will be a corrupt practice and not permissible. • **SC** sacked Anurag Thakur, President, BCCI and Secretary Ajay Shirke from their posts. • A seven-judge Constitution Bench of the Supreme Court has held that re-promulgation of ordinances is a fraud on the Constitution and a subversion of democratic legislative processes. So, placing of Ordinance before Legislature is mandatory. • A High Court cannot initiate contempt proceedings or punishment for contempt of the Supreme Court. A Bench headed by Chief Justice of India TS Thakur set aside an order of division bench of Delhi High Court, which found editors and cartoonists of Mid-Day newspaper guilty of contempt for maligning the former Chief Justice of India.	• Abhiram Singh vs. C.D. Commachen. • BCCI vs. Lodha Panel • Krishna Kumar Singh vs. State of Bihar. • Vitusah Oberoi vs. Court of Its Own Motion.
04-02-2017	**SC** declined to interfere in a Public Interest Litigation (PIL) for regulation of private coaching institutes.	The Student Federation of India (SFI) vs. Union of India & ors.
01-03-2017	**SC** directed all universities to verify certificates of law degree holders without charging a fee.	Ajayinder Sangwan vs. Bar Council of India & ors.
03-03-2017	**SC** notice to Centre, CBSE on plea to include urdu un NEET.	Through its Secretary & ors vs. Union of India.
07-03-2017	**SC** Tells High Courts not to keep review petetions pending for long.	Sasi (D) Through Lrs. vs. Aravindakshan Nari and Others.
08-03-2017	**SC** declared trust can't file complaint before consumer forum.	Pratibha Pratisthan vs. Manager, Canara Bank.
10-03-2017	**SC** ruled central PF authorities have no authority over 'exempted' establishments.	Yeshwant Gramin Shikshan Sanstha vs. Assistant Provident Fund Commissioner.
31-03-2017	**SC** ban sale of Bharat Stage III (BS III) vehicles from April 1, 2017	M.C. Mehta vs. Union of Indian & ORS.
31-03-2017	NEET 2017 Supreme Court verdict: Students aged above 25 years can now appear for exam	Rai Sabiasachi and ANR vs. Union of India and ORS.

Decriminalisation of Section 377

- In a landmark judgment, the Supreme Court on 6 September 2018 decriminalised homosexuality. The five-judge SC bench's decision to make gay sex legal has restored the LGBTIQ community members' faith in the Indian judicial system. While many take a sigh of relief that "they would not be seen as a criminal", Shashi Tharoor feels we all should "savour this victory".
- The Supreme Court decriminalised homosexuality between consenting adults by declaring Section 377, the penal provision which criminalised gay sex, as "manifestly arbitrary".

Reservation in Promotion for SC/ST Government Employees

- The Supreme Court turned down an appeal to reconsider its own earlier order that had rejected the idea of reservations for Scheduled Castes (SCs) or Scheduled Tribes (STs) in government job promotions on September 26.

Validity of Aadhaar

- The Supreme Court upheld the validity of Aadhaar on September 26, 2018 and struck down Section 57 of Aadhaar Act. It said, private companies cannot ask for Aadhaar. It won't be mandatory for opening of bank accounts, mobile connections.

Ram Janmabhoomi-Babri Masjid

- The Supreme Court turned down two pleas in the Ayodhya case on September 27, 2018. One that directly deals with the way the disputed land was split according to the 2010 Allahabad High Court ruling, and another that would have had a direct impact on the Supreme Court's final verdict in the case.

Adultery

- In a historic judgement, the Supreme Court quashed adultery as a criminal offence in India. The court underlined that Section 497 treats women as properties of their husbands and is hence manifestly discriminatory. It trashed the central government's defence of Section 497 that it protects the sanctity of marriages.

Sabarimala Verdict

- The Supreme Court lifted centuries' old prohibition of women between ages 10 and 50 from entering Sabarimala temple in Kerala on Friday. "The practice in Sabarimala temple violates the rights of Hindu women. It has to be in harmony with the Constitution" said Chief Justice of India Dipak Mishra.

Live Streaming of Court Hearing

- The Supreme Court on Wednesday decided to bring its courtroom proceedings under public glare by agreeing to live-streaming of court functioning, paving the way for people to watch the courtroom drama live as it unfolds on September 26, 2018.

Politicians with Criminal Antecedents

- In its unanimous verdict, a five-judge bench led by Chief Justice Mishra on Tuesday left it to Parliament to bar lawmakers facing trial for heinous and grievous offences from contesting elections by enacting a "strong law", while it observed that the criminalisation of politics is a bitter manifest truth and a "termite" to the citadel of democracy. Refusing to put a ban on candidates with criminal antecedents from entering the poll fray, the court said the law should also make it mandatory for political parties to revoke the membership of candidates facing serious criminal cases.

Triple Talaq

- The Supreme Court on August 22, 2017 banned a controversial Islamic practice of instant divorce as arbitrary and unconstitutional, in a landmark verdict for gender justice that will stop Muslim men calling off a marriage on a whim. The top court said Triple Talaq violates the fundamental rights of Muslim women as it irrevocably ends marriage without any chance of reconciliation.

State Judiciary High Court

- *Article 214* provides that there shall be a High Court for each state. However under Article 231 (1) Parliament can establish by law, a common High Court for two or more States or for two or more States and a UT. **There are 24 High Courts in India.** Out of them three are common High Courts.
- Calcutta High Court Madras High Court Bombay High Court and Allahabad High Court are the oldest four High Courts in India Among the four, the Calcutta High Court is the oldest, established on 2nd July 1862.
- Parliament may by law constitute a High Court for UT or declare any court in any such UT to be a High Court (Article 241).

- *Guwahati High Court* is the largest High Court in India; its territorial jurisdiction extends to seven states of the North East.
- Kolkata High Court has territorial jurisdiction over Andaman and Nicobar.
- Delhi has a separate high court but the other UTs come under the jurisdiction of various High Courts.

Appointment of Judges of High Court

- **Article 217 provides that every judge of a high court shall be appointed by the President.**
- President appoints Chief Justice of High Court after consultation with Chief Justice of India and the Governor of the state concerned. In case of appointment of others judges of the High Court he may consult the Chief Justice of High Court concerned.
- The strength of the judges of the High Courts is not the same.
- In Presidential Reference Case (popularly known as Appointment and Transfer of Judges Case), Supreme Court held that the Chief Justice of India should consult "a collegium of two senior most judges of the Supreme Court" for the appointment of a judge of Supreme Court or High Court.
- Further in case of transfer of High Court judges, in addition to the collegium of 4 judges of Supreme Court, the Chief Justice of India is required to consult Chief Justice of both the High Courts (one from where the judge is being transferred and the other, receiving him).
- Article 222 empowers the President (after consultation with Chief Justice of India) to transfer a judge from one High Court to another High Court.

Qualifications of a Judge of High Court

1. He must be a Citizen of India,
2. Have held a judicial office for at least 10 years or
3. Have been an advocate of one High Court or two or more High Courts in succession for at least 10 years.

Term of HC Judges

- Until he attains the age of 62 years.
- He may resign by writing to the President.
- He may be removed by the President on the grounds of proved misbehavior or incapacity on an address by both houses of parliament supported by the vote of 2/3rd of members present and voting in each house.
- Thus a judge of the HC can be removed in the same way as a judge of SC.

Emoluments

- Besides other facilities, Chief Justice and other Judges of High Court get a salary of ₹ 2.5 lakhs and ₹ 2,25,000 per month, respectively.
- The salaries and allowances of the judges of HC are charged on the Consolidated Fund of the State. These cannot be varied by the parliament to their disadvantage after their

appointment (except under financial emergency). The pensions of the judges are charged on the Consolidated Fund of India.

- After retirement, a permanent judge of HC cannot plead or act in a court of India except SC or HC other than the one in which he has held office.

Jurisdiction of high court

Original Jurisdiction

It means the power of a High Court to hear disputes in the first instance, not by way of appeal. It extends to the following:

(a) Matters of admirality, will, marriage, divorce, company laws and contempt of court.

(b) Disputes relating to the election of members of Parliament and state legislatures.

(c) Regarding revenue matter or an act ordered or done in revenue collection.

(d) Enforcement of fundamental rights of citizens.

(e) Cases ordered to be transferred from a subordinate court involving the interpretation of the Constitution to its own file.

(f) The four high courts (i.e., Calcutta, Bombay, Madras and Delhi High Courts) have original civil jurisdiction in cases of higher value.

Writ Jurisdiction

Article 226 of the Constitution empowers High Court to issue writs including *habeas corpus. mandamus, certiorari, prohibition* and *quo-warranto* for enforcement of the fundamental rights of the citizens and for any other purpose. The phrase 'for other purpose' refers to the enforcement of an ordinary legal right. The High Court can issue writs to any person, authority and government not only within its territorial jurisdiction but also outside its territorial jurisdiction if the cause of action arises within its territorial jurisdiction.

The writ jurisdiction of the High Court (under Article 226) is not exclusive but concurrent with the writ jurisdiction of the Supreme Court (under Article 32). It means, when the fundamental rights of a citizen are violated, the aggrieved party has the option of moving either the High Court or the Supreme Court directly. However, the writ jurisdiction of the High Court is wider than that of the Supreme Court. This is because, the Supreme Court can issue writs only for the enforcement of fundamental rights and not for any other purpose, that is, it does not extend to a case where the breach of an ordinary legal right is alleged."

Appellate Jurisdiction

A high court is primarily a court of appeal. It hears appeals against the judgements of subordinate courts functioning in its territorial jurisdiction. It has appellate jurisdiction in both civil and criminal matters. Hence, the appellate jurisdiction of a High Court is wider than its original jurisdiction.

- On the civil side, an appeal to the High Court is either a first appeal or a second appeal.

- The criminal appellate jurisdiction of the High Court includes appeals from the decisions of :
  (i) A Sessions Judge or an Additional Sessions Judge.
  (ii) An Assistant Sessions Judge.

Supervisory Jurisdiction

A high court has the power of superintendence over 'all courts and tribunals functioning in its territorial jurisdiction (except military courts or tribunals). Thus, it may—

(a) call for returns from them;

(b) make and issue, general rules and prescribe forms for regulating the practice and proceedings of them;

(c) prescribe forms in which books, entries and accounts are to be kept by them; and

(d) settle the fees payable to the sheriff, clerks, officers and legal practitioners of them.

This power of superintendence of a High Court is very broad because,

(i) it extends to all courts and tribunals whether they are subject to the appellate jurisdiction of the High Court or not;

(ii) it covers not only administrative superintendence but also judicial superintendence;

(iii) it is a revisional jurisdiction and

it can be *suo-motu* (on its own) and not necessarily on the application of a party.

However, this power does not vest the High Court with any unlimited authority over the subordinate courts and tribunals. It is an extraordinary power and hence has to be used most sparingly and only in appropriate cases. Usually, it is limited to,

(i) excess of jurisdiction,

(ii) gross violation of natural justice

(iii) error of law,

(iv) disregard to the law of superior courts,

(v) perverse findings, and

(vi) manitest injustice.

Control over Subordinate Courts

In addition to its appellate jurisdiction and supervisory jurisdiction over the subordinate courts as mentioned above, a High Court has an administrative control and other powers over them. These include the following:

(a) It is consulted by the Governor in the matters appointment, posting and promotion of district judges and in the appointments of persons in the judicial service of the state (other district judges).

(b) It deals with the matters of posting, promotion grant of leave, transfers and discipline of members of the judicial service of the state (other than district judges).

(c) It can withdraw a case pending in a subordinate court if it involves a substantial question of law that require the interpretation of Constitution. It can then either dispose of case itself or determine the question of law and return the case to the subordinate court with its judgement.

(d) Its law is binding on all subordinate courts functioning within its territorial jurisdiction in same sense as the law declared by the Supreme Court is binding on all courts in India.

Power of Judicial Review

Judicial review is the power of a High Court to examine the constitutionality of legislative enactments and executive orders of both the Central and state governments. On examination, if they are found to be violative of the Constitution (ultra-vires), they can be declared as illegal, unconstitutional and invalid (null and void) by the High Court.

Though the phrase 'judicial review' has no where been used in the Constitution, the provisions of **Articles 13 and 226** explicitly confer the power of judicial review on a High Court. The constitutional validity of a legislative enactment or an executive order can be challenged in a High Court on the following three grounds:

(a) It infringes the fundamental rights (Part III),

(b) It is outside the competence of the authority which has framed it, and

(c) It is repugant to the constitutional provisions.

The 42nd Amendment Act of 1976 curtailed the judicial review power of High Court. It debarred the High Courts from considering the constitutional validity of any central law. However, the 43rd Amendment Act of 1977 restored the original position.

Territorial Jurisdiction of a High Court : Except where Parliament establishes a Common High Court for two or more states or extends the jurisdiction of a High Court to a Union Territory, the jurisdiction of the High Court of a State is co-terminous with the territorial limits of that State.

Parliament has extended the jurisdiction of some of the High Courts to their adjoining Union Territories by enacting the States Re-organisation Act, 1956.

Jurisdiction of High Court

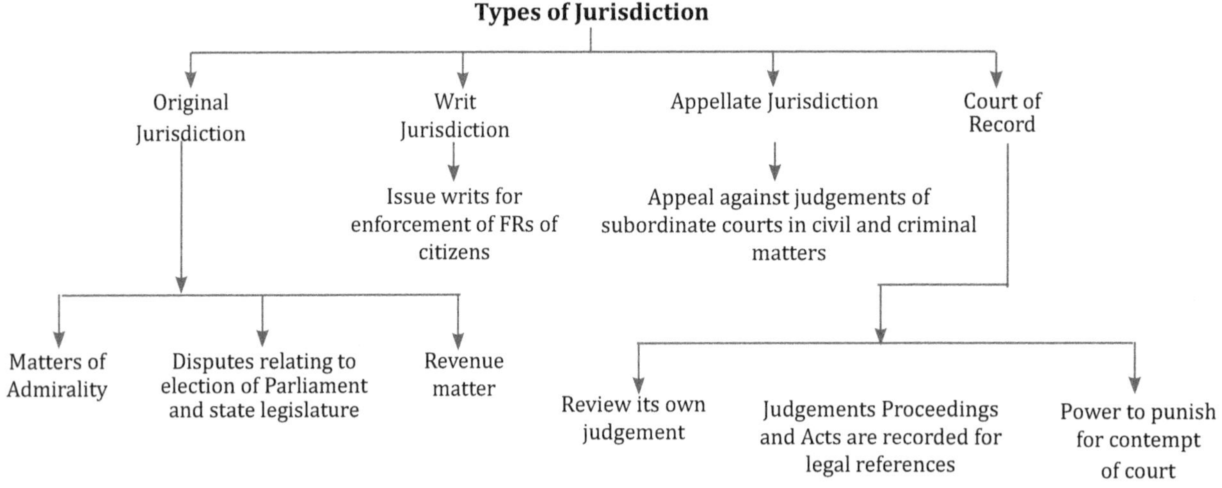

Comparison between Supreme Court and High Court

Supreme Court	High Court
1. This is the union court and the apex institution of the united court system.	1. The High Court is constituted in every State for a group of states.
2. All the Judges of the Supreme Court, retire on attaining the age of 65 years.	2. The Judge of the High Court retires after attaining the age of 62 years.
3. The Judges of the Supreme Court cannot do their practice after retirement. These are also restricted during their tenure.	3. The Judge of the High Court cannot do his legal practice during his tenure but we can do this after his tenure in any High Court or Supreme Court. He cannot do his legal practices in courts below High Court.
4. The Judges of the Supreme Court cannot be transferred and cannot be promoted.	4. The Judges of the High Courts are transferrable to the other high courts. They can be promoted upto Judge of the Supreme Court.
5. The Supreme Court is not bounded to obey the decisions of the High Courts or any other courts.	5. The High Courts are bounded to obey the decision of Supreme Court.
6. The Supreme Court only has the power to take decisions regarding constitutions.	6. The High Court has no power to take decisions regarding constitution.
7. The Chief Justice of the Supreme Court draws a salary of 2.8 lakhs Rupees per month while other Judges draw ₹ 2.5 lakhs per month.	7. The chief Justice of High Court draws a salary of ₹ 2.5 lakhs while other Judges draw ₹ 2,25,000 p.m.
8. The cases involving the interpretation of the Constitution are decided only by the Supreme Court.	8. The cases involving the interpretation of the Constitution are not decided by the High Court.
9. The Supreme Court can issue writs only for the enforcement of fundamental Rights.	9. High Court can issue writs not only for the enforcement of fundamental Rights but also for any other purpose.
10. A remedy under Article 32 in in Itself a Fundamental Right and hence, the Supreme Court may not refuse to exercise its writ jurisdiction.	10. A remedy under Article 226 is discretionary and hence, a High Court may refuse to exercise its writ jurisdiction.

The High Courts: Seats and Jurisdiction

The Calcutta High Court is the oldest High Court in the country, established on 2 July 1862. High Courts that handle a large number of cases of a particular region have permanent benches established there. Benches are also present in states which come under the jurisdiction of a court outside its territorial limits. Smaller states with few cases may have circuit benches established. Circuit benches (known as circuit courts in some parts of the world) are temporary courts which hold proceedings for a few selected months in a year. Thus cases built up during this interim period are judged when the circuit court is in session.

The Madras High Court in Chennai, Bombay High Court in Mumbai, Calcutta High Court in Kolkata and Allahabad High Court in Allahabad are the oldest four High Courts in India.

The following are the 24 High Courts of India sorted by name, year established, Act by which it was established, jurisdiction, headquarters, benches, the maximum number of judges sanctioned and the presiding Chief Justice of the High Court

Court name	Established	Act established	Jurisdiction	Seat	Benches
Allahabad High Court	11 June 1866	Indian High Courts Act 1861	Uttar Pradesh	Allahabad	Lucknow
Bombay High Court	14 August 1862	Indian High Courts Act 1861	Maharashtra, Goa, Dadra and Nagar Haveli, Daman and Diu	Mumbai	Aurangabad, Nagpur, Panaji
Calcutta High Court	2 July 1862	Indian High Courts Act 1861	West Bengal, Andaman and Nicobar Islands	Kolkata	Port Blair
Chhattisgarh High Court	1 November 2000	Madhya Pradesh Reorganisation Act, 2000	Chhattisgarh	Bilaspur	
Delhi High Court	31 October 1966	Delhi High Court Act, 1966	National Capital Territory of Delhi	New Delhi	
Gauhati High Court	1 March 1948	Government of India Act, 1935	Arunachal Pradesh, Assam, Nagaland, Mizoram	Guwahati	Aizwal, Itanagar, Kohima

Gujarat High Court	1 May 1960	Bombay Reorgansisation Act, 1960	Gujarat	Ahmedabad	
High Court of Judicature at Hyderabad	5 July 1954	Andhra State Act, 1953	Andhra Pradesh Telangana	Hyderabad	
Himachal Pradesh High Court	1971	State of Himachal Pradesh Act, 1970	Himachal Pradesh	Shimla	
Jammu and Kashmir High Court	28 August 1943	Letters Patent issued by then Maharaja of Kashmir	Jammu and Kashmir	Srinagar/ Jammu[6]	
Jharkhand High Court	15 November 2000	Bihar Reorganisation Act, 2000	Jharkhand	Ranchi	
Karnataka High Court	1884	Mysore High Court Act, 1884	Karnataka	Bengaluru	Dharwad, Gulbarga
Kerala High Court	1956	States Reorganisation Act, 1956	Kerala, Lakshadweep	Kochi	
Madhya Pradesh High Court	2 January 1936	Government of India Act, 1935	Madhya Pradesh	Jabalpur	Gwalior, Indore
Madras High Court	15 August 1862	Indian High Courts Act 1861	Tamil Nadu, Puducherry	Chennai	Madurai
Manipur High Court	25 March 2013	North-Eastern Areas (Reorganisation) and Other Related Laws (Amendment) Act, 2012	Manipur	Imphal	
Meghalaya High Court	25 March 2013	North-Eastern Areas (Reorganisation) and Other Related Laws (Amendment) Act, 2012	Meghalaya	Shillong	
Orissa High Court	3 April 1948	Orissa High Court Order, 1948	Odisha	Cuttack	
Patna High Court	2 September 1916	Government of India Act, 1915	Bihar	Patna	
Punjab and Haryana High Court	21 March 1919	High Court (Punjab) Order, 1947	Punjab, Haryana, Chandigarh	Chandigarh	
Rajasthan High Court	21 June 1949	Rajasthan High Court Ordinance, 1949	Rajasthan	Jodhpur	Jaipur
Sikkim High Court	16 May 1975	The 36th Amendment to the Indian Constitution	Sikkim	Gangtok	
Tripura High Court	26 March 2013	North-Eastern Areas (Reorganisation) and Other Related Laws (Amendment) Act, 2012	Tripura	Agartala	
Uttarakhand High Court	9 November 2000	Uttar Pradesh Reorganisation Act, 2000	Uttarakhand	Nainital	

H. Court by State/ U. Territory	Court	Principal Seat/(Bench having jurisdiction of the State)
Andaman and Nicobar Islands	Calcutta High Court	Kolkata (Bench at Port Blair)
Arunachal Pradesh	Gauhati High Court	Guwahati (Bench at Itanagar)
Andhra Pradesh	High Court of Judicature at Hyderabad	Hyderabad
Assam	Gauhati High Court	Guwahati
Bihar	Patna High Court	Patna
Chhattisgarh	Chhattisgarh High Court	Bilaspur
Chandigarh	Punjab and Haryana High Court	Chandigarh
Dadra and Nagar Haveli	Bombay High Court	Mumbai
Daman and Diu	Bombay High Court	Mumbai
National Capital Territory of Delhi	Delhi High Court	New Delhi

Goa	Bombay High Court	Mumbai (Bench at Panaji)
Gujarat	Gujarat High Court	Ahmedabad
Haryana	Punjab and Haryana High Court	Chandigarh
Himachal Pradesh	Himachal Pradesh High Court	Shimla
Jammu and Kashmir	Jammu and Kashmir High Court	Srinagar/Jammu
Jharkhand	Jharkhand High Court	Ranchi
Karnataka	Karnataka High Court	Bengaluru (Bench at Dharwad and Gulbarga)
Kerala	Kerala High Court	Kochi
Lakshadweep	Kerala High Court	Kochi
Madhya Pradesh	Madhya Pradesh High Court	Jabalpur (Bench at Gwalior and Indore)
Maharashtra	Bombay High Court	Mumbai (Bench at Aurangabad and Nagpur)
Manipur	Manipur High Court	Imphal
Meghalaya	Meghalaya High Court	Shillong
Mizoram	Gauhati High Court	Guwahati (Bench at Aizawl)
Nagaland	Gauhati High Court	Guwahati (Bench at Kohima)
Odisha	Orissa High Court	Cuttack
Puducherry	Madras High Court	Chennai
Punjab	Punjab and Haryana High Court	Chandigarh
Rajasthan	Rajasthan High Court	Jodhpur (Bench at Jaipur)
Sikkim	Sikkim High Court	Gangtok
Tamil Nadu	Madras High Court	Chennai (Bench at Madurai)
Telangana	High Court of Judicature at Hyderabad	Hyderabad
Tripura	Tripura High Court	Agartala
Uttarakhand	Uttarakhand High Court	Nainital
Uttar Pradesh	Allahabad High Court	Allahabad (Bench at Lucknow)
West Bengal	Calcutta High Court	Kolkata

Courts under High Court

- District Courts of India
- District Munsiff Court
- Courts of Judicial Magistrate of First Class
- Courts of Judicial Magistrate of Second Class

Subordinate Courts (part VI, Articles 233 to 237)

Under the High Court there are three types of courts in the districts. They are the *Civil Courts*, the *Criminal Courts* and the *Revenue Courts*. The highest Civil Court in a district is that of the district judge. They have the power to try civil cases and to hear appeals. The less important cases are decided by sub-judges and munsifs. The highest District Court to try criminal cases is that of the *Sessions Judge*. The criminal cases are heard by the Magistrates too. The district judge also acts as the Sessions Judge in a district. Appeal cases against the lower courts are heard by the District Courts and appeals against the decisions taken by the District Court can be made to the State High Court.

Appointment of District Judges

The appointment, posting and promotion of a District Judge is done under the Governor of the State in consultation with the High Court. The necessary qualifications for a person to be appointed as a District Judge are as follows:

- Article 233 strictly says that a person to be appointed as District Judge must not be in the service of the Central or the State Government.
- He should have been an advocate or a pleader for 7 years.
- He should be recommended by the High Court for appointment as a District Judge.

Other Local Courts

In addition to the three type of courts mentioned above, there are the *Panchayati Adalats* or *Nyaya Panchayats* which are also under the District Judge in some states. Four or Five Gram Sabha have one such Panchayati Court. They are established to try small cases of all kinds. Under this system the cases can be decided fast and need not in value much expenditure.

The Nyaya Panchayats function in ruler areas a similar concept introduced in some urban area this is called the '*Lok Adalat*'

National Legal Services Authority

In 1987 the Legal Services Authorities Act (LSAA) was enacted by the parliament, which came into force on November 9, 1995 to establish a nationwide uniform network for providing free and Competent Legal Services to the weaker section of the society on the basis of equal opportunity. **The National Legal Service Authority (NALSA) has been constituted under the Legal Services Authority Act 1987 to monitor and evaluate implementation of legal aid programmes and lay down policies and principles for making legal services available under the Act.**

In every state, a State Legal Services Authority and in every High Court a High Court legal services committee has been constituted. District legal services authorities and Taluka Legal Service Committees have been constituted in the district and most of the Talukas in order to give effect to the policies and directions of the NALSA and to provide free legal services to the people and conduct Lok Adalat in the states.

NALSA issues guidelines for the State Legal Services Authorities to implement, the legal aid programmes and schemes through out the country. Primarily, the state legal services authorities, district legal service authority, Taluka Legal service committee, etc. have been assigned the task of discharging the following two main functions on regular basis:

(i)   To provide free legal services to the eligible persons; and

(ii) To organise Lok Adalats for amicable settlement of disputes.

Mobile Courts

Mobile Court means a court set-up in a vehicle, which can move from one place to another, according to a well-prepared plan and schedule. Mobile Courts will be of great relief to the rural people. It would create greater awareness about the judicial system among rural masses, cut costs for them and render justice at their doorstep. These courts should see to that hearings are not unnecessarily postponed.

The Mobile Court is equipped to receive complaints, civil and criminal applications, grant bail and remand accused to custody, issue summons, receive police reports, record evidence, pronounce and execute decrees and judgements, pass sentences and can send convicts to prison. It also delivers certified copies of its orders and judgements. **The Country's first mobile court was launched at Mewat district in Haryana.**

Lok Adalat

It is a system of alternative dispute resolution developed in India. It roughly means People's court. They are governed by Legal Services Authorities Act of 1987. **The Award of the Lok Adalat is binding upon all the parties.** Lok Adalats are given certain powers of the Civil Courts. The Lok Adalats have wide jurisdiction that means any matter falling within the jurisdiction of Civil, Criminal, Revenue Courts or Tribunals are dealt by them.

Lok Adalat accepts the cases which could be settled by conciliation and in which, compromise was pending in the Regular Courts within their jurisdiction. The Lok Adalat is presided over by a sitting or Retired Judicial Officer or an other person of respect and legal knowledge as the Chairman, with two other members, usually a lawyer and a social worker.

The first Lok Adalat was held on March 14, 1982 at Junagarh in Gujarat.

Alternative Dispute Resolution (ADR)

It encompasses arrangement of means to resolve conflict without formal litigation. It seeks to reduce cost and delay and avoid the adversarial nature of litigation. ADR have following techniques:

- **Conciliation** is an informal process designed to create an environment where negotiations can take place. If the parties fail to reach an agreement, the case is referred to mediation.

- **Mediation** is voluntary and confidential process where a neutral third party assists negotiations. The parties are responsible for reaching an agreement and the negotiator cannot impose settlement. If the mediation fails to reach agreement, the case is referred to arbitration.

- **Arbitration** is form of private adjudication where a mutually acceptable third party hears arguments from either side in a dispute and renders a judgement. The judgement known as an **Award**, is confidential and binding.

- **Community-driven** resolution mechanism (**Lok Adalat**) literally means 'Peoples Court'. It is an alternative dispute settlement mechanism, which settles disputes. It helps in quick disposal of cases and the process is simple and carries no fees. Lok Adalats are statutory forums since the enactment of the **Legal Serivces Authorities Act, 1987.**

LEGAL TERMS	
Affidavit	This is a sworn statement made by a party, in writing, made in the presence of an oath commissioner or a notary public which is used either in support of applications to the Court or as evidence in court proceedings.
Alimony	The maintenance given by a husband to his divorced wife.
Amicus curiae	Translated from the Latin as 'friend of the Court'. An advocate appears in this capacity when asked to help with the case by the Court or on volunteering services to the Court.
Arbitration	Settling disputes by referring them to independent third parties as an alternative to court proceedings.

Audi alteram partem	This is a rule of natural justice which translates from the Latin as 'hear the other side' or 'hear both sides'.	**Locus Standi**	Translated from Latin as 'place of standing', locus standi gives the right to pursue a litigation. Under this rule, only a person or group of persons affected by the issue may **petition the Court.**
Bequeath	To dispose of personal property by Will.	**Ordinance**	A codified law made, as a temporary measure, by the President of India or the Governor of a State when the Parliament or legislature of a state is not in session.
Caveat	Where it is apprehended that an opposite party may file a case, a party may file a document requesting the court that no order be made in the case without hearing the caveator.		
		Perjury	This occurs when a person gives false evidence or false affidavit in a case.
Cognizable offence	An offence in which arrest can be made without a warrant.	**Petition**	A written document filed in a court asserting a claim or a right and seeking relief on legal grounds.
Dasti Notice	Dasti is a persian word, which means 'by hand'. Dast Notice means service of the notice by the Petitioner on the Respondent(s) in person, and not by the Registry through post.	**Pleadings**	A collective noun for all the petitions, affidavits, replies, rejoinders drafted by or on behalf of the parties to a case.
		Prima facie	At first sight; on the face of it.
Decree	The formal expression of an adjudication which, so far as regards the Court expressing it.	**Pro bono publico**	Translated from the Latin as 'for the public good'. In PIL, this refers to a petitioner acting bonafide in the public interest.
Estoppel	A legal principle that bars a party from denying or alleging a certain fact owing to that party's previous conduct, allegation, or denial.	**Respondent**	A party against whom a petition is filed. A proforma respondent is a party against whom no relief is sought.
Habeas Corpus	A writ requiring a person under arrest to be brought before a judge or into court, especially to secure the person's release unless lawful grounds are shown for their detention.	**Stare decisis**	The principle that decisions of Courts in previous cases must be followed in subsequent cases of similar nature.
		Statute	A codified law that is enacted by the Parliament or a State Legislature.
In pari delicto	When both the parties are equally in fault.	**Stay Order**	A party filing a petition may require some immediate relief, even before the respondents can be heard or a final decision given.
Interim Order	Any order by a court before a final order is made.		
Interlocutory Application	Petition seeking a relief even while the main petition remains in the Court.		
Intervenor	A person who is not a party to the proceedings may, with the permission of the court, intervene if it is shown that the outcome of the case will affect such person in some way.	**Suo Motu**	The Court may take action on its own when facts requiring legal intervention reach its notice. The Court is then said to be acting suo moto.
Judgment-debtor	Any person against whom a decree has been passed or an order capable of execution has been made.		
Judicial Review	A term that describes the function of the judiciary being able to examine and correct the actions of all the organs of State—the executive, the legislature and the judiciary itself.		
Justiciable	A matter is justiciable if it lends itself to adjudication by a court. This is determined by criteria laid down in law.		
Litigation	The totality of the legal proceedings in any dispute.		

Juvenile Justice Act 2015

Juvenile Justice (Care and Protection of Children) Act, 2015 of Ministry of Women and child Development came into force on 15th January 2016. This is an Act to consolidate and amend the Law relating to children in need of care and protection, by catering to their basic needs through development, treatment, and social re-integration, by adopting a child-friendly approach. This Act enhances the time and punishment for sale of tobacco products to minors. The Law for underage offenders also would Rave the way for trying those between 16 and 18 years of age, accused of heinous crimes as adults, punishable with a jail terms of upto 7 years.

Uniform Civil Code

What is uniform civil code?

- Uniform Civil Code generally refers to that part of law which deals with family affairs of an individual and denotes uniform law for all citizens, irrespective of his/her religion, caste or tribe.
- A Uniform Civil Code administers the same set of secular civil laws to govern different people belonging to different religions and regions. This supersedes the right of citizens to be governed under different personal laws based on their religion or ethnicity. The common areas covered by a civil code include:
  (I) Personal Status
  (II) Rights related to acquisition and administration of property
  (III) Marriage, divorce and adoption
- Uniform Civil Code will in the long run ensure Equality. Also, UCC will help to promote Gender equality.

What the constitution says?

Article 44 of the Constitution says that there should be a Uniform Civil Code. According to this article, "The State shall endeavor to secure for the citizens a uniform civil code throughout the territory of India". Since the Directive Principles are only guidelines, it is not mandatory to use them.

Historical background:

Uniform Civil Code was one of the key issues debated during the writing of the Constitution, with passionate arguments on both sides. However, unable to arrive at a solution, a directive principle was struck regarding this in the constitution.

- But, several members of the Constituent Assembly disagreed vehemently with the compromise and argued that one of the factors that have kept India back from advancing to nationhood has been the existence of personal laws based on religion which keep the nation divided into watertight compartments in many aspects of life.
- Though, after independence, few governments tried to have a UCC, religious conservative groups did not allow governments to proceed ahead in this regard.

India needs a Uniform Civil Code for the following reasons:

- A secular republic needs a common law for all citizens rather than differentiated rules based on religious practices.
- Another reason why a uniform civil code is needed is gender justice. The rights of women are usually limited under religious law, be it Hindu or Muslim. The practice of **Triple Talaq** is a classic example.
- Many practices governed by religious tradition are at odds with the fundamental rights guaranteed in the Indian Constitution.
- Courts have also often said in their judgments that the government should move towards a uniform civil code including the judgment in the **Shah Bano** case.

Why it is difficult to have a UCC?

India being a secular country guarantees its minorities the right to follow their own religion, culture and customs under Article 29 and 30. But implementing a Uniform Code will hamper India's secularism.

Concerns:

What is unfortunate is the demand for UCC has always been framed in the context of communal politics. Many see it as majoritarianism under the garb of social reform.

Way ahead:

The government cannot remain silent on the issue anymore. It is obvious that the government would have to face several challenges from many conservative groups on this front. But, it will have to work hard to build trust, and more importantly, make common cause with social reformers rather than religious conservatives, as has been the wont of previous governments.

- One strategic option is to follow the path taken after the fiery debates over the reform of Hindu civil law in the 1950s.
- Rather than an omnibus approach, the government could also bring separate aspects such as marriage, adoption, succession and maintenance into a uniform civil code in stages.
- A comprehensive review of several other laws in the context of gender justice would also do well.

Model of Uniform Civil Code in Goa:

The civil law in Goa—derived from the Portuguese Civil Procedure Code of 1939—could be a useful starting point for a national debate. Goa continued with its practice of treating all communities alike even after its entry into the Indian Union.

Conclusion:

Government's move to refer this matter to the law commission is hopefully the first step towards the implementation of something that has been delayed for far too long. It is now 66 years since the Constitution came into force. It is high time there was a decisive step towards a common civil code.

Exercise -1

1. The Supreme Court has suggested to give social service duties to those prisoners who have been sentenced to 6 months or 1 year.
   In this context, which of the following states has worst inmate to prison staff ratio?
   (a) Uttar Pradesh   (b) Jharkhand
   (c) Bihar   (d) Maharashtra
2. Judges of the Supreme Court are administered oath by
   (a) Chief Justice of India
   (b) President or Vice-President
   (c) President
   (d) None of the above
3. A judge of a High Court can be removed before the expiry of his time by:
   (a) President on the recommendation of the Supreme Court
   (b) Governor on the recommendation of the State legislature
   (c) President on the recommendation of the State legislature
   (d) President on the recommensdation of the Parliament
4. A judge of a High Court willing to resign addresses his letter or resignation to:
   (a) the President
   (b) the Chief Justice of his High Court
   (c) the Chief Justice of India
   (d) Governor of the State
5. Which among the following is not the power of a High Court?
   (a) Supervision over all courts under its jurisdiction
   (b) Jurisdiction over revenue matters
   (c) Supervision over tribunals constituted by law relating to armed forces
   (d) Issue writs for enforcing fundamental rights or for any other purpose
6. Oath to a High Court judge is administered by:
   (a) Chief Justice of India
   (b) Chief Justice of that High Court
   (c) Governor of the State
   (d) President of India
7. Public interest litigation applies to cases of public injury arising from:
   (a) Breach of public duty
   (b) Violation of a constitutional provision
   (c) Violation of law
   (d) all of the above
8. In Minerva Mills cases, the Supreme Court has further reaffirmed its decision pronounced in
   (a) Golakh Nath Case   (b) Keshavanand Bharati case
   (c) Sajjan Singh Case   (d) None of the above
9. District Judges are appointed by:
   (a) The Chief Justice of High Court
   (b) The State Public Service Commission
   (c) The Chief Minister of state
   (d) The Governor of state
10. The District and sessions Judge works directly under the control of:
    (a) District Collector
    (b) Governor of the state
    (c) Law Minister of the state
    (d) High Court of the state
11. If any question arises as to the age of a judge of a High Court, the question shall be decided by the President after consultation with:
    (a) The Chief Justice of the concerned High Court
    (b) The Governor of the concerned state
    (c) The Attorney-General of India
    (d) The Chief Justice of India
12. The Chief Justice of the High Court is appointed by
    (a) the Governor of the state
    (b) the President of India
    (c) the Chief Minister of the state
    (d) the Chief Justice of India
13. The Supreme Court of India tenders advice to the President on a matter of law or fact
    (a) on its own initiative
    (b) only if he seeks such advice
    (c) only if the matter relates to the fundamental righ of citizens
    (d) only if the issue poses a threat to the unity and integrity of the country
14. Which one of the following is directly related to the appellate jurisdiction of the Supreme Court of India ?
    (a) Appeals made in civil, criminal and constitutional cases
    (b) Appeals made in constitutional cases
    (c) Adjudication of disputes between the union and the states
    (d) Adjudication of disputes between the states
15. Which of the following statements is correct?
    (a) The President of India is the custodian of the Constitution of India
    (b) The Supreme Court of India can declare a law passed by any State/Union Legislature null and void if it encroaches upon the Fundamental Rights guaranteed by the Constitution of India
    (c) The number of judges in a High Court is to be determined from time to time by the Governor of the State concerned
    (d) The Chief Justice of a High Court is appointed by the Governor of the State concerned on the recommendation of the Chief Justice of India
16. Which of the following is covered under the original jurisdiction of the Supreme Court:
    (a) Dispute relating to civil matters
    (b) Dispute relating to criminal cases involving murder
    (c) Disputes between two states of the Indian Union
    (d) Disputes between two citizens from two different states
17. Who has the right to seek advisory opinion of the Supreme Court of India, on any question of Law?
    (a) Prime Minister
    (b) President
    (c) Any judge of the high court
    (d) All of the above
18. The power of the Supreme Court of India to decide disputes between the Centre and the State falls under its
    _____
    (a) Advisory jurisdiction
    (b) Appellate Jurisdiction
    (c) constitutional Jurisdiction
    (d) Original Jurisdiction

19. Sovereignty of Indian Parliament is restricted by:
    (a) Powers of the President of India
    (b) Judicial review
    (c) Powers of the Prime Minister of India
    (d) Leader of the opposition
20. Who of the following Chief Justice of India acted as the Presid0ent of India also?
    (a) Justice M. Hidayatullah
    (b) Justice P.N. Bhagwati
    (c) Justice Mehar Chand Mahajan
    (d) Justice B.K. Mukherjee
21. The Indian constitution provides for the appointment of Adhoc judges in:
    (a) Supreme Court
    (b) High Court
    (c) District and session Court
    (d) All of these
22. Which of the following State/Union territories have a common High Court?
    (a) Uttar Pradesh and Bihar
    (b) Punjab, Haryana and Chandigarh
    (c) Punjab and Jammu and Kashmir
    (d) Assam and Bengal
23. Which of the following High Courts has the largest number of Benches?
    (a) Kolkata High Court
    (b) Madhya Pradesh High Court
    (c) Bombay High Court
    (d) Guwahati High Court
24. The first High court/Supreme Court judge, who voluntarily made his assets public is
    (a) justice D.V.S. Kumar
    (b) justice K. Chandra
    (c) justice K. Kannan
    (d) justice V.C. srivastava
25. Which one of the following High Courts has the territorial jurisdiction over Andaman and Nicobar Islands?
    (a) Andhra Pradesh   (b) Calcutta
    (b) Madras   (d) Odisha
26. In the verdict of which case, Supreme Court has nullified Parliament, effort to establish preference of all the Directive Principles of state policy over Fundamental rights?
    (a) Keshvanand Bharti Vs. State of Kerala Case
    (b) Francis Coralie Mullin Vs. Union Territory of Delhi
    (c) Minerva Mills Vs. Union of India case
    (d) Indira Sawhani
27. Original jurisdiction of Supreme Court is mentioned in which of the following articles of Indian constitution?
    (a) Article 131   (b) Article 132
    (c) Article 143   (d) Article 148
28. Which of the following writs literally means 'we command'?
    (a) Habeas Corpus   (b) Mandamus
    (c) Prohibition   (d) Quo-Warranto
29. In which of the following cases Supreme Court of India enunciated the doctrine of basic structure?
    (a) Keshwanand Bharti case
    (b) Golaknath case
    (c) Minnerva Mills case
    (d) Gopalan case

30. In Indian constitution the power to issue a writ of 'Habeas corpus' is vested only in-
    (a) The Supreme Court
    (b) The High Court
    (c) The Supreme Court and the High Court
    (d) Lower Courts
31. The Provisions concerning the powers of the Union judiciary in the Constitution can be amended by
    (a) Simple majority of the parliament
    (b) Two-third majority of the parliament
    (c) Two-third majority of the parliament and the majority of states
    (d) None of the above
32. The Supreme Court of India declares by issuing a writ that "respondent was not entitled to an office he was holding or a privilege he was exercising". which writ is that?
    (a) Habeas Corpus   (b) Quo Warranto
    (c) Prohibition   (d) Certiorari
33. What is the objective advocated for appointment of the National judicial commission?
    (a) Training of the judges
    (b) Reforms in legal system
    (c) Bringing about transparency and impartiality in the appointment of judges of the highest level.
    (d) To examine the working period of the judges.
34. How can the number of judges in the Supreme Court in India be increased ?
    (a) Representation from the Supreme Court
    (b) By amendment of the constitution
    (c) By a Parliamentary Act
    (d) By Presidential notification
35. Which of the following cases cannot be filed directly in the Supreme Court ?
    (a) Cases against encroachment on Fundamental Rights
    (b) Both (a) and (b) above.
    (c) If one's property is forcefully occupied by the other
    (d) Disputes between two or more States
36. Which is not an eligibility criterion for appointment as a Judge of the High Court ?
    (a) Must have been an advocate of a High Court for not less than 10 years
    (b) Must be, in the opinion of the President, a distinguished jurist.
    (c) Must have attained the age of 55 years
    (d) Must have been a High Court Judge for at least 5 years
37. Judicial Review function of the Supreme Court means the power to
    (a) Review the functioning of judiciary in the country
    (b) Undertake periodic review of the Constitution.
    (c) Examine the constitutional validity of the laws
    (d) Review its own judgement
38. The High Courts in India were first started at
    (a) Bombay, Delhi, Madras
    (b) Madras and Bombay
    (c) Bombay, Madras, Calcutta
    (d) Delhi and Calcutta
39. Besides its permanent seat at Delhi, the Supreme Court can also meet at?
    (a) Any other Union Territory
    (b) Any other place as decided by the Chief Justice of India in consultation with the President
    (c) Any other metropolitan city
    (d) Any other major city

40. What is meant by a Court of Record?
    (a) The court that maintains records of all lower courts.
    (b) The court that is competent to give directions and issue writs.
    (c) The court that can punish for its contempt.
    (d) The court that preserves all its records.
41. Judges of the High Court are appointed by the
    (a) Chief Justice of the High Court
    (b) President
    (c) Governor
    (d) Chief Justice of India
42. After retirement, a Judge of a High Court can undertake practice in
    (a) Any other court except the same court
    (b) Wherever he intends to practice.
    (c) The same court
    (d) Lower courts only
43. Separation of the Judiciary from the Executive is enjoined by
    (a) VII Schedule to the Constitution
    (b) Judicial decision
    (c) Directive Principles
    (d) Preamble
44. The Chief Justice and other Judges of the High Court are appointed by the
    (a) Chief Justice of the Supreme Court
    (b) Chief Minister of the concerned state
    (c) Governor of the concerned state
    (d) President
45. Judicial Review signifies that the Supreme Court
    (a) Can impeach the President
    (b) Can declare a state law as unconstitutional
    (c) Can review cases decided by the High Courts.
    (d) Has final authority over all cases
46. Which one of the following comes under the jurisdiction of both the High Court and the Supreme Court ?
    (a) Disputes between two States
    (b) Protection against the violation of the Constitution
    (c) Protection of the Fundamental Rights
    (d) Disputes between the Centre and the States
47. Congnizable offence refers to an offence where
    (a) Arrests can be made without warrant
    (b) Police can register a case without formal complaints
    (c) Arrests can be made with warrant
    (d) It is under the jurisdiction of a court
48. Under the writ of Mandamus, the Court can
    (a) Ask the person to be produced
    (b) Order to transfer the case from one court
    (c) Ask to let a person free for a temporary period
    (d) Direct the Government to do or not to do a thing
49. Which of the following writs is a bulwark of personal freedom ?
    (a) Certiorari
    (b) Habeas Corpus
    (c) Mandamus
    (d) Quo Warranto
50. Appointment of officers and servants of a High Court are made by the
    (a) None of these
    (b) Chief Justice of the High Court
    (c) President
    (d) Governor

51. Salaries of the Judges of the Supreme Court are drawn from the
    (a) Grants-in-aid   (b) Public Accounts
    (c) Contingency Fund   (d) Consolidated Fund
52. Which of the following High Courts covers more than one State/ Union Territories ?
    (a) Allahabad   (b) Delhi
    (c) Guwahati   (d) None of these
53. Which of the following writs may be issued to enforce a Fundamental Right ?
    (a) Certiorari   (b) Habeas Corpus
    (c) Mandamus   (d) Prohibition
54. The Judges of the Supreme Court can be removed from office by the
    (a) President on request of Parliament
    (b) Chief Justice of India
    (c) President
    (d) Prime Minister
55. The authority competent to suspend the operation of Fundamental Rights guaranteed under the Constitution of India is
    (a) Supreme Court   (b) Prime Minister
    (c) Parliament   (d) President
56. Which is the highest and final judicial tribunal in respect of the Constitution of India ?
    (a) President   (b) Union Cabinet
    (c) Supreme Court   (d) Parliament
57. Which of the following is an extensive original jurisdiction given by the Constitution of India to the Supreme Court ?
    (a) Enforcement of Fundamental Rights
    (b) Advising the Chief Executive in legal matters
    (c) Hearing revenue cases of appeal
    (d) Hearing criminal cases of appeal
58. The High Court of West Bengal (Calcutta) has got the additional jurisdiction to hear cases from
    (a) Arunachal Pradesh (b) Mizoram
    (c) Tripura
    (d) Andaman and Nicobar islands
59. Which of the following is enforceable in a court of law ?
    (a) Fundamental Rights
    (b) Fundamental Duties
    (c) Directive Principles
    (d) Preamble
60. In whom are the powers of Judicial Review vested in India ?
    (a) All the courts
    (b) Supreme Court and all the High Courts
    (c) President
    (d) Parliament
61. The lowest court of revenue is that of a
    (a) Naib Tehsildar
    (b) Sub-judge
    (c) Third class magistrate
    (d) Munsif
62. To ensure impartiality, the retired Chief Justice and other Judges of the Supreme Court are debarred from practising law
    (a) In any court other than State High Courts
    (b) In any Criminal Court
    (c) In any court of India
    (d) In any court other than the Supreme Court
63. Who decides the number of Judges in a High Court ?
    (a) Governor of the State   (b) Parliament
    (c) President   (d) State Government

64. Who is appointed as an adhoc judge of the Supreme Court ?
    (a) A sitting judge of a High Court duly qualified for appointment as a Supreme Court Judge
    (b) A person fully qualified for appointment as a Judge of the Supreme Court
    (c) A retired judge of Supreme Court
    (d) An acting judge of the Supreme Court

65. Which of the following is covered under the original jurisdiction of the supreme court ?
    (a) Dispute relating to civil matters
    (b) Dispute between two citizens from two different states
    (c) Dispute relating to criminal cases involving murder
    (d) Disputes between two states of the Indian Union

66. A common High Court for two or more states and Union Territory may be established by
    (a) Parliament by Law   (b) Chief Justice of India
    (c) President   (d) Governer of the state

67. Under a single, integrated, hierarchical judicial system, the High Court in the states are directly under the
    (a) President   (b) Union Parliament
    (c) Governor of the state (d) Supreme Court

68. A Judge of a Supreme court may resign his office by writing under his hand addressed to the
    (a) Chief Justice of India
    (b) Senior most judge of the supreme court
    (c) Prime Minister
    (d) President

69. The Appellate Jurisdiction of the Supreme Court does not involve
    (a) Criminal Cases
    (b) Cases involving interpretation of the Constitution
    (c) Civil Cases
    (d) Disputes arising out of pre-Constitution treaties and agreements

70. When the chief justice of a High Court acts in an administrative capacity, he is subject to.
    (a) The writ jurisdiction of any of the other judges of the High Court.
    (b) Special control exercised by the chief justice of India.
    (c) Discretionary power of the Governor of the State
    (d) Special powers provided to the Chief Minister in this regard

71. Article 136 of Indian Constitution authorizes the Supreme Court to grant special leave to appeal. Which of the following statement is not correct with respect to 'Appeal by Special Leave'?
    (a) It is a discretionary power of the Supreme Court
    (b) It can be granted against any court or tribunal including the military court
    (c) It can be related to any matter
    (d) None of these

72. The power of the Supreme Court of India to decide disputes between the Centre and the States falls under its
    (a) advisory jurisdiction (b) appellate jurisdiction
    (c) original jurisdiction (d) writ jurisdiction

73. The power to increase the number of judges in the Supreme Court of India is vested in
    (a) the President of India
    (b) the Parliament
    (c) the Chief Justice of India
    (d) the Law Commission

74. Who among the following appoints the Judges of a High Court?
    (a) The President of India
    (b) The Chief Justice of India
    (c) The Governor of the State concerned
    (d) The Union Minister of Law

75. What is the number of Judges (including Chief Justice) in the Supreme Court of India as provided in the Constitution of India?
    (a) 20   (b) 24
    (c) 26   (d) 28

76. Public Interest Litigation (PIL) may be linked with
    (a) judicial review   (b) judicial activism
    (c) judicial intervention (d) judicial sanctity

77. The writ of certiorari is issued by a superior court to
    (a) an inferior court to stop further proceedings in a particular case
    (b) an inferior court to transfer the record of proceedings in a case for review
    (c) an officer to show his/her right to hold a particular office
    (d) a public authority to produce a person detained by it before the court within 24 hours

78. The Bombay High Court does not have a bench at which one of the following places?
    (a) Nagpur   (b) Panaji
    (c) Pune   (d) Aurangabad

79. Which one of the following jurisdictions of the Indian judiciary covers Public Interest Litigation?
    (a) Original Jurisdiction (b) Appellate Jurisdiction
    (c) Epistolary Jurisdiction (d) Advisory Jurisdiction

80. For which one of the following Judgements of the Supreme Court of India, the Kesavananda Bharati vs State of India case is considered a landmark?
    (a) The religion cannot be mobilised for political ends
    (b) Abolishing untouchability from the country
    (c) The basic structures of the Constitution, as defined in the preamble, cannot be changed
    (d) Right to life and liberty cannot be suspended under any circumstance

81. The original jurisdiction of the Supreme Court of India extends to
    (a) treaties and agreements signed by the Government of India
    (b) disputes between the Government of India and one or more States
    (c) disputes relating to implementation of the Directive Principles of State Policy
    (d) a bill passed by the Parliament which is violative of the Constitution

82. According to the Administrative Tribunal Act, 1985. the Central Administrative Tribunal adjudicates disputes and complaints with respect to the service of persons who are
    (a) appointed to pubic services and posts in connection with the affairs of the Union except members of the Defence services
    (b) official and servants of the Supreme Court or any High Courts
    (c) members of the Secretarial staff of the Parliament or any state legislatures
    (d) members of the Defence services

83. In which one of the following cases the Supreme Court of India gave verdicts which have a direct bearing on the Centre-State relations?
    (a) Keshavananda Bharati case
    (b) Vishakha case
    (c) S R Bommai case
    (d) Indira Sawhney case

84. With reference to Lok Adalats, which one among the following statements is correct?
    (a) Lok Adalats have the jurisdiction to settle the matters at pre-litigative state and not those matters pending before any court
    (b) Lok Adalats can deal with matters which are civil and not criminal in nature
    (c) Lok Adalats has not been given any statutory status so far
    (d) No appeal lies in a civil court against the order of the Lok Adalat

85. Power of the Supreme Court of India to decide the dispute between centre and state falls under
    (a) advisory jurisdiction
    (b) original jurisdiction
    (c) appellate jurisdiction
    (d) constitutional jurisdiction

86. The Judge of the High Courts in India is administered oath of office by
    (a) the Chief Justice of the High Court
    (b) the Governor of the State
    (c) the President of India
    (d) the Chief Justice of India

87. In the SR Bommai vs Union of India case, which one among the following features of the Constitution of India was upheld by the Supreme Court as a basic structure?
    (a) Liberalism
    (b) Secularism
    (c) Dignity of the human person
    (d) Freedom of religion

88. Which of the following statements about Indian Judiciary is not correct ?
    (a) The Constitution of India has not provided for double system of courts as in the United States
    (b) The organization of the subordinate judiciary in India varies slightly from State to State
    (c) Every State in India has separate High Court
    (d) The Supreme Court has issued direction to constitute an All India Judicial Service to bring about uniformity in designation of officers in criminal and civil side

89. In which of the following cases did the Supreme Court rule that Constitutional - Amendments were also laws under Article 13 of the Constitution of India, which could be declared void for being inconsistent with Fundamental Rights ?
    (a) Keshavanand Bharati Case
    (b) Golaknath Case
    (c) Minerva Mills Case
    (d) Maneka Gandhi Case

90. The concept of public Interest litigation originated in:
    (a) United Kingdom   (b) Australia
    (c) USA   (d) Canada

91. With reference to the Consumer Disputes Redressal at district level in India, which one of the following statements is not correct ?
    (a) A State Government can establish more than one District Forum in a district if it deems fit.
    (b) One of the members of the District Forum shall be a woman
    (c) The District Forum entertains the complaints where the value of goods or services does not exceed rupees fifty lakhs.
    (d) A complaint in relation to any goods sold or any service provided may be filed with a District Forum by the State Government as a representative of the interests of the consumers in general.

92. The power of the Supreme Court of India to decide disputes between the Centre and the State falls under its:
    (a) advisory jurisdiction
    (b) appellate jurisdiction
    (c) original jurisdiction
    (d) constitutional jurisdiction

93. When the Chief Justice of a High Court acts in an administrative capacity, he is subject to :
    (a) the writ jurisdiction of any other judges of the High Court
    (b) special control exercised by the Chief Justice of India
    (c) discretionary powers of the Governor of the state
    (d) special powers provided to the Chief Minister

94. According to the Constitution of India the term 'district judge' shall not include:
    (a) chief presidency magistrate
    (b) sessions judges
    (c) tribunal judge
    (d) chief judge of a small cause court

95. The Supreme Court of India tenders advice to the President on a matter of law or fact:
    (a) on its own initiative
    (b) only if he seeks such advice
    (c) only if the matter relates to the Fundamental Rights of citizens
    (d) only if the issue poses a threat to the unity and integrity of the country

96. The salaries and allowances of the Judges of the High Court are charged to the:
    (a) Consolidated Fund of India
    (b) Consolidated Fund of the State
    (c) Contingency Fund of India
    (d) Contingency Fund of the State

97. The power to enlarge the jurisdiction of the Supreme Court of India with respect to any matter included in the Union List of Legislative Powers rests with:
    (a) The President of India
    (b) The Chief Justice of India
    (c) The Parliament
    (d) The Union Ministry of Law, Justice and Company Affairs

98. Which one of the following is the correct sequence in the descending order of precedence in the warrant of precedence?
    (a) Attorney General of India–Judges of the Supreme Court–Members the of Parliament–Deputy Chairman of Rajya Sabha
    (b) Judges of the Supreme Court–Deputy Chairman of Rajya Sabha–Attorney General of India–Members of the Parliament
    (c) Attorney General of India–Deputy Chairman of Rajya Sabha–Judges of the Supreme Court–Members of Parliament
    (d) Judges of the Supreme Court–Attorney General of India–Deputy Chairman of Rajya Sabha–Members of Parliament

99. Who was the Chief Justice of India when Public Interest Litigation (PIL) was introduced to the Indian judicial system?
    (a) M. Hidayatullah (b) A. M. Ahmadi
    (c) A. S. Anand (d) P. N. Bhagwati

100. How many High Courts in India have jurisdiction over more than one State (Union Territories not included)?
    (a) 2 (b) 3
    (c) 4 (d) 5

101. With reference to Lok Adalats, which of the following statements is correct ?
    (a) Lok Adalats have the jurisdiction to settle matters at pre-litigating stage and not those matters pending before any court
    (b) Lok Adalats can deal with matters which are civil and not criminal in nature.
    (c) Every Lok Adalat consists of either serving or retired judicial officers only and not any other person.
    (d) None of the statements given above is correct.

102. The power of the Supreme Court of India to decide disputes between the Centre and the States falls under its **[IAS Prelims 2014]**
    (a) advisory jurisdiction (b) appellate jurisdiction
    (c) original jurisdiction (d) writ jurisdiction

103. The power to increase the number of judges in the Supreme Court of India is vested in **[IAS Prelims 2014]**
    (a) the President of India
    (b) the Parliament
    (c) the Chief Justice of India
    (d) the Law Commission

104. Which of the following is the custodian of the Constitution of India? **[IAS Prelims 2014]**
    (a) The President of India
    (b) The Prime Minister of India
    (c) The Lok Sabha Secretariat
    (d) The Supreme court of India

105. In India, Judicial Review implies **[IAS Prelims 2017]**
    (a) the power of the Judiciary to pronounce upon the constitutionality of laws and executive orders.
    (b) the power of the Judiciary to question the wisdom of the laws enacted by the Legislatures.
    (c) the power of the Judiciary to review all the legislative enactments before they are assented to by the President.
    (d) the power of the Judiciary to review its own judgements given earlier in similar or different cases.

106. Every Judge of the Supreme Court of India is appointed by
    (a) the Supreme Court Collegium **[NDA 2018]**
    (b) the Cabinet
    (c) the President of India
    (d) the Lok Sabha

Exercise -2

Statement Based MCQ

1. Consider the following statements :
   1. A retired judge of High court can be appointed as a judge of Supreme court.
   2. Ad hoc judges to the Supreme court are appointed by the chief justice of India.
   3. An Ad hoc judge of Supreme court enjoys same power and privileges as enjoyed by other judges of Supreme court.
   Choose the correct statement from the above.
   (a) 2 & 3 (b) 1 & 3
   (c) only 3 (d) All 1, 2, & 3

2. The Supreme Court has suggested to give social service duties to those prisoners who have been sentenced to 6 months or 1 year.
   In this context, which of the following states has worst inmate to prison staff ratio?
   (a) Uttar Pradesh (b) Jharkhand
   (c) Bihar (d) Maharashtra

3. Consider the following statements :
   1. Supreme court has power to review its own judgement.
   2. All authorities, civil and judicial shall act in aid of the Supreme court.
   Choose the correct statement/statements –
   (a) 1 only (b) 2 only
   (c) Both 1 & 2 (d) None of the Above

4. Article-32 gives Supreme court the right to issue writs for the restoration of fundamental rights of an aggrieved person.
   On which of the following grounds, a writ can be issued:
   1. An arrested person is not presented before court.
   2. A particular office holder is not doing legal duty.
   3. When a lower court has considered a case going beyond its jurisdiction.
   4. A person is holding office but is not entitled to hold that office.
   (a) 1, 2 and 3 only (b) 2, 3 and 4 only
   (c) 1, 2 and 4 only (d) All 1,2,3 and 4 are correct

5. Consider the following statements :
   1. Constitution declares Delhi as the seat of the Supreme court.
   2. The president can appoint other place or places as seat of the Supreme court.
   Which of the following are correct –
   (a) 1 only   (b) 2 only
   (c) Both 1 and 2   (d) None

6. Choose the correct statements:
   1. Supreme court can transfer a case pending in one high Court to another high court.
   2. Supreme court exercise power of superintendence over sub-ordinate courts and tribunals.
   (a) 1 only   (b) 2 only
   (c) Both 1 and 2   (d) None of the Above

7. Which among the following is/are among the legislative protection given to Judges?
   (a) Judges are exempted from the criminal proceedings for something said or done in the course of their judicial duties.
   (b) The government cannot initiate criminal proceedings against a sitting or former judge of a superior court.
   (c) Both (a) and (b)
   (d) None of the these.

8. 1. Expenses of the Supreme court are charged on the consolidated fund of India.
   2. Parliament is authorised to curtail the jurisdiction of the Supreme court.
   Choose the incorrect statements.
   (a) 1 only   (b) 2 only
   (c) Both 1 and 2   (d) None of the above

9. Consider the following statements.
   1. There is a division of judicial power between centre and states.
   2. The laws of parliament are not applicable to the Indian citizens living abroad.
   Select the correct statement/statements using the codes given below:
   (a) 1 only   (b) 2 only
   (c) Both 1 and 2   (d) Neither 1 nor 2

10. Which of the following statements highlights the need of Judicial Review:
    1. To uphold the principle of the Supremacy of constitution.
    2. To maintain federal equilibrium.
    3. To protect the fundamental rights of the citizens.
    (a) 1 and 2   (b) 2 and 3
    (c) 1 and 3   (d) 1, 2 and 3

11. Consider the following statements.
    1. High court is a court subordinate to Supreme court.
    2. Supreme court can hold a High court judge for contempt.
    Which of the above given statements are true
    (a) 1 only   (b) 2 only
    (c) Both 1 and 2   (d) None of the Above

12. Which of the following statements are true with reference to Indian Constitution:
    1. The constitution does not confer on High court the power to review its own judgement.
    2. As a court of record, a high court has the power to review and correct its own judgement.
    (a) Only 1   (b) Only 2
    (c) Both 1 and 2   (d) Neither 1 nor 2

13. Consider the following statements.
    1. The chief justice of India is appointed by the president after consulting Prime Minister and council of ministers.
    2. The judges of Supreme court are appointed by president after consultation with Chief Justice of India and such other Judges of Supreme Court and High court.
    Which of the above statements is/are correct.
    (a) 1 only   (b) 2 only
    (c) Both 1 and 2   (d) None of the Above

14. Consider the following statements:
    1. A motion regarding removal of a judge of Supreme court must be signed by atleast half of the strength of the house.
    2. The speaker/chairman may refuse to admit the motion regarding removal of a Supreme court judge.
    3. So far no judge of S.C has been removed by parliament.
    4. A motion regarding removal of a Supreme Court judge must be passed by each house of parliament by absolute majority.
    Choose the correct statements using the codes given below:
    (a) 1, 2, and 3 only   (b) 2 and 3 only
    (c) 3 and 4 only   (d) 2, 3, and 4 only

15. Consider the following statements:
    1. Constitution does not specify the strength of a high court.
    2. Supreme court is the final authority on decisions regarding establishment of common High court for 2 or more states.
    Select the correct statement/statements using the codes given below:
    (a) 1 only   (b) 2 only
    (c) Both 1 and 2   (d) Neither 1 nor 2

16. Which of the following statements is/are not true.
    1. Judiciary is not a part of the democratic political structure of the country.
    2. Judiciary is not accountable to the people of the country.
    Select the correct answer using the codes given below.
    (a) 1 only   (b) 2 only
    (c) Both 1 & 2   (d) None of the above.

17. Consider the following statements :
    1. President of India can refer any matter of public importance of Supreme court for its advice.
    2. Supreme court is bound to give such an advice to president.
    3. President is not bound to accept such an advice rendered by Supreme court.
    Choose the correct statement/statements using the codes given below:
    (a) 1 & 2 only   (b) 2 & 3 only
    (c) 1 & 3 only   (d) 1, 2 & 3 all

18. 1. The total sanctioned strength of Supreme court is 35.
    2. The present strength of Supreme court is 25.
    Choose the correct alternate/option.
    (a) 1 only   (b) 2 only
    (c) Both 1 & 2   (d) None of the above

19. Consider the following statements:
    1. The first high courts were set up at Calcutta, Bombay and Madras.
    2. Delhi is the only union territory that has a high court of its own (since 1966)
    Select the correct answer from the codes given below:
    (a) 1 only   (b) 2 only
    (c) Both 1 and 2   (d) Neither 1 nor 2

20. Which of the following ensures independence of judiciary?
    1. The judges have a fixed tenure.
    2. The legislature is not involved in the process of appointment of judges.
    3. The judiciary is not financially dependent on either the executive or legislature.
    4. Parliament cannot remove a judge of Supreme court.
    Select the correct answer using the codes given below:
    (a) 1 & 3 only   (b) 2, 3, & 4 only
    (c) 1, 2 & 3 only   (d) All the above are correct.

21. Consider the following statements with reference to the office of Attorney General of India (AGI).
    1. AGI is the highest law officer in the country.
    2. The term of office of the Attorney General is 5 years.
    3. AGI holds office during the pleasure of the president.
    4. The remuneration of the AGI is fixed by the constitution.
    Select the correct statement/statements using the codes given below:
    (a) 1, 2 and 3 only   (b) 1 and 4 only
    (c) 1 and 3 only   (d) 2 and 4 only

22. Consider the following statements:
    1. High Courts have power to examine the legislative enactments and executive orders of both the central and state governments.
    2. The phrase "Judicial review" is nowhere used in the constitution.
    Which of the statement/statements given above is/are correct:
    (a) 1 only   (b) 2 only
    (c) Both 1 and 2 only   (d) Neither 1 nor 2

23. Consider the following statements :
    1. A retired judge of High court can be appointed as a judge of Supreme court.
    2. Ad hoc judges to the Supreme court are appointed by the chief justice of India.
    3. An Ad hoc judge of Supreme court enjoys same power and privileges as enjoyed by other judges of Supreme court.
    Choose the correct statement from the above.
    (a) 2 & 3   (b) 1 & 3
    (c) only 3   (d) All 1, 2, & 3

24. Consider the following statements :
    1. Supreme court has power to review its own judgement.
    2. All authorities, civil and judicial shall act in aid of the Supreme court.
    Choose the correct statement/statements –
    (a) 1 only   (b) 2 only
    (c) Both 1 & 2   (d) None of the Above

25. Which of the following statements can be considered as a reason behind judicial delays in India.
    1. Poor judge-population ratio.
    2. Impasses over appointment of judges.
    3. Liberal adjournment of cases.
    4. Police lack scientific training.

Select the correct answer using the codes given below:
(a) 1, 2, 4 only   (b) 1, 2, 3 only
(c) 2, 3, 4 only   (d) 1, 2, 3, 4 All

26. Article-32 gives Supreme court the right to issue writs for the restoration of fundamental rights of an aggrieved person.
    On which of the following grounds, a writ can be issued:
    1. An arrested person is not presented before court.
    2. A particular office holder is not doing legal duty.
    3. When a lower court has considered a case going beyond its jurisdiction.
    4. A person is holding office but is not entitled to hold that office.
    (a) 1, 2 and 3 only   (b) 2, 3 and 4 only
    (c) 1, 2 and 4 only   (d) All 1, 2, 3 and 4 are correct

27. Choose the correct statements:
    1. Supreme court can transfer a case pending in one high Court to another hight court.
    2. Supreme court exercise power of superitendence over sub-ordinate courts and tribunals.
    (a) 1 only   (b) 2 only
    (c) Both 1 and 2   (d) None of the Above

28. 1. Expenses of the Supreme court are charged on the consolidated fund of India.
    2. Parliament is authorised to curtail the jurisdiction of the Supreme court.
    Choose the incorrect statements.
    (a) 1 only   (b) 2 only
    (c) Both 1 and 2   (d) None of the above

29. Which of the following statements highlights the need of Judicial Review:
    1. To uphold the principle of the Supremacy of constitution.
    2. To maintain federal equilibrium.
    3. To protect the fundamental rights of the citizens.
    (a) 1 and 2   (b) 2 and 3
    (c) 1 and 3   (d) 1, 2 and 3

30. With Reference advisory jurisdiction of the Supreme Court, which of the following statements is/ are Not Correct?
    1. It is obligatory for the Supreme Court to give its opinion if it is sought.
    2. The advice is not binding on the President.
    3. President may ask the Court's opinion on treaties and agreements made before the Constitution was framed.
    Select the correct answer from the codes given below:
    (a) 1 and 2   (b) 1, 2 and 3
    (c) 1 and 3   (d) 2 and 3

31. Supreme Court is a court of record. This implies that:
    1. It can punish for its contempt
    2. its decisions' are admitted as evidence and cannot be questioned by any court
    3. it has to keep a record of all the important cases in India
    4. its decisions, once taken, are binding upon it
    Which of the above statements is/are correct?
    (a) 1, 2 and 3   (b) 1 and 2
    (c) 1, 3 and 4   (d) 1, 2, 3 and 4

32. Which of the following _________ is/are the qualifications for a High Court judge?
    1. Citizenship of India
    2. Must have held a judicial office for at least ten years
    3. Must not be over 62 years of age
    4. Must have been an advocate of a High Court for at least ten years or be an eminent jurist
    Select the correct answer from the codes given below:
    (a) 1, 2 and 3   (b) 1 and 2
    (c) 1, 3 and 4   (d) 1, 2, 3 and 4
33. Chief Justice of a High Court is appointed by the President after consultation with?
    1. Chief Justice of India
    2. Governor of the State
    3. Chief Minister of the State
    Select the correct answer from the codes given below:
    (a) 1 only   (b) 1 and 2
    (c) 3 only   (d) 1, 2 and 3
34. In a criminal case, an appeal lies to the Supreme Court if the High Court:
    1. has convicted the accused and awarded him a death sentence
    2. has on appeal reversed an order for acquittal of an accused and sentenced him to imprisonment of ten years or more
    3. has withdrawn for trial before itself any case from a subordinate court and has convicted the accused and sentenced him to death
    Which of the above statements is/are correct?
    (a) 1 and 3   (b) 2 and 3
    (c) 3 only   (d) 1, 2 and 3
35. Consider the following statements :
    1. A person who has held office as a permanent Judge of a High Court cannot plead or act in any court or before any authority in India except the Supreme Court.
    2. A person is not qualified for appointment as a Judge of a High Court in India unless he has for at least five years held a judicial office in the territory of India.
    Which of the statements given above is/are correct?
    (a) 1 only   (b) 2 only
    (c) Both 1 and 2   (d) Neither 1 nor 2
36. Which of the following statements are incorrect about the difference between the writ jurisdiction of the Supreme Court and high courts in India ?
    1. The Supreme Court can issue writs not only for the purpose of enforcement of Fundamental Rights but also for any other purpose, whereas high courts can issue writs only for the purpose of enforcement of Fundamental Rights.
    2. High courts can issue the writ of Injunction, whereas the Supreme Court cannot issue the writ of Injunction.
    3. The Supreme Court can issue writs only in the case of appeal, whereas high courts can issue writs only when the party directly approaches it.
    4. High courts can issue writs not only for the purpose of enforcement of Fundamental Rights but also for any other purpose, whereas the Supreme Court can issue writs only for the purpose of enforcement of Fundamental Rights.

Select the correct answer using the codes given below:
(a) 1 and 2   (b) 1, 2 and 3
(c) 2 and 3   (d) 4 only
37. The Chief Justice of a High Court is appointed by the President after consultation with
    1. the Chief Justice of India
    2. the Governor of the state
    3. the Chief Minister of the state
    Select the correct answer using the codes given below:
    (a) 1 only   (b) 1 and 2
    (c) 3 only   (d) 1, 2 and 3
38. Consider the following statements regarding the advisory jurisdiction of the Supreme Court:
    1. The reference for advice may be made to the Supreme Court on a question of law of fact by the President of India
    2. Disputes arising out of pre-constitution treaties and agreements excluded from the original jurisdiction of the Supreme Court may also be referred to it.
    3. The advice given by the Supreme Court is binding on the government
    4. One of the cases referred to the Supreme Court for its advice was the constitutionally of the Kerala education bill.
    Which of the above statements is/are correct?
    (a) 1, 2 and 4   (b) 2 and 3
    (c) 1 and 2   (d) 3 and 4
39. In which of the following categories of cases the Supreme Court of India has the power to decide
    1. Reference made by the President on a question of law or fact
    2. A case involving interpretation of the constitution
    3. A case involving substantial question of law of general importance
    4. A case where the constitutionally of any law has been challenged
    Which of the following statements is/are correct?
    (a) 1, 2 and 3   (b) 1, 3 and 4
    (c) 1, 2 and 4   (d) 2, 3 and 4
40. Which of the following characteristics are essential to federal government ?
    1. A supreme and written constitution
    2. Separation of powers and the system of checks and balances
    3. Distribution of powers between the centre and states
    4. Fundamental Rights guaranteed to citizens
    Which of the following statements is/are correct?
    (a) 1 and 2   (b) 1 and 3
    (c) 2 and 4   (d) 2, 3 and 4
41. Consider the following statements regarding the High Courts in India:
    1. There are eighteen High Courts in the Country.
    2. Three of them have jurisdiction over more than one state.
    3. No Union territory has a High Court of its own.
    4. Judges of the High court hold office till the age of 62.
    Which of the above statements is/are correct?
    (a) 1, 2 and 4   (b) 2 and 4
    (c) 1 and 4   (d) 4 only

42. The Supreme Court of India issued certain guidelines to put a halt to eve-teasing. In this regard consider the following statements:
    1. women cops, in civil uniform, should be deputed at the public places
    2. The court also ordered the states and the UTs to form a uniform law
    3. The eve-teasing can lead to violation of the fundamental rights.
    Which of the above statement given above are correct?
    (a) 1and 2 only   (b) 1 and 3 only
    (c) 2 and 3 only   (d) 1, 2 and 3

43. Consider the following statements about the judicial system introduced by the British in India:
    1. It judicially unified India.
    2. The British established a new system of law through the process of enactment and relevant interpretation of customary laws.
    3. In general the British tended to avoid the customary laws of India.
    Which of the Statements given above are correct?
    (a) 1 and 2 only   (b) 2 and 3 only
    (c) 1 and 3 only   (d) 1, 2 and 3

44. With reference to National Legal Services Authority, consider the following statements:
    1. Its objective is to provide free and competent legal services to the weaker sections of the society on the basis of equal opportunity.
    2. It issues guidelines for the State Legal Services Authorities to implement the legal programmes and schemes throughout the country.
    Which of the statements given above is/are correct?
    (a) 1 only   (b) 2 only
    (c) Both 1 and 2   (d) Neither 1 nor 2

45. Consider the following statements :
    1. The Chief Justice of a High Court is appointed by the Governor of the state.
    2. Every Judge of a High Court including the Chief Justice holds office until he/she attains the age of 65 years.
    Which of the statements given above is/are correct ?
    (a) Only 1   (b) Only 2
    (c) Both 1 and 2   (d) Neither 1 nor 2

46. On which of the following grounds can a Judge of the Supreme Court or a High Court be impeached?
    1. Violation of the Constitution
    2. Proved misbehaviour
    3. Incapacity
    Select the correct answer using the codes given below:
    (a) 1 only   (b) 2 only
    (c) 1, 2 and 3   (d) 2 and 3

47. Which of the following statements with respect to the judiciary in India is/are correct?
    1. Unlike in the United States, India has not provided for a double system of courts.
    2. Under the Constitution of India, there is a single integrated system of courts for the Union as well as the states.
    3. The organisation of the subordinate judiciary varies slightly from state to state.

Select the correct answer using the codes given below
(a) Only 1   (b) 1 and 2
(c) 2 and 3   (d) All of these

48. Consider the following statements regarding e-courts, launched recently in India
    1. They will facilitate hearing of cases via video conferencing.
    2. They will follow the same procedures that are laid out for the bench for hearing appeals in an open court.
    Which of the statement(s) given above is/are correct?
    (a) Only 1   (b) Only 2
    (c) Both 1 and 2   (d) Neither 1 nor 2

49. Consider the following statements :
    The Supreme Court of India tenders advice to the President of India on matters of law or fact:
    1. on its own initiative (on any matter of larger public interest).
    2. if he seeks such an advice.
    3. only if the matters relate to the Fundamental Rights of the citizens.
    Which of the statements given above is/are correct ?
    (a) 1 only   (b) 2 only
    (c) 3 only   (d) 1 and 2

50. Consider the following statements regarding the High Courts in India:
    1. There are eighteen High Courts in the country
    2. Three of them have jurisdiction over more than one state
    3. No Union Territory has a High Court of its own
    4. Judges of the High Court hold office till the age of 62
    Which of these statements is/are correct?
    (a) 1, 2 and 4   (b) 2 and 3
    (c) 1 and 4   (d) 4 only

51. Consider the following statements:
    1. The highest criminal court of the district is the Court of District and Session Judge
    2. The District Judge are appointed by the Governor in consultation with the High Courts
    3. A person to be eligible for appointment as a District Judge should be an advocate or a pleader of seven years' standing or more, or an officer in judicial service of the Union or the State
    4. When the sessions judge awards a death sentence, it must be confirmed by the High Court before it is carried out
    Which of the statements given above are correct?
    (a) 1 and 2   (b) 2, 3 and 4
    (c) 3 and 4   (d) 1, 2, 3 and 4

52. Consider the following statements:
    1. There are 25 High Courts in India.
    2. Punjab, Haryana and the Union Territory of Chandigarh have a common High Court.
    3. National Capital Territory of Delhi has a High Court of its own.
    Which of the statements given above is/are correct?
    (a) 2 and 3   (b) 1 and 2
    (c) 1, 2 and 3   (d) 3 only

53. Consider the following statements:
    1. The Parliament cannot enlarge the jurisdiction of the Supreme Court of India as its jurisdiction is limited to that conferred by the Constitution.
    2. The officers and servants of the Supreme Court and High Courts are appointed by the concerned Chief Justice and the administrative expenses are charged on the Consolidated fund of India.
    Which of the statements given above is/are correct?
    (a) 1 only
    (b) 2 only
    (c) Both 1 and 2
    (d) Neither 1 nor 2

54. Consider the following statements:
    1. A person who has held office as a permanent Judge of a High Court cannot plead or act in any court or before any authority in India except of the Supreme Court.
    2. A person is not qualified for appointment as a Judge of a High Court in India unless he has for at least five years held a judicial office in the territory of India.
    Which of the statement(s) given above is/are correct?
    (a) 1 only
    (b) 2 only
    (c) Both 1 and 2
    (d) Neither 1 nor 2

55. Consider the following statements:
    1. The mode of removal of a Judge of a High Court in India is same as that of removal of a Judge of the Supreme Court.
    2. After retirement from the office, a permanent judge of a High Court cannot plead or act in any court or before any authority in India.
    Which of the statements given above is/are correct?
    (a) 1 only
    (b) 2 only
    (c) Both 1 and 2
    (d) Neither 1 nor 2

56. With reference to Lok Adalats, consider the following statements:
    1. An award made by a Lok Adalat is deemed to be a decree of a civil court and no appeal lies against there to any court.
    2. Matrimonial/Family disputes are not covered under Lok Adalat.
    Which of the statements given above is/are correct?
    (a) 1 only
    (b) 2 only
    (c) Both 1 and 2
    (d) Neither 1 nor 2

57. With reference to the Delimitation Commission, consider the following statements :
    1. The orders of the Delimitation Commission cannot be challenged in a Court of Law.
    2. When the orders of the Delimitation Commission are laid before the Lok Sabha or State Legislative Assembly, they cannot effect any modifications in the orders.
    Which of the statements given above is/are correct?
    (a) 1 only
    (b) 2 only
    (c) Both 1 and 2
    (d) Neither 1 nor 2

58. What is the provision to safeguard the autonomy of the Supreme Court of India?
    1. While appointing the Supreme Court Judges, the President of India has to consult the Chief Justice of India.
    2. The Supreme Court Judges can be removed by the Chief Justice of India only.
    3. The salaries of the Judges are charged on the Consolidated Fund of India to which the legislature does not have to vote.
    4. All appointments of officers and staffs of the Supreme Court of India are made by the Government only after consulting the Chief Justice of India.
    Select the correct answer using the codes given below?
    (a) 1 and 3
    (b) 3 and 4
    (c) 4 only
    (d) 1, 2, 3 and 4

59. With reference to National Legal Services Authority, consider the following statements:
    1. Its objective is to provide free and competent legal services to the weaker sections of the society on the basis of equal opportunity.
    2. It issues guidelines for the State Legal Services Authorities to implement the legal programmes and schemes throughout the country.
    Which of the statements given above is/are correct?
    (a) 1 only
    (b) 2 only
    (c) Both 1 and 2
    (d) Neither 1 nor 2

60. With reference to the 'Gram Nyayalaya Act', which of the following statements is/are correct? **[IAS Prelims 2016]**
    1. As per the Act, Gram Nyayalayas can hear only civil cases and not criminal cases.
    2. The Act allows local social activists as mediators/reconciliators.
    Select the correct answer using the code given below.
    (a) 1 only
    (b) 2 only
    (c) Both 1 and 2
    (d) Neither 1 nor 2

61. 1. The total sanctioned strength of Supreme court is 35.
    2. The present strength of Supreme court is 25.
    Choose the correct alternate/option.
    (a) 1 only
    (b) 2 only
    (c) Both 1 & 2
    (d) None of the above

62. Consider the following statements.
    1. High court is a court subordinate to Supreme court.
    2. Supreme court can hold a High court judge for contempt.
    Which of the above given statements are true
    (a) 1 only
    (b) 2 only
    (c) Both 1 and 2
    (d) None of the Above

63. Consider the following statements.
    1. The chief justice of India is appointed by the president after consulting Prime Minister and council of ministers.
    2. The judges of Supreme court are appointed by president after consultation with Chief Justice of India and such other Judges of Supreme Court and High court.
    Which of the above statements is/are correct.
    (a) 1 only
    (b) 2 only
    (c) Both 1 and 2
    (d) None of the Above

64. Which of the following statements is/are not true.
    1. Judiciary is not a part of the democratic political structure of the country.
    2. Judiciary is not accountable to the people of the country.
    Select the correct answer using the codes given below.
    (a) 1 only
    (b) 2 only
    (c) Both 1 & 2
    (d) None of the above.

Hints and Explanations

EXERCISE-1

1. (b) Jharkhand has the worst inmate to prison staff ratio, followed by Uttar Pradesh.
2. (c) 3. (d) 4. (a) 5. (c) 6. (c)
7. (d) 8. (b) 9. (d) 10. (d) 11. (d)
12. (b) 13. (b) 14. (a) 15. (b) 16. (c)
17. (b)
18. (d) The power of the Supreme Court of India to decide disputes between the centre and the states falls under its original jurisdiction. The original jurisdiction of a court is the power to hear a case for the first time, as opposed to appellate jurisdiction, when a court has the power to review a lower court's decision. In India, the Supreme Court has exclusive original jurisdiction on all cases between the Government and the States or between Government and states on side and one or more states on other side or cases between different states. In addition, Article 32 of the Constitution of India grants original jurisdiction to the Supreme Court on all cases involving the enforcement of fundamental rights of citizens.
19. (b) Sovereignty of Indian parliament is restricted by judicial review. Parliamentary sovereignty (also called parliamentary supremacy or legislative supremacy) is a concept in the constitutional law of some parliamentary democracies. It holds that the legislative body has absolute sovereignty, and is supreme over all other government institutions, including executive or judicial bodies. The concept also holds that the legislative body may change or repeal any previous legislation, and so that it is not bound by written law (in some cases, even a constitution) or by precedent. Parliamentary sovereignty may be contrasted with the doctrines of separation of powers, which limits the legislature's scope often to general law-making, and judicial review, where laws passed by the legislature may be declared invalid in certain circumstances.
20. (a)
21. (d) The Indian constitution provides for the appointment of adhoc judge in supreme court, high court and district and session court. If at any time there should not be a quorum of the Judges of the Supreme Court available to hold or continue any session of the Court, the Chief Justice of India may, with the previous consent of the President and after consultation with the Chief Justice of the High Court concerned, request in writing the attendance at the sittings of the Court, as an ad hoc Judge, for such period as may be necessary, of a Judge of a High Court duly qualified for appointment as a Judge of the Supreme Court to be designated by the Chief Justice of India.
22. (b)
23. (d) Guwahati high court has the largest number of Benches.

The principal seat of the Gauhati High Court is at Guwahati in Assam. The court has 3 outlying benches. These are:
The Kohima bench for Nagaland state.
The Aizawl bench for Mizoram state.
The Itanagar bench for Arunachal Pradesh state.
Former benches, now full fledged high courts:
The Imphal bench (established on 21 January 1972) (Converted to a High Court in March 2013)
The Agartala bench established on 24 January 1972) (Converted to a High Court in March 2013)
The Shillong bench established on 4 September 1974) (Converted to a High Court in March 2013)
24. (c)
25. (b) Calcutta High court has the territorial jurisdiction over Andaman and Nicobar island. The Calcutta High Court is the oldest High Court in India. It was established as the High Court of Judicature at Fort William on 1 July 1862 under the High Courts Act, 1861.
26. (c) In the verdict of Minerva Mills Vs. Union of India case, Supreme Court has nullified parliament's effort to establish preference of all the directive principles of state policy over Fundamental Rights.
27. (a)
28. (b) The writ *mandamus* literally means 'we command'. Mandamus is a judicial remedy in the form of an order from a superior court, to any government subordinate court, corporation, or public authority—to do (or forbear from doing) some specific act which that body is obliged under law to do (or refrain from doing)—and which is in the nature of public duty, and in certain cases one of a statutory duty. It cannot be issued to compel an authority to do something against statutory provision.
29. (a) In Keshvanand Bharti case the Supreme Court of India enunciated the doctrine of basic structure. The case originated in February 1970 when Swami HH Sri Kesavananda Bharati, Senior Pontiff and head of "Edneer Mutt" - a Hindu Mutt situated in Edneer, a village in Kasaragod District of Kerala, challenged the Kerala government's attempts, under two state land reform acts, to impose restrictions on the management of its property. Although the state invoked its authority under Article 31, a noted Indian jurist, Nanabhoy Palkhivala, convinced the Swami into fighting his petition under Article 26 (not Article 29), concerning the right to manage religiously owned property without government interference. Even though the hearings consumed five months, the outcome would profoundly affect India's democratic processes.
30. (c) In Indian constitution, the power to issue a writ of 'Habeas Corpus' is vested only in the supreme court and the High court. A writ of habeas corpus is a writ (court order) that requires a person under arrest to be brought before a judge or into court. The principle of habeas corpus ensures that a prisoner can be released

from unlawful detention—that is, detention lacking sufficient cause or evidence. The remedy can be sought by the prisoner or by another person coming to the prisoner's aid. This right originated in the English legal system, and is now available in many nations. It has historically been an important legal instrument safeguarding individual freedom against arbitrary state action.

31. (c)

32. (b) The above provision came under a writ quo warranto issued by the Supreme Court of India. Quo warranto (Medieval Latin for "by what warrant?") is a prerogative writ requiring the person to whom it is directed to show what authority they have for exercising some right or power (or "franchise") they claim to hold.

33. (c) The main objective advocated for appointment of the National judicial commission is bringing about transparency and impartiality in the appointment of judges of the highest level.

34. (b)	35. (d)	36. (a)	37. (c)	38. (c)
39. (b)	40. (d)	41. (b)	42. (a)	43. (c)
44. (d)	45. (c)	46. (c)	47. (b)	48. (d)
49. (b)	50. (b)	51. (d)	52. (c)	53. (b)
54. (a)	55. (d)	56. (c)	57. (a)	58. (d)
59. (a)	60. (b)	61. (a)	62. (c)	63. (d)
64. (a)	65. (d)	66. (a)	67. (d)	68. (d)

69. (d)

70. (c) According to Article 227(b), the Chief Justice of High Court when acts in an administrative capacity, any rule made by him shall not be inconsistent with the provision of any law in force and requires the previous approval of the governor.

71. (b) According to Article 136, 'Appeal by special leave' can be granted against any court or tribunal including the military court.

72. (c) It is under original jurisdiction the supreme court decides the disputes between centre and one or more states.

73. (b) It is the Parliament which has the power to increase the number of judges in the Supreme Court of India. Parliament increased the number of judges from the original eight in 1950 to eleven in 1956, fourteen in 1960, eighteen in 1978, twenty-six in 1986 and thirty-one in 2008.

74. (a)

75. (c) The Supreme Court originally consisted of a Chief-Justice and seven other judges. In 1985, the strength was increased. It comprises the chief justice and not more than 25 other judge.

76. (b) Public Interest litigation (PIL) may be linked with judicial activism in India.

77. (b) Literally 'certiorary' means 'to be certified'. It can be issued by the Supreme Court or the High Court for quashing the order already passed by an inferior court, tribunal or quasi-judicial authority.

78. (c) The Bombay High Court has benches in Nagpur, Aurangabad and Panaji.

79. (b) PIL (Public Interest Litigation) writ petition can be filed in Supreme Court under Article 32 only if a question concerning the enforcement of a fundamental right is involved. Under Article 226, a writ petition can be filed in a High court whether or not a Fundamental Right is involved. Thus, it comes under appellate jurisdiction.

80. (c) Kesavananda Bharati vs State of Kerala (1973)is a landmark decision of the Supreme Court of India that outlined the Basic Structure doctrine of the Constitution. In the case, the Supreme Court ruled that all provisions of the constitution, including Fundamental Rights can be amended. However, the Parliament cannot alter the basic structure of the constitution like secularism, democracy, federalism, separation of powers.

81. (b) The original jurisdiction of supreme court of India extends to all cases between the Government of India and the States of India or between Government of India and states on side and one or more states on other side or cases between different states.

82. (a) The Central Administrative Tribunal has been established for adjudication of disputes with respect to recruitment and conditions of service of persons appointed to public services and posts in connection with the affairs of the Union or other local authorities within the territory of India.

83. (c) S. R. Bommai Vs. Union of India was a landmark judgment of the Supreme Court of India regarding provisions of Article 356 of the Constitution of India and related issues. This case had huge impact on Centre-State Relations. The misuse of Article 356 was stopped after this judgment. Article 356 deals with imposition of President's Rule over a State of India.

84. (d) Award has the same effect as of a Civil Court decree. The Supreme Court has held that award of the Lok Adalat is as good as the decree of a Court. The award of the Lok Adalat is fictionally deemed to be decrees of Court and therefore the courts have all the powers in relation thereto as it has in relation to a decree passed by itself. It was the legal services authority act 1987, which gave statutory status to Lok Adalat.

85. (b) Original jurisdiction of the Supreme Court (Article 131): Supreme court has power to decide disputes
   • between the Government of India and one or more States.
   • between the Government of India and any State or States on one side and one or more other States on the other
   • between two or more States.

86. (b) According to Article 219 of Indian Constitution (Oath or affirmation by Judges of High Courts) every person appointed to be a Judge of a High Court shall, before he enters upon his office, make and subscribe before the Governor of the State, or some person appointed in that behalf by him, an oath or affirmation according to the form set out for the purpose in the Third Schedule.

87. (b) The case of S.R. Bommai vs Union of India is a landmark case in the purview of the Indian Constitutional history relating to the proclamation of emergency under Article 356 of the Constitution. The case mainly came up with the issue of the power of the President to issue proclamation under Article

356 of the Constitution including the power to dissolve State Legislative Assemblies and also issues relating to federalism and secularism as a part of basic structure.

88. **(c)** Every state in India does not have a separate High Court .The constitution provides that parliament may by law establish a common High Court for two or more states and a Union Territory.

89. **(a)** Kesavananda Bharati. vs. State of Kerala is a landmark decision of the Supreme Court of India that outlined the Basic Structure doctrine of the Constitution Upholding the validity of clause (4) of article 13 and a corresponding provision in article 368(3) inserted by the 24th Amendment. The Court settled in favour of the view that Parliament has the power to amend the Fundamental Rights also.

90. **(c)** PIL originated in USA. It seeks to protect and promote interest of the public at large.

91. **(c)** The District Forum entertains the complaints where the value of goods or services does not exceed rupees twenty lakhs.

92. **(c)** According to Article 131, The SC has original jurisdiction in any dispute - (a) between the Government of India & one or more States; or (b) between the Government of India and any State or States on one side and one or more other States on the other; or (c) between two or more States.

93. **(a)** It his administrative capacity he is subject to writ judiciary in (Article 1720–224).

94. **(c)** Under article 236 of the Constitution, The term "District Judge" includes judge of a city civil court, additional district judge, joint district judge, assistant district judge, chief judge of a small cause court, chief presidency magistrate, additional chief presidency magistrate, sessions judge and assistant sessions judge and additional sessions judge.

95. **(b)** As per provisions under Article 143

96. **(b)** The salaries and allowances of the Judges of the HC are charged to the Consolidated Fund of the state but their pensions are payable as Charged Expenditure / Art 112(3).

97. **(c)** Such is the prerogative of the Parliament.

98. **(b)** President comes first, Vice-President second, Prime Minister third and Governors of states with in their respective State comes fourth in the Warrant of Precedence.
According to Indian order of precedence,
Judges of the Supreme Court – Rank 9
Deputy Chairman of Rajya Sabha – Rank 10
Attorney General of India – Rank 11
Members of Parliament – Rank 21

99. **(d)** PN Bhagwati was CJI during July 1985–Dec 1986. During his tenure as CJI, PIL was introduced to the Indian judicial system.

100. **(b)** Bombay HC (Maharashtra & Goa); Guwahati (Assam, Manipur, Meghalaya, Nagaland, Tripura, Mizoram and Arunachal Pradesh); Punjab and Haryana HC (Punjab, Haryana)

101. **(d)** Cases that are pending in regular courts can be transferred to a Lok Adalat if both the parties agree. These are usually presided over by retired judges, social Activists, or other members of the legal profession. Lok Adalats can deal with any matter falling within the jurisdiction of civil, criminal etc.

102. **(c)** It is under original jurisdiction the supreme court decides the disputes between centre and one or more states.

103. **(b)** It is the Parliament which has the power to increase the number of judges in the Supreme Court of India. Parliament increased the number of judges from the original eight in 1950 to eleven in 1956, fourteen in 1960, eighteen in 1978, twenty-six in 1986 and thirty-one in 2008.

104. **(d)** The Supreme Court of India is the apex court in India. As stated by the Indian Constitution, the function of the Supreme Court of India is that of a custodian of the Constitution, a court established by the authority of a federal government, and the uppermost court of appeal.

105. **(a)** New NCERT, Std. 11, Indian Constitution at Work, Chapter-6 Judiciary, Page 139

106. **(a)** Judicial review means the power of SC or HC to examine the constitutionality of any law.

EXERCISE-2

1. **(d)** – At any given time, the chief justice of India can request a retired judge of the Supreme court or High court to act as an Ad hoc judge of the Supreme court.

   – When there is a lack of Quorum in the Supreme court, the chief justice of India can appoint a judge of High court as Ad hoc judge to the Supreme court.

   – Quorum: It is the minimum strength of the Supreme court which is required for Supreme court to function efficiently.

   – The Ad hoc judges enjoy all the jurisdiction, powers and privileges of a judge of the Supreme court.

2 **(b)** Jharkhand has the worst inmate to prison staff ratio, followed by Uttar Pradesh.

3. **(c)** **Article - 137:** Supreme court shall have the power to review any judgement pronounced or order made by it.
   Article - 144: All authorities, civil and judicial, in the territory of India shall act in aid of the Supreme court.

4. **(d)** Under Article-32: Supreme court can issue writs on all the above mentioned grounds i.e. the writ of Habeas Corpus, Mandamus, Prohibition, Quowarranto, Certiorari can be issued.

   Article-226: High Court can issue writs for the restoration of Fundamental Rights.

   The writ jurisdiction of high court is wider than supreme court, as it can issue writs not only for the restoration of Fundamental Rights but also on other grounds.

   Source: N.C.E.R.T- XIth (Indian Constitutionat Work)

5. **(a)** Chief Justice of India (Not President) has the power to appoint other seat of Supreme court. But he/she can do so only with the approval of president. Art – 130 deals with seat of the Supreme court.

6. (a) – Statement 1 is correct.
   – High court exercises power of supritendence over subordinate courts and tribunals. Supreme court has no such powers.
   – Article - 139 (A) deals with transfer of cases.

7. (a) The government can initiate criminal proceedings against a sitting or former judge of a superior court under sub-section (2) of section (3) of the Judges (Protection) Act,1985 if it can produce material evidence to show that a judgement or a judicial decision was passed after taking a bribe.

8. (b) The salaries, allowances and pensions of judges and all the administrative expenses of Supreme court are charged on consolidated fund of India. Thus they are non-votable by the parliament.

   The constitution has guaranteed to the Supreme court, jurisdiction of various kinds and therefore parliament is not authorised to curtail the jurisdiction and powers of the Supreme court.

   Source: M. Lakshmikant.

9. (d) There is no division of judicial power as the constitution has established an integrated judicial system to enforce both the central laws as well as state laws.

   Parliament alone can make extra-territorial legislation. Thus the laws of the parliament are also applicable to the Indian citizens and their property in any part of the world.

10. (d) All the Above statements highlight the need for Judicial Review.

11. (b) 1. While explaining the relation between High court and Supreme court, the apex court has time and again reiterated that " The High court is not a court subordinate to Supreme court". The constitution has clearly divided the jurisdiction between High court and Supreme court.
   2. Supreme court has the power to enlarge its jurisdiction (Article - 138) and also Article - 141 i.e law declared by Supreme court to be binding on all courts.
   3. Recently in 2017, Supreme court found the conduct of Kolkata High court judge, justice C.S. Karnan as "Unsound and erroneous" and sentenced him to 6 months of imprisonment.

12. (c) As a court of record, a high court also has the power to review and correct its own judgement or order or decision, even though no specific power of review is conferred on it by the constitution. The supreme court on the other hand has been specifically conferred with the power of review by the constitution.

13. (b) Constitution ensures independence of judiciary and legislature has no role in the appointment of judges, so first statement is wrong.
   – Chief Justice of Supreme court of India is appointed by president on consultation of such other judges of Supreme court and High court.
   – Other judges of Supreme court are appointed by president on consultation of chief Justice of India and other Judges of Supreme court and High court.

   Source – M Lakshmikant

14. (b) 1. A motion regarding removal of a judge of Supreme court must be signed by 100 members (in Lok Sabha) and 50 members (in Rajya Sabha).
   2. Second statement is true.
   3. Although impeachment process was initiated against justice V. Ramaswamy of Punjab High court and Justice Sukumar Sen of Kolkata High Court but couldn't be pursued further.
   4. Such a motion should be passed by special majority (Not by absolute majority).

15. (a) At present there are 21 high courts in the country. Out of them, three are common high courts.

   The constitution of India provides for a high court for each state, but the Seventh Amendment Act of 1956 authorised the parliament to establish a common high court for two or more states or for two or more and a union territory.

   Constitution does not specify the strength of a high court and leaves it to the discretion of the president. Accordingly the president determines the strength of a high court from time to time depending upon its workload.

16. (c) Judiciary is very much part of the democratic political structure and it is therefore accountable to the people.
   Source – N. C. E. R. T –XIth (Chap – 6)

17. (c) President can seek advice of Supreme court on any matter of public importance. However Supreme court is not bound to give such an advice and President is not bound to accept such an advice given by the Supreme court.
   Source – N.C.E.R.T – XIth (chap – 6).

18. (d) The parliament can by law increase or decrease the strength of Supreme court. The sanctioned strength of originally constituted Supreme court was 7. Now it stands at 31 (including (II). Against total sanctioned strength of 31, at present there are only 25 judges in Supreme court.

19. (c) 1. These three high courts were set up under the provisions of the Indian High Court Act, 1861. Also in 1866, a fourth high court was established at Allahabad.
   2. At present Delhi is the only UT that has a high court of its own (since 1966). The other union territories fall under the jurisdiction of different state high courts.
   e.g.: Lakshadweep – Ernakulam
   Puducherry – Chennai
   Daman and Diu – Mumbai
   Dadar and Nagar Haveli – Mumbai
   Andman and Nicobar islands – Kolkata
   Chandigarh – Chandigarh

20. (c) All the above statements except the last one are true. The judges of Supreme Court can be removed by parliament according to the provision mentioned in the constitution.
   Source: M. Lakshmikant.

21. (c) The constitution (Article-76) has provided for the office of the Attorney General of India. He is the highest law officer in the country.
   The Attorney General is appointed by the president. He must be a person who is qualified to be appointed as judge of the Supreme Court.

The term of office of the Attorney General is not fixed by the constitution. Further the constitution does not contain the procedure and grounds for his removal. He holds office during the pleasure of the president. The remuneration of the AG is not fixed by the constitution.

22. (c) Though the phrase 'Judicial review' has nowhere been mentioned in the constitution, the provision of Art-13 and 226 explicitly confer the power of judicial review on a high court.

23. (d) – At any given time, the chief justice of India can request a retired judge of the Supreme court or High court to act as an Ad hoc judge of the Supreme court.

– When there is a lack of Quorum in the Supreme court, the chief justice of India can appoint a judge of High court as Ad hoc judge to the Supreme court.

– Quorum: It is the minimum strength of the Supreme court which is required for Supreme court to function efficiently.

– The Ad hoc judges enjoy all the jurisdiction, powers and privileges of a judge of the Supreme court.

24. (c) **Article - 137**: Supreme court shall have the power to review any judgement pronounced or order made by it.

Article - 144: All authorities, civil and judicial, in the territory of India shall act in aid of the Supreme court.

25. (d) 1. India has only 17 judges per 10 lakh population which is very poor as compared to other European and American countries. eg. USA has 151 and China 170 judges per 10 lakh population.

2. Vacancies in High courts have reached nearly 50% of their sanctioned strength. Lower courts too have huge unfilled posts.

3. In efficient and time consuming procedures must be avoided.

4. Police often fail to collect vital evidences because of lack of scientific training.

Source – The Hindu.

26. (d) Under Article-32: Supreme court can issue writs on all the above mentioned grounds i.e. the writ of Habeas Corpus, Mandamus, Prohibition, Quowarranto, Certiorari can be issued.

Article-226: High Court can issue writs for the restoration of Fundamental Rights.

The writ jurisdiction of high court is wider than supreme court, as it can issue writs not only for the restoration of Fundamental Rights but also on other grounds.

Source: N.C.E.R.T- XIth (Indian Constitution at Work)

27. (a) – Statement 1 is correct.

– High court exercises power of superintendence over subordinate courts and tribunals. Supreme court has no such powers.

– Article - 139 (A) deals with transfer of cases.

28. (b) The salaries, allowances and pensions of judges and all the administrative expenses of Supreme court are charged on consolidated fund of India. Thus they are non-votable by the parliament.

The constitution has guaranteed to the Supreme court, jurisdiction of various kinds and therefore parliament is not authorised to curtail the jurisdiction and powers of the Supreme court.

Source: M. Lakshmikant.

29. (d) All the Above statements highlight the need for Judicial Review.

30. (d) 31. (b) 32. (a) 33. (b) 34. (a)
35. (d) 36. (b) 37. (b) 38. (a) 39. (a)
40. (b)

41. (b) There are 21 High Courts in the country, three having jurisdiction over more than one state. The Judge in the High Court holds office up to 62 years of age.

42. (d) The Supreme Court of India ordered the state governments and the UTs to depute female police officers in plain clothes at the public places to check the incidents of eve-teasing.

43. (a) In general the British observed customary laws of India.

44. (c) The National Legal Services Authority (NALSA) has been constituted under the Legal Services Authorities Act, 1987 to provide free Legal Services to the weaker sections of the society and to organize Lok Adalats for amicable settlement of disputes. In every state, State Legal Services Authority has been constituted to give effect to the policies and directions of the NALSA and to give free legal services to the people and conduct Lok Adalats in the State.

45. (d) The Chief Justice of the High Court is appointed by the President in consultation with the chief justice of India and Governor of the state concerned (Article 217). Every judge of a High Court including the Chief Justice holds office until he/she attain the age of 62 years.

46. (d) The Judge of the Supreme Court or a High Court can be impeached on the basis of proved misbehaviour and incapacity.

47. (d) The U.S. court system is divided into two administratively separate systems, the federal and the state, each of which is independent of the executive and legislative branches of government. One of the unique features of the Indian Constitution is that, notwithstanding the adoption of a federal system and existence of Central Acts and State Acts in their respective spheres, it has generally provided for a single integrated system of Courts to administer both Union and State laws. At the apex of the entire judicial system, exists the Supreme Court of India below which are the High Courts in each State or group of States. Below the High Courts, lies a hierarchy of Subordinate Courts.

48. (c) The E-courts project was established in 2005. According to the project, all the courts including taluk courts will get computerized. As per the project in 2008, all the District courts were initialised under the project. In 2010, all the District courts were computerized. The project also includes producing witnesses through video conferencing. The judicial service centres are available in all court campuses. The Public as well as the advocates can walk in directly and ask for the case status, stage and next hearing dates.

49. (b) According to Article 143 (Power of President to consult Supreme Court).

50. (d) There are 24 High Courts in India. Six (Bombay, Calcutta, Guwahati, Kerala, Madras and Punjab and

Haryana High Court) of them have jurisdiction over more than one state. National Capital Territory of Delhi has High Court of its own.

51. (d) These provisions are given under Article 233-235 in the chapter of Subordinate Courts in the Constitution of India.

52. (a) There were 21 High Courts in India with three new states created in 2000, having their own High Courts (Chattisgarh at Bilaspur, Uttarakhand at Nainital and Jharkhand at Ranchi). Punjab, Haryana and Chandigarh have a common HC at Chandigarh.

In the year 2013, three new High Courts in the northeast - Meghalaya, Manipur and Tripura were created taking the total number of High Courts in the country from 21 to 24.

National Capital Territory of Delhi has a High Court of its own which was established in the year 1966.

53. (b) The statement (1) is not correct as according to Article 138(1) of the Constitution, Parliament can enlarge the jurisdiction and powers of the SC w.r.t. to any of the matters in the Union List. Whereas SC's jurisdiction w.r.t. to any other matter can be enlarged by a special agreement between Government of India and government of the concerned State.

54. (d) Statement 1 is incorrect because after retirement a permanent judge of High Court shall not plead or act in a Court or before any authority in India, except the SC and a HC other than the HC in which he had held his office (Art 220).

Statement 2 is incorrect as according to Article 217, a person is not qualified for appointment as a judge of a High Court in India unless he has for at least ten years held a judicial office in the territory of India.

55. (a) Statement 2 is incorrect because after retirement a permanent judge of High Court shall not plead or act in a Court or before any authority in India, except the SC and a HC other than the HC in which he had held his office (Art 220).

56. (a) When statutory recognition had been given to Lok Adalat, it was specifically provided that the award passed by the Lok Adalat formulating the terms of compromise will have the force of decree of a court which can be executed as a civil court decree.

57. (c) Both are correct. Hence the option (c) is right.

58. (a) 1st and 3rd are correct statements thus option (a) is right.

59. (c) The National Legal Services Authority (NALSA) has been constituted under the Legal Services Authorities Act, 1987 to provide free Legal Services to the weaker sections of the society and to organize Lok Adalats for amicable settlement of disputes. In every state, State Legal Services Authority has been constituted to give effect to the policies and directions of the NALSA and to give free legal services to the people and conduct Lok Adalats in the State.

60. (b) Each gram Nyayalaya is a court of Judicial Magistrate of the first class and its presiding officer is appointed by the state government in consultation with the High court.

Gram Nyayalaya Act; 2008 came into force of Oct, 2, 2009. The objective of this Act is to Provide inexpensive justice to people in rural areas at their doorsteps.

• Gram Nyayalaya try criminal cases, civil suits, claims or disputes which are specified in the First Schedule and the Second Schedule of the Gram Nyayalaya Act the Act.The Gram Nyayalaya are supposed to try to settle the disputes as far as possible by bringing about conciliation between the parties and for this purpose, it can make use of the appointed conciliators.

• Reference- Page no. 601 of India year book 2016, under heading Judiciary it says- Panchayat Courts also function in some states under various names like Nyaya Panchayat, Panchayat Adalat, Gram Kachehri, etc., to decide civil and criminal disputes of petty and local nature. That means first statement is wrong.

• Under this act, District court with consultation of DM, prepares panel of social workers to act as councilors. Hence 2nd statement is right.
Ref: Original Act Page no 7; http://doj.gov.in

• Judicial review means the power of SC or HC to examine the constitutionality of any law. So, "A" is the most fitting option.

61. (d) The parliament can by law increase or decrease the strength of Supreme court. The sanctioned strength of originally constituted Supreme court was 7. Now it stands at 31 (including (II). Against total sanctioned strength of 31, at present there are only 25 judges in Supreme court.

62. (b) 1. While explaining the relation between High court and Supreme court, the apex court has time and again reiterated that " The High court is not a court subordinate to Supreme court". The constitution has clearly divided the jurisdiction between High court and Supreme court.

2. Supreme court has the power to enlarge its jurisdiction (Article - 138) and also Article - 141 i.e law declared by Supreme court to be binding on all courts.

3. Recently in 2017, Supreme court found the conduct of Kolkata High court judge, justice C.S. Karnan as "Unsound and erroneous" and sentenced him to 6 months of imprisonment.

63. (b) Constitution ensures independence of judiciary and legislature has no role in the appointment of judges, so first statement is wrong.

– Chief Justice of Supreme court of India is appointed by president on consultation of such other judges of Supreme court and High court.

– Other judges of Supreme court are appointed by president on consultation of chief Justice of India and other Judges of Supreme court and High court.

Source – M Lakshmikant

64. (c) Judiciary is very much part of the democratic political structure and it is therefore accountable to the people.

Source – N. C. E. R. T –XIth (Chap – 6)

STATE GOVERNMENT

Our constitution provides for a Federal Government, having separate system of administration for the Union and its units, namely the States. The Constitution contains provisions for the government of both.

The Constitution Makers had decided to adopt the same pattern of Parliamentary system of Government in the States i.e. a replica of Government at the Union.

- The only difference is that the Constitutional Head of the Government in the State (i.e. Governor) is not elected, either directly or indirectly, rather be is appointed by the President.
- The Constitution lays down a uniform structure for the State Government, in Part–VI of the Constitution, which is applicable to all the states except the state of Jammu & Kashmir which has a separate Constitution for the its State Government.
- Article 153 to 167 of Indian Constitution deals with the State executive.

Part-VI	
Articles	**Provisions**
Article 153-162	The Governor
Article 163-164	Council of Ministers
Article 165	Advocate General for the State
Article 166-167	Conduct of Government Business

The pattern of Government in the States is the same as that for the Union, namely a Parliamentary System — the executive had being a constitutional ruler who is to act according the advice of Ministers responsible to the State Legislature.

STATE EXECUTIVE

Governor

Article 153 states that there shall be a Governor for each state. Same person can be appointed as Governor for 2 or more states (7th amendment act 1956.)

Article 154 states that the executive power of the state is vested in him and is exercised by him either directly or through officers subordinate to him.

Appointment & Tenure (Article 155 & 156)

- Governor is the executive Head/Nominal Head of the State.
- Governor of a State is appointed by the President.
- Hold office during the pleasure of the President.
- May resign by submitting his resignation to the President. Otherwise the normal term of his office is 5 years.
- Grounds for removal of the Governor are not mentioned in the Constitution; however he must be involved in the gross deliquency like bribery, treason or violation of the Constitution for such an action.
- A President may transfer a Governor appointed to one State to another State for rest of the term.
- A Governor whose term has expired may be reappointed in the same State or any other State.

Qualifications & Conditions for office (article 157 & 158) of Governor

- He must be –
  - A citizen of India.
  - Has attained 35 years of age.
  - Not a member of parliament or state legislature.
  - Not hold any office of profit under the government.
- His emoluments, allowances and privileges are determined by parliament by law.
- The emoluments are charged on the Consolidated Fund of India and cannot be diminished during his term of office.
- If the same person acts as Governor of 2 or more states, the Constitution provides that President may decide about the allocation of emoluments of Governor among states proportion wise (Article 158(3A)).

Oath

Article 159 says that the Governor and every person discharging the functions of the Governor is to take an oath or affirmation before the Chief Justice of the High Court of that state, or in his absence, the senior-most judge of that court available.

Article 160 gives the president the power to make such provision as he thinks fit for the discharge of the functions of the Governor in any contingency not provided for in the Constitution.

Executive Powers of Governor

- **Article 166:** All executive actions of the state are to be taken in the name of the Governor. He acts as a representative of President in the state. He has power to recommend President that the government of the state cannot be carried on in accordance with the provisions of the Constitution. This leads to the imposition of **President rule** in the State under **Article 356**.
- All major appointments in the state are made by the Governor – those of CM, Ministers, and Advocate-General (and decide his remuneration), Chairman & members of State Public Service Commission (PSC), State Election Commissioner and Finance Commission. Members and Chairman of State PSC are however removed by President.
- He is the Chancellor of various universities in the state and appoints their Vice-Chancellors.

Legislative Powers of Governor

- He is an integral part of the state legislature, though not a member of it, he discharges some important legislative functions.
- He **summons** the house(s) of the legislature of state to meet at such a time and place as he thinks fit.
- He may **prorogue** the house(s) and **dissolve** the legislative assembly.
- He has right to reserve certain bills for the assent of the President [Article 200].
- He nominates 1/6th of the members of Legislative Council having special knowledge in literature, science, arts, cooperative movement and social service.
- He decides on the question of disqualification of a member of State Legislature in consultation with Election Commission.
- His most important power is the ordinance making power [Article 213].
- But the Governor cannot issue an ordinance without the previous instructions from the President in cases in which–
  - (a) Bill would have required his previous sanction.
  - (b) Required to be reserved under the Constitution for the assent of the President.
- The ordinances have to be approved by the state legislature, in the same way as the Parliament does in case of Presidential ordinances.
- The scope of the ordinance making power of the Governor is co-extensive with the legislative powers of the State Legislature and is confined to the subjects mentioned in state List and Concurrent List.

- Submission of reports from Auditor General, State Public Service Commission, State Finance Commission, etc. before the Legislature.

Discretionary Powers of Governor

- Discretion of the Governor is wider than that of the President. Article 163 (2) provides that as to the question of matter of discretion, it is the Governor himself who decides which matter falls in his discretion. And his action based on such discretion shall not be called in question.
- Though in most of the matters he has to act on the advice of Council of Ministers, but there are some matters in which he can act according to his discretion.
- He selects the CM if no party has clear-cut majority.
- Dismissal of Ministry if he is convinced that it has lost majority support. But SC in S.R. Bommai Vs UOI (1994) case directed that his opinion must not be subjective and compulsory floor-testing must be done.
- Dissolving the Legislative Assembly.
- Submission of report to the President regarding failure of constitutional machinery in the State.
- Reservation of certain bills for the consideration of the President (Article 200). He must reserve the bill that endangers the position of high court. In addition, he can also reserve the bills that are against the provisions of Constitution, are against larger national interest or DPSP and those which deal with compulsory acquisition of property under Article 31A.

Financial Powers of Governor

- A money bill cannot be introduced in the Legislative Assembly of the State without the recommendation of the Governor.
- No demand of grants can be made except on the recommendation of the Governor.
- **The Governor is required to cause to be laid before the house or houses of the legislature "annual financial statements", that is "Budget" [Article 202].**
- He constitutes a finance commission after every five years to review the financial position of the panchyats and the municipalities.

Judicial powers of governor

- Governor appoints judges of the courts below HC
- He is consulted by the President before appointing judges of the HC.
- Under Article 161 he can grant pardons, reprieves, remission of punishment to the persons convicted under state laws. However he has no power to pardon a sentence of death or remit sentence by the court martial (military court).

Other Powers

The Governor receives the report of the Auditor General and places it before the State Legislature. He places the report of the state Public Service Commission along with the observations of the Council of Ministers before the State Legislature.

Why an appointed Governor?

- It would save the country from another election, conducted on public money.
- If the Government were to be elected by direct vote, then there can be conflict of power between Governor and Chief Minister.
- Through an appointed Governor, the Union Government would be able to maintain intact its control over the states.
- The method of elections would encourage separatist tendencies. The stability and unity of the Governmental machinery of the country as a whole could be achieved only by adopting the system of nomination.
- In actual working it may be said that in states where one party has a clear majority, the part played by the Governor has been that of a constitutional and impartial head but in those States where there are multiple parties with an uncertain command over the Legislature, the Governor has acted as a mere agent of Centre.

Comparison between Powers and Position of the president and the Governor

President	Governor
The President is not only the Head of the State and the Government, he is also the Commander-in-Chief of the Armed Forces.	Each state has its own laws and the Governor, who looks after internal governance of every state. He finalises the budget of the state and also appoint judges in the courts.
The President cannot function without the aid and advise of the Council of Ministers.	Governor can exist without the aid and advice of the Council of Ministers.
The President can grant pardon, reprieve, respite, suspension, remission of commutation in respect to punishment or sentence by a Court Martial.	Governor can suspend, remit or commute a death sentence. The Governor does not enjoy power of pardoning a death sentence.
Every Ordinary Bill, after it is passed by both the houses of the Parliament is presented to the President for his assent.	Every Ordinary bill after it is passed by the Legislative Assembly in case of a Unicameral Legislature or both the Houses in case a Bicameral Legislature either in the first instance or in the second instance is presented to the Governor for his assent.
Every Money Bill after it is passed by both the House of the Parliament is presented to the President for his assent.	Every Money Bill after it is passed by the State Legislature is presented to the Governor for his assent.
A President needs no instructions for making an ordinance	Governor can make an ordinance without the instructions from the President in certain cases.

Chief Minister

The Governor is assisted in the discharge of his functions by a Council of Ministers headed by the Chief Minister. **He is the Real Executive Authority (de facto executive). The Chief Minister is appointed by the Governor**. Generally, the leader of the majority party in the State Assembly is appointed Chief Minister, who holds position identical to that of the Prime Minister at the Centre. He enjoys a term that runs parallel to that of the State Legislature i.e., five years. However, if the term of the State Legislature is extended, the tenure of the Chief Minister is also extended.

The Chief Minister recommends to the Governor the names of persons to be appointed as members of the Council of Ministers, and allocates portfolios among them. He can ask any minister to resign from the Council or drop him from the Council by reshuffling it. He coordinates the working of various ministers and ensures that the Council works as a team.

The Chief Minister is the link between the Governor and the Council of Ministers and keeps the former informed of all decisions of the Council. The Chief Minister takes active part in the deliberations of the State Legislature.

He makes all important policy announcements on the floor of the legislature and defends the policies of his government in the house. He can recommend dissolution of the Legislative Assembly to the Governor even before the expiry of its term. Generally this advise is accepted by the Governor.

Council of Ministers (COM)

- Article 163 (1) provides that there should be COM with Chief Minister as the head to aid and advise the Governor in exercise of his functions.
- The real executive authority of the state is vested in the COM, the Governor, however is not bound to act by the advice of COM in all cases, as he can exercise his discretionary powers.
- Any person may be appointed as a minister, but he ceases to be a minister if he doesn't become a member of the state legislature within 6 months (Article 164).
- Salaries and allowances of ministers are governed by laws made by the state legislature.
- Ministry which loses the confidence of the legislative assembly should resign. The Governor may choose to dismiss the ministry if it does not resign and ask the leader of opposition to constitute an alternative ministry, or if he feels that no stable ministry can be formed, recommend President's rule in the State.
- Like at the Centre, in the states too, the Council of Ministers consists of three categories-cabinet ministers, Ministers of State, & Deputy Minister.

- Article 164 states that the COM is collectively responsible to Legislative Assembly of state.
- The Ministers hold office till the pleasure of the Governor but, the Ministers can be removed only on the advice of CM. Thus the CM can hold Ministers individually responsible by removing them in case of non-performance.

Functions of Chief Minister & COM

The Constitution does not assign any formal powers to the Council of Ministers. However, in practice it has a wide range of functions. It formulates the policy of the Government and implements it. It assists the Governor in making all the important appointments. Most of the important bills are introduced in the legislature by members of the Council of Ministers. It formulates the State budget and submits it to the Legislature for its approval. It can present supplementary demands for grants whenever necessary. It also plays an important role in preparing and implementing State Plans.

Advocate General (Article 165)

- He is an official of State, corresponding to the Attorney-General of India (Art 76).
- He advices government of state upon legal matters.
- Appointed by the Governor, and holds office during his pleasure.
- **A person qualified to be a judge of a HC can be appointed as an Advocate General.**
- His remuneration is determined by the Governor.
- He can speak and take part in the proceedings of the Legislature of the State but he has no right to vote in it. (Article – 177)

STATE LEGISLATURE (PART VI, ART. 168-212)

- **Legislature of every State consists of Governor and House (state legislative assembly) or Houses (state legislative assembly and council).**
- **At present, only 7 states - Maharashtra, Karnataka, Telangana, Bihar, U.P, Andhra Pradesh, J&K have a bicameral (consisting of 2 houses) Legislature.**
- The above list is not permanent in the sense that the Constitution provides for the abolition of the Second Chamber in a state where it exists as well as for the creation of such a chamber in a state where there is none at present, by a simple procedure which does not involve an amendment of the Constitution. The procedure involves a resolution at the Legislative Assembly of the state concerned passed by a majority of the total membership of the Assembly not being less than two-thirds of the members actually present and voting, followed by an Act of Parliament (Article 169).

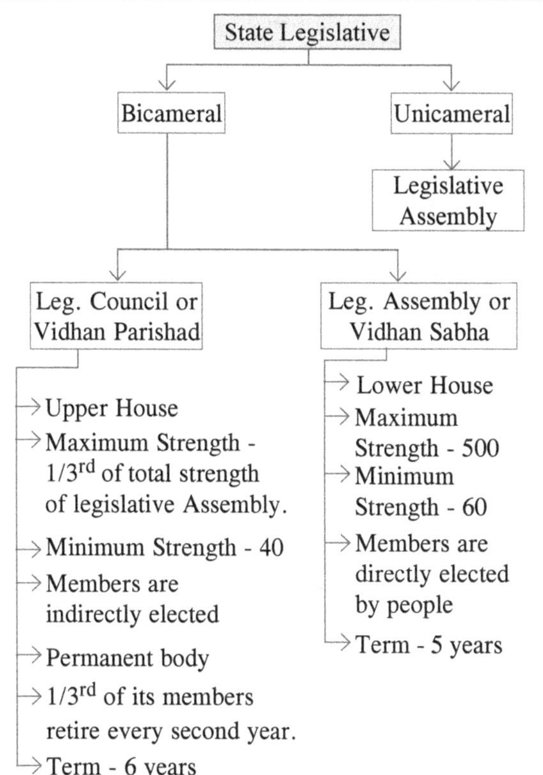

Legislative Assembly (Vidhan Sabha)

- It is the lower and popular house of the State. Members are chosen by direct election on the basis of adult suffrage from territorial constituencies (Article 170).
- The number of members varies between 60 and 500. However certain States like Sikkim, Goa, Mizoram and Arunachal Pradesh have less than 60 members.
- The Governor may nominate one Anglo-Indian to the house.
- The reservation of seats has been provided for SCs and STs on the basis of their population.
- According to Article 172, duration of assembly is normally 5 years. But it may be dissolved earlier by the Governor.
- Its term may also be extended by one year at a time by parliament during national emergency, though this can in no case be extended beyond 6 months after the proclamation has ceased to operate.

Legislative Council (Vidhan Parishad) (Article 169)

- It is the upper house.
- Parliament may by law create or abolish Legislative Council.
- It can be created, if the Legislative Assembly of the state passes a resolution to the effect by special majority.
- It is not an amendment to the Constitution and therefore it can be passed like an ordinary piece of legislation.
- Article 171 contains various categories of members. According to this:

- 1/3rd of its members are elected by legislative assembly.
- 1/3rd by local bodies.
- 1/6th nominated by the Governor.
- 1/12th are elected by teachers.
- 1/5th by university graduates.
- The maximum strength of Legislative Council can be 1/3rd of the total membership of Legislative Assembly, but in no case less than 40.
- Parliament has the final power to decide about its composition.
- It is not subject to dissolution. But 1/3rd of its members retire on the expiry of every 2nd year.

Qualifications

- Article 173 mentions the qualifications of members as:-
  - A citizen of India.
  - Not less than 25 years of age for legislative assembly and not less than 30 years of age for Legislative Council.
  - Possesses such other qualifications as may be prescribed by the Parliament.
  - Not hold any office under the Union or state government.
- **Article 190:** No person shall be a member of both houses of State Legislature and if anyone gets elected to both Houses, he has to vacate one seat.
- No person can become a member of legislature of 2 or more states.

Disqualifications for memberships:

- The disqualifications for memberships of a State Legislature as laid down in Article-191 of the Constitution are analogous to the disqualifications for membership of either House of Parliament (Article-102).

Presiding Officers of State Legislature

The Speaker

The Speaker is elected by the assembly itself from amongst its members and remains in office during the life of the assembly. However, he may vacate his office by writing to the Deputy Speaker or be removed by a resolution passed by a majority of all the then members of the assembly or he ceases to be a member of the assembly. Such a resolution can be moved only after giving 14 days prior notice.

Powers and Duties of Speaker

- His functions are similar to those of the Speaker of the Lok Sabha. He adjourns the assembly or suspends the meeting in the absence of a quorum and maintains order and decorum in the assembly for conducting its business and regulating its proceedings.
- He can allow a secret sitting of the house at the request of the leader of the house. He decides the questions of disqualification of a member of the assembly, arising on the ground of defection under the provisions of the Tenth Schedule of the Constitution. However, he also vacates his office earlier in any of the following three cases:

1. If he ceases to be a member of the assembly.
2. If he resigns by writing to the deputy speaker.
3. If he is removed by a resolution passed by a majority of all the members of the assembly. Such resolution can be moved only after giving 14 days advance notice.

- He appoints the Chairman of all the committees of the assembly and supervises their functioning. He himself is the Chairman of the Business Advisory Committee, the Rules Committee and the General Purpose Committee. The speaker decides whether a bill is a Money Bill or not.

Deputy Speaker

Like the speaker, the Deputy Speaker is also elected by the assembly itself from amongst its members. He is elected after the election of the Speaker has taken place. The Deputy Speaker performs the duties of the speaker's office when it is vacant. He also acts as the speaker when the latter is absent from the sitting of assembly. In both the cases, he has all the powers of the speaker.

Chairman of the Legislative Council

The Chairman is elected by the Council itself from amongst its members. He may vacate his office by resigning by writing to the Deputy Chairman or if he ceases to be a member of the Council. His powers and functions are comparable to the Speaker of the Assembly with few exceptions. Such as the speaker has one special power which is not enjoyed by the Chairman. The speaker decides whether a bill is a Money Bill or not and his decision on this question is final.

Deputy Chairman of Legislative Council

Like the Chairman, the Deputy Chairman also elected by the Council itself from amongst its members. The Deputy Chairman performs the duties of the Chairman's office when it is vacant. He also acts as the Chairman, when the latter is absent from the sitting of the Council. In both the cases, he has all the powers of the Chairman.

Comparison of Legislative Council and Legislative Assembly

- In the passage of an Ordinary Bill, both the houses enjoy equal status but in case of disagreement the will of the Assembly prevails over that of the Council and there is no provision of joint sitting in this regard.
- A Money Bill can be introduced only in Assembly not in Council.
- The Council has no participation in the election of the President.
- It also has no effective say in the ratification of the Constitutional Amendment Bill. Also, the existence of the Council depends on the will of the assembly.

Legislative Procedure

The legislative procedure in a State Legislature having two houses is broadly similar to that in Parliament except for some aspects.

Money Bill

The position is the same at Union and State Levels : the Bill can be introduced only in the Assembly; the will of the Assembly prevails; and the Assembly is not bound to accept any recommendation by the Council which may at the most withhold the bill for 14 days from the date of its receipt.

Ordinary Bill

The only power of the Council is to interpose some delay in the passage of the Bill for a period of three months at the most. Ultimately the will of the assembly prevails and when the bill comes to the Council a second time the Council can delay it for not more than a month.

Governor's Assent

When a bill is presented to the Governor after its passage by the houses of the legislature the Governor may (i) declare his assent to the bill, in which case, it would become a law at once; (ii) declare that he withholds his assent in which case the bill fails to become a law; (iii) return the bill, if it is not a money bill with a message; (iv) reserve the bill for the consideration of the President.

Comparing Legislative Procedure in the Parliament and State Legislature

Parliament	State Legislature
A. With Regard to Ordinary Bills	
1. It can be introduced in either house of the Parliament.	1. It can be introduced in either House of the state legislature.
2. It can be introduced either by a minister or by a private member.	2. It can be introduced either by a minister or by a private member.
3. It passes through first reading, second reading and third reading in the originating house.	3. It passes through first reading, second reading and third reading in the orginating house.
4. It is deemed to have been passed by the Parliament only when both the houses have agreed to it. either with or without amendments.	4. It is deemed to have been passed by the state legislature only when both the houses have agreed to it, either with or without amendments.
5. A deadlock between the two houses takes place when the second house, after receiving a bill passed by the first House, rejects the bill or proposes amendments that are not acceptable to the first House or does not pass the bill within six months.	5. A deadlock between the two houses takes place when the Legislative Council, after receiving a bill passed by the Legislative Assembly, rejects the bill or proposes amendments that are not acceptable to the Legislative Assembly or does not pass the bill within three months.
6. The Constitution provides for the mechanism of joint sitting of two houses of the Parliament to resolve a deadlock between them over the passage of a bill.	6. The Constitution does not provide for the mechanism of joint sitting of two houses of the state legislature to resolve a deadlock between them over the passage of a bill.
7. The Lok Sabha cannot override the Rajya Sabha by passing the bill for the second time and vice versa. A joint sitting is the only way to resolve a deadlock between the two houses.	7. The Legislative Assembly can override the Legislative Council by passing the bill for the second time and vice versa. When a bill is passed by the Assembly for the second time and transmitted to the Legislative Council, if the Legislative Council rejects the bill again or proposes amendments that are not acceptable to the Legislative Assembly, or does not pass the bill within one month, then the bill is deemed to have been passed by both the houses in the form in which it was passed by the Legislative Assembly for the second time.
8. The mechanism of joint sitting for resolving a deadlock applies to a bill whether originating in the Lok Sabha or the Rajya Sabha. If a joint sitting is not summoned by the President, the bill ends and becomes dead.	8. The mechanism of passing the bill for the second time to resolve a deadlock applies to a bill originating in the Legislative Assembly only. When a bill, which has originated in the Legislative Council and sent to the Legislative Assembly, is rejected by the latter, the bill ends and becomes dead.
B. With Regard to Money Bills	
1. It can be introduced only in the Lok Sabha and not in the Rajya Sabha.	1. It can be introduced only in the Legislative assembly and not in the Legislative Council.
2. It can be introduced only on the recommendation of the President.	2. It can be introduced only on the recommendation of the governor.
3. It can be introduced only by a minister and not by a private member.	3. It can be introduced only by a minister and not by a private member.
4. It cannot be rejected or amended by the Rajya Sabha. It should be returned to the Lok Sabha within 14 days, either with or without recommendations.	4. It cannot be rejected or amended by the Legislative Council. It should be returned to the legislative Assembly within 14 days, either with or without amendments.

5. The Lok Sabha can either accept or reject all or any of the recommendations of the Rajya Sabha.	5. The Legislative Assembly can either accept or rejedll all or any of the recommendations of the legislative council.
6. If the Lok Sabha accepts any recommendation, the bill is then deemed to have been passed by both the houses in the modified form.	6. If the legislative assembly accepts any recommendation, the bill is then deemed to have been passed by both the houses in the modified form.
7. If the Lok Sabha does not accept any recommendation, the bill is then deemed to have been passed by both the houses in the form originally passed by the Lok Sabha without any change.	7. If the Legislative Assembly does not accept any recommendation, the bill is then deemed to have been passed by both the houses in the form originally passed by the legislative Assembly without any change.
8. If the Rajya Sabha does not return the bill to the Lok Sabha within 14 days, the bill is deemed to have been passed by both the houses at the expiration of the said period in the form originally passed by the Lock Sabha.	8. If the Legislative Council does not return the bill to the Legislative Assembly within 14 days, the bill is deemed to have been passed by both the houses at the expiration of the said period in the form originally passed by the Legislative Assembly.
9. The Constitution does not provide for the resolution of any deadlock between the two houses. This is because, the will of the Lok Sabha is made to prevail over that of the Rajya Sabha.	9. The Constitution does not provide for the resolution of any deadlock between two houses. This is because, the will of the Legislative Assembly is made to prevail over that of Legislative Council.

Utility of the Second Chamber (Legislative Council)

- The very composition of the legislative council, renders its position work, being partly elected and partly nominated and representing various interests.
- Its very existence depends upon the will of the Legislative Assembly, because the latters has the power to pass a resolution for the abolition of the Second Chamber.
- The Council of Ministers is responsible only to due Legislative Assembly.
- Therefore, the Second Chamber in a state is not every a revising body like the second chamber in the Union Parliament.

Privileges of a State Legislature

The privileges of the Legislature of a state are similarly to those of the Union Parliament in as much as the constitutional provisions (Article-105 and Article-194) are identical.

- Each house of the State Legislature has the power to punish for breach of its privileges or for contempt.
- Each house is the sole judge of the questions of breach of its privileges and courts have no jurisdiction to interfere with the decision of the House on this point.
- Once a privilege is held to exist, it is for the House to judge the occasion and its manner of exercise.

The State of Jammu and Kashmir

The State of Jammu and Kashmir holds a special position under the Constitution of India. Though it is one of the states specified in the First Schedule and forms a part of the territory of India as defined in Article 1, all the provisions of the Constitution of India relating to the States do not apply to Jammu and Kashmir. The state alone of all the states of the Indian Union has its own Constitution.

The Article 370 in Part XXI of the Constitution grants a special status to state of Jammu and Kashmir. Accordingly, all the provisions of the Constitution of India do not apply to it. It is also the only state in the Indian Union which has its own separate state Constitution.

The 'Instrument of Accession of Jammu and Kashmir to India' was signed by Pandit Jawaharlal Nehru and Maharaja Hari Singh on 26 October 1947. Under this, the state surrendered only three subjects (defence, external affairs and communications) to the Dominion of India, the Government of India made a commitment that 'the people of this state, through their own Constituent Assembly, would determine the internal Constitution of this state and the nature and extent of the jurisdiction of the Union of India over the state, and until the decision of the Constitution of India could only provide an interim arrangement regarding the state.

In pursuance of this commitment, Article 370 was incorporated in the Constitution of India. It clearly states that the provisions with respect to the state of J & K are only temporary and not permanent. It became operative on 17 November 1952, with the following provisions:

In pursuance of the provisions of Article 370, an executive order was issued by the President on the constitutional position of the state and its relationship with the Union. At present, it is as follows:

1. Jammu and Kashmir is a constituent state of the Indian Union and has its place in Part I and Schedule I of the Constitution of India (dealing with the Union and its Territory). But its name, area or boundary cannot be changed by the Union without the consent of its legislature.

2. The state of J & K has its own Constitution. Hence, Part VI of the Constitution of India (dealing with state government) is not applicable to this state. The very definition of 'state' under this part does not include the state of J & K.

3. Parliament can make laws in relation to the state on most of the subjects enumerated in the Union List and on a good number of subjects enumerated in the Concurrent List. But, the residuary power belongs to the state legislature except in few matters like prevention of activities involving terrorist acts, questioning or disrupting the sovereignty and territorial integrity of India. Further, the power to make laws of preventive detention in the state belongs to the state legislature. This means that the preventive detention laws made by the Parliament are not applicable to the state.

4. Part III (dealing with Fundamental Rights) is applicable to the state with some exceptions and conditions. The fundamental right to property is still guaranteed in the state.

5. Part IV (dealing with Directive Principles of State Policy) and Part IV A (dealing with Fundamental Duties) are not applicable to the state.

6. A National Emergency declared on the ground of internal disturbance will not have effect in the state except with the concurrence of the state government.

7. The President has no power to declare a financial emergency in relation to the state of J & K.

Constitution of Jammu and Kashmir

The Constitution of Jammu and Kashmir was adopted on November 17, 1957 and came into effect from January 26, 1957.

Some of its important provisions are considered here.

The Legislative Assembly consists of 100 numbers elected directly from territorial constituencies of the state and two women members nominated by the Governor. Twenty-four seats are to remain vacant till filled by representatives of people in Pakistan occupied Kashmir (PoK).

The Legislative Council consists of 36 member, 11 of whom are elected by the Assembly from among the people of Kashmir provided that of the members elected at least one shall be a resident of Tehsil Ladakh and at least one a resident of Tehsil Kargil, and 11 elected by the Assembly from people of Jammu. The remaining 14 members are elected by various electorates, such as municipal councils and such other local bodies.

The High Court of the state consists of a Chief Justice and two or more other Judges. Every Judge is to be appointed by the President after consultation with the Chief Justice of India and the Governor.

The official language of the State is Urdu, but English will continue to be used for official purpose unless the State Legislature provides otherwise. And no amendment can be made to change any provision regarding the relationship of the state with the Union of India.

- There will be a Public Service Commission for the State. The Commission along with its Chairman will be appointed by the Governor.
- The State Constitution may be amended by introducing a Bill in the Legislative Assembly and getting it passed in each House by a majority of not less that two-third of total membership of that House.

Administration of Scheduled Areas

Article 244 in Part X of the Constitution envisages a special system of administration for certain areas designated as 'Scheduled areas' and 'tribal areas'.

The Constitution has made special provision for the administration of Scheduled Areas in a state other than Assam, Meghalaya, Tripura and Mizoram. The right to declare any area as a Scheduled Area rests with the President and is subject to legislation by the Parliament.

The Constitution contains special provisions regarding the administration of Scheduled Areas, which are contained in the *Fifth Schedule*.

The Union Government can also give directions to the respective State regarding administration of the Scheduled Areas. The Governor of the state, where such areas are located, has to submit reports to the President regarding the administration of such areas annually or whenever required by the President. To take care of the welfare and advancement of the Scheduled Tribes in the State, a **Tribes Advisory Council is constituted**. In addition, the Governor can also take certain steps to protect the interests of the Scheduled Tribes. Thus, he can direct that a particular Act of Parliament or state legislature shall not apply to the Scheduled Area. He can make regulations prohibiting or restricting transfer of land, allotment of land and money lending. However, all these actions of the governor need prior approval of the President.

Tribes Advisory Council

The Constitution of India provides for a Tribes Advisory Council (TAC) in each State having Scheduled areas and if the president so directs, also in any State having Scheduled Tribes but not Scheduled areas. TAC shall consists of not more than 20 members of whom three-fourths shall be the representatives of the Scheduled Tribes in the Legislative Assembly of the State.

The Governor makes rules prescribing or regulating as the case may be (i) the number of members of the Council, the mode of their appointment and the appointment of the Chairman of the Council and of the officers and servants thereof; (ii) the conduct of its meetings and its procedure in general; and (iii) all other incidental matters.

Tribal Areas

These areas are located in the states of Assam, Meghalaya, Mizoram and Tripura and have been specified in the Sixth Schedule of the Constitution. Though these areas fall within the executive authority of the state, provision has been made for the creation of district councils and regional councils for the exercise of certain legislative and judicial powers in these areas. **The district and regional councils are empowered to make laws in certain fields such as management of forests, marriage and social customs, inheritance of property, etc.** These councils can also impose certain taxes and collect land revenue.

Exercise -1

1. Governor can remove a minister (State Assembly) only on the advice of
   - (a) Chief Minister
   - (b) Prime Minister
   - (c) President
   - (d) His own discretion

2. A Governor holds office:
   - (a) for five years
   - (b) for a period specified by the Parliament
   - (c) during the pleasure of the President
   - (d) till he has the confidence of the Parliament

3. In appointing a Governor, the President consults the Chief Minister of the State as this is:
   - (a) constitutionally imperative
   - (b) a convention
   - (c) as Parliament has legislated to the effect
   - (d) A duty of the President

4. Dual role of the Governor means:
   - (a) Constitutional and real executive
   - (b) Head of a state and head of government under certain circumstances
   - (c) Belonging both to Central and State executive
   - (d) Constitutional ruler and represents the Centre

5. Governor of which State has been vested with special powers for scheduled tribes?
   - (a) Arunachal Pradesh (b) Assam
   - (c) Maharashtra (d) West Bengal

6. Who presides over meetings of Council of Ministers in a State?
   - (a) Governor (b) Chief Minister
   - (c) Senior ministers (d) Both (a) and (b)

7. To be a member of a State Council of Ministers, a person:
   - (a) must belong to the Legislative Assembly
   - (b) must get membership of the State Legislature within six months
   - (c) cannot be less than 35 years old
   - (d) an expert in some field if he is not a member of the Legislature

8. Chairman of Legislative Council is:
   - (a) appointed by the Governor
   - (b) the Governor
   - (c) elected by the members of the Legislative Council from among themselves
   - (d) appointed by the Speaker of the Assembly

9. Limitations on authority of the State Legislature EXCLUDES:
   - (a) Parliament's authority to make laws on subjects in the State List during an Emergency
   - (b) Parliament's authority to make laws on state subjects if Rajya Sabha passes a reso-lution
   - (c) Governor's discretionary power to dissolve the legislature
   - (d) Governors power to reserve bills for consideration of the President

10. The Constitution of J & K was framed by:
    - (a) Constituent Assembly which framed India's Constitution
    - (b) Constituent Assembly set up by the Parliament
    - (c) Constituent Assembly set up by the State
    - (d) the State Legislature

11. An amendment to the Constitution of India extends to J&K:
    - (a) automatically
    - (b) only if ratified by State Legislature
    - (c) by an order of the President under Article 370
    - (d) Can never be extended

12. If the State government fails to comply with the directions of the Centre in the exercise of administrative powers:
    - (a) Governor may be directed by the President to dismiss the ministry
    - (b) President can declare a national emergency and convert the federal structure into a unitary one
    - (c) Constitutional emergency can be declared and the President can assume the powers of the State government
    - (d) Supreme Court may be asked to intervene

13. Privileges of the State Legislature are mentioned in Article:
    - (a) 105 of the Constitution
    - (b) 194 of the Constitution
    - (c) chapter on Fundamental Rights under Article 19
    - (d) nowhere in the Constitution as they have evolved as part of parliamentary convention

14. Mizoram and Sikkim may have a maximum of :
    - (a) 7 ministers
    - (b) 12 ministers
    - (c) 15% of their lower house members
    - (d) 5 % of the lower house members

15. If in an election of State Legislative Assembly, the candidate who is not elected loses his deposit, it means that
    - (a) the polling was very poor
    - (b) the election was for a multi-member constituency
    - (c) the elected candidate's victory over his nearest rival was marginal
    - (d) he did not get the required number of minimum votes

16. The Constitution says that the state council of ministers hold office during the pleasure of the Governor. The words "during the pleasure of the Governor" in reality means :
    - (a) Pleasure of the President
    - (b) Pleasure of the Prime Minister
    - (c) Pleasure of the Chief Minister
    - (d) Pleasure of the Legislative Assembly

17. The Chief Minister of a state is
    - (a) elected by the State Legislature

(b)　appointed by the Governor
(c)　appointed by the President
(d)　None of the above

18.　The oath of office is administered to the members of the State Council of Ministers by the
(a)　Governor
(b)　Chief Minister
(c)　Chief Justice of the State High Court
(d)　Speaker of Legislative Assembly

19.　There is a constitutional requirement to have a minister of tribal welfare for the states of
(a)　Assam, Nagaland and Manipur
(b)　Himachal Pradesh, Haryana and Rajasthan
(c)　Bihar, Madhya Pradesh and Odisha
(d)　Manipur, Tripura and Meghalaya

20.　Who administers oath of office to the Governor of a State?
(a)　Chief Justice of India
(b)　President
(c)　Chief Justice of High Court Concerned
(d)　Speaker of Legislative Assembly of the Concerned State.

21.　As per the Constitution of India, what is the limit prescribed for the number of members in the Legislative Assembly of a State?
(a)　350 members　　　(b)　400 members
(c)　450 members　　　(d)　500 members

22.　The Legislative Council in a State in India can be created or abolished by the
(a)　Parliament on the recommendation of a Governor of the state.
(b)　Parliament alone
(c)　Parliament after the state assembly passes the resolution of that effect.
(d)　Governor of the state on the recommendation of the Council of Ministers.

23.　The State Government's responsibility for educational planning is shared by the
(a)　Ministery of Programme implementation
(b)　Ministry of Human Resource Development
(c)　Ministry of Planning
(d)　Ministry of Home Affairs

24.　The Union Legislature cannot legislate on a subject in the State List unless:
(a)　The President call upon it to do so
(b)　The Rajya Sabha passes a resolution that it is necessary in national interest to do so
(c)　The Speaker certifies that it is necessary
(d)　There is a national emergency

25.　If the States fail to carry out the directives of the Central Government with regard to exercise of their administrative powers:
(a)　the President can impose President's rule on the State and assume all the powers of the State Government
(b)　the President can send reserve police to the State for the implementation of these directives
(c)　the President can dispatch army for their implementation
(d)　the President can direct the Governor to dismiss the State Council of Ministers

26.　If in an election to a state Legislative Assembly the candidate who is declared elected losses his deposit, it means that:
(a)　A very large number of candidate contested the election
(b)　The elected candidate's victory over his nearest rival was very marginal
(c)　The election was for a multi-member constituency
(d)　All of the above

27.　As per the Constitution of India, what is the limit prescribed for the number of members in the Legislative Assembly of a State?
(a)　350 members　　　(b)　400 members
(c)　450 members　　　(d)　500 members

28.　The Legislative Council in a State in India can be created or abolished by the
(a)　Parliament on the recommendation of a Governor of the state.
(b)　Parliament alone
(c)　Parliament after the state assembly passes the resolution of that effect.
(d)　Governor of the state on the recommendation of the Council of Ministers.

29.　With respect to Article 371 A of the Constitution of India, the Governor of which one of the following States has special responsibility with respect to law and order of the State?
(a)　Assam　　　　　(b)　Manipur
(c)　Nagaland　　　　(d)　Andhra Pradesh

30.　According to Article 164(1) of the Constitution of India, in three States there shall be a Minister in charge of tribal welfare who may in addition be in charge of the welfare of the Scheduled Castes and Backward Classes. Which one of the following States is not covered by the Article?
(a)　Jharkhand　　　　(b)　Punjab
(c)　Madhya Pradesh　(d)　Odisha

31.　Who among the following recommends to the Parliament for the abolition of the Legislative Council in a State?
(a)　The President of India
(b)　The Governor of the concerned State
(c)　The Legislative Council of the concerned State
(d)　The Legislative Assembly of the concerned State

32.　Which one of the following states does not have Vidhan Parishad?
(a)　Bihar　　　　　(b)　Maharashtra
(c)　Tamil Nadu　　　(d)　Uttar Pradesh

33.　Which one among the following is not a recommendation of the Sarkaria Commission on the appointment of the Governor in a state?
(a)　He/She must not have participated in active politics at least for sometime before his/her appointment as Governor
(b)　The Chief Justice of the Supreme Court may be consulted by the President in selecting a Governor
(c)　The Governor's term of office of five years should not be disturbed except very rarely
(d)　The Governor should not be the native of the state

34. The Governor may recommend the imposition of the President's rule in the state
    (a) on the recommendation of the State Legislature
    (b) on the recommendation of the President
    (c) on the recommendation of the Chief Minister
    (d) if he is convinced thai the Government of the State cannot be carried on in accordance with the provisions of the Constitution of India

35. Which one of the following States of India does not have a Legislative Council even though the Constitution? (Seventh Amendment) Act, 1956 provides for it?
    (a) Maharashtra   (b) Bihar
    (c) Karnataka   (d) Madhya Pradesh

36. Which one of the following Articles of the Constitution of India says that the executive power of every State shall be so exercised as not to impede or prejudice the exercise of the executive power of the Union?
    (a) Article 257   (b) Article 258
    (c) Article 355   (d) Article 358

37. In which one of the following areas does the State Government not have control over its local bodies?
    (a) Citizens' grievances (b) Financial matters
    (c) Legislation   (d) Personnel matters

38. Which one of the following statements is correct?
    (a) In India, the same person cannot be appointed as Governor for two or more States at the same time
    (b) The Judges of the High Court of the States in India are appointed by the Governor of the State just as the Judges of Supreme Court are appointed by the President
    (c) No procedure has been laid down in the Constitution of India for the removal of a Governor from his/her post
    (d) In the case of a Union Territory having a legislative setup, the Chief Minister is appointed by the Lt. Governor on the basis of majority support

39. Which of the following constitutional Amendment Act provided for the appointment of the same person as Governor for two or more states?
    (a) 4th Amnd.   (b) 7th Amnd
    (c) 11th Amnd   (d) 24th Amnd

40. Article 154 states that the Governor can exercise his executive authority either directly of through officers subordiante to him. The word subordinates includes :
    (a) All the ministers and the Chief Minister
    (b) All the ministers except the Chief Minister
    (c) Only the Chief Minister and the Deputy Chief Minister
    (d) Only the Cabinet Minister

41. Which of the following is not correctly matched?
    (a) Article 153 - Office of the Governor
    (b) Article 156 - Term of the Governor
    (c) Article 154 - Executive authority of Governor
    (d) Article 155 - Removal of Governor

42. Who/Which of the following can abolish a State Legislative Council.
    (a) Parliament   (b) President
    (c) Governor   (d) State Assembly

43. Union Territories are administered by the:
    (a) Parliament
    (b) Union Council of Ministers
    (c) President through administrators
    (d) Prime Minister

44. Which one is not the component of the 'Pradhan Mantri Gramodaya Yojna'?
    (a) Elementary Education
    (b) Primary health
    (c) Rural Road
    (d) Nutrition

45. Which one of the following statements in respect of the States of India is not correct?   **[CDS 2018]**
    (a) States in India cannot have their own constitutions.
    (b) The State of Jammu and Kashmir has its own constitution.
    (c) States in India do not have the right to secede from the Union of India.
    (d) The maximum number of members in the Council of Ministers of Delhi can be 15 percent of the total

46. Which one among the following States of India has the largest number of seats in its Legislative Assembly?   **[CDS 2018]**
    (a) West Bengal   (b) Bihar
    (c) Madhya Pradesh   (d) Tamil Nadu

Exercise -2

Statement Based MCQ

1. Consider the following statements
   1. The constitution has given the states the option of establishing either a unicameral or bicameral legislature.
   2. At present only 5 states have bicameral legislature.
   Select the correct statement/statements using the codes given below.
   (a) 1 only   (b) 2 only
   (c) Both 1 and 2   (d) Neither 1 nor 2

2. Governor of a state can promulgate ordinances when the state legislature is not in session. After the re-assembly of state legislature, these ordinances must be approved by it within
   (a) 1 month   (b) Six months
   (c) 2 months   (d) Three weeks

3. Consider the following statements:
   1. Maximum strength of state legislative council is fixed at two-third of the total strength of the legislative assembly of concerned state.
   2. 5/6th of the total members of a legislative council are indirectly elected.

3. 1/6th of the total members of a legislative council are nominated by the governor.
Select the correct statement/statements using the codes given below:
(a) 1 only   (b) 2 and 3 only
(c) 1 and 3 only   (d) 1 and 2 only

4. Recently, the Punchhi Commission was set up to enquire into the role of Governor. Which of the following is/are not among the recommendations of this Commission?
(i) The Governor must be a person from inside the concerned state.
(ii) The tenure of the Governor must be fixed.
(iii) The Governor should be a detached person and not too intimately connected with the local politics of the state.
(iv) The Governor is eligible for further appointment as second term as Governor, or election as Vice President or President of India.
Select the correct answer using the codes given below:
(a) (ii), (iii) and (iv) are correct
(b) (i), (iii) and (iv) are correct
(c) (iii) and (iv) are correct
(d) all are correct

5. Consider the following statements.
1. All members of all the legislative assemblies are elected directly.
2. Constitution fixes the maximum strength of state legislative assembly at 500 and minimum strength at 60.
Select the correct statement/statements using from the codes given below:
(a) 1 only   (b) 2 only
(c) Both 1 and 2   (d) Neither 1 nor 2

6. Consider the following statements:
1. The number of members to be elected from each state to Rajya Sabha has been fixed by the Seventh Schedule of the constitution.
2. The term of the legislative assembly of Jammu and Kashmir is 4 years.
Select the correct answer from the codes given below:
(a) 1 only   (b) 2 only
(c) Both 1 and 2   (d) Neither 1 nor 2

7. Which of the following is a discretionary powers of the Governor?
1. Selecting a chief minister if no single party has a clear majority.
2. Dismissing the ministry at any time.
3. Reserving a bill for the President.
Select the correct answer using the codes given below:
(a) 1 and 3   (b) 1 and 2
(c) 3 only   (d) 1, 2 and 3

8. Legislative Council of a State:
1. is not subject to dissolution
2. can be abolished by the State Legislative Assembly
3. can be abolished by the President on Governor's recommendation

Which of the above statements is/are correct?
(a) 1 only   (b) 2 only
(c) 1 and 2   (d) 3 only

9. Which of the following is/are required for a Legislative Council in a State to be created or abolished?
1. Act of Parliament
2. Resolution of the Legislative Assembly of the State concerned
3. Recommendation by the Governor of the State concerned
4. Constitutional Amendment requiring States' ratification
Select the correct answer using the codes given below:
(a) 1 only   (b) 1 and 2
(c) 1, 2 and 3   (d) 2 and 4

10. Which of the following statements are true about the Governor of a state?
1. The executive power of the state is vested in him.
2. He must have attained 35 years of age.
3. He holds office during the pleasure of the President.
4. The grounds for his removal are laid down in the Constitution.
Select the correct answer using the codes given below:
(a) 1,2, and 4   (b) 1,2 and 3
(c) 1, 3 and 4   (d) 1, 2, 3 and 4

11. Consider the following in context of the ordinance making power of the Governor:
1. It is laid down in Article 213.
2. It can be issued by him after the advice of the President or state council of ministers.
3. It is co-extensive with the legislative power of the state legislature.
4. It can be issued only during the recess of State Legislative Assembly and not the Legislative Council.
5. It can not be withdrawn by him anytime.
Select the correct answer using the codes given below:
(a) 2,3 and 4   (b) 1,3 and 5
(c) 1, 2 and 3   (d) 2, 4 and 5

12. The Governor of state :
1. Possesses executive, legislative and judicial powers analogous to the President.
2. Has to act with the aid and advice of the council of ministers always.
3. Has the power to appoint and remove the members of State Public Service Commission.
4. Has the power to allocate business of the government among the various ministers.
Of the above, the correct statement are :
(a) 1 and 2   (b) 2, 3 and 4
(c) 1 and 4   (d) 1, 3 and 4

13. Article 156 of the Constitution of India provides that a Governor shall hold office for a term of 5 years from the date on which he enters upon his office. Which of the following can be deducted from this?
1. No Governor can be removed from office till the completion of his term.
2. No Governor can continue in office beyond a period of five years.

Select the correct answer using the codes given below:
(a) 1 only   (b) 2 only
(c) Both 1 and 2   (d) Neither

14. Which of the following are the discretionary powers given to the Governor of a State?
1. Sending a report to the President of India for imposing the President's rule
2. Appointing the Ministers
3. Reserving certain bills passed by the State Legislature for consideration of the President of India
4. Making the rules to conduct the business of the State Government
Select the correct answer using the code given below.
(a) 1 and 2 only   (b) 1 and 3 only
(c) 2, 3 and 4 only   (d) 1, 2, 3 and 4

15. While appointing a Lokayuka, the Governor in most of the states consults :
1. President of India
2. Speaker of the Legislative Assembly
3. Leader of the opposition in the Legislative Assembly
4. Chief justice of the State High Court.
5. Leader of the Opposition in the Legislative Council.
Select the correct answer using the codes given below:
(a) 1, 4 and 5   (b) 1, 2 and 4
(c) 3, 4 and 5   (d) 3 and 4

16. Under which of the following circumstances, the Governor can reserve a state bill for the consideration of the President?
1. If it is ultra vires.
2. It it is opposed to the Directive Principles of State Policy.
3. If it endangers the position of the state High Court.
4. If it is dealing with the compulsory acquisition of property under Article 31 A.
Select the correct answer using the codes given below:
(a) 1, 2 and 3   (b) 1, 2, 3 and 4
(c) 2, 3 and 4   (d) 1, 3 and 4

.17. The correct statements regarding the difference between the pardoning powers of President and Governor are :
1. The Governor can pardon sentences inficted by court martial while the President cannot.
2. The President can pardon death sentence while Governor cannot.
3. The Governor can pardon death sentence while the President cannot.
4. The President can pardon sentences inflicted by court martial while the Governor cannot.
Select the correct answer using the codes given below:
(a) 1 and 2   (b) 2 and 4
(c) 1 and 3   (d) 3 and 4

18. Select the constitutional duties of the Chief Minister from following by the codes given below
1. The Chief Minister communicates to the Governor all decisions of the Council of Ministers related to the administration of the affairs of the State.
2. The Chief Minister communicates to the Governor the proposals for legislation.

3. The Chief Minister participates in the meetings of National Development Council.
4. The Chief Minister submits for the consideration of the Council of Ministers any matter on which decision has been taken by a minister but which has not been considered by the council as if the Governor requires.
Select the correct answer using the codes given below:
(a) 1 and 2   (b) 1 and 4
(c) 1, 2 and 3   (d) 1, 2 and 4

19. Consider the following statements with respect to the powers of the Governor of a State :
1. The governor can summon, prorogue and dissolve the State Assembly.
2. The Governor can adjourn the sittings of the State Assembly.
3. The Governor addresses the first session of the Legislative Assembly after elections.
4. The Governor causes to lay the annual budget in the State Assembly.
Which of the statements given above are correct ?
(a) 1 and 2   (b) 1, 3 and 4
(c) 2 and 3   (d) 2 and 4

20. Consider the following statements:
The Governor of a State has the power to appoint:
1. Judges of the High Court
2. Members of the State Public Service Commission
3. Members of the State Finance Commission
4. The Accountant General
Which of the above statements are correct?
(a) 1 and 2   (b) 2 and 3
(c) 1, 3 and 4   (d) 1, 2, 3 and 4

21. Consider the following statements :
1. The Governor cannot function without the State Council of Ministers.
2. A person who is not a member of the State Legislature cannot be appointed as a minister.
3. The State Council of Ministers can function for sometime even after death or resignation of the Chief Minister.
4. In the absence of the Chief Minister, only the Home Minister can preside over emergency meetings of the State Council of Ministers.
Which of the above statements is / are correct ?
(a) Only 1   (b) 3 and 4
(c) 1, 2 and 4   (d) 1, 2, 3 and 4

22. Consider the following statements:
1. No person is eligible for appointment as Governor unless he has completed the age of thirty years.
2. The same person can be appointed as Governor for three States.
Which of the statements given above is/are correct?
(a) 1 only   (b) 2 only
(c) Both 1 and 2   (d) Neither 1 nor 2

23. Consider the following statements:
1. A bill pending in the Legislature of a State shall not lapse by reason of the prorogation of the House or House thereof.

2. A bill pending in the Legislative Council of a State which has not been passed by the Legislative Assembly shall not lapse on dissolution of the Assembly.

   Which of the statements given above is/are correct?
   - (a) 1 only
   - (b) 2 only
   - (c) Both 1 and 2
   - (d) Neither 1 nor 2

24. Which of the statements given below is/are correct?
    1. The Speaker immediately vacates his/her office whenever the State Legislative Assembly is dissolved.
    2. No Member of a State Legislative Assembly shall be liable to any proceeding in any court in respect of anything said or any vote given by him/her in the legislature.

    Select the correct answer using the code given below :
    - (a) 1 only
    - (b) 2 only
    - (c) Both 1 and 2
    - (d) Neither 1 nor 2

25. Under the provisions of Article 200 of the Constitution of India the Governor of a state may:
    1. Withhold his assent to a Bill passed by the state legislature.
    2. Reserve the Bill passed by the state legislature for consideration of the President.
    3. Return the Bill, other than a money Bill, for reconsideration of the legislature.

    Select the correct answer using the codes given below
    - (a) Only 1
    - (b) 1 and 2
    - (c) 2 and 3
    - (d) All of the above

26. Article 156 of the Constitution of India provides that a Governor shall hold office for a term of five year from the date on which he enters upon his office. Which of the following can be deduced from this?
    1. No Governor can be removed from office till completion of his term
    2. No Governor can continue in office beyond five years

    Select the correct answer using the codes given below:
    - (a) 1 only
    - (b) 2 only
    - (c) Both 1 and 2
    - (d) Neither 1 nor 2

27. Consider the following statements:
    The Constitution of India provides that:
    1. the Legislative Assembly of each State shall consist of not more than 450 members chosen by direct election from territorial constituencies in the State
    2. a person shall not be qualified to be chosen to fill a seat in the Legislative Assembly of a State if he/she is less than 25 years of age

    Which of the statements given above is/are correct?
    - (a) 1 only
    - (b) 2 only
    - (c) Both 1 and 2
    - (d) Neither 1 nor 2

28. Which of the following are matters on a which a Constitutional Amendment is possible only with the ratification of the legislatures of not less than one-half of the states?
    1. Election of the President
    2. Representation of states in Parliament
    3. Any of the lists in the seventh Schedule
    4. Abolition of the Legislative Council of a state

    Select the correct answer using the codes given below:
    - (a) 1, 2 and 3
    - (b) 1, 2 and 4
    - (c) 1, 3 and 4
    - (d) 2, 3 and 4

29. Govt. decided to add four new tribes, Abuj Maria, Korba, Hill Korba and Kodaku into the list of scheduled tribes. Which of the following is/are correct in regard to granting the status of scheduled tribe to a tribe?
    1. President has the authority to include or exclude a tribe from the list of schedule tribes.
    2. The criterion for a community to be recognized as scheduled tribe is not spelled out in the constitution

    Select the correct answer using the codes given below:
    - (a) 1 only
    - (b) 2 only
    - (c) Both 1 and 2
    - (d) Neither 1 nor 2

30. The legislative power of the Parliament includes making laws
    1. on matters not enumerated in the Concurrent List and State List.
    2. in respect of entries in the State List if two or more State Legislatures consider it desirable
    3. for implementing any treaty agreement or convention with any country even if it falls in the State List.

    Select the correct answer using the codes given below
    - (a) Only 2
    - (b) 1 and 2
    - (c) 1 and 3
    - (d) All of these

31. Consider the following statements with reference to State Election Commission ?
    1. The State Election Commissioner shall be appointed by the Governor of the State.
    2. The State Election Commission shall have the power of even preparing the electoral rolls besides the power of superintendence, direction and control of election to the panchayats.
    3. The State Election Commissioner cannot be removed in any manner from his office until he demits himself or completes his tenure.

    Which of the above statements is/are correct?
    - (a) 1, 2 and 3
    - (b) 1 and 2 only
    - (c) 2 and 3 only
    - (d) 1 only

32. Consider the following statements: **[IAS Prelims 2015]**
    1. The Legislative Council of a State in India can be larger in size than half of the Legislative Assembly of that particular State
    2. The Governor of a State nominates the Chairman of Legislative Council of that particular State.

    Which of the statements given above is/are correct?
    - (a) 1 only
    - (b) 2 only
    - (c) Both 1 and 2
    - (d) Neither 1 nor 2

33. Consider the following statements : **[IAS Prelims 2016]**
    1. The Chief Secretary in a State is appointed by the Governor of that State.
    2. The Chief Secretary in a State has a fixed tenure.

    Which of the statements given above is/are correct?
    - (a) 1 only
    - (b) 2 only
    - (c) Both 1 and 2
    - (d) Neither 1 nor 2

34. Which of the following statements about the Ordinance-making power of the Governor is/are correct? **[CDS 2018]**

1. It is a discretionary power.
2. The Governor himself is not competent to withdraw the Ordinance at any time.

Select the correct answer using the code given below.
(a) 1 only
(b) 2 only
(c) Both 1 and 2
(d) Neither 1 nor 2

35. Consider the following statements: **[IAS Prelims 2015]**
1. The Legislative Council of a State in India can be larger in size than half of the Legislative Assembly of that particular State
2. The Governor of a State nominates the Chairman of Legislative Council of that particular State.

Which of the statements given above is/are correct?
(a) 1 only
(b) 2 only
(c) Both 1 and 2
(d) Neither 1 nor 2

36. Which of the following are not necessarily the consequences of the proclamation of the President's rule in a State? **[IAS Prelims 2017]**
1. Dissolution of the State Legislative Assembly
2. Removal of the Council of Ministers in the State
3. Dissolution of the local bodies

Select the correct answer using the code given below:
(a) 1 and 2 only
(b) 1 and 3 only
(c) 2 and 3 only
(d) 1, 2 and 3

Matching Based MCQ

DIRECTIONS (Qs. 37 to 42): Match List-I with List-II and select the correct answer using the codes given below the lists.

37. Match List-I with List-II and select the correct answer using the codes given below the lists:

List-I (Local bodies)	List-II (States as in 1999)
A. Zila Parishads at the sub-divisional level	1. Andhra Pradesh
B. Mandal Praja Parishad	2. Assam
C. Tribal Councils	3. Mizoram
D. Absence of Village Panchayats	4. Meghalaya

Codes :
(a) A-2, B-1, C-4, D-3
(b) A-1, B-2, C-4, D-3
(c) A-3, B-2, C-1, D-4
(d) A-2, B-1, C-3, D-4

38.

List-I	List-II
(A) Governor	(1) Article 167
(B) Council of ministers	(2) Article 169
(C) Duties of Chief Minister	(3) Article 155
(D) Legislative Council	(4) Article 163

(a) A – 1 ; B – 2 ; C – 3 ; D – 4
(b) A – 4 ; B – 3 ; C – 2 ; D – 1
(c) A – 3 ; B – 2 ; C – 4 ; D – 1
(d) A – 3 ; B – 4 ; C – 1 ; D – 2

39.

List I (Article of the Constitution)	List II (Content)
(A) Article 54	(1) Election of the President of India
(B) Article 75	(2) Appointment of the Prime Minister and Council of Ministers
(C) Article 155	(3) Appointment of the Governor of a state
(D) Article 164	(4) Appointment of the Chief Minister and Council of Ministers of a state
	(5) Composition of Legislative Assemblies

(a) A – 1 ; B – 2 ; C – 3 ; D – 4
(b) A – 1 ; B – 2 ; C – 4 ; D – 5
(c) A – 2 ; B – 1 ; C – 3 ; D – 5
(d) A – 2 ; B – 1 ; C – 4 ; D – 3

40.

List-I	List-II
(A) Union List	(1) Banking
(B) State List	(2) Public order and police
(C) Concurrent	(3) Labour Wel-List fare

(a) A – 2 ; B – 1 ; C – 3
(b) A – 1 ; B – 2 ; C – 3
(c) A – 1 ; B – 3 ; C – 2
(d) A – 3 ; B – 1 ; C – 2

41.

List-I (States)	List-II (Governor's special responsibilities)
(A) Madhya Pradesh	(1) Law and order
(B) Gujarat	(2) Administration of tribal areas
(C) Nagaland	(3) Development of backward areas
(D) Assam	(4) Minister for Tribal Welfare
	(5) Hill Areas Committee working

Codes:

	A	B	C	D
(a)	3	4	2	5
(b)	2	1	4	3
(c)	4	3	1	2
(d)	5	3	2	4

42.

List-I	List -II
(A) Article 156	(1) Executive authority of Governor
(B) Article 154	(2) Tenure of Governor
(C) Article 153	(3) Appointment of Governor
(D) Article 155	(4) Office of Governor
	(5) Discretionary power of Governor

Codes:

	A	B	C	D
(a)	3	4	2	5
(b)	2	1	4	3
(c)	4	3	1	2
(d)	5	3	2	4

Hints and Explanations

EXERCISE-1

1. (a) 2. (c) 3. (b) 4. (d) 5. (a) 6. (b)
7. (b) 8. (c) 9. (c) 10. (c) 11. (c) 12. (c)
13. (b) 14. (b) 15. (d) 16. (d) 17. (b) 18. (a)
19. (d) 20. (c)

21. (d) The Legislative Assembly (the Vidhan Sabha) is the popular House of the State Legislative and its member are chosen by direct election on the basis of adult suffrage from territorial constituencies (Article 170).The number of members ranges between 60 and 500.

22. (c) 23. (b) 24. (b) 25. (d) 26. (a)

27. (d) The Legislative Assembly (the Vidhan Sabha) is the popular House of the State Legislative and its member are chosen by direct election on the basis of adult suffrage from territorial constituencies (Article 170).The number of members ranges between 60 and 500.

28. (c)

29. (c) Article 371A deals with the Special provision with respect to the State of Nagaland.

30. (b) According to Article 164(1) in the State of Bihar, Madhya Pradesh and Orissa, there shall be a Minister in charge of tribal welfare who may in addition be in charge of the welfare of the Scheduled Castes and backward classes or any other work. Punjab is not covered by the Article.

31. (d) The legislative assembly of the concerned state recommends to the parliament for the abolition of the legislative council in a state (Article 169).

32. (c) Up to 2014, seven (out of twenty-nine) states have a Legislative Council: Andhra Pradesh, Bihar, Jammu and Kashmir, Karnataka, Maharashtra, Telangana and Uttar Pradesh.Tamilnadu does not have Legislative Council.

33. (b) Sarkaria Commission was set up in June 1983 by the central government of India. According to the commission, Chief Minister should be consulted before appointing the Governor.

34. (d) President's rule refers to Article 356 of the Constitution of India deals with the failure of the constitutional machinery of an Indian state. In the event that government in a state is not able to function as per the Constitution, the state comes under the direct control of the central government, with executive authority exercised through the Governor instead of a Council of Ministers headed by an elected Chief Minister accountable to the state legislature.

Article 356 is invoked if there has been failure of the constitutional machinery in any states of India.

35. (d) The are only five states with bicameral legislature (Legislative assembly as well as Legislative Council)- UP, Bihar, Maharashtra, Karnataka and Jammu & Kashmir

36. (a) Article 257 in the Constitution states that the executive power of every State shall be so exercised as not to impede or prejudice the exercise of the executive power of the Union, and the executive power of the Union shall extend to the giving of such directions to a State as may appear to the Government of India to be necessary for that purpose. Article 258: Power of the Union to confer powers on the States in certain cases; Article 355: Duty of the Union to protect States against external aggression and internal disturbance; Article 358: Suspension of provisions of Article 19 during emergencies.

37. (a) The State government does not have control over its local bodies in matters of Citizens' grievances.

38. (d) A lieutenant Governor is in charge of a Union Territory whereas a Governor is in charge of a State. The rank of Lt.Governor is present only in the states of Delhi, Andaman and Nicobar Islands and Puducherry. So in the case of a Union Territory specified where there is a legislative setup, the Chief Minister is appointed by the Lieutenant Governor.

39. (b) 40. (a) 41. (d) 42. (a) 43. (c)

44. (d) Nutrition is not the component of the Pradhan Mantri Gramodaya Yojna. Pradhan Mantri Gramodaya Yojana' aims at -
1. meeting rural needs like primary education, health care, drinking water, housing, rural roads
2. alleviating employment in rural areas
3. generating employment in rural areas
4. strengthening Panchayati Raj system in rural areas

45. (d) Article 1 of the Constituion of India uses the word "Union of states" instead of "federation of states" thus states do not have right to secede. Jammu and kashmir has its own Constitution as per article 370. No other state has their own constitution. As per article 239AA of Indian Constitution, number of Cabinet Ministers cannot exceed ten percent of Delhi assembly seats.

46. (a) Total membership of legislative assembly varies according to the state's population. Uttar Pradesh have the highest membership- 403 followed by West Bengal- 294 and Maharashtra- 288.

EXERCISE-2

1. **(a)** At present only seven states have a bicameral legislature.

   State having a bicameral legislature.

   - Andhra Pradesh
   - Bihar
   - Jammu & Kashmir
   - Karnataka
   - Maharashtra
   - Telangana
   - Uttar Pradesh
   - The parliament can abolish a legislative council or create it if the legislative assembly of the concerned State passes a resolution to that effect.
   - Such a specific resolution must be passed by the state assembly by a special majority.

2. **(b)**

3. **(b)** The members of the legislative council are indirectly elected. The maximum strength of the council is fixed at one-third of the total strength of the assembly and the minimum strength is fixed at 40.

   It means that the size of the council depends on the size of the assembly of the concerned state.

4. **(a)** Statement (ii), (iii) and (iv) are correct. According to Puncchi Commission, The Governor must be a person from outside the concerned state. The Governor should, in the opinion of the President, be an eminent person. A provision may be made for the impeachment of the Governor by the state legislature on the same lines as the impeachment of the President by the Parliament.

5. **(d)** In case of Arunachal Pradesh, Sikkim and Goa, the minimum number is fixed at 30 and in case of Mizoram and Nagaland. It is 40 and 46 respectively. Also some members of the legislative assemblies in Sikkim and Nagaland are also elected indirectly. Therefore; while the maximum strength is fixed at 600, the minimum strength of state assembly depends on population of the state.

6. **(d)**
   - The number of members to be elected from each state to Rajya Sabha has been fixed by the Fourth Schedule of the constitution.
   - The term of the legislative assembly of Jammu and Kashmir is six years under its own state constitution.
   - Both the statements are therefore wrong.

7. (a)   8. (a)   9. (b)   10. (b)   11. (c)

12. (c)   13. (d)   14. (b)   15. (d)   16. (b)

17. (b)

18. **(d)** National Development Council is not constitutional

19. **(b)** The Governor is a part of the state legislative and can summon, adjourn or prorogue the state legislative. The governor can even dissolve the Vidhan Sabha. At the commencement of the first session after each general election to the Legislative Assembly and at the commencement of the first session of each year the Governor shall address the Legislative Assembly. As per Article 202 of the Constitution of India the Governor of a State shall, cause to be laid before the House or Houses of the Legislature of the State a Statement of the estimated receipts and expenditure of the State for a financial year. This estimated statement of receipt and expenditure for a financial year named in the Constitution as the "Annual Financial Statement" is commonly known as "Budget".

20. **(b)** The Governor has the power to appoint the Council of Ministers including the Chief Minister of the state, the Advocate General and the members of the State Public Service Commission. However, the Governor cannot remove the members of the State Public Service Commission as they can only be removed by an order of the President.

21. **(a)** The Constitution provides that there shall be a Council of Ministers with the Chief Minister at the head to aid and advice the Governor in the exercise of his functions except in so far as he is by or under the Constitution required to act in his discretion. The governor appoints the Chief Minister and other Ministers on the advice of the Chief Minister.

22. (b)   23. (c)

24. **(b)** members of state legislative assembly are not liable to any proceeding in any court.

25. **(d)** All of the above statements are correct.

26. **(d)** According to Article 156, the Governor shall hold office during the pleasure of the President, the Governor may, by writing under his hand addressed to the President, resign his office. Subject to the foregoing provisions of this article, a Governor shall hold for a term of five years from the date on which he enters upon his office. Provided that a Governor shall, notwithstanding the expiration of his term, continue to hold office until his successor enters upon his office.

27. **(b)** Statement 2 is correct as per provisions given under Article 173. Statement 1 is incorrect as according to article 170, the legislative assembly of each state shall consist of not more than 500 and not less than 60 members chosen by direct election from territorial constituencies in the state.

28. (a)

29. (b) According to article 342 of the constitution parliament, can decide on the inclusion and exclusion of a tribe into the list of schedule tribe. The President may with respect to any State or Union territory, and where it is a State, after consultation with the Governor thereof, by public notification, specify the tribes or tribal communities or parts of or groups within tribes or tribal communities which shall for the purposes of this Constitution be deemed to be Scheduled Tribes in relation to that State or Union territory, as the case may be.

30. (d) Article 248- Parliament has exclusive power to make any law with respect to any matter not enumerated in the Concurrent List or State List.

Article 252- If it appears to the Legislatures of two or more States to be desirable that any of the matters with respect to which Parliament has no power to make laws for the States except as provided in Articles 249 and 250 should be regulated in such States by Parliament by law.

Article 253- Legislation for giving effect to international agreements notwithstanding anything in the foregoing provisions of this Chapter, Parliament has power to make any law for the whole or any part of the territory of India for implementing any treaty, agreement or convention with any other country or countries or any decision made at any international conference, association or other body.

31. (b) The Election Commissioners in the each State shall be appointed by the Governor of the respective State from a panel of five names for each office forwarded by the Election Commission. Election Commissioner of a State can be removed by the Full Bench of State Judicial Commission on the basis of enquiry and investigation made by a judicial committee constituted for the purpose, consisting of two Chief Justices and one Judge from different High Courts.

32. (d) The maximum strength of the legislative council is fixed at one third of the total strength of the legislative assembly and the minimum strength is fixed at 40. The chairman of the legislative council is elected by the council itself from amongst its members.

33. (a) Zilla parishads at the sub-divisional level-Assam Mandal Praja parishad-Andhra Pradesh, Tribal Councils-Meghalaya and Absence of village panchayats-Mizoram

34. (d) The ordinance-making power of the governor under Article 214 is similar to that of the president under Article 123. The governor can issue ordinance only when two conditions are fulfilled ; (a) the governor can only issue ordinances when the legislative assembly of a state both houses in session or where there are two houses in a state both houses are not in session. (b) the governor must be satisfied that circumstance exist which render it necessary for him to take immediate action. The court cannot question the validity or the ordinance on the ground that there was no necessity or sufficient ground for issuing the ordinance by the governor. The existence of such necessity is not a justiciable discretionary. The exercise of ordinance-making power is not discretionary. The governor exercises this power on the advice of the cabinet. It is not a discretionary power and shall be exercised with aid and the advice of members. The Governor himself shall be competent to withdraw the ordinance at any time.

35. (d) The maximum strength of the legislative council is fixed at one third of the total strength of the legislative assembly and the minimum strength is fixed at 40. The chairman of the legislative council is elected by the council itself from amongst its members.

36. (b) MIND IT: you've to find the wrong statements here- they're the right answers.
   - when the President's Rule is imposed in a state, the President dismisses the state council of ministers headed by the chief minister. The state governor, on behalf of the President, carries on the state administration with the help of the chief secretary of the state or the advisors appointed by the President. Meaning "2" is definitely the consequence of proclamation. Hence all options involving "2" are wrong. Hence by elimination we are left with answer "B": 1 and 3 only.

37. (a) 1st statement is right. Because
   - Under Article 168 of the Constitution of India: All executive actions of the Governor of a State shall be expressed to be taken in the name of Governor. (which include transfer, posting, promotion of civil servants allotted to that state cadre) so, Yes, as such chief Secretary is "chosen" by Chief minister officially its expressed that chief Secretary is 'appointed' by the governor of the state.
   - Another way to look at it is- even state advocate general, university vice chancellors are 'chosen' by CM from among his favorite people-but officially they're 'appointed' by the Governor. Ref: Page 26.5- Indian Polity by M. Laxmikanth, 4th Edition (Macgrawhill Publication)

38. (d) 39. (a) 40. (b) 41. (c) 42. (b)

LOCAL GOVERNMENT

History of Local self-Government in India

India has a long history of local self-Goverment. Evidence suggests that during the Rig-vedic period (1700 BC), self governing village bodies collect "Sabha's and Samitis" existed.

- In the days of Maurya the village and the district were units of administration.
- During the time of Pandyas and the Pallavas (8th century) and early 9th century, a system of local self-Government existed but it was not so well developed as under the Cholas in later times.
- Nadu and Nagaram were the other Local self-Government institutions that existed in South India.
- History also find evidences of appointment of women to key positions in local bodies and active participation of women in local self Government.

Local Self-Government under British Rule

- The East India Company after taking over the administration continued the policy of the Mughals to curb the powers of the local institutions.
- The company slowly but steadily destroyed the local institutions, especially village panchayats.
- The modern system of local self Government began in 1687 when for the first time, a Municipal corporation was set up for the city of Madras.
- The Charter Act of 1793 established Municipal administration in three presidency town of Madras, Calcutta and Bombay.
- In 1842, Municipal administration was extended to district town in Bengal when the Bengal People's Act was passed.
- The years 1870 makes of further state in the evolution of local Government when Lord Mayo's famous resolution advocated a measure of decentralisation from the centre to the provinces, emphasiged the desirability of associating Indians in the administration.

Lord Ripon's Resolution on Local self-Government, 1882

- Lord Ripon is rightly regarded as the father of Local self-Government in Modern India.
- The resolution which his Government issued in 1882 embodies the idea that since the time was not ripe for giving them a share in the Central or Provincial Government, so they should be first trained in the sphere of local Government.
- The Process of strengthening of local self-Government institutions received further impetus with the appointment of the "Royal Commission on decentralisation in 1907" headed by C.E.H Hobhouse.

National Movement and the Local Self Government

- The importance of the village panchayats came to be recognised after 1909, when Royal Commission report was published.
- The Indian National Congress of its 24th session at Lahore in 1909 passed a resolution and urged the Government of India "to take early steps to make all local bodies from village panchayats upwards elective with elected non-official chairman and to support them with adequate financial aid.
- The Government of India Act : 1919 made Local Self Government a subject of responsibility for the popular ministry and this gave and impetus to the Government of local bodies.
- The non-co-operation resolution moved by Mahatma Gandhi and passed by the congress in its. Calcutta Session of September 1920, articulated the approach to rural development by recommending "hand spinning in every house".
- The introduction of Provincial Autonomy in 1937, under the Government of India Act; 1935, gave farther impetus to the development of local self Government and it was classified as a provincial subject.

- In 1927, an Indian Statuary Commission was appointed under the Chairmanship of Simon to go into the details of the working of local self-government and also to enquire into the system of responsible Government under the Act of 1919.

Local Self Government Post-Independence

- In 1949, the Government of India appointed the Local Finance Enquiry Committee, which made a number of recommendations for improving and stabilizing local finance.
- The Constitutions of India come into fence in 1950, which contained many provisions for local self-Government.
- Article-40 of the Constitution commits the state to organise village panchayats and endow them with adequate powers and authority to enable them to function as units of self-Government.
- Article-48 states that "the State shall endeavor to organize agriculture and animal husbandry on modern and scientific lines".
- Though the Constitution makes it the duty of the State to apply these principle in making laws, they are not and cannot be justifiable.

Indian Administrative Structure

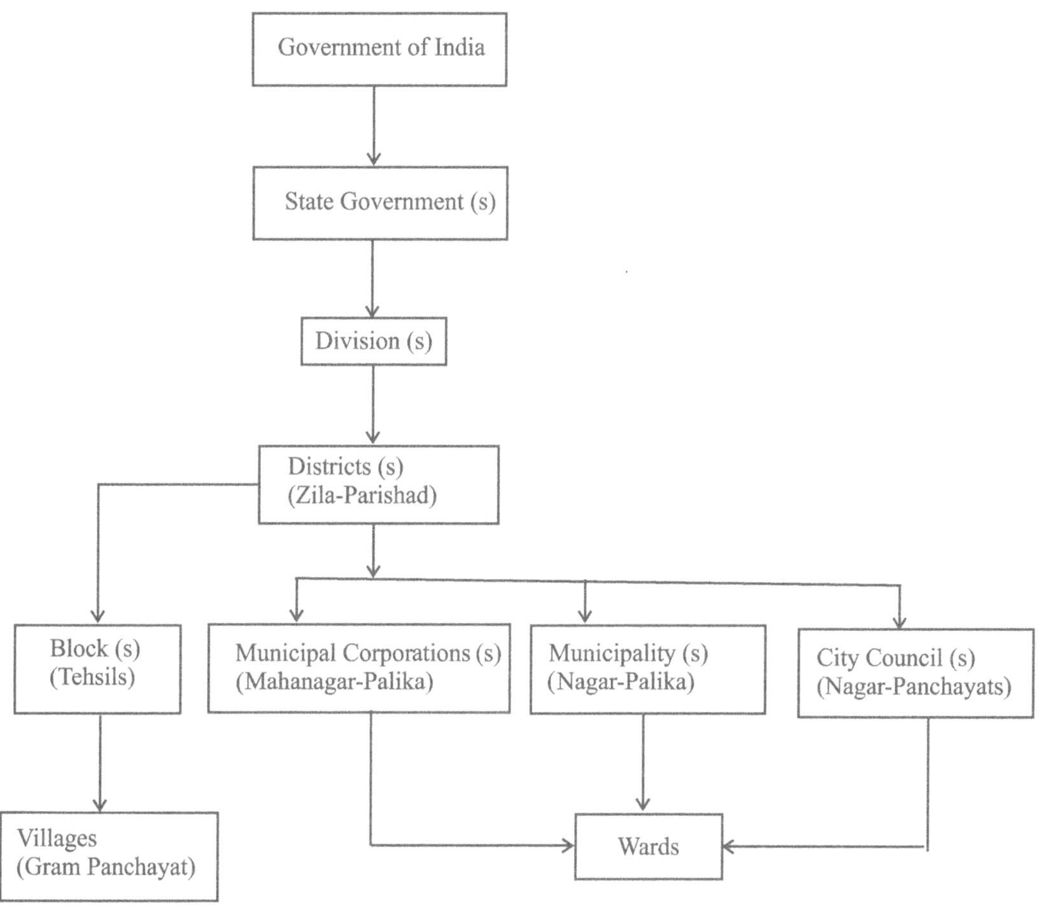

RURAL LOCAL GOVERNMENT

Panchayati Raj

The term Panchayti Raj in India signifies the system of rural local self-government. It has been established in all the states of India by the Acts of the State Legislatures to build democracy at the grass root level. It is entrusted with rural development. It was constituationlised through the 73rd Constitutional Amendment Act 1992.

A village or a group of villages, formed a panchayat of elected representatives, a few Panchayats formed a Panchayat Samiti and the various Panchayat Samities of a district were governed by a Zila Parishad and these three institutions had a three fold purpose :

(i) to be autonomous and self governing to some extent.

(ii) to play an effective role in drawing up the 5 year plans.

(iii) to have scope for initiative and readjustment in implementing the plans to suit local needs.

Evolution of Panchayati Raj

- The Narasimha Rao Government introduced the Constitutional Amendment Bill in the Lok Sabha in September, 1991.

- It was passed by the Parliament in 1992. Later it was approved by the 17 State Assemblies and received the assent of the President of India in, 1993.
- Thus, it emerged as the *73rd Constitutional Amendment Act, 1992* and came into force on 24th April, 1993.
- **Rajasthan was the first state to establish the institution of Panchayati Raj in Nagaur District in 1959. Rajasthan was followed by Andhra Pradesh.**

Balwant Rai Mehta Committee (1957)

- It was set up to examine the working of the Community Development Programme (1952) and the National Extension Service (1953).
- Recommendations:
  (i) **Three-tier Panchayati Raj system:** Gram Panchayat at the Village level, Panchayat Samiti at the block level, Zila Parishad at the district level.
  (ii) Village Panchayat is directly elected, while the Panchayat Samiti and Zila Parishad constituted with indirectly elected members.
  (iii) Panchayat Samiti is the executive body, while the Zila Parishad is the advisory, coordinating and supervisory body.
  (iv) The District Collector should be the Chairman of the Zila Parishad.
  (v) Sufficient resources should be transferred to these bodies to enable them to discharge their functions.

Note: The recommendations of Balwant Rai Mehta Committee (1957) were accepted by the National Development Council in 1958.

K Santhanam Committee

The K Santhanam Committee was appointed to look solely at the issue of PRI finance, in 1963.

Recommendations

- Panchayats should have special powers to levy special tax on land revenues, home taxes, etc.
- All grants and subventions at the state level should be mobilised and sent in a consolidate form to various PRIs.
- A Panchayati Raj finance corporation should be set-up to look into the financial resource of PRIs at all levels, provide loans and financial assistance to these grassroots level governments and also provide non-financial requirements of villages.

Ashok Mehta Committee

In **December 1977**, the Janata Government appointed a Committee on Panchayati Raj Institutions under the Chairmanship of Ashok Mehta. It submitted its report in August, 1978 and made recommendations to revive and strengthen the declining Panchayati Raj System in the country.

Recommendations

- The three-tier system of the Panchayati Raj should be **replaced by two-tier system, that is, the Zila Parishad at the district level and below it the Mandal Panchayat** consisting of a group of villages comprising a population upto 20,000.
- The Zila Parishad should be the executive body and be made responsible for planning at the district level.
- The *Panchayati Raj Institutions* should have Compulsory powers for taxation to mobilise their own financial resources.
- The **Nyaya Panchayats should be kept as separate bodies** from that of development Panchayats.
- A minister for the Panchayati Raj should be appointed in the State Council of Ministers to look after the affairs of the Panchayati Raj Institutions.
- **Seats for the SCs and the STs should be reserved** on the basis of their population.

G V K Rao Committee

The Committee on Administrative Arrangement for Rural Development and Poverty Alleviation Programmes under the chairmanship of G.V.K. Rao was appointed by the Planning Commission in 1985.

Recommendations

The Committee made the following recommendations to strengthen and revitalise the Panchayati Raj system:
- "The district is the proper unit for planning and development and the Zila Parishad should become the principal body for management of all development programmes which can be handled at that level".
- The Panchayati Raj institutions at the district and lower levels should be assigned an important role with respect to planning, implementation and monitoring of rural development programmes.
- A post of District Development Commissioner should be created.
- Elections to the Panchavati Raj institutions should be held regularly.

LM Singhvi Committee

In 1986, Rajiv Gandhi Government appointed a committee on the **"Revitalisation of the Panchayati Raj Institutions for democracy and development"** under the Chairmanship of LM Singhvi.

Recommendations

- The *Panchayati Raj Institutions* should be constitutionally recognised, protected and preserved. It also suggested some constitutional provisions to ensure regular, free and fair elections to the Panchayati Raj bodies.
- Nyaya Panchayats should be established for a cluster of villages.
- The villages should be organised to make the Gram Panchayats more viable.

- The Village Panchayats should have more financial resources.
- The judicial tribunals should be established in each state to eradicate controversies about election to the Panchayati Raj Institutions, their dissolution and other matters related to their functioning.

Attempts to Make Panchayats Mandatory

Rajiv Gandhi Government

In July 1989, Rajiv Gandhi Government introduced the 64th Constitutional Amendment Bill to constitutionalise PRIs, but it was not approved by Rajya Sabha.

VP Singh Government

In November 1989, Prime Ministers VP Singh proposed the introduction of a fresh Constitutional Amendment Bill and the bill was introduced in Lok Sabha in September 1990, but it lapsed due to the fall of government.

Narsimha Rao Government

In September 1991, Prime Minister P V Narsimha Rao introduced the modified proposal of Constitutional Amendment Bill, which finally emerged as the 73rd Constitutional Amendment Act, 1992 and came into force on 24th April, 1993.

73rd Amendment Act (1992)

- **Added to Part-IX (Articles 243 to 243-O) and the Eleventh Schedule to the Constitution.**
- **11th Schedule contains 29 functional items and deals with Article 243-G.**
- The Act has given a practical shape to Article 40. The Act has brought them under the purview of the justifiable part of the Constitution.
- State governments are under constitutional obligation to adopt the new Panchayati raj system in accordance with the provisions of the Act. However the Panchayati raj system in each state is created through its own Act.
- The main provisions of the Act are as follows:

Three-Tier System

- Three-tier system with panchayats at the village, intermediate, and district levels. Panchayat means an institution of self-government for rural areas.
- Act brings about uniformity in the structure of Panchayati raj throughout the country. However a state having a population not exceeding 20 lakhs may not constitute panchayats at the intermediate level.

Gram Sabha (Article 243A)

Gram sabha is the foundation of the Panchayati raj system. It shall exercise such powers & functions at the village level as the legislature of a state determines.

Elections to Panchayats (Article 243C)

- All the members of Panchayats at the village, intermediate and district levels shall be elected directly by the people.
- Chairperson of Panchayat at the village level shall be elected in such manner as the state legislature determines. However, the chairperson at the intermediate and district levels shall be elected indirectly; by and from amongst the elected members there of.

Qualifications

- A person seeking election to the panchayat must possess the qualifications prescribed for a member of state legislature.
- **Minimum age for contesting election to the panchayat is 21 year** (as against 25 years for State Legislature).

Disqualifications for Membership (Article 243F)

- A person shall be disqualified for being chosen as, and for being a member of a Panchayat-
    - (a) If he is so disqualified by or under any law for the time being in force for the purposes of election, to the Legislature of the State concerned.
    - (b) If he is so disqualified by or under any law made by the Legislature of the State.
- If any question arise as to whether a member of a Panchayat has become subject to any of the disqualifications mentioned in clause (1), the question shall be referred for the decision of such authority and in such manner as the legislature of a State may, by law, provide.
- No person shall be disqualified on the ground that he is less than twenty-five years, of age, if he has attained the age of twenty-one years.
- The question regarding disqualification of the members of panchayat are referred to such authority as may be provided by the state legislature by law.

State Election Commission

- The superintendence, direction and control of the preparation of lectoral rolls for, and the conduct of all election to the Panchayats shall be vested in a State Election Commission consisting of a *State Election Commissioner* to be appointed by the Governor.
- Subjects to the provisions of any law made by the legislature of a State, the conditions of service and tenure of office of the State Election Commissions shall be such as the Governor may by rule determine.
- The State Election Commissioner shall not be removed from the office except in the manner and on the grounds prescribed for the removal of a judge of the State High Court.

Reservation of Seats (Article 243D)

- Reservation of seats for SCs & STs in every Panchayat (at all levels) in proportion of their population to the total population in that area. State legislature shall provide for the reservation of offices of chairpersons in the Panchayat at the village or any other level for the SCs and STs.

- **Reservation of not less than one-third of the total number of seats for women** (including those reserved for women of SCs and the STs). Not less than one-third of the total number of offices of chairpersons in the Panchayats at each level shall be, reserved for women.
- For any backward classes, state legislature is authorized to make any provision for reservation.

State Finance Commission (Article 243I)

- Governor of the state shall constitute a Finance Commission to review the financial position of the Panchayats after each five year.
- State Legislature may provide for the composition of the Commission, the required qualifications of its members and the manner of their selection.
- They review the financial position of the panchayats and makes recommendations to the governor for the distribution of the net proceeds of taxes between the states and the panchayats. It also recommends grants-in-aid to the panchayats, from the *Consolidated Fund of the State*.
- Central Finance Commission shall also suggest the measures needed to augment the consolidated fund of a state to supplement the resources of the panchayats in the States.

Audit of Accounts of Panchayats

The legislature of a State may, by law, make provisions with respect to the maintenance of accounts by the Panchayats and the auditing of such accounts.

Duration of Panchayats (Article 243E)

- Fixed tenure of **Five-year**
- In case the panchayat is dissolved before its term of 5 years, fresh elections must be held within six months. The panchayat thus constituted are elected for the remaining period. It may be noted that if the remaining tenure of the dissolved panchayat is less than six months no elections need be held.

Application to Union Territories

- The President of India may direct that the provisions of this act shall apply to any Union territory subject to such exceptions and modifications as he may specify.

Exempted Areas

- The 73rd Amendment Act does not apply to the states of Jammu and Kashmir, Nagaland, Meghalaya and Mizoram and certain other areas.

Courts cannot Interfere

- The validity of any an relating to the delimitation of constituencies or the allotment of seats to such constituencies cannot be questioned in any Court.

Powers and Functions (Article 243G)

The State Legislature may endow the Panchayats, with such powers and authority as may be necessary to enable them to function as institutions of self government. Such a scheme may contain provisions for the devolution of powers and responsibilities upon Panchayats at the appropriate level with respect to

- Preparation of **plans** for economic development and social justice.
- the implementation of schemes for the economic development and social justice as may be entrusted to them, including those in relation to the 29 matters listed in the Eleventh Schedule.

The following 29 functional items placed within the purview of Panchayats are:

1. Agriculture, including agricultural extension.
2. Land improvement, implementation of land reforms, land consolidation and soil conservation.
3. Minor irrigation, water management and watershed development.
4. Animal husbandry, dairying and poultry.
5. Fisheries, social forestry and farm forestry.
6. Minor forest produce.
7. Small-scale industries, including food processing industries.
8. Khadi, village and cottage industries.
9. Rural housing.
10. Drinking water.
11. Fuel and fodder.
12. Roads, culverts, bridges, ferries, waterways and other means of communication.
13. Rural electrification, including distribution of electricity.
14. Non-conventional energy sources.
15. Poverty alleviation programme.
16. Education, including primary and secondary schools.
17. Technical training and vocational education.
18. Adult and non-formal education.
19. Libraries.
20. Cultural activities.
21. Markets and fairs.
22. Health and sanitation, including hospitals, primary health centres and dispensaries.
23. Family welfare.
24. Women and child development.
25. Social welfare, including welfare of the handicapped and mentally retarded.
26. Welfare of the weaker sections and in particular, of the Scheduled Castes and the Scheduled Tribes.
27. Public distribution system.
28. Maintenance of community assets.
29. The act gives a constitutional status to the Panchayati Raj Institutions.

All Provisions not compulsory

- Some of the Provisions of the 73rd constitutional Amendment Act are compulsory while some are voluntary in nature.

Examples of Compulsory Provisions

- Organisations of Gram Sabha in a village/groups of villages.
- Establishment of Panchayats at the village, intermediate and district levels.
- Direct elections to all seats in panchayats at village, intermediate and district levels.
- 21 years to be the minimum age for contesting elections to Panchayats.
- Fixing tenure of five years for panchayats at all levels.
- Holding fresh elections within six month in the event of super session of any panchayat.

Examples of Voluntary Provisions

- Giving representation to members of the Parliament (both the Houses) and the State Legislature (both the Houses) in the panchayats of different levels falling within their constituencies.
- Providing reservation seats for backward classes in Panchayats at any level.
- Granting financial power to the panchayats.

Major Problems and Shortcomings in the Working of PRIs

- Election not being held on a regular basis.
- Lack of adequate transfer of powers and resources to Panchayati institutions.
- Lack of Panchayati Raj bodies to generate their own resources such as tax on sale of land.
- Non-Representation of women and weaker sections on the elected bodies.
- The distribution of functions between the structures at different levels has not been made along scientific lines.
- There is incompatible relation between the three tiers.
- Lack of cordial relations between officials and people.
- Undemocratic compositions of various Panchayati Raj institutions.
- Administrative problems like tendency towards politicization of the local administration.

PESA Act, 1996

This act is called Provisions of the *Panchayats Extension to the Scheduled Areas* (PESA) Act, 1996. In this Act 'Scheduled Areas' means the Scheduled Areas as referred to in clause (1) of the Article 244 of the Constitution.

Bhuria Committee

- It was set-up in June 1994 to work out details as to how structures similar to Panchayati Raj Institutions can take shape in Tribal Areas and Scheduled Areas to define their powers. It submitted it's report in January 1995 and GOI made PESA, 1996.

- According to this act, under Part IX of the Constitution, the Legislature of a State shall not make any law under that part, which is inconsistent with the following features
  - A State Legislation on the Panchayats shall be in consonance with the customary law, social and religious practices and traditional management practices of community resources.
  - Reservation for the Scheduled Tribes shall not be less than one-half of the total number of seats. Reservation shall be in proportion to the population of the communities for whom reservation is sought. All seats of Chairpersons at all levels shall be reserved for the Scheduled Tribes.
  - Gram Sabha shall be consulted before making the acquisition of land in Scheduled Areas for development projects.
  - The recommendation of Gram Sabha shall be made mandatory to grant of prospecting licence or mining lease for minor minerals in the Scheduled Areas.
  - Powers of Panchayat in the Scheduled Areas to regulate, sale and consumption of intoxicant, ownership of minor forest produce, preventing alienation of land as per laws, manage village markets, exercise control over money lending, control over institutions and functionaries in social sectors and local plans and resources.
  - The act extended provisions of Panchayats to *tribal areas of 9 states* that are included in Fifth Schedule these are - Andhra Pradesh, Himachal Pradesh, Madhya Pradesh, Chhattisgarh, Jharkhand, Odisha, Gujarat, Maharashtra, and Rajasthan.

The Scheduled Tribes and other Traditional Forest Dwellers (Recognition of Forest Rights) Act, 2006

- The Scheduled Tribes and other Traditional Forest Dwellers (Recognition of Forest Rights) Act, 2006 is a result of the protracted struggle by the marginal and tribal communities of our country to assert their rights over the forest land over which they were traditionally dependent.
  - This act is crucial to the rights of millions of tribals and other forest dwellers in different parts of our country as it provides for the restitution of deprived forest rights across India. Including both individual rights to cultivated land in forest land and community rights over common property resources. The notification or rulers for the implementation of the Forest Right. Rights Act, 2006 on 1st January. 2008, has finally paved the way to undo the '*historical injustice*' done to the tribals and other forest dwellers.
  - The act is significant as it provides scope and historic opportunity of integrating conservation and livelihood rights of the people.

- This act will prove a potential tool
  - To empower and strengthen the local self-governance.
  - To address the livelihood security of the people, leading to poverty alleviation and pro-poor growth.
  - To address the issues of conservation and management of the Natural Resources and Conservation Governance of India.

Significance of the Act

- Community Rights or rights over common property resources of the communities in addition to their individual rights has been recognized.
- Rights over disputed land, rights of settlement and conversion of all forest villages, old habitation, unsurveyed villages and other villages in forests into revenue villages.
- Right to protect, regenerate or conserve or manage any community forest resource which the communities have been traditionally protecting and conserving for sustainable use.
- Right to intellectual property and traditional knowledge related to biodiversity and cultural diversity.
- Rights of displaced communities.
- Rights over developmental activities.

URBAN LOCAL GOVERNMENT

Evolution of Urban Local Government in India

- We have substantial evidence that the Indus valley civilization had a highly sophisticated and a well structured Urban culture.
- During the Mughal responsibility of administering a city was entrusted on the "Kotowal".
- Abul Fazal in his Ain-I-Akbari serialised as many as eight functions of a Kotowal.
- In the year 1688, the British administration for the first time introduced a Municipal corporation in the city of Madras by a charter granted in 1687.
- In 1726, the Municipal corporation was converted to a Mayor's Court empowering it with the judicial powers and thus it became a judicial body than an administrative entity.
- It was only in 1793, that the Municipal administration in India was given the statutory rank when the Charter Act of 1793 was passed.
- Lord Ripon is considered as the founding father of Urban Local Self Government.
- Ripon resolution of 1882 on local self government of with the bodies, their functions, finances and powers and set the ground work of local self-government in independent India.
- In 1906, the Royal commission on Decentralisation was set up which made public its report in 1908. The Commission made certain noteworthy recommendations concerning the Municipal bodies.

- The Government of Inida Act : 1919 made the local self government or the Municipalities a transferred topic incharge of the Ministers.
- After independence local bodies were shelkred in the state list and government by state statutes or in the Union Territories by the Union Parliament.
- **There are eight types of urban local governments in India** – Municipal Corporation, Municipality, Notified Area Committee, Town Area Committee, Cantonment Board, township, port trust, special purpose agency. At the Central level the subject of 'urban local government' is dealt with by the following three Ministries.
  - (i) Ministry of Urban Development created as a separate ministry in 1985.
  - (ii) Ministry of Defense in the case of cantonment boards.
  - (iii) Ministry of Home Affairs in the case of Union Territories.

74th Amendment Act (1992)

- 74th Amendment Act pertaining to urban local government was passed during the regime of P.V. Narsimha Rao's government in 1992. It came into force on 1st June, 1993.
- **Added Part IX -A and consists of provisions from articles 243-P to 243-ZG.**
- **Added 12th Schedule to the Constitution. It contains 18 functional items of Municipalities and deals with Article 243 W.**
- State governments are under constitutional obligation to adopt the new system of Municipalities in accordance with the provisions of the Act.

Municipalities

There are three types of municipalities which are as follows:
(i) **Nagar panchayat** for a transitional area from a rural area to urban area.
(ii) A **municipal council** for a smaller urban area
(iii) A **municipal corporation** for a larger urban area.

Municipal Corporation

It is created for the administration of big cities like Delhi, Mumbai, Kolkata, Hyderabad, Bangalore and others. Established in the States by the Acts of the concerned State Legislatures and in the UTs by the Acts of the Parliament of India.

Municipal Council

Municipal Council is established for the administration of towns and smaller cities. They are also set up in the States by the Acts of the concerned State Legislatures and in the UTs by the Acts of the parliament. They are also known by various other names like *Municipal Committee, Municipal Board, City municipality* and others.

Composition

- **Members shall be elected directly.** State legislature may provide the manner of election of the chairperson of a Municipality.
- For this purpose, **each Municipal area shall be divided into territorial constituencies to be known as Wards.** It may also provide for the representation of the following persons in a municipality.
  1. Persons having special knowledge or experience in municipal administration without the right to vote in the meetings of municipality.
  2. The members of the Lok Sabha and the state legislative assembly representing constituencies that comprise wholly or partly the municipal area.
  3. The members of the Rajya Sabha and the state Legislative Council registered as electors within the municipal area.
  4. The chairpersons of committees (other than wards committees).

Wards Committees

Wards committee, consisting of one or more wards, within the territorial area of a municipality having population of *three lakhs* or more.

Reservation of Seats (Art. 243 T)

- For SCs & STs, in proportion of their population to the total population in that area. For backward classes, state legislature may make provisions.
- Reservation of not less than one-third of the total number of seats for women (including those reserved for women belonging to the SCs and the STs)
- State legislature may provide for the manner of reservation of offices of chairpersons in the municipalities for the SCs, the STs and the women.

District Planning Committee

- Every state shall constitute a district planning committee to constitutes the plans prepared by panchayats and municipalities in the district and to prepare a draft development plan for the district as a whole.
- The Legislature of a state may, by law, make provision, with respect to —
  (a) The composition of the District Planning Committees;
  (b) Four-fifths of the members of a district planning committee should be elected by the elected members of the district panchayat and municipalities in the district from amongst themselves.
  (c) The function relating to district planning which may be assigned to such committees.
  (d) The manner in which the chairpersons of such committees shall be chosen.
- Every District Planning Committee shall, in preparing the draft development plan, have regard to
  (a) (i) matters of common interest between the panchayats and the municipalities including spatial planning sharing of water and other physical and natural resources, the integrated development of infrastructure and environmental conservation.
      (ii) the extent and type of available resources whether financial or otherwise.
  (b) Consult such institutions and organizations as the Governor may, by order specify.
- The chairperson of every District Planning Committee shall forward the development plan, as recommended by such committee, to the Government of the State.

Disqualifications for Membership

- A person shall be disqualified for being chosen as, and for being a member of a municipality-
  (a) If he is so disqualified by as under any law for the time being in force for the purposes of election to the legislature of the state concerned provided that no person shall be disqualified on the ground that he is less than twenty-five years of age, he has attained the age of twenty-one years;
  (b) If he is so disqualified by or under any law made by the legislature of the state.
- If any question arises as to whether a member of a municipality has become subject to any of the disqualifications mentioned in clause (1), the question shall be referred for the decision of such authority and in such manner as the legislature of a State may, by law, provide.

Bar to Interference by Courts in Electoral Matters

Not with standing anything in this constitution-

- The validity of any law relating to the delimitation of constituencies or the allotment of seats to such constituencies made or purporting to be made under article 243ZA, shall not be called in question in any court.
- No election to any municipality shall be called in question except by an election petition presented to such authority and in such manner as is provided for by or under any law made by the Legislature of a state.

Continuance of Existing Law and Municipality

Not with standing anything in this part, any provision of any law relating to municipalities in force in a state immediately before the commencement of the constitution (seventy-fourth amendment) Act, 1992, which is inconsistent with the provisions of this part, shall continue to be in force until amended or replaced by a competent legislature or other competent authority or until the expiration of are year from such commencement, whichever is earlier.

Provided that all the municipalities existing immediately before such commencement shall continue all the expiration of their duration, unless sooner dissolved by a resolution passed to that effect by the Legislative Assembly of that State or, in the case of a state having a Legislative Council, by each House of the Legislature of that state.

Duration of Municipalities

Five-year term. However, it can be dissolved before the completion of its term. Further, the fresh election to constitute a municipality shall be completed (i) before the expiry of its duration of five year; or (ii) in case of dissolution before the expiry of a period of six months from the date of its dissolution.

Powers and Functions

Under **Article 243(W),** subject to the provisions of this Constitution, the Legislature of a State may, by law, endow

- The municipalities with such powers and authority as may be necessary to enable them to function as institutions of self government and such law may contain provisions for the devolution of powers and responsibilities upon municipalities, subject to such conditions as may be specified therein, with respect to
  - the preparation of plans for economic development and social justice.
  - the performance of functions and the implementation of schemes as my be entrusted to them including those in relation to the matters listed in Twelfth Schedule.
- The committees with such powers and authority as may be necessary to enable them to carry out the responsibilities conferred upon them including those in relation to the matters listed in the Twelfth Schedule.

Twelfth Schedule

It contains 18 functional items which is covered in **Article 243 (W).** They are as follows

- Urban planning including town planning.
- Regulation of land use and construction of buildings.
- Planning for economic and social development.
- Roads and bridges.
- Water supply for domestic, industrial and commercial purposes.
- Public health, sanitation conservancy and solid waste management.
- Fire services.
- Urban forestry, protection of the environment and promotion of ecological aspects.
- Safeguarding the interests of weaker sections of society, including the handicapped and mentally retarded.
- Slum improvement and upgradation.
- Urban poverty alleviation.
- Provision of urban amenities and facilities such as parks, gardens, and playgrounds.
- Promotion of cultural, educational and aesthetic aspects.
- Burials and burial grounds; cremations, cremation grounds and electric crematoriums.
- Cattle pounds; prevention of cruelty to animals.
- Vital statistics including registration of births and deaths.
- Public amenities including street lighting, parking lots, bus stops and public conveniences.
- Regulation of slaughter houses and tanneries.

Finance Commission

- Consituted after every five years, review the financial position of municipalities and make recommendation to the Governor.
- The distribution of net proceeds of taxes, duties, tolls and fees between State Municipalities, which are levied by the State.
- Central Finance Commission shall also suggest the measures needed to augment the Consolidated Fund of a State to supplement the resources of the Municipalities in the State.

Application to Union Territories

- President of India may direct that the provisions of this act shall apply to any Union Territory subject to such exceptions and modifications as he may specify.

Areas Kept Out side 74th Amendment Act

- Scheduled areas and tribal areas referred in Article 244 of the Indian Constitution.
- It shall also not affect the functions and powers of the Darjeeling, Gorkha Hill Council of the West Bengal.

Structure of Urban Local Government in India

There are eight types of Urban Local bodies that are created in India for the administration of urban areas. These are as follows:

1. Municipal Corporation

Municipal Corporation are for the big cities like Delhi, Mumbai, Kolkata, Hyderabad, Bengaluru and others.

These are established by the Acts of State Legislature and the Parliament in case of Union Territories. A Municipal Corporation has three authorities.

(i) The Council

It is a deliberative and legislative wing of the corporation. It has councilors, directly elected by the people.

The council is headed by the Major and he/she is assisted by a Deputy Major who is elected for 1 year with renewable term.

(ii) The Standing Committees

It is created to facilitate the working of the Council. These committees deal with public works, education, health, taxation, finance, etc.

(iii) The Municipal Commissioner

The Commissioner is responsible for the implementation of the decisions taken by the Council and its standing committees. The Commissioner is appointed by the State Government. So, that he is the chief executive authority of the Municipal Corporation. Generally, the Commissioner is a member of the IAS cadre.

2. Municipality

The Municipalities are established for the administration of towns and small cities. Like the corporation, they are also established by the Act of State Legislature and the Parliament. Municipality has three authorities

(i)   The Council

(ii)   The Standing Committees

(iii) The Chief Executive Officer. All the authorities have same functions as the corporation has.

3. Notified Area Committee

It is any land area earmarked by legal provision for future development. It is set-up by government notification and not a legislation.

All its members and Chairman are appointed by the State Government and not elected. It is set-up in area where municipality is not feasible, but potential for fast development is there.

4. Town Area Committee

It is set-up by an Act of State Legislature and can have both elected and nominated members. It is quasi-municipality with limited number of Municipal functions like street/ lighting, sanitation, etc.

5. Cantonment Board

They are autonomous bodies functioning under the overall control of the Ministry of Defence. These boards comprise elected members besides ex-officio and nominated members with the station commander as the President of the Board.

The resources of these boards are limited as the bulk of the property is owned by government on, which no tax can be levied.

Thus, the Central Government provides financial assistance by way of grants-in-aid. The boards are responsible for discharging the mandatory duties like provision of public health, sanitation, primary education and street lighting etc.

6. Township

The township is established to provide civic amenities to its staff and workers who live in the housing colonies built near the plant by the large public enterprises.

The township is headed by the town administrator, appointed by the enterprises, he/she is assisted by some engineers and other technical and non-technical staff. It shows the bureaucratic structure of the enterprises.

7. Port Trust

The Port Trusts are established in the port areas such as Mumbai, Kolkata, Chennai, etc. These are established for the following purposes

–   To manage and protect the ports.

–   To provide civic amenities.

The port trust is established by an Act of the Parliament. It has both elected and nominated members. Its Chairman is an official and its civic functions are more or less similar to those of a municipality.

8. Special Purpose Agency

- Above all seven area based urban bodies, the states have set-up certain agencies to undertake designated activities or specific functions. The special purpose agencies are established for single purpose. Some such bodies are as follows :

- Town improvement trusts
    – Water supply and sewerage boards.
    – Urban development authorities.
    – Housing boards.
    – Pollution control boards.
    – Electricity supply boards.
    – City transport boards.

- These bodies are created as statutory bodies by an Act of State Legislature or as department by an executive resolution.

- They function as autonomous bodies and are not subordinate agencies of the local municipal bodies.

Co-operatives

In 1958, the National Development Council (NDC) had 'recommended a national policy on co-operatives. Jawaharlal Nehru had a strong faith in the co-operative movement. In 2011, the cooperatives were given constitutional status by the 97th Constitutional Amendment Act, 2011. Co-operatives have been inserted in Part IXB covering **Articles 243 ZH-ZT**.

Incorporation of co-operative societies (Article 243ZI) subject to the provisions of this part, the Legislature of a State may by law make provisions with respect to the incorporation, regulation and winding up of co-operative societies based on the principles of voluntary formation, democratic control, economic participation and autonomous functioning.

Audit of Accounts of Co-operative Societies (Article 243 ZM)

The Legislature of a State may by law, make provisions with respect to the maintenance of accounts by the cooperative societies and the auditing of such accounts atleast once in each financial year.

The accounts of every cooperative society shall be audited within 6 months of the close of the financial year to which such accounts relate.

Number and Term of Members of Board and its Office Bearers (Article 243 ZJ)

- The board shall consist of such number of directors as may be provided by the Legislature of a State by law. The maximum number of directors of a cooperative society shall not exceed *twenty-one*.

- The Legislature of a State shall by law provide for reservation of one seat for the Scheduled Castes or the Scheduled Tribes and two seats for women on board of every cooperative society.
- The term of office of elected members of the board and its office bearers shall be 5 years from the date of election.

The Legislature of a State shall, by law, make provisions for persons to be members of the board having experience in the fields of banking, management, finance or specialisation in any other field relating to the objects and activities undertaken by the cooperative society as members of the board.

Election of Members of Board (Article 243 ZK)

The superintendence, direction and control of the preparation of electoral rolls for and the conduct of all elections to a cooperative society shall vest in such an authority or body, as may be provided by the Legislature of a State by law.

Central Council of Local Government

- The Central Council of Local Government was set-up in 1954. It was constituted under Article 263 of the Constitution of India by an order of the President of India.
- The Council is an advisory body. It consists of the Minister for Urban Development in the Union and for local self-government in the state. The Chairman of the Council is the Union Minister. The Council has following functions
    - Considering and recommending the policy matters.
    - Making proposals for legislation.
    - Drawing up a common programme of action.
    - Examining the possibility of cooperation between the Centre and the States.
    - Recommending Central Financial Assistance.
    - Reviewing the work done by the local bodies with the Central Financial Assistance.

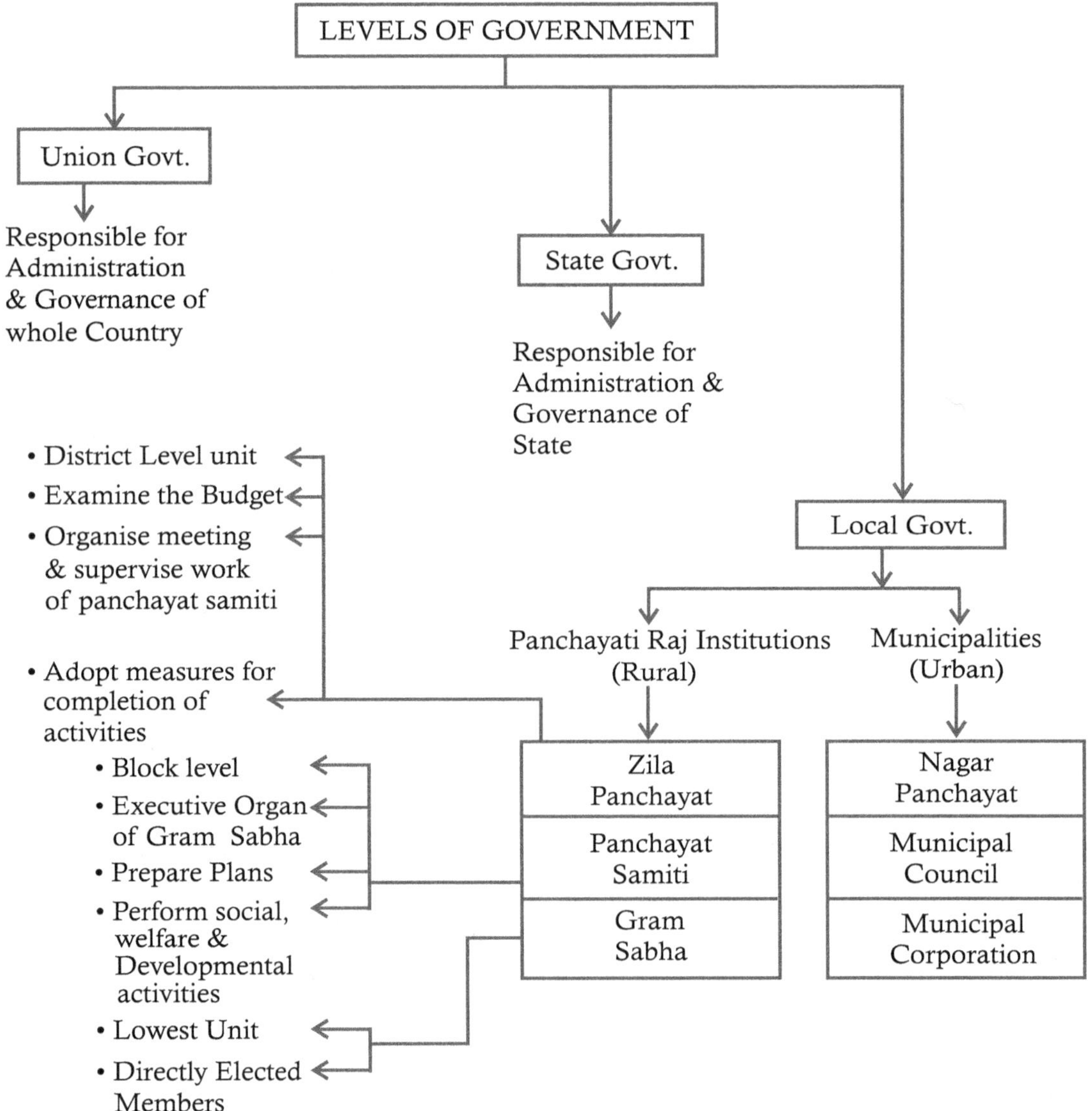

Exercise -1

1. Which of the following is not among recommendation of Balwant Rai Mehta Committee:
   - (a) Establishment of a three-tier panchayat.
   - (b) Village panchayat should be directly elected.
   - (c) Zila parishad should be the executive body.
   - (d) The district collector should be the chairman of the zila parishad.

2. In case of dissolution of panchayat before the completion of its term, fresh election is to be conducted within a period of
   - (a) 3 months
   - (b) 6 months
   - (c) 9 months
   - (d) 1 year

3. The superintendence, direction and control of the preparation of electoral rolls and the conduct of all elections to the Panchayats shall be vested in the
   - (a) Election Commission of India
   - (b) State Legislative Assembly decides the manner of Election
   - (c) State Election Commission
   - (d) As decided by the district executive

4. Who conducts elections to Panchayats and Municipalities?
   - (a) State Government
   - (b) Central Government
   - (c) State Election Commission
   - (d) Central Election Commission

5. Which of the following is incorrect reservation of seats in panchayats and municipalities?
   - (a) Seats are reserved for SC/ST in proportion to their number
   - (b) At least 1/3 of total number of seats are filled by direct elections and are reserved for women
   - (c) reservations for SC/ST are effective till 2010
   - (d) Unreserved seats cannot be contested by women

6. If the Governor of a State is appointed administrator of a Union Territory, he exercises his functions
   - (a) on advice of his Council of Ministers
   - (b) independently of Council of Ministers
   - (c) according to Parliament's directions
   - (d) on the directions of the State Legislature

7. Which of the following is not a provision of the constitution 73rd Amendment Act?
   - (a) 30% seats in all elected rural local bodies will be reserved for women
   - (b) States will constitute Finance Commissions to allocate resources to Panchayati Raj bodies
   - (c) Elected functionaries would be disqualified to hold offices if they have more than two children
   - (d) Elections will be held in six months' time if Panchayati Raj bodies are superseded or dissolved.

8. According to the Balwant Rai Mehta Committee, the District Collector should be:
   - (a) Kept out of the Zila Parishad
   - (b) A non-voting member of the Zila Parishad
   - (c) A member of the Zila Parishad with the right to vote
   - (d) The Chairman of the Zila Parishad

9. Panchayati Raj form of rural local government was adopted first by (in the order):
   - (a) Rajasthan and Madhya Pradesh
   - (b) Andhra Pradesh and West Bengal
   - (c) Rajasthan and Andhra Pradesh
   - (d) Andhra Pradesh and Rajasthan

10. "The state shall take steps to organise village Panchayats and endow them with such powers as may be necessary to enable them to function as units of self-government." This provision is mentioned in:
    - (a) Part I of the Constitution
    - (b) Part IV-A of the Constitution
    - (c) Part III of the Constitution
    - (d) Part IV of the Constitution

11. Which of the following is not correct about a cantonment board?
    - (a) It is created by an executive resolution.
    - (b) It works under the administrative control of the Union Defence Ministry.
    - (c) It is established for municipal administration for civilian population in the cantonment area.
    - (d) It is a statutory body

12. The committee appointed in 1977 to review working of the Panchayti Raj was chaired by
    - (a) Balwant Rai Mehta
    - (b) Ashok Mehta
    - (c) K.N. Katju
    - (d) Jagjivan Ram

13. If a Panchayat is dissolved, elections are to be held within:
    - (a) One month
    - (b) Three months
    - (c) Six months
    - (d) One year

14. Which of the following committees is not concerned with Panchayati Raj?
    - (a) Santhnam Committee
    - (b) Ashok Mehta Committee
    - (c) Balwant Rai Mehta Committee
    - (d) V.K.R.V. Rao Committee

15. Under 74th Amendment of the Constitution the local body for a transitional area is known as
    - (a) Nyaya Panchayat
    - (b) Municipal Panchayat
    - (c) Nagar Panchayat
    - (d) Gram Panchayat

16. 'Swaranajayanti Gram Swarozgar Yojna' came into being in:
    (a) April, 1995 (b) April, 1997
    (c) April, 1999 (d) July, 2001
17. The system of Panchayati Raj involves
    (a) The village block and district levels
    (b) The village and State levels
    (c) The village State and Union levels
    (d) None of these
18. The primary aim of the Panchayati Raj administration is:
    (a) to work for rural development
    (b) to ensure the upliftment of Harijans
    (c) to arouse in the people continuous interest in the community development programmes
    (d) to increase agricultural production through the involvement of the people in extension programmes
19. The lowest unit in the Panchayati Raj institutions is
    (a) a village panchayat (b) the Panchayat Samiti
    (c) Zilla Parishad (d) the Gram Sabha
20. The Committee on whose recommendation Panchayati Raj was introduced in the country was headed by
    (a) Jivraj Mehta (b) Ashok Mehta
    (c) Balwant Rai Mehta (d) None of these
21. When was the Panchayati Raj introduced in India?
    (a) 1950 (b) 1959
    (c) 1952 (d) 1962
22. Which of the following is not a part of Panchayati Raj Institutions?
    (a) District Board
    (b) Town Area Committees
    (c) Village Block
    (d) Panchayati Boards
23. The original Scheme of Panchayati Raj introduced in 1959, operates at (in descending order of tiers):
    (a) Zilla Parishad. Samiti, Gram Sabha
    (b) Panchayat Samiti, Gram Panchayat, Zilla Parishad
    (c) Gram Sabha, Zilla Parishad, Village Panchayat
    (d) Zilla Parishad, Panchayat Samiti, Village Panchayat
24. Who is known as the 'Father of Local Government in India'?
    (a) Lord Curzon (b) Lord Wellesly
    (c) Lord Mayo (d) Lord Ripon
25. A person to be qualified for standing in a Panchayat election must have attained the age of:
    (a) 21 years (b) 18 years
    (c) 25 years (d) 30 years
26. The Panchayati Raj institutions in India get their funds mainly from
    (a) voluntary contributions (b) property tax
    (c) local taxes (d) Government grants
27. What is main purpose of Panchayati Raj?
    (a) To increase agricultural production
    (b) To create employment
    (c) To make people politically conscious
    (d) To make people participate in developmental administration
28. Nyaya Panchayats are expected to
    (a) deal with all crimes committed in the villages
    (b) met out justice to villagers so that litigation is minimum
    (c) settle disputes through persuasion
    (d) try petty civil suits and minor offences
29. In which part of the Constitution is the State enjoined to establish Panchayati Raj institutions?
    (a) Preamble (b) Directive Principles
    (c) Fundamental Rights (d) Seventh Schedule
30. Which of the following is not one of the sources of revenue of village Panchayats?
    (a) Government Grants (b) House Tax
    (c) Income Tax (d) Local Taxes on land
31. Which of the following statement is incorrect?
    (a) The Gram Panchayat is headed by the Sarpanch
    (b) The Panchayat Samiti is headed by the Chairman
    (c) The Zila Parishad is headed by the Chairman
    (d) The Sarpanch and the Chairman are elected directly by the people
32. A Panchayat Samiti at the Block level is:
    (a) an advisory body
    (b) an administrative authority
    (c) a consultant committee
    (d) a supervisory authority
33. Who has representation on the Zilla Parishad?
    (a) Women
    (b) Scheduled Castes and Scheduled Tribes
    (c) Representatives of cooperative societies
    (d) All of the above
34. Panchayati Raj is
    (a) the functioning of village republics in a democracy
    (b) the self-government of the villagers in India
    (c) a complex system of rural local government
    (d) a hierarchical set up for rural administration
35. Balwant Rai Mehta team was set up in 1956 by the National Development Council for the purpose of:
    (a) reporting on the working of the village panchayats at that time
    (b) investigating the feasibility of setting up the new panchayat machinery
    (c) suggesting measures for democratic decentralization
    (d) suggesting measures for better efficiency in the implementation of the Community Development projects

36. Who are generally the members of Gram Sabha?
    (a) All the heads of families of the respective villages
    (b) All the voters in the respective villages
    (c) All adult males in the villages
    (d) Nominated members

37. Local government institutions:
    (a) can levy taxes with prior approval of the State government
    (b) can levy all taxes
    (c) propose taxes to the state governments
    (d) can levy taxes

38. In the three-tier Panchayati Raj structure the Block is:
    (a) the lowest structure
    (b) the intermediary structure
    (c) the highest structure
    (d) None of these

39. The members of the Panchayat are:
    (a) nominated by the District Officer
    (b) elected by the people
    (c) nominated by Local Self-Government and Ministers of the State
    (d) nominated by the Block Development Organisation

40. The Zilla Parishad is:
    (a) a co-ordinating and supervisory body
    (b) an implementing body
    (c) a judicial body
    (d) a combination of all the above

41. Which of the following States has no Panchayat Raj institution at all?
    (a) Assam   (b) Nagaland
    (c) Tripura   (d) Kerala

42. In the new Panchayati Raj Bill enacted in 1993, there are several fresh provisions deviating from the past. Which one of the following is not such provision?
    (a) A number of added responsibilities in the area of agriculture, rural development, primary education and social forestry among others
    (b) Elections being made mandatory for all posts at the time they are due
    (c) A statutory representation for women in the panchayats, upto a third of the strength
    (d) Regular remuneration to the Panchayat members, so as to ensure their punctuality and accountability

43. What is the system of goverance in the Panchayati Raj set up?
    (a) Single tier structure of local self government at the village level
    (b) Two tier system of local self government at the village and block levels
    (c) Three tier structure of local self government at the village, block and district levels
    (d) None of these

44. Which one of the following is incorrect in respect of local government in India?
    (a) According to the Indian Constitution, local government is not an independent tier in the federal system
    (b) 30% of the seats in local bodies are reserved for women
    (c) Local government finances are to be provided by a Commission
    (d) Elections to local bodies are to be determined by a Commission

45. The Government enacted the Panchayat Extension to Scheduled Areas (PESA) Act in 1996. Which one of the following is not identified as its objective?
    (a) To provide self-governance
    (b) To recognize traditional rights
    (c) To create autonomous regions in tribal areas
    (d) To free tribal people from exploitation

46. Which of the following is the main source of income for the Municipal Committee?
    (a) octroi duty
    (b) income tax
    (c) assistance from the centre
    (d) excise duty

47. Which one of the following statements regarding local government in India has been wrongly listed?
    (a) The election to local bodies are determined by a commission
    (b) 30 per cent of the seats in local bodies are reserved for the women
    (c) Finances to local governments are provided by a commission
    (d) None of the above

48. What is the system of governance in the Panchayati Raj set up?
    (a) Single tier structure of local self govt. at the village level
    (b) Two tier system of local self govt. at the village and block levels.
    (c) Three tier structure of local self govt. at the village, block and district levels.
    (d) Four tier system of local self govt. at the village, block, district and state levels.

49. Which one of the following was NOT proposed by the 73rd constitutional amendment in the area of Panchayati Raj?
    (a) Thirty percent seats in all elected rural local bodies will be reserved for women candidates at all levels.
    (b) The state will constitute their Finance Commissions to allocate resources to Panchayati Raj Institutions.
    (c) The Panchayati Raj elected functionaries will be disqualified to hold their offices if they have more than two children.
    (d) The elections will be held in six months time if Panchayati Raj bodies are superseded or dissolved by the state government.

50. The Balwant Rai Mehta Committee recommended which one of the following Panchayati Raj structures?
    (a) Gram Panchayat at the village level and Panchayat Samiti at the block level only
    (b) Panchayat Samiti at the block level and Zilla Parishad at the district level only
    (c) Gram Panchayat at the village level, Panchayat Samiti at the block level and Zilla Parishad at the district level
    (d) Gram Panchayat at the village level and Zilla Parishad at the district level only

51. Which of the following is not a recommendation of the Ashok Mehta Committee on Panchayati Raj ?
    (a) Open participation of political parties in Panchayati Raj affairs
    (b) Creation of a three-tier system
    (c) Reservation of seats for Scheduled Castes and Scheduled Tribes
    (d) Compulsory powers of taxation to Panchayati Raj Institution.

52. The tenure of every Panchayat shall be for five years from the date of
    (a) its first meeting
    (b) issue of notification for the conduct of elections to the Panchayat
    (c) declaration of the election results
    (d) taking oath of office by the elected members

53. The Parliament of India passed the Panchayats Extension to Scheduled Areas Law popularly known as PESA law. Which one among the following statements regarding PESA law is not correct?
    (a) PESA was meant to provide self-governance in the scheduled areas
    (b) PESA disempowers Gram Sabhas
    (c) PESA protects the interests of the tribals
    (d) PESA conducts public hearings to protect inheritance rights of the tribals

54. Which one of the following was not proposed by the 73rd Constitutional Amendment in the area of Panchayati Raj?
    (a) Thirty percent seats in all elected rural local bodies will be reserved for women candidates at all level
    (b) The States will constitute their Finance Commissions to allocate resources to Panchayati Raj institutions
    (c) The Panchayati Raj functionaries will be disqualified to hold their offices if they have more than two children
    (d) The elections will be held in six months time if Panchayati Raj bodies are superceded or dissolved by the State government

55. The 73rd Constitution Amendment Act, 1992 refers to the:
    (a) generation of gainful employment for the unemployed and the under employed men and women in rural areas
    (b) generation of employment for the able bodied adults who are in need and desirous of work during the lean agricultural season
    (c) laying the foundation for strong and vibrant Panchayati Raj institutions in the country
    (d) guarantee of right to life, liberty and security of person, equality before law and equal protection without discrimination

56. Which one of the following is incorrect in respect of Local Government in India?
    (a) According to the Indian Constitution, local government is not an independent tier in the federal system
    (b) 30% of the seats in local bodies are reserved for women
    (c) Local government finances are to be provided by a Commission
    (d) Elections to local bodies are to be determined by a Commission

57. What is the system of governance in the Panchayati Raj set up?
    (a) Single tier structure of local self government at the village level.
    (b) Two tier system of local self government at the village and block levels
    (c) Three tier structure of local self government at the village, block and district levels
    (d) Four tier system of local self government at the village block, district and in the state levels

58. Panchayat Raj was first introduced in India in October, 1959 in:
    (a) Rajasthan
    (b) Tamil Nadu
    (c) Kerala
    (d) Karnataka

59. In the new Panchayati Raj Bill enacted in 1993, there are several fresh provisions deviating from the past. Which one of the following is not one such provisions?
    (a) A number of added responsibilities in the area of agriculture, rural development, primary education and social forestry among other
    (b) Elections being made mandatory for all posts at the time they are due
    (c) A statutory representation for women in the panchayats, upto a third of the strength
    (d) Regular remuneration to the panchayat members, so as to ensure their punctuality and accountability

60. In India, the first Municipal Corporation was set up in which one among the following?
    (a) Calcutta
    (b) Madras
    (c) Bombay
    (d) Delhi

61. Under the Scheduled Tribes and Other Traditional Forest Dwellers (Recognition of Forest Rights) Act, 2006 who shall be the authority to initiate the process for determining the nature and extent of individual or community forest rights or both?
    (a) State Forest Department
    (b) District Collector / Deputy Commissioner
    (c) Tahsildar / Block Development Officer / Mandal Revenue Officer
    (d) Gram Sabha

62. Local self-government can be best explained as an exercise in **[IAS Prelims 2017]**
    (a) Federalism
    (b) Democratic decentralization
    (c) Administrative delegation
    (d) Direct democracy

Exercise -2

1. Consider the following statements:
   1. Lord Dalhousie is known as the father of local self government in India.
   2. Govt of India Act 1919 provided for the establishment of village panchayats.

   Select the correct statement/statements using the code given below:
   - (a) 1 only
   - (b) 2 only
   - (c) Both 1 and 2
   - (d) Neither 1 nor 2

2. Recently, an expert committee headed by Sumit Bose submitted its report to govt. In this report the committee highlighted the need for reforms in Panchayati Raj institutions.

   Which among the following forms the part of Sumit Bose Panel recommendations?
   - (i) Every village Panchayat should have a full time "Secretary".
   - (ii) The Secretary would be incharge of administration including service delivery.
   - (iii) Every Panchayat should have a technical assistance.

   Select the correct answer using the codes given below.
   - (a) (i) and (ii)
   - (b) (ii) and (iii)
   - (c) (i) and (iii)
   - (d) All are correct.

3. Which of the following is/are not the provision of the 73rd Amendment Act:
   1. All states shall compulsarily constitute the 3-tier system of Panchayati Raj.
   2. State legislature shall decide the manner of election of chairperson of a Panchayat at village level.
   3. One-third of the total number of offices of chairpersons in the Panchayats at each level shall be reserved for women.

   Select the incorrect statement/statements from the codes given below:
   - (a) 3 only
   - (b) 2 only
   - (c) 1 only
   - (d) 1 and 3 only

4. Which of the following is a cold current flowing in the north Atlantic ocean:
   - (a) North Atlantic Drift
   - (b) Kuroshio Current
   - (c) Canaries Current
   - (d) Augulhas Current

5. Consider the following statements for Urban Local Government:
   1. there is 50% reservation for women in the scats to be filled by direct elections
   2. grant-in-aid may be given to municipalities from the Consolidated Fund

   Which of the above statements is/are correct?
   - (a) 1 only
   - (b) 2 only
   - (c) Both 1 and 2
   - (d) Neither 1 nor 2

6. The recommendations of Balwant Rai Mehta Committee includes:
   1. Open participation of political parties in Panchayati Raj affairs.
   2. Genuine transfer of power and responsibility to the Panchayati Raj institutions.
   3. Constitutional protection for Panchayati Raj.
   4. District Collector should be the Chairman of the Zila Parishad.
   5. Panchayat Samlti to be the executIve body

   Which of the above statements is/are correct?
   - (a) 1, 2 and 5
   - (b) 2, 4 and 5
   - (c) 2, 3 and 4
   - (d) 1, 3 and 4

7. Which of the following is/are the compulsory provisions of the 73rd Amendment Act on Panchayati Raj?
   1. Indirect elections of the chairpersons of Panchayats at the intermediate and district levels.
   2. Fresh elections within six months in case of dissolution.
   3. Provision for reservation of seats for back-ward classes.
   4. Giving representation to MPs and MLAs in Panchayats.

   Select the correct answer using the codes given below:
   - (a) 1, 3 and 4
   - (b) 2 and 4
   - (c) 1 and 2
   - (d) 2,3 and 4

8. Consider the following statements :
   In India, a Metropolitan Planning Committee :
   1. is constituted under the provisions of the Constitution of India.
   2. prepares the draft development plans for metropolitan area.
   3. has the sole responsibility for implementing Government sponsored schemes in the metropolitan area.

   Which of the statements given above is/are correct?
   - (a) 1 and 2
   - (b) 2 only
   - (c) 1 and 3
   - (d) 2 and 3

9. Which of the following provisions about the Panchayati Raj in the Constitution of India is/are correct?
   1. All the members of Panchayats at the village, intermediate and district levels are elected directly by the voters.
   2. The Chairperson of Panchayats at the village, intermediate and district levels is elected directly by the voters.

   Select the correct answer using the codes given below:
   - (a) 1 only
   - (b) 2 only
   - (c) Both 1 and 2
   - (d) Neither 1 nor 2

10. Which one of the following is incorrect in respect of local government in India?
   - (a) According to the Indian constitution, local government is not an independent tier in the federal system.
   - (b) 30% of the seats in local bodies are reserved for women.
   - (c) Local government finances are to be provided by a commission.
   - (d) Elections to local bodies are to be determined by a commission.

11. Which among the following are true about the 73rd constitutional Amendment in the area of Panchayati Raj?
    1. Thirty per cent seats in all elected rural local bodies will be reserved for women candidates at all levels.
    2. The States will constitute their Finance Commissions to allocate resources to Panchayati Raj institutions.
    3. The Panchayati Raj elected functionaries will be disqualified to hold their offices if they have more than two children.
    4. The elections will be held in six months time if Panchayati Raj bodies are superceded or dissolved by the State government.
    Select the correct answer using the codes given below:
    (a) 2 and 4   (b) 1 and 4
    (c) 1, 3 and 4   (d) 1, 2 and 4

12. Which of the following features of Panchayati Raj, envisaged under the 73rd Amendment of the Constitution, are correctly listed?
    1. the elections to the Panchayats will be held by the Union Election Commission.
    2. there is mandatory reservation of seats for weaker sections and women.
    3. the Panchayats shall have a fixed term of five years and, if dissolved before the expiry of this term, the elections must be held within six months.
    Codes:
    (a) 1, 2 and 3   (b) 2 and 3
    (c) 2 only   (d) 1 and 2

13. Consider the following statements:
    1. Part IX of the Constitution of India contains provisions for Panchayats and was inserted by the Constitution (73rd Amendment) Act 1992.
    2. Part IX A of the Constitution of India contains provisions for municipalities and the Article 243 Q envisages two types of municipalities—a Municipal Council and a Municipal Corporation for every State.
    Which of the statements given above is/are correct?
    (a) 1 only   (b) 2 only
    (c) Both 1 and 2   (d) Neither 1 nor 2

14. Which of following are the features of 74th Amendment Act on muncipalties?
    1. Reservation of seats for SCs and Sts in Proportion of their population.
    2. Mandatory periodic elections every 5 years.
    3. The procedure for maintenance of accounts and audit would be decided by the state Governor.
    4. Constitution of Nagar-Panchayats for smaller Urban area:
    Select the correct answer using the codes given below:
    (a) 1, 2, and 3   (b) 2 and 3
    (c) 3 and 4   (d) 1 and 2

15. Which one of the following is not a feature of part IX of the Constitution of India?
    (a) Five year tenure for panchayats
    (b) Reservation of seats for Schedule Castes and Schedule Tribes for Panchayat membership
    (c) Indirect election for all panchayat seats (village/ intermediate level)
    (d) Reservation for not less than one-third of the seats for women

16. Point out the difference between the local government in India before and after the Constitutional Amendments in 1992:
    1. It has become mandatory to hold regular elections to the local government bodies.
    2. 1/3rd positions are reserved for women.
    3. Elected officials exercise supreme power in the government.
    Select the correct answer using the code given below.
    (a) 1 only   (b) 1 and 2 only
    (c) 1, 2 and 3   (d) 2 and 3 only

17. The 73rd Amendment of the Constitution provided constitutional status to the Panchayati Raj Institutions. Which of the following are the main features of this provision?
    1. A three-tier system of Panchayati Raj for all states.
    2. Panchayat election in every 5 years.
    3. Not less than 33% of seats are reserved for women.
    4. Constitution of district planning committies to prepare development plans.
    Select the correct answer using the codes given below
    (a) 1, 2 and 3 (b) 1, 3 and 4 (c) 1, 2 and 4 (d) 2, 3 and 4

18. Which among the following statements regarding Lord Ripon's plan for local self-government in India is/are correct?
    1. The district should be the maximum area served by one Committee or Local Board.
    2. The Local Boards should consist of a large majority of nominated official members and be presided over by an official member as Chairman.
    Select the correct answer using the codes given below
    (a) Only 1   (b) Only 2
    (c) Both 1 and 2   (d) Neither 1 nor 2

19. How does participatory budgeting seek to make the functioning of local governance institutions more transparent and accountable?
    1. By allowing citizens to deliberate and negotiate over the distribution of public resources.
    2. By allowing citizens to play a direct role in deciding how and where resources should be spent.
    3. By allowing historically excluded citizens with access to important decision-making venues.
    Select the correct answer using the codes given below:
    (a) 1 and 2   (b) 2 and 3
    (c) Only 3   (d) 1, 2 and 3

20. Consider the following statements about local government in India:
    1. Article 40 of Indian Constitution provides for the State to organize village panchayats and endow them with such powers and authority as may be necessary to make them function as units of self-government.
    2. The 73rd and 74th Constitution Amendments inserted Part IX and IX A in the Constitution.
    3. The provisions in Farts IX and IX A of Indian Constitution are more or less parallel and analogous.
    4. The 73rd Constitution Amendment is applicable to all states irrespective of size of population.
    Which of the statements given above are correct?
    (a) 1 and 2 only   (b) 1, 2 and 3 only
    (c) 3 and 4 only   (d) 1, 2, 3 and 4

21. Consider the following statements:
    1. Part IX of the Constitution of India provisions for Panchyats and was inserted by the Constitution (Amendment) Act, 1992.
    2. Part IX A of the Constitution of India contains provisions for Municipalities and the Article 243 Q envisages two types of Municipalities a Municipal Council and a Municipal Corporation for every State.

    Which of the statements given above is/are correct?
    (a) Only 1
    (b) Only 2
    (c) Both 1 and 2
    (d) Neither 1 nor 2

22. The Constitution (Seventy-Third Amendment) Act, 1992, which aims at promoting the Panchayati Raj Institutions in the country, provides for which of the following ?
    1. Constitution of District Planning Committees.
    2. State Election Commissions to conduct all panchayat elections.
    3. Establishment of State Finance Commission.

    Select the correct answer using the codes given below:
    (a) 1 only
    (b) 1 and 2 only
    (c) 2 and 3 only
    (d) 1, 2 and 3

23. In the areas covered under the Panchayat (Extension to the Scheduled Areas) Act, 1996, what is the role/power of Gram Sabha?
    1. Gram Sabha has the power to prevent alienation of land in the Scheduled Areas.
    2. Gram Sabha has the ownership of minor forest produce.
    3. Recommendation of Gram Sabha is required for granting prospecting licence or mining lease for any mineral in the Scheduled Areas.

    Which of the statements given above is/are correct?
    (a) 1 only
    (b) 1 and 2 only
    (c) 2 and 3 only
    (d) 1, 2 and 3

24. The fundamental object of Panchayati Raj system is to ensure which among the following ?
    (1) People's participation in development
    (2) Political accountability
    (3) Democratic decentralization
    (4) Financial mobilization

    Select the correct answer using the code given below.
    (a) 1, 2 and 3 only
    (b) 2 and 4 only
    (c) 1 and 3 only
    (d) 1, 2, 3 and 4

25. With reference to the 'Gram Nyayalaya Act', which of the following statements is/are correct?
    1. As per the Act, Gram Nyayalayas can hear only civil cases and not criminal cases.
    2. The Act allows local social activists as mediators/reconciliators.

    Select the correct answer using the code given below.
    (a) 1 only
    (b) 2 only
    (c) Both 1 and 2
    (d) Neither 1 nor 2

26. Consider the following statements.
    1. The minimum age prescribed for any person to be a member of Panchayat is 25 years.
    2. A Panchayat reconstituted after prenature dissolution continues only for the remainder period.

    Which of the statements given above is/are correct?
    (a) 1 only
    (b) 2 only
    (c) Both 1 and 2
    (d) Neither 1 nor 2

27. To be eligible to contest election under the Haryana Panchayati Raj (Amendment) Act, 2015, a candidate should **[CDS 2017]**
    1. have a functional toilet at home
    2. have payment slips of power bills
    3. not be a cooperative loan defaulter
    4. have studied minimum matriculation irrespective of category

    Select the correct answer using the code given below.
    (a) 1, 2 and 3 only
    (b) 1, 2 and 4 only
    (c) 1, 2, 3 and 4
    (d) 3 and 4 only

28. Which of the following statements with regard to Panchayats in India are correct? **[CDS 2017]**
    1. Seats in a Panchayat are filled by direct election from the territorial constituencies in the Panchayat area.
    2. The Gram Sabha is the body of persons registered in the electoral rolls relating to a village within the Panchayat area.
    3. The Panchayats work on the principle of constitutional autonomy.
    4. The State Legislature may by law endow the Panchayats with the power and authority to enable them to function.

    Select the correct answer using the code given below.
    (a) 1, 2 and 3
    (b) 2, 3 and 4
    (c) 1, 2 and 4
    (d) 1 and 4 only

Hints and Explanations

EXERCISE-1

1. (c) Balwant Rai Mehta Committee recommended that zila parishad should be the advisory, co-ordinating and supervisory body. While Ashok Mehta Committee recommended that zila parishad should be the executive body and made responsible for planning at the district level.

2. (b) The 73rd Amendment Act provides for a 5 year term of office to the panchayat at every level. However it can be dissolved before the completion of its term.

   Further fresh elections to constitute a panchayat shall be completed (a) before the expiry of the duration of five years. (b) In case of dissolution, before the expiry of a period of six months from the date of its dissolution.

3. (c) The superintendence, direction and control of the preparation of electoral rolls and the conduct of all elections to the panchayats shall be vested in the state election commission. It consists of a state election commissioner to be appointed by the governor. His conditions of service and tenure of office shall also be determined by the governor.

4. (c) 5. (d) 6. (b) 7. (c) 8. (d)
9. (c) 10. (d) 11. (a)

12. (b) The Committee appointed in 1977 to review working of the Panchayati Raj was chaired by Ashok Mehta. The committee submitted its report in August 1978 and made 132 recommendations to revive and strengthen the declining Panchayati Raj system in the country. As a result of this report, the Indian states of Karnataka, Andhra Pradesh, and West Bengal passed new legislations.

13. (c) 14. (a)

15. (c) Under 74th Amendment of the constitution the local body for a transitional area is known as Nagar Panchayat. This article provides that there be a Nagar Panchayat for transitional areas i.e. an area in transition from rural to urban, a municipality for a smaller urban area and a municipal corporation for a larger urban area.

16. (c) 'Swaranajayanti Gram Swarojgar Yojna' came into being in April, 1999. Swarnajayanti Gram Swarojgar Yojana (SGSY) is an initiative launched by the Government of India to provide sustainable income to poor people living in rural areas of the country.

The SGSY aims at providing self-employment to villagers through the establishment of Self-help groups.

17. (a) 18. (c) 19. (a) 20. (c) 21. (b) 22. (b)
23. (d) 24. (d) 25. (a) 26. (d) 27. (d) 28. (d)
29. (b) 30. (c) 31. (d) 32. (b) 33. (d) 34. (c)
35. (d) 36. (b) 37. (d) 38. (b) 39. (b) 40. (a)
41. (b) 42. (d) 43. (c) 44. (a)

45. (d) PESA Act does not identify the freedom of tribal people from exploitation as its objectives, but it automatically becomes a byproduct of its objectives.

46. (a) 47. (c)

48. (c) Part IX of the constitution envisages a 3-tier system of panchayats, namely (a) the village level (b) the district panchayat (district-level) (c) The intermediate panchayat (block-level)

49. (a) The act provides for the reservation of not less than one third(33%) of the total of seats for women at all levels.

50. (c) The Balwant Rai Mehta Committee was appointed by the Government of India in January 1957 to examine the working of the Community Development Programme(1952). It recommended a 3-tier Panchayati Raj system-Gram Panchayat at the village level, Panchayat Samiti at the block level, and Zila Parishad at the district level.

51. (b) Creation of a three-tier system was not the recommendation of Ashok Mehta Committee. According to this committee, the 3-tier system of Panchayati Raj should be replaced by the 2-tier system. Ashoka Mehta committee was appointed by the Janata Government under the chairmanship of Ashoka Mehta.

52. (a) According to Article 243(E), every Panchayat, unless sooner dissolved under any law for the time being in force, shall continue for five years from the date appointed for its first meeting and no longer.

53. (b) Panchayats Extension to Scheduled Areas Act(PESA) is a law enacted by the Government of India to cover the "Scheduled areas" which are not covered in the 73rd amendment or Panchayati Raj Act of the Indian Constitution. It was enacted on 24 December 1996 to enable Gram Sabhas to self-govern their natural resources.

54. (c) Statement given under option (c) is not mentioned in 73rd amendment act. But this norm is applied in Haryana, Rajasthan, MP, Odisha and Andhra Pradesh.

55. (c) 73rd Amendment Act added Eleventh Schedule to the Constitution and Part IX, which provides for the Panchayati Raj System.

56. (b) According to 73rd Amendment Act 1993, under Article 243D, not less than 1/3rd *i.e.* 33% seats should be reserved for women in local bodies.

57. (c) According to 73rd Amendment Act, three-tier system of Panchayats exists: Village level, District Panchayat at the district level, the intermediate Panchayat which stands between the village and District Panchayats in the States where the population is above 20 Lakhs.

58. (a) Panchayati Raj System was first introduced in Nagaur district of Rajasthan on October 2, 1959 followed by Andhra Pradesh in 1959.

59. (d) Provision given in option (d) is not included under 73rd Amendment Act 1993.

60. (b) In 1688, the first Municipal Corporation of India was set up in Madras.

61. (d) Section C of the Forest Dweller Act provides a transparent three step procedure for deciding on who gets rights.

    Firstly, the Gram Sabha makes a recommendation-i.e, who has been cultivating land for how long, which minor forest produce is collected; etc. The Gram Sabha's recommendation goes through two stages of screening committees- the Taluka and the District levels.

62. **(b)** Balwant Rai G Mehta Committee submitted its report in November 1957 and recommended the establishment of the scheme of 'democratic decentralisation', which ultimately came to be known as Panchayati Raj.

EXERCISE-2

1. (b) In modern times, elected local government bodies were created after 1882. Lord Ripon, who was the viceroy of India at that time, took the initiative in creating these bodies. They were called local boards.

    Government of India Act 1919 (Montagu Chelmsford) reforms provided for the establishment of village panchayats. Consequently village panchayats were established in a number of provinces. This trend continued after the government of India Act of 1935.

2. (d) All the statements given in the question are correct. The Sumit Bose Panel said that Panchayats are not equipped to handle the workload relating to three key areas–engineering, accounting and data entry which have increased manifold in recent years.

3. (c) Statement (2) and (3) are correct.
    The act provides for a three-tier system of Panchayati Raj in every state, that is Panchayats at the village, intermediate and district levels.

Thus the Act brings about uniformity in the structure of Panchayati Raj throughout the country.

However, a state having population not exceeding 20 lakh may not constitute panchayats at the intermediate level.

4. (c) Kuroshio current is a warm current in the North Pacific Ocean.
    - North Atlantic drift is a warm current in the North Atlantic Ocean.
    - Augul has current is a warm current in the South Indian Ocean.

5. (b) 6. (b) 7. (c) 8. (a)

9. (a) The Chairperson of Panchayats at inter-mediate and district levels are elected indirectly.

10. (b) Under Article 243, it has been mentioned that not less than 1/3rd (33%) seats in the local bodies shall be reserved for women.

11. (d) 12. (a) 13. (a) 14. (d) 15. (c)

16. (b) Not less than one-third (including the number of seats reserved for women belonging to the Scheduled Castes and the Scheduled Tribes) of the total number of seats to be filled by direct election in every Municipality shall be reserved for women and such seats may be allotted by rotation to different constituencies in a Municipality.

17. (a) The salient features of the 73rd Amendment Act, 1992 are: -
    - To provide 3-tier system of Panchayati Raj for all States having population of over 20 lakhs.
    - To hold Panchayat elections regularly every 5 years.
    - To provide reservation of seats for Scheduled Castes, Scheduled Tribes and women (not less than 33%)
    - To appoint State Finance Commission to make recommendations as regards the financial powers of the Panchayats.

18. (d) Lord Ripon's plan for local Self government in India is as follows:
    1. The sub-division, not the district, should be the maximum area served by one committee or local board with primary boards under it serving very small areas, so that each member of it might possess knowledge of and interest in its affairs.
    2. The local boards should consist of a large majority of elected non-official members, and they should be presided over by a non-official member.

19. (d) Participatory Budgeting is a democratic process of deliberation by citizens, civic officials and elected representatives on the issues that need attention and collectively arriving at decisions that would directly

be included in the budget of the government. Participatory budgeting empowers the citizens to present their demands and priorities for improvement and influence through discussions and negotiations the budget allocations made by their municipalities. It is an opportunity in which the common citizens can decide about the allocation and distribution of public expenditure in their areas or regions.

20. **(b)** 73rd constitution amendment is applicable to all states except Jammu & Kashmir.

21. **(a)** Part IX and Eleventh Schedule were added by 73rd Constitutional Amendment Act, 1992 which contain provisions for Panchayats, Part IX A. Twelfth Schedule were added by 74th Constitutional amendment act, 1992 which contain provisions for Municipalities but Article 243 Q envisages three types of municipalities: Nagar Panchayats for a transitional area, Municipal Council for smaller urban areas and Municipal Corporation for larger urban areas.

22. **(c)** District planning committee comes under 74th Amendment not in 73rd Amendment.

23. **(d)** According to Panchayat Extension to the Scheduled Areas) Act 1996, Gram Sabha has the power to prevent alienation of land in the Scheduled Areas, has the ownership of minor forest produce and the recommendation of Gram Sabha is required for granting prospecting licence or mining lease for any mineral in the Scheduled Areas.

24. **(a)** The fundamental object to Panchayati Raj system is to ensure people's participation in development, political accountability and democratic decentralization.

25. **(b)** • Gram Nyayalaya try criminal cases, civil suits, claims or disputes which are specified in the First Schedule and the Second Schedule to the Act. The Gram Nyayalaya are supposed to try to settle the disputes as far as possible by bringing about conciliation between the parties and for this purpose, it can make use of the appointed conciliators.

• Reference- Page no. 601 of India year book 2016, under heading Judiciary it says- Panchayat Courts also function in some states under various names like Nyaya Panchayat, Panchayat Adalat, Gram Kachehri, etc., to decide civil and criminal disputes of petty and local nature. That means first statement is wrong.

• Under this act, District court with consultation of DM, prepares panel of social workers to act as councilors. Hence 2nd statement is right.

26. **(b)** • For PRI Bodies minimum age is 21 years, to contest elections, so first statement is wrong.

• 2nd statement is correct-

27. **(a)** The Haryana Panchayati Raj (Amendment) Bill, 2015 is an amendment of the Haryana Panchayati Raj Act, 1994. The minimum eligibility of a candidate for contesting election are: having a functional toilet at home, having power bills payment slips, should not be a cooperative loan defaulter, and having minimum matriculation degree for people in the general category, middle standard or class 8th passed for the women (general) and Scheduled caste candidates, and class V passed for women SC candidates.

28. **(c)** Panchayati system functions as a system of governance in India in which gram panchayats acts as basic units of local administration. A village with population of 1500 and more forms Gram Sabha. Article 243G, empower State legislatures to provide Panchayats with powers and authority to enable them to function. Seats in a Panchayat are filled by persons chosen by direct election from territorial constituencies in the Panchayat area.

THE FEDERAL SYSTEM

CENTRE – STATE RELATIONS

Political scientists have classified government into unitary and federal on the basis of the nature of relations between the national government and the regional government.

A federal government is one in which powers are divided between the national government and the regional governments by the jurisdiction independently.

In a federal model, the national government is known as the Federal Government or the Central Government or the Union Government.

- The distribution of powers is an essential feature of federalism. A federal Constitution establishes the dual polity with the Union at the centre and the States at the periphery, each endowed with the sovereign powers to be exercised in the field assigned to them respectively by the Constitution. The one is not subordinate to the other in its own field; the authority of one is co-ordinate with the other.
- In the Indian federal set-up, the Constitution divides powers between centre and states as:-
  - Legislative
  - Administrative
  - Financial

Legislative Relations

- *Article 245 to 255 in part XI of the Constitution* deals with the Legislative relation between the Centre & the States.
- *Article 245(1)* of the Constitution of India provides that the Parliament has power to make laws for the whole or any part of territory of India. This includes not only the States but also the UTs or any other area, for the time being included in the territory of India. It also possesses the power of 'Extra-Territorial Legislation' which no State Legislature possesses.
- The State Legislature is competent only to make laws for the whole or any part of the state to which it belongs.

- For certain UTs like Andaman & Nicobar and Lakshadweep, regulations made by the President have the same force as the Acts of the Parliament and such regulations may repeal or amend a law made by Parliament in relation to such territory.
- The application of Acts of parliament to any Scheduled Area may be barred or modified by notifications made by the Governor.
- **In distributing the subject matters between Centre and states, our Constitution makers followed Canadian scheme.** However they added one more list to it, *Concurrent list*. (GOI Act 1935 had 3 fold enumeration – federal, provincial and concurrent) at present
  1. **Union List – 100 subjects**
  2. **State List – 61 subjects, originally 66 subjects**
  3. **Concurrent List –52 subjects, originally 47 subjects**
- Subjects mentioned in the *Union List* are of national importance and only Parliament is competent to make laws on these subjects.
- For *State List*, only the States have exclusive power to make laws.
- Concurrent list is a *"Twilight Zone"*, where both the Union and the states are competent to make law, without any conflict.
- **Residuary powers (Article 248): Parliament has exclusive power to make laws on the subjects not enumerated in any of the lists (Entry 97 of Union List).**
- Wherever the conflict arises as to a subject matter, the Union List predominates over the other lists.
- To determine whether a particular enactment falls under one entry or the other, it is the pith and substance of such enactment and not its legislative level that is taken account of.

- **Colorable Legislation** – The motives of the legislature are, otherwise, irrelevant for determining whether it has transgressed the constitutional limits of the legislative power. This principle is based on the maxim that you can not do indirectly what you can not do directly.
- Under Art 249, in the national interest, Parliament has the power to make laws w.r.t. any matter included in the State List, for a temporary period, if Rajya Sabha passes a resolution supported by 2/3rd of the members present and voting in that respect.
- Under the proclamation of emergency, Article 250 empowers the Parliament to make laws for the whole or any part of the territory of India w.r.t. all matters in the State List. Such a law however shall cease to effect on the expiration of 6 months after the proclamation of emergency has ceased to operate.
- Under Article 252, if the legislatures of two or more States pass a resolution to the effect that it is desirable to have a law passed by Parliament on any matters in the state list common to these states, Parliament can make laws in that respect.
- Under Article 253, Parliament has power to make any law for the whole or any part of the territory of India for implementing treaties and international agreements and conventions.
- Under Article 256, Parliament is empowered to make laws w.r.t. all matters in the state list when there is failure of constitutional machinery of the State under Article 356.

Administrative Relations

- During the time of emergency Indian Constitution works like a unitary government.
- In normal times, there are constitutional provisions which ensure the control of the union over the states. Some of the mechanisms are:
- Power to appoint and dismiss the Governor (articles 155-156), power to appoint judges of HC, members of state PSC (articles 217, 317)
- Article 256 provides that the executive power of the state shall be so exercised as to ensure compliance with the laws made by the parliament and executive power of the Union shall also extend to the giving of such directions to a state as it may deem essential for the purpose.
- Further article 257 provides that states must exercise their executive power in such a way so as not to impede or prejudice the exercise of the executive power of the Union in the state.
- The powers of the Union Government also extend to giving directions to a state in 2 specific matters:
  1. Construction and maintenance of means of communication which are declared to be of national or military importance.
  2. Measures to be taken for the protection of the railway within the states.
- The Constitution prescribes and coercive sanction for the enforcement of its directions through article 356.

Delegation of Union functions to the States

- *Under article 258 (1),* Parliament with the consent of the state government can entrust to it any matter falling with in the executive powers of the Union.
- Under article 258(2) Parliament is empowered to use state machinery for the enforcement of Union laws. For such purpose, it can confer powers or impose duties on state functionaries.
- Therefore under clause (1) delegation of power is made with the consent of the state, whereas consent of the state is not necessary under clause (2), and such delegation is done by the parliament by law. This implies that parliament can interfere in the state administration, even without the consent of the State.
- State government has also the power to delegate its functions to the Union and its officers. Article 258 (A) provides that Governor of the state with the consent of GOI, entrust to the government, such functions to which the executive power of State extends.
- All India services are common to both the Union and the states. The officers of these services are appointed and regulated by the Centre and are placed in various states.
- **Grants in-aid (Article 275):** Parliament has power to make such grants as it may deem necessary to give financial assistance to any state which is in need of such assistance (Article 275).
- Under Article 263, President has power to establish **Inter-State Councils**. These Councils have duty of inquiring into and advising upon disputes which arises between the states. These councils also investigate and discuss the subjects of common interest between the union and the States or between two or more states.
  - The President has so far established Central Council of health, a Central Council of local self-government and a Transport Development Council.
- Parliament has power to constitute an **Inter-State Commerce Commission** (Article 307) and empower it to execute such functions as it may deem fit.
- Article 261 provides that full faith and credit shall be given throughout the territory of India to public acts, records and judicial proceedings of the Union and every state.
- Article 261 (3) declares that final judgement or orders delivered or passed by civil courts in any part of territory of India can be executed anywhere in the country.
- *Article 262*: Adjudication of disputes relating to waters of inter-state rivers or river valleys. Article 262 (2) provides that parliament may by law provide that neither the SC nor any other court shall exercise jurisdiction in respect of any such dispute.

Financial Relations

- **Articles 268 to 293 in part XII deal with the financial relations.**
- These relations are related to the distribution of taxes as well as non-tax revenue and the power of borrowing.
- Grant-in-aid forms an important part of centre-state relations.

- Parliament can levy taxes on the subjects enlisted in the List - I (Union List) while the states can levy taxes on the subjects mentioned in the State List. (List II).
- There are no taxes on the subjects of the Concurrent List (List III).
- Finance Commission (Article 280) recommends to the President on the distribution of net proceeds of taxes between the Centre and states.

IMPORTANT SUBJECTS IN VARIOUS LISTS

Union List (List I)

6. Atomic energy and mineral resources.
18. Extradition.
45. Banking.
47. Insurance.
48. Stock exchanges and futures markets.
49. Patents, inventions and designs; copyright; trade-marks and merchandise marks.
69. Census.
85. Corporation tax.
97. Any other matter not enumerated in List II or List III including any tax not mentioned in either of those lists.

State List (List II)

1. Public order.
5. Local government.
6. Public health and sanitation.
12. Libraries, museums and other similar institutions.
14. Agriculture.
21. Fisheries.
25. Gas and gas-works.
28. Markets and fairs.
61. Captivation taxes.

Concurrent List (List III)

1. Criminal law.
2. Criminal procedure.
3. Preventive detention.
5. Marriage and divorce.
6. Transfer of property other than agricultural land.
7. Contracts.
13. Civil procedure.
14. Contempt of court, but not including contempt of the Supreme Court.
17. Prevention of cruelty to animals.
20. Economic and social planning.
26. Legal, medical and other professions.
38. Electricity.
40. Archaeological sites.

Administration of Union Territories

There is no uniform system of administration in the union territories. Parliament has been vested with the power to prescribe the structure of administration in the various union territories. The administrators of union territories are variously known as Lieutenant Governors, Chief Commissioners or Administrators. In Daman and Diu and Pondicherry, they are designated as Lieutenant Governors. In Andaman and Nicobar Islands and Chandigarh they are known as Chief Commissioners and in Lakshadweep as Administrator.

Similarly, some Union Territories possess Legislative Assemblies and Councils of Ministers such as Daman and Diu, Pondicherry, and Delhi (National Capital Territory), while others do not. It may be noted that in Union Territories with Legislative Assemblies, the right to legislate on subjects enumerated in the State List and Concurrent List vests with the Assembly. With respect to other union territories, the laws are enacted by the Parliament. The administrators of the union territories enjoy the right to issue ordinance within certain limitations. When the legislatures of the union territories are dissolved or suspended, responsibility for the peace, progress and good government of the territory falls on the President.

Commissions for the Improvement of Centre-State Relations

There have been several efforts for the improvement of Centre-State relations. Central Government have set-up many commissions to review and examine the Federal Relations from time to time, leading among them are

Sarkaria Commission

Sarkaria Commission was set-up in June, 1983 by the Central Government of India. The Sarkaria Commission's charter was to examine the relationship and balance of power between State and Central Governments in the country and suggest changes within the framework of Constitution of India. The commission was so named as it was headed by Justice Rajinder Singh Sarkaria, a retired Judge of the Supreme Court of India and other two members of the committee were Shri B Sivaraman and Dr SR Sen.

The Commission made 247 recommendations to improve Centre-state relations. The important recommendations are mentioned below:

1. A permanent *Inter-State Council* called the Inter-Governmental Council should be set up under Article 263.
2. Article 356 (President's Rule) should be used very sparingly, in extreme cases as a last resort when all the available alternatives fail.
3. The institution of All-India Services should be further strengthened and some more such services should be created.
4. The residuary powers of taxation should continue to remain with the Parliament, while the other residuary powers should be placed in the Concurrent List.
5. The National Development Council (NDC) should be renamed and reconstituted as the National Economic and Development Council (NEDC).
6. The Centre should consult the states before making a law on a subject of the Concurrent List.
7. The governor's term of five years in a state should not be disturbed except for some ex¬tremely compelling reasons.

8. The surcharge on income tax should not be levied by the Centre except for a specific purpose and for a strictly limited period.
9. When the president withholds his assent to the state bills, the reasons should to communicated to the state government.
10. The Union Government should consult the Government of the States before enacting any law related to a subject included in the Concurrent List.
11. As provided in Article 263, an Inter-State Council should be constituted to resolve differences between the Union and the States. The Chief Ministers of all the states should be Ex-officio Members of the Council.
12. The states should be given right to amend the "subjects included in State List, this requires an amendment to the Article 252 of the Constitution. An Expenditure Commission should be set-up at the Union level. The Corporation Tax should be distributed between Centre and States.

MM Punchhi Commission

A Commission on Centre-State Relations was set-up by the Government of India in April, 2007 under the Chairmanship of Madan Mohan Punchhi, Former Chief Justice of India to look into the issues of Centre-State Relations. Some of the recommendations given in its various reports are as below

- It recommended higher central transfers to backward states to enable them to improve their physical and human infrastructure.
- It recommended for the adoption of a multi-pronged strategy in the backward regions of the country comprising public investment in infrastructure development, proactive policies to attract private investment, higher public expenditure on social sectors, such as health and education and area specific strategy for the growth of agricultural production.
- There should be much better coordination between the Finance Commission and the Planning Commission. The synchronisation of the periods covered by the Finance Commission and the Five Year Plan will considerably improve such coordination. It recommended that another attempt be made to synchronise the periods.
- There should be mandatory devolution of functions to local government and it must be done by the year 2015. Priority should be given to items pertaining to basic needs. Articles *243 G* and *243 W* should be amended to mandate that devolution of functions as listed out in the Eleventh and Twelfth Schedules, together with the powers and authority to implement them, should be done by the year 2015.
- The Collector is overburdened and hence, there should be a separate administrative structure for the district Panchayat.
- The Constitution needs to be amended to provide a specific entry in List 1 (Union List) of the Seventh Schedule empowering the Union on matters concerning environment, ecology and climate change.

- The **National Water Resources Council** needs to play a greater role in integrating policy and programmes on a continuous basis.
- Government should ideally explore the possibilities of setting up a single regulator for tariff regulation of power, coal and gas.

Inter-State Water Disputes

- **Article 262 of the Constitution envisages the adjudication of inter-state water disputes** which make two provisions
  1. Parliament may by law provide for the adjudication of any dispute or complaint with respect to the use, distribution and control of waters of any inter-state river and river valley.
  2. Parliament may also provide that neither the Supreme Court nor any other court is to exercise jurisdiction in respect of any such dispute or complaint.
- **Under this provision,** the Parliament has enacted two laws i.e. the *River Boards Act of 1956* and the *Inter-State Water Disputes Act of 1956.*
- **The River Board Acts,** envisions the establishment of rivers boards for the regulation and development of inter-state river and river valleys. **The Inter-State Water Disputes Act empowers the federal government (i.e. Central Government) to set-up an adhoc tribunal for the adjudication of a dispute between two or more states in relation to the waters of an inter-state river or river valleys.**

Inter-State Water Dispute Tribunals

Name	Set-up in	State Involved
Krishna Water Disputes Tribunal	1969	Maharashtra, Karnataka and Andhra Pradesh
Godavari Water Disputes Tribunal	1969	Maharashtra, Karnataka, Andhra Pradesh, Madhya Pradesh and Odisha
Narmada Water Disputes Tribunal	1969	Rajasthan, Gujarat, Madhya Pradesh and Maharashtra
Ravi and Beas Water Disputes Tribunal	1986	Punjab and Haryana
Cauvery Water Disputes Tribunal	1990	Karnataka, Kerala, Tamil Nadu and Puducherry
Second Krishna Water Disputes Tribunal	2004	Maharashtra, Karnataka and Andhra Pradesh
Vansadhara Water Disputes Tribunal	2010	Odisha and Andhra Pradesh
Mahadayi Water Disputes Tribunal	2010	Goa, Karnataka and Maharashtra

Inter-State Councils

- The power of the President to set-up Inter-State Councils may be exercised not only for advising upon disputes, but also for the purpose of investigating and discussing subjects, in which some or all of the States or the Union and one or more of the States or the Union have a common interest.
- In the exercise of this power the President has already constituted the Central Council of Health, the Central Council of Local Self-Government, the Central Council of Indian Medicine, the Central Council of Homeopathy the changing role of Inter-State Council.
- **The Inter-State Council was set-up under Article 263 of the Constitution of India in May, 1990.** The council charged with the duty of
  - inquiring into and advising upon disputes, which may have arisen between states;
  - investigating and discussing subjects in which some or all of the States or the Union and one or more of the states, have a common interest or
  - making recommendations upon any such subject and in particular recommendations for the better coordination of policy and action with respect to that subject;
- It shall be lawful for the President by order to establish such a council and to define the nature of the duties to be performed by it and its organisation and procedure.

Composition of Inter-State Council

The Composition of the Inter-State Council includes the Prime Minister, Chief Ministers of all States, Chief Ministers of Union Territories having Legislative Assemblies and Administrators of Union Territories not having Legislative Assemblies, Governors of states under President Rule, six Ministers of Cabinet rank in the Union Council of Ministers' to be nominated by the Prime minister and two Ministers of Cabinet rank in the Union Council of Ministers to be nominated by the Prime Minister permanent invites.

Duties of the Council

- To investigate and discuss subjects of common interest.
- Make recommendations for the better coordination of policy and actions on such subjects; and
- Deliberate on such matters of general interest to the states referred by the Chairman to the Council. It shall have its own Secretariat.

INTER-STATE TRADE AND COMMERCE

Articles 301 to 307 in Part XIII of the Constitution deal with the trade, commerce and intercourse within the territory of India.

Article 301 declares that trade, commerce and intercourse throughout the territory of India shall be free. The object of this provision is to break down the border barriers between the states and to create one unit with a view to encourage the free flow of trade, commerce and intercourse in the country. The freedom under this provision is not confined to inter-state trade, commerce and intercourse but also extends to intra-state trade, commerce and intercourse. Thus, Article 301 will be violated whether restrictions are imposed at the frontier of any state or at any prior or subsequent stage.

The freedom guaranteed by Article 301 is a freedom from all restrictions, except those which are provided for in the other provisions (Articles 302 to 305) of Part XIII of the Constitution itself. These are explained below:

(i) Parliament can impose restrictions on the freedom of trade, commerce and intercourse between the states or within a state in public interest. But, the Parliament cannot give preference to one state over another or discriminate between the states except in the case of scarcity of goods in any part of India.

(ii) The legislature of a state can impose reasonable restrictions on the freedom of trade, commerce and intercourse with that state or within that state in public interest. But, a bill for this purpose can be introduced in the legislature only with the previous sanction of the president. Further, the state legislature cannot give preference to one state over another or discriminate between the states.

(iii) The legislature of a state can impose on goods imported from other states or the union territories any tax to which similar goods manufactured in that state are subject. This provision prohibits the imposition of discriminatory taxes by the state.

(iv) The freedom (under Article 301) is subject to the nationalisation laws (i.e. laws providing for monopolies in favour of the Centre or the states). Thus, the Parliament or the state legislature can make laws for the carrying on by the respective government of any trade, business, industry or service, whether to the exclusion, complete or partial, of citizens or otherwise.

The Parliament can appoint an appropriate authority for carrying out the purposes of the above provisions relating to the freedom of trade, commerce and intercourse and restrictions on it. The Parliament can also confer on that authority the necessary powers and duties. But, no such authority has been appointed so far.

ZONAL COUNCILS

The Zonal Councils are the statutory (and not the constitutional) bodies. They are established by an Act of the Parliament, that is, States Reorganisation Act of 1956. The act divided the country into five zones (Northern, Central, Eastern, Western, Southern) and provided a zonal council for each zone.

Each zonal council consists of the follow members:

(a) Home Minister of Central government.

(b) Chief Ministers of all the States in the zone.

(c) Two other ministers from each state in the zone.

(d) Administrator of each Union Territory in the zone.

The Home Minister of Central Government is the common chairman of the five zonal councils. Each Chief Minister acts as a vice-chairman of the council by rotation, holding office for a period of one year at a time.

The Zonal Councils aim at promoting cooperation and coordination between states, union territories and the Centre. They discuss and make recommendations regarding matters like economic and social planning, linguistic minorities, border disputes, inter-state transport, and so on. They are only deliberative and advisory bodies.

The objectives (or the functions) of the Zonal Councils, in detail, are as follows:

- To achieve an emotional integration of the country.
- To help in arresting the growth of acute state- consciousness, regionalism, linguism and particularistic trends.
- To help in removing the after-effects separation in some cases so that the process of reorganisation, integration and economic advancement may synchronise.
- To enable the Centre and states to cooperate with each other in social and economic matters and exchange ideas and experience in order to evolve uniform policies.
- To cooperate with each other in the successful and speedy execution of major development projects.
- To secure some kind of political equilibrium between different regions of the country.

North-Eastern Council

In addition to the above Zonal Councils, **a North-Eastern Council was created by a separate Act of Parliament– the North-Eastern Council Act of 1971**. Its members include Assam, Manipur, Mizoram, Arunachal Pradesh, Nagaland, Meghalaya, Tripura and Sikkim.

Zonal Councils at a glance

Name	Members	Headquarters
1. Northern Zonal Council	Jammu and Kashmir, Himachal Pradesh, Haryana, Punjab, Rajasthan, Delhi, and Chandigarh	New Delhi
2. Central Zonal Council	Uttar Pradesh, Uttarakhand, Chhattisgarh, and Madhya Pradesh	Allahabad
3. Eastern Zonal Council	Bihar, Jharkhand, West Bengal and Orissa	Kolkata
4. Western Zonal Council	Gujarat. Maharastra, Goa, Dadra and Nagar Haveli and Daman and Diu	Mumbai
5. Southern Zonal Council	Andhra Pradesh, Karnataka, Tamil Nadu, Kerala and Puducherry	Chennai

Articles Related to Inter-State Relations at a Glance

Article No.	Subject-matter
	Mutual Recognition of Public Acts, etc.
261.	Public acts, records and judicial proceedings
	Disputes Relating to Waters
262.	Adjudication of disputes relating to waters of Inter-State Rivers or river valleys
	Co-ordination between States
263.	Provisions with respect to an inter-state council
	Inter-State Trade and Commerce
301.	Freedom of trade, commerce and intercourse
302.	Power of Parliament to impose restrictions on trade, commerce and intercourse
303.	Restrictions on the legislative powers of the Union and of the states with regard to trade and commerce
304.	Restrictions on trade, commerce and intercourse among states
305.	Saving of existing laws and laws providing for state monopolies
306.	Power of certain states in Part B of the First Schedule to impose restrictions on trade and commerce (Repealed)
307.	Appointment of authority for carrying out the purposes of Articles 301 to 304

Exercise -1

1. With reference to Inter State Council, which among the following statements stands false?

    (a) Its functions are complementary to Supreme Court's Jurisdiction under Art 131 to decide a legal controversy between the state governments.

    (b) Composition of Inter State Council also includes Six Central Cabinet Ministers, including Home Minister.

    (c) It is a recommendatory body and not a permanent constitutional body.

    (d) All the Chief Ministers except those of Union Territories are included in the composition of Inter State Council.

2. With reference to Inter State Council, which among the following statements stands false?

    (a) Its functions are complementary to Supreme Court's Jurisdiction under Art 131 to decide a legal controversy between the state governments.

    (b) Composition of Inter State Council also includes Six Central Cabinet Ministers, including Home Minister.

    (c) It is a recommendatory body and not a permanent constitutional body.

    (d) All the Chief Ministers except those of Union Territories are included in the composition of Inter State Council.

3. Which of the following is not a condition when parliament can legislate on the matters of state list:

    (a) When Rajya Sabha declares that it is necessary for parliament to make laws on matter of state list.

    (b) During the proclamation of national emergency in the state.

    (c) When two or more states pass resolutions in this regard.

    (d) When there is no clear majority in the state legislative assembly.

4. A government is federal or unitary on the basis of relation between the:

    (a) three organs of the government

    (b) Centre and the States

    (c) Legislature and the Executive

    (d) Constitution and the States

5. Grant in aid are provided every year to States in need of assistance as recommended by the

    (a) President

    (b) Parliament

    (c) Finance Commission

    (d) None of the above

6. Which statements regarding the levying, collection and distribution of Income Tax is correct?

    (a) Union levies, collects and distributes the collection between itself and the states

    (b) Union levies, collects and keeps all the proceeds of income tax

    (c) Union levies and collects the tax but the proceeds are allocated among the states

    (d) Only the surcharge levied on income tax is shared between the Union and the states

7. Which one of the following is charged upon the Consolidated Fund of India and can be spent without authorization by the Parliament?

    (a) Debit charges for which the Government of India is liable

    (b) Salary and allowances of President

    (c) Salaries, allowances and pensions of the judges of Supreme Court and High Courts

    (d) all the above

8. The entry "Public health and Sanitation" is included in the Constitution of India in

    (a) Union List   (b) State List

    (c) Concurrent List   (d) None of these

9. The Parliament can legislate on the subjects in the State List if the

    (a) President issues an order authorizing it to do so

    (b) Supreme Court gives authority to the Parliament in this regard

    (c) Rajya Sabha passes a resolution by two-thirds of its members present and voting, declaring it expedient to legislate on a State matter in the national interest

    (d) Prime Minister issues a special order

10. The Sarkaria Commission Report deal with which one the following?

    (a) Corruption in India (b) Centre-state relations

    (c) local governance   (d) Inter-river dispute

11. Sarkaria Commission was established to study

    (a) President and Governoers' relations

    (b) Centre-State relations

    (c) State and Panchayat body relations

    (d) President and Prime Minister' relations

12. Which one among the following pairs of level of government and legislative power is not correctly matched ?

    (a) Central Government   : Union List

    (b) Local Governments   : Residuary powers

(c) State Governments : State List

(d) Central and State Government : Concurrent List

13. With reference to the Constitution of India, which one of the following pairs is not correctly matched?

    (a) Forests : Concurrent List

    (b) Stock Exchange : Concurrent List

    (c) Post Office Savings Bank : Union List

    (d) Public Health : State List

14. Which one of the following subjects is under the Union List in the Seventh Schedule of the Constitution of India?

    (a) Regulation of labour and safety in mines and oilfields

    (b) Agriculture

    (c) Fisheries

    (d) Public Health

15. Which one of the following is not a feature of Indian federalism? **[IAS Prelims 2017]**

    (a) There is an independent judiciary in India.

    (b) Powers have been clearly divided between the Centre and the States.

    (c) The federating units have been given unequal representation in the Rajya Sabha.

    (d) It is the result of an agreement among the federating units.

16. Local self-government can be best explained as an exercise in **[IAS Prelims 2017]**

    (a) Federalism

    (b) Democratic decentralization

    (c) Administrative delegation

    (d) Direct democracy

Exercise -2

1. In which of the following bodies, does the Chief Minister of a State hold membership?
    1. National Integration Council
    2. National Development Council
    3. Inter-State Council
    4. Zonal Council
    Select the correct answer from the codes given below :
    (a) 1, 3 and 4   (b) 2 and 3
    (c) 1, 2, 3 and 4   (d) 2, 3 and 4

2. India's is a federal system of government as:
    1. Union Legislature is bicameral
    2. provision of single citizenship
    3. Constitution is supreme
    4. there is an independent judiciary
    Which of the above statements is/are correct?
    (a) 1, 3 and 4   (b) 1, 2 and 3
    (c) 2 and 4   (d) 1, 2, 3 and 4

3. Which of the following are the features of Indian federal system?
    1. Division of powers between the centre and the units
    2. Residuary powers vested with the centre
    3. Existence of the nominal and real executive
    Which of the following statements is/are correct?
    (a) 1, 2 and 3   (b) 1 and 2
    (c) 1 and 3   (d) 2 and 3

4. The Inter-State Council consists of
    1. Prime Minister
    2. Chief Ministers of all states
    3. Chief Ministers of union territories with legislatures
    4. Eight Union Cabinet Ministers
    5. Administrators of union territories with legislatures
    Select the correct answer using the codes given below:
    (a) 1, 2, 3, 4 and 5   (b) 1, 2, 3 and 4
    (c) 1, 2 and 3   (d) 1, 2, 3 and 5

5. The Prime Minister of India recently ruled out the decision of the Cauvery River Authority, in which Karnataka was ordered to release water to Tamil Nadu. Which of the following statement(s) is/are correct?
    1. The Cauvery River Authority comprises of the Chief Ministers of Puducherry, Kerala, Tamil Nadu and Karnataka along with the PM as chairman.
    2. Inter-state water disputes are excluded from the primary jurisdiction of the Supreme Court of India.
    Select the correct answer using the codes given below:
    (a) 1 only   (b) 2 only
    (c) Both 1 and 2   (d) Neither 1 nor 2

6. Which of the following can be associated with MGNREGA programme?
    1. It provides wage employment to every household whose adult members volunteer to do unskilled manual work.
    2. It focuses on strengthening of natural resource management.
    3. It encourages sustainable development.
    Select the correct answer using the codes given below:
    (a) 1 only   (b) 1 and 2 only
    (c) 1 and 3 only   (d) 1, 2 and 3

7. Which of the following is among the main provisions of the 'MGNREGA'?
    1. There is no time bound limit to provide employment to the beneficiaries registered under the act
    2. There is a provision for daily unemployment allowance in cash to be paid.
    3. Employment is limited and confined within a limited radius.
    4. At least one-third beneficiaries have to be women
    State the correct answer using the codes given below:
    (a) 1, 2 and 3 only   (b) 2, 3 and 4 only
    (c) 1, 3 and 4 only   (d) 1, 2, 3 and 4

8. Which of the following statements with regard to Inter-State Council is/are correct?
    1. It was established under the provisions of the Constitution of India.
    2. The Council is a recommendatory body.
    3. There is a standing committee of the Council under the Chairmanship of the Prime Minister of India to process matters for consideration of the Council.
    Select the correct answer using the codes given below
    (a) Both 1 and 3   (b) Only 2
    (c) 1 and 2   (d) All of these

9. Consider the following statements with reference to finance commission:
    1. It is a quast-judicial body.
    2. It ascertains and certifies the net proceeds of a tax in any area.
    Which of the above statements is/are correct?
    (a) 1 only   (b) 2 only
    (c) Both 1 and 2   (d) Neither 1 nor 2

10. While the proclamation of financial emergency is in operation, the centre can give directions to the states for?
    1. To reduce the salaries and allowances of all class of persons serving in the state.

2. To reserve all money bills for the consideration of President.

   Select the correct answer using the codes given below:

   (a) 1 only   (b) 2 only

   (c) Both 1 and 2   (d) Neither 1 nor 2

11. Consider the following statements with reference to Government of India Act to 1935:

    1. It gave three-fold enumeration of subject.

    2. Residuary powers were given to federal legislature.

    Which of the above statements is/are correct?

    (a) 1 only   (b) 2 only

    (c) Both 1 and 2   (d) Neither 1 nor 2

12. Which of the following is/are features of unitary government?

    1. No division of powers

    2. Single Government

    3. Rigid Constitution

    Select the correct answer from the codes given below?

    (a) 1 only   (b) 1 and 2 only

    (c) 2 and 3 only   (d) 1, 2 and 3

13. Consider the following statements:

    1. Indian judicial system enforce only Central laws.

    2. The Parliament alone can make "extra-territorial legislation.

    Which of the above statements is/are correct?

    (a) 1 only   (b) 2 only

    (c) Both 1 and 2   (d) Neither 1 nor 2

14. Parliament can legislate with respect to matters in the state list when?

    1. Rajyasabha powers a resolution.

    2. During national emergency.

    3. On the request of states.

    Select the correct answer from the codes given below:

    (a) 1 only   (b) 2 only

    (c) Both 1 and 2   (d) Neither 1 nor 2

Hints and Explanations

EXERCISE-1

1. **(d)** Inter State Council is a recommendatory body on issues relating to inter-state, centre-state and centre and Union Territory relations, composition of Inter State Council includes Prime Minister as the Chairman, Chief Ministers of all states, Chief Ministers of Union Territories having legislative Assemblies, Governors of the States under the President's rule and Six Central Cabinet Ministers, including Home Minister to be nominated by the P.M.

2. **(d)** Inter State Council is a recommendatory body on issues relating to inter-state, centre-state and centre and Union Territory relations, composition of Inter State Council includes Prime Minister as the Chairman, Chief Ministers of all states, Chief Ministers of Union Territories having legislative Assemblies, Governors of the States under the President's rule and Six Central Cabinet Ministers, including Home Minister to be nominated by the P.M.

3. **(d)** Parliament can legislate on the matters of state list on the situations mention in options (a), (b) and (c).

    – Lack of majority in the state assembly is no ground for parliament to make laws on state list.

4. **(b)**   5.   **(b)**   6.   **(a)**   7.   **(d)**

8. **(b)** The entry "public health and sanitation" is included in the state list of the constitution of India.

9. **(c)** State list consists of 61 items (previously 66 items). Uniformity is desirable but not essential on items in this list: maintaining law and order, police forces, healthcare, transport, land policies, electricity in state, village administration, etc. The state legislature has exclusive power to make laws on these subjects. But in certain circumstances, the parliament can also make laws on subjects mentioned in the State list. Then the parliament has to pass a resolution with 2/3rd majority that it is expedient to legislate on this state list in the national interest. Though states have exclusive powers to legislate with regards to items on the State list, articles 249, 250, 252, and 253 state situations in which the federal government can legislate on these items.

10. **(b)** Sarkaria Commission was set up in June 1983 to examine the relationship and balance of power between state and central government.

11. **(b)** Sarkaria Commission was set up by the central government of India in June 1983 to examine the relationship and balance of power between state and central governments in the country and suggest changes within the framework of Constitution of India.

12. **(b)** The State list contains 66 subjects of local or state importance. The state governments have the authority to make laws on these subjects. These subjects include police, local governments, trade, commerce and agriculture. Parliament has exclusive power to make any law with respect to any matter not enumerated in the Concurrent List or State List.

    Note: Residuary Power retained by a governmental authority after certain powers have been delegated to other authorities.

13. **(b)** Stock Exchanges are listed in the Seventh Schedule (Article 246) List I-Union List, item no. 90 that reads, taxes other than stamp duties on transactions in stock exchanges and futures markets. Forests-Concurrent List, 17-A, Post Office Savings Bank -Union List-3, Public health and sanitation; hospitals and dispensaries - State List -6.

14. **(a)** Agriculture (Entry 14), Fisheries (Entry 21), Public Health (Entry 6) are in the State List. Regulation of Labour and safety in mines and oil fields is in the Union list under Entry 55 (Art 246).

15. **(d)** Indian federation is not the result of an agreement among the states unlike the American federation. So, "D" is not the feature of Indian federalism.

16. **(b)** Balwant Rai G Mehta Committee submitted its report in November 1957 and recommended the establishment of the scheme of 'democratic decentralisation', which ultimately came to be known as Panchayati Raj.

EXERCISE-2

1. **(c)**   2.   **(a)**   3.   **(b)**   4.   **(c)**

5. **(c)** The Cauvery River authority comprises of the CMs of puducherry, Kerala, Tamil Nadu and Karnataka. Inter-State water disputes are excluded from the primary jurisdiction of the supreme court of India. On 20 February 2013, based on the directions of the Supreme Court, the Indian Government has notified the final award of the Cauvery Water Disputes Tribunal (CWDT). The Tribunal, in a unanimous decision in 2007, determined the total availability of water in the Cauvery basin at 740 thousand million cubic (tmc) feet at the Lower Coleroon Anicut site, including 14 tmcft for environmental protection and seepage into the sea. The final award makes an annual allocation of 419 tmcft to Tamil Nadu in the entire Cauvery basin, 270 tmcft to Karnataka, 30 tmcft to Kerala and 7 tmcft to Puducherry.

6. (d) MGNREGA Programme provides employment to every household adult members to do unskilled manual work, focuses on natural resources management and encourages sustainable development. The statute is hailed by the government as "the largest and most ambitious social security and public works programme in the world".

7. (b) Under this act, there is a time bound limit to provide employment to the beneficiaries registered under the act.

8. (c) The Inter-State Council was established under Article 263 of the Constitution of India through a Presidential Order, 1990. As the article 263 makes it clear that the Inter-State Council is not a permanent constitutional body for coordination between the States of the Union. It can be established 'at any time' if it appears to the President that the public interests would be served by the establishment of such a Council. The Council is a recommendatory body. The Council shall consist of Prime Minister (Chairman), Chief Ministers of all States and union territories (Member), Administrators (UT) and Six Ministers of Cabinet rank to be nominated by the Prime Minister (Member). This is not a standing committee.

9. (a) Article 280 provides for a Finance Commission as 9 quast- judicial body. It is constituted by the President every fifth year on even earlier.

    The net proceeds of a tax or a duty in any area is to be ascertained and certified by the comptroller and Auditor- General of India.

10. (c) While the proclamation of financial emergency (Article-360) is in operation, the Centre can give directions to the States:
    (i) To observe the specified canons of financial propriety.
    (ii) To reduce the salaries and allowances of all class of persons serving in the state.
    (iii) To reserve all money bills and other financial bills for the consideration of the President.

11. (a) The GoI Act: 1935 provided for a three-fold enumeration i.e. federal, provincial and concurrent. The residuary powers were given neither to the federal legislature nor to the provincial legislature but to the Governor- General of India.

12. (b) Features of unitary government.
    - Single government.
    - Constitution may be written or unwritten.
    - No division of power.
    - Constitution may be rigid or flexible.
    - Legislature may be bicameral (Britain) or unicameral (China).

13. (b) There is no division of judicial power as the Constitution has established an integrated judicial system to enforce both the Central laws as well as State laws.
    The Parliament alone can make 'extra-territorial legislation'. Thus the laws of the Parliament are also applicable to the Indian citizens and their property in any part of the world.

14. (d) The Constitution empowers the Parliament to make laws on any matter enumerated in the state list in all the above mentioned cases.

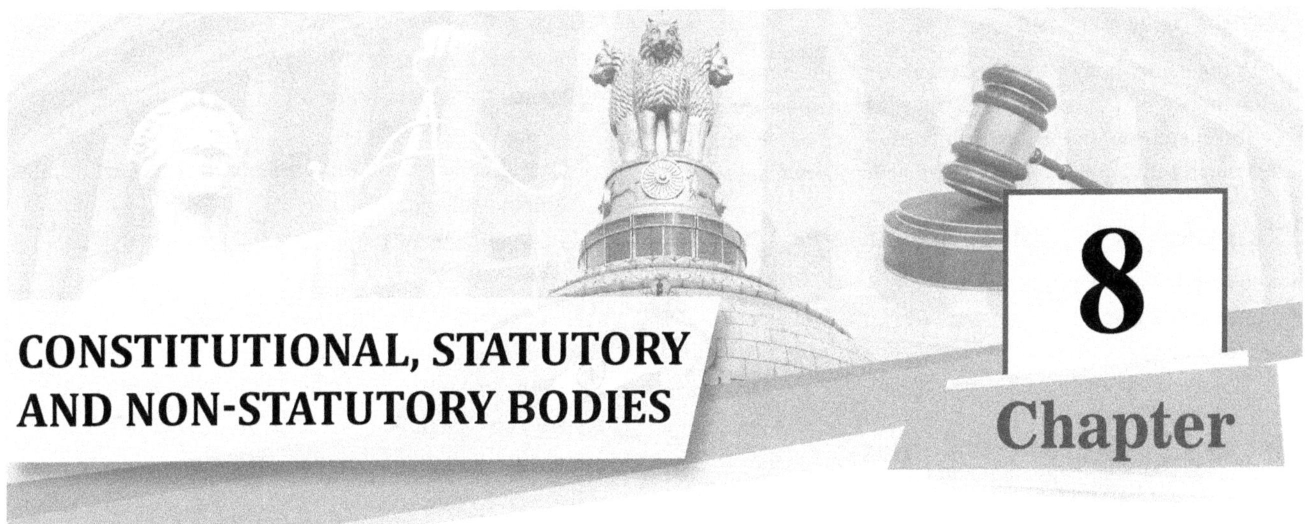

CONSTITUTIONAL, STATUTORY AND NON-STATUTORY BODIES

Chapter 8

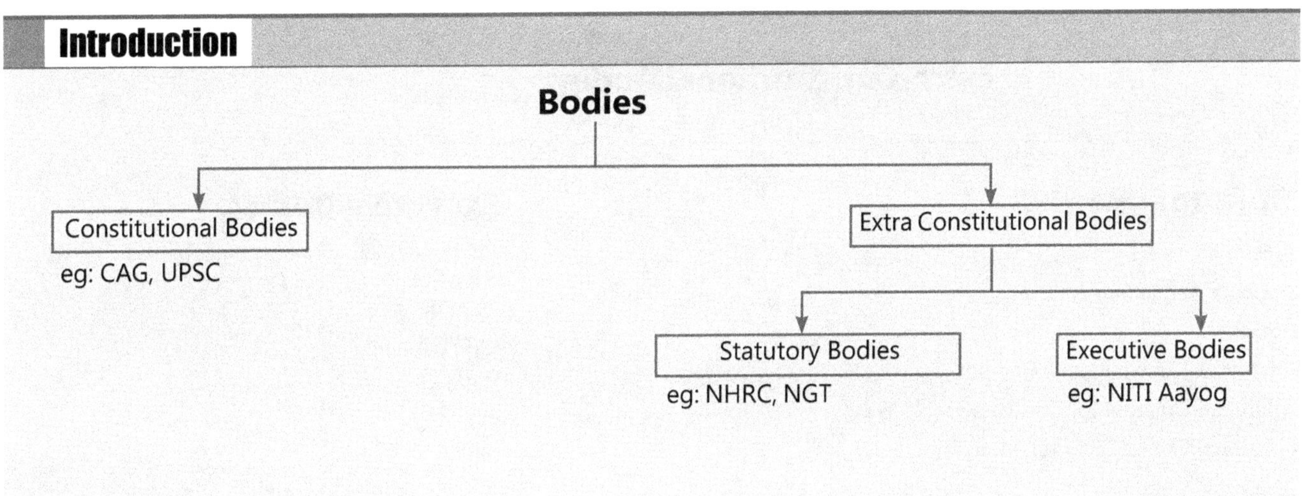

Constitutional Bodies

- Constitutional Bodies derive their authority from the constitution. Such bodies or institutions are written into the constitution of a nation and can't be abolished without amending that part of the constitution which Sometimes also requires the consert of the states.
- All the constitutional bodies have dedicated article in the constitution.
- The chief of the constitutional bodies are appointed by either the president or the Prime Minister.

  Examples of the Constitutional Bodies mentioned in the constitution of India are:
- UPSC (Art - 315)
- CAG (Art - 148)
- Election Commission of India (Art - 324)
- Finance Commission of India (Art - 280)

Statutory, Regulatory and Various Quasi Judicial Bodies

Statutory bodies are established by acts which parliament and state legislature can pass.

Basically, a statutory body is an organisation of government which is not demarcated in constitution of India but it gets its power, service rules, authority by an act of parliament or state legislatures.

Examples of Statutory Bodies

- National Human Rights Commission.
- National Commission for women.
- National commission for minorities.
- National Commission for Backward Classes.
- Armed Forces Tribunal.

Regulatory Bodies

- A regulatory body also called regulatory agency is a public authority or a government agency which is accountable for exercising autonomous authority over Some area of human activity in a regulatory or supervisory Capacity.

Examples of Regulatory Bodies

- Competition commission of India.
- Advertising Standards council of India.
- Press council of India.
- Reserve Bank of India.

List of Constitutional Bodies

- Union Public Service Commission (UPSC) (Article -3/5)
- The Comptroller and Auditor General of India (Article - 148)

- Election Commission of India (Article - 324)
- Finance Commission of India (Article - 280)
- National Commission For Scheduled Castes (NCSC, (Art - 338)
- National Commission for Scheduled Tribes (Art - 338 A)
- Attorney-General of India (Article - 76)
- Special Officer for Linguistic Minorities (Article - 350-B)

Extra-Constitutional Bodies

- An extra Constitutional body is an institution of government which is not defined in Constitution of India.

There are two type of extra- constitutional bodies.

1. Statutory Bodies.
2. Executive Bodies.

Extra-Constitutional Bodies

Statutory Bodies

A Body that derives its
existence and authority from
a State.

- National Human Rights Commission. (NHRC)
- National Commission for women (NCW)
- National Commission for Minorities.
- National Commission for Backward Classes.
- National Green Tribunal (NGT).
- The Telecom Regulatory Authority of India (TRAI).
- Central Information Commission (CIC)
- Central Vigilance commission (CVC)
- Armed Forces Tribunal.

Executive Bodies

Bodies Which are created by an executive order of any ministry of union or state.

- NITI Aayog.
- UIDAI

Planning Commission

- Constituted in March 1950 by a resolution of the Government of India on the recommendation of the Advisory Planning Board in 1946 under the chairmanship of K.C. Neogi.
- Planning Commission was neither a constitutional body nor a statutory body. It is a **non-constitutional or extra-constitutional or a non-statutory body.**
- Objective is to formulate 5 year plans for economic and social development and to advice Central government in this regard.

NITI Aayog

The Government of India has **replaced Planning Commission** with a new institution named NITI Aayog (National Institution for Transforming India).

The institution will serve as *'Think Tank'* of the Government - a directional and policy dynamo.

NITI Aayog will provide Governments at the Central and State Levels with relevant strategic and technical advice across the spectrum of key elements of policy, which includes matters of national and international importance on the economic front, dissemination of best practices from within the country as well as from other nations, the infusion of new policy ideas and specific issue-based support.

Composition

NITI Aayog will have Prime Minister as its chairman, one Vice-Chairman cum chief-executive officer, 3 full time members and 2 part time members, apart from 4 Central Government ministers.

NITI Aayog (National Institution for Transforming India)

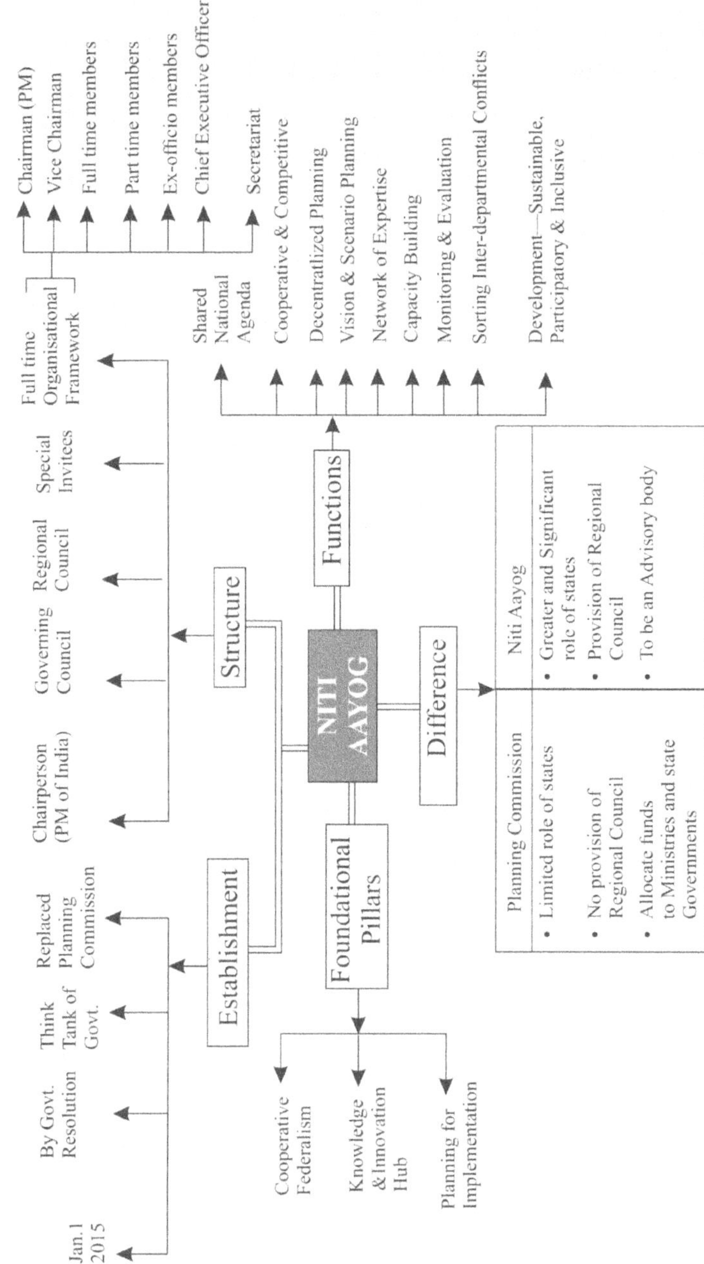

COMPOSITION OF NITI AAYOG

Chairperson

- Prime Minister

Governing Council

- CMs (States) and It Governors (UTs)

Regional Councils

- Formed on need-basis, Comprising CMs and Lt Govs of the region

Members

- Full-time basis.

Part-time members.

- Max 2, rotational, from relevant institutions

Ex- Officio members

- Max 4 from council of ministers, nominated by PM.

Special Invites.

- Experts, Specialists, practitioners with domain knowledge.

Chief Executive officer

- Appointed by PM for fixed tenure, Sectretary rank.

Secretariat

- As deemed necessary.

Difference Between Planning Commission and NITI Aayog

S.No	Points of Difference	NITI Aayog	Planning Commission
1.	Financial clout	To be an advisory body, or a think-tank. The powers to allocate fund vested in the finance ministry.	Enjoyed the powers to allocate funds to ministries and state governments
2.	Full-time members	Three full-time members.	Had eight full-time members
3.	States' role	Includes the Chief Ministers of all States and the Lieutenant Governors of all Union territories in its Governing Council, devolving more power to the States of the Union.	States' role was limited to the National Development Council and annual interaction during plan meetings
4.	Member secretary	To be known as the CEO and to be appointed by the Prime Minister	Secretaries or member secretaries were appointed through the usual process
5.	Part-time members	To have a number of part time member, depending on the need from time to time	Full Planning Commission had no provision for part time members
6.	Constitution	Governing Council has state Chief Ministers and lieutenant governors.	The Commission reported to National Development Council that had State Chief Ministers and lieutenant governors.
7.	Organization	New posts of CEO, of secretary rank, and vice Chairperson. Will also have two full-time members and part-time members as per need. Four cabinet ministers will serve as ex-officio members.	Had deputy chairperson, a member secretary and 8 full time members.
8.	Participation	Consulting states while making policy and deciding on funds allocation. Final policy would be a result of that.	Policy was formed by the Commission and states were then consulted about allocation of funds.
9.	Allocations	No power to allocate funds	Had power to decide allocation of government funds for various programs at national and state levels.
10.	Nature	NITI is a think-tank and does not have the power to impose policies.	Imposed policies on states and tied allocation of funds with projects it approved.

National Development Council (NDC)

- It was **established in August 1952** by an executive resolution of the Government of India on the recommendation of the First Year Plan.
- It is neither a constitutional body nor a statutory body.
- **Sarkaria Commission** recommended for its constitutional status under article 263 of the Constitution and should be renamed as 'National Economic and Development Council'.

Composition

- The NDC is composed of the following members.
  - Prime Minister of India as its chairman /head.
  - All Union cabinet ministers (since 1967).
  - Chief ministers of all states.
  - Administrators of all Union territories.
  - Members of the Planning Commission.
- Secretary of the Planning Commission acts as the secretary to the NDC.

Objectives

- Chief objective –To secure cooperation of states in the execution of the plan.
- To strengthen and mobilize the efforts and resources of the nation in support of the plan.
- To promote common economic policies.
- To ensure balanced and rapid development of all parts of the country.

Functions

- Prescribe guidelines for preparation of the national plan.
- Consider the national plan as prepared by Planning Commission.
- Make an assessment of the resources required for implementing the plan.
- Consider important questions of social and economic policy affecting national development.
- Review the working of the national plan from time to time.
- Recommend measures for achievement of the aims and targets set out in plan.
- NDC is the highest body, below the Parliament. However it (the NDC) is listed as an *advisory body* **and its recommendations are not binding**.
- It should meet at least **twice every year**.

STAGES IN MAKING OF A PLAN
Drafting of Five-Year Plan

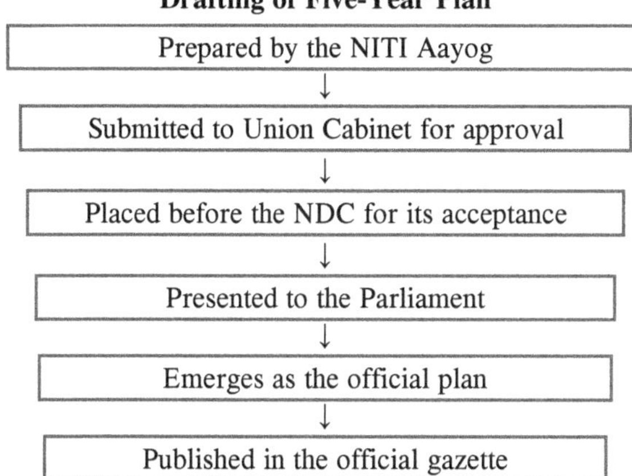

Finance Commission

- Article 280 provides Finance Commission as a **quasi-judicial** body constituted by the President every fifth year or at such earlier time as he considers necessary.
- Recommendations made by the Finance Commission are only of advisory nature and not binding upon the government.

Composition

- A chairman and four other members appointed by the President.
- They hold office for such period as specified by the President in his order. The are Eligible for reappointment.
- The Constitution authorises Parliament to determine the qualifications of the members and the manner in which they should be selected. Accordingly, the Parliament enacted *Finance Commission Act of 1951*, specifying the qualifications of the chairman and its members.
- *Chairman* should be a person having experience in public affairs.
- The *four other members* should be selected from the following :
  - *A Judge of high court* or one to be qualified to be appointed as one.
  - A person having specialized *knowledge of finance* and *accounts* of the government.
  - A Person having Wide experience in financial matters and in administration.
  - A person who has Special knowledge of economics.

Functions

- The Finance Commission is required to make recommendations to the President of India on the following matters:
  - Distribution of the net proceeds of taxes to be shared between the Centre and the States.
  - Principles that should govern the grants-in-aid to the states by the Centre (i.e. out of the Consolidated Fund of India).
  - The measures needed to augment the Consolidated Fund of a State to supplement the resources of the Panchayats and the Municipalities in the state on the basis of the recommendations made by the State Finance Commission. This function is added by the 73rd and 74th Constitutional Amendment 1992.
  - Any other matter referred to it by the President in the interests of sound finance.
- Commission also suggests the amounts to be paid to Assam, Bihar, Orissa and West Bengal in lieu of assignment of any share of the net proceeds in each year of export duty on jute and jute products (Article 273).
  - **Commission submits its report to the President.** He lays it before both the Houses of Parliament along with an explanatory memorandum as to the action taken on its recommendations (Article 281).

Finance Commission	Chairman	Operational Duration
First	K. C. Neogy	1952–57
Second	K. Santhanam	1957–62
Third	A. K. Chanda	1962–66
Fourth	P. V. Rajamannar	1966–69
Fifth	Mahaveer Tyagi	1969–74
Sixth	K. Brahmananda Reddy	1974–79
Seventh	J. M. Shelat	1979–84
Eighth	Y. B. Chavan	1984–89
Ninth	N. K. P. Salve	1989–95
Tenth	K. C. Pant	1995–2000
Eleventh	A. M. Khusro	2000–2005
Twelfth	C. Rangarajan	2005–2010
Thirteenth	Dr. Vijay L. Kelkar	2010–2015
Fourteenth	Dr. Y. V. Reddy	2015–2020

Financial Stability and Development Council

- With a view to strengthening and institutionalizing the mechanism for maintaining financial stability, enhancing inter-regulatory coordination and promoting financial sector development, the FSDC was set up by the Government as the upper level forum in December 2010.

- The chairman of the Council is the Union Finance Minister.
- It monitors macro prudential supervision of the economy. It also focuses on financial literacy and financial inclusion.
- Recommendations for such a super regulatory body were first mooted by Raghuram Rajan.
- FSDC has replaced the High Level co-ordination committee on Financial Markets (HLCCFM).

Election Commission

- It is a permanent and an independent body established by the Constitution of India directly to ensure free and fair elections in the country (Art. 324).
- Elections to Parliament, State legislatures, President and Vice-President are vested in it.

Composition (Article 324)

- Election Commission shall consist of Chief Election Commissioner and such number of other Election Commissioners, as the President may from time to time fix.
- The Appointment of the Chief election commissioner and other election commissioners Shall be made by the President.
- When any other Election Commissioner is appointed the Chief Election Commissioner shall act as the Chairman of the Election Commission.
- President may also appoint after consultation with the Election Commission, regional commissioners to assist the Election Commission.
- Conditions of service and tenure of office shall be determined by the President.
- Since its inception in 1950 and till oct 1989, the election commission functioned as a single member body consisting of the chief Election commissioner. In 1989, two more members were added to cope with the increased work on account of lowering of the voting age from 21 to 18 years by the 61st Amendment 1989.
- Chief Election Commissioner and other Election Commissioners have equal powers and receive equal salary, allowances and other prerequisites.
- All entitled to the same salary and other facilities as a judge of the Supreme Court.
- Term is six years or until they attain the age of 65 years, whichever is earlier.

Independence Of The Election Commission

- Article 324 of the Constitution safeguard –
  - (i) *Security of tenure* i.e. Chief Election Commissioner is removed in same manner and on the same grounds as a judge of the Supreme Court, ie by Parliament with special majority, either on the ground of proved misbehaviour or incapacity. Thus, he does not hold his office till the pleasure of the President, though appointed by the President.
  - (ii) Service conditions cannot be varied to his disadvantage after his appointment.
  - (iii) Other election commissioner or a regional commissioner removed only on the recommendation of the chief Election Commissioner.
- Constitution has not prescribed the qualifications (legal, educational, administrative or judicial), term and has not debarred the retiring Election Commissioners from any further appointment by the government.

Powers and Functions

- The powers and function of the Election Commission with regard to elections to the Parliament, State Legislatures and offices of President and Vice-President can be classified into three categories, :
  - Administrative
  - Advisory
  - Quasi-Judicial

In details, these powers and functions are :

- To determine the territorial areas of the electoral constituencies throughout the country on the basis of the Delimitation Commission Act of Parliament.
- Decide delimitation of constituencies, allocation of seats in Parliament and state legislatures.
- To constitute administrative machinery for conducting elections, election disputes, by-elections, etc.
- Not concerned with the elections to panchayats and municipalities in the states. For this, the Constitution of India (Art 243K and 243 AZ) provides for a separate state election commission.
- To prepare and periodically revise electoral rolls and to register all eligible voters.
- To notify the dates and schedules of elections and to scrutinise nomination papers.
- To grant recognition to political parties and allot election symbols to them.
- To act as a court for settling disputes related to granting of recognition to political parties and allotment of election symbols to them.
- To appoint officers for inquiring into disputes relating to electoral arrangements.
- To determine the code of conduct to be observed by the parties and the candidates at the time of elections.
- To advise the president on matters relating to the disqualifications of the members of Parliament.
- To advise the governor on matters relating to the disqualifications of the members of State Legislature.
- To cancel polls in the event of rigging, booth capturing, violence and other irregularities.
- To request the President for requisitioning the staff necessary for conducting elections.
- To supervise the machinery of elections throughout the country to ensure free and fair elections.
- To advise the President whether elections can be held in a state under President's rule in order to extend the period of emergency after one year.
- To register political parties for the purpose of elections and grant them the status of national or state parties on the basis of their poll performance.

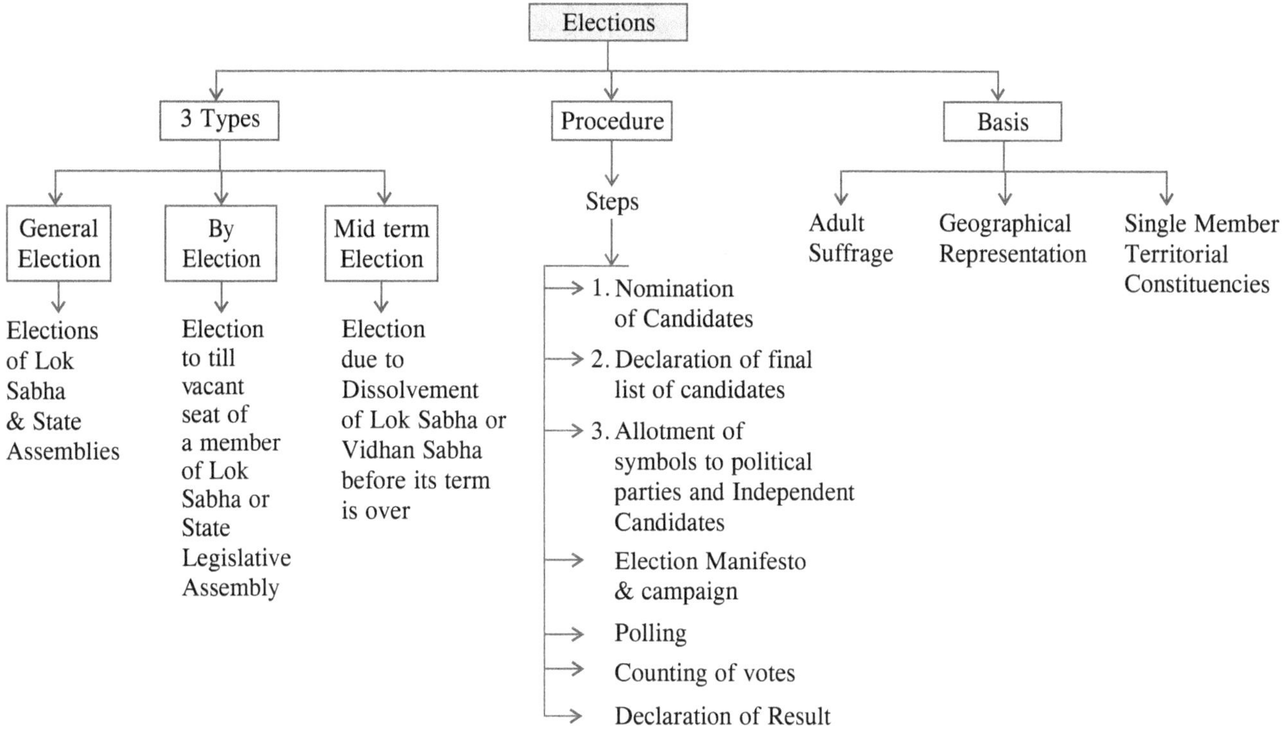

16th LOK SABHA ELECTION, 2014

Major Facts–

- The elections were conducted in 9 phases from 7th April, 2014 to 12th may 2014.
- The BJP (of the NDA) achieved an absolute majority with 282 seats out of 543.
- Its PM condidate, Narendra Modi, took office on the 26th of May, 2014 as the 15th prime minister of independent India.
- The India National Congress (of the UPA) could only manage 44 seats.
- The All India Anna Dravide Munnetra Kazhagam (AIADMK) party from Tamil Nadu Came a close 3rd with 37 seats.
- Name of states and No. of seats acquired:

	States	NDA	UPA	Other
1.	Bihar	31	7	2
2.	NCT of Delhi	7	0	0
3.	Haryana	7	1	2
4.	Himachal Pradesh	4	0	0
5.	Jammu and Kashmir	3	0	3
6.	Madhya Pradesh	27	2	0
7.	Punjab	6	3	4
8.	Utter Pradesh	73	2	5
9.	Uttarakhand	5	0	0
10.	Arunachal Pradesh	1	0	0
11.	Assam	7	3	4
12.	Chattisgarh	10	1	0
13.	Jharkhand	13	1	0
14.	Manipur	0	2	0
15.	Meghalaya	1	1	0
16.	Mizoram	0	1	0
17.	Nagaland	1	0	0
18.	Odisha	1	0	20
19.	Sikkim	0	0	1
20.	Tripura	0	0	2
21.	West Bengal	2	4	36
22.	Andhra Pradesh	19	2	21
23.	Karnataka	17	9	2
24.	Kerala	0	10	10
25.	Tamil Nadu	02	00	37
26.	Goa	02	00	00
27.	Gujarat	26	00	00
28.	Maharashtra	42	06	00
29.	Rajasthan	25	00	00

New Happenging in this Election

(1) NOTA – NOTA (None of the above) was a category introduced this time for voters who could raise their voice not to choose any representative if they dislike any of the above.

(2) Spread Out – This was the longest tenured election that lasted in India.

(3) Aam Aadmi Party – A new born party become a major challenge to BJP and Congress reaching a National Support base for the first time.

(4) BJP won majority (282 seats) of the total seats declaring a clear single party majority win with a lowest vote share of 31% of total valid vote casted. But this win marked as a least percentage win as compared to the Previous years. The previous lowest vote share for a single party majority was in 1967, when congress won 283 out of 520 seats with 40.8% of total valid votes polled.

- There was an approximate turn out at 66.4% among the Indians.

- Govt. spent 131% more on organising elections more than what was spent in the 2009 election.

- The total expenditure in this election was Rs. 3426 crore.

- Cash and 2.25 crore litres of illicit liquor was seized by the pool panel.

Voters Turn out

- India recorded the highest number of voters this time during Election 2014.

- The voting percentage was recorded at 66.38% with 551 million people casting their ballot.

- Voter turnout in Varanasi was 55.56%, which is a massive improvement from 44% in 2009.

- Turn out Numbers voters:

East India – 75%

South India – 72%

North India – 60%

West India – 62%

List of member of the 16th Lok Sabha.

- Speaker – Sumitra Mahajan.

- Deputy Speaker – Thambinduri

- Leader of the House – Narendra Modi

- Leader of the Opposition – Mallikarjun Kharge

Leader of the House in the Rajya Sabha – Arun Jaitley

- Secretary General – P. Sreedharan.

About NOTA

The Election Commission of India asked the Supreme Court that to offer the voter a 'NOTA' option at the ballot as its would give voters the freedom of not selecting any undeserving candidate. The Government was not in favour of such an idea. 'The people's Union for civil Liberties' which is an NGO, filed a PIL to favour NOTA. Finally on 27th September 2013, the right to register a 'NOTA' vote in elections was applied by the supreme court of India, which then ordered the election commission that then ordered the election Commission that all voting machines should be provided with a NOTA button so as to give voters the option to choose 'None of the above'. The Symbol for NOTA, a ballot paper with a black cross, is designed by National Institute of Design, Ahmedabad. In the Indian general election, 2014, NOTA polled 1.1% of the votes, counting to over 6 million.

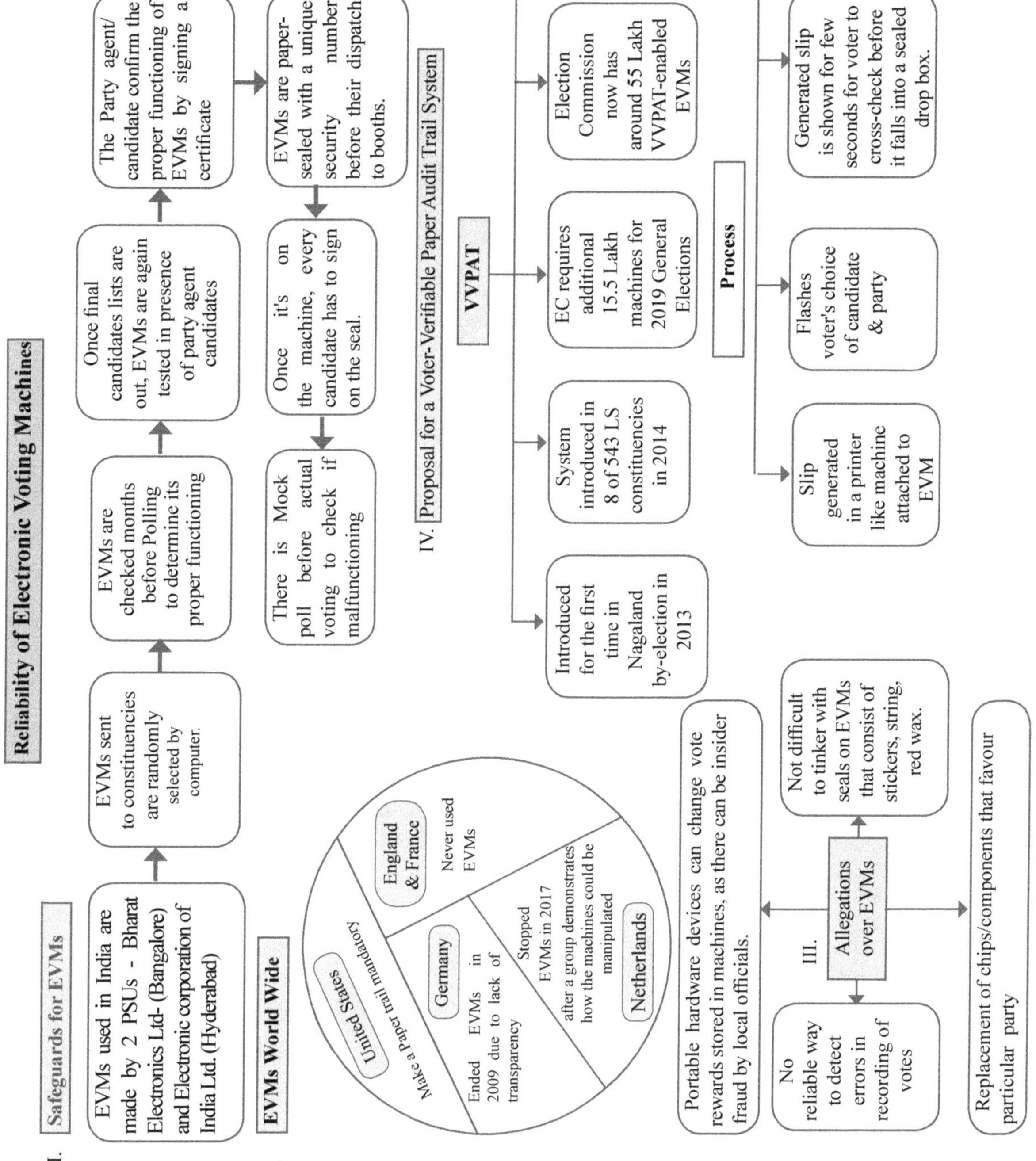

Political Parties

Political Party is a group of persons who agree on some ideology and seek to capture the power and form the government on the basis of collective leadership.

Type of Party System in India - Multi Party System

Functions-

(i) Recruitment of leaders.

(ii) To contest election

(iii) Formation of government

(iv) Formulation of laws when in power.

(v) Role of oppositions

(vi) Shaping public opinion.

(vi) Provide political stability.

Category of Political Party in India:

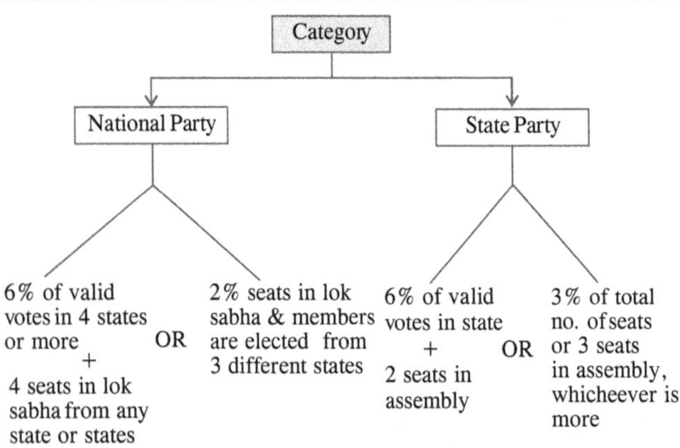

Swaraj India's Common Symbol & Delhi MCD Election 2017

Yogendra Yadav-led Swaraj India's plea for a common symbol in the upcoming MCD polls was dismissed by the Delhi High Court on 29th March 2017.

The high court dismissed the party's plea, saying since the electronic voting machines would now carry photographs of the candidates, it would not be put to any disadvantage if there was no common symbol.

As the plea was filed after several steps in the electoral process had started, it was "very late in the day for the court to interfere," Justice Hima Kohli noted.

Earlier, on 23 March, the high court had asked the Delhi poll panel whether it intends to give a common symbol to political parties like Yogendra Yadav-led Swaraj India, which are registered but unrecognised.

The court had posed the query to the Commission after senior advocate Shanti Bhushan, appearing for Swaraj India, submitted that a letter was sent to the Delhi government to consider amending the rules for allotment of common symbols to registered but unrecognised political parties.

Bhushan had made the submissions during arguments on a plea challenging the Commissions's decision not to allot a common symbol to Swaraj India to contest the upcoming MCD polls.

Swaraj India claimed that non-allotment of a common symbol to a registered party amounted to discrimination as the Aam Aadmi Party was granted such a relief when it had contested for the first time.

Swaraj India has sought quashing of the panel's 14 March, 2017 notification and an April 2016 order which said the nominees of such parties would be treated as independent candidates for allotment of symbols.

Swaraj India was floated in October last year by Yadav and advocate Prashant Bhushan, who were expelled from the AAP after they questioned Arvind Kejriwal's leadership.

The party, registered by the Election Commission of India (ECI) in February 2017, has contended that the Delhi symbols order was "wholly illegal, arbitrary, capricious, unreasonable and selective, destroying the very fairness of the proposed electoral process itself".

It has said that providing it a common symbol will create a level playing field among all the political parties, whether recognised or not, and ensure free and fair election.

It has also challenged the 21 February, 2017 and 7 March, 2017, orders of the poll panel declining the party's request for a common symbol.

The party has contended that the panel rejected its request for a symbol despite a provision in the ECI rules to provide a common symbol to a registered but unrecognised political party like Swaraj India, which is set to make its election debut in the 23 April MCD polls.

The party said the ECI's Election Symbols (Reservation and Allotment) (Amendment) Order allows newly registered political parties to have a common symbol for all their candidates for contesting their first election.

The party has claimed that states like Maharashtra, Andhra Pradesh, Haryana, West Bengal, Kerala, Sikkim and Tripura follow the rule.

Pressure Groups

- Represents socio-economic and political interests of a particular section in political system. For examples. farmers, industrial workers, etc.
- Organised on the basis of common goals and share similar values.
- Seek support of party leaders, legislators and bureaucracy in vigorous pursuit of their goals.
- Exert pressure on government in order to obtain laws and administrative measures in favour of their specific interests.
- Termed as a *"Anonymous Empire"*.

Types of Pressure Group in India

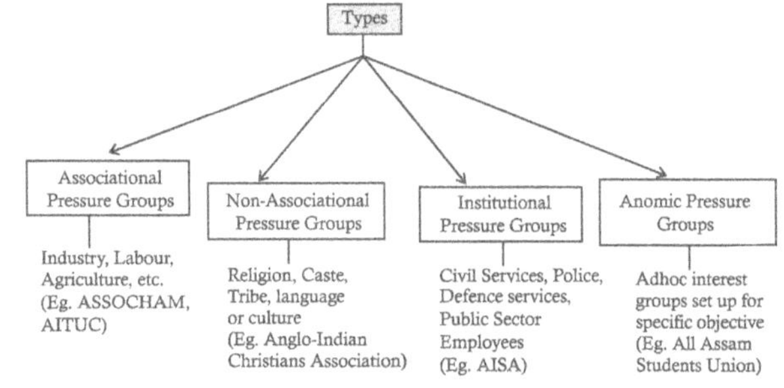

Distinction between Political Parties and Pressure Groups

Political Parties	Pressure Groups
They are political as they are part of political system.	They are non-political as they are part of social system.
They contest elections & form either the government or the opposition.	They do not contest elections, nor do they participate in the working of the government
They seek political power and as such their object is general.	They seek specific objects
They are outward oriented, too formal, and too open.	They are inward-oriented, too secretive.

Attorney-General of India (Article 76)

- The President shall appoint a person who is qualified to be appointed a judge of the Supreme Court to be Attorney-General of India. He is the highest law officer in the Country.

- He must be a citizen of India and he must have been a judge of some high court for five years or an advocate of some high court for ten years or an eminent Jurist, in the opinion of the President.

- The term of office of the AG is not fixed by the Constitution. Further, the Constitution does not contain the procedure and grounds for his removal. He holds office during the pleasure of the President. This means that he may be removed by the President at any time. He may also quit his office by submitting his resignation to the President. Conventionally, he resigns when the Government (Council of Ministers) resigns or is replaced, as he is appointed on its advice.

- It shall be the duty of the Attorney General to give advice to the Government of India upon such legal matters, and to perform such other duties of a legal character, as may from time to time be referred or assigned to him by the President and to discharge the functions conferred on him by or under this Constitution or any law for the time being in force.

- The President has assigned the following duties to the AG :
  - To appear on behalf of the Government of India in all cases in the Supreme Court in which the Government of India is concerned.
  - To represent the Government of India in any reference made by the President to the Supreme Court under Article 143 of the Constitution.
  - To appear (when required by the Government of India) in any high court in any case in which the Government of India is concerned).

- In the performance of his duties the Attorney General shall have right of audience in all courts in the territory of India.

- He has the right to speak and to take part in the proceedings of both the Houses of Parliament of their joint sitting and any committee of the Parliament of which he may be named a member, but without a right to vote. He enjoys all the privileges and immunities that are available to a member of parliament.

- The Attorney-General shall hold office during the pleasure of the President, and shall receive such remuneration as the President may determine.

- He does not fall in the category of government servants. Further, he is not debarred from private legal practice.

Official Language of the Union (Article 343)

The official language of the Union shall be **Hindi in Devanagri script.** The form of numerals to be used for the Official purposes of the Union shall be the international form of Indian numerals.

Notwithstanding anything in clause (1), for a period of fifteen years from the commencement of this Constitution, the English language shall continue to be used for all the official purposes of the Union for which it was being used immediately before such commencement:

Provided that the president may, during the said period, by order authorise the use of the Hindi language in addition to the English language and of the Devanagri form of numerals in addition to the international form of Indian numerals for any of the official purposes of the Union.

Notwithstanding anything in this Article, Parliament may by law provide for the use, after the said period of fifteen years, of:

(a) the English language or,

(b) the Devanagri form of numerals for such purposes as may be specified in law.

Comptroller and Auditor-General of India

- The Constitution of India (Article 148) provides for an independent office of the Comptroller and Auditor General of India (CAG). He is the head of the Indian Audit and Accounts Department. He is the guardian of the public purse and controls the entire financial system of the country at both the levels, the Centre and the state.

- The CAG is appointed by the President of India by a warrant under his hand and seal. He holds office for a period of six years or up to the age of 65 years, whichever is earlier. He can resign any time from his office by addressing the resignation letter to the President. He can also be removed by the President on same grounds and in the same manner as a judge of the Supreme Court.

- *The Constitution has made the following provisions to safeguard and ensure the independence of CAG:*
  - He is provided with the security of tenure. He can be removed by the President only in accordance with the procedure mentioned in the Constitution. Thus, he does not hold his office till the pleasure of the President, though he is appointed by him.
  - He is not eligible for further office, either under the Government of India or of any state, after he ceases to hold his office.
  - His salary and other service conditions are determined by the Parliament. His salary is equal to that of a judge of the Supreme Court.
  - Neither his salary nor his rights in respect of leave of absence, pension or age of retirement can be altered to his disadvantage after his appointment.
  - The conditions of service of persons serving in the Indian Audit and Accounts Department and the administrative powers of the CAG are prescribed by the President after consultation with the CAG.
  - The administrative expenses of the office of the CAG, including all salaries, allowances and pensions of persons serving in that office are charged upon the Consolidated Fund of India. Thus, they are not subject to the vote of Parliament.

- The duties and functions of the CAG as laid down by the Parliament and the Constitution are:
    - He audits the accounts related to all expenditure from the Consolidated Fund of India, consolidated fund of each state and consolidated fund of each union territory having a Legislative Assembly.
    - He audits all expenditure from the Contingency Fund of India and the Public Account of India as well as the contingency fund of each state and the public account of each state.
    - He audits all trading, manufacturing, profit and loss accounts, balance sheets and other subsidiary accounts kept by any department of the Central Government and state governments.
    - He audits the receipts and expenditure of the Centre and each state to satisfy himself that the rules and procedures in that behalf are designed to secure an effective check on the assessment, collection and proper allocation of revenue.
    - He audits the receipts and expenditure of the following :
    (a) All bodies and authorities substantially financed from the Central or state revenues
    (b) Government companies; and
    (c) Other corporations and bodies, when so required by related laws.
    - He audits all transactions of the Central and governments related to debt, sinking funds, deposits, advances, suspense accounts and remittance business. He also audits receipts, stock accounts and others, with approval of the President, or when required by the President.
    - He audits the accounts of any other authority when requested by the President or Governor. For example, the audit of local bodies.
    - He advises the President with regard to prescription of the form in which the accounts of the Centre and the states shall be kept (Article 150).
    - He submits his audit reports relating to the accounts of the Centre to President, who shall in turn, place them before both the Houses of Parliament (Article 151).
    - He submits his audit reports relating to the accounts of a state to governor, who shall, in turn, place them before the state legislature (Article 151).
    - He ascertains and certifies the net proceeds any tax or duty (Article 279). His certificate is final. The 'net proceeds' means the proceeds of a tax or a duty minus the cost of collection.
    - He acts as a guide, friend and philosopher of Public Accounts Committee of the Parliament.
    - He compiles and maintains the accounts of the state governments. In 1976, he was relieved of his responsibilities with regard to the compilation and maintenance of accounts of the Central Government due to the separation of accounts from audit, that is, departmentalisation accounts.

The CAG submits three audit reports to the president—audit report on appropriation accounts, audit report on finance accounts, and audit report before on public undertakings. The President lays these reports before both the Houses of Parliament. After this, the Public Accounts Committee examines them and reports its findings to the Parliament.

National Commission for Scheduled Castes and Scheduled Tribes

(I) **The National Commission for Scheduled Castes (SCs)**

It is a constitutional body in the sense that it is directly established by Article *338* of the Constitution. On the other hand, the other national commissions like the National Commission for Women (1992), the National *Commission for Minorities (1993)*, the National *Commission for Backward Classes (1993)*, the National Human Rights Commission (1993) and the National Commission for protection of Child Rights (2007) are statutory bodies in the sense that they are established by acts of the Parliament.

- Originally, Article 338 of the Constitution provided for the appointment of a Special Officer for Scheduled Castes (SCs) and Scheduled Tribes (STs) to investigate all matters relating to the constitutional safeguards for the SCs and STs and to report to the President on their working. He was designated as the Commissioner for SCs and STs and assigned the said duty.
- Later the 65th Constitutional Amendment Act of 1990 provided for the establishment of a high level multi-member National Commission for SCs and STs in the place of a single Special Officer for SCs and STs. This constitutional body replaced the Commissioner for SCs and STs as well as the Commission set up under the Resolution of 1987.

Again, the 89th Constitutional Amendment Act of 2003[6] bifurcated the combined National Commission for SCs and STs into two separate bodies, namely. National Commission for Scheduled Castes (under Article 338) and National Commission for Scheduled Tribes (under Article 338-A).

- The separate National Commission for SCs came into existence in 2004. It consists of a chairperson, a vice-chairperson and three other members. They are appointed by the President by warrant under his hand and seal. Their conditions of service and tenure of office are also determined by the President.
- The functions of the Commission are :
    - To investigate and monitor all matters relating to the constitutional and other legal safeguards for the SCs and to evaluate their working;
    - To inquire into specific complaints with respect to the deprivation of rights and safeguards of the SCs;
    - To participate and advise on the planning process of socio-economic development of the SCs and to evaluate the progress of their development under the Union or a state;
    - To present to the President, annually and at such other times as it may deem fit, reports upon the working of those safeguards;
    - To make recommendations as to the measures that should be taken by the Union or a state for the

effective implementation of those safeguards and other measures for the protection, welfare and socio-economic development of the SCs; and

- To discharge such other functions in relation to the protection, welfare and development and advancement of the SCs as the president may specify.

• **The commission presents an annual report to the President.**

The president places all such reports before the Parliament.

The President also forwards any report of the Commission pertaining to a state government to the state governor. The governor places it before the state legislature.

(II) National Commission for Scheduled Tribes like the National Commission for Schedules Castes (SCs), **the National Commission for Scheduled Tribes (STs) is** also a constitutional body in the sense that it is directly established by Article 338-A of the Constitution.

• Geographically and culturally, the STs are different from the SCs and their problems are also different from those of SCs. In 1999, a new Ministry of Tribal Affairs was created to provide a sharp focus to the welfare and development of the STs.

• Hence, in order to safeguard the interests of the STs more effectively, it was proposed to set up a separate National Commission for STs by bifurcating the existing combined National Commission for SCs and STs. This was done by passing the 89th Constitutional Amendment Act of 2003. This Act further amended Article 338 and inserted a new Article 338-A in the Constitution.

• The separate National Commission for STs came into existence in 2004. It consists of a chairperson, a vice-chairperson and three other members. They are appointed by the President by warrant under his, hand and seal. Their conditions of service and tenure of office are also determined by the President.

• The Functions of the Commission are:

- To investigate and monitor all matters relating to the constitutional and other legal safeguards for the STs and to evaluate their working;

- To inquire into specific complaints with respect to the deprivation of rights and safe guards of the STs.

- To participate and advise on the planning process of socio-economic development of the STs and to evaluate the progress of their development under the Union or a state;

- To present to the President, annually and at such other times as it may deem fit, reports upon the working of those safeguards;

- To make recommendations as to the measures that should be taken by the Union or a state for the effective implementation of those safeguards and other measures for the protection, welfare and socio-economic development of the STs; and

- To discharge such other functions in relation to the protection, welfare and development and advancement of the STs as the President may specify.

• **The Commission presents an annual report to the President.**

The President places all such reports before the Parliament.

The President also forwards any report of the Commission pertaining to a state government to the state governor. The governor places it before the state legislature.

National Commission for Backward Classes

A Statutory Body under the Ministry of Social Justice & Empowerment

The Supreme Court of India in – Indra Sawhney & Ors. Vs. Union of India and Ors., directed the Govt. of India, State Governments and Union Territory Administrations to constitute a permanent body of the nature of a Commission or Tribunal for entertaining, examining and recommending upon requests for inclusion and complaints of over-inclusion and under-inclusion in the list of OBCs.

The Act came into effect on the 2nd April, 1993. Section 3 of the Act provides that the Commission shall consist of five Members, comprising of a Chairperson who is or has been a judge of the Supreme Court or of a High Court; a social scientist; two persons, who have special knowledge in matters relating to backward classes; and a Member-Secretary, who is or has been an officer of the Central Government in the rank of a Secretary to the Government of India.

Recently, the NCBC has demanded that the government introduce quotas for OBCs in private sector.

National Commission for Minorities

The Union Government set up the National Commission for Minorities (NCM) under the National Commission for Minorities Act, 1992. Five religious communities, viz; Muslims, Christians, Sikhs, Buddhists and Zoroastrians (Parsis) have been notified as minority communities by the Union Government. Further vide notification detail 27th Jan 2014, Jains have also been notified as minority community. The Commission has one Chairperson and five Members represented five minority communities.

Andhra Pradesh, Assam, Bihar, Chattisgarh, Delhi, Jharkhand, Karnataka, Maharashtra, Madhya Pradesh, Manipur, Rajasthan, Tamil Nadu, Uttarakhand, Uttar Pradesh and West Bengal have also set up State Minorities Commissions in their respective States. Their offices are located in the State capitals. The functions of these Commissions, inter-alia, are to safeguard and protect the interests of minorities provided in the Constitution and laws enacted by Parliament and the State Legislatures.

National Commission for Women (NCW)

NCW is a statutory body for women established in 1992 by Government of India as per provisions made in **National Commission for Women Act, 1990.**

Composition of Commission

The commission consists of

- A Chairperson, to be nominated by the Central Government.
- Five members to be nominated by the Central Government from amongst persons of ability, integrity and standing, who have had experience in law or legislation, trade unionism, management of an industry or organisation committed towards increasing the employment potential of women, women's voluntary organisations (including women activists), administration, economic development, health, education or social welfare provided that atleast one member each shall be from amongst persons belonging to the Scheduled Castes and Scheduled Tribes respectively.
- Member-Secretary to be nominated by the Central Government who shall be an expert in the field of Management Organisational Structure or Sociological Movement or an Officer, who is a member of a Civil Service of the Union or of All India Service or holds a Civil Post under the Union with appropriate experience.

Functions of the Commission

- National Commission for Women Act, 1990 has below mentioned provisions regarding the functions of National Commission for Women. The Commission performs all or any of the following functions, namely
  - Investigate and examine all matters relating to the safeguard provided for women under the Constitution and other laws.
  - Present to the Central Government, annually and at such' other times as the Commission may deem fit, reports upon the working of those safeguards.
  - Make in such reports recommendations for the effective implementation of those safeguards for improving the conditions of women by the Union or any State.
  - Review, from time to time, the existing provisions of the Constitution and other laws affecting women and recommend amendments there to so as to suggest remedial legislative measures to meet any lacuna, inadequacies or shortcomings in such legislations.
  - Take up the cases of violation of the provisions of the Constitution and of other laws relating to women with the appropriate authorities.
  - Look into complaints and take suo motu notice of matters relating to
    - (a) deprivation of women's rights.
    - (b) non-implementation of laws enacted to provide protection to women and also to achieve the objective of equality and development.
    - (c) non-compliance of policy decisions, guidelines or instructions aimed at mitigating hardships and ensuring welfare and providing relief to women and take up the issues arising out of such matters with appropriate authorities.
  - Call for special studies or investigations into specific problems or situations arising out of discrimination and atrocities against women and identify the constraints so as to recommend strategies for their removal.
  - Undertake promotional and educational research so as to suggest ways of ensuring due representation of women in all spheres and identify factors responsible for impeding their advancement, such as, lack of access to housing and basic services, inadequate support services and technologies for reducing drudgery and occupational health hazards and for increasing their productivity.
  - Participate and advise on the planning process of socio-economic development of women.
  - Evaluate the progress of the development of women under the union and any state.
  - Inspect or cause to be inspected a jail, remand home, women's institution or other place of custody where women are kept as prisoners or otherwise and take up with the concerned authorities for remedial action, of found necessary.
  - Fund litigation involving issues affecting a large body of women.
  - Make periodical reports to the government on any matter pertaining to women on various difficulties under which women toil.
  - Any other matter which may be referred to it by Central Government.

National Human Rights Commission (NHRC)

The National Human Rights Commission is an expression of India's concern for the protection and promotion of human rights. It came into being in, October 1993. In terms of Section 2 of the Protection of Human Rights Act, 1993 "human rights" means the rights relating to life, liberty, equality and dignity of the individual guaranteed under the Constitution or embodied in the International Covenants and enforceable by courts in India. "International Covenants" means the International Covenant on Civil and Political Rights and the International Covenant on Economic, Social and Cultural Rights adopted by the General Assembly of the United Nations on the 16th December, 1966.

The Commission performs all or any of the following functions, namely

(a) Inquire, on its own initiative or on a petition presented to it by a victim or any person on his behalf, into complaint of-
  - i) Violation of human rights or abetment or
  - ii) Negligence in the prevention of such violation, by a public servant.

(b) Intervene in any proceeding involving any allegation of violation of human rights pending before a court with the approval of such court.

(c) Visit, under intimation to the State Government, any jail or any other institution under the control of the State Government. Where persons are detained or lodged for purposes of treatment, reformation or protection to study the living condition of the inmates and make recommendations thereon.

(d) Review the safeguards by or under the Constitution or any law for the time being in force for the protection of human rights and recommend measures for their effective implementation.

(e) Review the factors, including acts of terrorism that inhibit the enjoyment of human rights and recommend appropriate remedial measures.

(f) Study treaties and other international instruments on human rights and make recommendations for their effective implementation.

(g) Undertake and promote research in the field of human rights.

(h) Spread human rights literacy among various sections of society and promote awareness of the safeguards available for the protection of these rights through publications, the media, seminars and other available means.

(i) Encourage the efforts of non-Government organisations and institutions working in the field of human rights.

(j) Such other functions as it may consider necessary for the promotion of human rights

While inquiring into complaints under the Act, the Commission shall have all the powers of a civil court trying a suit under the Code of Civil Procedure, 1908, and in particular the following.

a) Summoning and enforcing the attendance of witnesses and examining them on oath;

b) discovery and production of any document;

c) receiving evidence on affidavits;

d) requisitioning any public record or copy there of from any court of office;

e) issuing commissions for the examination of witnesses or documents;

f) any other matter which may be prescribed.

The autonomy of the Commission derives, inter-alia, from the method of appointing its Chairperson and Members, their fixity of tenure, and statutory guarantees thereto, the status they have been accorded and the manner in which the staff responsible to the Commission - including its investigative agency - are appointed and conduct themselves. The financial autonomy of the Commission is spelt out in Section 32 of the Act.

The Chairperson and Members of the Commission are appointed by the President on the basis of recommendations of a Committee comprising the Prime Minister as the Chairperson, the Speaker of Lok Sabha, the Home Minister, the leaders of the opposition in the Lok Sabha and Rajya Sabha and the Deputy Chairman of the Rajya Sabha as Members.

Inquiring into complaints is one of the major activities of the Commission.

However, the Commission also actively seeks out issues in human rights which are of significance, either suo motu, or when brought to its notice by the civil society, the media, concerned citizens, or expert advisers.

The commission's purview covers the entire range of civil and political, as well as economic, social and cultural rights.

Areas facing terrorism and insurgency, custodial death, rape and torture, reform of the police, prisons, and other institutions such as juvenile homes, mental hospitals and shelters for women have been given special attention. The Commission has urged the provision of primary health facilities to ensure maternal and child welfare essential to a life with dignity, basic needs such as potable drinking water, food and nutrition, and highlighted fundamental questions of equity and justice to the less privileged, namely the Scheduled Castes and Scheduled Tribes and the prevention of atrocities perpet, Acted against them.

Union Public Service Commission (Part XIV, Article 315-323)

- UPSC is a central recruiting agency. It is independent constitutional body. Apart from UPSC, Constitution provides provisions for State Public Service Commission and Joint State Public Service Commission.

- JSPSC can be created for two or more states by an Act of Parliament on the request of the legislatures of the States concerned.

- The UPSC can also serve the needs of a State on the request of the State Governor and with the approval of the President.

Article 315 – Public Service Commissions for Union and states.
Article 316 – Recruitment and Conditions of Service of Persons Serving the Union or a State
Article 317 – Removal and Suspension of a Member of Public Service Commission
Article 319 – Prohibition as to the Holding of Offices by Members of the Commission on Ceasing to be such Members.
Article 320 – Functions of Public Service Commission
Article 321 – To Extend Functions of Public Service Commission
Article 323 – Reports of Public Service Commissions

Composition

- Constitution does not specify the strength of the Commission but has left the matter to the discretion of the President. Usually, the Commission consists of 9 to 11 members including the Chairman.

- Chairman and members have tenure of six years or until age of 65 years, in the case of SPSC or JSPSC age limit is 62 years.

Removal

- Removed on the grounds of insolvent bankrupt, paid employment, infirmity of mind.

- President can also remove him on the grounds for his misbehaviour. However, in this case, President has to refer the matter to the Supreme Court for an enquiry. If the Supreme Court, upholds the cause President can remove him. The advice tendered by the Supreme Court in this regard is binding on the President. During the course of enquiry by the Supreme Court, the President can suspend the chairman or the member of UPSC.

Independence

- Security of tenure.
- Conditions of service determined by the President, cannot be varied to his disadvantage after his appointment.
- Entire expenses are charged on the consolidated fund of India.
- Chairman is not eligible for further employment in the Government of India or any state.
- Members eligible for appointment as the chairman of UPSC or a SPSC.
- Chairman or members are not eligible for reappointment for second term.

Functions

- The UPSC performs the following functions:
- Assists the states (if requested by two or more states so to do) in framing and operating schemes of joint recruitment.
- Serves all or any of the needs of a state on the request of the state Governor and with the approval of the President of India.
- It advises the President of India –
  - All matters relating to methods of recruitment civil services and for civil posts.
  - Suitability of candidates for appointments for promotions.
  - On all disciplinary matters regarding person serving under the Government of India.
- The UPSC presents a report, annually, to the President on its performance. The President places this report before both the houses of parliament.
- The President can exclude posts, services and matters from the purview of the UPSC.

Role

- UPSC is only a central recurring agency while the department of personnel and training is the central personnel agency in India.
- Role of UPSC is not only limited, but also recommendations made by it are only of advisory nature and hence, not binding on the government.
- The emergence of central vigilance commission (CVC) in 1964 affected the role of UPSC in disciplinary matters.
  This is because both are consulted by the government while taking disciplinary action against a civil servant.

Law Commission

Law Commission of India is a non-statutory body constituted by the Government of India from time to time. The Commission was originally constituted in 1955 and is reconstituted every 3 years. The Reports of the low commission are considered by Ministry of law in consultation with the concerned administrative Ministries and are submitted to parliament.

First	1955-1958	MC Setalvad
Second	1958-1961	Justice TV Venkatarama Aiyar
Third	1961-1964	Justice JL Kapur
Fourth	1964-1968	Justice JL Kapur
Fifth	1968-1971	KVK Sundaram, ICS
Sixth	1971-1974	Justice Dr PB Gajendragadkar
Seventh	1974-1977	Justice Dr PB Gajendragadkar
Eighth	1977-1979	Justice HR Khanna
Ninth	1979-1980	Justice PV Dixit
Tenth	1981-1985	Justice KK Mathew
Eleventh	1985-1988	Justice DA Desai
Twelfth	1988-1991	Justice MP Thakkar
Thirteenth	1991-1994	Justice KN Singh
Fourteenth	1995-1997	Justice K Jayachandra Reddy
Fifteenth	1997-2000	Justice BP Jeevan Reddy
Sixteenth	2000-2001	Justice BP Jeevan Reddy
Seventeenth	2003-2006	Justice M Jagannadha Rao
Eighteenth	2006-2009	Justice AR Lakshmanan
Nineteenth	2009-2012	Justice PV Reddy
Twentieth	2012-2015	DK Jain

21th Law commission

- It was constituted through a Government Order with effect from 31st September, 2015. It has a three - year term, ending on 31st August, 2018.
- The terms of reference are as follows:
  (a) Review/Repeal of obsolete laws.
  (b) Law and Poverty:-
  Examine the laws which affect the poor and carry out post -audit for socio-economic
  (c) Simplification of procedure to reduce and eliminate technicalities and devices for delay so that it operates not as an end in itself but as a means of achieving justice.
  (d) Examine existing laws in the light of DPSP & to suggest ways of improvement and reform.
  (e) Examine existing laws with a view for promoting gender equality and suggesting amendments thereto.
  (f) Revise the central Acts to remove anomalies, ambiguities and inequities.
  (g) Consider and convey to the Government its views on low and judicial administration related subjects, specifically referred to it through Ministry of Law and Justice.
  (h) Consider the requests for providing research to any foreign countries.
  (i) Examine the input of globalization on food security, unemployment and recommend measures for the protection of interests of the marginalized.
  Justice Balbir Singh Chauhan has been appointed as chairman of 21st Law commission.
  (j) Keep under review the system of judicial administration to ensure that it is responsive to the reasonable demands of the times.

Evolution of the Civil Services in India

The beginning of a more organised form of the Civil Services started when **Lord Cornwallis** in 1793, started covenanted services. Indians were virtually disallowed to join these services and only lower posts were kept open for the Indians. Another serious effort was made by Lord Wellesley, who established a college at Fort William to train civil servants in India for a period of 3 years before assigning them any administrative duties.

In 1854 **lord Macaulay Committee** recommended for conducting exams for recruitment into the Civil Service.

Consequently, first ever competitive exam was held in 1855 in London. Indians could not find their way into Indian Civil Services due to several hurdles like the entry age was kept very low, exams were not conducted in India, cost of living in London was relatively expensive.

In 1864, **Satyendranath Tagore** became the first Indian to qualify for the covenanted Civil Services. The British Parliament passed an Act in 1870, authorising the appointment of any Indian (of proved merit and ability) to any office or the Civil Services without reference to the Act of 1861, which reserved specific appointments to the covenanted service.

Later on various committees (Aitchison Committee, Islington Committee, Lee Committee, etc.) recommended for increasing the representation of Indians in Civil Services. As provided in **Government of India Act, 1919** (later recommended by the Lee Commission also) the Federal Public Service Commission was set-up in 1926. This Commission went on to become the Union Public Service Commission after Independence.

Three types of services viz, **All India Services Central Services** and **State Services** were created. The original Constitution of India had recognised only two All India Services namely Indian Administrative Service and Indian Police Service.

In 1966, another All India Service i.e. the Indian Forest Service was created. Presently, there are three all India Civil Services namely

1. Indian Administrative Service (IAS)
2. Indian Police Service (IPS) and
3. Indian Forest Service (IFS)

- While IAS and IPS existed at the time of independence IFS came into existence in 1966.
- Administrative control of different services is as under:
  - IAS - Ministry of Personnel
  - IPS - Ministry of Home
  - IFS - Ministry of Environment and Forest
- **An All India Service can be created by parliament under Article 312 on the basis of a resolution passed by Rajya Sabha.** Thus an All India Service can be created only by an act of parliament and not by the resolution of Rajya Sabha, though such a resolution is must before enacting such an Act.

Constitutional Safeguards to Civil Servants

- *Doctrine of Pleasure* (*English Common Law Doctrine*) – A civil servant holds office during pleasure of crown and his services can be terminated at any time without giving reasons. Not bound by any contract of employment.
- Same doctrine has been embodied in Article 310 (not absolute) subject to the expressed provisions of Constitution (Article 311).
- *Article 310:* All persons (members of defense/civil service/ all india service) hold office during the pleasure of President.
- *Restrictions on doctrine of pleasure:*
  - Certain constitutional offices have been excluded from application of the doctrine like that of SC/ HC Judges, CAG, Chief Election Commissioner, Chairman and members of UPSC.
  - The doctrine cannot be exercised in derogation of fundamental rights

- Article 311 provides safeguards to civil servants.
- *Safeguards under Art 311:*
  (1) There shall be no removal by subordinate authority. Removing authority can be of coordinate rank/higher than the appointing authority.
  (2) Reasonable opportunity to defend himself.
- *Principle of Natural Justice:*
  - No bias,
  - Can't be Judge in his own case,
  - Both parties are heard,
  - Notice given.
- *Exceptions to natural justice:*
  - Person dismissed/removed/reduced in rank on account of misconduct which has led to conviction/ criminal charges.
  - Where it is impracticable to give civil servant such an opportunity. But in such a case, the authority taking such action has to record reasons.
  - If President/ Governor satisfied that in the interest of security of State, it is expedient to hold such an inquiry.

Administrative Reforms

The nodal agency of the Government for administrative reforms as well as redressel of public grievances relating to the states and Central Government agencies is the Department of Administrative Reforms and Public Grievances (DARPG). The Department comes under the Ministry of Personnel, Public Grievances and Pensions.

ARC at a Glance		
Appointed by	Government of India.	
Objective	Recommendations for reforming Indian public administration system.	
Two commis-sion	First ARC	Second ARC
	• Set up in Jan. 1966. • Initially chaired by Morarji R Desai. • Later chaired by K. Hunmanthaiya. • Submitted 20 reports contained 537 major recommendations.	• Set up in Aug. 2005. • Initially chaired by Mr. Veerappa Moily. • Later chaired by Ramachandran. • Submitted 15 reports.

Citizens' Charter

- First articulated and implemented in the UK by Conservative Government of John Major in 1991.
- Represents the commitment of the organization towards standard, quality and time frame of service delivery, grievance redressal mechanism, transparency and accountability.
- It is basically a set of commitments made by an organization regarding the standards of service which it delivers.
- In India it was first introduced simultaneously in Central departments and in all state governments in May 1997.

- 2nd ARC has recommended adoption of the "Seven Step Model for Citizen Centricity—Sevottam", for making citizen's Charters effective.
- The Right to Public Service Delivery Act, based on Sevottam model, guaranteeing the delivery of certain time bound services to the citizens have been enacted by many state governments.

Governance

Governance generally means 'the act or process of governing, specifically authoritative direction and control . The World Bank document, "Governance and Development defines governance as 'the manner in which power is exercised in management of a country's economic and social resources for development'.

Good Governance is about making sure that the exercise of power by the government helps improve quality of life enjoyed by all citizens.

At the constitutional level, good governance requires change that will strengthen the rule of law and decentralise political authority. At the political and organizational level, good governance requires three at tributes-political pluralism, opportunities for extensive participation and incorruptibility in the use of public powers and offices by servants of the state.

The UNDP defined good governance as - "the exercise of political, economic and administrative authority to manage a nation's affairs at all levels. It comprises the mechanism, process and institutions, through which citizen and group articulate their interests, exercise their legal rights, met their obligations and mediate their differences."

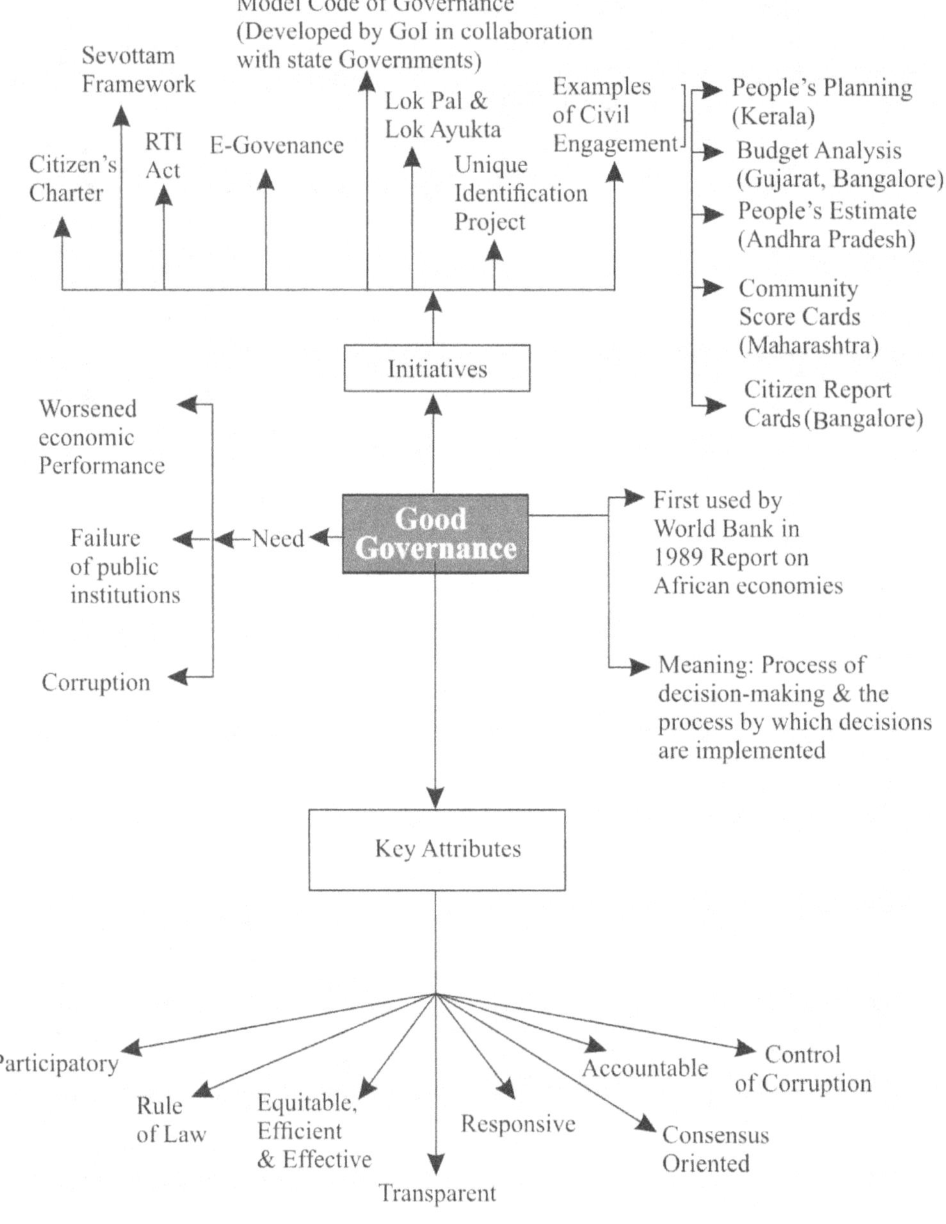

	Governance Performance				Index	
Dimensions	Infrastructure service delivery	Social service Delivery	Fiscal Performance	Law & Order	Judicial Service Delivery	Quality of Legislature
	Water supply & sanitation	Health	Development Expenditure as percentage of total expenditure	Rate of violent crimes	Trials completed in 1-3 years as % of total trials in all courts	Proportion of MLA's with serious criminal charges pending(%)
Indicators	Per captia power consumption	Education	Own Revenve GSDP Ratio	Complaints registered against police per person		Proportion of women MLA's (%)
	Road length per square kilometer			Police strength per lakh poulation		

Table 1: INDICATORS OF QUALITY OF GOVERNANCE

E-Governance

In the context of globalization, the recent conceptualization of 'e-governance' or "digital governance" is of significance in administrative reforms Drawn on the latest ICT, the aim of e-governance is to open up government processes and enable greater public access to information. Digital/e-governance refers to the use of the emerging ICT like the internet, web page, and mobile phones to deliver information and services to citizens. It can include Publication of information about government services on web sites and citizens can download the application forms for these services. It can also deliver services, such as filling of a tax form, renewal of licence, and processing on-line payments as well. The Appropriate use of various techniques of ICT will usher in a new era in public administration by seeking to make to make the governmental functioning and processes more transparent and accessible.

So e-governance through a technological innovation 'has changed the basic character of governance - its operational methodology, functional style, ideological orientation, even the spirit, heart and soul'. In the developed countries, e-goverance is a well-established mode in which governmental services are made available to the citizens through online portals. In India, digital governance has been legalized by the Information Technology Act of 2000. This Act provides:

- Legal recognition for transaction carried out by means of electronic data interchange and other means of electronic communication, commonly referred to as 'electronic commerce' which involve use of alternatives to paper-based methods of communication and storage of information,
- To facilitate electronic filling of documents with the government agencies.
- Defining **'electronic form'** as 'any information generated, sent, received or stored in media, magnetic, optical, computer memory, microfilm, computer-generated microfiche or similar device', the act accords legal sanction to following devices which are:
  - (a) the filling of any form, application or any other document with any office, authority, body or agency owned or controlled by appropriate government in a particular manner;
  - (b) the issue or grant of any license, permit, sanction or approval by whatever name called in a particular manner; and
  - (c) the receipt or payment of money in a particular manner.
- Legally endorsed, this Act is a watershed in conceptualizing administrative reform in India.
- More importantly, e-governance is certainly an attack on bureaucratic red tapism causing unnecessary delay and corruption.
- Further more, it also creates a space for regular involvement of citizens who, as customers of public services, have now direct access to governmental activities through the ICT.
- So, the citizens can not only view online the governmental acts, they can also provide significant inputs to the government through e-mails and electronic devices. Technology is, thus, an important tool integrating citizens' input and transparency into one model.
- The ICT-based e-governance has ushered in a new era in government innovations with improved capacities to
  - (a) reduce the cost of government
  - (b) increase citizens input into government,
  - (c) improve public decision-making, and
  - (d) increase the transparency of government transactions.

In view of these well-defined functional characteristics, e-governance is also a very meaningful step in combating corruption. Not only does it take any discretion, thereby curbing opportunities for arbitrary action, e-government also empowers the citizens by making their intervention in the transactions of governmental business regular through ICT.

Drawn on the ICT, e-governance articulates public administration in a refreshingly new way. The public sector cannot opt for e-governance to replace people for two reasons. First, access to internet is still limited even in the developed countries. Thus, while transactions through ICT cost less than they are by conventional devices, the government has to maintain both the old and new systems to sustain its 'public' character; otherwise, a large portion of the 'people' will remain outside governmental transactions. Second, downsizing and reducing public sector employment in many countries result in economic hardship of those losing jobs, which, for obvious reasons, has severe political repercussions. Thus, for the leadership, this is not a desirable option unless there is no option available.

In other words, given the obvious adverse consequences of e-governance both in developed and developing countries, its applicability is both uncertain and limited.

The Lokpal and Lokayuktas

The *Scandinavian* institution of *Ombudsman* created in *Sweden* in 1809 is the earliest democratic institution in the world for the redressal of citizens' grievances. The Ombudsman in India is called as Lokpal/Lokayukta.

The idea of creating an anti-corruption ombudsman, in the form of a Lokpal, was first conceptualised in 1968 in the fourth Lok Sabha. Thereafter in 1971, 1977, 1985, 1989, 1996, 1998 and 2001 efforts were made to enact legislation to create the institution of Lokpal, but these efforts remained unsuccessful.

The historic Lokpal and Lokayuktas Bill, 2011 passed by Parliament 2013 paves the way for setting up of the institution of Lokpal at the Centre and Lokayuktas in States by law enacted by the respective State Legislatures within one year of coming into force of the Act.

Lokpal and Lokayuktas to inquire into allegations of corruption against certain public functionaries and for matters connected therewith or incidental thereto. The new law provides for a mechanism for dealing with complaints of corruption against public functionaries, including those in high places.

Salient Features of the Act

- Establishment of the institution of Lokpal at the Centre and Lokayuktas at the level of the States, thus providing a uniform vigilance and anti-corruption road-map for the nation, both at the Centre and the States.
- The Lokpal to consist of a Chairperson and a maximum of eight members, of which 50% shall be judicial Members. 50% of members of Lokpal shall be from amongst SC, ST, OBCs, Minorities and Women.
- The selection of Chairperson and Members of Lokpal shall be through a Selection Committee consisting of
  - Prime Minister;
  - Speaker of Lok Sabha;
  - Leader of Opposition in the Lok Sabha;
  - Chief Justice of India or a sitting Supreme Court Judge nominated by CJI;

- An eminent jurist to be nominated by the President of India.
- A Search Committee will assist the Selection Committee in the process of selection. 50% of members of the Search Committee shall also be from amongst SC, ST. OBCs. Minorities and Women.
- Prime Minister was brought under the purview of the Lokpal with subject matter exclusions and specific process for handling complaints against the Prime Minister.
- Lokpal's jurisdiction will cover all categories of public servants including Group 'A', 'B', 'C' & D officers and employees of government. On complaints referred to CVC by Lokpal, CVC will send its report of preliminary enquiry in respect of Group A' and 'B' officers back to Lokpal for further decision. With respect to Group 'C' and 'D' employees, CVC will proceed further in exercise of its own powers under the CVC Act subject to reporting and review by Lokpal.
- All entities receiving donations from foreign source in the context of the Foreign Contribution Regulation Act (FCRA) in excess of ₹ 10 lakhs per year are brought under the jurisdiction of Lokpal.
- Lokpal will have power of superintendence and direction over any investigation agency including CBI for cases referred to them by Lokpal.
- A high powered committee chaired by the Prime Minister will recommend selection of the Director, CBI.
- Attachment and confiscation of property of public servants acquired by corrupt means, even while prosecution is pending.
- *Clear time lines for*
  - Preliminary enquiry - three months extendable by three months.
  - Investigation - six months which may be extended by six months at a time.
  - Trial - one year extendable by one year and, to achieve this, special courts to be set up.
- Enhancement of maximum punishment under the Prevention of Corruption Act from 7 years to 10 years. The minimum punishment under sections 7, 8, 9 and 12 of the Prevention of Corruption Act will now be 3 years and the minimum punishment under section 15 (punishment for attempt) will now be 2 years.
- The Lokpal and Lokayuktas Act., 2013 come in to force w.e.f 16.10.2014. The government initiated the process for appointment by convening the Selection Committee meting.
- The Bill was rfeared to the Department-related justice for examination and report.

The said committee has submitted its report in the Parliament on 2015.

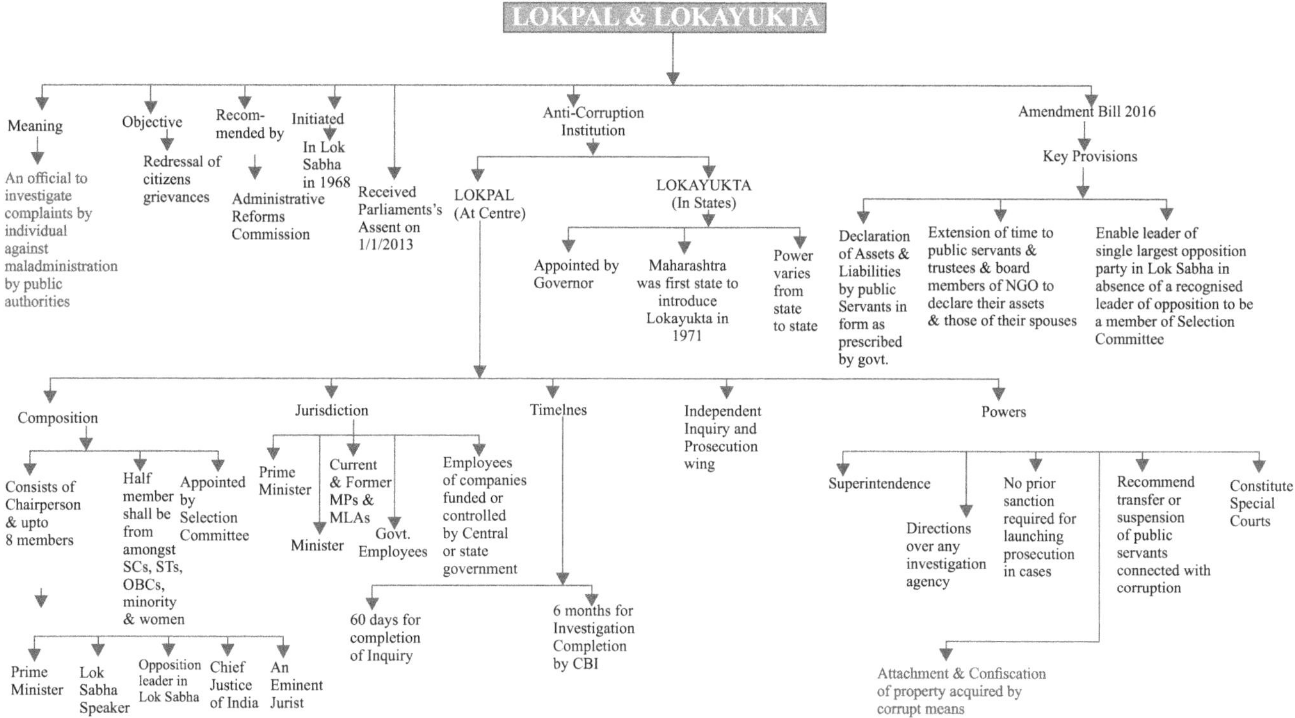

Special Lokpal Courts

- The Central Government shall constitute a number of special courts as recommended by the Lokpal, to hear and decide the cases arising out of the Prevention of Corruption Act, 1988 or under this Act. These special courts are supposed to ensure completion of each trial within a year of the filing of the case.
- The Lokpal is not meant to inquire into any complaint made against the Chairperson or any member and any complaint against the Chairperson or a member shall be made by an application by the party aggrieved, to the president. If on trial a public servant is seen to have been involved in some corrupt practice, then he or she will be liable of making up for the loss to the exchequer if any.
- Whoever makes a false or frivolous complaint under this Act shall, on conviction, be punished with imprisonment for at least two. The term of imprisonment can extend to 5 years and with a fine not less than 25 thousand which can be raised to 2 lakhs.

ANTI-DEFECTION LAW

The 52nd Amendment Act of 1985 provided for the disqualification of the members of Parliament and the state legislatures on the ground of defection from one political party to another. For this purpose, it made changes in four articles of the Constitution and added a new schedule (the Tenth Schedule) to the Constitution. This Act is often referred to as the 'Anti-defection Law'.

Later, **the 91st amendment act of 2003** made one change in the provisions of the Tenth Schedule. It omitted an exception provision, i.e. disqualification on ground of defection not to apply in case of split.

Provisions of the Act

The Tenth Schedule contains the following provisions with respect to the disqualification of members of parliament and the State Legislatures on the ground of defection:

1. **Disqualification of Members Of Political Parties**

   A member of a house belonging to any political party becomes disqualified for being a member of the house, (a) if he voluntarily gives up his membership of such political party; or (b) if he votes or abstains from voting in such house contrary to any direction issued by his political party without obtaining prior permission of such party and such act has not been condoned by the party within 15 days.

   From the above provisions it is clear that a member elected on a party ticket should continue in the party and obey the party directions.

   Independent Members

   An independent member of a house (elected without being set up as a candidate by any political party) becomes disqualified to remain a member of the house if he joins any political party after such election.

   Nominated Members

   A nominated member of a house becomes disqualified for being a member of the house if he joins any political party after the expiry of six months from the date on which he takes his seat in the house. This means that he may join any political party within six months of taking his seat in the house without inviting this disqualification.

2. **Exceptions**

   The above disqualification on the ground of defection does not apply in the following two cases:

(a) If a member goes out of his party as a result of a merger of the party with another party. A merger takes place when *two-thirds* of the members of the party have agreed to such merger.

(b) If a member, after being elected as the presiding officer of the house, voluntarily gives up the membership of his party or rejoins it after he ceases to hold that office. This exemption has been provided in view of the dignity and impartiality of this office.

3. Deciding Authority

Any question regarding disqualification arising out of defection is to be decided by the presiding officer of the house. Originally, the act provided that the decision of the presiding officer is final and cannot be questioned in any court. The Supreme Court declared this provision as unconstitutional on the ground that it seeks to take away the jurisdiction of the Supreme Court and the high courts. It held that the presiding officer, while deciding a question under the Tenth Schedule, function as a tribunal. Hence, his decision like that of any other tribunal, is subject to judicial review on the grounds of mala fides, perversity, etc.

4. Rule-Making Power

The presiding officer of a house is empowered to make rules to give effect to the provisions of the Tenth Schedule. All such rules must be placed before the house for 30 days. The house may approve or modify or disapprove them. Further, he may direct that any willful contravention by any member of such rules may be dealt with in the same manner as a breach of privilege of the house.

According to the rules made so, the presiding officer can take up a defection case only when he receives a complaint from a member of the house. Before taking the final decision, he must give the member (against whom the complaint has been made) a chance to submit his explanation. He may also refer the matter to the committee of privileges for inquiry. Hence, defection has no immediate and automatic effect.

Evaluation of the Act

The Tenth Schedule of the Constitution (which embodies the Anti-defection Law) is designed to prevent the evil or mischief of political defections motivated by the lure of office or material benefits or other similar considerations. It is intended to strengthen the fabric of Indian parliamentary democracy by curbing unprincipled and unethical political defections.

Advantages

The following can be cited as the advantages of the Anti-defection Law:

(a) It provides for greater stability in the body politic by checking the propensity of legislators to change parties.

(b) It facilitates democratic realignment of parties in the legislature by way of merger of parties.

(c) It reduces corruption at the political level as well as non-developmental expenditure incurred on irregular elections.

(d) It gives, for the first time, a clear-cut constitutional recognition to the existence of political parties.

Criticism

Though the Anti-defection Law been hailed as a bold step towards cleansing our political life and started as new epoch in the political life of the country, it has revealed many lacunae in its operation and failed to prevent defections in toto. It came to be criticised on the following grounds:

1. It does not make a differentiation between dissent and defection. It curbs the legislator's right to dissent and freedom of conscience.

2. Its distinction between individual defection and group defection is irrational. In other words, 'it banned only retail defections and legalised wholesale defections'[5].

3. It does not provide for the expulsion of a legislator from his party for his activities outside the legislature.

4. Its discrimination between an independent member and a nominated member is illogical. If the former joins a party, he is disqualified while the latter is allowed to do the same.

5. Its vesting of decision-making authority in the presiding officer is criticised on two grounds. Firstly, he may not exercise this authority in an impartial and objective manner due to political exigencies. Secondly, he lacks the legal knowledge and experience to adjudicate upon the cases.

The National Green Tribunal

The National Green Tribunal has been **established on 18th October, 2010** under the **National Green Tribunal Act, 2010** for effective and expeditious disposal of cases relating to environment protection and conservation of forests and other natural resources including enforcement of any legal right relating to environment and giving relief and compensation for damages to persons and property and for matters connected therewith or incidental thereto.

It is a specialised body equipped with the necessary expertise to handle environmental disputes involving multi- disciplinary issues. The tribunal shall not be bound by the procedure laid down under the **Code of Civil Procedure, 1908,** but shall be guided by principles of natural justice.

The tribunal's dedicated jurisdiction in environmental matters shall provide speedy environmental justice and help reduce the burden of litigation in the higher courts. The tribunal is mandated to make endeavour for disposal of applications or appeals finally within 6 months of filing of the same. Initially, the NGT is proposed to be set-up at five places of sittings and will follow circuit procedure for making itself more accessible. New Delhi is the Principal place of sitting of the Tribunal and Bhopal, Pune, Kolkata and Chennai shall be the other four places of sittings of the tribunal.

Members

The sanctioned strength of the tribunal is currently 10 expert members and 10 judicial members, although the act allows for upto 20 of each. The Chairman of the tribunal, who is the administrative head of the tribunal, also serves as a judicial member. Every bench of the tribunal must consist of atleast one expert member and one judicial member. The Chairman of the tribunal is required to be a serving or retired Chief justice of a High Court or a Judge of the Supreme Court of India.

On 18th October, 2010, **Justice Lokeshwar Singh Panta** became its first Chairman. Currently, it is chaired by **Justice Adarsh Kumar Goel**.

Telecom Regulatery Authority of India (TRAI)

- TRAI is a statutory body set up by the Government of India under Section 3 of the Telecom Regulatory Authority of India Act, 1997. It is a regulator of the telecommunications Sector in India.
- TRAI is an indesendent regulator of Telecom Business in India.
- TRAI fixes or revises the tariffs for telecom Services in india.
- The TRAI Act was amended by an ordinance in 2000 to establish a Telecommunications Dispute Settlement and Appellate Tribunal (TDSAT) to take over the adjudicatery and disputes functions from TRAI

State Public Service Commission

- There Shall be a State Public Service Commission (SPSC) in a state on the lines of UPSC (Article - 315 to 323).
- A state public Service Commission consists of a chairman and other members appointed by the governor of the state.
- The constitution does not Specify the strength of the commission but has left the matter to the discretion of the Governor.
- The constitution also authorises the governor to determine the conditions of Service of the chairman and members of the commission.
- Although the chairman and members of a SPSC are appointed by the governor, they can be removed only by the president (and not by the governor).
- The chairman and members of the commission hold office for a term of six years or untill they attain the age of 62 years.
- A State public Service commission performs all those functions in respect of the state services as the UPSC does in relation to the central services.

Central Vigilance Commission

The CVC is the main agency for preventing corruption in the central government.

- It was established in 1964 by an executive resolution of the central government.
- Its establishment was recommended by the Santhanam committee on prevention of corruption (1962-64).
- The CVC is a multi-member body consisting of a Central Vigilance Commissioner (Chairperson) and not more than two Vigilance commissioners.
- They are appointed by president on recommendation of a three member committee.
- They hold office for a term of four years or until they attain the age of Sixty five years.
- They are not eligible for further employment under the central or a state government.
- The Salary, allowances and other conditions of service of the central vigilance commissioner are similar to those of the chairman of UPSC and that of the Vigilance commissioner are Similar to those of a member of UPSC.

Central Information Commission

- The CIC was established by the central Government in 2005.
- CIC is a Statutory body.
- The commission consists of a chief Information Commissioner and not more than ten information commissioners.
- They are appointed by the President on the recommendation of a committee consisting of the Prime Minister as its. chairperson
- Members of CIC Sould not be a member of Parliament or member of the Legislature of any state or Union Territory.
- The CIC hold office for a term of 5 Years or untill they attain the age of 65 Years, Which ever is earlier.
- They are not eligible for re-appointment.
- The President can remove the CIC on certain grounds.
- The CIC can order Suo-moto inquiry into any matter if there are reasonable grounds.
- While inquiring the commission has the powers of a civil court in respect of certain matters.

Exercise -1

1. In case of national emergency, the State Government
   - (a) cannot legislate
   - (b) can legislate only on subjects in the Concurrent List
   - (c) can legislate on the subjects in the State List
   - (d) Legislative power is suspended
2. Chairman of the Finance Commission must be:
   - (a) Qualified to be a High Court judge
   - (b) A person with background of economics
   - (c) A person in public affairs
   - (d) All of the above
3. President's Rule can be declared
   - (a) on the written advice of the Union Cabinet
   - (b) only on the recommendation of the Governor of the concerned State
   - (c) if the President is satisfied that the government of a state cannot be carried on in accordance with the provisions of the Constitution
   - (d) if a State ministry is defeated on the floor of the Legislative Assembly
4. Impact of financial emergency excludes
   - (a) Union getting the power to issue directions to State to observe canons of financial propriety
   - (b) President's power to direct a reduction in the salaries of Supreme Court and High Court judges
   - (c) President's right to direct States to reserve even money bills for his consideration
   - (d) President's power to suspend fundamental rights in Article 19
5. The Constitution envisages
   - (a) two types of civil services administrative and police
   - (b) two types of civil services Indian and provincial
   - (c) three types of civil services : all-India, central and regional
   - (d) three types of civil services : all-India, central and state
6. Composition of the UPSC is
   - (a) laid down in the Constitution
   - (b) determined by Parliament
   - (c) determined by the President
   - (d) determined by the Chairman of UPSC
7. Members of a State Public Service Commission can be removed by the
   - (a) Governor on a report by the Supreme Court
   - (b) Governor on a resolution passed by the Parliament
   - (c) President on a report by the Supreme Court
   - (d) President on a resolution passed by the Parliament
8. Resignation letter of a State Public Service Commission member is addressed to the
   - (a) President
   - (b) Governor of the state
   - (c) Chief Justice of India
   - (d) Chief Minister of the state
9. A Joint Public Service Commission may be set up for two or more states
   - (a) if the Parliament provides for it after Rajya Sahha resolves to that effect
   - (b) only if the States are very small
   - (c) if the State Legislatures approve of the decision
   - (d) if the Parliament provides for it after a resolution to that effect is passed by the State
10. Which of the given statement is not correct ?
    - (a) Supreme Court can appoint officers of the Court after consulting the UPSC
    - (b) Joint Public Service Commission member retires at 62 years
    - (c) UPSC may in case of a parliament resolution agree to serve the needs of a State
    - (d) Public Service Commissions are to be consulted on matters relating to system of recruitment to civil posts
11. System of representation used in India for elections of the Lok Sabha and State Assemblies is
    - (a) proportional representation
    - (b) territorial representation
    - (c) functional representation
    - (d) none of the above
12. Constitution stipulates that
    - (a) Election Commission may consist of a Chief Election Commissioner and not more than three other Election Commissioners
    - (b) when any other Election Commissioner is appointed the Chief Election Commissioner shall act as Chairman of the Election Commission
    - (c) Election Commissioners can be removed only on the recommendation of the Supreme Court
    - (d) Supreme Court may set aside an election on the ground that the electoral roll was defective
13. Permission for the use of English for official purposes was extended beyond the fifteen years initially allowed by the Constitution through
    - (a) a Constitutional amendment
    - (b) an act of Parliament
    - (c) President's order
    - (d) a government order
14. The Constitution protects the interests of the Anglo-Indian community by
    - (a) Reserving seats for them in the defence forces
    - (b) Reserving seats for them in the services and legislatures
    - (c) Reserving seats for them in the Indian Army
    - (d) authorizing the President to nominate two members of the community to the Lok Sabha
15. Election Commission holds election for the:
    - (a) Parliament
    - (b) Parliament and State Legislative Assemblies
    - (c) Parliament, State Legislative Assemblies and State Legislative Councils
    - (d) Parliament, State Legislatures and elections of President and the Vice President
16. Who, under the anti-defection Act, is the final authority to decide whether a member of Lok Sabha has incurred disqualification?
    - (a) Speaker of the House
    - (b) President of India
    - (c) Central Election Commission
    - (d) High Court of the State

17. After the Constitutional Amendment to the Anti-Defection Act in 2003,
    (a) A merger is no longer valid even if 2/3 of the members of a political party join another party
    (b) A split of a legislature party is invalid even if 1/3 of the party leaves
    (c) A defector has to resign and cannot stand for re-election till the term of the legislature ends
    (d) All the above have been legislated
18. National Commission for Backward Classes
    (a) has been set up by a Constitutional decree
    (b) has three members
    (c) has the powers of a civil court
    (d) is a permanent body whose members enjoy a four-year term
19. A political party that loses recognition still retains its symbol
    (a) for two years
    (b) for six years
    (c) till the next elections
    (d) only so far as another party does not claim it
20. For recognition as a state party, a political party
    (a) must secure at least 6% of valid votes in the general elections in the state plus two seats in the State Assembly
    (b) must win at least six seats in the State Assembly
    (c) must secure at least 2% of the valid votes polled in the state's elections to the Lok Sabha
    (d) get at least 11 MPs in the Lok Sabha
21. Which statement correctly describes the 4th Schedule of the Constitution of India?
    (a) It lists the distribution of powers between the Union and the states
    (b) It contains the languages listed in the Constitution
    (c) It contains the provisions relating to administration of tribal areas
    (d) It allocates seats in the Council of States
22. Proclamation of emergency by the President
    (a) Do not apply to J&K
    (b) Is effective in J&K only with concurrence of the State Legislature
    (c) Apply to J&K after endorsement by the Governor
    (d) Has to be separately issued
23. State Election Commissioner can be removed from office
    (a) only by the Governor
    (b) in the same manner and grounds as a Judge of the Supreme Court
    (c) only the President on the advice of the Chief Justice of the state
    (d) in the same manner as the Vice President of India
24. Single-member constituency system means
    (a) a constituency having only one candidate
    (b) there can be only one voter in the constituency
    (c) a constituency which elects only one representative though there can be many candidates.
    (d) a constituency having only one political party to contest election
25. For which one of the following reforms was a Commission set up under the Chairmanship of Veerappa Moily by the Government of India?
    (a) Police Reforms
    (b) Tax Reforms
    (c) Reforms in Technical Education
    (d) Administrative Reforms
26. The personnel system of any local authority, corporate body or public institution can be placed within the jurisdiction of the UPSC by
    (a) President of India
    (b) Central Ministry of Personnel
    (c) Parliament
    (d) Supreme Court
27. A Joint Public Service Commission can be created by:
    (a) An order of the President
    (b) A resolution of the Rajya Sabha
    (c) An act of Parliament
    (d) A resolution of the concerned state legislatures
28. According to the constitution of India, a new all India service can be instituted with the initiative taken by
    (a) more than two-thirds of the states
    (b) The inter-states council
    (c) the Lok Sabha
    (d) The Rajya Sabha
29. Which one of the following is not explicitly stated in the Constitution of India but followed as a convention?
    (a) The Finance Minister is to be a member of the lower House
    (b) The Prime Minister has to resign if he loses majority in the lower house
    (c) All the parts of India are to be represented in the Council of Ministers
    (d) In the event of both the President and the Vice-President deemitting office simultaneously before the end of the their tenure, the Speaker of the lower house of the Parliament will officiate as the President.
30. The finance commission is constituted to recommend criteria for
    (a) Framing a finance bill
    (b) preparing the annual budget of union government
    (c) Distribution of financial resources between union and the states
    (d) Auditing the receipts and expenditures of the union government
31. Which of the following expenditures shall be charged on the Consolidated Fund of India?
    (a) The emoluments and allowances of the President and other expenditure relating to his office
    (b) The emoluments and allowances of the Prime Minister and other expenditure relating to this office
    (c) The salaries and allowances of the chairman and the deputy chairman of the council of states
    (d) The salaries and allowances of the speaker and the deputy speaker of the Lok Sabha
32. Whose duty is it to recommend to the President of India on the issue of the distribution and allocation of the net proceeds of taxes in the context of Centre-State fiscal relations?
    (a) Planning commission
    (b) National Development Council
    (c) Union Ministry of Finance
    (d) Finance Commission

33. With reference to Indian polity, which one of the following statements is correct?
    (a) Planning Commission is accountable to the Parliament
    (b) President can make ordinance only when either of the two Houses of Parliament is not in session
    (c) The minimum age prescribed for appointment as a Judge of the Supreme Court is 40 years
    (d) National Development Council is constituted of Union Finance Minister and the Chief Ministers of all the States

34. From time to time, the Government of India approves various Foreign Direct Investment (FDI) proposals. Which among the following bodies recommends this approval prior to the ministry of Finance/Cabinet Committee on Economic Affairs?
    (a) National Development Council
    (b) Foreign Investment Promotion Board
    (c) Central Economic Intelligence Bureau
    (d) Ministry of Commerce, Govt. of India

35. The Primary function of the Finance Commission in India is
    (a) Distribution of revenue between the centre and the states
    (b) Preparing the Annual Budget
    (c) Advise the President on financial matters
    (d) Allocate funds to various ministries of the Union and State Governments

36. With reference to Indian polity, which one of the following statements is correct?
    (a) National Development Council (NDC) is constituted of Union Finance Minister and the Chief Minister of all the States
    (b) Planning Commission is accountable to State Legislature
    (c) President can make ordinance even when both house is in session
    (d) The minimum age to contest election for Member of Parliament is 35 years

37. Five year plans in India are finally approved by:
    (a) Union Cabinet
    (b) President
    (c) Planning Commission
    (d) National Development Council

38. Financial distribution between the Union and the States takes places on the basis of the recommendation of
    (a) The Planning Commission
    (b) The National Development Council
    (c) Inter-State Council
    (d) The Finance Commission

39. The jurisdiction of the Finance Commission does not extends to:
    (a) recommendation of the allocation of funds among the various heads of expenditure in the Union and State budgets
    (b) recommendation of the distribution between the Union and the States of the net proceeds of taxes
    (c) recommendation of the allocation to the States of the respective shares of such tax proceeds
    (d) recommendation of the principles which govern the Grants-in-Aid of the revenue of the States out of the Consolidated Fund of India.

40. The strength of the UPSC
    (a) has been permanently fixed by the Constitution
    (b) was determined by the Presidential Ordinance in 1952
    (c) is determined by the Parliament
    (d) is determined by the President from time to time

41. The members of UPSC hold office:
    (a) for a term of six years or till they attain the age of 65 years
    (b) for a term of five years irrespective of the upper age limit
    (c) for a term of six years or till they attain the age of 62 years
    (d) during the pleasure of the President

42. The members of the UPSC can be removed from their office during their tenure by
    (a) the President
    (b) the Parliament
    (c) the President on the report of the Parliament
    (d) the President on the report of the Supreme Court of India

43. The functions of the UPSC include
    (a) conduct of examination for appointment to services of the Union
    (b) tendering of advice to the President in matters relating to the methods recruitment to civil services including promotion and disciplinary actions
    (c) tendering of advice to the President regarding the claims of a person regarding costs incurred by him in defending legal proceedings instituted against him in respect of acts done in execution of duties
    (d) all the above

44. The UPSC submits an annual report of its work to
    (a) the President   (b) the Cabinet Secretariat
    (c) the Home Minister   (d) Parliament

45. A State PSC member resigns by writing a letter addressed to the:
    (a) President   (b) UPSC Chairman
    (c) Governor   (d) Chief Minister

46. Why does the Constitution debar the Chairman of the UPSC from further employment either under the Government of India or the Government of a State?
    (a) Because one cannot take up government post after the age of sixty-five years
    (b) To ensure the independence of the Commission
    (c) To ensure the dignity of the office of Chairman, UPSC
    (d) To make sure that the Commission does not become corrupt

47. Which one of the following is not an All India Service?
    (a) Indian Forest Service
    (b) Indian Economic Service
    (c) Indian Administrative Service
    (d) Indian Police Service

48. The Comptroller and Auditor General acts as friend, philosopher and guide of:
    (a) the Public Accounts Committee
    (b) the Estimate Committee
    (c) the Committee on Public Undertaking
    (d) All of the above

49. The independence of the Election Commission has
    (a) by making the removal of the Chief Election Commissioner difficult
    (b) by not permitting any change in the salary and other service conditions of the Election Commissioner during his term
    (c) Both the above provisions
    (d) by none of the above provisions

50. The power to decide a petition pertaining to election is vested in the
    (a) Parliament
    (b) Supreme Court
    (c) Administrative Tribunal
    (d) Election Commissioner

51. The power to set up a Administrative Tribunal for the adjudication of disputes relating to elections vested in:
    (a) presidential proclamation
    (b) the appropriate legislature
    (c) special ordinances made for the purpose
    (d) any law made by the Election Commission

52. The term of office, salaries, allowances and other conditions of the Chairman and other members of Finance Commission:
    (a) have been specified in the Constitution
    (b) are determined by the President
    (c) are specified by the Finance Ministry
    (d) are determined by the Parliament from time to time

53. In which of the following states, it is constitutionally obligatory for the state to have a Minister for Tribal Welfare?
    (a) Bihar   (b) Madhya Pradesh
    (c) Orissa   (d) Both (b) & (c)

54. The recommendations of the Finance Commission are:
    (a) binding on the President
    (b) not binding on the President
    (c) generally accepted as a matter of convention
    (d) None of the above

55. Which of the following Central Pay Commission recommended that the membership of an unrecognized association by an employee should not be considered as disciplinary offence?
    (a) Single Commission
    (b) Veradachariar Commission
    (c) Rabhubir Dayal Commission
    (d) Jagannath Das Commission

56. In the constitution of India, the budget has been mentioned as:
    (a) Annual Financial Statement
    (b) Annual Budget Statement
    (c) Annual Revenues Statement
    (d) Annual Expenditure Statement

57. Who prepares the Appropriation Accounts?
    (a) The Planning Commission
    (b) The Public Accounts Committee
    (c) The Comptroller and Auditor-General
    (d) The Finance Minister.

58. Under the Comptroller and Auditor General of India there Shall be an ____in each state.
    (a) Accountant General
    (b) Audit Chief General
    (c) Comptroller Accountant
    (d) Chief of the state Accounts

59. What are the functions of the Finance Commission?
    (a) The distribution between the union and states, on the net proceeds of taxes which are to be, or may be divided between them and the allocation between the states, of the respective shares of such proceeds.
    (b) Regarding the principles which should govern the grants-in-aid of the revenue of the states in need of such assistance out of the consolidated fund of India.
    (c) Any other matter referred to the Commission by the President in the interest of sound finance.
    (d) All of the above

60. State funding of elections takes place in:
    (a) U.S.A and Canada
    (b) Britain and Switzerland
    (c) France and Italy
    (d) Germany and Austria

61. Who among the following has a right to speak and otherwise take part in proceedings of either House of Parliament without the right to vote ?
    (a) Chairman, Finance Commission
    (b) The Attorney General
    (c) The Comptroller and Auditor General
    (d) The Chief Election Commissioner

62. Which one among the following is not a function of the Comptroller and Auditor General of India?
    (a) Auditing the transactions of Centre and state Governments relating to contingency funds and public accounts
    (b) Compiling the accounts of Defence
    (c) Auditing the accounts of institutions financed by the Government
    (d) Compiling the accounts of States

63. Who of the following constitutes a Finance Commission for a State in India?
    (a) The President of India
    (b) The Governor of the State
    (c) The Union Finance Minister
    (d) The Union Cabinet

64. Who among the following can be the Chairperson of the National Human Rights Commission?
    (a) A Member of either House of Parliament
    (b) A Chief Justice of the Supreme Court of India
    (c) A social worker actively involved in the promotion of human rights
    (d) Any sitting Judge of High Court or Supreme Court

65. Financial distribution between the Union and the State takes place on the basis of the recommendations of which one of the following?
    (a) The National Development Council
    (b) The Inter-State Council
    (c) The Planning Commission
    (d) The Finance Commission

66. Department of Official Language (Raj Bhasha Vibhag) comes under which one of the following Ministries?
(a) Ministry of Culture
(b) Ministry of Home Affairs
(c) Ministry of Human Resource Development
(d) Ministry of Information and Broadcasting

67. Which one of the following Commissions is not provided in the Constitution of India?
(a) Planning Commission
(b) UPSC
(c) Finance Commission
(d) Election Commission

68. The Chief Election Commissioner of India holds office for a period of
(a) six years
(b) during the pleasure of the President
(c) for 6 years or till the age of 65 years, whichever is earlier
(d) for 5 years or till the age of 60 years, whichever is earlier

69. Which one among the following is the distinguishing factor between a pressure group and a political party?
(a) Pressure groups are confined to a few, while political parties involve larger number of people
(b) Pressure groups do not seek active political power, political parties do
(c) Pressure groups do not politically motivate people, while political parties do
(d) Political parties take political stance, while pressure groups do not bother about political issues

70. Under which law it is prescribed that all proceedings in the Supreme Court of India shall be in English language?
(a) The Supreme Court Rules, 1966
(b) A Legislation made by the Parliament
(c) Article 145 of the Constitution of India
(d) Article 348 of the Constitution of India

71. Delimitation of constituencies and determination of constituencies reserved for Scheduled Castes and Scheduled Tribes are done by
(a) Election Commission
(b) Delimitation Commission
(c) Planning Commission
(d) Election Commission with the assistance of Delimitation Commission

72. Which one among the following statements about the functioning of political parties in a democracy is not correct?
(a) Political parties give political education to the people
(b) Political parties serve as a link between the government and the people
(c) Political parties fight elections and try to get the maximum number of their candidates elected
(d) None of the above

73. Electoral disputes arising out of Presidential and Vice-Presidential Elections are settled by
(a) Election Commission of India
(b) Joint Committee of Parliament
(c) Supreme Court of India
(d) Speaker of Lok Sabha

74. The power to decide the date of an election to a State Legislative Assembly rests with the
(a) President of India
(b) Chief Minister and his/her Cabinet
(c) Election Commission of India
(d) Parliament

75. The primary function of the Finance Commission in India is to:
(a) distribution of revenue between the Centre and the States
(b) prepare the Annual Budget
(c) advise the President on financial matters
(d) allocate funds to various ministries of the Union and State Governments

76. Which Article of the Constitution provides that it shall be the endeavour of every state to provide adequate facility for instruction in the mother tongue at the primary stage of education?
(a) Article 349   (b) Article 350
(c) Article 350-A   (d) Article 351

77. Which one of the following duties is not performed by Comptroller and Auditor general of India?
(a) To audit and report on all expenditure from the Consolidated Fund of India
(b) To audit and report on all expenditure from the Contingency Funds and Public Accounts
(c) To audit and report on all trading, manufacturing, profit and loss accounts
(d) To control the receipt and issue of public money, and to ensure that the public revenue is lodged in the exchequer

78. With reference to Indian polity, which one of the following statements is correct?
(a) Planning Commission is accountable to the Parliament
(b) President can make ordinance only when either of the two Houses of Parliament is not in session
(c) The minimum age prescribed for appointment as a Judge of the Supreme Court is 40 years
(d) National Development Council is constituted of Union Finance Minister and the Chief Ministers of all the States

79. Which of the following bodies does not/do not find mention in the Constitution?
1. National Development Council
2. Planning Commission
3. Zonal Councils
Select the correct answer using the codes given below.
(a) 1 and 2 only   (b) 2 only
(c) 1 and 3 only   (d) 1, 2 and 3

80. Which one of the following is correct in respect of the commencement of the election process in India?
(a) The recommendation for election is made by the government and the notification for election is issued by the Election Commission
(b) The recommendation for election is made by the Election Commission and the notification for election is issued by the Home Ministry at the Centre and Home Departments in the States

(c) The recommendation for election is made by the Election Commission and the notification for election is issued by the President and Governors of the States concerned

(d) Both the exercises of making a recommendation for election and that of issuing a notification in respect of it are done by the Election Commission

81. If in an election to a State legislative assembly, the candidate who is declared elected loses his deposit, it means that:
   (a) the polling was very poor
   (b) the election was for a multi-member constituency
   (c) the elected candidate's victory over his nearest rival was very marginal
   (d) a very large number of candidates contested the election

82. Proportional representation is not necessary in a country where:
   (a) there are no reserved constituencies
   (b) a two-party system has developed
   (c) the first past-post system prevails
   (d) there is a fusion of presidential and parliamentary forms of government

83. Which one of the following statements with regard to the Comptroller and Auditor General (CAG) of India is NOT correct? **[NDA 2018]**
   (a) He is appointed by the President of India
   (b) He can be removed from office in the same way as the judge of the Supreme Court of India
   (c) The CAG is eligible for further office under the Government of India after he has ceased to hold his office
   (d) The salary of the CAG is charged upon the Consolidated Fund of India

84. The Superintendence, direction and control of elections in India is vested in
   (a) The Supreme Court of India
   (b) The Parliament of India
   (c) The Election Commission of India
   (d) The Chief Election Commissioner

85. The Central Vigilance Commission was established on the recommendation of which one of the following Committees?
   (a) Santhanam Committee
   (b) Dinesh Goswami Committee
   (c) Tarkunde Committee
   (d) Narasimham Committee

Exercise -2

Statement Based MCQ

1. Consider the following statements:
   1. Finance Commission is a 5 member body (including the chairman)
   2. Finance Commission submits its report to parliament.
   Which of the above statements is/are correct.
   (a) 1 only
   (b) 2 only
   (c) Both 1 and 2
   (d) None of the above

2. Consider the following statements with reference to the National Human Rights Commission (NHRC):
   1. The chairman should be a retired chief justice of India.
   2. The chairman and members are not eligible for further employment under the central/state government post retirement.
   Select the correct statement/statements using the codes given below:
   (a) 1 only
   (b) 2 only
   (c) Both 1 and 2
   (d) Neither 1 nor 2

3. With reference to "National Commission for Scheduled Tribes" consider the following questions.
   1. It found place in the original constitution as imple-mented on 26-Jan 1950.
   2. It consists of a chairperson, a vice-chairperson and 3 other members.
   3. The commission is vested with the power to regulate its own procedure.
   Which of the above statement is/are true.
   (a) 1 and 2 only
   (b) 2 and 3 only
   (c) 1 and 3 only
   (d) 1, 2 and 3 all are correct

4. Consider the following statements regarding the functioning of National Human Rights Commission (NHRC):
   1. It has all the powers of a civil court and its proceedings have a judicial character.
   2. It has power to punish the violators of human rights.
   3. It can award any relief including monitory relief to the victim.
   Select the correct statement/statements using the codes given below:
   (a) 1 and 2 only
   (b) 2 and 3 only
   (c) 1 only
   (d) 3 only

5. 1. The 15th Finance Commission has been constituted under the chairmanship of N.K. Singh.
   2. The term of 15th Finance Commission will from 2020–2025.
   Choose the correct statements.
   (a) 1 only
   (b) 2 only
   (c) Both 1 and 2
   (d) None of these

6. 1. Parliament can establish a tribunal for the adjudication of election disputes.
   2. Orders of Delimitation Commission can be challenged in court.
   Choose the correct statements:
   (a) 1 only
   (b) 2 only
   (c) Both 1 and 2
   (d) Neither 1 nor 2

7. Consider the following statements:
   1. All states have constituted respective State Human Rights Commissions.
   2. A State Human Rights Commission can inquire into violation of human rights only in respect of subjects mentioned in the State List of the Seventh Schedule of the Constitution.
   Select the correct statement/statements using the codes given below:
   (a) 1 only
   (b) 2 only
   (c) Both 1 and 2
   (d) Neither 1 nor 2

8. Consider the following statements with reference to elections in India:
   1. The chief election commissioner may appoint such "Regional Commissioners" as he may consider necessary to assist the election commission.
   2. The conditions of service and tenure of regional commissioners shall be determined by the president.
   Select the correct statement/statements.
   (a) Only 1
   (b) Only 2
   (c) Both 1 and 2
   (d) None of the above

9. Consider the following statements:
   1. State election commissioner is appointed by the president.
   2. State election commissioner can be removed by the governor only.
   Select the correct statement/statements using the codes given below:
   (a) 1 and 2 both
   (b) 1 only
   (c) 2 only
   (d) Neither 1 nor 2

10. Consider the following statements:
    1. CAG is responsible only to the parliament.
    2. CAG has no control over the issue of money from the consolidated fund of India.
    3. CAG submits audit reports to parliament.
    Choose the correct statments:
    (a) All 1, 2 and 3
    (b) Only 1 and 2
    (c) Only 2 and 3
    (d) Only 1 and 3

11. Which of the following is/are duties and functions of the CAG as laid down by the parliament:
    1. He audits the account related to expenditure from consolidated fund of each state and each union territory
    2. He audits all expenditure from public account of India as well as the public account of each state.
    3. He audits all bodies and authorities substantially financed from the state revenue.
    4. He compiles and maintains the accounts of state government.
    (a) 1, 2 and 3 only   (b) 2, 3 and 4 only
    (c) 1, 3 and 4 only   (d) All 1, 2, 3 and 4

12. With reference to the National Commission for Scheduled Castes, consider the following statements.
    1. It is appointed by the president.
    2. The commission presents an annual report to parliament.
    3. The commission while investigating any matter has all the powers of a civil court.
    Which of the above given statements is/are correct.
    (a) 1 and 2 only   (b) 1 and 3 only
    (c) 2 and 3 only   (d) 1, 2 and 3 all are correct

13. 1. The EVMs were used for the first time in 1998 in Assembly elections of Bihar and U.P.
    2. The EVMs were used for the first time in General elections (entire state) to the Assembly of Goa in 1999.
    Which of the statements given above is/are correct?
    (a) 1 only   (b) 2 only
    (c) Both 1 and 2   (d) None of the above

14. Consider the following statements regarding office of CAG:
    1. Comptroller and Auditor general of India can hold office up to the age of 65 years.
    2. CAG holds office for a period of 6 years.
    3. He can be removed on the same grounds as a judge of the Supreme Court.
    4. Parliament shall decide salary and other conditions of work for CAG.
    Choose the correct statement:
    (a) 1 and 3 only   (b) 2, 3 and 4 only
    (c) 1, 2, 3 and 4 All   (d) 1, 2 and 3 Only

15. Consider the following statements:
    1. Central information commission (CIC) is not a constitutional body.
    2. Members of CIC should not be a member of parliament or of the legislature of any state/UT.
    Select the correct statement/statements using the codes given below
    (a) 1 only   (b) 2 only
    (c) Both 1 and 2   (d) Neither 1 nor 2.

16. Which of the following can be inferred as true with reference to "pressure groups":
    1. Pressure groups neither contest elections nor try to capture political power.
    2. Pressure groups influence the policy making and policy implementation in the government.
    3. Business groups, Trade unions, Student organisations are examples of pressure groups.
    Select the correct answer from the codes given below
    (a) 1 and 2 only   (b) 2 and 3 only
    (c) All the above   (d) 1 and 3 only

17. With reference to the National Human Rights Commission, consider the following statements:
    1. The NHRC can't initiate an inquiry on its own.
    2. The NHRC does not have the power of prosecution.
    Choose the correct statement/statements from the codes given below
    (a) 1 only   (b) 2 only
    (c) Both 1 and 2   (d) None of above

18. Which of the following elections are conducted by Election Commission of India:
    1. Election of president.
    2. Election of vice-president
    3. Election of Lok Sabha as well as Rajya Sabha
    4. Election to Panchayati Raj institutions
    5. Election to state legislatures as well as legislative councils.
    Select the correct answer using the codes given below:
    (a) 1, 2 and 3 only   (b) 1, 2, 3 and 5 only
    (c) 2, 3, 4 and 5 only   (d) All the above

19. Consider the following statements:
    1. Central Vigilance Commission (CVC) is a non-statutory body.
    2. The Central Vigilance Commissioner can be removed by the president.
    3. Prime Minister has no role in the appointment of Central Vigilance Commissioner.
    Select the correct statement/statements using the given codes:
    (a) 1 and 2 only   (b) 2 only
    (c) 1 and 3 only   (d) 1, 2 and 3 all

20. With reference to the constitution of India consider the following statements:
    1. There should be a special officer for Linguistic Minorities.
    2. The Special officer for linguistic minorities shall report to the president.
    3. The president should place all such reports before each house of parliament.
    Which of the above statements is/are true:
    (a) 1 and 2 only   (b) 2 and 3 only
    (c) 1 and 3 only   (d) All 1, 2 and 3 are correct

21. Consider the following statements:
    1. The members of defence forces are not covered under the jurisdiction of Central Administrative Tribunal (CAT).
    2. Members of CAT are appointed by president.
    Select the correct statement/statements from the given codes:
    (a) 1 only
    (b) 2 only
    (c) Both 1 and 2
    (d) Neither 1 nor 2

22. Consider the following statements with reference to NITI Aayog:
    1. Prime Minister is the chairman of NITI Aayog.
    2. Administrators of all the Union Territories are membrs of NITI Aayog's Governing Council.
    3. The vice-chairperson of the NITI Aayog is appointed by president.
    Select the correct statement/statements using the given codes:
    (a) 1 and 2 only
    (b) 2 and 3 only
    (c) 1 and 3 only
    (d) 1, 2 and 3 all

23. Who appoints the Advocate General of a State?
    (a) President of India
    (b) Governor of the state concerned
    (c) Chief minister of the state concerned
    (d) High court of the state concerned

24. Consider the following statements:
    1. The All-India services are controlled jointly by the central and state governments.
    2. Any disciplinary action against officers of all-India services can be taken by the concerned state governments only.
    Select the correct statement/statements using from the codes given below:
    (a) 1 only
    (b) 2 only
    (c) Both 1 and 2
    (d) Neither 1 nor 2

25. Which of the following comes under powers and functions of Election Commission as mentioned in the constitution?
    1. Determine the territorial areas of the electoral constituencies.
    2. To prepare electoral rolls.
    3. To determine code of conduct to be observed by the parties.
    4. To advise president on matters relating to disqualification of members of parliament.
    5. To register political parties for the purpose of elections.
    Select the correct answer using the codes given below:
    (a) 1, 2, 3 only
    (b) 2, 3, 4, 5 only
    (c) 1, 2, 3, 5 only
    (d) All the above are correct

26. With reference to the Attorney General of India, consider the following statements:
    1. He does not fall in the category of government servants.
    2. He has right to take part in the proceedings of both houses of parliament.
    Choose the correct statement/statements using the codes given below:
    (a) 1 only
    (b) 2 only
    (c) 1 and 2 both
    (d) None of the above

27. Finance Commission recommends:
    1. Determination of and principles guiding grant-in-aid
    2. Economy in expenditure
    3. Distribution of net proceeds of tax collection between Centre and States
    Which of the above statements is/are correct?
    (a) 1 and 2
    (b) 1, 2 and 3
    (c) 3 only
    (d) 1 and 3

28. UPSC holds examinations for
    1. Central Services
    2. All India Services State
    3. services
    4. State services for two or more States jointly
    Which of the above is/are correct?
    (a) 1, 2 and 3
    (b) 2 and 4
    (c) 1 only
    (d) 1 and 2

29. A person is eligible to vote in the general elections if he or she
    1. is a citizen of India
    2. is not less than 21 years
    3. does not hold any office of profit under the Government
    4. is not disqualified on grounds of unsound mind
    Select the correct answer using the codes given below.
    (a) 1, 2 and 3
    (b) 1 and 4
    (c) 1 and 2
    (d) 1, 2 and 4

30. A political party is recognised by the Election Commission only if
    1. it has engaged in political activity continuously for five years
    2. has returned at least one member of the Lok Sabha for every 25 members of that House or any fraction of that number elected from that State
    3. polled not less than 6% of total number of valid votes polled by its candidates during elections
    4. has contested elections in four or more states in three consecutive general elections
    Which of the above statements is/are correct?
    (a) 1 and 2
    (b) 1, 3 and 4
    (c) 3 and 4
    (d) 1, 2, 3 and 4

31. Which of the following are national political parties ?
    1. Congress (I)
    2. All India Muslim League
    3. Dravida Munnetra Kazhagam
    4. All India Forward Bloc
    Select the correct answer using the codes given below:
    (a) 1 only
    (b) 1, 2 and 4
    (c) 1 and 2
    (d) 1, 3 and 4

32. Which of the following political parties came into being before independence?
    1. Communist Party of India (Marxist)
    2. Communist Party of India
    3. Dravida Munnetra Kazhagam
    4. Bharatiya Janata Party
    Select the correct answer using the codes given below:
    (a) 1 and 2
    (b) 2 only
    (c) 1, 2 and 3
    (d) 2 and 4

33. The Constitution seeks to protect the interests of the Scheduled Castes/Scheduled Tribes by
    1. reservation of seats for them in the legislatures
    2. bestowal of special rights on the state to impose special restrictions on their rights for their advancement
    3. National Commission for the Scheduled Castes and Scheduled Tribes
    Which of the above statements is/are correct?
    (a) 1 and 2   (b) 2 and 3
    (c) 1, 2 and 3   (d) 1 only

34. Consider the following statements about the recent amendments to the Election Law by the Representation of the People (Amendment) Act, 1996 :
    1. Any conviction for insulting the Indian National flag or the Constitution of India shall entail disqualification for contesting elections to Parliament and state legislatures for six years from the date of conviction.
    2. There is an increase in the security deposit which a candidate has to make to contest the election to Lok Sabha.
    3. A candidate cannot stand for election from more than one parliamentary constituency.
    4. No election will now be countermanded on the death of a contesting candidate.
    Which of the above statements is/are correct?
    (a) 2 and 3   (b) 1, 2 and 4
    (c) 1 and 3   (d) 1, 2, 3 and 4

35. Which statements are correct about the rights of the District Council of an autonomous district?
    Council may make regulations to
    1. license money-lending business
    2. prescribe the maximum rate of interest to be charged by a money-lender
    3. prevent non-Schedule Tribe residents from carrying on business without a license
    4. do any of the above provided it is passed by a majority of 2/3 of the total membership of the District Council
    Which of the above statements is/are correct?
    (a) 1 and 2   (b) 1, 2 and 3
    (c) 2 and 3   (d) 1, 2, 3 and 4

36. National Commission of Scheduled Castes:
    1. has a chairperson, a vice chairperson and four other members
    2. the tenure of office of the chairperson is fixed as three years
    3. conditions of service of the members are as the President may by rule determine
    Which of the following statements is/are correct?
    (a) 1 and 2   (b) 2 only
    (c) 1 and 3   (d) 3 only

37. National Commission for Scheduled Tribes
    1. is a constitutional body
    2. inquires into specific complaints with respect to deprivation of rights and safeguards of the Scheduled Tribes

    3. has a chairman, vice-chairman and three other members
    4. is to present to Parliament, an annual report upon the working of safeguards of the Scheduled Tribes
    Which of the above statements is/are correct?
    (a) 1, 2 and 3   (b) 2, 3 and 4
    (c) 1 and 2   (d) 1, 2, 3 and 4

38. Consider the following statements about the minorities in India:
    1. The Government of India has notified five communities, namely, Muslims, Sikhs, Christians, Buddhists and Zoroastrians as Minorities.
    2. National Commission for Minorities was given statutory status in 1993.
    3. The smallest religious minority in India are Zoroastrians.
    4. Constitution of India recognises and protects religious and linguistic minorities.
    Which of these statements are correct?
    (a) 2 and 3   (b) 1 and 4
    (c) 2, 3 and 4   (d) 1, 2 and 4

39. Article 164 of the Constitution provides for a minister in charge of tribal welfare in:
    1. Bihar   2. Chhattisgarh
    3. Madhya Pradesh   4. Odisha
    Which of the above is/are correct?
    (a) 1, 2 and 3   (b) 2, 3 and 4
    (c) 2 and 3 only   (d) 1, 2, 3 and 4

40. A political party becomes a national party if:
    1. It is recognised as a State party in at least three States
    2. It wins 2% of seats in the Lok Sabha from at least three different States
    Which of the above statements is/are correct?
    (a) 1 and 2   (b) 1 only
    (c) Neither 1 nor 2 (d) 2 Only

41. To be recognised as a State party, a political party should:
    1. win at least one seat for every 25 Lok Sabha seats, or any fraction thereof.
    2. secure 6% of valid votes polled in that State at a general election to the House of the People
    Which of the following statements is/are correct?
    (a) 1 only   (b) 2 only
    (c) Both 1 and 2   (d) Neither 1 nor 2

42. According to the anti-defection law:
    1. It is not possible for 1/3 of a legislature party to go over to an-other party claiming a 'split'.
    2. All disputes arising out of interpretation of the anti-defection law are decided by the Election Commission.
    Which of the above statements is/are correct?
    (a) 1 only   (b) 2 only
    (c) Both 1 and 2   (d) Neither 1 nor 2

43. The UPSC derives its functions from which of the following sources?
    1. Constitution
    2. Parliamentary laws

3. Executive rules and orders
4. Conventions
Which of the above is/are correct?
(a) 1 only   (b) 1 and 2
(c) 1 and 3   (d) 1,2,3 and 4

44. Which of the following statements is/are correct?
1. The Constitution does not fix the number of members of the UPSC.
2. One-half of the members of the UPSC should be persons who have held office under the Government of India or of a state atleast for five years.
3. The Chairman and members of the UPSC hold office for a term of five years or until they attain the age of 60 years.
4. The salaries and allowances of the members of the UPSC are determined by the Parliament.
5. The entire expanses of UPSC are charged on the Consolidated Fund of India.
Select the correct answer using the codes given below:
(a) 2, 4 and 5   (b) 1 and 5
(c) 2, 3 and 4   (d) 1, 4 and 5

45. Which of the following statements are correct with regard to the prohibition as to the holding of offices by members of Public Service Commissions on ceasing to be such members?
1. The Chairman of the UPSC shall be ineligible for further employment either under the Government of India or under the government of a state.
2. The Chairman of a SPSC shall be eligible for appointment as Chairman or any other memeber of the UPSC or as Chairman of any other SPSC, but not for any other employment either under the Government of India or under the government of a state.
3. A member other than Chairman of the UPSC shall be eligible for appointment as Chairman of the UPSC or as Chairman of a SPSC, but not for any other employment, either under the Government of India or under the government of a state.
4. A member other than Chairman of the SPSC shall be eligible for appointment as Chairman or any other member of the UPSC or as Chairman of that or any other SPSC, but not for any other employment either under the Government of India or under the government of a state.
Select the correct answer using the codes given below:
(a) 1 only   (b) 2 and 4
(c) 1 and 3   (d) 1, 2, 3 and 4

46. Consider the following statements with reference to the Central Administrative Tribunal are correct?
1. It is a statutory body.
2. Its members are drawn from administrative background only.
3. It is not bound by the procedure prescribed in the code of civil procedure.
4. Its jurisdiction covers the members of All India Services as well as Central Services and Central Government posts.
5. It was setup in 1985.
Which of the above statements is/are correct?
(a) 2, 3 and 5   (b) 1 and 4
(c) 1, 3, 4 and 5   (d) 2 and 3

47. Which of the following civil services find mention in the Constitution?
1. Indian Administrative Service
2. Indian Forest Service
3. Indian Police Service
4. All-India Judicial Service
5. Indian Foreign Service
Select the correct answer using the codes given below:
(a) 1 and 3   (b) 1,2 and 3
(c) 1, 3 and 5   (d) 1,3 and 4

48. Which of the following is/are not the concerns of the UPSC?
1. Classification of services
2. Promotion
3. Training
4. Disciplinary matters
5. Talent hunting
Which of the above is/are correct?
(a) 2, 4 and 5   (b) 1, 3 and 4
(c) 1 and 3   (d) 1 and 4

49. Which of the following are correct with regard to the functions of the UPSC?
1. To conduct examinations for appointments to the services of the Union.
2. To assist states, if requested, in framing and operating schemes of joint recruitment for any services for which candidates possessing special qualifications are required.
3. To advise the Union and state governments on all matters relating to methods of recruitment to civil services and for civil posts.
4. To present, annually, to the President a report as to the work done by it.
Select the correct answer using the codes given below:
(a) 1, 2 and 3   (b) 1, 3 and 4
(c) 1, 2 and 4   (d) 1, 2, 3 and 4

50. Consider the following functionaries:
1. Cabinet Secretary
2. Chief Election Commissioner
3. Union Cabinet Ministers
4. Chief Justice of India
The correct sequence, in order of precedence is
(a) 3, 4, 2, 1   (b) 4, 3, 1, 2
(c) 4, 3, 2, 1   (d) 3, 4, 1, 2

51. Consider the following statements about the minorities in India:
1. The government of India has notified five communities, namely, Muslims, Sikhs, Christians, Buddhists and Zoroastrians as Minorities.

2. The National Commission for Minorities was given statutory status in 1993.
3. The smallest religious minority in India are the Zoroastrians.
4. The Constitution of India recognizes and protects religious and linguistic minorities.
Which of the above statements is/are correct?
(a) 2 and 3　　　　(b) 1 and 4
(c) 2, 3 and 4　　　(d) 1, 2 and 4

52. Consider the following statements regarding the National Human Rights Commission of India:
1. Its Chairman must be retired Chief Justice of India.
2. It has formations in each state as State Human Rights Commission
3. Its powers are only recommendatory.
4. It is mandatory to appoint a woman as a member of the Commission.
Which of the above statements is/are correct?
(a) 1, 2, 3 and 4　　(b) 2 and 4
(c) 2 and 3　　　　(d) 1 and 3

53. Consider the following statements regarding the political parties in India.
1. The representation of the People's Act, 1951 provides for the registration of political parties.
2. Registration of political parties is carried out by the Election Commission.
3. A national level political party is one which is recognized in four or more states.
4. During the 1999 general elections, there were 6 national and 48 state level parties recognized by the Election Commission.
Which of the above statements are correct ?
(a) 1, 2 and 4　　(b) 1 and 3
(c) 2 and 4　　　(d) 1, 2, 3 and 4

54. Consider the following statements with reference to India.
1. The Chief Election Commissioner and other election commissioners enjoy equal powers but receive unequal salaries.
2. The Chief Election Commissioner is entitled to the same salary as is provided to a judge of the Supreme Court.
3. The Chief Election Commissioner shall not be removed from his office except in like manner and on like grounds as a judge of the Supreme Court.
4. The term of office of the Election Commissioner is 5 years from the date he assumes his office or till the day he attains the age of 62 years, whichever is earlier.
Which of the above statements are correct ?
(a) 1 and 2　　　(b) 2 and 3
(c) 1 and 4　　　(d) 2 and 4

55. Which of the following have recommended the establishment of public sector corporations ?
1. Administrative Reforms Commission
2. Krishna Menon Committee
3. Estimates Committee
4. Arjun Sengupta Committee

Select the correct answer using the codes given below:
(a) 1 only　　　　(b) 1 and 3
(c) 1 and 4　　　(d) 1 and 2

56. Consider the following statements :
1. Central Administrative Tribunal (CAT) was set up during the Prime Ministership of Lal Bahadur Shastri.
2. The Members for CAT are drawn from both judicial and administrative streams.
Which of the statements given above is/are correct ?
(a) 1 only　　　　(b) 2 only
(c) Both 1 and 2　(d) Neither 1 nor 2

57. Which of the following can be said to be essentially the parts of 'Inclusive Governance'?
1. Permitting the Non-Banking Financial Companies to do banking
2. Establishing effective District Planning Committees in all the districts
3. Increasing the government spending on public health
4. Strengthening the Mid-day Meal Scheme
Select the correct answer using the codes given below :
(a) 1 and 2　　　(b) 3 and 4
(c) 2, 3 and 4　　(d) 1, 2, 3 and 4

58. Consider the following:
1. Disputes with mobile cellular companies
2. Motor accident cases
3. Pension cases
For which of the above are Lok Adalats held?
(a) 1 only　　　　(b) 1 and 2
(c) 2 only　　　　(d) 1, 2 and 3

59. Which of the following is/are extra-constitutional and extra-legal device(s) for securing cooperation and coordination between the States in India?
1. The National Development Council
2. The Governor's Conference
3. Zonal Councils
4. The Inter-State Council
Select the correct answer using the codes given below:
(a) 1 and 2　　　(b) 1, 2 and 3
(c) 1, 2 and 4　　(d) 2 only

60. Arrange the following stages in recruitment process in proper order—
1. Selection　　　　2. Appointment
3. Placement　　　　4. Certification
5. Probation　　　　6. Orientation
Select the correct answer using the codes given below:
(a) 1, 4, 2, 6, 3, 5　　(b) 4, 1, 2, 6, 3, 5
(c) 4, 1, 2, 5, 3, 6　　(d) 1, 2, 4, 6, 3, 5

61. Consider the following statements
1. Report of the Administrative Reforms Commission, headed by late Morarji Desai, recommended the establishment of Lokpal and Lokayukta institutions.
2. Lokpal is the highest institution in India to investigate corruption at higher places in Government.
Which of the statements given above is/are correct?
(a) 1 only　　　　(b) 2 only
(c) Both 1 and 2　(d) Neither 1 nor 2

62. Which among the following statements with respect to the Comptroller and Auditor General of India is/are correct?
    I.   The procedure and grounds for his removal from the office are the same as of a Judge of Supreme Court.
    II. He prescribes the form in which accounts of the Union and the States are to be kept.
    Select the correct answer using the code given below
    (a) I only   (b) II only
    (c) Both I and II   (d) Neither I nor II

63. Assertion (A) The number of the Members of the Union Public Service Commission is preserved in the Constitution of India.
    Reason (R) The Union Public Service Commission was constituted under the provisions in the Constitution of India.
    Codes:
    (a) Bath A and R are true and R is the correct explanation of A
    (b) Both A and R are true, but R is not the correct explanation of A
    (c) A is true, but R is false
    (d) A is false, but R is true

64. Consider the following statements
    1.   The maximum number of the Judges of the Supreme Court of India is prescribed in the Constitution of India.
    2.   The maximum number of the Members of the Union Public Service Commission is prescribed in the Constitution of India.
    Which of the statements given above is/are correct?
    (a) Only 1   (b) Only 2
    (c) Both 1 and 2   (d) Neither 1 nor 2

65. Consider the following statements
    1.   The Chairman and the Members of the UPSC are appointed by the President.
    2.   The Chairman and the Members of the UPSC are eligible for further employment under the Government.
    Which of the statements given above is/are correct?
    (a) Only 1   (b) Only 2
    (c) Both 1 and 2   (d) Neither 1 nor 2

66. Consider the following statements with respect to the Attorney General of India
    1.   He is appointed by the President.
    2.   He must have the same qualifications as are required by a Judge of High Court.
    3.   In the performance of his duties he shall have the right of audience in all courts of India.
    Which of the statements given above is/are correct?
    (a) Only 1   (b) 1 and 3
    (c) 2 and 3   (d) 1, 2 and 3

67. Consider the following statements with respect to the Comptroller and Auditor General of India
    1.   He shall only be removed from office in like manner and on the ground as a Judge of the Supreme Court.
    2.   He shall not be eligible for further office either under the Government of India or under the Government of any State after he has ceased to hold his office.

Which of the statements given above is/are correct?
(a) Only 1   (b) Only 2
(c) Both 1 and 2   (d) Neither 1 nor 2

68. Consider the following statements
    1.   The Anti-Defection Law bans an elected member from voting against the explicit mandate of his/her party.
    2.   The Anti-Defection provisions do not apply if one-third of the members of a party disobey the mandate of the party and constitute themselves as a separate party.
    Which of the statement(s) given above is/are correct?
    (a) Only 1   (b) Only 2
    (c) Both 1 and 2   (d) Neither 1 nor 2

69. Which one among the following is not a constitutional body in India?
    (a) Comptroller and Auditor General
    (b) National Commissioner for religious and Linguistic Minorities
    (c) National Commission for Scheduled Castes
    (d) National Human Rights Commission in the eyes of the law.

70. Which of the following statements relating to Comptroller and Auditor General in India is/are correct?
    1.   He/She is not an officer of the Parliament but an officer under the President.
    2.   He/She is an independent constitutional authority not directly answerable to the House.
    Select the correct answer using the codes given below
    (a) Only 1   (b) Only 2
    (c) Both 1 and 2   (d) Neither 1 nor 2

71. Which of the following is/are extra-constitutional and extralegal device(s) for securing cooperation and coordination between the States in India?
    1.   The National Development Council
    2.   The Governor's Conference
    3.   Zonal Councils
    4.   Inter-State Council
    Select the correct answer using the codes given below:
    (a) 1 and 2   (b) 1, 2 and 3
    (c) 3 and 4   (d) 4 only

72. Consider the following statements about the Attorney General of India:
    1.   He is appointed by the President of India
    2.   He must have the same qualifications as are required for a judge of the Supreme Court
    3.   He must be a member of either House of Parliament
    4.   He can be removed by impeachment by Parliament
    Which of the above statements is/are correct?
    (a) 1 and 2   (b) 1 and 3
    (c) 2, 3 and 4   (d) 3 and 4

73. Consider the following statements:
    1.   National Development Council is an organ of the Planning Commission.
    2.   The Economic and Social Planning is kept in the Concurrent List in the Constitution of India.

3. The Constitution of India prescribes that Panchayats should be assigned the task of preparation of plans for economic development and social justice.
Which of the statements given above is/are correct?
(a) 1 only
(b) 2 and 3 only
(c) 1 and 3 only
(d) 1, 2 and 3

74. Which of the followings political parties is/are national political parties?
1. Muslim League
2. Revolutionary Socialist Party
3. All India Forward Block
4. Peasants and Workers Party of India
Select the correct answer using the codes given below:
(a) 1, 2 and 3
(b) 2 and 4
(c) 3 only
(d) None

75. Consider the following statements regarding the political parties in India:
1. The Representation of the People Act, 1951 provides for the registration of political parties
2. Registration of political parties is carried out by the Election Commission
3. A national level political party is one which is recognized in four or more states
4. During the 1999 general elections, there were six national and 48 state level parties recognised by the Election commission
Which of the above statement is/are correct?
(a) 1, 2 and 4
(b) 1 and 3
(c) 2 and 4
(d) 1, 2, 3 and 4

76. Consider the following statements with reference to India:
1. The Chief Election Commission and other Election Commissioners enjoy equal powers but receive unequal salaries
2. The Chief Election Commissioner is entitled to the same salary as is provided to a judge of the Supreme Court
3. The Chief Election Commissioner shall not be removed from his office except in like manner and on like grounds as a judge of the Supreme Court
4. The term of office of the Election Commissioner is five years from the date he assumes his office or till the day he attains the age of 62 years, whichever is earlier
Which of the above statements is/are correct?
(a) 1 and 2
(b) 2 and 3
(c) 1 and 4
(d) 2 and 4

77. Consider the following statements:
The function(s) of the Finance commission is/are:
1. to allow the withdrawal of the money out of the Consolidated Fund of India
2. to allocate between the States the shares of proceeds of taxes
3. to consider applications for grants-in-aid from States
4. to supervise and report on whether the Union and State governments are levying taxes in accordance with the budgetary provisions
Which of the above statements is/are correct?
(a) Only 1
(b) 2 and 3
(c) 3 and 4
(d) 1, 2 and 4

78. Consider the following tasks:
1. Superintendence, direction and conduct of free and fair elections
2. Preparation of electoral rolls for all elections to the Parliament, state Legislatures and the Office of the President and the Vice-President
3. Giving recognition to political, parties and allotting election symbols to political parties and individuals contesting the election.
4. Proclamation of final verdict in case of election disputes
Which of the above are the functions of the Election Commission of India?
(a) 1, 2 and 3
(b) 2, 3 and 4
(c) 1 and 3
(d) 1, 2 and 4

79. Consider the following statements:
1. The Advocate General of a State in India is appointed by the President of India upon the recommendation of the Governor of the concerned State.
2. As provided in Civil Procedure Code, High Courts have original, appellate and advisory jurisdiction at the State level.
Which of the statements given above is/are correct?
(a) 1 only
(b) 2 only
(c) Both 1 and 2
(d) Neither 1 nor 2

80. In India, other than ensuring that public funds are used efficiently and for intended purpose, what is the importance of the office of the Comptroller and Auditor General (CAG)?
1. CAG exercises exchequer control on behalf of the Parliament when the President of India declares national emergency/financial emergency.
2. CAG reports on the execution of projects or programmes by the ministries are discussed by the Public Accounts Committee.
3. Information from CAG reports can be used by investigating agencies to frame charges against those who have violated the law while managing public finances.
4. While dealing with the audit and accounting of government companies, CAG has certain judicial powers for prosecuting those who violate the law.
Which of the statements given above is/are correct?
(a) 1, 3 and 4 only
(b) 2 only
(c) 2 and 3 only
(d) 1, 2, 3 and 4

81. Consider the following statements : Attorney General of India can
1. take part in the proceedings of the Lok Sabha
2. be a member of a committee of the Lok Sabha
3. speak in the Lok Sabha
4. vote in the Lok Sabha

Which of the statements given above is/are correct?
(a) 1 only   (b) 2 and 4
(c) 1, 2 and 3   (d) 1 and 3 only

82. The Departmental Committee of the Parliament of India on the welfare of the Schedule Castes (SCs) and the Scheduled Tribes (STs) shall
   1. examine whether the Union Government has secured due representation of the SCs and the STs in the services and posts under its control.
   2. report on the working of the welfare programmes for the SCs and the STs in the Union Territories.
   Select the correct answer using the codes given below
   (a) Only 1
   (b) Only 2
   (c) Both 1 and 2
   (d) Neither 1 nor 2

83. With reference to 'Finacnial Stability and Development Council', consider the following statements.
   (IAS Prelims 2016)
   1. It is an organ of NITI Aayog.
   2. It is headed by the Union Finance Minister.
   3. It monitors macro-prudential supervision of the economy.
   Which of the statements given above is/are correct?
   (a) 1 and 2 only
   (b) 3 only
   (c) 2 and 3 only
   (d) 1,2 and 3

84. Which of the following is / are Constitutional Body/ Bodies?   **[CDS 2016]**
   1. National Commission for Scheduled Tribes
   2. National Commission for Women
   3. National Commission for Minorities
   4. National Human Right Commission
   Select the correct answer using the code given below
   (a) 1 only   (b) 1, 3 and 4 only
   (c) 3 and 4 only   (d) 1, 2, 3 and 4

85. Which of the following statement about Comptroller and Auditor General of India (CAG) are correct?
   [CDS 2016]
   1. The CAG will hold office for a period of six years from the date he assumes the office, He shall vacate office on attaining the age of 65 years, if earlier than the expiry of the 6 years term
   2. The powers of CAG are derived from the Constitution of India
   3. The CAG is a multi-member body appointed by the President of India in constitution with the prime Minister and the Council of Ministers
   4. The CAG may be removed by the President only on an address from both Houses of Parliament, on the grounds of proved misbehavior or incapacity
   Select the correct answer using the code given below :
   (a) 1, 2 and 4   (b) 1, 2 and 3
   (c) 3 and 4   (d) 1 and 2 only

86. Which of the following are the functions of the National Human Rights Commission (NHRC)?   **[CDS 2018]**
   1. Inquiry at its own initiative on the violation of human rights.
   2. Inquiry on a petition presented to it by a victim.
   3. Visit to jails to study the condition of the inmates.
   4. Undertaking and promoting research in the field of human rights.
   Select the correct answer using the code given below.
   (a) 1 and 2 only
   (b) 2, 3 and 4 only
   (c) 1, 3 and 4 only
   (d) 1, 2, 3 and 4

87. Consider the following statements: **[CDS 2017]**
   1. The Election Commission of India is a five-member body.
   2. Union Ministry of Home Affairs decides the election schedule for the conduct of both general elections and by-elections.
   3. Election Commission resolves the disputes relating to splits/mergers of recognized political parties.
   Which of the statements given above is/are correct?
   (a) 1 and 2 only   (b) 2 only
   (c) 2 and 3 only   (d) 3 only

88. How is the National Green Tribunal (NGT) different from the Central Pollution Control Board
   1. The NGT has been established by an Act whereas the CPCB has been created by an executive order of the Government.
   2. The NGT provides environmental justice and helps reduce the burden of litigation in the higher courts whereas the CPCB promotes cleanliness of streams and wells, and aims to improve the quality of air in the country.
   Which of the statements given above is/are correct:
   (a) 1 only   (b) 2 only
   (c) Both 1 and 2   (d) Neither 1 nor 2

Matching Based MCQ

DIRECTIONS (Qs. 89-92) : Match List-I with List-II and select the correct answer using the codes given below the lists.

89.

List-I	List-II
(A) Schedule	(1) Oath or affirmation
(B) Schedule Three	(2) Details of seat allotted to States in Rajya Sabha
(C) Schedule Four control	(3) Administration and control of scheduled areas
(D) Schedule Five	(4) Salaries of President

   (a) A – 1 ; B – 2 ; C – 3 ; D – 4
   (b) A – 2 ; B – 3 ; C – 4 ; D – 1
   (c) A – 4 ; B – 1 ; C – 2 ; D – 3
   (d) A – 4 ; B – 2 ; C – 1 ; D – 3

90.

	List I (Events)		List II (Years)
(A)	Formation of the Bharatiya Janata Party	(1)	1990
(B)	Acceptance of the Mandal Commission report	(2)	1980
(C)	Formation of the first communist government in an Indian state	(3)	1957
(D)	Passing of the 42nd Amendment Act	(4)	1976
		(5)	1947

	A	B	C	D
(a)	1	2	4	5
(b)	1	2	3	4
(c)	2	1	3	4
(d)	2	1	4	5

91. Match the following–

	List-I		List-II
A.	Third Pay Commission	1.	Varadachariar
B.	First Pay Commission	2.	Raghubir Dayal
C.	Fourth Pay Commission	3.	Jagannath Das
D.	Second Pay Commission	4.	Singhal Rajamannar

Codes:

	A	B	C	D
(a)	1	3	4	2
(b)	3	2	1	4
(c)	2	1	4	3
(d)	2	3	4	1

92. Consider the following statements about the Attorney-General of India?
1. He is appointed by the President of India
2. He has the right to take part in the proceeding of the Parliament.
3. He has the right of audience in all courts in India.

Which of the statements given above are correct?
(a) 1 and 2 (b) 1 and 3
(c) 2 and 3 (d) All of these

Hints and Explanations

EXERCISE-1

1.	(d)	2.	(c)	3.	(c)	4.	(d)	5.	(d)
6.	(c)	7.	(c)	8.	(b)	9.	(d)	10.	(c)
11.	(b)	12.	(b)	13.	(b)	14.	(d)	15.	(d)
16.	(a)	17.	(b)	18.	(c)	19.	(b)	20.	(a)
21.	(d)	22.	(b)	23.	(b)	24.	(c)	25.	(d)
26.	(c)	27.	(c)	28.	(d)	29.	(c)	30.	(c)
31.	(c)								

32. **(d)** An instrument which the constitution has evolved for the purpose of distributing financial resources between the centre and the states is the finance commission. According to Article 280 of the constitution, it is to be constituted by the president once five year and consist of a chairman and four other members appointed by the president.

33.	(a)	34.	(b)	35.	(a)	36.	(a)	37.	(d)
38.	(d)	39.	(a)	40.	(d)	41.	(a)	42.	(d)
43.	(d)	44.	(a)	45.	(c)	46.	(b)	47.	(b)
48.	(a)	49.	(c)	50.	(c)	51.	(b)	52.	(d)
53.	(d)	54.	(c)	55.	(d)	56.	(a)	57.	(c)
58.	(a)	59.	(d)						

60. **(d)** Party funding in Austria has been subject to public regulation and public subsidies since 1975. Party finance in Germany is the subject of statutory reports, which up to 35 parties file annually with the administration of the German parliament.

61. **(b)** The Attorney General for India is the Indian government's chief legal advisor, and its primary lawyer in the Supreme Court of India. He is appointed by the President of India under Article 76(1) of the Constitution and holds office during the pleasure of the President. He must be a person qualified to be appointed as a Judge of the Supreme Court.

62. **(b)** The Comptroller and Auditor General (CAG) of India is an authority, established by the Constitution of India under Chapter V, who audits all receipts and expenditure of the Government of India and the state governments, including those of bodies and authorities substantially financed by the government. The CAG is also the external auditor of government-owned companies.

63. **(b)** According to Article 243 (I) the governor of the state shall set up the Finance Commission within the period of one year. State Finance Commissions receive grants from the Finance Commission that is set up by the central government.

64. **(b)** The Human Right Commission consists of a chairman and other four members. The chairman should be a retired chief justice of India.

65. **(d)** The Finance Commission is constituted by the President under article 280 of the Constitution, mainly to give its recommendations on distribution of tax revenues between the Union and the States and amongst the States themselves.

66. **(b)** Department of Official language(Raj Bhasha Vibhag) comes under Ministry of Home affairs.

67. **(a)** The Planning Commission was set up by a Resolution of the Government of India in March 1950.It is not provided in the constitution of India.

68. **(c)** The Chief Election Commissioner holds office for a term of six years or until they attain the age of 65 years, whichever is earlier.

69. **(b)** Pressure groups do not seek active political power, political parties do. Political parties exist to gain power over governmental policy by winning elections for political office. Interest groups do not necessarily have their members run for office and they vote in a nonpartisan way, supporting candidates who promote their point of view.

70. **(d)** Article 348 of Indian Constitution mentions the language to be used in Supreme Court and the High Courts. According to the article 348, the language of all proceedings in the Supreme court and in every high court shall be English.

71. **(b)** Delimitation commission of India is a Commission established by Government of India under the provisions of the Delimitation Commission Act. In India, such Delimitation Commissions have been constituted 4 times - in 1952 under the Delimitation Commission Act, 1952, in 1963 under Delimitation Commission Act, 1962, in 1973 under Delimitation Act, 1972 and in 2002 under Delimitation Act, 2002. The main task of the commission is to redraw the boundaries of the various assemblyand Lok Sabha constituencies based on a recent census. The representation from each state is not changed during this exercise. However, the number of SC and ST seats in a state have been changed in accordance with the census.

72. **(a)** "Political parties give political education to the people" is not the function of political parties in a democracy.

73. **(c)** All doubts and disputes arising out of or in connection with the election of a President or Vice-President shall be inquired into and decided by the Supreme Court whose decision shall be final (Article 71(a)).

74. **(c)** The power to decide the date of an election a state legislative assembly rests with the election commission of India.

75. **(a)** According to Article 280 it shall be the duty of the Commission to make recommendations to the President as to (1) the distribution between the Union and the States of the net proceeds of taxes

which are to be, or may be, divided between them under this Chapter and the allocation between the States of the respective shares of such proceeds; (2) the principles which should govern the grants in aid of the revenues of the States out of the Consolidated Fund of India; (3) any other matter referred to the Commission by the President in the interests of sound finance; (4) The Commission shall determine their procedure and shall have such powers in the performance of their functions as Parliament may by law confer on them.

76. (c) Article 350A was inserted by 7th Constitutional Amendment act 1956. It says, it shall be the endeavour of every State and of every local authority within the State to provide adequate facilities for instruction in the mother-tongue at the primary stage of education to children belonging to linguistic minority groups; and the President may issue such directions to any State as he considers necessary or proper for securing the provision of such facilities. Article 349 – Special Procedure for enactment of certain laws relating to language; Article 350 – Language to be used in representations for redress of grievances; Article 351 – Directive for development of the Hindi language.

77. (d) As per provisions under Article 149, the Comptroller and Auditor General shall perform such duties and exercise such powers in relation to the accounts of the Union and of the States and of any other authority or body as may be prescribed by or under any law made by Parliament and, until provision in that behalf is so made, shall perform such duties and exercise such powers in relation to the accounts of the Union and of the States as were conferred on or exercisable by the Auditor General of India immediately before the commencement of this Constitution in relation to the accounts of the Dominion of India and of the Provinces respectively.

78. (b) President can issue an ordinance only when both houses of parliament are not in session (Art 123). No minimum age is prescribed for appointment as a judge of the Supreme Court in the Constitution. The age of a Judge of the SC shall be determined by such authority and in such manner as parliament may by law provide. NDC is composed of the PM as its head, all Union Cabinet ministers, the CMs of all states, CMs/Administrators of all UTs and the members of the Planning Commission. There is no constitutional provision regarding the accountability of the planning commission the parliament.

79. (d) National Development council is not a constitutional body. It is an extra-constitutional body. Planning Commission is a non-constitutional and non-statutory body. It was created by the Govt. of India in 1950 by a resolution. Zonal councils have been recognized in the 74th Constitutional Amendment Act of 1992.

80. (a) Elections in India are conducted according to the constitutional provisions, supplemented by laws made by Parliament. The major laws are Representation of the People Act, 1950, which mainly deals with the preparation and revision of electoral rolls, the Representation of the People Act, 1951 which deals, in detail, with all aspects of conduct of elections and post election disputes.

81. (d) A defeated candidate who fails to secure more than one sixth of the valid votes polled in the constituency will lose his security deposit. When a very large number of candidates contest the election, due to distribution of votes, the winning candidate may get less than 1/6 th of valid voters.

82. (b) Political scientists speculate that proportional representation leads logically to multi-party systems, since it allows new parties to build a niche in the legislature.

83. (c)
84. (c)
85. (a)

EXERCISE-2

1. (a) Finance Commission consists of a chairman and four other members to be appointed by the president.

   – The commission submits its report to the president. He lays it before both the houses of parliament.

2. (c) The NHRC is a multi-member body consisting of a chairman and four members. The chairman should be a retired chief justice of India and other members should be a serving or retired judge of the Supreme Court or of High Court.

   The chairman and members hold office for a term of 5 years or until they attain the age of 70 years, whichever is earlier. After their tenure, the chairman and members are not eligible for further employment under the central or a state government.

3. (b) In order to Safeguard the interests of the STs more effectively, it was proposed to set up a separate National Commission for STs by bifurcating the existing combined National Commission for SCs and STs.

   This was done by passing the 89th constitutional Amendment Act of 2003.

   – It consists of a chairperson, a vice-chairperson and 3 other members, all appointed by president.
   – The commission is vested with the power to regulate its own procedure.

4. (c) NHRC is vested with the power to regulate its own procedure. It has all the powers of a civil court and its proceedings have a judicial character.

   Functions of NHRC are mainly recommendatory in nature. It has no power to punish the violators of human rights, nor to award any relief including monetary relief to the victim.

The recommendations of NHRC are not binding on the concerned government or authority.

5. (c) The 15th finance commission has been set up by the government under the chairmanship of N.K. Singh. The Operational Duration of the commission will be 2020-2025.

6. (a) Article-323(B) empowers the appropriate legislature (Parliament or state legislature) to establish a tribunal for the adjudication of election disputes.

   The constitution declares that the validity of any law relating to the delimination of constituencies or the allotments of seats to such constituencies cannot be questioned in any court.

7. (d) The protection of Human Rights Act of 1993 provides for the creation of not only the National Human Rights Commission but also a State Human Rights Commission.
   – So far (2011) 20 states have constituted the State Human Rights Commissions through official Gazette Notifications.
   – A State Human Rights Commission can also inquire into violation of Human Rights in respect of Subjects mentioned in the concurrent list.
   – Therefore both statements are wrong.

8. (b) Article-324(4): The president may also appoint after consulation with the election commission such regional commissioners as he may consider necessary to assist the election commission.

   Article-324(5): The conditions of service and tenure of office of the election commissioners and the regional commissioners shall be determined by the president.

9. (d) The state election commissioner, though appointed by the governor of the state, can be removed by the president only.

   State election commission is a constitutional body which is entrusted with the task of conducting elections for the Panchayati Raj institutions or local governments.

10. (b) 1. CAG is an agent of the parliament and conducts audit of expenditure on behalf of the parliament. Therefore it is responsible only to the parliament.
    2. The Constitution of India visualises the CAG to be comptroller as well as Auditor General. However in practice, the CAG is fulfilling the role of an Auditor-General only and not that of a comptroller.
    3. The CAG submits audit reports to the president: The president lays these reports before both houses of parliament.
    Source: M. Lakshmikant

11. (b) CAG has the mandate to audit accounts related to expenditure from consolidated fund of India, that of states and consolidated fund of only those union territories that have a Legislative Assembly (that is Delhi and Pondicherry).

– All other statements are correct.
– Besides CAG also audits other corporations and bodies when so required by related laws.
Source: M. Lakshmikant.

12. (b) The National Commission for Scheduled Castes is appointed by the president by warrant under his hand and seal. Their conditions of service and tenure of office are also determined by president.

   The commission presents an annual report to the president.

   The president places all such reports before the parliament.

   The commission, while investigating any matter or inquiring into any complaint, has all the powers of a civil court trying a suit.

13. (b) – In 1989 a provision was made to facilitate the use of Electronic Voting Machine (EVMs) in elections.
    – The EVMs were used for the first time in 1998 on experimental basis in selected constituencies in the elections to the Assemblies of Rajasthan, Madhya Pradesh and Delhi.
    – The EVMs were used for the first time in the general elections (entire state) to the Assembly of Goa in 1999.
    Source: M. Lakshmikant

14. (c) CAG is appointed by the president of India by a warrant under his hand and seal.
    – He holds office for a period of 6 years or upto the age of 65 years whichever is earlier.
    – CAG can be removed by the president on same grounds and in the same manner as a judge of Supreme Court.
    – Art-148: There shall be a CAG of India who would be appointed by president.
    – Art-148 (3): The salary and other conditions of service of the comptroller and Auditor General shall be such as may be determined by parliament by law.
    Source: M. Lakshmikant

15. (c) The central information commission was established by the central government in 2005. It was constituted through an official Gagette Notification under the provisions of the Right to Information Act (2005). Hence it is not a constitutional body.

   The commission consists of a chief information commissioner and not more than ten information commissioners. They should not be a Member of Parliament or of legislature of any state or Union Territory.

16. (c) The term 'pressure group' originated in the USA. A pressure group is a group of people who are organised actively for promoting and defending their common interest.
    – The pressure groups are also called interest groups or vested groups. They are different from political parties

in that they neither contest elections nor try to capture politial power.

– The pressure groups influence the policy-making and policy-implementation in the government through legal and legitimate methods like lobbying, correspondence, publicity, petitioning etc.

– Some of the examples of pressure groups are Business Groups, Trade unions, Agrarian Groups, Student Organisations, Religious organisations, Caste groups, Tribal Organisations etc.

17. **(b)** The NHRC's functions include inquiry on its own initiative or on a petition presented to it by victim into complaint of violation of human rights; visits to jails to study the condition of the inmates,undertaking and promoting research in the field of human rights etc. However, the commission does not have the power of prosecution. It can merely make recommendations to the government or recommend to the courts to initiate proceedings based on the inquiry that it conducts.

Source: N.C.E.R.T- XIth [Indian Constitution at Work].

18. **(b)** Elections to Panchayati Raj institutions are conducted not by Election Commission of India but by the concerned State Election Commission.

Besides the above given matters, Election Commission of India is entrusted with following matters:
– Reservation of seats in Lok sabha and state legislatures.
– Qualifications of the MPs and MLAs.
– Determination of population for purposes of election.

19. **(b)** Originally the CVC was neither a constitutional body nor a statutory body. In 2003, the Parliament enacted a law conferring statutory status on the CVC.

The CVC is a multi-member body consisting of a Central Vigilance Commissioner and not more than two Vigilance Commissioners. They are appointed by the president. The president can remove the Central Vigilance Commissioner under certain circumstances.

The president appoints CVC officials (commissioners and members) on the recommendation of a three-member committee consisting of the Prime Minister as its head.

20. **(d)** All the given statements are true.
In pursuance of the provision of Article-350-B of the constitution, the office of the special officer for Linguistic Minorities was created in 1957. He is designated as the commissioner for Linguistic Minorities.

The Commission has its headquarters at Allahabad (UP).

Note: At the central level, the commissioner falls under the Ministry of Minory Affairs. Hence he submits the annual reports or other reports to the President through the Union Minority Affairs Ministry.

21. **(c)** The CAT exercises original jurisdiction in relation to recruitment and all service matters of public servants covered by it. Its jurisdiction extends to all-India services, the central civil services, civil posts under the centre and civilian employees of defence services. However, the members of the defence forces, officers and servants of the supreme court and the secretarial staff of the parliament are not covered by it.
The CAT is a multi-member body. Members of CAT are drawn from both judicial and administrative streams and are appointed by the president. They hold office for a term of five years or untill they attain the age of 65 years (chairman-62 years).

22. **(a)** Composition of NITI Aayog:
Chairperson – Prime Minister
Governing Council – Its members are chief ministers and administrators of the union territories.
Regional Councils – These are created as per need and its members would be chief Ministers and administrators of UTs of respective regions.
Vice-Chairperson – The vice-chairperson of the NITI-Aayog is appointed by Prime Minister.

23. **(b)** Governor appoints the Advocate General of a state and determines his remuneration. The advocate general holds office during the pleasure of the governor.

24. **(a)** The All-India services are controlled jointly by the central and state governments. The ultimate control lies with the central government while the immediate control is vested in the state governments.
Any disciplinary action (imposition of penalties) against these officers can only be taken by the central government.

25. **(c)** – All the above statements except (4) are correct.
– Election Commission advises to the governor (and not to the president) regarding disqualification of members of state legislature.
Besides Election Commission has many other powers:
– To advice the president regarding disqualification of the members of parliament.
– To notify the dates and schedules of elections.

26. **(c)** Attorney General has the right of audience in all courts in the territory of India. Further he has the right to speak and to take part in the proceedings of both the houses of parliament or their joint sitting and any committee of the parliament of which he is a member.
– However, the Attorney General is not a full time counsel for the government. He does not full in the category of government servants. Further he is not debarred from private legal practice.

27. (d)	28. (d)	29. (b)	30. (c)	31. (a)
32. (b)	33. (c)	34. (b)	35. (b)	36. (d)
37. (a)	38. (d)	39. (b)	40. (d)	41. (b)
42. (a)	43. (d)	44. (b)	45. (d)	46. (c)
47. (d)	48. (c)	49. (c)	50. (c)	51. (c)
52. (a)	53. (d)	54. (b)	55. (d)	56. (b)
57. (c)	58. (d)	59. (b)	60. (c)	

61. (c) Lokpal and Lokayukta are established under the report of the administrative reforms commission headed by Morarji Desai to investigate corruption at higher places in government.

62. (c)

63. (d) A is false because the constitution without specifying the strength of the Commission has left the matter to the discretion of the president, who determines its composition. According to article 315, the UPSC consists of a chairman and other members appointed by the president of India. Articles 315 to 323 of Part XIV of the constitution provide for a Public Service Commission for the Union and for each state.

64. (a) Article 124 (a) of the Indian Constitution stipulates that "There shall be a Supreme Court of India constituting of a Chief Justice of India and, until Parliament by law prescribes a larger number, of not more than seven other Judges". At present the Supreme Court consists of thirty one judges (one chief justice and thirty other judges).
Under article 315 the UPSC consists of a chairman and other members appointed by the president of India. The constitution without specifying the strength of the Commission has left the matter to the discretion of the president, who determines its composition.

65. (a) According to Article 316(a)of the Indian Constitution, the chairman and the members of the UPSC are appointed by the president. Under Article 316(c) a person who holds office as a member of a Public Service Commission shall, on the expiration of his term of office, be ineligible for re-appointment to that office.

66. (b) The Attorney General of India is the chief legal advisor of Indian government. He is appointed by the President of Indiaunder Article 76(a) of the Constitution. He must be a person qualified to be appointed as a Judge of the Supreme Court. The Attorney General has the right of audience in all Courts in India as well as the right to participate in the proceedings of the Parliament. He holds office during the pleasure of the President. The current Attorney General is Mukul Rohatgi(14th Attorney General).

67. (c) Under Article 148 of the Indian Constitution the Comptroller and Auditor General (CAG) of India audits all receipts and expenditure of the Government of India and the state governments, including those of bodies and authorities substantially financed by the government. The CAG shall only be removed from office in like manner and on the like grounds as a judge of the Supreme Court of India :Article148(a)
The Comptroller and Auditor General shall not be eligible for further office either under the Government of India or under the Government of any State after he has ceased to hold his office :Article 148(d)

68. (a) The grounds for disqualification under the Anti-Defection Law are as follows:
If he votes or abstains from voting in such House contrary to any direction issued by his political party or anyone authorised to do so, without obtaining prior permission. As a pre-condition for his disqualification, his abstention from voting should not be condoned by his party or the authorised person within 15 days of such incident. As per the 1985 Act, a 'defection' by one-third of the elected members of a political party was considered a 'merger'. Finally, the 91st Constitutional Amendment Act, 2003, changed this. So now at least two-thirds of the members of a party have to be in favour of a "merger" for it to have validity in the eyes of the law.

69. (b) National Commission for Religious and Linguistic Minorities was constituted by Government on 29 October 2004 to look into various issues related to Linguistic and Religious minorities in India. It is also called Ranganath Misra Commission because it was chaired by former Chief Justice of India Justice Ranganath Misra.

70. (b) The Comptroller and Auditor-General of India is appointed by the President of India. CAG is an authority that was established by the Constitution of India under article 148. Report of CAG of Union Accounts to be submitted to President who causes them to be laid before each house of parliament.

71. (a) Best answer is 1, 2 and 3. Because only Inter State Council is a constitutional body under article 263. So option 4 should not be included.

72. (a) Under Article 76, impeachment procedure of the Attorney-General is not provided. He shall hold office during the pleasure of the President. He must not be a member of either House of Parliament.

73. (b) Out of 52 items on the concurrent list, Economic and Social Planning is placed under Article 40 of the Constitution. Directive Principles of State Policy lays down that the State shall take steps to organize village panchayats and endow them with such powers and authority as may be necessary to enable them to function as units of self government. Planning for economic development and social justice is one such power given to village panchayats.

74. (d) All the parties mentioned are state level parties.

75. (d) All the statements are correct.

76. (b) The Chief Election Commissioner and other Election Commissioners enjoy equal powers and salaries. The term of office of the Election Commissioner is 6 years or till he attains the age of 65 years or whichever is earlier.

77. (b) Article 280 of the Constitution of India provides for a Finance Commission as a quasi-judicial body. It is constituted by the President of India every fifth year or at such earlier time as he considers necessary. The commission makes recommendations to the

president with regard to the distribution of the proceeds of taxes between the union and the states. The principles which should govern the grants-in-aid to be given to the states. Any other matter referred to the Commission by the President in the interest of sound finance.

78. (a) The High Court (and not the Election Commission) is the final authority to give a final verdict in case of election disputes. In the alternative special election benches may be constituted in high courts and earmarked exclusively for the disposal of election petitions and disputes.

79. (d) Statement 1 is incorrect as Advocate General of the state is appointed by the governor of the State. Statement 2 is incorrect as High Courts have Original, Appellate and Writ jurisdiction (not advisory jurisdiction).

80. (c) Only 2nd and 3rd are correct statements.
   (2) CAG reports on execution of projects or programmes by the ministries are discussed by the Public Accounts Committee.
   (3) Information from CAG reports can be used by investigating agencies to press charges against those who have violated the law while managing public finance.

81. (c) The Attorney General of India has a post parallel to any minister in Parliament. He can take part in the proceedings of either house. He can be a member of any committee of Parliament. He has the right to speak in the Parliament but he has no right to vote.

82. (a) The main functions of the Committee is to consider all matters concerning the welfare of the Scheduled Castes and Scheduled Tribes, falling within the purview of the Union Government and the Union Territories, to consider the reports submitted by the National Commission for Scheduled Castes and Scheduled Tribes and to examine the measures taken by the Union Government to secure due representation of the Scheduled Castes and Scheduled Tribes in services and posts under its control.

83. (c)

84. (d) Constitutional bodies are formed by the constitution which helps the government to run properly.

85. (a) The CAG is an authority, established by the constitution. Who audits all receipts and expenditure of the Government of India and the State Governments.

86. (d) All are correct.

87. (d) Election Commission has three election Commissioners.
   Election Commission decides the election schedule for the conduct of both general elections and bye-elections. It also decides the disputes relating to splits/mergers of recognized political parties.
   Hence answer "D" only 3.

88. (b) • Central Pollution Control Board (CPCB), is statutory organization, was constituted in September, 1974 under the Water (Prevention and Control of Pollution) Act, 1974. So #1 is wrong.
   • Principal functions of the CPCB, as spelt out in the Water (Prevention and Control of Pollution) Act, 1974, and the Air (Prevention and Control of Pollution) Act, 1981, (i) to promote cleanliness of streams and wells in different areas. So last part of sentence #2 is right.
   • Environment: National Green Tribunal (NGT) was set up in 2010 under the NGT Act, 2010, for the purpose of effective and expeditious disposal of cases relating to environmental protection. The Tribunal shall not be bound by the procedure laid down under the Code of Civil Procedure, 1908, but shall be guided by principles of natural justice. The Tribunal is mandated to make an endeavor for disposal of applications or appeals finally within 6 months of filing. So first part of sentence #2 is right.

89. (c) 90. (c) 91. (c)

92. (d) Attorney General of India is appointed by the President of India under Article 76(a) of the Constitution and holds the office during the pleasure of the President.

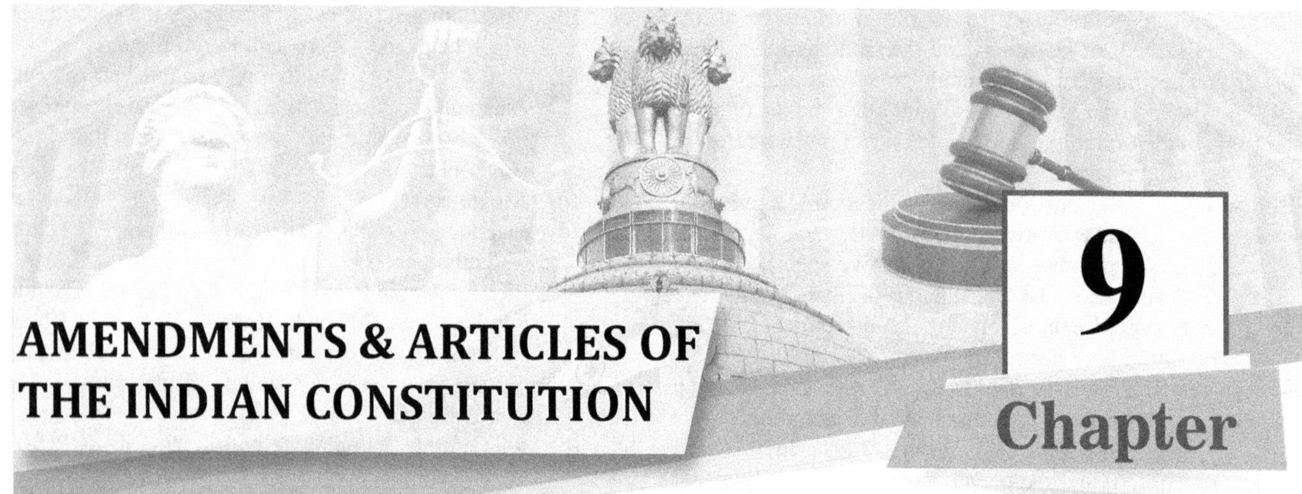

AMENDMENTS & ARTICLES OF THE INDIAN CONSTITUTION

Amendment Procedures Under Indian Constitution

Indian Constitution is a balanced Constitution. The farmers of the constitution desired to secure balance and moderation in incorporating various provision in our Constitution. As far as the amendments of the Constitution is concerned, a balance has been strucked in making the Constitution *partly rigid* and *partly flexible. A flexible Constitution* is one, which can be easily amended like ordinary law of the land. On the contrary, a rigid Constitution is one whose amendment is very difficult and where there is a distinction between the amendment of the Constitutional law and ordinary law. Both the types of Constitutions had their merits and demerits.

The proposal for amending the Constitution can be initiated only in the Union Legislature and the state legislatures have no such power. But the farmers of the Indian Constitution did not go to the extreme. They incorporated a unique procedure of amendment which combines both rigidity and flexibility. In this connection, it is world while to quote Pandit Nehru who clearly stated, "While one wants this constitution to be solid and permanent as we can make it, there is no permanence in the Constitution. There should be certain flexibility. If you make anything rigid and permanent you stop the nation's growth, the growth of a living vital organic people.

Methods of Amendments

Article 368 in part XX of the constitution deals with the Power of Parliament to amend the constitution and its procedure. However, the Parliament cannot amend those provisions which form the "basic - structure" of the constitution.

This was ruled by the supreme court in the Kesavananda a Bharti case (1973).

1. An amendment of the Constitution may be initiated only by the introduction of a bill for the purpose in either house of Parliament and when a bill is passed in each house.

    (i)   By a majority of total membership of that house.

    (ii) By a majority of not less than two-thirds of the members of that house present and voting, it shall be presented to the President who shall give his assent to the Bill and there upon the Constitution shall stand amended in accordance with the term of the Bill.

    Most of the provisions of the Constitution can be amended by this procedure.

2. For amending certain provisions a special procedure is to be followed, i.e.

    (i)   A Bill for the purpose must be passed in each house of parliament by a majority of total membership of the house.

    (ii) By a majority of not less than two-third of the members of that house present and voting and

    (iii) It should be notified by the legislatures of not less than one-half of the states before the Bill is presented to the President for assent.

    The provisions requiring this special procedure to be followed include:

    (a) Manner of the election of the President.

    (b) Matters relating to the executive power of the Union and of the state.

    (c) Representation of the states in Parliament.

    (d) Matters relating to the Union Judiciary and High Courts in the states.

    (e) Distribution of legislative powers between the Union and the States.

    (f) any of the list in the Seventh Schedule.

    (g) Provisions of Article 368 relating to the procedure for amendment of the Constitution, etc.

3. There are certain provisions which require simple majority for amendments. They can be amended by the ordinary law making process they include:

    (a) formation of new states and alteration of areas, boundaries or names of existing ones.

    (b) creation or abolition of legislative councils in the states.

    (c) administration and control of scheduled areas and tribal areas.

    (d) the salaries and allowances of the Supreme Court and High Court Judges.

    (e) laws regarding citizenship, etc. It is significant that the laws passed by Parliament to change the above provisions would not be deemed to be amendments of the Constitution for the purpose of Article 368.

    (f) Use of english language in the Parliament.

    (g) Delimitation of constituencies.

    (h) Union territories.

    (i) Use of official Parliament.

    (j) Quorum in the Parliament.

    (k) Election to the Parliament and state legislature.

Scope of Amendability: Basic Features

How far can the constitution be amended? Can any of its provisions be amended? Over the years, there has been some confusion over this issue. Until the **Golak Nath Case (1967),** the Supreme Court had been holding the view that no part of the Constitution is unamendable. In the Golak Nath case it was held that the Fundamental Rights cannot be amended. The decision was over turned in the **Keshavananda Bharti Case (1973).** However, it was also held by the Supreme Court that there are certain basic features of the Constitution that cannot be altered in the course of Parliament exercising its amending power under **Article 368**. As to what these basic features are, there seems to be no unanimous opinion. One may only reach certain broad conclusion on the matter, as pointed out by **Dr. D. D. Basu** in his Introduction to the Constitution of India:

– that any part of the Constitution may be amended after complying with the procedure laid down in Article 368;

– a reference to a Constituent Assembly or a referendum is not required to amend any part of the Constitution;

– however, no provision of the Constitution can be amended if it takes away or destroys any of the basic features of the Constitution.

While no list of *'basic features'* has been drawn up by the court, different judgements lead one to view the 'basic features' as –

(i)　Supremacy of the Constitution,

(ii)　Rule of law,

(iii)　Separation of powers,

(iv)　Objectives mentioned in the Preamble,

(v)　Judicial review,

(vi)　Federalism,

(vii)　Securalism,

(viii)　Soverign, democratic and republician structure,

(ix)　Principle of equality and the essence of other Fundamental Rights,

(x)　Social and economic justice,

(xi)　balance between Part III and Part IV,

(xii)　Concept of free and fair elections,

(xiii)　independence of the judiciary,

(xiv)　effective access of justice,

(xv)　Limitations on the amending power, conferred by Article 368.

List of Amendments of the Constitution of India

C.A. Acts	Coverage	Date of Assembly Enforced since	Objectives
1st C.A. Act 1951	Amended articles 15, 19, 85, 87, 174, 176, 341, 342, 372 and 376. Inserted articles 31A and 31B. Inserted Schedule 9.	18 June 1951	To fully secure the constitutional validity of zamindari abolition laws and to place reasonable restriction on freedom to speech. A new constitutional device, called Schedule Ninth introduced to protect laws that are contrary to the Constitutionally guaranteed.
2nd C.A. Act 1952	Amended article 81(1)(b).	1 May 1953	Removed the upper population limit for a parliamentary constituency by amending Article 81 (1) (b).
3rd C.A. Act 1954	Amended schedule 7.	22 February 1955	Re-enacted entry 33 of the Concurrent List in the Seventh Schedule with relation to include trade and commerce in, and the production, supply and distribution of 4 classes of essential commodities, viz, foodstuffs, including edible oil seeds and oils; cat.
4th C.A. Act 1955	Amended articles 31, 35 and 305. Amended 9th Schedule.	27 April 1955	Restriction on property rights and inclusion of related bills in 9th Schedule of the Constitution.
5th C.A. Act 1955	Amended article 3.	24 December 1955	Empowered the President to prescribe a time limit of a State Legislature to convey its views on proposed Central laws relating to the formation of new States and alteration of areas, boundaries or names of existing States.
6th C.A. Act 1956	Amended articles 269 and 286. Amended 7th Schedule. Amended articles 1, 3, 49, 80, 81, 82, 131, 153, 158, 168, 170, 171, 216, 217, 220, 222, 224, 230, 231 and 232.	11 September 1956	Amended the Union and State Lists with respect to raising of taxes.
7th C.A. Act 1956	Inserted articles 258A, 290A, 298, 350A, 350B, 371, 372A and 378A. Amended part 8. Amended schedules I, II, III and IV.	1 November 1956	Reorganization of states on linguistic lines, abolition of Class A, B, C, D states and introduction of Union Territories.

8th C.A. Act 1959	Amended article 334.	5 January 1960	Extended the period of reservation of seats for the Scheduled Castes and Scheduled Tribes and Anglo-Indians in the Lok Sabha and State Legislative Assemblies till 1970.
9th C.A. Act 1960	Amended I Schedule.	28 December 1960	Minor adjustments to territory of Indian Union consequent to agreement with Pakistan for settlement of disputes by demarcation of border villages, etc.
10th C.A. Act 1961	Amended article 240. Amended 1st Schedule.	11 August 1961	Incorporation of Dadra, Nagar and Haveli as a Union Territory, consequent to acquisition from Portugal.
11th C.A. Act 1961	Amended articles 66 and 71.	19 December 1961	Election of Vice President by Electoral College consisting of members of both Houses of Parliament, instead of election by a Joint Sitting of Parliament, Indemnify the President and Vice President Election procedure from challenge on grounds of existence.
12th C.A. Act 1962	1st Amended article 240. Amended Schedule.	20 December 1961	Incorporation of Goa, Daman and Diu as a Union Territory, consequent to acquisition from Portugal.
13th C.A. Act 1962	Amended article 170. Inserted new article 371A.	1 December 1963	Formation of State of Nagaland, with special potection under Article 371A
14th C.A. Act 1962	Amended articles 81 and 240. Inserted article 239A. Amended schedules 1 and 4.	28 December 1962	Incorporation of Pondicherry into the Union of India and creation of Legislative Assemblies for Himachal Pradesh, Tripura, Manipur and Goa.
15th C.A. Act 1963	Amended articles 124, 128, 217, 222, 224, 226, 297, 311 and 316. Inserted article 224A. Amended 7th Schedule.	5 October 1963	Raise retirement age of High court judges from 60 to 62 and other minor amendments for rationalizing interpretation of rules regarding judges, etc.
16th C.A. Act 1963	Amended articles 19, 84 and 173. Amended 3rd Schedule.	5 October 1963	Make it obligatory for seekers of public office to swear their allegiance to the Indian Republic and prescribe the various obligtory templates.
17th C.A. Act 1964	Amended article 31A. Amended 9th schedule.	20 June 1964	To secure the constitutional validity of acquisition of Estates and place land acquisition laws in 9th Schedule of the Constitution.
18th C.A. Act 1966	Amended article 3.	27 August 1966	Technical Amendment to include Union Territories in Article 3 and hence permit reorganisation of Union Territories
19th C.A. Act 1966	Amended article 324.	11 December 1966	Abolish Election Tribunals and enable trial of election petitions by regular High Courts.
20th C.A. Act 1966	Inserted article 233A.	22 December 1966	Indemnity and validate judgements, decrees, orders and sentences passed by judges and to validate the appoinment, posting, promotion and transfer of judges barring a few who were not eligible for appointment under article 233.
21st C.A. Act 1967	Amended 8th Schedule.	10 April 1967	Include Sindhi as an Official Language.
22nd C.A. Act 1969	Amended article 275. Inserted articles 244A and 371B.	25 September 1969	Provision to form Autonomous states within the State of Assam.
23rd C.A. Act 1969	Amended articles 330, 332, 333 and 334.	23 January 1970	Discontinued reservation of seats for the Scheduled Tribes in Nagaland, both in the Lok Sabha and State Legislative Assembly and stipulated that not more than one Anglo-Indian could be nominated by the Governor to any State Legislative Assembly. Extend reservation for SC/ST and Anglo Indian members in the Lok Sabha and State Assemblies for another ten years, i.e. up to 1980.
24th C.A. Act 1971	Amended articles 13 and 369.	5 November 1971	Enable parliament to dilute fundamental rights through amendments to the Constitution.

Act	Changes	Date	Description
25th C.A. Act 1971	Amended article 31. Inserted article 31C. Inserted article 31C.	20 April 1972	Restrict property rights and compensation in case the state takes over private property.
26th C.A. Act 1971	Amended article 366. Inserted article 363A. Remove articles 291 and 362.	28 December 1971	Abolition of privy purse paid to former rulers of princely states which were incorporated into the Indian Republic.
27th C.A. Act 1971	Amended articles 239A and 240. Inserted articles 239B and 371C.	15 February 1972	Reorganization of Mizoram into a Union Territory with a legislature and Council of Ministers.
28th C.A. Act 1972	Inserted article 312A. Remove article 314.	29 August 1972	Rationalize Civil Service rules to make it uniform across those appointed prior to independence and post independence.
29th C.A. Act 1972	Amended 9th Schedule.	9 June 1972	Place land reform acts and amendments to these act under 9th Schedule of the Constitution.
30th C.A. Act 1972	Amended article 133.	27 February 1973	Change the basis for appeals in Supreme Court of India in case of Civil Suits from value criteria to one involving substantial question of law.
31th C.A. Act 1973	Amended articles 81, 330 and 332.	17 October 1973	Increase size of Lok Sabha from 525 to 545 seats. Increased seats going to the new states formed in North East India and minor adjustment consequent to 1971 Delimitation exercise.
32nd C.A. Act 1973	Amended article 371. Inserted articles 371D and 371E. Amended 7th Schedule.	1 July 1974	Protection of regional rights in Telengana and Andhra regions of State of Andhra Pradesh.
33rd C.A. Act 1974	Amended articles 101 and 190.	19 May 1974	Prescribes procedure for resignation by members of Parliament and state legislature and the procedure for verification and acceptance of resignation by house speaker.
34th C.A. Act 1974	Amended 9th Schedule	7 September 1974	Place land reform acts and amendments to these act under 9th Schedule of the Constitution.
35th C.A. Act 1974	Amended articles 80 and 81. Inserted article 2A. Inserted schedule 10.	1 March 1974	Terms and Conditions for the incorporation of Sikkim into the Union of India.
36th C.A. Act 1975	Amended articles 80 and 81. Inserted article 371F. Amended 1st and 4th Schedules. Remove Schedule 10.	26 April 1975	Formation of Sikkim as a State within the Indian Union
37th C.A. Act 1975	Amended articles 239A and 240.	3 May 1975	Formation of Arunachal Pradesh legislative assembly.
38th C.A. Act 1975	Amended articles 123, 213, 239B, 352, 356, 359 and 360.	1 August 1975	Enhances the powers of President and Governors to pass ordinances.
39th C.A. Act 1975	Amended articles 71 and 329. Inserted article 329A. Amended schedule 9.	10 August 1975	Amendment designed to negate the judgement of Allahabad High Court invalidating Prime Minister Indira Gandhi's election to Parliament. Amendment placed restrictions on judicial scrutiny of post of Prime Minister.
40th C.A. Act 1976	Amended article 297. Amended 9th Schedule.	27 May 1976	Enable Parliament to make laws with respect to Exclusive Economic Zone and vest the mineral wealth with Union of India. Placed land reform & other acts and amendments to these act under 9th Schedule of the Constitution.
41st C.A. Act 1976	Amended article 316.	7 September 1976	Raise Retirement age Limit of Chairman and Members of Joint Public Service Commissions and State Public Service Commissions for sixty to sixty two.

42nd C.A. Act 1976	Amended articles 31, 31C, 39, 55, 74, 77, 81, 82, 83, 100, 102, 103, 105, 118, 145, 150, 166, 170, 172, 189, 191, 192, 194, 208, 217, 225, 226, 227, 228, 311, 312, 330, 352, 353, 356, 357, 358, 359, 366, 368 and 371F. Inserted articles 31D, 32A, 39A, 43A, 48A, 131A, 139A, 144A, 226A, 228A and 257A. Inserted parts 4A and 14A. Amended 7th Schedule.	1 April 1977	Amendment passed during internal emergency by Indira Gandhi. Provides for curtailment of fundamental rights, imposes fundamental duties and changes to the *basic structure* of the Constitution by making India a *"Socialist Secular"* Republic
43rd C.A. Act 1977	Amended articles 145, 226, 228 and 366 Removed articles 31D, 32A, 131A, 144A, 226A and 228A.	13 April 1978	Amendment passed after revocation of internal emergency in the Country. Repeals some of the 'Anti-Freedom' amendments enacted through 42nd Amendment Bill.
44th C.A. Act 1978	Amended articles 19, 22, 30, 31A, 31C, 38, 71, 74, 77, 83, 103, 105, 123, 132, 133, 134, 139A, 150, 166, 172, 192, 194, 213, 217, 225, 226, 227, 239B, 329, 352, 356, 358, 359, 360 and 371F. Inserted articles 134A and 361A. Removed articles 31, 257A and 329A. Amended part 12. Amended 9th Schedule.	6 September 1978	Amendment passed after revocation of internal emergency in the Country. Provides for human rights safeguards and mechanisms to prevent abuse of executive and legislative authority. Annuls some Amendments enacted in 42nd Amendment Bill 42
45th C.A. Act 1980	Amended article 334.	25 January 1980	Extend reservation for SC/ST and nomination of Anglo Indian members in Parliament and State Assemblies for another ten years, i.e. upto 1990.
46th C.A. Act 1982	Amended articles 269, 286 and 366 Amended 7th Schedule.	2 February 1983	Amendment to negate judicial pronouncements on scope and applicability on Sales Tax.
47th C.A. Act 1984	Amended 9th Schedule.	26 August 1984	Place land reform acts and amendments to these act under 9th Schedule of the Constitution.
48th C.A. Act 1984	Amended article 356.	1 April 1985	Article 356 amended to permit President's rule up to two years in the state of Punjab.
49th C.A. Act 1984	Amended article 244. Amended 5th and 6th Schedules.	11 September 1984	Recognized Tripura as a Tribal State and enable the creation of a Tripura Tribal Areas Autonomous District Council.
50th C.A. Act 1984	Amended article 33.	11 September 1984	Technical Amendment to curtailment of Fundamental Rights as per Part III as prescribed in Article 33 to cover Security Personnel protection property and communication infrastructure.
51st C.A. Act 1984	Amended articles 330 and 332.	16 June 1986	Provided reservation to Scheduled Tribes in Nagaland, Meghalaya, Mizoram, Arunachal Pradesh Legislative Assemblies.
52nd C.A. Act 1985	Amended articles 101, 102, 190 and 191. Inserted schedule 10.	1 March 1985	Anti Defection Law - Provide disqualification of members from Parliament and assembly in case of defection from one party to other.
53rd C.A. Act 1986	Inserted article 371G.	20 February 1987	Special provision with respect to the State of Mizoram.

54th C.A. Act 1986	Amended articles 125 and 221. Amended 2nd Schedule.	1 April 1986	Increase the salary of Chief Justice of India & other Judges and to provide for determining future increases without the need for constitutional amendment.
55th C.A. Act 1986	Inserted article 371H.	20 February 1987	Special powers to Governor consequent to formation of state of Arunachal Pradesh.
56th C.A. Act 1987	Inserted article 371I.	30 May 1987	Transition provision to enable formation of state of Goa.
57th C.A. Act 1987	Amended article 332.	21 September 1987	Provided reservation to Scheduled Tribes in Nagaland, Meghalaya, Mizoram, Arunachal Pradesh Legislative Assemblies.
58th C.A. Act 1987	Inserted article 394A. Amended part 22.	9 December 1987	Provision to public authentic Hindi translation of constitution as on date and provision to public authentic Hindi translation of future amendments.
59th C.A. Act 1988	Amended article 356. Inserted article 359A.	30 March 1988	Article 356 amended to permit President's rule up to three years in the state of Punjab, Articles 352 and Article 359A amended to permit imposing emergency in state of Punjab or in specific districts of the state of Punjab.
60th C.A. Act 1988	Amended article 276.	20 December 1988	Profession Tax increased from a minimum of ₹ 250/- to a maximum of ₹ 2500/-
61st C.A. Act 1988	Amended article 326.	28 March 1989	Reduced voting age from 21 to 18.
62nd C.A. Act 1989	Amended article 334.	20 December 1989	Extend reservation for SC/ST and nomination of Anglo Indian members in Parliament and State Assemblies for another ten years, i.e. upto 2000.
63rd C.A. Act 1989	Amended article 356. Removed article 359A.	6 January 1990	Emergency powers application to State of Punjab, accorded in Article 359A as per amendment 59th repealed.
64th C.A. Act 1990	Amended article 356.	16 April 1990	Article 356 amended to permit President's rule up to three years and six months in the state of Punjab.
65th C.A. Act 1990	Amended article 338.	12 March 1990	National Commission for Scheduled Castes and Scheduled Tribes formed and its statutory powers specified in the Constitution.
66th C.A. Act 1990	Amended 9th Schedule.	7 June 1990	Place land reform acts and amendments to these act under 9th Schedule of the Constitution.
67th C.A. Act 1990	Amended article 356.	4 October 1990	Article 356 amended to permit President's rule up to four years in the state of Punjab.
68th C.A. Act 1991	Amended article 356.	12 March 1991	Article 356 amended to permit President's rule up to five years in the state of Punjab.
69th C.A. Act 1991	Inserted articles 239AA and 239AB.	1 February 1992	To provide for a legislative assembly and Council of ministers for Federal National Capital of Delhi. Delhi continues to be a Union Territory.
70th C.A. Act 1992	Amended articles 54 and 239AA.	21 December 1991	Include National Capital of Delhi and Union Territory of Pondicherry in electoral college for Presidential Election.
71st C.A. Act 1992	Amended 8th Schedule.	31 August 1992	Include Konkani, Manipuri and Nepali as Official Languages.
72nd C.A. Act 1992	Amended article 332.	5 December 1992	Provide reservation to Scheduled Tribes in Tripura State Legislative Assembly.
73rd C.A. Act 1992	Inserted part 9.	24 April 1993	Statutory provisions for Panchayat Raj as third level of administration in villages.
74th C.A. Act 1992	Inserted part 9A.	1 June 1993	Statutory provisions for Local Administrative bodies as third level of administration in urban areas such as towns and cities.
75th C.A. Act 1993	Amended article 323B.	15 May 1994	Provisions for setting up Rent Control Tribunals.

76th C.A. Act 1994	Amended 9th Schedule.	31 August 1994	Enable continuance of 69% reservation in Tamil Nadu by including the relevant Tamil Nadu Act under 9th Schedule of the constitution.
77th C.A. Act 1995	Amended article 16.	17 June 1995	A technical amendment to protect reservation to SC/ST Employees in promotions.
78th C.A. Act 1995	Amended 9th Schedule.	30 August 1995	Place land reform acts and amendments to these act under 9th Schedule of the Constitution.
79th C.A. Act 2000	Amended article 334.	25 January 2000	Extend reservation for SC/ST and nomination of Anglo Indian members in Parliament and State Assemblies for another ten years, i.e. up to 2010.
80th C.A. Act 2000	Amended articles 269 and 270. Remove article 272.	9 June 2000	Implement Tenth Finance Commission recommendation to simply the tax structures by pooling and sharing all taxes between states and the Centre.
81st C.A. Act 2000	Amended article 16.	9 June 2000	Protect SC/ST reservation in filling backlog of vacancies.
82nd C.A. Act 2000	Amended article 335.	8 September 2000	Permit relaxation of qualifying marks and other criteria in reservation in promotion for SC/ST candidates.
83rd C.A. Act 2000	Amended article 243M.	8 September 2000	Exempt Arunachal Pradesh from reservation for Scheduled Castes in Panchayati Raj institutions.
84th C.A. Act 2001	Amended articles 55, 81, 82, 170, 330 and 332.	21 February 2002	Extend the usage of 1971 national census population figures for statewise distribution of Parliamentary seats.
85th C.A. Act 2002	Amended article 16.	4 January 2002	A technical amendment to protect Consequential seniority in case of promotions of SC/ST Employees
86th C.A. Act 2002	Amended articles 45 and 51A. Inserted article 21A.	12 December 2002	Provides Right to Education until the age of fourteen and Early childhood care until the age of six.
87th C.A. Act 2003	Amended articles 81, 82, 170 and 330.	22 June 2003	Extend the usage of 2001 National Census population figures for statewise distribution of parliamentary seats.
88th C.A. Act 2003	Amended article 270. Inserted article 268A. Amended 7th Schedule.	15 January 2004	To extend statutory cover for levy and utilization of Service Tax.
89th C.A. Act 2003	Amended article 338. Inserted article 338A.	28 September 2003	The National Commission for Scheduled Castes and Scheduled Tribes was bifurcated into the National Commission for Scheduled Castes and the National Commission for Scheduled Tribes.
90th C.A. Act 2003	Amended article 332.	28 September 2003	Reservation in Assam Assembly relating to Bodoland Territory Area.
91st C.A. Act 2003	Amended articles 75 and 164. Inserted article 361B. Amended 10th Schedule.	1 January 2004	Restrict the size of council of Ministers to 15% of legislative members and to strengthen Anti Defection laws.
92nd C.A. Act 2003	Amended 8th Schedule.	7 January 2004	Include Bodo, Dogri, Santhali, Maithali as official languages.
93rd C.A. Act 2005	Amended article 15.	20 January 2006	To enable provision of reservation (27%) for Other Backward Classes (O.B.C.) in government as well as private educational institutions.
94th C.A. Act 2006	Amended article 164.	12 June 2006	To provide for a Minister of Tribal Welfare in newly created Jharkhand and Chhattisgarh States including Madhyapradesh, Orrissa.
95th C.A. Act 2009	Amended article 334.	25 January 2010	To extend the reservation of seats for SCs and STs in the Lok Sabha and states assemblies from Sixty years to Seventy years.
96th C.A. Act 2011	Amended schedule 8.	23 September 2011	Substituted "Odia" for "Oriya"

97th C.A. Act 2011	Amended Art 19 and added Part IXB.	12 January 2012	Added the words "or co-operative societies" after the word "or unions" in Article 19(I) (c) and insertion of article 43B, i.e. Promotion of Co-operative Societies and added Part-IXB, i.e. the Co-operative Societies. The amendment objective is to encourage economic activities of cooperatives which in turn help progress of rural India. It is expected to not only ensure autonomous and democratic functioning of cooperatives, but also the accountability of the management to the members and other stakeholders.
98th C.A. Act 2012	Inserted Article 371J in the Constitution	2 January 2013	To empower the Governor of Karnataka to take steps to develop the Hyderabad-Karnataka Region.
99th C.A. Act 2014	Amended Article 127,128 Inserted new Articles 124 A, 124 B & 124 C.	13 April 2015	Amendment provides for the formation of a National Indician Appointments Commission.
100th C.A. Act 2015	Amendment of First Schedule to Constitution.	1 August 2015	To operationalise the land Boundary Agreement between India and Bangladesh.
101st Amendment Act : 2016	Amendment of Arts 248-250, 268-271, 286, 366, 368 Deleted Art. 268A & [107] Amended Schedule VI & VII. Inserted Act 246A, 279A	8 September 2016	To implement Goods & Service Tax (GST).
102nd Amendment Act : 217	This Bill was introduced alongside the National Commission for Backward Classes (Repeal) Bill, 2017 that seeks to repeal the National Commission for Backward Classes Act, 1993	11 August 2018	Constitutional status to National Commission for Backward Classes: The NCBC is a body set up under the National Commission for Backward Classes Act, 1993, It has the power to examine complaints regarding inclusion or exclusion of groups within the list of backward classes, and advise the central government in this regard. The Bill seeks to establish the NCBC under the Constitution, and provide it the authority to examine complaints and welfare measures regarding socially and educationally backward classes.

Article List

Part / Schedule	Chapter	Articles	Subject matter
I		1-4	The Union and its Territory
II		5-11	Citizenship
III		12-35	Fundamental Rights
IV		36-51	Directive Principles of State Policy
IVA		51A	Fundamental Duties
V		**52-151**	**The Union**
	I	52-78	The Executive – The President and Vice President, Council of Ministers, The Attorney-General for India, Conduct of Government Business, Duties of Prime Minister as respects the furnishing of information to the President, etc.
	II	79-122	Parliament, Conduct of business, Disqualifications of Members, Legislative procedure etc.
	III	123	Legislative powers of the President.
	IV	124-147	The Union Judiciary.
	V	148-151	Comptroller and Auditor-General of India.

VI		**152-237**	**The States**
	I	152	Definition
	II	153-167	The Executive - The Governor, Council of Ministers, The Advocate-General for the State, Conduct of Government business, Duties of Chief Minister in respects of furnishing of information to Governor, etc.
	III	168-212	The State Legislature, Disqualification of Members, Legislative Procedure, etc.
	IV	213	Legislative power of the Governor.
	V	214-232	The High Courts in the States.
	VI	233-237	Subordinate Courts.
VII		238	Repealed.
VIII		239-242	The Union Territories – administration, High Courts for Union Territories etc.
IX		243-243O	The Panchayats.
IXA		243P-243ZG	The Municipalities.
X		244-244A	The Scheduled and Tribal Areas.
XI		**245-263**	**Relations between the Union and the States**
	I	245-255	Legislative Relations – distribution of legislative powers, residuary powers of legislation, etc.
	II	256-263	Administrative Relations.
XII		**264-300A**	**Finance, Property, Contracts and Suits**
	I	264-291	Finance – taxes, grants, Finance Commission, recommendations of Finance Commission, exemption from taxes etc.
	II	292-293	Borrowing – by the Government of India and by States.
	III	294-300	Property, Contracts, Rights, Liabilities, Obligations and Suits and proceedings.
	IV	300A	Right to Property.
XIII		301-307	Trade, Commerce and Intercourse within theterritory of India.
XIV		**308-323**	**Services under the Union and the States**
	I	308-314	**Services** – recruitment and conditions of service of persons serving the Union or State,
	II	315-323	Public Service Commissions.
XIVA		323A-323B	Tribunals.
XV		324-329A	Elections.
XVI		330-342	Special Provisions relating to certain Classes- Scheduled Castes and Scheduled Tribes in House of the People, etc. Scheduled Castes and Scheduled Tribes
XVII		**343-351**	**Official Language**
	I	343-344	Language of the Union.
	II	345-347	Regional Languages.
	III	348-349	Language of the Supreme Court, High Court, etc.
	IV	350-351	Special Directives,
XVIII		352-360	Emergency Provisions,
XIX		361-367	Miscellaneous – protection of President, Governors and Rajpramukhs, abolition of privy purses, special provisions as to major ports and aerodromes, etc.
XX		368	Amendment of the Constitution - Power of Parliament and procedure.
XXI		369-392	Temporary, Transitional and Special Provisions.
XXII		393-395	Short Title, Commencement, Authoritative text in Hindi and Repeals.

Articles of the Indian Constitution

Part I : The Union And Its Territory

1   Name and territory of the Union.

2   Admission or establishment of new States.

2A   [Repealed.]

3   Formation of new States and alteration of areas, boundaries or names of existing States.

4   Laws made under articles 2 and 3 to provide for the amendment of the First and the Fourth Schedules and supplemental, incidental and consequential matters.

Part II : Citizenship

5 Citizenship at the commencement of the Constitution.
6 Rights of citizenship of certain persons who have migrated to India from Pakistan.
7 Rights of citizenship of certain migrants to Pakistan.
8 Rights of citizenship of certain persons of Indian origin residing outside India.
9 Persons voluntarily acquiring citizenship of a foreign State not to be citizens.
10 Continuance of the rights of citizenship.
11 Parliament to regulate the right of citizenship by law.

Part III : Fundamental Rights

General

12 Definition.
13 Laws inconsistent with or in derogation of the fundamental rights.

Right to Equality

14 Equality before law.
15 Prohibition of discrimination on grounds of religion, race, caste, sex or place of birth.
16 Equality of opportunity in matters of public employment.
17 Abolition of Untouchability.
18 Abolition of titles.

Right to Freedom

19 Protection of certain rights regarding freedom of speech, etc.
20 Protection in respect of conviction for offences.
21 Protection of life and personal liberty.
22 Protection against arrest and detention in certain cases.

Right against Exploitation

23 Prohibition of traffic in human beings and forced labour.
24 Prohibition of employment of children in factories, etc.

Right to Freedom of Religion

25 Freedom of conscience and free profession, practice and propagation of religion.
26 Freedom to manage religious affairs.
27 Freedom as to payment of taxes for promotion of any particular religion.
28 Freedom as to attendance at religious instruction or religious worship in certain educational institutions.

Cultural and Educational Rights

29 Protection of interests of minorities.
30 Right of minorities to establish and administer educational institutions.
31 [Repealed.]

Saving of Certain Laws

31A Saving of Laws providing for acquisition of estates, etc.
31B Validation of certain Acts and Regulations.
31C Saving of laws giving effect to certain directive principles.
31D [Repealed.]

Right to Constitutional Remedies

32 Remedies for enforcement of rights conferred by this Part.
32A [Repealed.]

33 Power of Parliament to modify the rights conferred by this Part in their application to Forces, etc.
34 Restriction on rights conferred by this Part while martial law is in force in any area.
35 Legislation to give effect to the provisions of this Part.

Part IV : Directive Principles Of State Policy

36 Definition.
37 Application of the principles contained in this Part.
38 State to secure a social order for the promotion of welfare of the people.
39 Certain principles of policy to be followed by the State.
39A Equal justice and free legal aid.
40 Organisation of village panchayats.
41 Right to work, to education and to public assistance in certain cases.
42 Provision for just and humane conditions of work and maternity relief.
43 Living wage, etc., for workers.
43A Participation of workers in management of industries.
44 Uniform civil code for the citizens.
45 Provision for free and compulsory education for children.
46 Promotion of educational and economic interests of Scheduled Castes, Scheduled Tribes and other weaker sections.
47 Duty of the State to raise the level of nutrition and the standard of living and to improve public health.
48 Organisation of agriculture and animal husbandry.
48A Protection and improvement of environment and safeguarding of forests and wild life.
49 Protection of monuments and places and objects of national importance.
50 Separation of judiciary from executive.
51 Promotion of international peace and security.

Part IVA : Fundamental duties

51A Fundamental duties.

Part V : The Union

Chapter I. The Executive

The President and Vice-President
52 The President of India.
53 Executive power of the Union.
54 Election of President.
55 Manner of election of President.
56 Term of office of President.
57 Eligibility for re-election.
58 Qualifications for election as President.
59 Conditions of President's office.
60 Oath or affirmation by the President.
61 Procedure for impeachment of the President.
62 Time of holding election to fill vacancy in the office of President and the term of office of person elected to fill casual vacancy.
63 The Vice-President of India.
64 The Vice-President to be ex officio Chairman of the Council of States.

Part X : The Scheduled and Tribal Areas

Part XI : Relations Between The Union and The States

Chapter I: Legislative Relations

Distribution of Legislative Powers

Chapter II. Administrative Relations

General

Part XIII Finance, Property, Contracts And Suits

Chapter I. Finance

General

340	Appointment of a Commission to investigate the conditions of backward classes.
341	Scheduled Castes.
342	Scheduled Tribes.

Part XVII: Official Language

Chapter I. Language of the Union

343	Official language of the Union.
344	Commission and Committee of Parliament on official language.

Chapter II. Regional Languages

345	Official language or languages of a State.
346	Official language for communication between one State and another or between a State and the Union.
47	Special provision relating to language spoken by a section of the population of a State.

Chapter III. Language of the Supreme Court, High Courts, Etc.

348	Language to be used in the Supreme Court and in the High Courts and for Acts, Bills, etc.
349	Special procedure for enactment of certain laws relating to language.

Chapter IV. Special Directives

350	Language to be used in representations for redress of grievances.
350A	Facilities for instruction in mother-tongue at primary stage.
350B	Special Officer for linguistic minorities.
351	Directive for development of the Hindi language.

Part XVIII: Emergency Provisions

352	Proclamation of Emergency.
353	Effect of Proclamation of Emergency.
354	Application of provisions relating to distribution of revenues while a Proclamation of Emergency is in operation.
355	Duty of the Union to protect States against external aggression and internal disturbance.
356	Provisions in case of failure of constitutional machinery in States.
357	Exercise of legislative powers under Proclamation issued under article 356.
358	Suspension of provisions of article 19 during emergencies.
359	Suspension of the enforcement of the rights conferred by Part III during emergencies.
359A	[Repealed.]
360	Provisions as to financial emergency.

Part XIX : Miscellaneous

361	Protection of President and Governors and Rajprakukhs.
361A	Protection of publication of proceedings of Parliament and State Legislatures.
361B	Disqualification for appointment on remunerative political post.
362	[Repealed.]
363	Bar to interference by courts in disputes arising out of certain treaties, agreements, etc.

363A	Recognition granted to Rulers of Indian States to cease and privy purses to be abolished.
364	Special provisions as to major ports and aerodromes.
365	Effect of failure to comply with, or to give effect to, directions given by the Union.
366	Definitions.
367	Interpretation.

Part XX: Amendment of the Constitution

368	Power of Parliament to amend the Constitution and procedure therefor.

Part XXI: Temporary, Transitional and Special Provisions

369	Temporary power to Parliament to make laws with respect to certain matters in the State List as if they were matters in the Concurrent List.
370	Temporary provisions with respect to the State of Jammu and Kashmir.
371	Special provision with respect to the States of Maharashtra and Gujarat.
371A	Special provision with respect to the State of Nagaland.
371B	Special provision with respect to the State of Assam.
371C	Special provision with respect to the State of Manipur.
371D	Special provisions with respect to the State of Andhra Pradesh.
371E	Establishment of Central University in Andhra Pradesh.
371F	Special provisions with respect to the State of Sikkim.
371G	Special provisions with respect to the State of Mizoram.
371H	Special provision with respect to the State of Arunachal Pradesh.
371-I	Special provision with respect to the State of Goa.
372	Continuance in force of existing laws and their adaptation.
372A	Power of the President to adapt laws.
373	Power of President to make order in respect of persons under preventive detention in certain cases.
374	Provisions as to Judges of the Federal Court and proceedings pending in the Federal Court or before His Majesty in Council.
375	Courts, authorities and officers to continue to function subject to the provisions of the Constitution.
376	Provisions as to Judges of High Courts.
377	Provisions as to Comptroller and Auditor-General of India.
378	Provisions as to Public Service Commissions.
378A	Special provision as to duration of Andhra Pradesh Legislative Assembly.
379-391	[Repealed.]
392	Power of the President to remove difficulties.

Part XXII: Short Title, Commencement, Authoritative Text

In Hindi and Repeals

393	Short title.
394	Commencement.
394A	Authoritative text in the Hindi language.
395	Repeals.

Exercise -1

1. With reference to "Prevention of Cruelty to Animals Rules, 2017", which among the following stands false?
   (a) The Union Government has banned the sale of cattle for slaughter.
   (b) The cattle can only be purchased for "agricultural purposes."
   (c) The Union Government has reduced the paperwork for both buyer and seller.
   (d) No animal market can be organised within 50 km of an international border and 25 km of a state border.

2. Which of the following fundamental duties was added to constitution by the 86th Amendment Act.
   (a) To protect and improve the natural environment including forests, lakes, rivers and wildlife.
   (b) To provide opportunities for education to his child or ward between the age of six and fourteen years.
   (c) To strive towards excellence in all spheres.
   (d) To value and preserve the rich heritage of the country's composite culture.

3. The constitution 114th Amendment Bill of 2010 pertains to:
   (a) Increasing the retirement age of Supreme Court judges from 65 to 67.
   (b) Increasing retirement age of High Court judges from 62 to 65.
   (c) National Judicial Appointment commission.
   (d) Provisions regarding removal of judges.

4. The Constitution (43rd Amendment) Act:
   (a) Ensured Press freedom
   (b) Restored to the Supreme Court and the High Courts the power to consider the constitutional validity of Central or State laws
   (c) prescribed serious limitations on the Government's power to proclaim internal emergency
   (d) removed the right to property from the Constitution

5. The majority of the provisions of the Indian Constitution can be amended:
   (a) by the State Legislature alone
   (b) the Parliament alone
   (c) with the joint approval of the Parliament and State Legislatures
   (d) only on ratification of half the States

6. Which of the following is not of the methods for amending the different categories of provisions in the Constitution?
   (a) Certain provisions may be amended by a simple majority in Parliament
   (b) Certain other provisions may be amended only by a two-thirds majority
   (c) Certain provisions may be amended only by a three-fourths majority
   (d) Certain amendments require to be ratified by one-half of the States after being passed in Parliament

7. Which one of the following amendments has been described as Mini Constitution?
   (a) Forty-third
   (b) Forty-second
   (c) Fifty-second
   (d) Thirty-ninth

8. Which among the following constitutional amendment provided for state reorganisation on linguistic basis?
   (a) Third Amendment
   (b) Fourth Amendment
   (c) Sixth Amendment
   (d) Seventh Amendment

9. Which one of the following may be said to constitute the basic structure of the Constitution?
   (a) Federal character of Constitution
   (b) Secular nature of polity
   (c) Mandate to build a welfare state
   (d) all of them

10. One of the following amendments imposed restrictions on the fundamental rights of the citizens with a view to protect the sovereignty and integrity of India. It was the:
    (a) Sixteenth Amendment
    (b) Twentieth Amendment
    (c) Fifteenth Amendment
    (d) Forty-second Amendment

11. Simple majority in voting is enough to amend provisions relating to:
    (a) citizenship
    (b) creation and abolition of a State
    (c) administration of Scheduled Castes and Schedules Tribes
    (d) all the above

12. Constitutional safeguards to civil servants are ensured by:
    (a) Article 310
    (b) Article 315
    (c) Article 312
    (d) Article 311

13. Which Article of the Indian Constitution provides for the setting up of the Consolidated Fund of India?
    (a) Article 278 (1)
    (b) Article 283 (1)
    (c) Article 267 (1)
    (d) Article 301 (1)

14. Which one of the following Amendments of the Constitution of India deals with the issue of strengthening of the Panchayati Raj?
    (a) 42nd
    (b) 44th
    (c) 73rd
    (d) 86th

15. Which of the following Constitutional Amendments have added Article 15 (5) in the Constitution of India providing for reservation in educational institutions in the private sector also ?
    (a) 81st Amendment
    (b) 86th Amendment
    (c) 9lst Amendment
    (d) 93rd Amendment

16. The Constitution (74th) Amendment Act makes mention of the
    (a) composition of the National Development Council
    (b) structure of the Planning Commission of India
    (c) functions of the State Finance Commission
    (d) functions of the Kaveri Water Authority

17. Which one of the following amendments to the Indian Constitution empowers the President to send back any matter for reconsideration by the Council of Ministers?
    (a) 39th (b) 40th
    (c) 42nd (d) 44th
18. The 93rd Constitution Amendment deals with the:
    (a) continuation of reservation for backward classes in government employment
    (b) free and compulsory education for all children between the age of 6 and 14 years
    (c) reservation of 30 percent posts for women in government recruitments
    (d) allocation of more number of parliamentary seats for recently created States
19. Which of the following Constitutional Amendments are related to raising the number of Members of Lok Sabha to be elected from the States?
    (a) 6th and 22nd (b) 13th and 38th
    (c) 7th and 31st (d) 11th and 42nd
20. The Constitution (98th Amendment) Act is related to:
    (a) empowering the Centre to levy and appropriate service tax
    (b) the constitution of the National Judicial Commission
    (c) readjustment of electoral constituencies on the basis of the population census 2001
    (d) the demarcation of new boundaries between States.
21. Which of the following Constitution Amendment Acts seeks that the size of the Councils of Ministers at the Centre and in a State must not exceed 15 per cent of the total number of members in the Lok Sabha and the total number of members of the Legislative Assembly of that State, respectively?
    (a) 91st (b) 93rd
    (c) 95th (d) 97th
22. Which Article mentions disqualification of members in the Parliament"
    (a) Article 101 to Article 104
    (b) Article 101 to Articles 105
    (c) Article 102 to Article 106
    (d) Article 106 to Article 110
23. Which Constitutional Article lays down the reservation of seats for Scheduled Castes and Scheduled Tribes in the Lok Sabha ?
    (a) Article 330 (b) Article 332
    (c) Article 333 (d) Article 334
24. Which Constitutional Article deals with `Representation of the Anglo-Indian Community' with House of the People ?
    (a) Article 334 (b) Article 331
    (c) Article 332 (d) Article 333
25. Which of the following is correct about the Constitution (First Amendment) Act, 1950
    (a) provides new grounds of restrictions to the right to freedom of speech and expression
    (b) Provides new grounds of restrictions to the right to practice any profession or to carry on any trade or business

    (c) Inserted two new Articles 31A and 31B and the Ninth Schedule to give protection from challenge to land reform laws
    (d) All the above
26. By the Constitution (Sixth Amendment) Act,1956 by.
    (a) Articles 269 and 286 were amended regarding taxes in the course of interstate trade and commerce
    (b) 92A was added to the Union List of Seventh Schedule
    (c) (a) and (b)
    (d) Inserted two new Articles 31A and 31B and the Ninth Schedule to give protection from challenge to land reform laws
27. The Constitution (Seventh Amendment) Act, 1956
    (a) Giving effect to the recommendations of the State Reorganisation Commission
    (b) Two fold classification of States and Union Territories
    (c) (a) and (b)
    (d) Act 92A was added to the Union List of Seventh Schedule
28. The Constitution (Eighth Amendment) Act, 1960
    (a) Article 31(2) of Constitution was amended to provide state power of compulsory acquisition of private property
    (b) Extenstion of reservations to SC and ST and Anglo Indians
    (c) Substituted entry 33 of Concurrent List of 7th Schedule
    (d) Act 92A was added to the Union List of Seventh Schedule
29. Which of the following Amendment Act of the Constitution imposed certain restrictions on the right to property?
    (a) The Constitution (Thirty-seventh Amendment) Act, 1975
    (b) The Constitution (Thirty-eighth Amendment) Act, 1975
    (c) The Constitution (Forty-First Amendment) Act, 1976
    (d) The Constitution (Forty-Second Amendment) Act, 1976
30. Which of the following is true about the Constitution (Twenty Furth Amendment) Act, 1971
    (a) Parliament has the power to amend any part of the Constitution including fundamental rights
    (b) The President is bound to assent Constitution amendment bill
    (c) Education was transferred to the Concurrent List\
    (d) All the above
31. Which of the following amendment of the Constitution increased the elective strength of Lok Sabha from 525 to 545?
    (a) 31st amendment (b) 30th amendment
    (c) 25th amendment (d) 21st amendment
32. Which of the following amendment was passed during the period of emergency?
    (a) 45th amendment (b) 50th amendment
    (c) 42nd amendment (d) 47th amendment
33. Which of the following is true about the Constitution (Forty Second Amendment) Act, 1976?
    (a) Precedence to Directive Principles over Fundamental Rights
    (b) Fundamental Duties are included
    (c) Constitutional Amendment should not be questioned in any court
    (d) All the above

34. In which of the following amendments the term of Lok Sabha is increased from 5 to 6 years?
    (a) 40th amendment   (b) 42nd amendment
    (c) 44th amendment   (d) 46th amendment

35. Which of the following Amendment Act of the constitution deleted the right to property from the list of fundamental rights?
    (a) The Constitution (Thirty-seventh Amendment) Act, 1975
    (b) The Constitution (Thirty-eighth Amendment) Act, 1975
    (c) The Constitution (Forty-Fourth Amendment) Act, 1978
    (d) The Constitution (Forty-Second Amendment) Act, 1976

36. Article 352 of the Constitution of India contains provisions related to **[NDA 2018]**
    (a) financial emergency
    (b) failure of constitutional machinery in States
    (c) suspension of the enforcement of right conferred in Part III of the Constitution
    (d) general emergency

37. The Right to Education was added to the fundamental Rights in the Constitution of India through the **[CDS 2016]**
    (a) Constitution (86th Amendment) Act, 2002
    (b) Constitution (93th Amendment) Act, 2005
    (c) Constitution (87th Amendment) Act, 2003
    (d) Constitution (97th Amendment) Act, 2011

38. Which one of the following statements with regard to the Ninth Schedule of the Constitution of India is not correct? **[CDS 2016]**
    (a) It was inserted by the Constitution (First Amendment) Act, 1951.
    (b) The Acts and Regulations specified in the Ninth Schedule shall become void on the ground that it violates a fundamental right in Part III of the Constitution.
    (c) The Supreme Court has the power of judicial review of an Act included in the Ninth Schedule on the doctrine of basic structure.
    (d) The appropriate Legislature can repeal or amend an Act specified in the Ninth Schedule.

39. Which one of the following Amendments to the Constitution of India has prescribed that the Council of Ministers shall not exceed 15 percent of total number of members of the House of the People or Legislative Assembly in the States? **[CDS 2018]**
    (a) 91st Amendment   (b) 87th Amendment
    (c) 97th Amendment   (d) 90th Amendment

40. Under which one of the following Amendment Acts was Sikkim admitted into the Union of India? **[CDS 2018]**
    (a) 35th   (b) 36th
    (c) 37th   (d) 38th

Exercise -2

1. The 52nd Amendment Act pertains to the process by which legislators may be disqualified on grounds of defection: In this context consider the following statements.
   1. A legislator is to be disqualified if he/she voluntarily resigns from his/her party.
   2. If an independent member joins a political party, he/she is to be disqualified.
   Choose the correct statement/statements using the codes given below.
   (a) 1 only (b) 2 only
   (c) Both 1 and 2 (d) None of the above

2. Read the following statements with reference to Indian Surrogacy (Regulation) Bill, 2016.
   1. Surrogacy would be allowed only for Infertile Indian married heterosexual couples
   2. The age of female partner in case of heterosexual couples should be between 23-50 years
   3. The issueless women is ineligible to be a surrogate mother
   Select the correct answer using the codes given below:
   (a) 1 only (b) 3 only
   (c) 2 and 3 only (d) 1, 2 and 3

3. Consider the following statements:
   1. The power to initiate an amendment to the constitution lies only with the centre.
   2. President enjoys suspensive veto over state bills.
   Select the correct answer from the codes given below
   (a) 1 only (b) 2 only
   (c) Both 1 and 2 (d) Neither 1 nor 2

4. Consider the following statements:
   1. The term "minority" has not been defined anywhere in the constitution.
   2. The central government has notified five communities as religious minorities at the national level.
   Which of the above given statements is/are correct:
   (a) 1 only
   (b) 2 only
   (c) Both 1 and 2
   (d) Neither 1 nor 2

5. Consider the following statements with reference to the Armed Forces Special Powers Acts (AFSPA):
   1. It empowers governor to declare an area as "disturbed area".
   2. At present, the AFSPA has been enforced in 6 states only.
   Select the correct statement/statements using the codes given below:
   (a) 1 only (b) 2 only
   (c) Both 1 and 2 (d) Neither 1 nor 2

6. Which of the following provisions of the Constitution of India need the ratification by the legislatures of not less than one-half of the states to effect amendment?
   1. The manner of election of the President of India.
   2. Extent of the executive power of the Union and the states.
   3. Powers of the Supreme Court and High Courts.
   4. Any of the Lists in the 7th Schedule.
   Select the correct answer using the codes given below
   (a) 1, 2, 3 and 4 (b) 1, 2 and 3
   (c) 3 and 4 (d) 1 and 2

7. There are provisions in the Constitution of India which empower the Parliament to modify or annuel the operation of certain provisions of the Constitution without actually amending them.
   They include
   1. any law made under Article 2 (relating to admission or establishment of new states)
   2. any law made under Article 3 (relating to formation of new states)
   3. amendment of First Schedule and Fourth Schedule.
   Select the correct answer using the codes given below
   (a) 1 and 2 (b) 2 and 3
   (c) 2 and 3 (d) None of these

8. Which of the following are matters on which a constitutional amendment is possible only with the ratification of the legislature of not less than one-half of the states?
   1. Election of the President
   2. Representation of states in the Parliament
   3. Lists in the 7th Schedule
   4. Abolition of the Legislative Council in a State
   Select the correct answer using the codes given below.
   (a) 1, 2 and 3 (b) 1, 2 and 4
   (c) 1, 3 and 4 (d) 2, 3 and 4

9. Consider the following statements:
   An amendment to the Constitution of India can be initiated by the:
   1. Lok Sabha 2. Rajya Sabha
   3. State Legislature 4. President
   Which of the above statements is/are correct?
   (a) Only 1 (b) 1, 2 and 3
   (c) 2, 3 and 4 (d) 1 and 2

10. Consider the following statements about the recent amendments to the elections law by the Representation of the People (Amendment) Act 1996:
    1. Any conviction for the offence of insulting the Indian National flag or the Constitution of Indian shall entail disqualification for contesting elections to Parliament and State Legislatures for six year from the date of conviction
    2. There is an increase in the security deposit which a candidate has to make to contest the election to the Lok Sabha
    3. A candidate cannot now stand for election from more than one Parliament Constituency
    4. No election will now be countermanded on the death of a contesting candidate.
    Which of the above statements is/are correct?
    (a) 2 and 3 (b) 1, 2 and 4
    (c) 1 and 3 (d) 1, 2, 3 and 4

11. Consider the following statements:
    1. An amendment to the Constitution of India can be initiated by an introduction of a bill in the Lok Sabha only.
    2. If such an amendment seeks to make changes in the federal character of the Constitution, the amendment also requires to be ratified by the legislature of all the States of India.
    Which of the statements given above is/are correct?
    (a) 1 only (b) 2 only
    (c) Both 1 and 2 (d) Neither 1 nor 2

12. Consider the following provisions-
    1. Free & compulsory education to all children below 14 years of age.
    2. Right to elementary Education.
    3. Ban on employment of children below the age of 14 in hazardous industries & factories.
    Which of the above provision comes under Article 24?
    (a) 1 & 2 (b) 2 & 3
    (c) only 3 (d) None of the above

13. The National Green Tribunal Act, 2010 was enacted in consonance with which of the following provisions of the Constitution of India?
    (1) Right to healthy environment, construed as a part of Right to life under Article 21.
    (2) Provision of Grants for raising the level of administration in the scheduled Areas for the welfare of Scheduled Tribes under Article 275 (1)
    (3) Powers & functions of gram sabha as mentioned under Article 243 (A)
    Select the correct answer using the codes given below:
    (a) 1 only (b) 2 & 3 only
    (c) 1 & 3 only (d) 1, 2 & 3

14. Which of the following is correct statement?
    1. The universal Adult franchise is guaranteed under the Constitution.
    2. The 61st Amendment brought the age for voting to 18 years.
    (a) (1) only (b) (2) only
    (c) 1 and 2 (d) Neither 1 nor 2

15. Article 358 & 359 describe the effect of a National emergency on the fundamental right which of the following statements are correct with regard to article 358 & 359.
    1. Article 358 operates only in the case of External emergency & not in the case of internal emergency.
    2. Article 359 operates in case of both External & Internal emergency.
    3. Article 358 suspends FR under Article 19 for the entire duration of emergency.
    4. Article 358 extends to the entire coutry whereas Article 359 may extend to entire country or part of it.
    Select the correct answer using the codes given below.
    (a) 1 & 2 only (b) 1, 2 & 3 only
    (c) 2, 3 & 4 only (d) 1, 2, 3 & 4

Matching Based MCQ

16. Match the following columns

List-I	List-II
A. Reorganisation of States	1. Seventh Amendment
B. Sikkim became 22nd State of Indian Union	2. Thirty-sixth Amendment
C. Ninth Schedule added	3. First Amendment
D. Abolition of Titles of Princes	4. Twenty-sixth Amendment

    (a) A-1, B-2, C-3, D-4 (b) A-2, B-1, C-3, D-4
    (c) A-3, B-2, C-1, D-4 (d) A-3, B-1, C-4, D-2

17. Which of the following articles are correctly matched:
    1. Election Commission – Article 338.
    2. Finance Commission – Article 280.
    3. National Commission for SCs – Article. 324
    4. CAG – Article 148.
    5. Attorney General of India – Article 76.
    Select the correct answer using the codes given below:
    (a) All except 1 & 5.
    (b) All except 1 & 3.
    (c) All except 2 & 5.
    (d) None of the above options are correct.

18. Match List-I with List-II and select the correct answer using the codes given below the lists:

List-I	List-II (Amendments to the Constitution)
A. The Constitution (Sixty-ninth Amendment) Act, 1991	1. Establishment of state level Rent Tribunals
B. The Constitution (Seventy-fifth Amendment) Act. 1994	2. No reservations for Scheduled Castes in Panchayats in Arunachal Pradesh
C. The Constitution (Eighteenth Amendment) Act, 2000	3. Constitution of Panchayats in Villages or at other local level
D. The Constitution (Eighty-third Amendment) Act, 2000	4. Accepting the recommendations of the Tenth Finance Commission
	5. According the status of National Capital Territory of Delhi

Select the correct answer using the codes given below:
(a) A-5, B-1, C-4, D-2
(b) A-1, B-5, C-3, D-4
(c) A-5, B-1, C-3, D-4
(d) A-1, B-5, C-4, D-2

19. Which of the following are constitutional provisions and laws for the protection of the rights of the Scheduled Castes in India?　　**[CDS 2016]**
1. Article 17 of the Constitution of India
2. The Protection of Civil Rights Act, 1955
3. The Scheduled Castes and the Scheduled Tribes (Prevention of Atrocities) Act, 1989

Select the correct answer using the code given below.
(a) 1 and 3 only
(b) 1 and 2 only
(c) 1, 2 and 3
(d) 2 and 3 only

20. Which of the following statements regarding Article 21 of the Constitution of India is/ are correct? **[CDS 2017]**
1. Article 21 is violated when the under-trial prisoners are detained under judicial custody for an indefinite period.
2. Right to life is one of the basic human rights and not even the State has the authority to violate that right.
3. Under Article 21, the right of a woman to make reproductive choices is not a dimension of personal liberty.

Select the correct answer using the code given below.
(a) 1, 2 and 3
(b) 1 and 2 only
(c) 1 and 3 only
(d) 2 only

Hints and Explanations

1. (c) The union government has recently notified prevention of cruelty to animals (Regulation of Livestock Markets) Rules, 2017 under prevention of cruelty to Animal Act, 1960, for restricting trade in cattle. Key provisions in new formulated rules include introducing lot of paperwork for both buyer and seller, prohibition of cruel practices like slaughter, painting of horns and cutting the ears of buffaloes. Approval of District Animal Market Monitoring Committee (DAMMC) is required to run the market. Other provisions such as no sale of young and unfit animals, certification of veterinary inspector and separate facilities for sick animals in these markets are also included.

2. (b) To provide opportunities for education to his child or ward between the age of six and fourteen years was made a fundamental duty by the 86th Constitutional Amendment Act-2002.

3. (b) The constitution (114th Amendment Bill); 2010 seeks to amend Articles – 217 and 224 of the constitution relating to judges of the High court.
The Bill seeks to increase the retiring age of High court judges from 62 to 65 years.
Source: The Hindu.

4. (b)   5. (b)   6. (c)   7. (d)   8. (c)
9. (d)   10. (a)   11. (d)   12. (d)   13. (c)

14. (c) The 73rd Amendment (1992) of Indian constitution provided for constitution of municipalities, reservation of seats in every municipality for the SC and ST women and backward classes.

15. (d) The reservation in educational institutions in the private sector was provided in the 93rd Amendment under the article 15 (5) of the constitution of India.

16. (c) Article 243(I) of the Indian Constitution prescribes that the Governor of a State shall, as soon as may be within one year from the commencement of the Constitution (73rd Amendment Act, 1992), and thereafter at the expiration of every fifth year, constitute a Finance Commission to review the financial position of the Panchayats.

17. (d) Before the 42nd amendment, Article 74(1) stated that, "there shall be a Council of Ministers with the Prime Minister at the head to aid and advise the President in the exercise of his functions". However, there was a slight ambiguity whether the advice of the Council of Ministers is binding on the President. Forty-second Amendment of the 42nd Constitutional Amendment (1976) made it explicit that the President shall, "act in accordance with such advice". The amendment went into effect from 3 January, 1977. The 44th Amendment (1978) however added that the President can send the advice back for reconsideration once. But if the Council of Ministers sends the same advice again to the President then the President must accept it. The amendment went into effect from 20 June, 1979.

18. (b) According to 93rd Amendment every Child of the age group of 6-14 years shall have right to free and compulsory Education. No child is liable to pay any kind of fee/ capitation fee/ charges. A collection of capitation fee invites a fine up to 10 times the amount collected.

19. (c) 7th Amendment Act 1956 provides for composition of the House of the People and re-adjustment after every census. 31st amendment act 1973 provides for raising the upper limit for the representation of states in the Lok Sabha from 500 to 525 and reducing the upper limit for the representation of UTs from 25 to 20.

20. (b) The Constitution 98th Amendment Bill, 2003, seeks to constitute a National Judicial Commission (NJC) by including Chapter IV-A in Part V of the Constitution which will be in charge of appointing judges to the higher judiciary and for transferring High Court Judges.

21. (a) The above provision has been added by 91st constitutional Amendment Act, 2003.

22. (a)   23. (a)   24. (b)   25. (d)   26. (c)
27. (c)   28. (b)   29. (d)   30. (d)   31. (a)
32. (c)   33. (d)   34. (b)   35. (c)   36. (c)

37. (a) In 2002, through the 86th amendement act, the Right to Education was added to the Fundamental Rights.

38. (b) Article 31-B was inserted by the First Constitutional (Amendment) Act 1951 which states that without prejudiced to the generality of the provisions contained in Article 31-A, none of the Acts and Regulations specified in the Ninth Schedule of the constitution of India nor any of the provisions thereof shall be deemed to be void.

39. (a) Amendments to the Constitution of India has prescribed that the Council of Ministers shall not exceed 15 percent of total number of members of the House of the People or Legislative Assembly in the States.

40. (b) Sikkim became a state of India via the Thirty-sixth Amendment Act, 1975 on 26th April, 1975. The Sikkim State day is observed on 16th May of every year because this was the day when the first Chief Minister of Sikkim assumed office.

EXERCISE-2

1. (c) Through 52 Amendment Act: Articles-101, 102, 190 and 191 were changed. It laid down the process by which legislators may be disqualified on grounds of defection. A member of parliament may be disqualified if:

    – He/She voluntarily resigns from the party on whose ticket he/she has been elected.

    – Does not vote/abstain as per party's whip.

    – If an independent member joins a political party.

    A nominated member who was not member of a party could join a party within 6 months, after that period.

2. (d) As per Indian Surrogacy Bill surrogacy would be allowed only for infertile Indian married heterosexual couples where the woman is between 23 to 50 years. The age of male partner in case of heterosexual couples should be between 26 to 55 years. Issue less of unmarried women are prohibited under the Bill to be surrogate mothers.

3. (a) The bulk of the constitution can be amended by the unilateral action of the parliament either by simple majority or by special majority.

    Further, the power to initiate on amendment to the constitution lies only with the centre.

    – The governor is empowered to reserve certain types of bills passed by the state legislature for the consideration of the president.

    – The president can withhold his assent to such bills not only in the first instance but also in the second instance.

    – Thus the president enjoys absolute veto (and not suspensive veto) over state bills.

    – Suspensive veto: A veto by which a law is merely suspended until reconsidered by the legislature and becomes a law if repassed by the legislature.

4. (c) The constitution refers to two types of minorities, namely religious minorities and linguistic minorities. However the term 'minority' has not been defined anywhere in the constitution.

The central government has notified five communities namely, Muslims, Sikhs, Christians, Buddhists and Zoroastrians as religious minorities at the national level.

5. (c) The AFSPA was enacted in 1958 to bring declared disturbed areas under control of the Armed forces for the sake of restoration of law and order.

    The Section (3) of the Act empowers governor of state/ UT to issue an official notification in Gazette of India, following which centre has authority to send in armed forces for civilian aid. Once declared 'disturbed', the region has to maintain status quo for a minimum of three months.

    At present, the AFSPA has been enforced in 6 states viz. Assam, Nagaland, Arunachal Pradesh (certain areas only), Manipur (except Imphal), Meghalaya and Jammu and Kashmir.

6. (a) Bills that have to be passed by Special Majority and also to be ratified by not less than one-half of the State Legislatures . This comprises of Constitutional Amendment Bills which seek to make any change in articles relating to:

    · The Election of the President.
    · The extent of the Executive Power of the Union and the States.
    · The Supreme Court and the High Courts.
    · Any of the Lists in the Seventh Schedule.
    · The representation of States in Parliament.
    · The provisions of Article 368 itself.

7. (c) Representation of states in the Parliament does require a constitutional amendment only with the ratification of the legislature of not less than one-half of the states. Other given options require the same.

8. (d) An amendment to the Constitution of India can be initiated by either House of Parliament under article 368. It does not require the President's recommendation.

9. (b) Statement 3 is incorrect as a candidate shall not be allowed to contest from more than two constituencies, it also adds options 1 and 2.

10. (a)

11. (d) An amendment to the constitution of India is introduced as a bill in the Parliament. It then must be approved by both the houses of Parliament. The amendments must then be ratified by the legislatures of at least one half of the states (not all the states). Once all these stages are complete the amendment is bound to receive the assent of the President of India.

12. (c) 13. (a) 14. (c) 15. (d) 16. (a)

17. (a) Article 2- (Admission or establishment of new States) Parliament may by law admit into the Union, or establish new States on such terms and conditions as it thinks fit.

Article 3- Formation of new States and alteration of areas, boundaries or names of existing States.

Amendment in the First and Fourth schedule can be done through constitution amendment bill.

18. (a)

19. (c) Article 17 of the constitution of India deals with untouchability and enforcement of any disability arising out of Untouchability is an offence punishable in accordance with law. The protection of civil rights act, 1955 deals with punishment for the preaching and practice of untouchability and for matters connected with it. The scheduled castes and the scheduled tribes (prevention of atrocities) act, 1989 forbids any atrocities against them and any offence under this act is punishable.

20. (b) Supreme Court of India has ruled that it is the violation of Article 21 of the Indian Constitution if an under-trial prisoner is held in custody for long period, and such prisoner has the right to get bail. Article 21 also ensures woman's right to make reproductive choices and is considered as personal liberty of women.